9th International Natural Language Generation Conference (INLG 2016)

Edinburgh, United Kingdom
5-8 September 2016

ISBN: 978-1-5108-3116-2

INLG 2016

The 9th International
Natural Language Generation conference

Proceedings of the Conference

September 5-8, 2016
Edinburgh, UK

Introduction

Welcome to the 9th International Natural Language Generation Conference (INLG 2016)! INLG is the biennial meeting of the ACL Special Interest Group on Natural Language Generation (SIGGEN). The INLG conference provides the premier forum for the discussion, dissemination, and archiving of research and results in the field of Natural Language Generation (NLG). Previous INLG conferences have been held in Ireland, the USA, Australia, the UK, and Israel. Prior to 2000, INLG meetings were held as international workshops with a history stretching back to 1983. In 2016, INLG is organized in Edinburgh, UK.

The INLG 2016 program includes presentations of substantial, original, and previously unpublished results on all topics related to natural language generation. This year, INLG received 65 submissions (29 full papers, 30 short papers and 6 demo proposals) from 12 different countries. 16 submissions were accepted as full papers (10 presented orally, 6 as posters), 20 as short papers (4 presented orally, and 16 as posters), and 3 demos. In addition, INLG 2016 includes an invited talk by Yejin Choi (University of Washington) and Vera Demberg (Saarland University).

The organizing committee would like to offer their thanks to our invited speakers for agreeing to join us and to the authors of all submitted papers. We have also received sponsorship from Arria and WebNLG, for which we are extremely grateful. Finally, we would like to welcome you to Edinburgh and hope that you have an enjoyable and inspiring visit!

Amy Isard, Verena Rieser and Dimitra Gkatzia
INLG 2016 Co-Chairs

Organizers:

Amy Isard
Verena Rieser
Dimitra Gkatzia
Jekaterina Novikova
Simon Keizer

Program Committee:

Anja Belz
Aoife Cahill
Nina Dethlefs
Katja Filippova
Claire Gardent
Albert Gatt
Pablo Gervás
Alistair Knott
Ioannis Konstas
Emiel Krahmer
Guy Lapalme
David McDonald
Cecile Paris
Paul Piwek
Ehud Reiter
Kristina Striegnitz
Mariët Theune
Ielka van der Sluis
Keith Vander Linden
Leo Wanner
Michael White
Sandra Williams
Helen Hastie
Barbara Di Eugenio
Vera Demberg
Laura Perez-Beltrachini
Saad Mahamood
Andreas Vlachos
Kees van Deemter
David Howcroft
Yejin Choi
Kathy McKeown
Diana Bental

François Portet
Simon Mille
Cyril Labbe
John Kelleher
Sander Wubben
Somayajulu Sripada
Nikolaos Engonopoulos
Amanda Stent
David Schlangen
Sina Zarrieß

Invited Speakers:

Yejin Choi (University of Washington)
Vera Demberg (Saarland University)

Table of Contents

Conference Program

Wednesday, September 7, 2016

8:00–9:15   **Registration**

9:15–9:30   **Welcome / Opening remarks**

9:30–10:30   **Oral Session: Summarisation / Narrative**

09:30–10:00   *Summarising News Stories for Children*
Iain Macdonald and Advaith Siddharthan

10:00–10:30   *Discourse-Driven Narrative Generation With Bipartite Planning*
David Winer and R. Michael Young

10:30–11:00   **Coffee break**

11:00–12:20   **Oral Session: short papers**

11:00–11:20   *Generating English from Abstract Meaning Representations*
Nima Pourdamghani, Kevin Knight and Ulf Hermjakob

11:20–11:40   *Generating summaries of hospitalizations: A new metric to assess the complexity of medical terms and their definitions*
Sabita Acharya, Barbara Di Eugenio, Andrew D Boyd, Karen Dunn Lopez, Richard Cameron and Gail M Keenan

11:40–12:00   *Designing Algorithms for Referring with Proper Names*
Kees van Deemter

12:00–12:20   *When to Plummet and When to Soar: Corpus Based Verb Selection for Natural Language Generation*
Charese Smiley, Vassilis Plachouras, Frank Schilder, Hiroko Bretz, Jochen Leidner and Dezhao Song

Wednesday, September 7, 2016 (continued)

12:20–13:30   Lunch

13:30–14:30   *Invited Talk*
Yejin Choi, session chair: Amy Isard

–13:30   *Sketch-to-Text Generation: Toward Contextual, Creative, and Coherent Composition*
Yejin Choi

14:30–16:00   Posters and Demos with coffee

15:00–15:30   *Abstractive Compression of Captions with Attentive Recurrent Neural Networks*
Sander Wubben, Emiel Krahmer, Antal van den Bosch and Suzan Verberne

15:00–15:30   *Infusing NLU into Automatic Question Generation*
Karen Mazidi and Paul Tarau

15:00–15:30   *Automatic label generation for news comment clusters*
Ahmet Aker, Monica Paramita, Emina Kurtic, Adam Funk, Emma Barker, Mark Hepple and Rob Gaizauskas

15:00–15:30   *Improving Fluency in Narrative Text Generation With Grammatical Transformations and Probabilistic Parsing*
Emily Ahn, Fabrizio Morbini and Andrew Gordon

15:00–15:30   *The Multilingual Affective Soccer Corpus (MASC): Compiling a biased parallel corpus on soccer reportage in English, German and Dutch*
Nadine Braun, Martijn Goudbeek and Emiel Krahmer

15:00–15:30   *Challenges of Argument Mining: Generating an Argument Synthesis based on the Qualia Structure*
Patrick Saint-Dizier

15:00–15:30   *Tense and Aspect in Runyankore Using a Context-Free Grammar*
Joan Byamugisha, C. Maria Keet and Brian DeRenzi

15:00–15:30   *Task demands and individual variation in referring expressions*
Adriana Baltaretu and Thiago Castro Ferreira

15:00–15:30   *Category-Driven Content Selection*
Rania Mohammed, Laura Perez-Beltrachini and Claire Gardent

12:45–13:45   **Lunch**

13:45–15:15   **Posters and demos with coffee**

14:45–15:15   *On the verbalization patterns of part-whole relations in isiZulu*
C. Maria Keet and Langa Khumalo

14:45–15:15   *SimpleNLG-IT: adapting SimpleNLG to Italian*
Alessandro Mazzei, Cristina Battaglino and Cristina Bosco

14:45–15:15   *Don't Mention the Shoe! A Learning to Rank Approach to Content Selection for Image Description Generation*
Josiah Wang and Robert Gaizauskas

14:45–15:15   *Good Automatic Authentication Question Generation*
Simon Woo, Zuyao Li and Jelena Mirkovic

14:45–15:15   *Automatic Generation of Student Report Cards*
Amy Isard and Jeremy Knox

14:45–15:15   *Collecting Reliable Human Judgements on Machine-Generated Language: The Case of the QG-STEC Data*
Keith Godwin and Paul Piwek

14:45–15:15   *Ranking Automatically Generated Questions Using Common Human Queries*
Yllias Chali and Sina Golestanirad

14:45–15:15   *Towards proper name generation: a corpus analysis*
Thiago Castro Ferreira, Sander Wubben and Emiel Krahmer

14:45–15:15   *An Analysis of the Ability of Statistical Language Models to Capture the Structural Properties of Language*
Aneiss Ghodsi and John DeNero

14:45–15:15   *Enhancing PTB Universal Dependencies for Grammar-Based Surface Realization*
David L. King and Michael White

14:45–15:15   *Effect of Data Annotation, Feature Selection and Model Choice on Spatial Description Generation in French*
Anja Belz, Adrian Muscat, Brandon Birmingham, Jessie Levacher, Julie Pain and Adam Quinquenel

Summarising News Stories for Children

Iain Macdonald
Computing Science
University of Aberdeen
Scotland, U.K.
iain.j.macdonald.12@aberdeen.ac.uk

Advaith Siddharthan
Computing Science
University of Aberdeen
Scotland, U.K.
advaith@abdn.ac.uk

Abstract

This paper proposes a system to automatically summarise news articles in a manner suitable for children by deriving and combining statistical ratings for how important, positively oriented and easy to read each sentence is. Our results demonstrate that this approach succeeds in generating summaries that are suitable for children, and that there is further scope for combining this extractive approach with abstractive methods used in text simplification.

1   Introduction

Automatic text summarisation is a research area with half a century of history, with Luhn (1958) discussing as far back as 1958 the task he called "auto-abstracting of documents". This field has evolved considerably with a large number of unsupervised and supervised techniques for summarising documents reported in the literature (see Nenkova and McKeown (2012) for an overview). The vast majority of publications focus on sentence selection based on notions of information content and topicality; such methods are referred to collectively as extractive summarisation. We adapt one such well understood notion of informativeness to incorporate other desirable characteristics such as how positive or optimistic sentences are and how difficult they are to read, with the goal of generating news summaries that are suitable for children.

We are targeting a similar demographic of children as that of the British Broadcasting Cor-poration's CBBC Newsround[1], a television pro-gramme and website dedicated to providing children in the age range of 6–12 years with news suitable for them (Newsround, 2011). This is primarily motivated by two factors: the importance of young people engaging with current affairs and the potential benefits of automating the creation of children's news articles.

Multiple studies have highlighted potential links between youth civic engagement (defined by Adler and Goggin (2005) as active participation in the life of a community to improve conditions for others or to help shape the community's future) with the use of various forms of news media (see Boyd and Dobrow (2010) for a good overview). However, while children's news sources exist, possibly the best known being the aforementioned Newsround, they are time consuming to maintain, and as a result very few news stories are made available through them. For instance, Newsround has only six journalists working to maintain the website (Newsround, 2008), who focus more on multimedia content, so only around five articles a day are published for children. While the guidelines used to produce Newsround articles are not public, we have observed that they are shorter than those that appear on the main news site, use simpler language, and also try to stay upbeat, avoiding upsetting news where possible. Our primary objective is to automate the generation of such news stories for children using an extractive approach, though the further potential for abstractive ap-

---

[1] http://www.bbc.co.uk/newsround

proaches such as text simplification is also discussed. In order to achieve this objective, there are four key components described in this paper:

- A measure of how informative a sentence is.
- A measure of how positive or negative a sentence is.
- A measure of how difficult a sentence is to read and understand.
- A formula for combining the combining the previous measures.

We describe these components and our evaluation methodology in §2 and our results in §3 before discussing our contributions with respect to related work in §4 and presenting our conclusions in §5.

2 Method

We based our summariser on SumBasic, a contemporary summariser that has been shown to perform well in evaluations in the news domain (Nenkova and Vanderwende, 2005) and is easy to adapt. SumBasic is a greedy algorithm that incrementally selects sentences to create a summary with a similar distribution of words as the input document(s). It begins by estimating the probability of seeing each word w_i in the input as $p_{input}(w_i) = n/N$, where n is the frequency of w_i in the input and N is the total number of words in the input. It then assigns a score to each sentence S_j which is the average probability of all the words in the sentence $Score_{SumBasic}(S_j) = \sum_{w_i \in S_j} p(w_i)/length(S_j)$. Sentences are selected in decreasing value of the score, and each time a sentence is incorporated in the summaries, the probabilities of words contained in the sentence are discounted to reduce the chance of selecting redundant sentences. We extended this algorithm to incorporate sentiment and ease of language as described below.

2.1 Information Score

We based our information metric on the SumBasic metric proposed by Nenkova and Vanderwende (2005):

$$Score_{SumBasic}(S_j) = \frac{1}{|\{w_i | w_i \in S_j\}|} \sum_{w_i \in S_j} p_{input}(w_i)$$

where the denominator denotes the number of words in the sentence. We adapted this metric in two ways:

1. A list *Stop* of 173 common stop words (University of Washington, 2012) was incorporated, and these were discounted in the calculations.

2. A peculiarity of news reporting in English is that the central information is often summarised within the first two sentences; this is sometimes referred to as the inverted pyramid structure, widely believed to have been developed in the 19th century (Pöttker, 2003), and the most common structure for print, broadcast and online news articles in English (Rich, 2015, p. 162). To account for this, we increased the score of the first sentence by a factor of 2 and the second by a factor of 1.5.

Our implemented information score is:

$$Score_{info}(S_j) = \frac{IPW}{|\{w_i|_{w_i \notin Stop}^{w_i \in S_j}\}|} \sum_{\substack{w_i \in S_j \\ w_i \notin Stop}} p_{input}(w_i)$$

where IPW, the inverted pyramid weight, is 2 for first sentence, 1.5 for second sentence and 1 otherwise.

2.2 Sentence Difficulty Score

Sentence difficulty is often assessed as some combination of lexical and syntactic difficulty. Typical heuristics such as readability formulae (Dale and Chall, 1948; Kincaid et al., 1975; Gunning, 1952; Mc Laughlin, 1969) are intended for scoring entire texts, rather than individual sentences. Alternately, psycholinguistic data for vocabulary such as the Bristol Norms (Stadthagen-Gonzalez and Davis, 2006; Gilhooly and Logie, 1980) exist for age of acquisition, familiarity, etc., but are relatively small (the Bristol Norms contain only 3,394 words).

To more directly assess linguistic suitability for children, we used a language model derived from historical BBC Newsround stories. Text-STAT (Hüning, 2002) was used to acquire 1000 Newsround URLs and ICEweb (Weisser, 2013) was used to extract the text from these web page. The probability of every word in the corpus was calculated, resulting in a lexicon of over

12,500 words. Lexical difficulty was then estimated in the same manner as importance in the section above; i.e. as the average probability of the words in the sentence, but this time according to the Newsround model. We excluded names from the calculation by matching words against a large collection of names (Ward, 1993):

$$Score_{lex}(S_j) = \frac{1}{|\{w_i|_{\substack{w_i \in S_j \\ w_i \notin Names}}\}|} \sum_{\substack{w_i \in S_j \\ w_i \notin Names}} p_{newsround}(w_i)$$

We used a simple sentence length heuristic for syntactic difficulty, to give a combined difficulty score:

$$Score_{diff}(S_j) = \frac{Score_{lex}(S_j)}{|\{w_i|w_i \in S_j\}|}$$

2.3 Sentiment score

We implemented hybrid of a statistical and a rule based sentiment analysis component.

Supervised sentiment classifier: The statistical component was implemented as a supervised Naïve Bayes classifier with unigram, bigram and trigram features. We first experimented with training it on a large corpus of positive and negative movie reviews (Pang and Lee, 2004). We were however not satisfied with the quality of classifications for news stories. The key issue was the difference in vocabulary usage in the two genres; e.g. a word such as "terrifying" features prominently in positive movie reviews, but should no predict positive sentiment in a news story. For genre adaptation, a new dataset was created specifically for our purpose by taking a pre-existent dataset of 2,225 BBC articles assembled for topic classification (Greene and Cunningham, 2006). These articles were then manually labelled as positive, negative or neutral based just on the topic of the story, and the sentences from the positive and negative articles were added to the training data from the movie review dataset. This augmentation was observed to produce better results on new stories, but no formal evaluation was carried out on this particular aspect. For a sentence with n words, Naïve Bayes returns conditional probabilities for each class (Pos and Neg), calculated as:

$$p(Pos|w_{1..n}) = p(Pos) \prod_{i=1..n} p(w_i|Pos)$$
$$p(Neg|w_{1..n}) = p(Neg) \prod_{i=1..n} p(w_i|Neg)$$

From these, we calculate a sentiment score as:

$$Score_{nb}(S_j) = \frac{p(Pos|w_{1..n})}{p(Pos|w_{1..n}) + p(Neg|w_{1..n})}$$

Dictionary based approach: In an effort to further overcome vocabulary issues with the statistical system, we also incorporated a dictionary-based approach. We used a sentiment dictionary with around 2000 positive and 4800 negative words respectively (Liu et al., 2005). The classifier simply starting with a sentiment score of 0.5 and incremented or decremented by 0.1 for every word in a sentence found in the positive or negative dictionary respectively.

$$Score_{dict}(S_j) = 0.5 + \sum_{\substack{w_i \in S_j \\ w_i \in Dict_{pos}}} 0.1 - \sum_{\substack{w_i \in S_j \\ w_i \in Dict_{neg}}} 0.1$$

2.4 Combining Scores

In order to combine scores, we first converted each individual score into its standard score (also called z-score); a renormalisation that gives each score a mean of 0 and a standard deviation of 1 over all sentences in the input. Following this step, a score for each sentence was computed as follows. First, the statistical and dictionary based (standardised) sentiment scores were combined in the ratio three is to one to give a single sentiment score:

$$Score_{sent}(S_j) = \frac{2}{3} Score_{nb}(S_j) + \frac{1}{3} Score_{dict}(S_j)$$

The final sentence score was then computed as a linear function of the scores for informativeness, difficulty and sentiment:

$$\begin{aligned} Score_{children}(S_j) &= 5 \times Score_{info}(S_j) \\ &+ 5 \times Score_{sent}(S_j) \\ &+ 2 \times Score_{diff}(S_j) \end{aligned}$$

The weightings were set by hand based on manual experimentation. We found that within a single news report, there was limited variation in sentence difficulty; this score could be assigned a higher weight in a multi-document summarisation task.

2.5 Experimental Setup

Evaluation platform: Amazon's Mechanical Turk service[2] was utilised to create a survey to compare different summaries of news articles. Various studies have been carried out into the quality of data provided by Mechanical Turk with the general consensus of these seeming to be that, provided the questions are clear and that the instructions are intuitive, the data generated from Mechanical Turk is of a high quality (Ramsey et al., 2016; Buhrmester et al., 2011; Rand, 2012).

Summariser settings: We compared two summariser settings, the original SumBasic score for informativeness ($S_{SumBasic}$), and the other that combined informativeness with ease of reading and sentiment ($S_{children}$). For both settings, we set the required summary length to either one hundred words or half the length of the original article, whichever was smaller. With respect to how this was implemented in the iterative summariser described at the top of §2, any sentence that would cause the summary to exceed this length was ignored and the next highest rated sentence was given a chance in its place. Further, to prevent poorly scoring sentences being included, a minimum z-score limit was set to -0.25 below which sentences would be rejected. For both summarisers, sentences in the summary were reordered to correspond to their original ordering in the news article.

Evaluation data: We sampled 9 news articles to summarise, six from the BBC and one each from The Guardian, The Independent and Sky News. For the BBC articles, we generated a corpus of 1000 Newsround stories using Text-STAT (Hüning, 2002), and iteratively picked one using a random number generator, and then

[2]http://www.mturk.com/

checked that it was based on an article on the main BBC webpage (we did this in order to conduct a further comparison to the manually written Newsround story [c.f.§3.1]). The first six articles found to meet this criteria were used. An additional article was taken from each of The Guardian, The Independent and Sky News, again by sampling at random from a corpus of 1000 articles generated using TextSTAT.

These articles were then split into three surveys each with two BBC articles and one of the other three articles. For each article participants were presented with the two summaries produced by NSFC and GS, side by side, labelled 'A' and 'B', in a randomised order and without any information on how they were produced. They were provided a link to the original news report, but not forced to read it. Examples of summaries used in the evaluation are provided in Table 1. Participants were then asked to answer a four comparison questions on a five point scale ["A is significantly more X", "A is slightly more X", "Not sure, or equally X", "B is slightly more X" and "B is significantly more X"], where X is the word in bold font in the questions below:

Q1 Which of these summaries is more **informative**?

Q2 Which of these summaries is more **positive**?

Q3 Which of these summaries is more **easy** to read and understand?

Q4 Overall, which of these summaries do you believe is more **suitable** for a child?

Finally, we asked a single non-comparison question for each summary on a five point scale ["Strongly disagree", "Disagree", "Not sure", "Agree", "Strongly Agree"]:

Q5 I would consider showing summary {A|B} to a child if I wanted them to know more about this news story.

Design: We solicited nine participants for each survey, twenty-seven in total, resulting in each question being answered eight-one times (twenty-seven participants, three articles each).

NSFC	GS
A blaze that swept through a dogs' home has now claimed the lives of 60 animals, police have said. More than 150 dogs were rescued from the fire, which broke out at Manchester Dogs' Home in Moss Brook Road in Harpurhey on Thursday evening. Greater Manchester Fire and Rescue Service (GMFRS) tweeted its thanks to people who have donated money, saying: "One hundred and fifty dogs rescued. Thousands of pounds donated. Thank you Greater Manchester." The RSPCA described the fire as "heartbreaking". The Manchester home was established in 1893 and cares for more than 7,000 dogs every year.	The newspaper has also captured aerial footage showing the extent of the damage caused by the blaze. In the aftermath of the fire, the manager of the home said 60 dogs had been housed in the worst-affected building. Hundreds of messages of sympathy have been left on the JustGiving page, as the amount of money donated continues to rise. A number of people, including police officers and staff were quickly on the scene and put their life on the line to help with the rescue effort. The RSPCA described the fire as "heartbreaking".
Doctors have warned that almost half of all adults in Britain will be classified as obese within the next 20 years. They predict that on current trends an extra 11 million people will be severely overweight by 2030, bringing the total to 26 million. Only tough government action, including a tax on unhealthy food, can slow the trend, they say. At the top is a 10% tax on high-calorie food and drink. "People know obesity is a real problem. People don't know, as individuals, what to do about it."	The doctors have produced a league table of possible actions that could be taken to curb the epidemic. At the top is a 10% tax on high-calorie food and drink. "People know obesity is a real problem. People don't know, as individuals, what to do about it." "Governments do know what to do about it and if they could persuade people, as they easily could, it would be a popular action." Tam Fry, of the National Obesity Forum, said: "Children are born thin. It's what we do to children that makes them obese."
A new species of titanosaur unearthed in Argentina is the largest animal ever to walk the Earth, palaeontologists say. Based on its huge thigh bones, it was 40m (130ft) long and 20m (65ft) tall. A film crew from the BBC Natural History Unit was there to capture the moment the scientists realised exactly how big their discovery was. This giant herbivore lived in the forests of Patagonia between 95 and 100 million years ago, based on the age of the rocks in which its bones were found. There have been many previous contenders for the title "world's biggest dinosaur".	A new species of titanosaur unearthed in Argentina is the largest animal ever to walk the Earth, palaeontologists say. By measuring the length and circumference of the largest femur (thigh bone), they calculated the animal weighed 77 tonnes. "Given the size of these bones, which surpass any of the previously known giant animals, the new dinosaur is the largest animal known that walked on Earth," the researchers told BBC News. "It will be named describing its magnificence and in honour to both the region and the farm owners who alerted us about the discovery," the researchers said.

Table 1: Sample summaries used in the evaluation

3   Results

We will refer to the two summarisers being compared as NSFC (News Summariser for Children), which uses $Score_{children}$ as the metric and GS (Generic Summariser), which uses $Score_{SumBasic}$. The quantitative data for the four comparison questions are reported in Table 2, with pie charts for each question in Fig. 1.

For statistical analysis of significance, we used the *Sign Test*, by ignoring the 'Not Sure' counts and aggregating counts for 'slightly' and 'significantly' more. The family significance level was set at $\alpha = 0.05$; with $m = 6$ null hypotheses (that the two summaries are equal on Q1–4 and that for Q5 neither summariser would be considered suitable for children). We used the Bonferroni Correction (α/m), giving an individual significance threshold of $0.05/6 = 0.00833$.

Informative: News Summariser for Children outperformed the generic summariser by a sig-

	Q1 Info	Q2 Pos	Q3 Easy	Q4 Overall
GS Significant	7	1	7	6
GS Slight	12	12	9	14
Not Sure	6	32	14	4
NSFC Slight	26	20	34	32
NSFC Significant	30	16	17	25

Table 2: Responses to comparison questions

nificant margin of 56 to 19 ($p < 0.0001$), with only 14 instances of "Not Sure". This suggests that the potentially negative effect on informativeness of incorporating sentiment and reading ease into the sentence score was more than offset by our adaptation of the SumBasic score to incorporate increased weight for the first two sentences and ignore stop words.

Positive: While the News Summariser for Children still outperformed the generic summariser by a significant margin of 36 to 13 ($p = 0.0014$), the most common response was "Not Sure"(40% of responses).

Easy: News Summariser for Children outperformed the generic summariser by a significant margin of 51 to 16 ($p < 0.0001$), with only 14 instances of "Not Sure".

Overall: News Summariser for Children outperformed the generic summariser by a significant margin of 57 to 20 ($p < 0.0001$), with only 4 instances of "Not Sure".

Non-comparison question: The final question Q5 simply asked the participant to rate whether they would show each summary to a child on a Likert scale. This question was necessary as the News Summariser for Children could have radically outperformed the generic summariser whilst still not have produced a particularly good summary in and of itself. Table 3 presents the quantitative data for the non-comparison question. While the generic summariser (GS) produced output deemed suitable for being shown to children for slightly fewer than half the cases (38 out of 58 where an opinion was expressed; not significant with $p = 0.0124$), the news summariser for children

(NSFC) produced output deemed suitable for the vast majority of cases (69 out of 74 where an opinion was expressed; $p < 0.0001$).

Overall, these results were deemed to be tremendously positive and indicating that the News Summariser for Children has the potential to be an excellent tool in creating news summaries for children. To gain further insights, we also asked an expert in education to provide some qualitative feedback, as reported below.

3.1 Qualitative Comparison to BBC Newsround

In order to get qualitative feedback on the strengths and weaknesses of our summariser (NSFC), we selected the summaries of BBC news reports from the previous experiment for which NSFC received the highest and the lowest overall ratings. These were shown to a faculty member from our University's School of Education, alongside the text from the corresponding BBC Newsround article. The Newsround article and NSFC summary were labelled A or B in each case and no indication was given as to the identity of either. For the NSFC summary rated highest, the qualitative feedback from the expert indicated that the summary created by the NSFC ("B" in the following quote) was actually preferable to the article featured on Newsround ("A" in the following quote):

> "While A provides more information about the [e]vent, it does not necessarily make the news clearer or understandable. Children up to the age of 10 generally find it difficult to deal with big numbers and with metaphorical words... The level of information [in B] is kept to a minimum. It is very factual and therefore easy to understand

	GS	NSFC
Disagree Strongly	4	1
Disagree	16	4
Not Sure	23	7
Agree	29	44
Agree Strongly	9	25

Table 3: Responses to non-comparison question

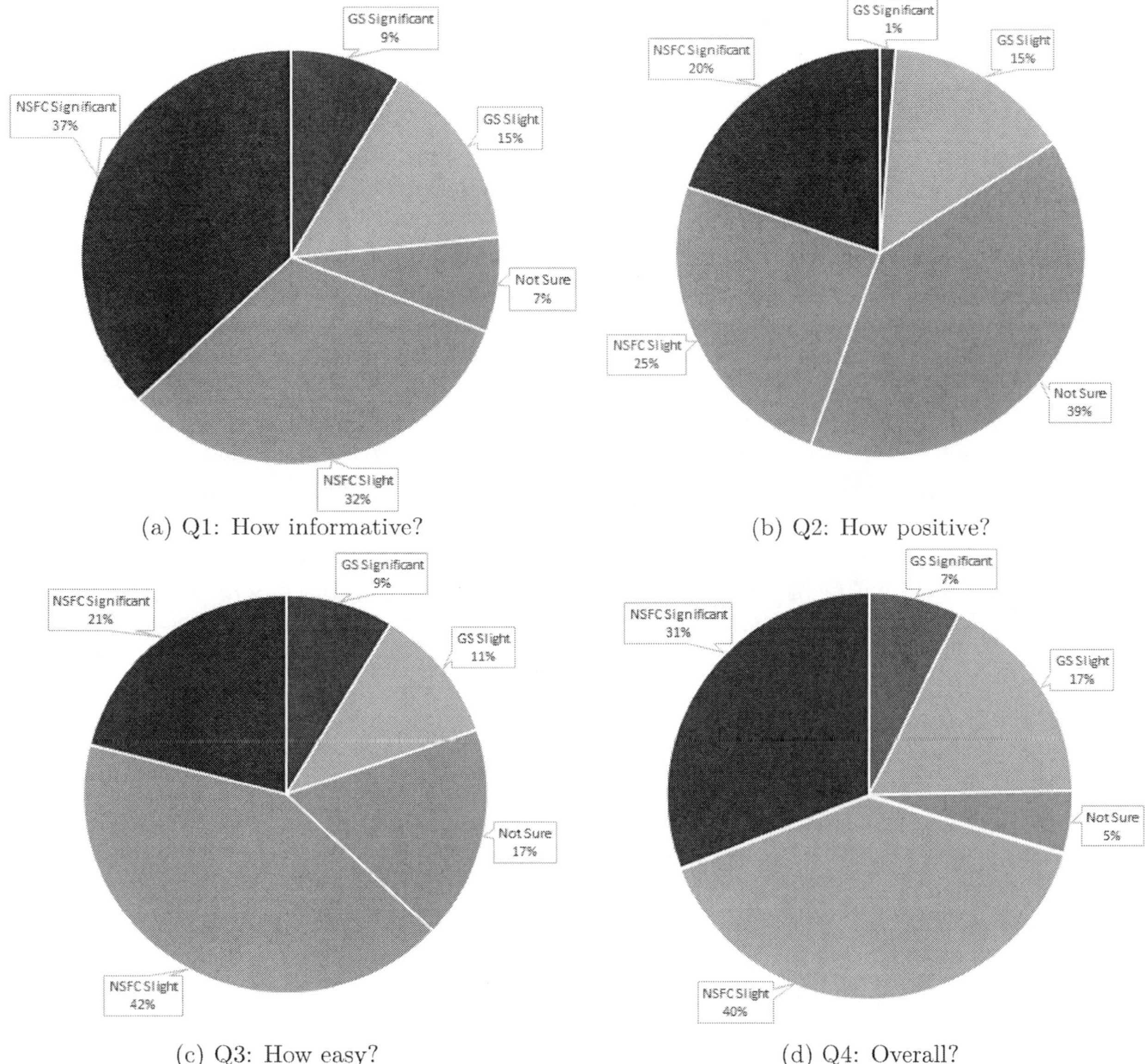

(a) Q1: How informative?   (b) Q2: How positive?

(c) Q3: How easy?   (d) Q4: Overall?

Figure 1: Responses to comparison questions

and to recall. Generally, the usage of common words, short sentences and factual description helps understanding of the news items."

For the NSFC summary rated lowest, the qualitative feedback from the expert indicated that the summary created by the NSFC ("A" in the following quote) was inferior to the article featured on Newsround ("B" in the following quote):

"A is shorter but 'denser' due to the use of scientific jargon, anthropomorphised usage of non-human subjects and presence of metaphorical terms.... B is longer and it also includes elements of scientific jargon and metaphorical terms. However the sentences are describing facts effectively by means of clear stating of the subjects, their actions captured by verbs in the active form and places/time"

4 Discussion

While there is considerable work in automatic text summarisation (Nenkova and McKeown,

2012), sentiment analysis (Liu and Zhang, 2012) and computational assessment of text readability (Collins-Thompson, 2014), as well as related fields such as text simplification (Siddharthan, 2014), we are unaware of any work directly targeting the task of summarising news stories for children. Perhaps the most closely related work is De Belder and Moens (2010), who describe a system for *simplifying* news stories in a manner that is suitable for children, splitting sentences up into smaller simpler ones and replacing difficult words with easier synonyms. Related ideas have also been explored in Information Retrieval research, with Collins-Thompson et al. (2011) describing how search results can be reranked by readability to make them suitable for different reading skills, and Enikuomehin and Rahman (2015) describing how sentiment analysis could be incorporated into an IR engine for children.

In the real world, news reporting for children is done manually at considerable cost. The BBC's CBBC Newsround is a news source with a long history, with its first episode airing in 1972 and regular episodes continuing to broadcast to this day. The primary demographic for these summaries is children aged six to twelve years old (Newsround, 2011). Today a website provides manually written news stories for children. In reality, these stories are often edited versions of an article on the main BBC webpage, but considerably shorter, with easier to read sentences and by and large an optimistic outlook. This is the sort of news story we were attempting to emulate in this paper.

Our quantitative results suggest that our summariser is successful in identifying sentences that are informative while still being upbeat and easy to read. However, there are clearly limitations of our current work. These come through clearly in the qualitative feedback we received from the expert, who made references to "big numbers", "metaphorical words", "clear stating of the subjects", "verbs in the active form", etc. None of these are captured by our score. Even if they were, it is doubtful whether alternative sentences that are equally informative can be found in a single document summarisation context. The expert also made various specific observations about vocabulary, highlighting words and phrases such as 'blaze', 'flash floods', 'arson' and 'aid agencies' as examples that may be difficult for a child to understand, and approving of Newsround defining terms like 'arson' clearly within the text. The solution it would appear is to combine the purely extractive approach described in this paper with more abstractive approaches used in research on text simplification. This will be explored in future work. For instance, numerical simplification (Power and Williams, 2012; Bautista et al., 2011), accurate conversion of passive to active voice (Siddharthan, 2010), sentence shortening to preferentially remove difficult words (Angrosh et al., 2014), lexical simplification (De Belder and Moens, 2010; Yatskar et al., 2010), explanatory descriptions of named entities (Siddharthan et al., 2011), simplifying causality and discourse connectives (Siddharthan, 2003; Siddharthan and Katsos, 2010) and defining terminology (Elhadad, 2006) have all been demonstrated for text simplification systems.

5   Conclusions

Our goal was to create an automatic news summarisation system capable of producing summaries suitable for children by combining scores for sentence informativeness, sentiment and difficulty. Our evaluation confirmed that our summariser outperforms a generic summariser focused only on informativeness in each of the aspects of informativeness, positivity and simplicity. Additionally, an overwhelming majority of experimental participants rated the summaries created by this system as being suitable for being shown to children. An expert in the field of education further confirmed that when the system worked well, the summaries were of a high standard and indeed superior to that created by a professional journalist. The expert also analysed reasons for poor performance of the system on other stories. As discussed in the previous section, there is potential for overcoming these by combining the extractive methods described here with abstractive methods from research on automatic text simplification.

References

Richard P Adler and Judy Goggin. 2005. What do we mean by "civic engagement"? *Journal of Transformative Education*, 3(3):236–253.

Mandya Angrosh, Tadashi Nomoto, and Advaith Siddharthan. 2014. Lexico-syntactic text simplification and compression with typed dependencies. In *Proceedings of COLING 2014, the 25th International Conference on Computational Linguistics: Technical Papers*, pages 1996–2006, Dublin, Ireland, August. Dublin City University and Association for Computational Linguistics.

Susana Bautista, Raquel Hervás, Pablo Gervás, Richard Power, and Sandra Williams. 2011. How to make numerical information accessible: Experimental identification of simplification strategies. *Human-Computer Interaction–INTERACT 2011*, pages 57–64.

Michelle J Boyd and Julie Dobrow. 2010. Media literacy and positive youth development. *Advances in child development and behavior*, 41:251–271.

Michael Buhrmester, Tracy Kwang, and Samuel D Gosling. 2011. Amazon's mechanical turk a new source of inexpensive, yet high-quality, data? *Perspectives on psychological science*, 6(1):3–5.

Kevyn Collins-Thompson, Paul N Bennett, Ryen W White, Sebastian de la Chica, and David Sontag. 2011. Personalizing web search results by reading level. In *Proceedings of the 20th ACM international conference on Information and knowledge management*, pages 403–412. ACM.

Kevyn Collins-Thompson. 2014. Computational assessment of text readability: A survey of current and future research. *ITL-International Journal of Applied Linguistics*, 165(2):97–135.

Edgar Dale and Jeanne S Chall. 1948. A formula for predicting readability: Instructions. *Educational research bulletin*, pages 37–54.

Jan De Belder and Marie-Francine Moens. 2010. Text simplification for children. In *Prroceedings of the SIGIR workshop on accessible search systems*, pages 19–26. ACM.

Noemie Elhadad. 2006. Comprehending technical texts: Predicting and defining unfamiliar terms. In *AMIA Annual Symposium proceedings*, volume 2006, page 239. American Medical Informatics Association.

AO Enikuomehin and MA Rahman. 2015. A quantum based web summarizer for childrenâĂŹs news rendering. *International Journal of Internet of Things*, 4(1):6–10.

Ken J Gilhooly and Robert H Logie. 1980. Age-of-acquisition, imagery, concreteness, familiarity, and ambiguity measures for 1,944 words. *Behavior Research Methods & Instrumentation*, 12(4):395–427.

Derek Greene and Pádraig Cunningham. 2006. Practical solutions to the problem of diagonal dominance in kernel document clustering. In *Proc. 23rd International Conference on Machine learning (ICML'06)*, pages 377–384. ACM Press.

Robert Gunning. 1952. The technique of clear writing.

Matthias Hüning. 2002. Textstat. http://neon.niederlandistik.fu-berlin.de/static/textstat/TextSTAT-Doku-EN.html#7.

JP Kincaid, RP Fishburne, RL Rogers, and BS Chissom. 1975. Derivation of new readability formulas. Technical report, Technical report, TN: Naval Technical Training, US Naval Air Station, Memphis, TN.

Bing Liu and Lei Zhang. 2012. A survey of opinion mining and sentiment analysis. In *Mining text data*, pages 415–463. Springer.

Bing Liu, Minqing Hu, and Junsheng Cheng. 2005. Opinion observer: analyzing and comparing opinions on the web. In *Proceedings of the 14th international conference on World Wide Web*, pages 342–351. ACM.

Hans Peter Luhn. 1958. A business intelligence system. *IBM Journal of Research and Development*, 2(4):314–319.

G Harry Mc Laughlin. 1969. Smog grading-a new readability formula. *Journal of reading*, 12(8):639–646.

Ani Nenkova and Kathleen McKeown. 2012. A survey of text summarization techniques. In *Mining Text Data*, pages 43–76. Springer.

Ani Nenkova and Lucy Vanderwende. 2005. The impact of frequency on summarization. *Microsoft Research, Redmond, Washington, Tech. Rep. MSR-TR-2005-101*.

CBBC Newsround. 2008. Cbbc newsround - "who we are". http://news.bbc.co.uk/cbbcnews/hi/help/default.stm. Accessed: 16th November, 2015.

CBBC Newsround. 2011. Cbbc newsround - frequently asked questions. http://www.bbc.co.uk/newsround/13927399. Accessed: 13th April, 2016.

Bo Pang and Lillian Lee. 2004. A sentimental education: Sentiment analysis using subjectivity summarization based on minimum cuts. In *Proceedings of the ACL*.

Horst Pöttker. 2003. News and its communicative quality: the inverted pyramidâĂŤwhen and why did it appear? *Journalism Studies*, 4(4):501–511.

Richard Power and Sandra Williams. 2012. Generating numerical approximations. *Computational Linguistics*, 38(1):113–134.

Sarah R Ramsey, Kristen L Thompson, Melissa McKenzie, and Alan Rosenbaum. 2016. Psychological research in the internet age: The quality of web-based data. *Computers in Human Behavior*, 58:354–360.

David G Rand. 2012. The promise of mechanical turk: How online labor markets can help theorists run behavioral experiments. *Journal of theoretical biology*, 299:172–179.

Carole Rich. 2015. *Writing and reporting news: A coaching method.* Cengage Learning, eighth edition.

Advaith Siddharthan and Napoleon Katsos. 2010. Reformulating discourse connectives for non-expert readers. In *Proceedings of the 11th Annual Conference of the North American Chapter of the Association for Computational Linguistics (NAACL-HLT 2010)*, Los Angeles, CA.

Advaith Siddharthan, Ani Nenkova, and Kathleen McKeown. 2011. Information status distinctions and referring expressions: An empirical study of references to people in news summaries. *Computational Linguistics*, 37(4):811–842.

Advaith Siddharthan. 2003. Preserving discourse structure when simplifying text. In *Proceedings of the European Natural Language Generation Workshop (ENLG), 11th Conference of the European Chapter of the Association for Computational Linguistics (EACL'03)*, pages 103–110, Budapest, Hungary.

Advaith Siddharthan. 2010. Complex lexico-syntactic reformulation of sentences using typed dependency representations. In *Proceedings of the 6th International Natural Language Generation Conference*, pages 125–133. Association for Computational Linguistics.

Advaith Siddharthan. 2014. A survey of research on text simplification. *ITL-International Journal of Applied Linguistics*, 165(2):259–298.

Hans Stadthagen-Gonzalez and Colin J Davis. 2006. The bristol norms for age of acquisition, imageability, and familiarity. *Behavior research methods*, 38(4):598–605.

University of Washington. 2012. Stopword.list. `http://courses.cs.washington.edu/courses/cse573/12sp/A2/`.

Grady Ward. 1993. Names.txt. `http://www.gutenberg.org/ebooks/3201`.

Martin Weisser. 2013. Iceweb. `http://martinweisser.org/ling_soft.html#iceweb`.

Mark Yatskar, Bo Pang, Cristian Danescu-Niculescu-Mizil, and Lillian Lee. 2010. For the sake of simplicity: Unsupervised extraction of lexical simplifications from wikipedia. In *Human Language Technologies: The 2010 Annual Conference of the North American Chapter of the Association for Computational Linguistics*, pages 365–368. Association for Computational Linguistics.

Discourse-Driven Narrative Generation with Bipartite Planning

David R. Winer and **R. Michael Young**
Department of Computer Science
North Carolina State University
`drwiner@ncsu.edu, rmyoung@ncsu.edu`

Abstract

During content planning, a typical discourse generation system receives as input a library of facts and selects facts to include as the content for utterances. However, storytellers do not need to be completely constrained by a set of facts and instead can invent facts which support the storytellers goals, subsequently constructing the storyworld around those facts. We present a discourse-driven approach to narrative generation leveraging automated planning which can interleave construction of story and discourse while preserving modularity.

Introduction

Artificial intelligence (AI) automated planning research (Ghallab et al., 2004) is a popular source of data structures and algorithms for understanding, generating, and reasoning about stories (Young et al., 2014). Narratologists frequently distinguish the fabula (i.e., story) of narrative from the discourse (e.g., the narration of the story to a spectator) (Genette and Lewin, 1983; Bruner, 1991; Herman, 2013), and plans have proven useful for modeling both story and discourse (Young, 2007); they are effective for modeling discourse because a coherent sequence of communicative actions is plan-like (Cohen and Perrault, 1979; Lambert and Carberry, 1991; Young and Moore, 1994), and plans are effective for modeling stories because stories are composed of events with cause-effect relations and characters also form plans to achieve their goals (Trabasso and Sperry, 1985; Riedl and Young,

2010). Behavioral research demonstrates that plans capture many key features that spectators use to understand narrative discourse (Trabasso and Sperry, 1985; Christian and Young, 2004; Ware et al., 2014; Radvansky et al., 2014; Cardona-Rivera et al., 2016).

A typical approach to discourse generation is to supply a program with a library of facts about the domain of interest from which to select content for utterances (Meteer, 1991; Reiter and Dale, 1997). *Narrative* discourse generation systems are usually no different (Lönneker, 2005; Callaway and Lester, 2002); story is generated to meet some user-provided goals (i.e., a *story plan* solves a *story problem*) and passed through a pipeline as input for generating discourse and narration (e.g., text or animation) to solve a *discourse problem* (Callaway and Lester, 2002; Young et al., 2004; Jhala and Young, 2010; Cheong and Young, 2015) (see also (Young et al., 2014)). This pipeline architecture is amenable to the task of generating different discourse plans about the same set of events.

However, analysis of these programs reveals that if there are story constraints associated with discourse planning operations, an input plan that solves a story problem may not meet those constraints needed to solve the discourse problem (i.e., the story plan is *incompatible* with the discourse goals), even though a compatible solution to the story problem exists. For example, to tell stories about characters who courageously navigate a dangerous terrain, one discourse action might be to convey that an obstacle, such as a bridge, is dangerous and has the constraint that some character dies at this obstacle; if the discourse planner receives as input a story where no character dies, the discourse planner would be unable to meet the discourse goal or subgoal to convey an obstacle is dangerous, even though in the space of possible stories, there exists at least one story where at least one character dies. The discourse plan may depend on describing the obstacle as dangerous as a causal antecedent for conveying that the main protagonist is in danger because the protagonist is at the obstacle. A planner which generates both story and discourse plans from story and discourse problems is considered *bipartite complete* if the planner will find a compatible pair of story and discourse solutions if one exists.

Storytellers needn't be completely limited by existing facts and can invent facts to support their storytelling goals, subsequently building the storyworld around those facts. For example, a screenwriter may add an event to the story (e.g., a non-central character slips to his death from a narrow bridge), in order to elicit a discourse effect (e.g., believing the bridge is a dangerous obstacle for the protagonist). Following this idea, our approach to narrative generation is discourse-driven; as a discourse planner constructs a discourse plan, constraints on the scenarios in the story are added to the story plan so that a story planner constructs a story plan which is compatible with the discourse plan. Our representation of planning formalisms enables constraints to be *flexible* (they need not completely specify the underlying scenario), *narrative theoretic* (they can refer to high-level phenomena such as character intentionality and conflict), and to be *path pruning* (they can speed up the search for a solution by limiting exploration to just those plans which are consistent with the constraints).

In most classic NLG systems, generation of both the story and discourse would fall under the task of content determination (Reiter and Dale, 1997). However, our criticism of the story-then-discourse pipeline architecture is reminiscent of past discussions on the drawbacks of using a modular pipeline in NLG systems (Reiter, 2000) such as the well-known "generation gap" between text planning and realization (Meteer, 1991). We introduce *bipartite planning* which preserves modularity of story and discourse, allowing users to plug in different story and discourse problems and potentially different generation systems, but which interleaves construction of story and discourse to enable bipartite completeness.

Related Work

Narrative planning benefits from a rich history of AI research. The first story generation system to use planning is TALESPIN (Meehan, 1977), which generates stories about woodland creatures that take actions to satisfy simple needs in accordance with rules of the world. Another early story generation system UNIVERSE (Lebowitz, 1983) represents plot fragments as plans and selects a fragment to execute if it satisfies an authorial goal. MINSTREL (Turner, 1993) uses planning to create an outline of a story and case-based reasoning to fill in details from a story library. Cavazza and colleagues use forward state-space character-centric planning but cannot guarantee authorial goal conditions are achieved (Cavazza et al., 2002; Porteous et al., 2010). Plan-space search is used as a top-down approach to story generation; a user specifies initial and goal states of a story world and the solution space is restricted to just those story plans which are causally sound (Young et al., 2014), and narrative-theoretic extensions (e.g., IPOCL (Riedl and Young, 2010) and CPOCL (Ware et al., 2014)) further limit the solution space just to plans where characters act believably.

Narrative discourse generation systems (NDGS) typically take story as input from a library of facts such as from a story planner or from collected data and produce a plan for narrating the story. STORYBOOK (Callaway and Lester, 2002) is an end-to-end narrative prose generation system with four parts: 1) a narrative organizer which takes as input a story plan, 2) a sentence planner which creates a proto-sentence outline, 3) a revision module which produces prose paragraphs from proto-sentences, and 4) a surface realizer which makes some grammatical edits and formats the story in a file. However, STORYBOOK expects decisions about discourse, such as the order to tell events or how to describe elements of the story, such as from a particular character perspective (focalization), to be provided as part of the input (in the story plan). A distinct discourse module for content determination has been proposed as an amendment to this architecture (Lönneker, 2005). This more closely mirrors the way narratologists partition narrative into story and discourse (Genette and Lewin, 1983; Young, 2007).

Later NDGSs have included a discourse content determination module which structures events in story plans provided as input. Suspenser (Cheong and Young, 2015) and Prevoyant (Bae and Young, 2014) systems arrange the events in a story into an ordering which elicits suspense or surprise, respectively, based on cognitive-computational definitions inspired by psychological theory). These systems first determine which events from the story are worth telling by measuring their causal importance (Young, 1999), and include less important events when they can help maximize a suspense/surprise function by increasing the distance between important events. Darshak (Jhala and Young, 2010) is a cinematic discourse generation system in which dramatic patterns decompose into camera shot patterns to convey events from an input story plan which are animated in a virtual environment. These systems use a discourse planner adapted from the DPOCL (decompositional) algorithm (Young et al., 1994).

One drawback about these systems is that the communicative actions are all *inform* speech acts (suspense and surprise decompose into inform actions) and lack representation for evaluative description (e.g., a *brave* character, an *honorable* action, a *dangerous* location, etc.). An interesting approach by Li, Thakker, Wang, and Riedl (2014) is to learn the most probable sentiment of a story word from a corpus of annotated words and from crowdsourced stories involving a similar scenario to the story. The words used in the text can then be replaced to make the story more descriptive and to reflect the mood of the scene. Our vision of discourse generation more closely aligns with the properties described by Grosz and Sidner (1986): discourse reasoning ought to be goal-oriented, such that descriptions causally enable subsequent descriptions about the story. Bae, Cheong, and Young (2011) produce narrative plans with focalization by using different plan libraries for different characters which have built-in descriptions of the story based on the character's persona. The events are reconstructed with the plan library

representing the character who's perspective the story is being told from. However, tailoring these descriptions for a particular story is time consuming, and a modular, domain-independent approach is preferred where a user can swap out description knowledge and tell the same kind of narrative with different storyworlds and characters.

Problem Formulation

Our discourse-driven narrative planning approach is a search for solutions to two problems, a story problem and discourse problem, where a solution is a plan of actions to bring an initial state to a goal state. At the story level, the solution represents the actions of characters in the storyworld, whereas at the discourse level, the solution represents the communicative actions by a narrator agent to inform and describe elements in the story to a spectator agent. A pair of compatible story and discourse solutions to story and discourse problems is a *bipartite solution*. With prior approaches to story and discourse generation, a story solution is supplied as input to a discourse planner. In this approach, elements in a story solution become required as part of the search for a discourse solution. These requirements are prerequisite criteria about the story for the story and discourse plans to be a bipartite solution to the story and discourse problems.

Narrative Plans

Partial-order causal link (POCL) planning is a type of *planning as refinement search* (Kambhampati et al., 1995), involving search through plan-space such that each child node in the search is a refinement to the (potentially flawed) plan represented at its parent node. Through an iterative process of identifying flaws in the plan and repairing them in a least-commitment manner (Weld, 1994), plans with no flaws are selected and returned as solutions to the planning task. A **planning problem** or task consists of an initial state, a set of goal conditions, a set of action types, and a set of logical **constants**; in a storyworld, constants are characters, items, and locations, whereas at the discourse level, constants refer to elements of the story (e.g. a character, a character's plan, a conflict, etc.).

Figure 1 Example story action operators and planning problem

```
                 Miniature Story Planning Problem

"move" story operator
variables = {                        Constants: Indy, Sapito,
    ?c - character                   cliff1, cliff2, bridge
    ?from ?to - location}            Operators:{
precond(move, (at ?c ?from))             move,
precond(move, (adj ?from ?to))           fall-from}
precond(move, (alive ?c))            Initial: {
effect(move, (at ?c ?to))                (at Indy cliff1),
effect(move, ¬(at ?c ?from))             (at Sapito cliff1),
                                         (adj cliff1 bridge),
"fall-from" story operator               (adj bridge cliff2),
variables = {                            (intends Sapito
    ?c - character                           (at Sapito cliff2)),
    ?from - location}                    (intends Indy
precond(fall-from, (at ?c ?from))            (at Indy cliff2))}
precond(fall-from, (high-up ?from)) Goal: {
precond(fall-from, (alive ?c))           (at Indy cliff2),
effect(fall-from, ¬(alive ?c))           (alive Indy)}
effect(fall-from, ¬(at ?c ?from))
```

Action Operators

STRIPS-style **operators** (Fikes and Nilsson, 1972) depict action types that can occur, and a **step** is an instance of an action operator. Each operator has **preconditions**, describing what must be true for the step to occur, and **effects**, representing how the world will change after the step occurs. Preconditions and effects are described in a language of function-free first-order predicate literals. These literals have variables which must be assigned to constants in the planning problem. For instance, consider a story action operator type "fall-from" which may be found in a story problem (see Figure 1). The operator has variables ?character and ?from, preconditions that ?character is at ?from, ?character is alive, and that ?from is high-up, and effects that ?character is not at ?from and is not alive, reflecting the change in the world after the action executes. Figure 1 shows two example action operators written in a format amenable for understanding operations we discuss later.

At the discourse level, the world state is a conjunction of literals indicating what a spectator agent believes is true and not true about the story (denoted with *bel* before the believed literal). Discourse actions are communicative actions taken by a narrator agent to add or remove the spectator's beliefs. In addition to preconditions and effects, discourse action operators have **requirements** and **restrictions** on the variables used in its preconditions and effects. A discourse action cannot be used if one of its set of restrictions are detected in the story, and the story plan is considered incompatible if any set of restrictions from discourse actions are detected during its construction. When a discourse action is used as a step in a discourse plan, the requirements are matched to existing elements of the story plan and/or are added to the story plan.

When the variable in a requirement is a step in the story plan, the step might only be partially defined, called a **partial step**. The planner must select some action operator which is consistent with the step and its requirements and add components to the partial step so that the step is an instance of the operator. For example, a discourse action to convey that a location is dangerous (see Figure 2) has the requirements that some story action occurs with the precondition that a character is at this location and the effect that this character is not alive. The fall-from action operator (see Figure 1) would be considered consistent with these requirements. The rest of this step would be added to the story plan such as the preconditions that the location is high-up and the character is alive (see Figure 3). At some point, the variable representing the high-up location would be assigned to a constant from the story problem with the desired property, such as the bridge. Figure 2 shows two example discourse operators including the example discussed here.

The variable in a discourse action can have a type associated with any element of a story plan, such as a variable, step, set of steps, ordering of steps, causal link between steps, character plan, character goal, etc. This enables discourse actions to post requirements and restrictions about many aspects of the story and thus enables a wide range of descriptions to be readily supported in discourse actions. Each discourse action could also include communicative actions (e.g., camera shots, text operators, etc) that are designed by artists/writers to narrate the story content, similar to the design in DARSHAK (Jhala and Young, 2010) in which the communicative effects of a scene are decomposed into primitive camera shots.

Causal Soundness

Each plan has one placeholder **start step** whose effects express the initial state, and one placeholder **end step** whose only preconditions are the goal conditions that must be true at the end of the plan. All steps in a solution are goal-oriented; each step's

Figure 2 Example discourse action operators and planning problem

```
                Miniature Discourse Planning Problem

Constants: hero
Operators:{                      "convey-in-danger"
    convey-danger-at,              variables:(
    convey-in-danger}                ?hero ?c - actor
Init: None                           ?dloc - variable
Goal: (bel-in-danger hero)           ?move ?dstep - step)
                                   precondition: (
"convey-danger-at"                     bel-danger-at ?dloc ?dstep)
  variables:(                      effect: (bel-in-danger ?hero)
    ?death - step,                 requirements: {
    ?victim - actor                  ordering(?dstep, ?move),
    ?loc - variable)                 effect(?move, (at ?hero ?dloc))}
  precondition: None               restrictions={ exists ?m2 (
  effect:                            effect(?m2, ¬(at ?c ?dloc) and
    (bel-danger-at ?loc ?death)      not-effect(?m2, ¬(alive ?c)) and
  requirements: {                    ordering(?m2, ?move))}
    effect(?death, ¬(alive ?victim)),
    precond(?death, (at ?victim ?loc))}
```

preconditions are causally linked to one or more effects from prior steps. A **causal link** between steps s and t, denoted $s \xrightarrow{p} t$, indicates that s has an effect p which co-designates with a precondition p of step t. Step s is an *ancestor* of step t, and t is a *descendant* of step s. A step's *causal ancestors* are all steps in the transitive closure of the ancestor relationship. A step's *causal descendants* are all steps in the transitive closure of the descendant relationship.

A precondition which is not yet make true by another step (i.e., an **open precondition flaw**) is resolved by finding an action operator which has an effect that can become the needed precondition. When a step can possibly undo one of the effects of a prior step which is needed as a precondition of a later step (i.e., a **threatened causal link flaw**), the planner attempts to reorder steps or add constraints to the steps involved so that no conflict can arise. The plan is *causally sound* just when for every total ordering of steps, each step's preconditions are met when that step is executed.

Intentional Coherence

Another requirement adopted for story plans is that each character should only intentionally take actions which can be explained as part of a character plan to achieve one of that character's goals. An **intention frame** includes the elements needed to represent why a character adopts a goal and her actions to achieve it. It is a tuple $\langle a, g, m, s_f, S_f \rangle$ where a is an actor, g is some literal that a wishes to make true, m is a motivating step whose effects include $intends(a, g)$, s_f is the satisfying step whose effects include g, and S_f is a subplan for a to satisfy g such that all steps in S_f are causal ancestors of s_f and have the consent of a. An action which does not require a "volunteer", such as an accident or a force of nature, is called a **happening**. The solution is considered *intentionally coherent* just when when all voluntary actions are part of a character's intention frame. Characters do not always achieve their goals and may take the first n steps of the subplan. For example, a character a may not finish a plan because some other step undoes one of the effects of a step that a took to enable a subsequent step. The different ways that a character's plan can become thwarted by another step has been studied in prior work as a definition of narrative conflict (Ware et al., 2014). In story problems supporting character intentionality, characters either have goals in the initial state or adopt goals as the effects of actions taken in the story (e.g., a character who finds a treasure map might adopt the goal to have the treasure).

Solution

To solve the planning problems (one story problem and one discourse problem), the planner iteratively selects flaws from either plan and selects some method to resolve the flaw. The solutions are plans: a plan is a tuple $\langle S, B, O, L \rangle$ where S is a set of steps, B is a set of bindings between variables in S, O is a set of ordering constraints overs steps in S, and L is a set of causal links between steps in S. The plan is *valid* just when the plan is causally sound and all constants have an assigned variable. Additionally, story plans include a set of character intention frames. The story plan is *valid* just when the base plan is valid plus the plan is intentionally coherent and all variables are assigned to a constant[1]. The two plans are structurally similar but conceptually distinct. In the story plan, the steps are actions taken by characters. In the discourse plan, steps are communicative actions taken by a narrator agent to add or remove the spectator's beliefs. Once a compatible pair of solutions are constructed, the

---

[1]Stories are limited by the constants provided as input, whereas discourse variables may refer to elements created during story planning

Figure 3 Partial story step (and discourse variable) ?death in the discourse action "convey-danger-at" becomes an instance of the "fall-from" operator in the story plan. The solid arrows indicate which requirements are matched to elements of "fall-from". The hollow arrows indicate which elements of the operator are added to the requirements, so that ?death becomes an instance of "fall-from".

```
        "fall-from" story operator              "convey-danger-at" requirements
     precond(fall-from, (at ?c ?from))      precond(?death, (at ?victim ?loc))
     precond(fall-from, (high-up ?from))    effect(?death, ¬(alive ?victim))
     precond(fall-from, (alive ?c))         precond(?death, (high-up ?loc))
     effect(fall-from, ¬(alive ?c))         precond(?death, (alive ?victim))
     effect(fall-from, ¬(at ?c ?from))      effect(?death, ¬(at ?victim ?loc))

          bindings: <?loc = ?from>, <?victim = ?c>, <?death = fall-from>
```

solutions can be sent down the NLG pipeline to be realized as text or some in some other medium. For instance, the story could be used to animate avatars in a virtual world and the discourse actions could be mapped to camera actions to film the events.

Algorithm

The bipartite planning algorithm **BiPOCL** for generating story and discourse solutions to story and discourse problems is presented in Algorithm 1. In discourse planning (lines 3-8), flaws are added for requirements needed in the story plan. Story planning (lines 9-14) involves a combination of approaches from prior work (Riedl and Young, 2010; Ware, 2014) which are not provided in detail here (such as those involving intention frames). In addition, story planning involves selecting requirements to add to the story plan and partial steps in the story plan to make into instances of story action operators. Threats to causal links (lines 15-19) are resolved, with the exception that some threats are okay to leave in the story plan if they can represent conflict. The algorithm terminates when bindings or orderings are inconsistent in either plan, or when there are no flaws in either plan.

Example: The Dangerous Bridge

To help explain the bipartite planning approach to narrative generation, a miniature example is presented consisting of story and discourse problems and a bipartite solution. The story domain and problem for this example is inspired by Indiana Jones (see Figure 1). Agents in this domain can move between adjacent locations and fall by accident from high locations. The discourse problem contains actions for describing story elements as dangerous

(see Figure 2). The discourse action "convey-danger-at" describes a location as dangerous by virtue that some character dies as a consequence of being at this location. The discourse action "convey-in-danger" describes a character as being in danger by virtue that this character is at a dangerous location (precondition, requirement), and no other character before this has safely moved from this location and left without dying (restriction). Both problems are provided as input by users.

An instance of a bipartite solution to the story and discourse problems is presented in Figure 4. Space limitations prevent us from including figures to demonstrate the construction of this solution. For details on the construction of intention frames, see (Ware, 2014). To start, the BiPOCL is called with the initial plans, each containing a start and end step. In the story plan, there are two empty intention frames motivated by the start step which must explain how Indy and Sapito will achieve their goal to be across the bridge at cliff2. Open precondition flaws are added for every goal condition of both plans. Flaws can be selected in any order.

The open precondition `(at Indy cliff2)` is repaired by adding a causal link from a new step `move Indy bridge cliff2` which has the new open precondition `(at Indy bridge)` (the bridge is the only location adjacent to cliff2). The open precondition that `(bel-in-danger hero)` is repaired by adding a causal link from a new step `convey-in-danger hero` which has new open precondition `(bel-danger-at ?dloc)`. The requirements for this discourse action can be added to the story immediately or at some later iteration. The story action `move Indy bridge`

Algorithm 1 The BiPOCL (Bipartite Partial Order Causal Link) Algorithm

 1: **Termination**: If either plan is inconsistent, backtrack. Otherwise, return the plans.
 2: **Plan Refinement**: Non-deterministically select a flaw in either plan
 3:     **Discourse Planning:**
 4:         Choose a precondition of a step not yet established through a causal link and either:
 5:             **Reuse:** Find a step which already establishes the precondition.
 6:             **New:** Create the step from an operator which establishes the precondition.
 7:                 Add flaws for the step's requirements which need to be added to the story.
 8:         Add a causal link between the new/old step and the step with the precondition.
 9:     **Story Planning:** Do one of the following:
10:         Choose a flaw in the story and resolve with associated refinement method.
11:         Choose a discourse requirement not yet added to the story, and either:
12:             **Reuse:** Find a story element which already satisfies the requirement.
13:             **New:** Create the requirement and add it to the plan.
14:         Choose a partial step, select a consistent action operator, and add the step's missing components.
15: **Threat Resolution:**
16:     Find a step which may threaten to undo a causal link. Choose how to prevent the threat:
17:         **Promotion:** If possible, move the threatened steps to occur before the threat in the plan.
18:         **Demotion:** If possible, move the threatened steps to occur after the threat in the plan.
19:         **Restriction:** If possible, add constraints to the steps involved so that no conflict can arise.
20: **Recursive Invocation** Call the planner recursively with the new plan structure.

Figure 4 On the left is a discourse plan; boxes are discourse steps, arrows are causal links, and variables of interest are in ovals. On the right is a compatible story plan; boxes are steps, a dashed arrow is a threatened causal link, a solid arrow is a causal link, a dotted bounding box is an intention frame, the source of a hollow arrow is a motivating step and the sink is an intention frame, the dashed box in an intention frame indicates a step not taken (but which completes the character's plan), and an oval surrounds an element bound to the labeled discourse variable.

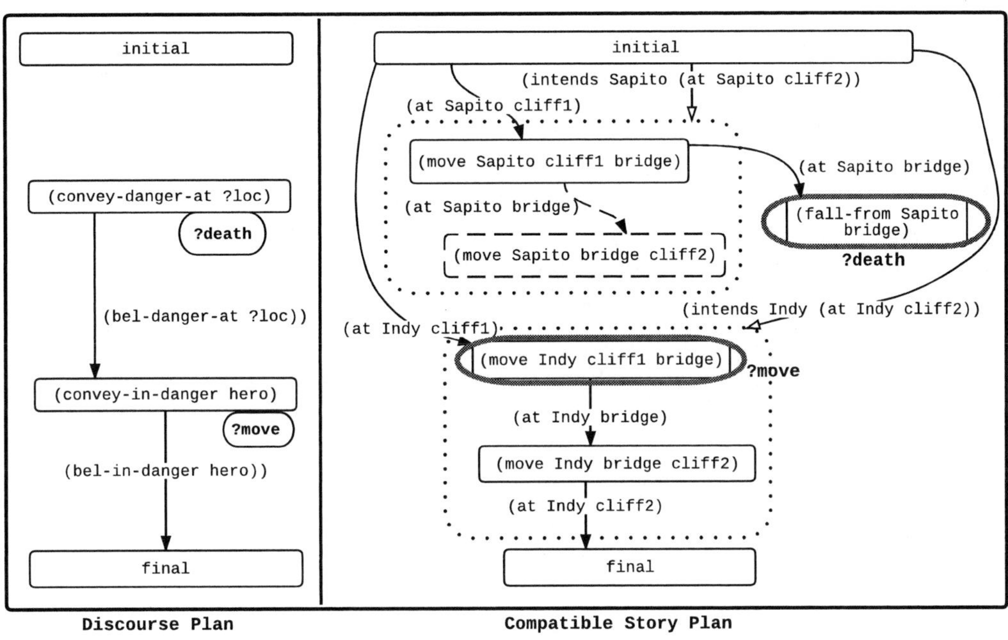

`cliff2` is a candidate for discourse variable ?move, making the dangerous location (?dloc) cliff2. The search would fail in this case because in our miniature universe, there exists no action that can bring death to a character at cliff2 (since cliff2 is not high-up). Alternatively, a new partial step could be added to the story plan, leaving the location yet unspecified. The partial step is only consistent with the "move" operator, creating step instance `move ?c ?from ?to` which floats in the plan ordered between the start and end steps. The open precondition `(at Indy bridge)` can be repaired by adding a causal link from this floating step, which becomes `move Indy ?from bridge`. The open precondition flaw for this step can be repaired by adding a causal link from the start step with effect `(at Indy cliff1)`, transforming the required step into `move Indy cliff1 bridge`. Since this step is bound to the discourse variable ?move, the bridge is the dangerous location ?dloc.

The open precondition `(bel-danger-at bridge)` (since now ?dloc=`bridge`) is repaired by a causal link from new step `convey-danger-at bridge`. Its requirement is that ?death is a step ordered before ?move (via binding to variable ?dstep in `convey-in-danger`) with the effect that ?victim is not alive. Only Sapito is a valid candidate to be ?victim. The requirement can be fulfilled by adding step `fall-from Sapito bridge`. Sapito's plan to be at cliff2 can be constructed like Indy's. Either Sapito can cross the bridge to cliff2 (fulfilling his goal) and then move back to the bridge, or he can get to the bridge and fall there without ever completing the goal. There is a restriction about the bridge from action `convey-in-danger` that no character can move from the bridge alive if that move occurs before Indy's action of moving to the bridge. Thus, Sapito must fall from the bridge without reaching cliff2.

Some of the relationships between discourse variables and story elements are marked in the figure. The bindings between discourse variables and story elements include ⟨hero, `Indy`⟩, ⟨?victim, `Sapito`⟩, ⟨?loc, `bridge`⟩, ⟨?move, `move Indy cliff1 bridge`⟩, and ⟨?death, `fall-from Sapito bridge`⟩.

The resulting narrative is that Sapito tries to cross the bridge but accidentally falls and dies so that the spectator believes the bridge is dangerous. Then, Indy moves to the bridge so that we believe he is in danger. Finally Indy safely crosses the bridge and achieves his goal. Medium-specific realization depends on system goals and can be as simple as filling slots in templates associated with discourse actions.

Discussion and Future Work

Typically, NDGSs accept as input a set of propositions or a database of facts from which to select for utterances in a communicative plan and are not bipartite complete. Our discourse-driven approach is likely bipartite complete because requirements limit the solution space for stories during discourse plan refinement rather than limiting the solution space for discourse plans during discourse plan refinement, avoiding the possibility for inconsistencies between requirements and existing story elements.

We call our narrative generation approach *discourse-driven* because the propositions about the domain of facts (i.e., the story world and character actions) are created to support the storyteller's goals. This shift of responsibility is appropriate for storytelling where an author/narrator may not be reporting on real events and instead invents scenarios for her characters to elicit a desired effect. With our approach, a story generation system accommodates these scenarios in a causally sound and intentionally coherent world. We presented an example motivated by Indiana Jones where the narrative planner adds an event to the story level (i.e., a non-central character slips off a bridge), in order to construe the bridge as dangerous.

Prior approaches to discourse planning have focusing on what order to inform events to a spectator (presentation order), rather than on describing events in a goal-oriented way. Research on discourse comprehension demonstrates that causal reasoning is biased by the recency of narrative events in text, which may have implications for timing (Winer et al., 2015) and recallability of events (Cardona-Rivera et al., 2012). Bipartite planning could set up good timing through a specification of minimum distances between steps in a story that are relevant for the discourse plan, or by structuring parallel plot lines to enable juxtaposition editing.

The story-then-discourse approach may not be well suited for "description planning" because it is unlikely that the propositions provided as input to the discourse planner contain the scenario or context needed for a particular description to be applicable. Our approach depends on the assumption that descriptions can have causal relationships, an assumption that ought to be evaluated empirically. In prior work, generated story plans have been automatically mapped to a psychological model of question-answering and shown to have representational accuracy on some key question types (Christian and Young, 2004; Cardona-Rivera et al., 2016). This model may be extended to include question types about a spectator's interpretation via information described at the discourse level. For example, if a story element is evidence for some belief (e.g., the death of Sapito is evidence that the bridge is dangerous), then our model may predict which elements of the story ought to be used to justify that belief (e.g., *Q*: "When did you begin to believe that the bridge is dangerous?" *A*: "When Sapito fell from the bridge.").

References

Byung-Chull Bae and R Michael Young. 2014. A computational model of narrative generation for surprise arousal. *Computational Intelligence and AI in Games, IEEE Transactions on*, 6(2):131–143.

Byung-Chull Bae, Yun-Gyung Cheong, and R Michael Young. 2011. Automated story generation with multiple internal focalization. In *2011 IEEE Conference on Computational Intelligence and Games (CIG'11)*, pages 211–218. IEEE.

Jerome Bruner. 1991. The narrative construction of reality. *Critical inquiry*, pages 1–21.

Charles B Callaway and James C Lester. 2002. Narrative prose generation. *Artificial Intelligence*, 139(2):213–252.

Rogelio E Cardona-Rivera, Bradley A Cassell, Stephen G Ware, and R Michael Young. 2012. Indexter: A computational model of the event-indexing situation model for characterizing narratives. In *The Workshop on Computational Models of Narrative at the Language Resources and Evaluation Conference*, pages 32–41.

Rogelio E Cardona-Rivera, Thomason Price, David R Winer, and R Michael Young. 2016. Question answering in the context of stories generated by computers. *Journal of Advances in Cognitive Systems.*

Marc Cavazza, Fred Charles, and Steven J Mead. 2002. Character-based interactive storytelling. *IEEE Intelligent systems.*

Yun-Gyung Cheong and R Michael Young. 2015. Suspenser: A story generation system for suspense. *Computational Intelligence and AI in Games, IEEE Transactions on*, 7(1):39–52.

David B Christian and R Michael Young. 2004. Comparing cognitive and computational models of narrative structure. In *AAAI*, pages 385–390.

Philip R Cohen and C Raymond Perrault. 1979. Elements of a plan-based theory of speech acts. *Cognitive science*, 3(3):177–212.

Richard E Fikes and Nils J Nilsson. 1972. Strips: A new approach to the application of theorem proving to problem solving. *Artificial intelligence*, 2(3):189–208.

Gérard Genette and Jane E Lewin. 1983. *Narrative discourse: An essay in method.* Cornell University Press.

Malik Ghallab, Dana Nau, and Paolo Traverso. 2004. *Automated planning: theory & practice.* Elsevier.

Barbara J Grosz and Candace L Sidner. 1986. Attention, intentions, and the structure of discourse. *Computational linguistics*, 12(3):175–204.

David Herman. 2013. *Storytelling and the Sciences of Mind.* MIT press.

Arnav Jhala and R Michael Young. 2010. Cinematic visual discourse: Representation, generation, and evaluation. *Computational Intelligence and AI in Games, IEEE Transactions on*, 2(2):69–81.

Subbarao Kambhampati, Craig A Knoblock, and Qiang Yang. 1995. Planning as refinement search: A unified framework for evaluating design tradeoffs in partial-order planning. *Artificial Intelligence*, 76(1):167–238.

Lynn Lambert and Sandra Carberry. 1991. A tripartite plan-based model of dialogue. In *Proceedings of the 29th annual meeting on Association for Computational Linguistics*, pages 47–54. Association for Computational Linguistics.

Michael Lebowitz. 1983. Creating a story-telling universe. *Proceedings of the Eighth International Joint Conference on Artifiial intelligence*, 1:63–65.

Boyang Li, Mohini Thakkar, Yijie Wang, and Mark O Riedl. 2014. Data-driven alibi story telling for social believability. *Social Believability in Games.*

Birte Lönneker. 2005. Narratological knowledge for natural language generation. In *Proceedings of the 10th European Workshop on Natural Language Generation (ENLG-05)*, pages 91–100. Citeseer.

James R Meehan. 1977. Tale-spin, an interactive program that writes stories. In *IJCAI*, volume 77, pages 91–98.

Marie W Meteer. 1991. Bridging the generation gap between text planning and linguistic realization. *Computational Intelligence*, 7(4):296–304.

Julie Porteous, Marc Cavazza, and Fred Charles. 2010. Applying planning to interactive storytelling: Narrative control using state constraints. *ACM Transactions on Intelligent Systems and Technology (TIST)*, 1(2):10.

Gabriel A Radvansky, Andrea K Tamplin, Joseph Armendarez, and Alexis N Thompson. 2014. Different kinds of causality in event cognition. *Discourse Processes*, 51(7):601–618.

Ehud Reiter and Robert Dale. 1997. Building applied natural language generation systems. *Natural Language Engineering*, 3(01):57–87.

Ehud Reiter. 2000. Pipelines and size constraints. *Computational Linguistics*, 26(2):251–259.

Mark O Riedl and R Michael Young. 2010. Narrative planning: Balancing plot and character. *Journal of Artificial Intelligence Research*, 39(1):217–268.

Tom Trabasso and Linda L Sperry. 1985. Causal relatedness and importance of story events. *Journal of Memory and language*, 24(5):595–611.

Scott R Turner. 1993. Minstrel: a computer model of creativity and storytelling.

Stephen G Ware, R Michael Young, Brent Harrison, and David L Roberts. 2014. A computational model of plan-based narrative conflict at the fabula level. *Computational Intelligence and AI in Games, IEEE Transactions on*, 6(3):271–288.

Stephen G Ware. 2014. *A Plan-Based Model of Conflict for Narrative Reasoning and Generation*. North Carolina State University.

Daniel S Weld. 1994. An introduction to least commitment planning. *AI magazine*, 15(4):27.

David R. Winer, Adam A. Amos-Binks, Camille Barot, and R. Michael Young. 2015. Good Timing for Computational Models of Narrative Discourse. In *6th Workshop on Computational Models of Narrative (CMN 2015)*, volume 45, pages 152–156.

R Michael Young and Johanna D Moore. 1994. Dpocl: A principled approach to discourse planning. In *Proceedings of the Seventh International Workshop on Natural Language Generation*, pages 13–20. Association for Computational Linguistics.

R Michael Young, Martha E Pollack, and Johanna D Moore. 1994. Decomposition and causality in partial-order planning. In *AIPS*, pages 188–194.

R Michael Young, Mark O Riedl, Mark Branly, Arnav Jhala, RJ Martin, and CJ Saretto. 2004. An architecture for integrating plan-based behavior generation with interactive game environments. *Journal of Game Development*, 1(1):51–70.

R Michael Young, SG Ware, BA Cassell, and Justus Robertson. 2014. Plans and planning in narrative generation: a review of plan-based approaches to the generation of story, discourse and interactivity in narratives. *SDV. Sprache und Datenverarbeitung.*

R Michael Young. 1999. Using grice's maxim of quantity to select the content of plan descriptions. *Artificial Intelligence*, 115(2):215–256.

R Michael Young. 2007. Story and discourse: A bipartite model of narrative generation in virtual worlds. *Interaction Studies*, 8(2):177–208.

Generating English from Abstract Meaning Representations

Nima Pourdamghani , Kevin Knight , Ulf Hermjakob
Information Sciences Institute
Department of Computer Science
University of Southern California
`{damghani,knight,ulf}@isi.edu`

Abstract

We present a method for generating English sentences from Abstract Meaning Representation (AMR) graphs, exploiting a parallel corpus of AMRs and English sentences. We treat AMR-to-English generation as phrase-based machine translation (PBMT). We introduce a method that learns to linearize tokens of AMR graphs into an English-like order. Our linearization reduces the amount of distortion in PBMT and increases generation quality. We report a Bleu score of 26.8 on the standard AMR/English test set.

1 Introduction

Banarescu et al. (2013) introduce Abstract Meaning Representation (AMR) graphs to represent sentence level semantics. Human annotators have created a dataset of more than $10,000$ AMR/English string pairs.

AMRs are directed acyclic graphs, where leaves are labeled with concepts, internal nodes are labeled with variables representing instances of those concepts, and edges are labeled with roles that relate pairs of concepts. For instance, the sentence *The boy wants to go* is represented as:

```
(w :instance-of want-01
    :arg0 (b :instance-of boy)
    :arg1 (g :instance-of go-01
            :arg0 b))
```

Colons discriminate roles from concepts. In this paper, *:instance-of* is our way of writing the slash (/) found in the AMR corpus.

Because AMR and English are highly cognate, the AMR-to-English generation problem might seem similar to previous natural language generation (NLG) problems such as bag generation (Brown et al., 1990), restoring order to unordered dependency trees (Guo et al., 2011) or generation from logical form (Corston-Oliver et al., 2002). However, AMR's deeper logic provides a serious challenge for English realization. AMR also abstracts away details of time, number, and voice, which must be inserted.

Langkilde and Knight (1998) introduced Nitrogen, which used a precursor of AMR for generating English. Recently, Flanigan et al. (2016) presented the first trained AMR-to-English generator. They generate spanning trees from AMR graphs and apply tree-to-string transducers to the trees to generate English.

We attack AMR-to-English generation using the tools of phrase-based machine translation (PBMT). PBMT has already been applied to natural language generation from simple semantic structures (Mairesse et al., 2010), but deep semantic representations such as AMR are more challenging to deal with. PBMT expects strings for its source and target languages, so we cannot work with AMR graphs as input. Therefore, we develop a method that *learns to linearize AMR graphs* into AMR strings. Our linearization strives to put AMR tokens roughly into English word order, making the transformation to English easier.

It may seem surprising that we ignore much of the structure of AMR, but we follow string-based statistical MT, which ignored much of the structure of

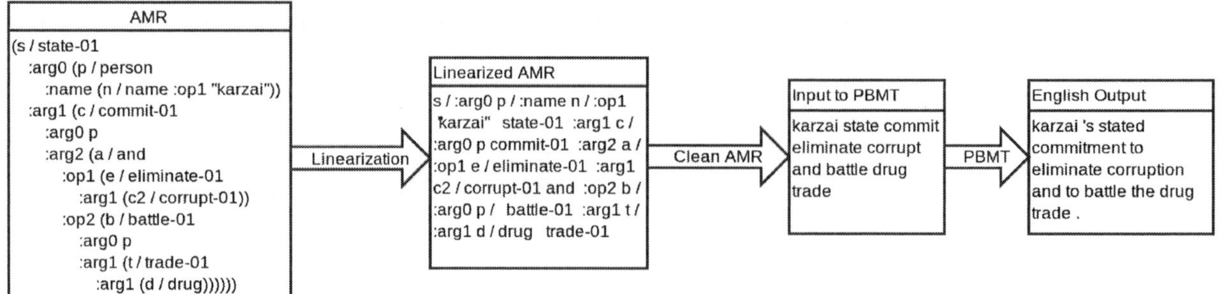

Figure 1: AMR-to-English generation pipeline.

language but nonetheless provided a strong baseline.

Figure 1 shows our pipeline for generating English from AMR. Our contributions are:

1. We present a strong baseline method for AMR-to-English generation.
2. We introduce a method that learns to linearize AMR tokens into an order resembling English.
3. We obtain a Bleu score of 26.8 on the standard AMR/English test set, which is 4.9 points higher than previous work.

2 Method

Given a set of AMR/English pairs, divided into train, development, and test sets, we follow these steps:

Construct token-level alignments: We use the method proposed in (Pourdamghani et al., 2014) to construct alignments between AMR and English tokens in the training set.

Extend training data: We use special realization components for names, dates, and numbers found in the dev/test sets, adding their results to the training corpus.

Linearize AMR graphs: We learn to convert AMR graphs into AMR strings in a way that linearized AMR tokens have an English-like order (Section 3).

Clean AMR strings: We remove variables, quote marks, and sense tags from linearized AMRs. We also remove *-quantity and *-entity concepts, plus these roles: *:op**, *:snt**, *:arg0*, *:arg1*, *:arg2*, *:name*, *:quant*, *:unit*, *:value*, *:year*, *:domain-of*.

Phrase-Based Machine Translation: We use Moses (Koehn et al., 2007) to train and tune a PBMT system on string/string training data. We then use this system to produce English realizations from linearized development and test AMRs.

3 Linearization

When we linearize AMR, we would like—at a minimum—for semantically-related tokens to stay close together. A straightforward, pre-order depth first search (DFS) accomplishes this (Pourdamghani et al., 2014). For instance, linearizing

```
(w :instance-of want-01
    :arg0 (b :instance-of boy)
    :arg1 (g :instance-of go-01
            :arg0 b))
```

yields "*w :instance-of **want-01** :arg0 b :instance-of boy :arg1 g :instance-of **go-01** :arg0 b*".

Of course, we are free to visit AMR sister nodes in any order. For instance, if we visit sisters in order *(:arg0, :instance-of, :arg1)*, we get this string instead: "*w :arg0 b :instance-of **boy** :instance-of **want-01** :arg1 g :instance-of **go-01** :arg0 b*", which more resembles English word order.

We therefore induce an ordering function that takes any set of edge labels as input and produces a permutation of those labels. We call this the *linearization function*.

The input to this function is a sequence consisting of the concept under the *:instance-of* edge (e.g., *want-01*) followed by the other edges sorted alphabetically (e.g., *:arg0 :arg1*). The output is a permutation of the input (e.g., *(2, 1, 3)*).

Because *:instance-of* concepts often have no equivalent in English, e.g.:

```
(n :instance-of name
    :op1 "Pierre"        -> Pierre Vinken
    :op2 "Vinken")
```

we additionally allow the first component of the output to be "-1", indicating deletion.

Our linearization function therefore has the following form:

$$p : \{c, r_1, r_2, ..., r_{k-1}\} \rightarrow (\pi_1, \pi_2, ..., \pi_k) \qquad (1)$$

where c is a concept token, r_i are role tokens, $\pi_{i>1} \in \{1, 2, ..., k\}$ and $\pi_1 \in \{-1, 1, 2, ..., k\}$.

Here are sample input/output pairs for the linearization function:

```
(want-01, :arg0, :arg1) -> (2, 1, 3)
(name, :op1, :op2) -> (-1, 1, 2)
(and, :op1, :op2) -> (2, 1, 3)
(area-quantity, :quant, :unit) -> (-1, 1, 2)
(win-01, :arg0, :arg1, :time) -> (2, 1, 3, 4)
```

Our overall objective is to minimize the number of crossings in the alignment links after linearization. We use our token-aligned AMR/English data to produce training examples for the function (1). We assign each outgoing AMR edge a position equal to the median of the alignment points of all tokens in its subtree, including the edge itself. We assign -1 to an edge if none of its subtree tokens are aligned. Then we extract all sets of sibling edges in the AMR graph, and sort them based on these numbers. We use these sorted sets to create training instances.

We now describe three linearization methods.

3.1 Pre-order DFS

This baseline method linearizes AMR by simple pre-order traversal, ignoring the data just described.

3.2 Majority Method

The majority method memorizes the most common order for each role set in the data. If no match is found, we use the ordering given in the original, human-annotated AMR, with the *:instance-of* edge first.

3.3 Classifier Method

The classifier method breaks the problem into learning three binary classifiers over inputs of the form $(c, r_1, r_2, ..., r_{k-1})$:

1. Should the *:instance-of* edge be dropped?
   - Features: k, c, (c, r_i), whether c is a Propbank frameset, and whether c is a "special keyword" as defined by Banarescu et al. (2013).
2. Should edge r_i appear before *:instance-of*?
   - Features: r_i, (c, r_i), (r_i, r_j) for all $j \neq i$
3. Should edge r_i appear before r_j?
   - Features: (c, r_i, r_j)

We use the toolkit of Zhang (2004) to learn a maximum entropy classifier for each task.

	AMR/English pairs	English word tokens
Train	10,313	218,021
Dev	1,368	29,848
Test	1,371	30,263

Table 1: Data for AMR-to-English generation.

After training, for a given input query, we consult the first classifier on whether or not to drop the *:instance-of* edge.

If we drop this edge, we consider the rest of the edges as one group; otherwise, we divide them into two groups each appearing on one side of the *:instance-of* edge, using the second classifier.

Next, we order the edges within each group. Let $P(r_i < r_j)$ be the probability—according to the third classifier—that r_i precedes r_j. For each edge r_i, we assign it a "left-leaning" score, which is the product of all $P(r_i < r_j)$, for all $j \neq i$. We remove the edge with the highest left-leaning score. We then recursively process the remaining edges in the group.

We were inspired by Lerner and Petrov (2013) to break the problem down this way. Because their dependencies are ordered, while our AMRs edges are not, we defined a different set of features and classifiers.

4 Experiments

We use AMR/English data from the AMR 1.0 corpus,[1] along with the provided train/development/test split (Table 1).

We implement the method of Pourdamghani et al. (2014) to construct alignments for the training set. We train the linearization function introduced in Section 3 on the aligned training set and use it to re-linearize that training set, maintaining the alignment links. This gives us aligned string-to-string training data for PBMT. We use the same trained linearization function to linearize development and test AMRs.

To measure the quality of linearization, we make calculations on the development set, using alignments to references (these alignments are used only for this experiment, and not for decoding).

A good linearization function should: (a) reduce the number of crossings in the alignment links, and (b) correctly identify concepts to be dropped.

---

[1] LDC Catalog number 2014T12.

	Crossings	Adj. crossings
Pre-order DFS	46671	7409
Majority Method	33772 (72%)	4850 (65%)
Classifier Method	35603 (76%)	4015 (54%)

Table 2: Total alignment crossings, and crossings between adjacent links after linearizing development AMRs with different methods. Numbers in parentheses show the reduction compared to Pre-order DFS.

	Dev Bleu	Test Bleu
1: Pre-order DFS	17.7	16.6
1a: 1 + clean AMRs	21.6	21.0
1b: 1a + name/number/date	23.5	22.5
2: Majority Method	26.5	25.6
3: Classifier Method	27.2	26.9
Flanigan et al. (2016)	22.7	22.0

Table 3: Results for AMR-to-English generation on development and test data. Experiments 2 and 3 include cleaning AMRs and name/number/date translations. Bleu scores are single-reference, case insensitive, $\{1..4\}$-grams.

Table 2 shows the total number of crossings and number of crossings between adjacent alignment links after linearizing development AMRs with the three methods introduced in Section 3. Both advanced methods highly reduce the number of crossings. The Classifier Method reduces the number of adjacent crossings much more than the Majority Method, helping to enhance locality. End-to-end experiments (Table 3) show that the Classifier Method outperforms the Majority Method in improving Bleu score.

With respect to concept dropping, 97% of the concepts dropped by the Classifier Method are in fact not aligned, and the method correctly drops 87% of the unaligned concepts.

Next, we use the Moses (Koehn et al., 2007) system for our PBMT implementation. Phrase extraction, limited to maximum phrase length 9, yields 1.2m phrase pairs. We use a 5-gram language model trained on 1.7b tokens of Gigaword English. We use MERT for tuning, and we decode linearized AMRs into English with a maximum stack size of 1000.

Table 3 shows our results. We find that better linearization methods lead to better Bleu scores. The Majority Method outperforms Pre-order DFS by 3.1 Bleu on test data, and the Classifier Method adds another 1.2 Bleu. We also find that steps of cleaning

and specialized name/number/date generators significantly improve Bleu. Compared to (Flanigan et al., 2016) our best system achives 4.5 Bleu points improvement on dev and 4.9 points improvement on test data.

Here is a small-sized input/output example from the automatic AMR-to-English generation system:

Input AMR:

```
(s / state-01
  :arg0 (p / person
    :name (n / name :op1 "fan"))
  :arg1 (c / concern-01
    :arg1 (c3 / commission)
    :arg2 (t / term
      :mod (i / invest-01
        :arg2 (c2 / country
          :name (n3/name :op1 "taiwan"))
        :time (f / future)))
    :manner (p2 / primary)))
```

Linearized, Cleaned AMR: fan state commission :manner primary concern invest taiwan :time future term

System Output: fans who have stated that the commission is primarily concerned with the terms of the investment in taiwan in the future .

Gold English: fan stated the commission is primarily concerned with the term of future investment in taiwan .

5 Conclusion

We introduce a method for learning to generate English from AMR. We use phrase-based machine translation technology and carry out experiments to compare different AMR linearization methods. We show that our method outperforms prior work by a large margin. We consider our results to form a strong baseline for future work.

References

Laura Banarescu, Claire Bonial, Shu Cai, Madalina Georgescu, Kira Griffitt, Ulf Hermjakob, Kevin Knight, Philipp Koehn, Martha Palmer, and Nathan Schneider. 2013. Abstract Meaning Representation for sembanking. In *Proc. ACL Linguistic Annotation Workshop (LAW)*.

Peter F. Brown, John Cocke, Stephen A. Della Pietra, Vincent J. Della Pietra, Fredrick Jelinek, John D. Lafferty, Robert L. Mercer, and Paul S. Roossin. 1990. A statistical approach to machine translation. *Computational linguistics*, 16(2):79–85.

Simon Corston-Oliver, Michael Gamon, Eric Ringger, and Robert Moore. 2002. An overview of Amalgam: A machine-learned generation module. In *Proc. INLG*.

Jeffrey Flanigan, Chris Dyer, Noah A. Smith, and Jaime Carbonell. 2016. Generation from abstract meaning representation using tree transducers. In *Proc. NAACL*.

Yuqing Guo, Haifeng Wang, and Josef Van Genabith. 2011. Dependency-based n-gram models for general purpose sentence realisation. *Natural Language Engineering*, 17(4):455–483.

Philipp Koehn, Hieu Hoang, Alexandra Birch, Chris Callison-Burch, Marcello Federico, Nicola Bertoldi, Brooke Cowan, Wade Shen, Christine Moran, Richard Zens, et al. 2007. Moses: Open source toolkit for statistical machine translation. In *Proc. ACL Poster and Demonstration Sessions*.

Irene Langkilde and Kevin Knight. 1998. Generation that exploits corpus-based statistical knowledge. In *Proc. ACL*.

Uri Lerner and Slav Petrov. 2013. Source-side classifier preordering for machine translation. In *Proc. EMNLP*.

François Mairesse, Milica Gašić, Filip Jurčíček, Simon Keizer, Blaise Thomson, Kai Yu, and Steve Young. 2010. Phrase-based statistical language generation using graphical models and active learning. In *Proc. ACL*.

Nima Pourdamghani, Yang Gao, Ulf Hermjakob, and Kevin Knight. 2014. Aligning English strings with Abstract Meaning Representation graphs. In *Proc. EMNLP*.

Le Zhang. 2004. Maximum entropy modeling toolkit for Python and C++. http://bit.ly/1DGnb2p.

Generating summaries of hospitalizations: A new metric to assess the complexity of medical terms and their definitions

Sabita Acharya, Barbara Di Eugenio, Andrew D. Boyd, Karen Dunn Lopez,
Richard Cameron, Gail M Keenan
University of Illinois at Chicago
Chicago, IL, USA

Abstract

Our system generates summaries of hospital stays by combining information from two heterogenous sources: physician discharge notes and nursing plans of care. It extracts medical concepts from both sources; concepts that are identified as "complex" by our metric are explained by providing definitions obtained from three external knowledge sources. Finally, relevant concepts (with or without definition) are realized by SimpleNLG.

1 Introduction

In the US, about 42 million people are hospitalized every year (Adams et al., 2013). When patients are released, they often do not understand their discharge instructions and what happened to them in the hospital (Haatainen et al., 2014). Our solution is to generate a concise summary that integrates the separate physician and nursing documentations, since in current hospital practice, no comprehensive record exists of the care provided to a patient.

After summarizing our baseline work previously reported in (Di Eugenio et al., 2014), we focus on medical term complexity. The novelty of our work consists in the multiprong approach underlying our complexity metric, that includes linear regression and clustering; and in applying the metric not just to the term in question, but to its many available definitions, so as to choose the simplest one to refer the patient to.

2 Related Work

Only few NLG systems generate personalized information from medical data for the *patient*, as opposed to health care personnel (Williams et al., 2007; Mahamood and Reiter, 2011). As concerns identifying difficult terms, some applications search for them in vocabularies or in specific corpora (Ong et al., 2007; Kandula et al., 2010). The drawback of these approaches is that they make an underlying assumption that all the terms that appear in such resources are *complex* and need to be explained further. Moreover, since none of the currently available vocabularies/corpora are exhaustive enough, this method is not reliable. Our approach for identifying complex terms is closer to (Shardlow, 2013), but we are interested in medical terms and use five times as many features, and a two-step approach, not their single SVM model. Similar to (Ramesh et al., 2013), we provide definitions for terms; but Ramesh et al. consider every term whose semantic type falls within a set of 16 types derived from the Unified Medical Language System[1] (UMLS) as complex, while we don't make such assumptions.

3 System Workflow

In our previous work (Di Eugenio et al., 2014), we set up the core of the NLG pipeline represented by *Component 1* in Figure 1. We also computationally demonstrated that doctor and nurses focus on different aspects of care (Di Eugenio et al., 2013; Roussi et al., 2015), and hence, that both perspectives need to be included. The first input to the system is the *hospital course* section of the doctor's free text discharge notes.[2] Medical concepts are extracted from the discharge notes by MedLEE (Friedman et al., 2004), a medical information extraction tool that maps entities to concepts in UMLS. UMLS includes 2.6 million concepts, identified by Concept Unique Identifiers (CUIs). A concept is described by either

---

[1] http://www.ncbi.nlm.nih.gov/books/NBK9676/
[2] The de-identified notes come from our hospital.

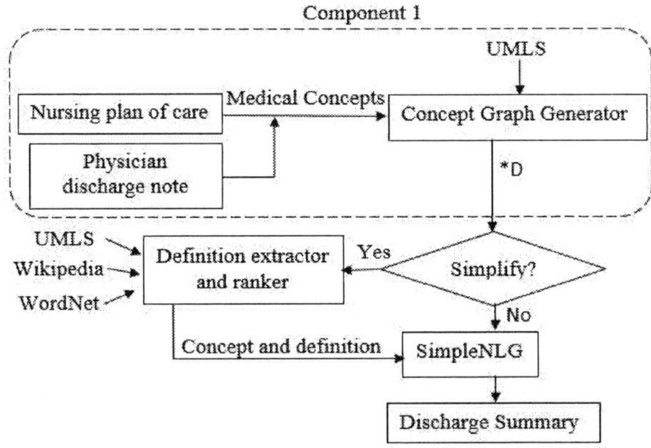

Figure 1: Schematic representation of the system

a single word or multiple words; eg., *Cerebrovascular accident* is a concept with CUI *C0038454*.

The second input to our system is structured nursing documentation as recorded via the HANDS tool (Keenan et al., 2002). HANDS employs structured nursing taxonomies (NNN, 2014):NANDA-I for nursing diagnoses, NOC for outcomes and NIC for interventions. HANDS also uses a scale from 1 to 5 to indicate the initial state of the patient for that outcome when s/he was admitted, and the expected rating at discharge. Since the nursing terminologies are already included within UMLS, they also have corresponding CUIs.

To generate the summary, for each patient, we build a graph, starting from two sets of CUIs: those extracted from the discharge notes; and those corresponding to the NANDA-I, NIC and NOC terms from HANDS. We grow the graph by querying UMLS for CUIs that are related to each of the CUIs in the initial sets. From the graph, we select those CUIs that either belong to one of the source lists, or are required to form a connection between a doctor-originated concept and a nurse-originated concept that would otherwise remain unconnected. In Figure 2, *difficulty walking* is a NANDA-I diagnosis that is related to *nervous system disorder*, which is an intermediate node discovered by our graph building procedure. Concepts corresponding to the selected CUIs are candidates for inclusion in our summary. First, a filter identifies whether the concept is *Simple* or *Complex*. If it is identified as *Complex*, it is sent to the *Definition extractor and ranker*

module that retrieves definitions of the concept from three external knowledge sources (see Section 5), ranks them according to their increasing complexity, and returns the simplest definition. These concepts, along with relevant verbs (that are supplied depending upon whether the concept is a diagnosis/ intervention/ treatment/ intermediate node) are couched as features of phrasal constituents via the operations provided by the SimpleNLG API (Gatt and Reiter, 2009), which then assembles grammatical phrases in the right order.

Our running example summary is shown in Figure 3. So far, we have generated discharge summaries for 58 patient cases; the average number of concepts in a summary is 33. Out of all the concepts that appear in our 58 summaries, 20% consist of a single word, 52% of two words, 16% of three words, and 12% of more than 3 words. Instead of explaining each word in a concept, we provide a definition for the concept as a whole. In the following, we will more specifically refer to concepts as "terms".

4 Term complexity assessment

Most of the earlier work assumes that every medical term is complex, and maps it to a simpler term via lexica (Ong et al., 2007). First, it is too simplistic to assume that every medical term is complex, however no measure exists to assess the complexity of a medical term. Tools for assessing health literacy (REALM, TOFHLA, NAALS) and reading level (Flesch, Fry Graph, SMOG) work only on sentences and not on words (CHIRR, 2012).

Second, as concerns the coverage of existing vocabularies for replacing complex terms, we started by assessing the foremost resource currently available, the Consumer Health Vocabulary (CHV) (Doing-Harris and Zeng-Treitler, 2011), which maps medical terms to plain language expressions. We found out that CHV provides a simplified alternative for only 14% of our terms, most of which we contend are not "simple" enough. We also compiled several vocabulary sources found online: MedicineNet[3], eMedicine[4], MedlinePlus[5] into a single lexicon, but only 2.17% of the medical terms

---

[3] www.medicinenet.com/ medterms-medical-dictionary
[4] www.emedicinehealth.com/medical-dictionary-definitions
[5] www.nlm.nih.gov/medlineplus

You were admitted for acute subcortical cerebrovascular accident. Difficulty walking related to nervous system disorder was treated with body mechanics promotion. Mobility as a finding has improved significantly and outcome has met the expectation. Risk for Ineffective Cerebral Tissue Perfusion was treated with medication management and administration:oral.[...] As a result, risk control behavior: cardiovascular health has improved slightly. Verbal impairment related to communication impairment was treated with speech therapy. [...] As a result, fall prevention behavior and knowledge level: fall prevention have improved slightly. Disease Process, Medication, and Disease Process (Heart disease) were taught.

Figure 2: Part of version 1 of the summary for Patient 149

You were admitted for acute subcortical cerebrovascular accident. During your hospitalization, you were monitored for chances of ineffective cerebral tissue perfusion, risk for falls, problem in verbal communication and walking. We treated difficulty walking related to nervous system disorder with body mechanics promotion. Mobility as a finding has improved appreciably. We provided treatment for risk for ineffective cerebral tissue perfusion with medication management and medication administration. As a result, risk related to cardiovascular health has reduced slightly. We worked to improve verbal impairment related to communication impairment with speech therapy. As a result, communication has improved slightly. We treated risk for falls by managing environment to provide safety. We provided information about fall prevention. As a result, fall prevention behavior and fall prevention knowledge have improved slightly. With your nurse and doctors, you learned about disease process and medication.

Figure 3: Version 2 of the summary for Patient 149

from our summaries were present in them.

4.1 Measuring term complexity

In order to develop a metric for determining the complexity of terms, we need a training set of *Simple* and *Complex* terms. For this purpose: 1) We randomly selected 300 terms from the *Dale-Chall List*, which consists of 3,000 terms that are known to be understood by more than 80% of 4th grade students (DC , 2016) and labeled them as *Simple*. 2) We randomly selected 300 medical terms present in our database of 3164 terms explored by the *Concept Graph Generator* in Figure 1 for 58 patients. Two non-native undergraduate students who have never had any medical conditions were asked to annotate the 300 terms taken from our database as *Simple* or *Complex* (Cohen's Kappa k=0.786). Disagreements between the annotators were resolved via mutual consultation.

Several features were extracted for each of the 600 terms: a) Lexical features: number of vowels, consonants, prefixes, suffixes, letters, syllables per word. b) Count of each type of POS, i.e. number of nouns, verbs, adjectives, prepositions, conjunctions, determiners, adverbs, numerals (extracted by the Stanford parser) c) whether the term is present in Wordnet d) UMLS derived features: number of semantic types, synonyms, and CUIs that are identified for the term; whether the term is present in CHV; whether the entire term has a CUI; whether the semantic type of the term is one of the 16 semantic types from (Ramesh et al., 2013).

As a first step, linear regression was performed on the 600 terms with *Complexity* (0-Simple, 1-Complex) as the dependent variable. This process filtered out unimportant features for predicting complexity: number of letters, consonants; number of prepositions, conjunctions; 4 out of the 16 semantic types discussed above: *Cell or Molecular Dysfunction, Experimental Model of Disease, Finding,* and *Physiologic Function*. It also provided a linear regression function that hence includes only the important features, which we will collectively call **F**.

As a second step, Expectation-Maximization clustering was performed on the remaining 2864 terms from our database, using the earlier collected 600 terms as *cluster seeds*. This resulted in 3 clusters. Of the 600 cluster seeds, 70% of those in Cluster1 had *Simple* label; 79% of those in Cluster3 had *Complex* label; 58% of those in Cluster2 had *Simple* label and 42% had *Complex* label. This indicates the presence of three categories of terms: some that can be identified as *Simple* (Cluster1), some that are *Complex* (Cluster3), and the rest for which there is no clear distinction between *Simple* and *Complex* (Cluster2). For the terms in each of these clusters, we further supplied feature values from the set $\mathbf{F}$ to the linear regression function and analyzed the corresponding scores. We found out that across all clusters, 88% of the terms labeled as *Simple* have scores below 0.4 while 96% of the terms whose score was above 0.7 were labeled *Complex*. For the terms whose score was between 0.4 and 0.7, no clear majority of *Simple* or *Complex* labeled terms was observed in any of the clusters. This further verifies the observation made during clustering that our dataset consists of three categories of terms. The thresholds of 0.4 and 0.7 were obtained by sorting the scores of the terms within each cluster and looking for the highest difference in consecutive scores.

Hence, given a new term to assess, our system will: a) Extract features $\mathbf{F}$ b) Supply feature values to the linear regression function c) If the score is below 0.4, the term is considered *Simple*; if score is above 0.7, the term is considered *Complex* and a definition is provided. For scores between 0.4 and 0.7, definition will be provided only if the term's semantic type falls within our list of 47 semantic types, obtained after removing non-medical types like *Organization* from the list of 133 semantic types in UMLS.

5 Choosing an appropriate definition

For the terms that are identified as *Complex* by our metric, we will extract definitions from three external knowledge sources: Wikipedia (extract only the first sentence), WordNet, and UMLS. Since more than 60 vocabulary sources are integrated into UMLS, a single term might have multiple definitions. Hence, definitions from all the three sources are obtained and for each definition, medical concepts present in it are extracted. Using our metric for determining complexity (Section 4.1), we obtain scores for each of the concepts in a definition and add them together to get a single score. The definition with the lowest score is eventually chosen.

For instance, for a term *Cerebrovascular accident*, 1) our metric returns a score of *0.801*, which indicates that a definition needs to be supplied. 2) *Definition extractor and ranker* module extracts definitions of the term from three knowledge sources and ranks them. 3) The definition from Wikipedia has the lowest score and hence the first occurrence

of the term *Cerebrovascular accident* in our summary will have the definition *when poor blood flow to the brain results in cell death* attached to it. All the terms that have been highlighted in Figure 3 are found to be *Complex* and a corresponding definition is provided by the system. These definitions can be presented in different forms (like *footnote* or *tooltip text*) depending upon the medium in which the summary is going to be presented. Whereas we have not run a formal evaluation, two of our patient advisors observed that our current summaries have vastly improved compared to the baseline.

6 Current and Future Work

Currently, some of the terms like *central venous* and *organism strain* are identified as *Simple* by our metric. In order to improve the accuracy of our metric, we plan to add a feature that represents the frequency of a term in Google-ngram corpus as is done in (Grabar et al., 2014; Kauchak and Leroy, 2016) and evaluate its effectiveness in predicting complexity. This could also be useful in disambiguating the complexity of terms with score between 0.4-0.7.

Our next immediate goal is to include the patient's perspective in our summaries, similarly to Gkatzia et al. (2014). We are collecting open-ended interviews with 40 patients and have interviewed four so far. We are currently transcribing the recordings; we will code them for features of interests, and plan to mine them with methods appropriate for *small data* (Smith et al., 2014). Once summaries can be personalized, we plan to perform first, controlled evaluations, and eventually longer-term assessments of whether our summaries engender better health, i.e., by better adherence to medications.

References

P.F. Adams, W.K. Kirzinger, and Martinez M. 2013. *Summary Health Statistics for the U.S. Population: National Health Interview Survey, 2012*, volume 10 of *Vital and Health Statistics*. Centers for Disease Control and Prevention.

CHIRR. 2012. Health literacy. Consumer health informatics research resource, https://chirr.nlm.nih.gov/health-literacy.php.

2016. Readability Formulas. readabilityformulas.com.

Barbara Di Eugenio, Camillo Lugaresi, Gail M. Keenan, Yves A. Lussier, Jianrong Li, Mike Burton, Carol

Friedman, and Andrew D. Boyd. 2013. HospSum: Integrating physician discharge notes with coded nursing care data to generate patient-centric summaries. In *AMIA 2013, American Medical Informatics Association Annual Symposium*, Washington D.C., November. Abstract.

Barbara Di Eugenio, Andrew D. Boyd, Camillo Lugaresi, Abhinaya Balasubramanian, Gail Keenan, Mike Burton, Tamara Goncalves Rezende Macieira, Jianrong Li, Yves Lussier, and Carol Friedman. 2014. PatientNarr: Towards generating patient-centric summaries of hospital stays. In *Proceedings of the 8th International Natural Language Generation Conference (INLG)*, pages 6–10, Philadelphia, Pennsylvania, U.S.A., June. Association for Computational Linguistics.

K.M. Doing-Harris and Q. Zeng-Treitler. 2011. Computer-assisted update of a consumer health vocabulary through mining of social network data. *Journal of Medical Internet Research*, 13(2).

C. Friedman, L. Shagina, Y. Lussier, and G. Hripcsak. 2004. Automated encoding of clinical documents based on natural language processing. *Journal of the American Medical Informatics Association*, 11(5):392.

A. Gatt and E. Reiter. 2009. SimpleNLG: A realisation engine for practical applications. In *Proceedings of the 12th European Workshop on Natural Language Generation*, pages 90–93. Association for Computational Linguistics.

D. Gkatzia, V. Rieser, A. McSporran, A.R. McGowan, A.R. Mort, and M. Dewar. 2014. Generating verbal descriptions from medical sensor data: A corpus study on user preferences. *BCS Health Informatics Scotland. Glasgow, UK*.

Natalia Grabar, Thierry Hamon, and Dany Amiot. 2014. Automatic diagnosis of understanding of medical words. *EACL 2014*, pages 11–20.

K. M. Haatainen, Ta. Tervo-Heikkinen, and K. Saranto. 2014. Adult patients' experiences of discharge education in an emergency department: a systematic review protocol. *The JBI Database of Systematic Reviews and Implementation Reports*, 12(5):80–87.

S. Kandula, D.y Curtis, and Q. Zeng-Treitler. 2010. A semantic and syntactic text simplification tool for health content. In *AMIA Annu Symp Proc*, volume 2010, pages 366–70.

David Kauchak and Gondy Leroy. 2016. Moving beyond readability metrics for health-related text simplification. *IT Professional*, 18(3):45–51.

G.M. Keenan, J.R. Stocker, A.T. Geo-Thomas, N.R. Soparkar, V.H. Barkauskas, and J.A.N.L. Lee. 2002. The HANDS Project: Studying and Refining the Automated Collection of a Cross-setting Clinical Data set. *CIN: Computers, Informatics, Nursing*, 20(3):89–100.

S. Mahamood and E. Reiter. 2011. Generating affective natural language for parents of neonatal infants. In *Proceedings of the 13th European Workshop on Natural Language Generation*, pages 12–21, Nancy, France, September. Association for Computational Linguistics.

2014. NNN: Knowledge-based terminologies defining nursing. http://www.nanda.org/nanda-i-nic-noc.html.

E.l Ong, J. Damay, G. Lojico, K. Lu, and D. Tarantan. 2007. Simplifying text in medical literature. *Journal of Research in Science, Computing and Engineering*, 4(1):37–47.

Balaji Polepalli Ramesh, Thomas K Houston, Cynthia Brandt, Hua Fang, and Hong Yu. 2013. Improving patients' electronic health record comprehension with noteaid. In *MedInfo*, pages 714–718.

Khawllah Roussi, Vanessa Soussa, Karen V Dunn Lopez, Abhinaya Balasubramanian, Gail M Keenan, Michel Burton, Neil Bahroos, Barbara Di Eugenio, and Andrew Boyd. 2015. Are we talking about the same patient? In *IOS Press*.

Matthew Shardlow. 2013. A comparison of techniques to automatically identify complex words. In *ACL (Student Research Workshop)*, pages 103–109. Citeseer.

G. CS Smith, S. R Seaman, A. M Wood, P. Royston, and I. R White. 2014. Correcting for optimistic prediction in small data sets. *American Journal of Epidemiology*.

S. Williams, Pa.l Piwek, and R. Power. 2007. Generating monologue and dialogue to present personalised medical information to patients. In *Proceedings of the Eleventh European Workshop on Natural Language Generation*, pages 167–170, Saarbrücken, Germany, June.

Designing Algorithms for Referring with Proper Names

Kees van Deemter

Computing Science Department, University of Aberdeen

`k.vdeemter@abdn.ac.uk`

Abstract

Standard algorithms for attribute choice in the generation of referring expressions have little to say about the role of Proper Names in referring expressions. We discuss the implications of letting these algorithms produce Proper Names and expressions that have Proper Names as parts.

1 Introduction

Reference – the production and comprehension of referring expressions – has been studied intensively throughout the cognitive sciences. Computational Linguists are no exception, often paying particular attention to the *generation* of referring expressions (REs, (Krahmer and Van Deemter, 2012) for a survey). This area of Natural Language Generation is known as Referring Expressions Generation (REG). An important strand of REG focusses on "one-shot" REs, which do not rely on any linguistic context (precluding anaphoric and other attenuated REs); these are also the primary focus of this paper.[1]

One of the classic algorithm coming out or REG is the Incremental Algorithm (IA) (Dale and Reiter, 1996). Simplifying slightly, the IA starts by ordering properties in a sequence known as the Preference Order. The algorithm starts with an empty RE, then examines the first property from the Preference Order. If this property is true of the referent r and rules out one or more distractors, it is added to the RE; otherwise it is not added, and the next property in the Preference Order is examined. The algorithm terminates when properties $P_{i_1}, .., P_{i_k}$ have

been selected that jointly identify the referent (i.e., $[\![P_{i_1}]\!] \cap ... \cap [\![P_{i_k}]\!] = \{r\}$). Different Preference Orders tend to generate different REs, so finding a good one is important.

Proper Names (PNs) are among the most widely studied REs in cognitive science (see e.g., (van Langendonck, 2007), *passim*; (van Deemter, 2016), chapters 2 and 7), and a crucial area of applied work in Information Extraction (e.g., (Jurafsky and Martin, 2009) chapter 22 on Named Entities). Yet REG[2] has neglected PNs, presumably because names could easily trivialise REG: suppose the KB contained a set of people. If only one of the people in the KB is named Obama, then it is easy to identify him, by referring to him by his name. Since PNs tend to make excellent REs, REG would become trivial – so the presumed argument goes.

We argue that this line of reasoning misses some important points and that PNs deserve more attention from researchers in REG.

2 Generating REs that contain a PN

Observe that:

- Name are often ambiguous. "Obama", for instance (not to mention "Smith") could refer to many different people.
- A referent can have many names ("Barack", "Obama", "Barack Obama", etc.) or none.
- A name can combine with other properties and epithets, as in "Mr Barack Obama, America's current president".

---

[1] See, however, section 2.1 on the use of salience.

[2] An early exception is the *ad hoc* treatment of PNs in (Winograd, 1972)'s SRDLU; recently the possibility of a systematic treatment was suggested as part of (van Deemter, 2014); an exploratory experimental study is (de Oliveira et al., 2015).

– A name can be part of an expression that refers to another referent. The process is recursive, e.g., "The height of the income of Obama's Secretary of State".

So how might PNs be given a place in REG?

2.1 Incorporating Proper Names into REG

Received views of REG suggest that the process contains two steps (Reiter and Dale, 2000): Step 1 decides what general syntactic type of RE to use (e.g., a full description, a PN, a pronoun, or some other type); once this decision is taken, Step 2 (discussed in section 1 above) makes more fine-grained decisions, for example, in case of a full description, this step decides what properties should be expressed in the description. The observations of the previous section make this two-step approach problematic, for example because (in some situations) no PN may be available for a given referent, or because PNs and descriptions must be combined (in other situations). In what follows, we explore a radical alternative, showing that if a suitable representation scheme is used, it is possible to incorporate all decisions related to PNs within Step 2.

Suppose each individual in the KB comes not just with a number of descriptive properties but with 0 or more PNs as well, where a PN is regarded as a property that is true of all individuals who bear this name.

– (being named) Joe Klein is a property of all individuals named Joe Klein
– (being named) Joe is a property of all those individuals named Joe
– (being named) Klein is a property of all those individuals named Klein

The idea that a PN can be viewed as a property of its bearer deviates from a long tradition of work in philosophy and logic that regards PNs as *rigid designators* (Kripke, 1980), yet it enjoys considerable support. (Burge, 1973), for example, observes that PNs can behave like common nouns, as in "There are relatively few Alfreds in P", and "An Alfred joined the club today" (see (Larson and Segal, 1995) and (Elbourne, 2005) for further support).

A simple KB containing PNs as well as ordinary properties could look like this:

JOB: political commentator, commentator
NATIONALITY: American
NAMES: Mr Joe Klein, Joe Klein, Joe, Klein

Because longer versions of a person's name are applicable to only some of the individuals to whom a shorter version is applicable, the values of the NAMES attribute often *subsume* each other: all people who are called Mr Joe Klein are also called Joe Klein, and so on. These properties can be dealt with using the mechanism for subsumption in the Incremental Algorithm (which would also state that all *political commentators* are *commentators*, for instance) (Dale and Reiter, 1996).

Of course if Joe Klein is the only Joe in the room, we can refer unambiguously to him saying "Joe". This is accounted for by making the REG algorithm that operates on the KB above salience aware in one of the standard ways, e.g., (Krahmer and Theune, 2002). Salience also suggests a way in which REG can extend beyond one-shot REs to cover reference in extended discourse or dialogue: if x is introduced by means of the PN "Joe Klein" in a text, then if x is the only Joe so far mentioned, then this makes x the most salient of all Joe's, licencing the short RE "Joe".

In short:

– Each object has an attribute NAMES.
– The set of values of NAMES can be empty (no name is available), singleton (one name), or neither (several names).
– A subsumption (i.e., subset) relation can be defined among these values.
– Different objects can share some or all of their names.

If names are the "canonical" way of referring to an entity, then standard mechanisms could be invoked to favour names at the expense of other properties. One option is to Dale and Reiter's Preference Order (Dale and Reiter, 1996), making NAMES the most highly preferred attribute in an Incremental Algorithm. Alternatively, a new type of brevity-based algorithm might be used that generates the RE that contains the smallest number of *syllables*.[3] Assuming that PNs are brief (as they often are), this type of approach would favour PNs, and it would favour shorter PNs over longer ones (e.g., "Klein" over "Joe Klein"). It would also predict that PNs are avoided

---

[3]Note that this approach would measure brevity as a surface property of a string, unlike the Full Brevity algorithm of (Dale, 1989), which sees brevity as a semantic property, letting REG choose the RE composed by the smallest number of *properties*.

where large sets are enumerated (compare the RE "the citizens of China" with an enumeration of all the elements of this set).

To see how REG could work in an Incremental Algorithm, consider a simple KB, where each individual has 1 name:

> TYPE: woman $\{w_1, w_2, w_3\}$, man $\{m1\}$, dog $\{d_1, d_2\}$
> NAMES: mary $\{w_1\}$, shona $\{w_2, w_3\}$, rover $\{d_1\}$, max $\{m_1, d_2\}$
> ACTION: feed $\{(w_1, d_1), (w_2, d_2), (w_2, d_1)\}$
> AFFECTION: love $\{(w_1, d_1), (w_3, d_1)\}$

This approach generates REs such as:

> d_1: "Rover"
> d_2: "The dog called Max"
> w_3: "Shona, who loves a dog"

With the above representation scheme in place, classic REG algorithms can be applied without modifications. However, the scheme does not allow PNs to have properties (e.g., "is a posh name", "has 5 characters" ,"is common in Scotland"). If names are *reified*, then this becomes possible; what's more, PNs themselves could be referred to (e.g., "the name his friends call him"): a name is just another object linked (on the one hand) to the things it names and (on the other hand) to the ways in which it manifests itself in spelling, pronunciation, etc. For example, n_2 may name both a man and a dog, and it may be written as "Max":

> Type: woman $\{w_1, w_2, w_3\}$, man $\{m_1\}$, dog $\{d_1, d_2\}$, name $\{n_1, n_2, n_3, n_4\}$
> Action: feed $\{(w_1, d_1), (w_2, d_2), (w_2, d_1)\}$
> Affection: love $\{(w_1, d_1), (w_3, d_1)\}$
> Naming: name $\{(d_1, n_1), (d_2, n_2),$
> $(w_1, n_3), (w_2, n_4), (w_3, n_4), (m_1, n_2)\}$
> Spelling: written $\{(n_1, Rover), (n_2, Max),$
> $(n_3, Mary), (n_4, Shona)\}$

Standard REG algorithms can use this KB to generate "The name shared by a man and a dog" (i.e., "Max"). If n_4 is Scottish, we obtain "women with a Scottish name" as well. A slight drawback of this approach, which treats names as objects, is that subsumption can no longer be used to compare names.

2.2 Challenges facing this approach

This approach works, but it puts a spotlight on some difficult issues, some of which affect the generation of *descriptive* REs as well:

1. PNs are *not* always preferred. For example, if the Director of Taxes is Mrs X, this does not mean that "Contact the Director of Taxes" is always better worded as "Contact Mrs X", since her job title may be relevant. The lack of a computational theory of *relevance* affects all of REG but becomes very noticeable in the choice between PNs and descriptions.

2. There is no reason for limiting reification to PNs. Colours too could be reified, for example, to generate "the colour of grass". The traditional dichotomy between objects and properties limits the range of REs that these algorithms can generate.

3. REG algorithms are ignorant about social relations between speaker, hearer, and referent. Consider a couple with a son and a daughter. Speaking to his mother, the son could say "my sister", "your daughter", etc., yet in most situations a PN would be better. Titles and epithets like "Dr" and "Aunt(y)", complicate matters further.

4. As elsewhere in REG, questions about overspecification need to be faced. When, for example, is it useful to add an *appositive* to a PN, as in "Mr Barack Obama, *America's current president*"? Furthermore, Linguistic Realisation will have to decide about the surface order of the PN and the appositive, perhaps depending on whether the PN and/or the appositive (by itself) refers uniquely.

5. If PNs are properties of the referent, then this leaves room for expressing one and the same PN with a different string. (For example, "Doctor" may be worded as "Doctor", "Dr.", or "Dr".) The desirability of this use of Linguistic Realisation would need to be investigated.

6. It is often difficult for the speaker to assess whether the hearer knows who a given PN refers to. The hearer may never have heard of Joe Klein, for example, and this would cause the RE "Joe Klein" to mis-fire. Lack of shared knowledge is a problem for *descriptive* REs as well, but it is exacerbated in the case of PNs, because names are highly conventional: once I've learned what "red" means, I can apply the word to any red object, but learning your name does not teach me to apply this name to anyone else.

The last point has important implications. Imagine a programmer wanting to implement the algorithm of section 2.1, aiming to mimic human language use. If she decides to implement an Incremental Algorithm, then how to choose its free pa-

Figure 1: *A trial in the "people" part of the* TUNA *experiment*

rameter, the Preference Order? She could learn one via an elicitation experiment, but how does she find a generic REG algorithm that works for all PNs?

Consider a scene from an experiment where speakers referred to stimuli on a screen (van Deemter et al., 2012). Participants called the man in the top right "the man with the white beard", etc. They *might* have said "Samuel Eilenberg", yet no-one did, because participants didn't know his name. Participants could have been trained to be familiar with every individual's name, but this could easily have *primed* the use of names at the expense of descriptions; the same happens when names are visible as captions, as was done in (de Oliveira et al., 2015) using fictitious names of geographical areas; see also (Anderson et al., 1991). Such an approach does not give reliable information on how REG algorithms should choose between PNs and descriptions. The problem is not just that PNs are conventional, but that their conventional meaning can be entrenched to different degrees, varying from short-lived "conceptual pacts" (Brennan and Clark, 1996) to names that are very widely known and used.

2.3 Lessons from situations where PNs are avoided

Suppose someone asks "Who is Joe Klein?" (cf., section 2.2, point 6). Would it make sense to respond "(He is) the author of the bestselling political novel of the 1990s?" It depends on the importance of this fact and how widely it is known.

To model answers to "Who is?" questions (see (Boër and Lycan, 1986) for a theoretical study),

(Kutlak et al., 2013) designed a REG algorithm that employs the following Heuristic: Based on the frequency with which a name n co-occurs with a property P, the Heuristic estimates how likely the proposition $P(n)$ is to be known by an arbitrarily chosen hearer. Evaluation studies suggest that this Heuristic goes a long way towards estimating how many people know a fact, and the complete REG algorithm (which involves 2 other heuristics) outperforms its competitors in terms of its ability to generate descriptions that allow hearers to guess correctly the name of the referent. Although the authors focussed on the WWW, the approach can use any corpus that represents the ideas of a community (e.g., a company's intranet).

This approach suggests a promising handle on the conventionality of PNs. It allows us to estimate, for example, the likelihood that a name like "Joe Klein" is known by hearers to refer to the commentator and novelist of that name, and this would allow us to limit the KB of section 2 to names that are well enough known. We hypothesise that PNs have a *higher likelihood* of being uttered as part of REs by members of a community (e.g., users of the WWW) the more frequently these PNs occur as names of this referent in documents produced by that community. Further experiments could flesh out how the use of PNs depends on a number of factors, including the Knowledge Heuristic. Essentially, PNs would be treated as properties of a referent that may or may not be known to the hearer, analogous to the descriptive properties of (Kutlak et al., 2013).

3   Conclusion

We have shown how, given appropriate semantic representations, standard attribute algorithms are able to generate REs that contain PNs, thereby solving problems with the standard 2-step perspective on REG that separates choosing the general syntactic type of RE from more fine-grained decisions about the content of the RE. However, our approach raises difficult questions about the choices that a REG algorithm needs to make between PNs and descriptive REs. We argue that some of the trickiest questions in this area may be solved if large corpora are employed as a source of insight into the degree to which a PN is likely to be known by the recipient of the RE.

References

Anne A. Anderson, Miles Bader, Ellen Gurman Bard, Elizabeth Boyle, Gwyneth Doherty, Simon Garrod, Stephen Isard, Jacqueline Kowtko, Jan McAllister, Jim Miller, Catherine Sotillo, Henry Thompson, and Regina Weinert. 1991. The HCRC map task corpus. *Language and Speech*, 34:351–366.

Steven E. Boër and William G. Lycan. 1986. *Knowing Who*. MIT Press, Cambridge, Mass.

Susan Brennan and Herbert H. Clark. 1996. Conceptual pacts and lexical choice in conversation. *Journal of Experimental Psychology*, 22(6):1482–1493.

Tyler Burge. 1973. Reference and proper names. *The Journal of Philosophy*, 70:425–439.

Robert Dale and Ehud Reiter. 1996. The role of the gricean maxims in the generation of referring expressions. In *AAAI–96 Spring Symposium on Computational Models of Conversational Implicature*.

Robert Dale. 1989. Cooking up referring expressions. In *Proceedings of the 27th Annual Meeting of the Association for Computational Linguistics (ACL)*, pages 68–75.

Rodrigo de Oliveira, Somayajulu Sripada, and Ehud Reiter. 2015. Designing an algorithm for generating named spatial references. In *Proceedings of 15th European Workshop on Natural Language Generation (ENLG-2015)*, pages 127–135, Brighton, UK.

Paul Elbourne. 2005. *Situations and Individuals*. MIT Press, Cambridge, Mass.

Daniel Jurafsky and James H. Martin. 2009. *Speech and Language Processing (second edition)*. Pearson, Upper Saddle River, NJ.

Emiel Krahmer and Mariët Theune. 2002. Efficient context–sensitive generation of descriptions in context. In Kees van Deemter and Rodger Kibble, editors, *Information Sharing: Givenness and Newness in Language Processing*, pages 223–264, CSLI Publications, CSLI, Stanford.

Emiel Krahmer and Kees Van Deemter. 2012. Computational generation of referring expressions: a survey. *Computational Linguistics*, 38(1):173–218.

Saul Kripke. 1980. *Naming and Necessity*. Harvard University Press, Cambridge, Mass.

Roman Kutlak, Kees van Deemter, and Chris Mellish. 2013. Generation of referring expressions in large domains. In *Proceedings of the workshop Production of Referring Expressions, associated with the 35th Meeting of the Cognitive Science Society*.

Richard Larson and Gabriel Segal. 1995. *Knowledge and Meaning. An Introduction to Semantic Theory*. MIT Press, Cambridge, Mass.

Ehud Reiter and Robert Dale. 2000. *Building Natural Language Generation Systems*. Cambridge University Press.

Kees van Deemter, Albert Gatt, Ielka van der Sluis, and Richard Power. 2012. Generation of referring expressions: Assessing the incremental algorithm. *Cognitive Science*, 36(5):799–836.

Kees van Deemter. 2014. Referability. In A. Stent and S. Bangalore, editors, *Natural Language Genetration in Interactive Systems*, pages 95–125. Cambridge University Press.

Kees van Deemter. 2016. *Computational Models of Referring: a Study in Cognitive Science*. MIT Press, May 2016.

Willy van Langendonck. 2007. *Theory and Typology of Proper Names*. Mouton de Gruyter, The Hague.

Terry Winograd. 1972. *Understanding Natural Language*. Academic Press, New York.

When to Plummet and When to Soar: Corpus Based Verb Selection for Natural Language Generation

Charese Smiley[1], Vassilis Plachouras [2], Frank Schilder[1], Hiroko Bretz[1],
Jochen L. Leidner[2], Dezhao Song[1]

[1] Thomson Reuters, Research & Development, 610 Opperman Drive, Eagan, MN, USA
[2] Thomson Reuters, Research & Development, 1 Mark Square, London, EC2A 4EG, UK
firstname.lastname@thomsonreuters.com

Abstract

For data-to-text tasks in Natural Language Generation (NLG), researchers are often faced with choices about the right words to express phenomena seen in the data. One common phenomenon centers around the description of trends between two data points and selecting the appropriate verb to express both the direction and intensity of movement. Our research shows that rather than simply selecting the same verbs again and again, variation and naturalness can be achieved by quantifying writers' patterns of usage around verbs.

1 Introduction

In April 2016, the headline "GoPro's stock rocketed up 19 percent after it poached top Apple designer" was splashed across the top of the Business Insider Tech pages [1]. The authors of stories such as these often use descriptive language such as verbs like *rocketed up* to convey both the direction of motion of a percentage change along with its intensity. Although it is appropriate to use a more neutral verb like *increase* or *decrease* as is the case with most previous research, a more natural sounding text can be generated if we can incorporate the intensity of change.

This paper discusses the use of a large scale news corpus to quantify which verb to use in data-to-speech generation. In this work, we propose that the verb can be collocated to the percentage change such that certain types of trends can be described using a

narrow set of verbs while other trends lend themselves to wider variation. We have developed the proposed method in the context of Thomson Reuters Eikon, an NLG system for macro-economic indicator and merger & acquisition deals data (Plachouras et al., 2016). However, the proposed method can be used for other domains with an appropriate corpus. The major contributions of this work are, to the best of our knowledge, the first large scale corpus study of lexical choice for perceptual change verbs with an evaluation using Amazon Mechanical Turk.

This article is structured as follows. Related work is discussed in the next section. Section 3 covers methods. Experiments and Discussion are discussed Section 4. Finally, Section 5 concludes the paper.

2 Related Work

Previous corpus based studies on the relationship between numbers and surrounding context for generation purposes have concentrated on the generation of appropriate numbers for a text in terms of roundness (e.g. 25 vs. 25.9) and format (such as preference for fraction vs. percentages) (Power and Williams, 2012) and hedging and rounding in conjunction with numerical expressions (e.g. less than 25%) (Williams and Power, 2013).

Several studies have explored generation of descriptions of times series data. The TREND system (Boyd, 1998) focuses on the generation of descriptions of historical weather patterns concentrating primarily on the detection of upward and downward trends in the data and using a limited set of verbs (*rose, dropped sharply*) to describe the direction and intensity of movement. More recently,

---

[1] http://uk.businessinsider.com/
gopro-stock-rocketed-up-19-percent-2016-4

Ramos-Soto et al. (2013) also address the surface realization of weather trend data. They create an "intermediate language" for temperature, wind etc. and then consider 4 different ways to verbalize temperatures based on the minimum, maximum and trend in the time frame considered. In contrast, our method selects the verb based on the trend without hard-wiring the mapping at system development, as the associations are learned from a corpus. NLG systems for the visually impaired have also explored the generation of text for trend data (Moraes et al., 2014) around the adaptation of generated descriptions to users' reading levels.

Perhaps the most similar work to ours is that of word choice in SUMTIME-MOUSAM (Reiter et al., 2005). This research conducted an empirical corpus-based study of human-written weather forecasts. One aspect of the research focused on verb selection in weather forecasts. They built a classifier to predict the choice of verb based on type (speed vs. direction), information content (change or transition from one wind state to another) and near-synonym choice. They found that verbs were chosen based upon the most salient semantic information such as whether wind speed, direction, or both constituted the most significant change. After a post-edit analysis where forecasters were asked to edit computer generated texts, they found that lexical choice was highly idiosyncratic based on the individual writer's idiolect. Our research shows that although there is an aspect of variability, writers may be operating within a more limited scope of possible lexical choice depending on factors such as the intensity of change.

3   Methods

For this study, we use the Reuters News Archive, a large corpus of 14 million news articles on a variety of topics collected from the Reuters News Agency[2]. Documents within the corpus were part-of-speech tagged using Stanford Core NLP (Manning et al., 2014). Then phrases that contained an expression of a percentage change in the form (subject, verb, number, percent) were extracted using a simple function in the format shown below:

[GoPro's stock] [rocketed up] [19 percent]

We elected to use percentage changes over absolute numbers as a way of minimizing some of the issues surrounding absolute numbers. An absolute number might be considered relatively small in one instance but large in another. For example, a 10 minute walk might be considered short while a 10 mile walk might be long. On the other hand, a \$3 rise in a car priced at \$30,000 would be a 0.01% increase whereas a \$3 rise in gas priced at \$3 would be a 100% increase thus suitably registering the magnitude of the change. Also, when dealing with precise numbers we have to consider the scale on which the number lies (e.g. 24 hours, 7 days, 60 minutes, etc.) (Krifka, 2007). This problem is avoided with percentages. Movements in the form of percentage changes are readily available in our news corpus and can be easily identified and extracted. Also, percentage change can be easily calculated given two data points and then the verb selection algorithm applied making this is useful for data-to-text systems.

After extracting a set of 1.7 million candidate phrases for a total of 5,417 verb types and 182,245 verb tokens, we eliminate rare verbs by removing phrases containing verbs that appear less than 50 times and phrases with noun-verb pairs that occur less than 2 times. We remove all modal and auxiliary verbs and keep only the bare form of the verb. Finally, we manually annotate the motion of the verb as rising or falling removing verbs such as *rebound* which imply a rising motion but have additional meaning of returning from a low to some previous high point. We also remove verbs such as *trade down* which are specific to a particular domain such as the stock market. After preprocessing, we are left with 49 verb types: 22 rising and 27 falling.

For each verb, we calculated the median, standard deviation, and interquartile range (IQR) for all instances of the verb in the corpus. Figure 1 (a) and (b) shows boxplots of the remaining verbs organized along the x-axis in order of ascending IQR with respect to the magnitude of change.

We find that verbs with a small IQR (e.g. *edge up* and *nudge up* are used with very low percentage changes. Verbs with larger IQRs are associated with more extreme changes (e.g. *skyrocket* and *rocket*). This pattern holds for both rising and falling verbs.

---

[2]A smaller version of this corpus is available at http://trec.nist.gov/data/reuters/reuters.html

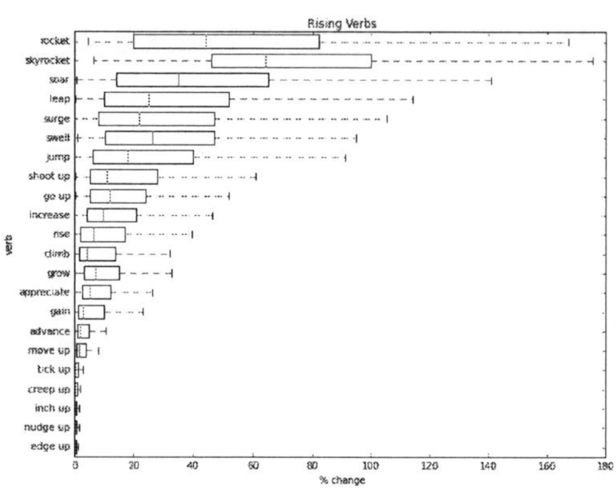
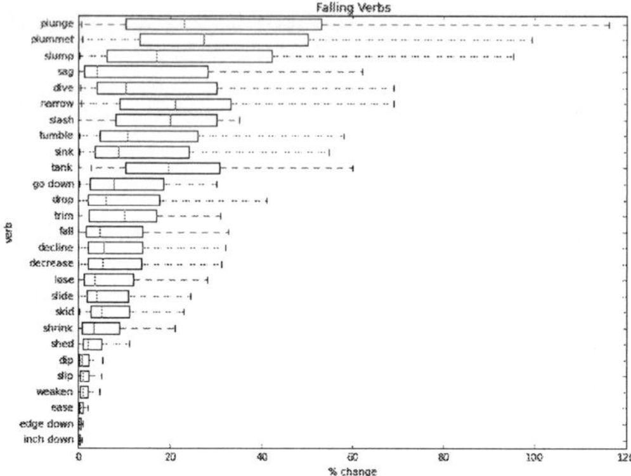

(a) Boxplot of 22 rising verbs, ordered by interquartile range.

(b) Boxplot of 27 falling verbs, ordered by interquartile range.

Figure 1: Rising and Falling Verbs

4 Experiments

The goal of our evaluation is to test whether our verb generator outperforms a random baseline. That is, if verb selection is truly idiosyncratic, we would expect that raters will have no preference for one verb over another such that their responses cannot be distinguished from chance in the aggregate.

In order to compare our verb selections against human judgements of naturalness, we evaluate using multiple choice questions on Amazon Mechanical Turk (AMT). AMT is a platform which allows requesters to post questions and tasks in order to obtain crowdsourced answers from anonymized workers. Requesters can filter workers on a variety of criteria including location, approval rate and number of Human Intelligence Tasks (HITs) approved. We restricted raters to those located in the United States, with an approval rating above 95% and 1,000 or more HITs approved.

For each question, we asked raters to select the most natural sounding sentence from a pair of sentences that varied only in verb choice. Each question was set up as a HIT (for a total of 2,000 HITs) asking raters to make quick judgements about the naturalness of a sentence. The random baseline is 50% (the chance of arbitrarily choosing either (a) or (b)). An example HIT is shown in Figure 2.

The sentences were generated using 3 topics: *gross domestic product*, *net profits*, and *share prices*, chosen from the most popular subjects in our corpus. We chose 3 noun phrases in the subject position of the sentence in order to reduce the effect of subject on verb selection while somewhat minimizing the repetitiveness of completing multiple HITs. The effect of subject on verb selection will be explored in depth in future research. Percentages were randomly selected from the corpus data. The verbs were generated by randomly selecting a verb where the percentage in question fell within the IQR of the verb. This decision is made to avoid atypical uses of a particular verb. When the percentage change fell within the IQR there were often multiple verbs to choose from. For example, with a 2% increase, our generator would select from among: *move up*, *rise*, *gain*, *advance*, and *climb*. We assume that the specific choice of verb within that range is up to the writer depending on personal preference, writing context, and other factors. To simulate this, we randomly select among the verbs.

The second question was generated by randomly choosing a verb from the list where the percentage did not fall within the IQR. We randomly generated 1,000 question pairs for each of sets of verbs (rising and falling) for a total of 2,000 questions.

For the falling verbs, raters agreed with our selection in 663 / 1,000 instances. For rising verbs, raters agreed in 709 / 1,000 instances. Both findings are statistically significant above the chance baseline of 50% ($p < 0.0001$ two-tail binomial test).

Disagreements between raters and our system were well distributed across all percentages. To keep the task simple for the raters, we did not ask them to justify their rationale for choosing one verb over the other. One limitation of the study, then, is that

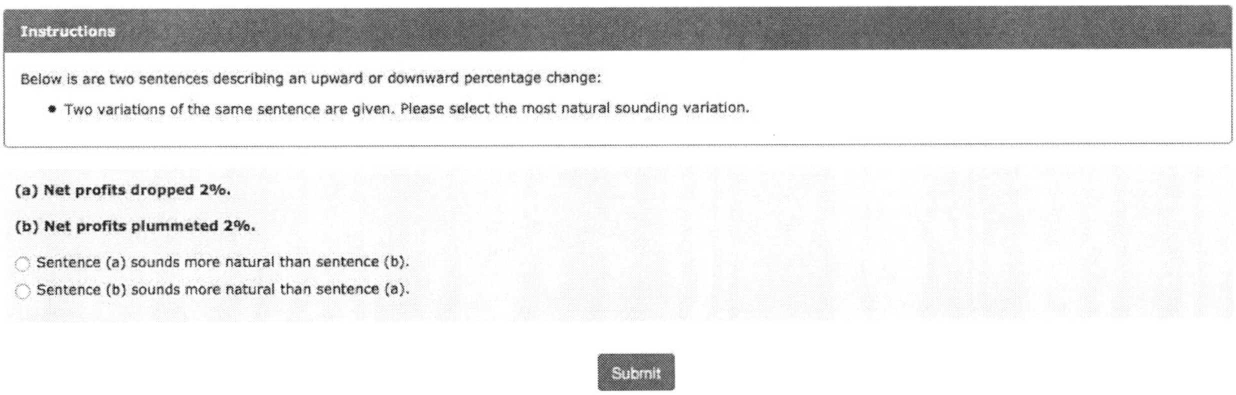

Figure 2: Example Verb Selection HIT on AMT

we cannot reliably distinguish raters who truly disagreed with our system's verb choice and those who are simply chose at random. However, we find it promising that we were able to reach statistical significance in spite of this.

5 Conclusion

We demonstrate verb selection for Thomson Reuters Eikon using a large news corpus. We find that verb selection can be quantified and that the results match our intuitions about which verbs express small and large rates of change. These results are further confirmed using an Amazon Mechanical Turk study of the naturalness of our generated texts.

Acknowledgments

We would like to thank Thomson Reuters F&R including Albert Lojko, Alex Tyrell, Sidd Shenoy, Rohit Mittal, and Jessica Tran as well as Tom Zielund and Khalid Al-Kofahi from Thomson Reuters R&D for their support and discussions. This work received financial support from Thomson Reuters Global Resources.

References

Sarah Boyd. 1998. Trend: a system for generating intelligent descriptions of time series data. In *IEEE International Conference on Intelligent Processing Systems (ICIPS1998)*. Citeseer.

Manfred Krifka. 2007. Approximate interpretation of number words: A case for strategic communication. *Cognitive foundations of interpretation*, pages 111–126.

Christopher D. Manning, Mihai Surdeanu, John Bauer, Jenny Finkel, Steven J. Bethard, and David McClosky. 2014. The Stanford CoreNLP natural language processing toolkit. In *Association for Computational Linguistics (ACL) System Demonstrations*, pages 55–60.

Priscilla Moraes, Kathleen McCoy, and Sandra Carberry. 2014. Adapting graph summaries to the users? reading levels. *INLG 2014*, page 64.

Vassilis Plachouras, Charese Smiley, Hiroko Bretz, Ola Taylor, Jochen L. Leidner, Dezhao Song, and Frank Schilder. 2016. Interacting with financial data using natural language. In *Proceedings of the 39th International ACM SIGIR conference on Research and Development in Information Retrieval*, pages 1121–1124. ACM.

Richard Power and Sandra Williams. 2012. Generating numerical approximations. *Computational Linguistics*, 38(1):113–134.

Alejandro Ramos-Soto, Alberto Bugarín, Senén Barro, and Juan Taboada. 2013. Automatic generation of textual short-term weather forecasts on real prediction data. In Henrik Legind Larsen, Maria J. Martín-Bautista, M. Amparo Vila, Troels Andreasen, and Henning Christiansen, editors, *Flexible Query Answering Systems - 10th International Conference, FQAS 2013, Granada, Spain, September 18-20, 2013. Proceedings*, volume 8132 of *Lecture Notes in Computer Science*, pages 269–280. Springer.

Ehud Reiter, Somayajulu Sripada, Jim Hunter, Jin Yu, and Ian Davy. 2005. Choosing words in computer-generated weather forecasts. *Artificial Intelligence*, 167(1):137–169.

Sandra Williams and Richard Power. 2013. Hedging and rounding in numerical expressions. *Pragmatics & Cognition*, 21(1):193–223.

Invited Speaker

Yejin Choi
University of Washington

Sketch-to-Text Generation: Toward Contextual, Creative, and Coherent Composition

Abstract

The need for natural language generation (NLG) arises in diverse, multimodal contexts: ranging from describing stories captured in a photograph, to instructing how to prepare a dish using a given set of ingredients, and to composing a sonnet for a given topic phrase. One common challenge among these types of NLG tasks is that the generation model often needs to work with relatively loose semantic correspondence between the input prompt and the desired output text. For example, an image caption that appeals to readers may require pragmatic interpretation of the scene beyond the literal content of the image. Similarly, composing a new recipe requires working out detailed how-to instructions that are not directly specified by the given set of ingredient names.

In this talk, I will discuss our recent approaches to generating contextual, creative, and coherent text given a relatively lean and noisy input prompt with respect to three NLG tasks: (1) creative image captioning, (2) recipe composition, and (3) sonnet composition. A recurring theme is that our models learn most of the end-to-end mappings between the input and the output directly from data without requiring manual annotations for intermediate meaning representations. I will conclude the talk by discussing the strengths and the limitations of these types of data-driven approaches and point to avenues for future research.

Abstractive Compression of Captions
with Attentive Recurrent Neural Networks

Sander Wubben[1,2], Emiel Krahmer[1], Antal van den Bosch[2], Suzan Verberne[2]
[1]Tilburg Center for Cognition and Communication (TICC)
Tilburg University
The Netherlands
[2]Centre for Language and Speech Technology (CLS)
Radboud University
The Netherlands
{s.wubben,e.j.krahmer}@uvt.nl
{a.vandenbosch,s.verberne}@let.ru.nl

Abstract

In this paper we introduce the task of abstractive caption or scene description compression. We describe a parallel dataset derived from the FLICKR30K and MSCOCO datasets. With this data we train an attention-based bidirectional LSTM recurrent neural network and compare the quality of its output to a Phrase-based Machine Translation (PBMT) model and a human generated short description. An extensive evaluation is done using automatic measures and human judgements. We show that the neural model outperforms the PBMT model. Additionally, we show that automatic measures are not very well suited for evaluating this text-to-text generation task.

1 Introduction

Text summarization is an important, yet challenging subfield of Natural Language Processing. Summarization can be defined as the process of finding the important items in a text and presenting them in a condensed form (Mani, 2001; Knight and Marcu, 2002). Summarization on the sentence level is called sentence compression. Sentence compression approaches can be classified into two categories: extractive and abstractive sentence compression. Most successful sentence compression models consist of extractive approaches that select the most relevant fragments from the source document and generate a shorter representation of this document by stitching the selected fragments together. In contrast, abstractive sentence compression is the process of producing a representation of the original sentence in a bottom-up manner. This results in a summary that may contain fragments that do not appear as part of the source sentence. While extractive sentence compression is an easier task, the challenges in abstractive sentence compression have gained more and more attention in recent years (Lloret and Palomar, 2012).

Extractive sentence compression entails finding a subset of words in the source sentence that can be dropped to create a new, shorter sentence that is still grammatical and contains the most important information. More formally, the aim is to shorten a sentence $x = x_1, x_2, ..., x_n$ into a substring $y = y_1, y_2, ..., y_m$ where all words in y also occur in x in the same order and $m < n$. A number of techniques have been used for extractive sentence compression, ranging from the noisy-channel model (Knight and Marcu, 2002), large-margin learning (McDonald, 2006; Cohn and Lapata, 2007) to Integer Linear Programming (Clarke and Lapata, 2008). (Marsi et al., 2010) characterize these approaches in terms of two assumptions: (1) only word *deletions* are allowed and (2) the word order is fixed. They argue that these constraints rule out more complicated operations such as reordering, substitution and insertion, and reduce the sentence compression task to a word deletion task. This does not model human sentence compression accurately, as humans tend to paraphrase when summarizing (Jing and McKeown, 2000), resulting in an abstractive compression of the source sentence.

Recent advances in Recurrent Neural Networks (RNNs) have boosted interest in text-to-text generation tasks (Sutskever et al., 2014). In this paper we focus on abstractive sentence compression with RNNs. In order to be applied to sentence compression, RNNs typically need to be trained on large data sets of aligned sequences. In the domain of abstractive sentence compression, not many of such data sets are available. For the related task of sentence simplification, data sets are available of aligned sentences from Wikipedia and Simple Wikipedia (Zhu et al., 2010; Coster and Kauchak, 2011). Recently, (Rush et al., 2015) used the Gigaword corpus to construct a large corpus containing headlines paired with the article's first sentence.

Here, we present a data set compiled from scene descriptions taken from the MSCOCO dataset (Lin et al., 2014). These descriptions are generally only one sentence long, and humans tend to describe photos in different ways, which makes this task suitable for abstractive sentence compression. For each image, we align long descriptions with shorter descriptions to construct a corpus of abstractive compressions .

We employ an Attentive Recurrent Neural Network (aRNN) to the task of sentence compression and compare its output with a Phrase-based Machine Translation (PBMT) system (Moses) and a human compression. We show through extensive automatic and human evaluation that the aRNN outperforms the Moses system and even performs on par with the human generated description. We also show that automatic measures such as ROUGE that are used generally to evaluate compression tasks do not correlate with human judgements.

2   Related work

A large body of work is devoted to extractive sentence compression. Here, we mention a few. (Knight and Marcu, 2002) propose two models to generate a short sentence by deleting a subset of words: the decision tree model and the noisy channel model, both based on a synchronous context free grammar. (Turner and Charniak, 2005) and (Galley and McKeown, 2007) build upon this model reporting improved results.

(McDonald, 2006) develop a system using large-margin online learning combined with a decoding algorithm that searches the compression space to produce a compressed sentence. Discriminative learning is used to combine the features and weight their contribution to a successful compression.

(Cohn and Lapata, 2007) cast the sentence compression problem as a tree-to-tree rewriting task. For this task, they train a synchronous tree substitution grammar, which dictates the space of all possible rewrites. By using discriminative training, a weight is assigned to each grammar rule. These grammar rules are then used to generate compressions by a decoder.

In contrast to the large body of work on extractive sentence compression, work on abstractive sentence compression is relatively sparse. (Cohn et al., 2008) propose an abstractive sentence compression method based on a parse tree transduction grammar and Integer Linear Programming. For their abstractive model, the grammar that is extracted is augmented with paraphrasing rules obtained from a pivoting approach to a bilingual corpus (Bannard and Burch, 2005). They show that the abstractive model outperforms an extractive model on their dataset.(Cohn and Lapata, 2013) follow up on earlier work and describe a discriminative tree-to-tree transduction model that can handle mismatches on the structural and lexical level.

There has been some work on the related task of sentence simplification. (Coster and Kauchak, 2011; Zhu et al., 2010) develop models using data from Simple English Wikipedia paired with English Wikipedia. Their models were able to perform rewording, reordering, insertion and deletion actions. (Woodsend and Lapata, 2011) use Simple Wikipedia edit histories and an aligned Wikipedia–Simple Wikipedia corpus to induce a model based on quasi-synchronous grammar and integer linear programming. (Wubben et al., 2012) propose a model for simplifying sentences using monolingual Phrase-Based Machine Translation obtaining state of the art results.

Recently, significant advances have been made in sequence to sequence learning. The paradigm has shifted from traditional approaches that are more focused on optimizing the parameters of several subsystems, to a single model that learns mappings between sequences by learning fixed representations end to end. This approach employs large recurrent neural networks (RNNs) and has been successfully applied to machine translation (Cho et al., 2014; Sutskever et al., 2014), image captioning (Vinyals et

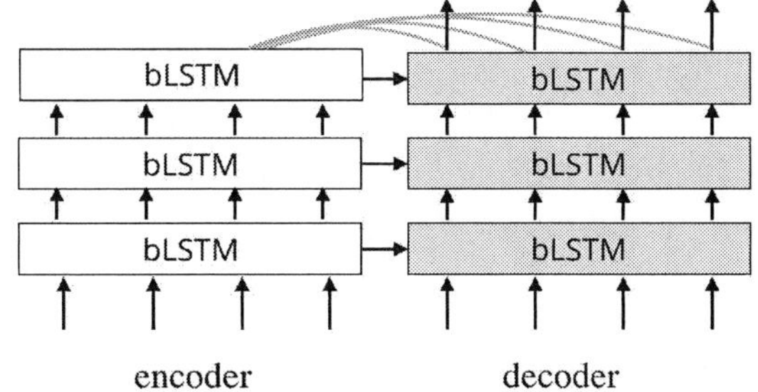

Figure 1: Schematic overview of the attentive bi-directional LSTM.

al., 2015) and extractive summarization (Filippova et al., 2015).

This encoder-decoder approach encodes a source sequence into a vector with fixed length, which the decoder decodes into the target sequence. The model is trained as a whole to maximize the probability of a correct transduction given the source sentence. While normal RNNs can have difficulties with long term dependencies, the Long Short-Term Memory (LSTM) is an extension that can handle these dependencies well and which can avoid vanishing gradients (Hochreiter and Schmidhuber, 1997).

Source vocabulary:	30,000
Target vocabulary:	10,000
Number of units per layer:	512
Number of layers:	3
Optimization:	SGD
Learning rate:	0.5
Batch size:	64

Table 1: Parameters used in the aRNN model

RNN encoders create a single representation of the entire source sequence from which the target sequence is generated by the decoder. (Bahdanau et al., 2014) claim that this fixed-length vector prevents improving the performance of encoder-decoder systems. This is particularly the case when the RNN needs to deal with long sentences. They propose an extension that allows a model to automatically search for parts of a source sentence that are relevant to predicting a target word. So, each time a target word is generated by the decoder, the model tries to find the places in the source sentence where the most relevant information is concentrated. This ar-

chitecture differs from the basic encoder-decoder in that it encodes the input sentence into a sequence of vectors and chooses a subset of these vectors while decoding. This means that not all information needs to be stored in one fixed-length vector, allowing for better performance on for instance longer sentences. In this way the model can learn soft alignments between source and target segments. This approach is called soft attention and the resulting model is an attention-based Recurrent Neural Network (aRNN). For a more detailed description of the model, see (Bahdanau et al., 2014).

A similar model is used by (Rush et al., 2015) to generate headlines. They train the model on a data set compiled from the GigaWord corpus, where longer sentences from news articles are paired with the corresponding headline of the article. They compare the performance of an attention-based RNN with a collection of other systems. They find that the vanilla attention-based RNN is unable to outperform a Moses system. Only after additional tuning on extractive compresssions do they get better ROUGE scores. This can be attributed to the fact that additional extractive features bias the system towards retaining more input words, which is beneficial for higher ROUGE scores.

Following this work, we employ an attentive Recurrent Network as described in (Bahdanau et al., 2014) to the task of abstractive summarization of scene descriptions.

3 Data set

To construct the data set to train the models on, we use the image descriptions in the MSCOCO[1] and FLICKR30K[2] (Young et al., 2014) data sets. These data sets contain images paired with multiple descriptions provided by human subjects. The FLICKR30K data set contains 158,915 captions describing 31,783 images and the MSCOCO data set contains over a million captions describing over 160,000 images. For this work, we assume that the shorter descriptions of the images are abstractive summaries of the longer descriptions. We constrain the long-short relation by stating that a short description should be at least 10 percent shorter than a long

[1]http://mscoco.org/dataset/

[2]http://shannon.cs.illinois.edu/DenotationGraph/

descriptions. Pairing the long and short sentences gives us 1,161,056 aligned sentence pairs where we consider the long sentence the source and the short sentence the target. On average, the source sentence contains 14.71 tokens and 73.23 characters and the target sentence 11.17 words and 54.77 characters. We use 900,000 pairs as our training set and the rest of the data are split into the development and test sets[3].

3.1   aRNN

The neural network model we train is based on the bidirectional sequence to sequence paradigm with attention (Bahdanau et al., 2014). The model is conditioned to maximize the probability of an output given the input sequence. We learn a model with parameters θ for each training pair (X, Y):

$$\theta = arg \max_{\theta} \sum_{X,Y} \log p(Y|X; \theta)$$

The probability p is modeled using the aRNN architecture, which was implemented in TensorFlow[4]. We set the vocabulary of the source to 30,000 and of the target to 10,000 as this covers most of the vocabularies. As we have less data and fewer output classes than earlier work in neural machine translation, we select a lower number of units than in this earlier work, namely 512 instead of 1024 (Sutskever et al., 2014). 512 dimensional word embeddings are jointly learned during training. We stack three LSTM layers on top of each other in order to learn higher level representations. Between the LSTM layers we apply dropout of nodes with probability of 0.3 for regularization of the network to prevent overfitting. Furthermore, we use a sampled softmax layer for the prediction of the words. Bucketing is used to more efficiently handle sentences of different lengths and the sentences are padded up to the maximum length in the bucket. Out of vocabulary words are replaced by an UNK token and the sentences receive special tokens for beginning (START) and end of the sequence (STOP). As soon as the decoder encounters STOP token, it stops outputting tokens. We use Stochastic Gradient Descent to maximize the training objective. We train the aRNN model on the training set and monitor perplexity on train and development data. As soon as the perplexity on the development set remains higher than on the development set we stop training to prevent overfitting.A schematic overview of the system is displayed in Figure 1

The training parameters that we choose can be found in Table 1.

A greedy search approach is used and no extra tuning is performed on the parameters of the model.

3.2   Moses

We use the Moses software package[5] to train a PBMT model (Koehn et al., 2007). A statistical machine translation model finds a best translation $\tilde{Y}$ of a sentence in one language X to a sentence in another language Y by combining a translation model that finds the most likely translation $P(X|Y)$ with a language model that outputs the most likely sentence $P(Y)$:

$$\tilde{Y} = arg \max_{Y \in Y^*} P(X|Y)P(Y)$$

Moses augments this model by regarding $log P(X|Y)$ as a loglinear model with added features and weights. During decoding, the sentence X is segmented into a sequence of I phrases. Each phrase is then translated into a phrase to form sentence Y. During this process phrases may be reordered. The GIZA++ statistical alignment package is used to perform the word alignments, which are later combined into phrase alignments in the Moses pipeline (Och and Ney, 2003) and the KenLM (Heafield, 2011) package is used to do language modelling on the target sentences.

Because Moses performs Phrase-based Machine Translation where it is often not optimal to delete unaligned phrases from the source sentence, we pad the source sentence with special EMPTY tokens until the source and target sentences contain equally many tokens. We train the Moses system with default parameters on the 900,000 padded training pairs. Additionally, we train a KenLM language model on the target side sentences from the training set. We perform MERT tuning on the development set and manually set the word penalty weight to 1.5 in order to obtain compressions that are roughly

---

[3]Data can be found at https://github.com/swubb/capcomp

[4]https://www.tensorflow.org/

[5]https://github.com/moses-smt/mosesdecoder

Original	a man flipping in the air with a snowboard above a snow covered hill
aRNN	A snowboarder is doing a trick on a snowy slope .
Moses	a person jumping a snow board jumping a hill
Human	a snow skier in a brown jacket is doing a trick
Original	many toilets without its upper top part near each other on a dark background
aRNN	A row of toilets sitting on a tiled floor .
Moses	a toilet with its top on a roof top near other
Human	An array of toilets sit crowded in a dark area .
Original	Three black cows are eating grass on the side of a hill above the city .
aRNN	Three cows are grazing in a grassy field .
Moses	Three cows grazing on a hill above a city
Human	Three cows are eating grass on the hillside .
Original	A table with three place settings with meat , vegetables and side dishes on it
aRNN	A table topped with plates of food and a glass of wine .
Moses	A table with plates of meat and vegetables with rice
Human	A dinner table filled with different dishes of food .
Original	A black cat posing on the arm of a couch and facing away from the camera .
aRNN	A black cat sitting on top of a couch .
Moses	A cat sitting on the couch behind
Human	A black cat sitting on a red sofa .
Original	A woman is leaning over a toilet , while her arms are inside a lawn and garden trash bag .
aRNN	A woman is cleaning a toilet in a park .
Moses	A woman is in a yard with a hand bag and garden
Human	A person crouched over on open lid toilet

Table 2: Example long descriptions with generated compressions and a human short description

equally long as the compressions the aRNN system generates. We also set the distortion limit to 9 to allow reordering. Our approach is similar to (Rush et al., 2015) and differs from (Wubben et al., 2012) in that they didn't change any parameters and chose heuristically from the n-best output from Moses.

model	CCR	Source BLEU
aRNN	0.62	0.08
Moses	0.61	0.09
Human	0.71	0.05

Table 3: Character compression rates and similarity to the source sentence

4 Experimental setup

Here we describe the experiment we performed in order to evaluate our models.

4.1 Materials

Out of the test set, we select only those descriptions that were aligned with four shorter descriptions. This yields a dataset of 10.080 long descriptions paired with 4 shorter descriptions each. For each of the long descriptions, we select one shorter description at random to serve as the human compression, and the remaining three are used as reference compressions for the BLEU and ROUGE metrics. This ensures the automatic measures we use can deal with variation by comparing to multiple references.

4.2 Evaluation

To evaluate the output of our systems we collect automatic scores (BLEU scores, various ROUGE scores and character compression rates) as well as human judgements on two different dimensions (Fluency and Importance).

model	BLEU	ROUGE 1	ROUGE 2	ROUGE 3	ROUGE 4	ROUGE SU4
ARNN	**0.21**	0.70	0.40	**0.28**	**0.22**	0.49
Moses	0.13	0.69	0.38	0.25	0.19	0.48
Human	0.17	**0.72**	**0.41**	**0.28**	0.21	**0.50**

Table 4: BLEU and ROUGE scores

4.2.1 Automatic Evaluation

First, we perform automatic evaluation using regular summarization and text generation evaluation metrics, such as BLEU (Papineni et al., 2002), which is generally used for Machine Translation and variants of ROUGE (Lin, 2004), which is generally used for summarization evaluation. Both take into account reference sentences and calculate overlap on the n-gram level. ROUGE also accounts for compression. ROUGE 1-4 take into account unigrams up to four-grams and ROUGE SU4 also takes into account skipgrams.

For BLEU we use `multi-bleu.pl`, and for ROUGE we used `pyrouge`. We also compute compression rate on the character level, as this tells us how much the source sentence has been compressed. We simply compute this by dividing the number of characters in the target sentence by the number of characters in the source sentence. We call this measure Character Compression Rate (CCR). Besides those measures, we additionally compute Source BLEU, which is the BLEU score of the output sentence if we take the source sentence as reference. This tells us something about how similar the sentence is compared to the source, or in other words, how aggressively the system had transformed the sentence.

4.2.2 Human Evaluation

In order to gain more insight in the quality of the generated compressions we let human subjects rate the generated compressions. Because we can only compare compressions in a meaningful way if the compression rates are similar (Napoles et al., 2011), we selected only those cases with rougly equal character compression rate (we limited this by selecting within a 0.1 CCR resolution). From this selection, we randomly selected 30 source sentences with their corresponding system outputs and one short human description which served as the human compression.

We used Crowdflower[6] to perform the evaluation study. CrowdFlower is a platform for data annotation by the crowd. We allowed only native English speakers with a trust level of minimally 90 percent to partcipate.

Following earlier evaluation studies (Clarke and Lapata, 2008; Cohn and Lapata, 2008; Wubben et al., 2012) we asked 25 participants to evaluate Fluency and Importance of the target compressions on a seven point Likert scale. Fluency was defined in the instructions as the extent to which a sentence is in proper, grammatical English. Importance was defined as the extent to which the sentence has retained the important information from the source sentence. The order of the output of the various systems was randomized. The participants saw 30 source descriptions and for each source description they evaluated all three compressions: the aRNN, Moses and Human compression. They were asked to rate the Importance and Fluency of each compression on a seven point scale with 1 being very bad and 7 very good.

5 Results

5.1 Automatic measures

As can be seen in Table 3, The aRNN and Moses systems compress at about the same rate. This was expected, as Moses has been tuned to generate compressions at a similar length as the aRNN system. Surprising is that the systems are actually compressing at a higher rate than the Human compression. If we look at Source BLEU, we see another picture. Here, we see that the Human compression generally has less overlap with the long description as the two computational models. Table 4 displays the BLEU and ROUGE scores, computed over three reference compressions. Generally we see that the aRNN and Human compression score best, with the Moses system scoring slightly worse. However, the differences

---

[6]http://www.crowdflower.com/

in ROUGE scores are not very pronounced.

model	Importance	Fluency
aRNN	4.34 CI[4.04-4.63]	5.62 CI[5.18-5.89]
Moses	3.82 CI[3.44-4.26]	3.75 CI[3.24-4.36]
Human	4.22 CI[3.83-4.58]	5.61 CI[5.24-5.80]

Table 5: Mean scores assigned by human subjects, with bootstrapped 95 percent confidence intervals between brackets

model	Correlation Imp./Flc.
aRNN	0.61*
Moses	0.82*
Human	0.36

Table 6: Pearson correlation between Importance and Fluency for the three systems. Scores marked * are significant at $p < .001$. The Human score approaches significance at $p < .06$

5.2 Human judgements

In this section we report on the human judgments of the output of the aRNN and Moses systems, compared to the human reference, in terms of Importance and Fluency. Table 5 summarizes the means and bootstrapped confidence intervals. For this, the confidence intervals were estimated using the Bias-corrected Accelerated bootstrapping method[7].Figures 2 and 3 visualize the results for Importance and Fluency respectively. The results paint a clear picture: the Moses PBMT system is rated lower than the aRNN system on both measures and the aRNN system scores nearly identical to the human description. Closer inspection of Figure 2 (Importance) shows that for this measure the difference in means is relatively small (roughly half a point on a seven point scale) and the range of scores is relatively large, indicating that there is considerable variation between sentences. The general pattern for Fluency, in Figure 3, is comparable, but much more pronounced: Fluency scores for Moses are (much) lower than for aRNN, and the latter are very similar to those for the Human descriptions.

5.3 Correlations

Interestingly, we found no significant correlations between the automatic measures and the human

---

7https://github.com/cgevans/scikits-bootstrap

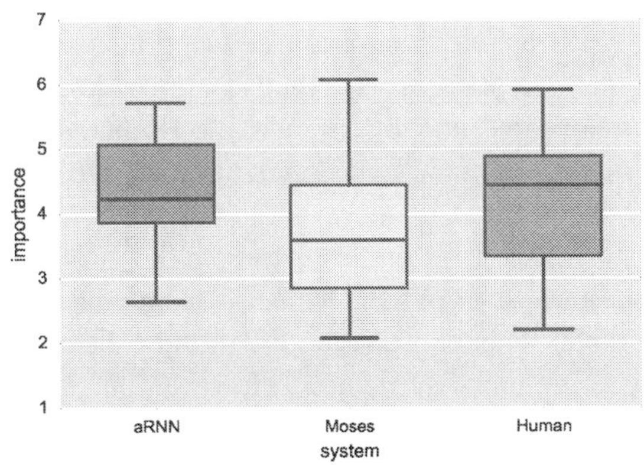

Figure 2: Importance scores given by human subjects to the two systems and human description.

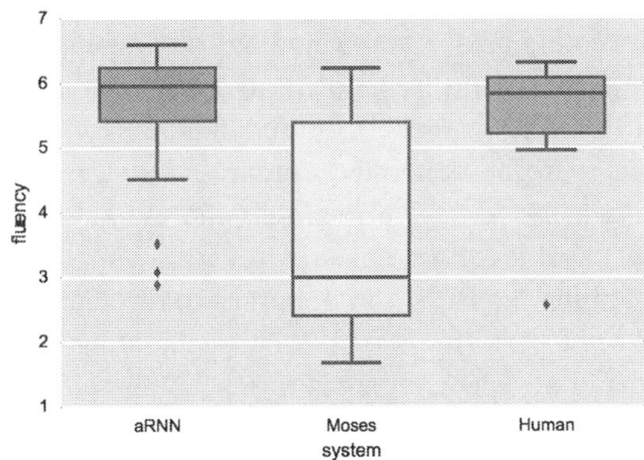

Figure 3: Fluency scores given by human subjects to the two systems and human description.

judgements. This is in line with earlier findings (Dorr et al., 2005). We did find correlations between human judgements, as can be observed in Table 6. Strong correlations are reported between the Fluency and Importance for the systems, and moderate correlation for the Human compression. This indicates some difference in the nature of the errors the systems and the humans make.

5.4 Qualitative analysis

When we look at the output in Table , we can observe a few interesting things. First, the human written descriptions sometimes contain errors, i.e. 'many toilets without its upper top part'. The aRNN system is robust to these errors as it can abstract away from them, but the Moses system copies words or phrases that are unknown from its input to its output. Another issue is that the systems base their compression on the source description, while the Human compression is actually another description of the original image. As such, the Human description might in some cases contain other information than the original sentence. Note that the system can do this as well: in the last example the aRNN adds a glass of wine and the Moses system adds rice to the table. This is probably due to the cooccurences of specific items in pictures. However, on closer inspection we find that in the great majority of cases the shorter sentence does not contain any conflicting or extra information compared to the longer sentence.

In general the aRNN model is capable of generating shorter paraphrases of longer source phrases ("are eating grass" ¿ "are grazing"). In many cases it is also successful in omitting adverbs("small , fluffy , ruffled bird" ¿ "bird") and redundant prepositional phrases in the generated compression (" throwing through the air" ¿ "throwing"). Remarkably, it is also capable of completely rewriting a sentence, something the PBMT system fails to do. The aRNN does not perform as well when generating lists of items in the scene. It tends to repeat items it has already listed ("A bathroom with a shower , toilet , and shower")

6 Discussion

In this paper we have described a method for generating abstractive compressions of scene description using attention-based bidirectional LSTMs (aRNN) trained on a new large dataset created from paired long and short image descriptions. We compared our system to a Phrase-based Machine Translation system (Moses) and a Human written short scene description. Following extensive automatic and human evaluation, we can conclude that the aRNN system generally outperforms the Moses system in terms of how much original information the compression retains and how grammatical the sentence is. In this sense the aRNN generated summaries are comparable with human ones. We also investigated the correlation between automatic measures and human judgements and found no significant correlation. Although the automatic measures paint a similar picture (although weaker), we must conclude and agree with earlier work that it is doubtful if these automatic metrics can be adequately used to measure the performance of language generation systems. If we look at correlation between the two human judgement dimensions (Importance and Fluency), we see a strong correlation between them in the automatic systems and a lower one in the human case. This might be due to the fact that when systems make a mistake, they are more likely to produce texts that are not Fluent and not Important, while humans tend to make mistakes in either of the dimensions, for instance making a spelling error or describing another part of the original picture. We should also note that the shorter sentences are not strictly summaries of the longer ones, as the annotators were not tasked with summarizing a longer sentence, but rather describe an image. As such, different descriptions might be focused detailing different parts of the image. Nevertheless, we believe the image description is a decent proxy of a summary and an aggregation of these long-short pairs can be used effectively to train an abstractive summarization system. We note that in general quality control of aligned sentences is a problem that is prevalent in and inherent to the automatic creation of large parallel corpora. While the domain is somewhat limited, we believe our contribution is valuable in that we show that the aRNN system can be successfully trained to generate true abstractive compressions, and we see many applications in typical NLG tasks and real world applications. We would like to extend the system to handle larger portions of text, moving from sentence compression to sentence fusion and paragraph compression. We are also interested in applying this model to other domains, such as sentence simplification, paraphrasing and news article compresson. We would additionally like to explore possibilities of improving caption generation system output.

Acknowledgements

This work is part of the research programmes Discussion Thread Summarization for Mobile Devices and The Automated Newsroom, which are financed by the Netherlands Organisation for Scientific Research (NWO). We thank the reviewers for their valuable comments.

References

Dzmitry Bahdanau, Kyunghyun Cho, and Yoshua Bengio. 2014. Neural machine translation by jointly learning to align and translate. *arXiv preprint arXiv:1409.0473*.

Colin Bannard and Chris C. Burch. 2005. Paraphrasing with bilingual parallel corpora. In *ACL '05: Proceedings of the 43rd Annual Meeting on Association for Computational Linguistics*, pages 597–604, Morristown, NJ, USA. Association for Computational Linguistics.

Kyunghyun Cho, Bart van Merrienboer, Caglar Gulcehre, Dzmitry Bahdanau, Fethi Bougares, Holger Schwenk, and Yoshua Bengio. 2014. Learning phrase representations using rnn encoder–decoder for statistical machine translation. In *Proceedings of the 2014 Conference on Empirical Methods in Natural Language Processing (EMNLP)*, pages 1724–1734, Doha, Qatar, October. Association for Computational Linguistics.

James Clarke and Mirella Lapata. 2008. Global inference for sentence compression an integer linear programming approach. *Journal of Artificial Intelligence Research*, 31:399–429.

Trevor Cohn and Mirella Lapata. 2007. Large margin synchronous generation and its application to sentence compression. In *Proceedings of EMNLP-CoLing*.

T. Cohn and M. Lapata. 2008. Sentence compression beyond word deletion. In *Proceedings of the 22nd International Conference on Computational Linguistics-Volume 1*, pages 137–144. Association for Computational Linguistics.

Trevor Cohn and Mirella Lapata. 2013. An abstractive approach to sentence compression. *ACM Transactions on Intelligent Systems and Technology (TIST)*, 4(3):41.

Trevor Cohn, Chris Callison-Burch, and Mirella Lapata. 2008. Constructing corpora for development and evaluation of paraphrase systems. *Computational Linguistics*, 34(4):597–614.

Will Coster and David Kauchak. 2011. Learning to simplify sentences using Wikipedia. In *Proceedings of the Workshop on Monolingual Text-To-Text Generation*, pages 1–9, Portland, Oregon, June. Association for Computational Linguistics.

Bonnie Dorr, Christof Monz, Stacy President, Richard Schwartz, and David Zajic. 2005. A methodology for extrinsic evaluation of text summarization: does rouge correlate? In *ACL Workshop on Intrinsic and Extrinsic Evaluation Measures for Machine Translation and/or Summarization*, pages 1–8.

Katja Filippova, Enrique Alfonseca, Carlos A Colmenares, Lukasz Kaiser, and Oriol Vinyals. 2015. Sentence compression by deletion with lstms. In *Proceedings of the 2015 Conference on Empirical Methods in Natural Language Processing*, pages 360–368.

Michel Galley and Kathleen McKeown. 2007. Lexicalized Markov grammars for sentence compression. In *Human Language Technologies 2007: The Conference of the North American Chapter of the Association for Computational Linguistics; Proceedings of the Main Conference*, pages 180–187, Rochester, New York, April. Association for Computational Linguistics.

Kenneth Heafield. 2011. Kenlm: Faster and smaller language model queries. In *Proceedings of the Sixth Workshop on Statistical Machine Translation*, pages 187–197. Association for Computational Linguistics.

Sepp Hochreiter and Jürgen Schmidhuber. 1997. Long short-term memory. *Neural computation*, 9(8):1735–1780.

Hongyan Jing and Kathleen McKeown. 2000. Cut and paste based text summarization. In *Proceedings of the 1st Conference of the North American Chapter of the Association for Computational Linguistics*, pages 178–185, San Francisco, CA, USA.

Kevin Knight and Daniel Marcu. 2002. Summarization beyond sentence extraction: a probabilistic approach to sentence compression. *Artif. Intell.*, 139(1):91–107.

Philipp Koehn, Hieu Hoang, Alexandra Birch, Chris C. Burch, Marcello Federico, Nicola Bertoldi, Brooke Cowan, Wade Shen, Christine Moran, Richard Zens, Chris Dyer, Ondrej Bojar, Alexandra Constantin, and Evan Herbst. 2007. Moses: Open source toolkit for statistical machine translation. In *ACL*. The Association for Computer Linguistics.

Tsung-Yi Lin, Michael Maire, Serge Belongie, James Hays, Pietro Perona, Deva Ramanan, Piotr Dollr, and C. Lawrence Zitnick. 2014. Microsoft coco: Common objects in context. In *European Conference on Computer Vision (ECCV)*, Zrich.

Chin-Yew Lin. 2004. ROUGE: A package for automatic evaluation of summaries. In *Proc. ACL workshop on Text Summarization Branches Out*, page 10.

Elena Lloret and Manuel Palomar. 2012. Text summarisation in progress: a literature review. *Artificial Intelligence Review*, 37(1):1–41.

Inderjeet Mani. 2001. *Automatic Summarization*. John Benjamins Publishers.

Erwin Marsi, Emiel Krahmer, Iris Hendrickx, and Walter Daelemans. 2010. On the limits of sentence compression by deletion. In Emiel Krahmer and Mariët Theune, editors, *Empirical methods in natural language generation*, pages 45–66. Springer-Verlag, Berlin, Heidelberg.

Ryan McDonald. 2006. Discriminative sentence compression with soft syntactic evidence. In *Proceedings of EACL*.

Courtney Napoles, Chris Callison-Burch, and Benjamin Van Durme. 2011. Evaluating sentence compression: Pitfalls and suggested remedies. In *Workshop on Monolingual Text-To-Text Generation*.

Franz Josef Och and Hermann Ney. 2003. A systematic comparison of various statistical alignment models. *Computational Linguistics*, 29(1):19–51.

Kishore Papineni, Salim Roukos, Todd Ward, and Wei-Jing Zhu. 2002. BLEU: a method for automatic evaluation of machine translation. In *Proceedings of ACL*.

Alexander M. Rush, Sumit Chopra, and Jason Weston. 2015. A neural attention model for abstractive sentence summarization. In Llus Mrquez, Chris Callison-Burch, Jian Su, Daniele Pighin, and Yuval Marton, editors, *EMNLP*, pages 379–389. The Association for Computational Linguistics.

Ilya Sutskever, Oriol Vinyals, and Quoc V Le. 2014. Sequence to sequence learning with neural networks. In *Advances in neural information processing systems*, pages 3104–3112.

Jenine Turner and Eugene Charniak. 2005. Supervised and unsupervised learning for sentence compression. In *Proceedings of the 43rd Annual Meeting of the Association for Computational Linguistics*, pages 290–297, Ann Arbor, Michigan, June.

Oriol Vinyals, Alexander Toshev, Samy Bengio, and Dumitru Erhan. 2015. Show and tell: A neural image caption generator. In *Proceedings of the IEEE Conference on Computer Vision and Pattern Recognition*, pages 3156–3164.

Kristian Woodsend and Mirella Lapata. 2011. Learning to simplify sentences with quasi-synchronous grammar and integer programming. In *Proceedings of the 2011 Conference on Empirical Methods in Natural Language Processing*, pages 409–420, Edinburgh, Scotland, UK., July. Association for Computational Linguistics.

Sander Wubben, Antal van den Bosch, and Emiel Krahmer. 2012. Sentence simplification by monolingual machine translation. In *Proceedings of the 50th Annual Meeting of the Association for Computational Linguistics (Volume 1: Long Papers)*, pages 1015–1024, Jeju Island, Korea, July. Association for Computational Linguistics.

Peter Young, Alice Lai, Micah Hodosh, and Julia Hockenmaier. 2014. From image descriptions to visual denotations: New similarity metrics for semantic inference over event descriptions. *Transactions of the Association for Computational Linguistics*, 2:67–78.

Zhemin Zhu, Delphine Bernhard, and Iryna Gurevych. 2010. A monolingual tree-based translation model for sentence simplification. In *Proceedings of the 23rd International Conference on Computational Linguistics (Coling 2010)*, pages 1353–1361, Beijing, China, August. Coling 2010 Organizing Committee.

Infusing NLU into Automatic Question Generation

Karen Mazidi and **Paul Tarau**

Department of Computer Science and Engineering
University of North Texas, Denton TX 76207 USA
`karenmazidi@my.unt.edu, paul.tarau@unt.edu`

Abstract

We present a fresh approach to automatic question generation that significantly increases the percentage of acceptable questions compared to prior state-of-the-art systems. In our evaluation of the top 20 questions, our system generated 71% more acceptable questions by informing the generation process with Natural Language Understanding techniques. The system also introduces our DeconStructure algorithm which creates an intuitive and practical structure for easily accessing sentence functional constituents in NLP applications.

1 Introduction

Question generation has been described as a dialogue and discourse task, drawing on both Natural Language Understanding and Natural Language Generation (Rus et al., 2012). However, current state-of-the-art question generation systems pay scant attention to the NLU aspect, an issue we address in this work. The question generator we present explores means of infusing NLU analysis (Allen, 1995) into the task of automatically generating questions from expository text for educational purposes. Ginzburg's work on Questions Under Discussion (2012) frames discourse as a series of questions to be addressed. Expository text could be viewed from this perspective: it is a monologue from which the author hopes the reader would be able to answer a set of questions. Automatic question generation, then, could be viewed as a process of discovering unasked questions within the monologue.

2 Prior work in question generation

Pioneering work in QG dates back to Wolfe (1976) who not only demonstrated the feasibility of automatically generating questions from text but also that automatically generated questions could be as effective as human-authored questions (Wolfe, 1977). Question generation has received revived interest in recent years, spurred in part by a series of workshops on question generation, the last one of which occurred in 2010 (Boyer and Piwek, 2010).

2.1 Common approaches to QG

Apart from a few outliers in specialized domains with limited results, the majority of question generation systems input a text source, parse the sentences, and transform sentences into questions. Two major design decisions are: (1) selecting a parser, and (2) deciding whether to use external templates or internal rules for sentence-to-question transformation. In a recent survey of question generation approaches for educational applications, Le et al. (2014) observed that template-based approaches tended to perform better than systems that syntactically rearrange the source text. Our observation is that generating any question type is theoretically possible in any approach, but that some approaches make some types easier to generate than others.

One of the most popular QG approaches involves parsing text with a PSG (phrase structure grammar) parser and then forming questions using templates (Rus et al., 2007; Wyse and Piwek, 2009; Liu et al., 2010; Liu et al., 2012) or transformation rules and tree manipulation tools (Gates, 2008; Heilman, 2011; Ali et al., 2010). Heilman notes (2011)

Sentence	ArgN	Dep. Label	Meaning
1. John broke *the window.*	Arg1	dobj	second entity in relation
2. John was *angry.*	Arg1	acomp	property of subject
3. John felt *that everyone always ignored him.*	Arg1	ccomp	proposition of subject
4. John is *an angry man.*	Arg1	attr	definition of subject
5. John wanted *to make his presence heard.*	Arg1	xcomp	purpose
6. John began *bleeding profusely.*	Arg1	xcomp	action

Table 1: Arg1 versus Dependency Labels

that these purely syntactic approaches do not allow higher-level abstractions that may be possible with more semantically informed approaches.

An alternative to the phrase-structure parse is the SRL (semantic role label) parse which identifies for each predicate in a sentence, its associated arguments and modifiers, and specifies their semantic roles. A QG system can then extract arguments and modifiers for question construction (Mannem et al., 2010; Lindberg et al., 2013; Mazidi and Nielsen, 2014; Chali and Hasan, 2015). These systems are able to generate a wider variety of questions than the phrase structure approach and are not as closely bound to the sentence source text.

A third type of parse used in QG systems is the dependency parse, which connects words in a sentence in a graphical structure based on their grammatical and functional relations. Although the SRL parse is sometimes referred to as a shallow semantic parse, certain dependency relations give greater insight into semantics than the SRL parse. The italicized portions of the sentences in Table 1 were all parsed as `Arg1` by the SRL parser. In contrast, the labels provided by the dependency parser are quite varied, and provide opportunities to glean varied meanings from what is simply `Arg1` in the SRL parse. Although the dependency parse had been used as an ancilliary tool and for sentence simplification, Mazidi et al. (2015) was the first to fully exploit dependency relations in question generation.

Another recent innovative approach (Labutov et al., 2015) used crowd sourcing to develop QG templates by leveraging the structure of their source data, Wikipedia. As an example, articles about persons have similar subsections such as Eary Life, Influences, and so forth, so that templates formed for one person should transfer reasonably well to others. It remains to be seen how this innovative but source-specific approach would transfer to other text sources such as textbooks on a wide range of topics. Interestingly, the approach relies on the observation that expository text tends to be rather redundant in structure, an observation that has parallels with the observations we offer in this paper.

2.2 NLU: the missing piece of the puzzle

Most prior work in QG views a sentence as a string of constituents and proceeds to rearrange those constituents into as many questions as possible according to grammar rules. In contrast, the work we present here first classifies what a sentence is communicating by examining the pattern of constituent arrangement. As described below, the identification of this *sentence pattern* is key to determining what type of question should be asked about that sentence, as opposed to generating questions on every possible sentence constituent. This sentence identification process is part of the DeconStructure algorithm.

3 DeconStructure algorithm

The DeconStructure algorithm has one major objective: a sentence is taken apart to be restructured in such a way that reveals what it is trying to communicate. This involves two major phases: deconstruction, then structure formation, In the deconstruction phase, the sentence is parsed with both a dependency parse and an SRL parse. Additionally, word lemmas and parts of speech are gathered, along with named entity information. In the structure formation phase, the algorithm first divides the sentence into independent clauses, then utilizes output from all parses to identify clause components and assigns each a label that represents its function within the clause. Before delving into the specifics of these two phases, we justify the approach with theoretical foundations.

Token	PSG	SRL	Dependency
1 The	(S(NP*	B-A0	det(algorithm-3,the-1)
2 DeconStructure	*	I-A0	compmod(algorithm-3,DeconStructure-2)
3 algorithm	*)	E-A0	nsubj(creates-4,algorithm-3)
4 creates	(VP*	S-V	ROOT(root-0,creates-4)
5 a	(NP(NP*	B-A1	det(representation-7,a-5)
6 functional-semantic	*	I-A1	amod(representation-7,functional-semantic-6)
7 representation	*)	I-A1	dobj(creates-4,representation-7)
8 of	(PP*	I-A1	adpmod(representation-7,of-8)
9 a	(NP*	I-A1	det(sentence-10,a-9)
10 sentence	*)))	E-A1	adpobj(of-8,sentence-10)
11 by	(PP*	B-AM-MNR	adpmod(creates-4,by-11)
12 leveraging	(S(VP*	I-AM-MNR	adpcomp(by-11,leveraging-12)
13 multiple	(NP*	I-AM-MNR	amod(parses-14,multiple-13)
14 parses	*)))))	E-AM-MNR	dobj(leveraging-12,parses-14)

Table 2: Comparing Parser Outputs: Phrase Structure Grammar, Semantic Role Label, Dependency

Constituent	Text	Head	Governor
predicate	creates	4	0
subject	the DeconStructure algorithm	3	4
dobj	a functional-semantic representation of a sentence	7	4
MNR	by leveraging multiple parses	11	4

Table 3: Front End DeconStructure for Sentence in Table 2

3.1 Theoretical Foundations

The Cambridge Grammar of the English Language (Huddleston et al., 2002) identifies three essential concepts in the analysis of sentences: (1) Sentences have parts, which may themselves have parts, (2) The parts of sentences belong to a limited range of types, and (3) The parts have specific roles or functions within the larger parts they belong to. Kroeger (2004) identifies three aspects of sentence structure: (1) argument structure, (2) constituent structure, and (3) functional structure. With these concepts in mind, the DeconStructure algorithm was designed with three desiderata: (1) Identify sentence constituents in a manner that is intuitive yet consistent with linguistic foundations, (2) Classify constituents from a set of types indicating the semantic function of constituents within sentences, and (3) Determine the sentence pattern: a sequence consisting of the root predicate, its complements and adjuncts.

3.2 Parser Comparisons

In prior work, we determined that no one parse tells us everything we would like to know about a sentence, as each of the three parser types gives its own particular viewpoint. Table 2 compares parser outputs. The PSG (phrase structure grammar) parse identifies sentence constituents and labels phrases with the appropriate phrase label such as VP, NP, and so forth. The SRL parse (semantic role label parse, also called predicate-argument parse) identifies numbered arguments of the predicate as well as modifiers. The dependency parse provides a representation of the grammatical relations between individual words in a sentence. Table 3 shows the front end of the DeconStructure created by the algorithm. The DeconStructure algorithm gleans the most important aspects from each of the parsers and combines them in to a structure that is both intuitive and practical, thus making sentence elements readily available for downstream NLP applications, such as the question generation system presented in this paper. Although Table 3 shows the front end of the DeconStructure, it is important to note that all of the parsing information from Table 2, as well as generated information such as sentence type, is available in the DeconStructure sentence object.

Pattern	Meaning	Frequency
S-V-acomp	adjectival complement that describes the subject	8%
S-V-attr	nominal predicative complement defining the subject	14%
S-V-ccomp	clausal complement indicating a proposition of subject	7%
S-V-dobj	indicates the relation between two entities	28%
S-V-iobj-dobj	indicates the relation between three entities	$< 1\%$
S-V-parg	phrase describing the how/what/where of the action	17%
S-V-xcomp	non-finite clause-like complement	8%
S-V	indicates an action of the entity	14%
other	combinations of constituents	4%

Table 4: Typical Sentence Pattern Distribution in Expository Text

3.3 Advantages of Multiple Parsers

The DeconStructure algorithm is encoded in a Python program that first parses sentences with Microsoft Research's SPLAT [1] (Quirk et al., 2012), which provides constituency parsing, dependency parsing using universal dependency labels (McDonald et al., 2013), semantic role labeling, tokenizing, POS tagging, lemmatization, and other NLP functions through a JSON (JavaScript Object Notation) request. It should be noted that the DeconStructure algorithm can be implemented with any parser that provides an SRL and dependency parse. Hence it does not require a custom parser as do other representations such as AMR (Banarescu et al., 2012).

The DeconStructure algorithm (see Algorithm 1) exploits synergies between the SRL and dependency parses. For example, a prepositional phrase that is dependent on the verb can be an argument or an adjunct. Knowing what role the PP is playing is crucial for NLP applications but the dependency parse does not identify this information. However, the SRL will label PPs with numbered arguments if they are arguments of the verb. By checking if a PP dependent on a root verb is also a numbered argument in the SRL parse, the PP can be identified as an argument; otherwise it will be considered to be an adjunct.

Complements are words, phrases and clauses that complete the meaning of the verb, including the objects of traditional grammar (Carnie, 2013; Huddleston et al., 2002). The universal dependency label set has six distinct labels that may be internal complements of the VP: direct object, indirect object, attr (attribute), acomp (adjectival complement),

ccomp (clausal complement) and xcomp (non-finite clause-like complement) (McDonald et al., 2013). Including the PP-argument and the case in which there are no internal VP arguments, this gives eight distinct patterns for major constituents in clauses. Table 4 provides pattern distribution data observed from collections of expository text. Table 7 provides sample sentences for each structure, along with generated questions. Note that all modifiers and PP that are not core arguments are available in the DeconStructure for placement in generated questions.

4 Question generation

As seen in Table 4, these *sentence patterns* fall into a surprisingly small number of categories. For each sentence, the QG system classifies its sentence pattern prior to the question generation phase. The sentence pattern is key to determining what type of question should be asked about that sentence. This analysis was based on text extracted from open source textbooks as well as Wikipedia passages, where each text passage consisted of the text of one chapter section, or Wikipedia text of equivalent length. In order to identify patterns to be included in the QG system, the following criteria was used: (1) Does the sentence pattern occur frequently across passages in different domains? (2) Is the semantic information conveyed by the sentence pattern consistent across different instances? and (3) Does the sentence pattern identify important content in source sentences so that generated questions will be meaningful and not trivial?

An independent clause can be viewed as a proposition, and the predicate identifies the relationship, property or state of the entities participating in the

---

[1] http://research.microsoft.com/en-us/projects/msrsplat/

proposition. The predicate determines the number of participants, or arguments, that are allowed (Kroeger, 2005). In the S-V-iobj-dobj pattern, for example, there must be 3 entities identified in the sentence. The predicate is often the main verb but there are other constructions in which the predicate can be found in other syntactic categories. The `acomp` constituent follows a copula verb which has negligible semantic content in this construction. The meaning is carried by the `acomp`, which may be an adjective or a noun. Linguists often used the term `xcomp` to denote predicate complements of various syntactic categories (Kroeger, 2005). In contrast, the universal dependency relations divide the complements into `acomp` for AP, `attr` for NP, `ccomp` for subordinate clauses, leaving `xcomp` for VP. It matters what syntactic category a complement belongs to because this provides important semantic indications of what the clause is saying. Take for instance a `ccomp` compared to a `dobj`. They differ syntactically in that the `ccomp` is a clause whereas the `dobj` is a phrase. Semantically, the `dobj` identifies the second entity in the predicate relation whereas the `ccomp` can be viewed as an independent proposition either indicated by or about the subject.

4.1 Templates and question generation

After a sentence object is created for each independent clause of each sentence via the DeconStructure algorithm, the sentence pattern is compared against approximately 60 templates. If a template matches the pattern, a question can be generated. Templates are designed to ask questions related to the major point of the sentence as identified in the pattern (see Table 7). Templates also contain filter conditions which are checked. Filter conditions may check for the presence or absence of particular verbs (particularly be, do and have), whether the sentence is in active or passive voice, and other conditions that are documented in the template file. More information is available[2] for those interested in implementation details.

4.2 Ranking question importance

A question generation system can increase its utility by ranking the output questions in order to iden-

---

Algorithm 1 DeconStructure Algorithm

S ← set of parsed sentences
for each sentence s ∈ S **do**
    DIVIDEINDEPCLAUSES(s)
    for each indepClause ic ∈ s: **do**
        Step 1: Add predicate complex
        ic[pred.label] ← predicate
        icRoot = pred.index
        Step 2: Add constituents
        for each dep ∈ dependencies **do**
            if dep.gov == icRoot **then**
                ic[const.label] ← dp
        Step 3: Add ArgMs to IC
        for each AM in ArgMs for icRoot **do**
            ic[AM.label] ← ArgM
        Step 4: Determine pp type
        for each pp in PPs **do**
            if pp == ArgN **then**
                pp.label = ppArg
            else
                pp.label = ppMod
        Step 5: Determine ic structure
        Determine ic type (passive, active, ...)
        Classify ic pattern
        Flag sentences with questionable parse

---

tify which questions are more likely to be acceptable. Heilman and Smith used a logistic regression question ranker which focused on linguistic quality. The ranker more than doubled the percentage of acceptable questions in the top 20% of generated questions, from 23% to 49% (2011). The logistic regression approach has also attempted by others, but with less success. One system (Lindberg et al., 2013) was able to identify with 86% precision that a question was not acceptable; however, their annotator considered 83% of the questions to be unacceptable questions so the utility of the classifer is unclear.

Given that our system typically outputs questions that are grammatically correct, we decided to evaluate the question importance, an often overlooked criterion (Vanderwende, 2008). To that end we employed the TextRank algorithm (Mihalcea and Tarau, 2004) for keyword extraction. For a given input passage, the top 25 nouns were identified by TextRank. Then each generated question was given

---

[2]http://www.karenmazidi.com/

Figure 1 box:

Figure 1: Sample Amazon Mechanical Turk HIT (Human Intelligence Task).

a score based on the percentage of top TextRank words it contained, with a penalty for very short questions such as *What is* `keyword`? Our evaluation demonstrated that outputting *important* questions also increases their acceptability scores.

5 Evaluation

There is no standard way to evaluate automatically generated questions. Recent work in QG and other NLP applications favors evaluation by crowdsourcing which has proven to be both cost and time efficient and to achieve results comparable to human evaluators (Snow et al., 2008; Heilman and Smith, 2010). We compared our system performance to the most-frequently cited prior question generation system by Heilman and Smith (2011). The evaluation was conducted using Amazon's Mechanical Turk Service. Workers were selected with at least 90% approval rating and who were located in the US and proficient in US English. To monitor quality, work was submitted in small batches, manually inspected, and run through software to detect workers whose ratings did not correspond well with fellow workers. Each question was rated on a 1-5 scale by 4 workers. The four scores were averaged. Figure 1 shows a sample HIT. Agreement between each set of workers and the average had a Pearson's correlation $r = .71$, showing high agreement.

5.1 Test data

Test data consists of 10 science and humanities passages, one each from 10 open source textbooks from OpenStax and Saylor. All text sources are written at an early college reading level with an average of 83 sentences per passage. Each passage represents the text of one textbook chapter section, chosen at random. Table 5 lists the topics in the test data set, along with the number of sentences in each file and the number of questions generated by the Heilman & Smith system and our system. The H&S system takes an overgenerate-and-rank approach, generating almost 5 questions per input sentence. In contrast, our system generates an average closer to one question per every 2 input sentences by focusing on the important content in each sentence but not generating questions when conditions are not favorable for generating a good question.

Table 5: Test Data and Questions Generated

Topic	Sents	H&S	M&T
Epithelial Tissue	148	600	77
Protists	118	545	76
Bankruptcy	37	159	23
Network Layers	79	267	55
Monetary Policy	90	431	37
Uzbekistan	71	351	52
Legislature	73	375	55
Jackson Era	46	279	24
Stages of Sleep	72	339	44
Education	103	715	50
Average	83	406	50
Generation Percents		488%	60%

5.2 Results

The evaluation looked at the top 20 questions output from each system for each input file, with each system performing its own internal ranking. Table 6 compares the average MTurk worker ratings for each file for the two systems. Our system had a higher rating for every topic. When averaging all 200 questions, the Heilman & Smith system had an average rating of 2.9. Our system had an average rating of 3.7. The results are statistically significant, $p < 0.001$, as determined by the Student's t-Test. Figure 2 shows a side-by-side histogram of the score distributions between the two systems. The histogram demonstrates that the majority of the Heilman and Smith system questions are below the midpoint of 3.0 and that the majority of our questions are above this mid-point. Using > 3.0 as the acceptability threshold, 72% of our questions are acceptable whereas only 42% of the Heilman and Smith questions pass this threshold. This is an increase in the acceptablity percentage of the top questions of 71%. Interestingly, the Heilman and Smith percentage of 42% found in our evaluation of their top 20 questions is close to the 49% acceptable percentage they found in their analysis of the top 20 *percent* of their generated questions.

Table 6: Average Scores for Top 20 Questions

Topic	H&S	M&T
Epithelial Tissue	2.6	3.9
Protists	2.6	4.1
Bankruptcy	2.7	3.5
Network Layers	3.0	3.9
Monetary Policy	2.8	3.8
Uzbekistan	3.3	3.6
Legislature	3.0	3.1
Jackson Era	3.4	3.7
Stages of Sleep	3.0	4.0
Education	2.6	3.1
Average	2.9	3.7

5.3 Error analysis

Analysis of unacceptable questions revealed both sources of errors and areas for future work. Some errors are caused by idiomatic langauge. For example the sentence: *Few members spend time in the*

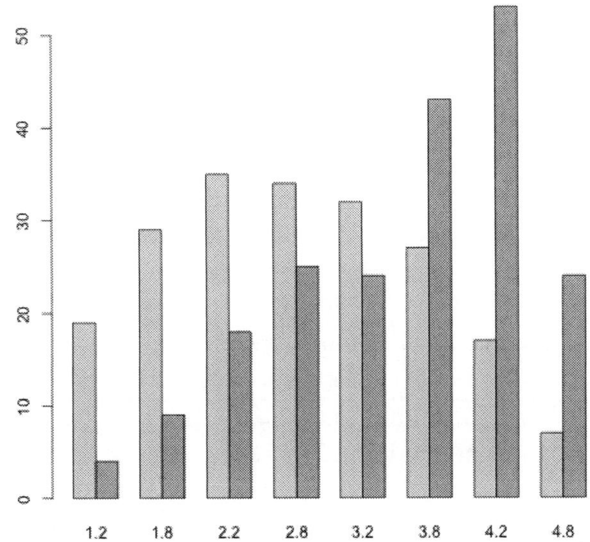

Figure 2: Score Distributions. Light:H&S, Dark:M&T

chamber other than when they are speaking or voting, resulted in the generated question: *What do few members spend?* In this case *time* grammatically is the direct object which is why this question was generated, but *spend time* is an idiom. One way to avoid generating this question would be to look for specific idiomatic phrases and rephrase them, essentially translating the idiomatic language into more direct language.

Another issue is that some templates work better with some topics other than others. For example, a template that matches the S-V-attr pattern is *How would you describe* `subject`*?* which generated the question: *How would you describe a gland?* with the answer: *a structure made up of one or more cells modified to synthesize and secrete chemical substances.* However in another passage it generates the question: *How would you describe the sea?* from the sentence: *The sea was once the fourth-largest body of water in the world.* Techniques need to be employed to identify noun phrases that are suitable for definition questions, a task to be explored in future work.

Another problem is insufficient preprocessing to remove sentences such as: *Different episodes of monetary policy are indicated in the figure,* which generated the question: *Where are different episodes of monetary policy indicated?* Our system prepro-

Pattern and Sample

1. `S-V-acomp` Adjectival complement that describes the subject.
S: Brain waves during REM sleep appear similar to brain waves during wakefulness.
Q: Indicate characteristics of brain waves during REM sleep.
2. `S-V-attr` Nominal predicative complement following copula, often defining the subject.
S: The entire eastern portion of the Aral sea has become a sand desert, complete with the deteriorating hulls of abandoned fishing vessels.
Q: How would you describe the entire eastern portion of the Aral sea?
3. `S-V-ccomp` Clausal complement indicates a proposition of or about the subject.
S: Monetary policy should be countercyclical to counterbalance the business cycles of economic downturns and upswings.
Q: What evidence could support the notion that monetary policy should be countercyclical?
4. `S-V-dobj` Indicates the relation between two entities.
S: The early portion of stage 1 sleep produces alpha waves.
Q: What does the early portion of stage 1 sleep produce?
5. `S-V-iobj-dobj` Indicates the relation between three entities.
S: The Bill of Rights gave the new federal government greater legitimacy.
Q: What gave the new federal government greater legitimacy?
6. `S-V-pparg` Prepositional phrase that is required to complete the meaning.
S: REM sleep is characterized by darting movement of closed eyes.
Q: What is REM sleep characterized by?
7. `S-V-xcomp` Non-finite clause-like complement.
S: Irrigation systems have been updated to reduce the loss of water.
A: For what purpose have the irrigation systems been updated?
8. `S-V` May contain phrases that are not considered arguments such as ArgMs.
S: The 1828 campaign was unique because of the party organization that promoted Jackson.
Q: Why was the 1828 campaign unique?

Table 7: Sample Questions by Sentence Type

cessing unit removes most but not all references to figures and tables.

Yet another issue is with text that conveys a sequence of events, in which case a given sentence in isolation may be vague. For example the sentence: *Political authority appeared to rest with the majority as never before*, generated the question: *What did political authority appear to do?* This question is vague out of context. This problem suggests that certain topics require features not available in general-purpose question generators. And indeed, there is an inherent conflict in designing a general-purpose question generation system as opposed to one targeted for a specific topic or source text.

6 Discussion

The question generation system presented here introduced a fresh approach to question generation by analyzing intrasentential structure and meaning with the DeconStructure algorithm. The pattern of the constituent structure indicates what meaning can be inferred from the sentence. This enables generation of questions relevant to the central point of a sentence and avoids the overgeneration problem of prior work. The approach can be implemented with off-the-shelf parsers that provide both a dependency and an SRL parse. The QG system achieved a 71% increase in the percentage of acceptable questions from among the top system-ranked questions compared to the most cited prior state-of-the-art system. This improvement is due in part to the internal NLU analysis of what the sentence is communicating and to the application of the TextRank algorithm to identify the most important questions.

References

Husam Ali, Yllias Chali, and Sadid A Hasan. 2010. Automation of question generation from sentences. In *Proceedings of QG2010: The Third Workshop on Question Generation*, pages 58–67.

James Allen. 1995. *Natural language understanding*. The Benjamin/Cummings Publishing Company.

Laura Banarescu, Claire Bonial, Shu Cai, Madalina Georgescu, Kira Griffitt, Ulf Hermjakob, Kevin Knight, Philipp Koehn, Martha Palmer, and Nathan Schneider. 2012. Abstract meaning representation (amr) 1.0 specification. In *Parsing on Freebase from Question-Answer Pairs. In Proceedings of the 2013 Conference on Empirical Methods in Natural Language Processing. Seattle: ACL*, pages 1533–1544.

Kristy Elizabeth Boyer and Paul Piwek. 2010. Proceedings. In *Proceedings of QG2010: The Third Workshop on Question Generation. Pittsburgh: questiongeneration. org*.

Andrew Carnie. 2013. *Syntax: A generative introduction*. John Wiley & Sons.

Yllias Chali and Sadid A Hasan. 2015. Towards topic-to-question generation. *Computational Linguistics*.

D Gates. 2008. Generating look-back strategy questions from expository texts. In *The Workshop on the Question Generation Shared Task and Evaluation Challenge, NSF, Arlington, VA. http://www. cs. memphis. edu/~ vrus/questiongeneration//1-Gates-QG08. pdf*.

Jonathan Ginzburg. 2012. *The interactive stance*. Oxford University Press.

Michael Heilman and Noah A Smith. 2010. Rating computer-generated questions with mechanical turk. In *Proceedings of the NAACL HLT 2010 Workshop on Creating Speech and Language Data with Amazon's Mechanical Turk*, pages 35–40. Association for Computational Linguistics.

Michael Heilman. 2011. *Automatic factual question generation from text*. Ph.D. thesis, Carnegie Mellon University.

Rodney Huddleston, Geoffrey K Pullum, et al. 2002. The cambridge grammar of english. *Language. Cambridge: Cambridge University Press*, pages 1–23.

Paul Kroeger. 2004. *Analyzing syntax: a lexical-functional approach*. Cambridge University Press.

Paul R Kroeger. 2005. *Analyzing grammar: An introduction*. Cambridge University Press.

Igor Labutov, Sumit Basu, and Lucy Vanderwende. 2015. Deep questions without deep understanding. In *Proceedings of the 53rd Annual Meeting of the Association for Computational Linguistics*.

Nguyen-Thinh Le, Tomoko Kojiri, and Niels Pinkwart. 2014. Automatic question generation for educational applications–the state of art. In *Advanced Computational Methods for Knowledge Engineering*, pages 325–338. Springer.

David Lindberg, Fred Popowich, John Nesbit, and Phil Winne. 2013. Generating natural language questions to support learning on-line. In *Proceedings of the 14th European Workshop on Natural Language Generation*. Association for Computational Linguistics.

Ming Liu, Rafael A Calvo, and Vasile Rus. 2010. Automatic question generation for literature review writing support. In *Intelligent Tutoring Systems*, pages 45–54. Springer.

Ming Liu, Rafael A Calvo, and Vasile Rus. 2012. G-asks: An intelligent automatic question generation system for academic writing support. *Dialogue and Discourse: Special Issue on Question Generation*, 3(2):101–124.

Prashanth Mannem, Rashmi Prasad, and Aravind Joshi. 2010. Question generation from paragraphs at upenn: Qgstec system description. In *Proceedings of QG2010: The Third Workshop on Question Generation*, pages 84–91.

Karen Mazidi and Rodney D Nielsen. 2014. Linguistic considerations in automatic question generation. In *Proceedings of the 52nd Annual Meeting of the Association for Computational Linguistics. Baltimore, Maryland: Association for Computational Linguistics*.

Karen Mazidi and Rodney D Nielsen. 2015. Leveraging multiple views of text for automatic question generation. In *Artificial Intelligence in Education, Springer LNCS*.

Ryan T McDonald, Joakim Nivre, Yvonne Quirmbach-Brundage, Yoav Goldberg, Dipanjan Das, Kuzman Ganchev, Keith B Hall, Slav Petrov, Hao Zhang, Oscar Täckström, et al. 2013. Universal dependency annotation for multilingual parsing. In *ACL (2)*, pages 92–97. Citeseer.

Rada Mihalcea and Paul Tarau. 2004. Textrank: Bringing order into texts. Association for Computational Linguistics.

Chris Quirk, Pallavi Choudhury, Jianfeng Gao, Hisami Suzuki, Kristina Toutanova, Michael Gamon, Wen-tau Yih, Lucy Vanderwende, and Colin Cherry. 2012. Msr splat, a language analysis toolkit. In *Proceedings of the 2012 Conference of the North American Chapter of the Association for Computational Linguistics: Human Language Technologies: Demonstration Session*, pages 21–24. Association for Computational Linguistics.

Vasile Rus, Zhiqiang Cai, and Arthur C Graesser. 2007. Experiments on generating questions about facts. In *Computational Linguistics and Intelligent Text Processing*, pages 444–455. Springer.

Vasile Rus, Brendan Wyse, Paul Piwek, Mihai Lintean, Svetlana Stoyanchev, and Cristian Moldovan. 2012. A detailed account of the first question generation shared task evaluation challenge. *Dialogue and Discourse*, 3(2):177–204.

Rion Snow, Brendan O'Connor, Daniel Jurafsky, and Andrew Y Ng. 2008. Cheap and fast—but is it good?: evaluating non-expert annotations for natural language tasks. In *Proceedings of the conference on empirical methods in natural language processing*, pages 254–263. Association for Computational Linguistics.

Lucy Vanderwende. 2008. The importance of being important: Question generation. In *Proceedings of the 1st Workshop on the Question Generation Shared Task Evaluation Challenge, Arlington, VA*.

John H Wolfe. 1976. Automatic question generation from text-an aid to independent study. In *ACM SIGCUE Outlook*, volume 10, pages 104–112. ACM.

John H Wolfe. 1977. Reading retention as a function of method for generating interspersed questions. Technical report, DTIC Document.

Brendan Wyse and Paul Piwek. 2009. Generating questions from openlearn study units.

Automatic label generation for news comment clusters

Ahmet Aker, Monica Paramita, Emina Kurtic, Adam Funk, Emma Barker
Mark Hepple and **Robert Gaizauskas**
University of Sheffield, UK
`ahmet.aker@ m.paramita@ e.kurtic@ a.funk@ e.barker@`
`m.hepple@ r.gaizauskas@ sheffield.ac.uk`

Abstract

We present a supervised approach to automatically labelling topic clusters of reader comments to online news. We use a feature set that includes both features capturing properties local to the cluster and features that capture aspects from the news article and from comments outside the cluster. We evaluate the approach in an automatic and a manual, task-based setting. Both evaluations show the approach to outperform a baseline method, which uses tf*idf to select comment-internal terms for use as topic labels. We illustrate how cluster labels can be used to generate cluster summaries and present two alternative summary formats: a pie chart summary and an abstractive summary.

1 Introduction

In many application domains such as search engine snippet clustering (Scaiella et al., 2012), summarising YouTube video comments (Khabiri et al., 2011) or online comments to news (Ma et al., 2012), grouping unlinked text segments by topic has been identified as a major requirement towards enabling efficient search or exploration of text collections.

In the online news domain, thousands of reader comments are produced daily. Identifying topics in comment streams is vitally important to providing an overview of what readers are saying. However, merely clustering comments is not enough: topic clusters should also be given labels that accurately reflect their content, and that are accessible to users.

Producing "good labels" is challenging, as what constitutes a good label is not well defined. A common method of labelling topic clusters with the top-n key terms characterising the topic is reported as less suitable than generating "textual labels" not consisting of key terms, to meaningfully represent the topic (Lau et al., 2011; Mei et al., 2007).

In most studies, such textual labels are still extractive, i.e. the methods rely on labels being present within the textual sources (Lau et al., 2011; Mei et al., 2007). To overcome this limitation, many studies use external resources, most notably Wikipedia, for deriving topic labels. Hulpus et al. (2013), for example, present a graph-based approach to labeling using DBpedia concepts. An advantage of such approaches is the potential to provide labels that are more abstract, and hence more akin to labels humans might produce. Aker et al. (2016) apply such an approach to the online news domain, and evaluate it via an information retrieval task (similar to the evaluation in Aletras et al. (2014)). However, low recall figures were reported due to the abstractedness of the labels. Joty et al. (2013) also argue that external resources like Wikipedia titles are too broad for their e-mail and blog domain, as shown by the fact that none of the human-created labels in their development set appears in a Wikipedia title. Chang et al. (2015) use human generated labels for social media posts in Google+, suggesting that post-internal information is not suitable for deriving labels.

In our work, we investigated label extraction from both the comments and from external sources, in our case the news article itself. This is motivated by two factors. First, in this domain, the news article triggers the comments, so it is plausible that the article will contain terms suitable for labelling the topics of some comment clusters. Second, comments do not only discuss topics from the article, but may drift away from them. Hence, using comment-internal terms as labels may be useful too. Thus we hypothesise that combining these two resources for label extraction should lead to a better performance. We test this hypothesis using a baseline that extracts labels from the comment clusters only. We adopt phrase or term as the most suitable linguistic unit to represent labels as evidenced by several previous studies (Mei et al., 2007; Joty et al., 2013; Aker et al., 2016).

This paper is organised as follows. Section 2 describes our dataset. Section 3 discusses our labeling approach. The experimental setup as well the description of our baseline method are reported in Section 4. In Section 5 we present and discuss the results. Section 6 presents how labels are used generate cluster summaries. Section 7 concludes the paper and outlines directions for future work.

2 Data

We used the gold-standard (GS) dataset reported in Barker et al. (2016). The dataset contains human-generated comment clusters for the first 100 associated comments of 18 online news articles from *The Guardian*. Fifteen articles were annotated by 2 annotators, and the remaining three by 3 annotators, resulting in 39 annotation sets. Annotators were asked to write summaries of the first 100 comments of each article, and created the comment clusters to facilitate them in this task. Annotators also provided a label for each cluster, to describe its content in terms of, e.g., topics, arguments or propositions, and different viewpoints. The resulting labels include a range of descriptors, from key words (e.g. "Climate change"), to full propositions or questions (e.g. "Why use the fine on wifi?").

Annotators were allowed to create sub-clusters if necessary; each sub-cluster also being assigned a label. For example, a cluster labelled "Climate change" has sub-clusters, such as "Natural or man-made", "Facts and statistics" and "Global warming". For this study, we flattened the clustering levels by treating each sub-cluster as an independent cluster.[1] Each sub-cluster label is concatenated with that of

---

[1]A parent cluster is also treated as an independent cluster if it includes any comments not included in any of its sub-clusters.

	Automatic Evaluation	Manual Evaluation
Number of clusters	415	20
Cluster labels (no. of words)	Min: 1 Max: 55 Mean: 8.88 Median: 7	Min: 1 Max: 9 Mean: 5.7 Median: 6
Cluster size (no. of comments)	Min: 1 Max: 37 Mean: 7.45 Median: 6	Min: 4 Max: 14 Mean: 7.9 Median: 8

Table 1: Dataset statistics

its parent cluster, e.g. in the above example, the sub-cluster "Global warming" becomes an independent cluster labelled "Climate change: Global warming". In total, the dataset contains 514 clusters, containing an average 7.88 comments (min: 1, max: 69, median: 6), with 8.53 words on average per label (min: 1, max: 55, median: 6).

We further filtered this data, by eliminating clusters whose labels do not reflect the *topic* of the cluster, e.g. labels such as "Jokes", "Personal attacks to commenters or empty sarcasm", "Miscellaneous" or "criticisms". This resulted in a set of 415 clusters that were used for the automatic evaluation.

For the manual evaluation, we further reduced the pool of clusters to those with a maximum of 14 comments (so that annotators could read all the comments prior to assessing the labels), and a minimum of 4 comments (so that annotators had enough data to determine the content of the comments). Lastly, only clusters whose labels contained at most 10 words were allowed, as it is not relevant to compare labels with significant length differences. From this pool, 20 comment clusters were randomly selected. Table 1 provides statistics on the two evaluation sets.

3 Method

Our labeling approach is supervised and we refer to it as *SCL* (Supervised Cluster Labeler). Using the entire set of manually annotated *Guardian* articles, we collect training data to build a regression model for extracting labels for automatic clusters.

To do this we first extract terms[2] from the arti-

---

[2]Terms are noun phrase-like word sequences and are extracted using POS-tag grammars such as *NN NN*. We use the automatically generated POS-tag grammars reported by Aker et al. (2014).

cle as well as comments and represent them with features. Each term is assigned a score between 0 and 1, where 0 indicates a term that is a poor label for a cluster, and 1 a term that makes an excellent label. We obtain the score using human summaries generated for the *Guardian* articles. For these human summaries we have the information about which sentences in the summary links to which human clusters. If the question is to answer whether the term X is a good label for the Y cluster, then we collect the sentences from the human summaries that are linked to that Y cluster and compare that term X with terms extracted from the summary sentences. The comparison is based on Word2Vec (Mikolov et al., 2013) similarity computation and results in a score that varies between 0 and 1. Following this approach we collect training data consisting of terms represented by features and the similarity score to be predicted. Once we have such training data we use linear regression[3] to train a regression model where the combination of the features is based on weighted linear combination.

In the test case, i.e., running the cluster labeling approach on a cluster to generate a new label, we again determine terms from the article and the comments, extract features, use the regression model to score the terms and select the best scoring term as the label for that cluster. The next section gives a detailed description of the features we used for representing candidate labels.

3.1 Features

In the cluster labeling approach we use several features extracted from the news article and the comments. To investigate to what extent our intuition about the relevance of the news article for labelling comment clusters is justified and craft features, we analysed a set of 1.7K *Guardian* news articles along with their user generated comments. On average we have 206 comments per news article. From each news article we extracted terms and analysed whether they are also used in the comments. Our analysis shows that 35% of the terms extracted from the news article also occur in the comments. We also found out that on average 55% of terms from

the title, and 60% of terms from the first sentence, were mentioned in the comments. Terms extracted from other parts of the news article (sentences 2 to 6 and sentences after the 6th) were mentioned in the comments in only around 45% and 33% of cases respectively. Around 43% of comments mentioned at least one term that was found in the article.

Based on this analysis we derived the following features:

- **#Term in title**: the number of occurrences of a term in the article title.
- **#Term in first sentence**: the number of occurrences of a term in the first sentence of the article.
- **#Term in sentences 2–6 (first paragraph)**: the number of occurrences of a term in the article sentences 2–6.
- **#Term in sentences after 6 (main text body)**: the number of occurrences of a term in the final portion of the article (from the 7th sentence to the end of the article).
- **#Term in the entire article**: the number of occurrences of a term in the entire article.
- **Article centroid similarity**: the cosine similarity (Salton and Lesk, 1968) between the term and the article centroid. The similarity is based on Word2Vec word embeddings: each word is represented by a 400-dimensional word embedding. We use the vectors published by Baroni et al. (2014). To compute the similarity of term:document pair, we remove stop-words and punctuation from each, then query for each remaining word's vector representation using the Word2Vec, and create a sum of the word vectors. We use the resulting sum vectors to compute their cosine similarity.

In addition to these article-related features, we also compute the following features:

- **Term length**: the number of words in the term.
- **#Term in all comments**: the frequency of a term in all comments given to the article.
- **#Term in all comments of cluster**: the number of occurrences of a term in all comments of a cluster.
- **Cluster centroid similarity**: the cosine similarity between the term and the cluster centroid. The similarity is based on Word2Vec.
- **#Term in article + comments**: the count of occurrences of a term in the article and its comments.

4 Evaluation

To assess the quality of automatic labels, we used two different evaluations: automatic and manual. In

---

[3]We use Weka's implementation of linear regression. `http://www.cs.waikato.ac.nz/ml/weka/`

both, we compare the performance of our proposed method *SCL* to our baseline method of tf*idf-based labeling, which is described below.

4.1 Baseline: *tf*idf*-based labeling

In the baseline approach we extract labels from the cluster using the *tf*idf* metric from information retrieval. In our case *tf* (term frequency) is the number of times a candidate label occurs in a cluster. The *idf* is computed based on the number of 'documents' in which the label occurs, where the document set comprises the article's comment plus an additional 4 documents created by splitting the article into the following parts: title, first sentence, (rest of) first paragraph and the remaining text body (as motivated by the observations in Section 3). The candidate labels for a cluster are scored by *tf*idf*, and the top scoring one selected as the cluster label. For comparability with the proposed approach (Section 3) we use terms to represent labels.

4.2 Automatic evaluation

For the automatic evaluation we compare the gold standard labels to the machine generated ones. For this purpose we use cosine similarity with and without Word2Vec word embeddings. We chose this approach for two reasons. First, when humans and machine select labels that are the same or very similar, this can be captured by cosine similarity without Word2Vec word embeddings. Second, humans and machine labels could have similar meaning but use different words, due to synonymy, in which case the use of Word2Vec word embeddings will help cosine to capture the semantic similarity between the labels. Because of these reasons we use cosine with and without Word2Vec word embeddings. The cosine similarity between two labels L_1 and L_2 is computed as follows:

$$cosine(L_1, L_2) = \frac{V(L_1) \cdot V(L_2)}{|V(L_1)| * |V(L_2)|} \quad (1)$$

where $V(.)$ is – depending on whether Word2Vec embeddings are used – either the word vector holding the frequency counts of the words in the respective label or the 400 dimension Word2Vec vector holding the word embeddings. Stop-words are removed before computing this metric. The metric returns a value from 0 (no similarity) to 1 (100% sim-

Metric	SCL	Baseline
Word-based	0.084	0.092
Word2Vec	0.37	0.30

Table 2: Automatic evaluation results

ilar). Overall performance is computed as the average, across all 415 clusters of the evaluation set, of the similarity scores between the automatically selected gold standard labels of the cluster

4.3 Manual evaluation

In our manual evaluation, we used an online interface where the assessors could first read the news article and assess the quality of the labels based on the scenario shown in Figure 1. Four assessors took part in the evaluation; all were fluent in English and had a background in Computer Science. All assessors evaluated the entire set of 20 clusters.

The manual evaluation was divided into three parts. In the first part, assessors were asked to read the comments in the given cluster and to suggest a relevant label to this cluster (referred to as "*assessor labels*"). In the second part, three different labels (gold standard label, baseline label, and the label generated using our SCL method) were then shown in a random order. For each label, assessors were asked to answer three questions using a 5-point Likert Scale (1: strongly disagree, 5: strongly agree): i) Q1: I can understand this label, ii) Q2: This label is a complete phrase, and iii) Q3: This label accurately reflects the content of the comment cluster. Lastly, assessors were asked to provide any comments of all the labels they have assessed.

> *Imagine you want to gain a quick overview of what is said in the comments of the news article, but have only a limited amount of time (e.g. a coffee break). The system groups comments into clusters (relating to the same topic), and provides a label, which is a word or phrase that briefly indicates the content of the cluster. A good label should give you a sense of the topics discussed in a cluster, perhaps helping you to decide whether or not to read those comments.*

Figure 1: Manual evaluation scenario

5 Results

5.1 Automatic evaluation results

The results of the automatic evaluation are shown in Table 2. From the table we can see that both baseline and the proposed approach achieve very similar scores measured using cosine without Word2Vec embeddings. Both scores are below 10% indicating that they have very little word overlap between the gold standard labels. When Word2Vec embeddings are used we see the SCL method achieves higher Word2Vec cosine similarity than the baseline method. The difference between the methods is also significant ($p < 0.05$).[4] According to this SCL is a better choice in terms of automatic cluster labeling.

5.2 Manual evaluation results

We gathered judgments of 20 cluster labels from each method: gold-standard (GS), baseline, and SCL. This results in the judgments of 60 cluster labels given by each assessor. These labels were evaluated on three aspects as described in Section 4.3. Figure 2 shows the average scores given by the four assessors for the evaluation questions, where Q1 identifies whether the label can be understood, Q2 represents the phrase completeness of the label, and Q3 represents the accuracy of the label. As we can see from the results the average scores with respect to the Q1 and Q2 are for both the baseline and our SCL method close to the gold label scores. This shows that both automatic labels can be understood and that they are both complete phrases. The results for the Q3, however, are for both systems much lower than the gold label figures. The baseline system achieves on average 1.98, the SCL 2.43 and the gold labels 4.26. The results between the baseline and SCL present a stable bias across all questions towards the SCL method. In all questions the SCL method outperforms the baseline approach by on average 0.27-0.45 points.

We measure inter-assessor agreement using Krippendorff's alpha coefficient.[5] Agreements in Q1 and Q2 are 0.423 and 0.372, respectively, while, higher

---

[4] Signficance was computed using a one-tailed Student t-test.

[5] Scores were computed using R, with the default 'ordinal' weighting that punishes larger disagreements more than smaller ones. For example, a disagreement between scores 1 and 3 is punished more than that between 1 and 2.

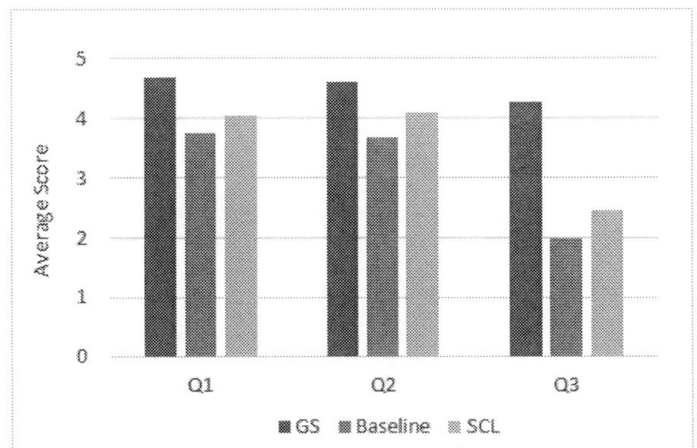

Figure 2: Average scores (4 assessors) on a scale 1:strongly disagree to 5:strongly agree. Questions: Q1:I can understand this label, Q2:This label is a complete phrase, Q3:This label accurately reflects the content of the comment cluster.

agreement of $\alpha = 0.699$ is achieved in Q3. Overall, 91.67% cases in Q3 were assigned the identical or a majority score by the four assessors. These figures were 88.3% and 85% for Q1 and Q2, respectively.

Disagreements in Q1 occurred when the labels included errors or were grammatically incorrect, such as 'threat so network rail'. The assessors differed in their judgment as to whether the error was relevant to their understanding of the label. A further source of disagreement in Q1 were general labels ('design stage'), or abstract labels ('bath of snobbery').

5.3 Discussion

The automatic comparison between the machine generated labels and the gold standard ones shows that our proposed method significantly outperforms the baseline approach and is a better choice for automatic cluster labeling. This is also confirmed by the manual evaluation figures where again the SCL method outperforms the baseline approach. The correspondence between automatic and manual evaluation results shows that the Word2Vec based cosine similarity is able to capture the performance differences between different labelling systems.

On the manual evaluation side, Figure 2 shows that both the baseline and the SCL methods perform similar to the gold standard labels with respect to questions Q1 and Q2. However, in case of the Q3 their results substantially differ from the gold standard figures.

We have manually performed an error analysis

to understand the reasons for this. The error analysis reveals that labels which summarise the overall discussion in the cluster have been more-highly rated than labels that pick up only a specific mention of that discussion. For instance, row 1 of Table 3 shows labels generated for a cluster talking about sewage workers. The gold standard (GS) label captures the essence of the discussion that they should be rewarded for their job, and so provides a good summary of the overall discussion. The automatic methods also capture that the discussion is about the sewage workers, but are not able to abstract it to summarise the entire discussion. From the assessor labels provided by our four judges during evaluation we can see that they label clusters using the same strategy followed by the annotators who generated the gold standard labels.[6] The labels shown in rows 2 and 3 of the table display the same tendency. Again the automatic labels capture a specific part of a discussion and fail to summarise it, while manually generated labels (both GS and assessor labels) provide a gist of the discussion. This clearly shows that good labels go beyond mere extraction of specific facts, and that automatic labeling systems should seek to more abstractly characterise content.

The performance difference between the SCL and the baseline method is most of the time due to the ability of capturing the topic discussed. Although in most cases the baseline method is able to pick up a specific topic relevant key word from a discussion, it fails to do this in few cases. Rows 3 and 4 of Table 3 show examples of such case. We can see that the baseline labels are somewhat related to the discussion however, it is not clear what they refers to. On the other hand the SCL labels do cover a specific part of a discussion completely.

Another reason is that the lengths of the automatically generated labels are generally shorter than the gold-standard labels, as shown in Table 4. The average number of words in the baseline labels and SCL labels are 2.7 and 4.55, whilst the human-proposed labels, i.e. the GS and assessor labels were much longer: an average of 5.7 and 6 words, respectively. This finding shows that additional words are needed to summarise the comment clusters more accurately.

------

[6]Note that the assessors did not see any labels before providing these labels for comment clusters.

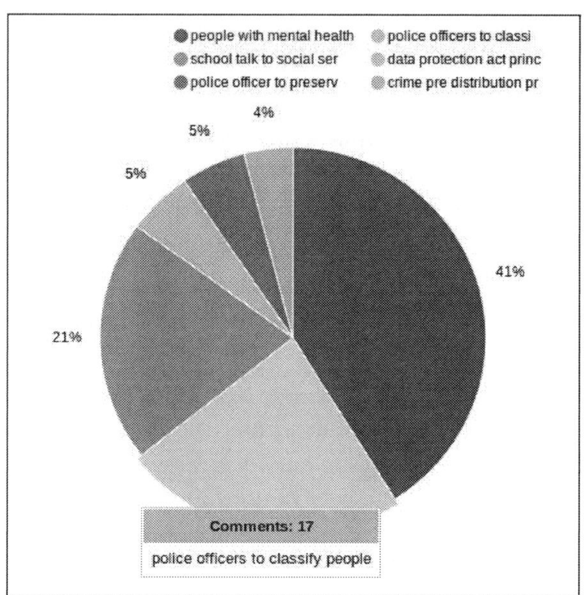

Figure 3: Pie chart

6 Application of cluster labels

Cluster labels can be used for various applications. In this section we describe how cluster labels can be used for summarisation, and we present two alternative summary formats: a pie chart summary and an abstractive summary. Both summary types could be used by readers of online news to quickly access the content of reader comments instead of browsing through entire comment threads, as in the current set up of commenting forums.

6.1 Pie chart summary

We use a pie chart to present a graphical summary of the clusters. The slices represent the clusters with the labels marking the slices. Figure 3 shows a typical pie chart with 6 clusters.

The pie chart is dynamically generated using PHP, JavaScript, and the D3 graphics library, and the cluster labels in the legend are truncated so they all fit neatly on the page. The chart is usually displayed plain with only percentages, but when the user hovers the mouse over a slice of the pie chart, that slice is emphasised and a box with the number of comments and the full text of the cluster label appears. Clicking on the slice causes a scrollable list of the comments in the cluster to appear in another section of same web page (not shown here). The pie chart gives an indicative summary of the clusters by

Method	Label	Score
GS	thanking sewerage workers: sewerage workers should be rewarded	4.75
SCL	people who work down sewers	3
Baseline	sewage worker	3
Assessor Labels	praise for the sewage workers; Praise for sewage workers; gratitude for the sewer workers; Appreciation for sewage workers	NA
GS	comparison between sewerage workers and declogging medication	4
SCL	cholesterol in your cells	2
Baseline	remove cholesterol	1.75
Assessor Labels	statin metaphors and jokes; Analogy for the sewage workers; sewage workers; sewage workers analogised as statins	NA
GS	planes for the carriers	4.25
SCL	ballistic anti carrier missiles	1.75
Baseline	thousands of miles	1
Assessor Labels	planes, especially aboard ships; Inefficient usage as a ship carrier; planes on ship; lack of planes to carry	NA
GS	plain packaging: plain packaging in Australia	4.5
SCL	sales of tobacco per person in Australia	3.75
Baseline	target for measures	1
Assessor Labels	effects of plain packaging on smoking rates in Australia; Plain-packaging reduced smoking in Australia; statistics regarding smoking habits after similar moves in Australia; Decline in smoking (or not?) after introducing plain packaging	NA

Table 3: Error analysis: example labels along with their average judgment scores. 'Assessor Labels' lists the labels proposed by each of the four assessors, separated by ";".

	Min	Max	Avg	Median
GS	1	9	5.7	6
SCL	3	7	4.55	4
Baseline	2	5	2.7	2
Assessor Labels	1	13	6	6

Table 4: Comparison of label lengths

first showing only the label and the proportion of the comments that fall in each cluster, but it also enables the user to access the full content of the cluster by just clicking the slice.

6.2 Abstractive summary

In addition to the pie chart summary we also generate an abstractive summary. Similar to the pie chart summary the cluster information is used to generate the abstractive summary. The input to the abstractive summariser are the clusters along with their labels. Using this input our summariser applies the following steps to generate the summary:

1. **Ordering the labels**: Each cluster comes with a label generated by the SCL method (see Section 3). The clusters are sorted according to their size, i.e. the number of comments.

2. **Selecting patterns in which to embed labels**: In this setup our aim is to write a sentence for each label. For this we have written a pool of patterns such as "Most of the comments talk about the topic ...", or "A good amount of contributors discuss the matter ...", etc. Based on the size of the cluster a pattern from the pattern pool is automatically selected and expanded with the label of that cluster. This process proceeds through cluster labels in descending order of cluster size.

3. **Selecting example sentences from the cluster**: Finally, we select for each cluster label an example sentence extracted from the comments of that cluster. To do this we construct the centroid vector representation of the entire cluster. The vector is based on Word2Vec and sums the vectors of all candidate labels within that label. This sum vector is then compared to Word2Vec vectors of individual sentences using cosine. The sentence that has the highest cosine similarity to the centroid is selected as the example sentence. In the summary the sentences extracted as example follow the generated sentences containing the pattern and the cluster label.

Figure 4 shows an example summary. Compared to the pie chart this abstractive summary also provides an example sentence about the label/topic used to mark the cluster. This is a useful feature to highlight what the discussion within the cluster looks like. Of course, similar to the pie chart, the labels in the summary can be coded as hyperlinks to provide

Most of the comments talk about the topic *"people with mental health issues"*. For example people say "My brother in law has a number of mental health issues including paranoid schizophrenia."

A good amount of contributors discuss the matter *"police officers to classify people"*. An example of such discussion is "The police aren't doctors and they shouldn't try to be."

Some people also share their opinions about the topic *"police access"*. An example of such opinion is "This is sadly what can happen when the police become involved with the vulnerable." Moreover what difference would it have made had the police access to his records?"

Furthermore, a few discussions entail the subject "school talk to social services". E.g. "Do you actually know what data social services and the police hold about you and whether it's accurate?"

Another few mention the topic about *"data protection act principles"*. A good example for this is the comment extract "Don't forget we are talking about sensitive personal data here."

In addition, some minor discussions are about the topic "police officer to preserve freedom". An examplar of such discussion is "It should be recognised as the duty of every police officer to preserve freedom."

Figure 4: Example abstractive summary.

access to the associated comment set. In the future we plan to expand the summary with two example sentences to each cluster label to also encode stance (agreement/disagreement) information. We aim to include an agreeing and a disagreeing sentence with respect to the cluster label.

7 Conclusions

In this paper we investigated cluster labeling for clusters containing reader comments to online news. Our labeling approach employs a feature set that includes both features capturing properties local to the cluster and features that capture aspects from the news article and from comments outside the cluster. The features are weighted and linearly combined. Feature weights are trained using gold standard data and linear regression. To assess the quality of the proposed approach (SCL) we compared it against a *tf*idf* based baseline using an automatic and a manual evaluation. Both evaluations showed that the SCL outperforms the baseline system. We also demonstrated how cluster labels can be used to provide cluster summaries and presented a pie chart and abstractive summary generated directly from the clusters and their labels.

In future we will focus on the limitations of the current studies: We aim to improve our proposed SCL method and aim to generate labels that take into consideration the entire discussion rather than picking a specific fact from it. With respect to the application areas we aim to enhance our comment cluster summaries with stance information. Similarly we aim to include sentiment information to capture the emotions expressed in the comments. On the manual evaluation track we aim to increase our gold standard data. This will help us to draw more reliable conclusions about the different methods.

Acknowledgments

This work was carried out as part of the EU-funded FP7 SENSEI project, grant number FP7-ICT-610916.

References

Ahmet Aker, Monica Lestari Paramita, Emma Barker, and Robert J Gaizauskas. 2014. Bootstrapping term extractors for multiple languages. In *LREC*, pages 483–489.

Ahmet Aker, Emina Kurtic, Balamurali A R, Monica Paramita, Emma Barker, Mark Hepple, and Rob Gaizauskas. 2016. A graph-based approach to topic clustering for online comments to news. In *Proceedings of the 38th European Conference on Information Retrieval*.

Nikolaos Aletras, Timothy Baldwin, Jey Han Lau, and Mark Stevenson. 2014. Representing topics labels for exploring digital libraries. In *Proceedings of the 14th ACM/IEEE-CS Joint Conference on Digital Libraries*, pages 239–248. IEEE Press.

Emma Barker, Monica Paramita, Ahmet Aker, Emina Kurtic, Mark Hepple, and Robert Gaizauskas. 2016. The SENSEI annotated corpus: Human summaries of reader comment conversations in on-line news. In *Proceedings of The 17th Annual SIGdial Meeting on Discourse and Dialogue (SIGDIAL 2016)*.

Marco Baroni, Georgiana Dinu, and Germán Kruszewski. 2014. Don't count, predict! a systematic comparison of context-counting vs. context-predicting semantic vectors. In *ACL (1)*, pages 238–247.

Shuo Chang, Peng Dai, Jilin Chen, and Ed H Chi. 2015. Got many labels?: Deriving topic labels from multiple sources for social media posts using crowdsourcing and ensemble learning. In *Proceedings of the 24th International Conference on World Wide Web Companion*, pages 397–406. International World Wide Web Conferences Steering Committee.

Ioana Hulpus, Conor Hayes, Marcel Karnstedt, and Derek Greene. 2013. Unsupervised graph-based topic labelling using dbpedia. In *Proceedings of the sixth ACM international conference on Web search and data mining*, pages 465–474. ACM.

Shafiq Joty, Giuseppe Carenini, and Raymond T Ng. 2013. Topic segmentation and labeling in asynchronous conversations. *Journal of Artificial Intelligence Research*, pages 521–573.

Elham Khabiri, James Caverlee, and Chiao-Fang Hsu. 2011. Summarizing user-contributed comments. In *ICWSM*.

Jey Han Lau, Karl Grieser, David Newman, and Timothy Baldwin. 2011. Automatic labelling of topic models. In *Proceedings of the 49th Annual Meeting of the Association for Computational Linguistics: Human Language Technologies-Volume 1*, pages 1536–1545. Association for Computational Linguistics.

Zongyang Ma, Aixin Sun, Quan Yuan, and Gao Cong. 2012. Topic-driven reader comments summarization. In *Proceedings of the 21st ACM international conference on Information and knowledge management*, pages 265–274. ACM.

Qiaozhu Mei, Xuehua Shen, and ChengXiang Zhai. 2007. Automatic labeling of multinomial topic models. In *Proceedings of the 13th ACM SIGKDD international conference on Knowledge discovery and data mining*, pages 490–499. ACM.

Tomas Mikolov, Ilya Sutskever, Kai Chen, Greg S Corrado, and Jeff Dean. 2013. Distributed representations of words and phrases and their compositionality. In *Advances in neural information processing systems*, pages 3111–3119.

G. Salton and M. Lesk, E. 1968. Computer evaluation of indexing and text processing. In *Journal of the ACM*, volume 15, pages 8–36, New York, NY, USA. ACM Press.

Ugo Scaiella, Paolo Ferragina, Andrea Marino, and Massimiliano Ciaramita. 2012. Topical clustering of search results. In *Proceedings of the fifth ACM international conference on Web search and data mining*, pages 223–232. ACM.

Improving Fluency in Narrative Text Generation With Grammatical Transformations and Probabilistic Parsing

Emily Ahn
Wellesley College
eahn@wellesley.edu

Fabrizio Morbini and **Andrew S. Gordon**
Institute for Creative Technologies, University of Southern California
morbini@ict.usc.edu, gordon@ict.usc.edu

Abstract

In research on automatic generation of narrative text, story events are often formally represented as a causal graph. When serializing and realizing this causal graph as natural language text, simple approaches produce cumbersome sentences with repetitive syntactic structure, e.g. long chains of "because" clauses. In our research, we show that the fluency of narrative text generated from causal graphs can be improved by applying rule-based grammatical transformations to generate many sentence variations with equivalent semantics, then selecting the variation that has the highest probability using a probabilistic syntactic parser. We evaluate our approach by generating narrative text from causal graphs that encode 100 brief stories involving the same three characters, based on a classic film of experimental social psychology. Crowdsourced workers judged the writing quality of texts generated with ranked transformations as significantly higher than those without, and not significantly lower than human-authored narratives of the same situations.

1 Narrative Text Generation

Across several academic disciplines, it has become common to represent narratives as causal graphs. In the *causal network model* of psychologists Trabasso and van den Broek (1985), vertices in the graph structure represent settings, events, goals, attempts and outcomes of a narrative, linked via directed edges that encode cause/effect relationships. In computer science, similar causal graphs have been used to model and manipulate narrative elements including suspense (Cheong and Young, 2014), conflict (Ware and Young, 2011), flashback and foreshadowing (Bae and Young, 2008). Elson (2012) elaborates the causal network model by relating it to both the temporal ordering of story-world events and an author's textual realization, creating a three-layer Story Intention Graph.

Causal graph representations of narrative create new opportunities for natural language generation (NLG) of narrative text. For example, Lukin et al. (2015) describe a narrative NLG pipeline for Story Intention Graphs, generating variations of an original text that can be parameterized for particular discourse goals. When serializing and realizing a causal graph structure as natural language text, some care must be taken to avoid the generation of cumbersome sentences with repetitive syntactic structure, e.g. as a long chain of "because" clauses. Lukin et al. (2015) directly compared readers' overall preferences for certain causal connectives over others, finding that no single class of variations will produce sentences that are preferable to a human author's stylistic choices.

We hypothesize that the policies used by native speakers to select among lexical-syntactic variations are complex and content-dependent, and are best described in statistical models trained on natural language corpora. In this paper, we explore a new approach to narrative NLG that integrates rule-based and statistical methods to produce fluent realizations of storylines encoded as causal graphs. Beginning with the output of a simple baseline system, we show that the fluency of narrative text generated

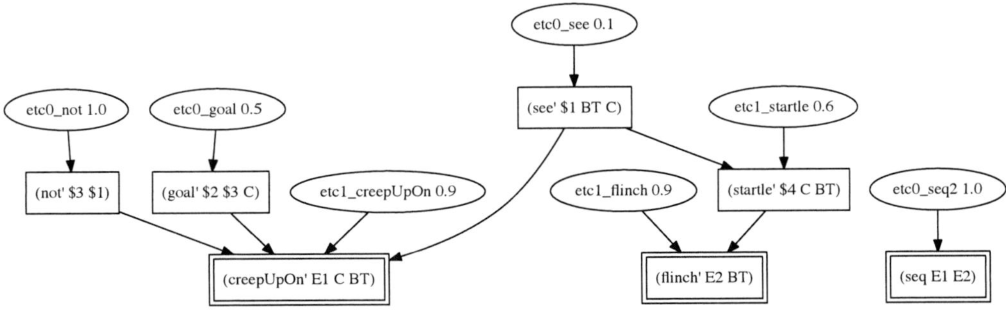

Figure 1: Causal graph output for Triangle-COPA question 1, where a circle (C) creeps up on a big triangle (BT), who then flinches.

from causal graphs can be improved by applying rule-based grammatical transformations to generate many sentence variations with equivalent semantics, then selecting the variation that has the highest probability using a probabilistic syntactic parser. Our software implementation is available online.[1]

2 Triangle-COPA Causal Graphs

As a corpus of causal graphs for use as input for our NLG experiments, we used a set of solutions to the 100 interpretation problems in the Triangle-COPA evaluation.[2] This evaluation set is based on a film from 1958 created by Fritz Heider and Marianne Simmel for use in early social psychology experiments (Heider and Simmel, 1944), depicting the movements of geometric shapes (two triangles and a circle) moving in and around a box with a door. The Triangle-COPA evaluation consists of 100 short movies in the same style, with both natural language and formal descriptions of their content. The evaluation tests a system's ability to select the most human-like interpretation of the observed behavior among two choices (Maslan et al., 2015).

Gordon (2016) demonstrated that Triangle-COPA questions could be solved by automatically constructing causal graphs that explain the behavior of the moving shapes in terms of their underlying goals, emotions, and social relationships. The approach pairs a hand-authored knowledge base of commonsense causal axioms with an abductive reasoning engine that finds the most-probable set of assumptions that logically entail the observed behavior.[3] Forward-chaining from these assumptions us-

ing the knowledge base axioms produces a directed causal graph, where the goals, emotions, and social relationships of the characters are intermediate inferences in proving the observations.

In our own research, we generated causal graphs for each of the 100 Triangle-COPA questions using the abduction engine and knowledge base of Gordon (2016), for use as input in our NLG experiments. An example causal graph solution appears in Figure 1 (for Triangle-COPA question 1). In our evaluations, we also used the human-authored narrative included with each question in the Triangle-COPA question set, which represents the realization of the writer's own interpretation of the events depicted in a given Triangle-COPA movie. For the same movie that produced the interpretation represented in Figure 1, the following is the human-authored narrative:

> *A circle stealthily stalks a big triangle. It does not want to be seen so it moves very slowly and quietly and then suddenly startles the triangle.*

3 Baseline NLG System

We developed a baseline NLG system that transforms our causal graphs into narrative texts. Our approach was to first divide the input graph into sections containing exactly one timeline event (*creep-up-on* and *flinch*, in Figure 1) along with its causal antecedents. Each of these sections becomes a sentence in the generated output, ordered by any sequence information provided in the input (*seq* in Figure 1). Each sentence is structured as a chain of "because" clauses, beginning with the timeline event and followed by each of its causal antecedents. These structures are then realized as text using the

---

[1]https://github.com/fmorbini/hsit-generation

[2]https://github.com/asgordon/TriangleCOPA

[3]https://github.com/asgordon/EtcAbductionPy

SimpleNLG engine (Gatt and Reiter, 2009) with the support of a custom lexicon for the specific predicates used in Triangle-COPA's representations.

Below is an example of the output of this Baseline NLG system, generated from the causal graph depicted in Figure 1. As expected, this text exhibits cumbersome phrasing and repetitive structure.

> *The circle creeps up on the big triangle because the circle wants that the big triangle does not see the circle. The big triangle flinches because the circle startles the big triangle because the big triangle sees the circle.*

4 Grammatical Transformations

We sought to improve the fluency of our baseline NLG system by generating many variations of each sentence through domain-independent grammatical transformations, then ordering these variations to select the best one. In this section, we describe the set of 24 hand-authored rules for grammatical transformations used in our experiments, of 7 types:

Sentential arguments: These transformations improve the fluency of verb phrases with sentential arguments. Example input: *A wants that B does C.* Output: *A wants B to do C.*

Causality: These transformations realize the causality relation in ways other than the default "because" connective. Example input: *A does B because A wants C.* (where the subject of C is A) Output: *A does B to C.*

Conjunction introduction: These transformations simplify neighboring structures that share some components (e.g. a subject). Example input: *A does B and A does C.* Output: *A does B and C.*

Repetitions: Identical timeline events in sequences are combined. Example input: *A does B. A does B. A does B.* Output: *A does B repeatedly.*

Intermediate deletion: These transformations remove intermediate vertices in causal chains, under the assumption that some causal links are intuitive and can be left implicit. Example input: *A ignores B because A dislikes B because B annoys A.* Output: *A ignores B because B annoys A.*

Pronoun introduction: These transformations replace proper nouns with pronouns when it is unambiguous to do so. Example input: *A ignores B because B annoys A.* Output: *A ignores B because A annoys it.*

Lexical fixes: These transformations handle special cases of lexical-syntactic patterns not easily handled by the realization engine. Example input: *A knocks the door in order to B.* Output: *A knocks on the door in order to B.*

Each of the 24 hand-authored rules in our system is applied recursively and exhaustively to the syntactic structures used in our baseline NLG system, generating tens to hundreds of variations for each input sentence. We explored the use of a large-scale paraphrase database (Ganitkevitch et al., 2013) as a source of transformation rules, but found that it contained none that were equivalent to those in our hand-authored set. The advantage our hand-authored rules is that they strictly preserve the semantics of the original input.

5 Probabilistic Parsing

To select the best variation for each sentence in the output narrative, we parse each variant using a probabilistic syntactic parser and rank according to the probability of the generated parse tree. For this purpose, we use the constituency parser of Charniak and Johnson (2005) without the built-in reranker, using model SANCL2012-Uniform. Each variant is grammatically correct, so our interest is solely the assigned probability score for the typicality of the lexical-syntactic structure in the training data. Here the parser serves the same role as n-gram language models in machine translation or speech recognition systems, but should be better suited for our task where intra-sentence long-range dependencies are factors in the quality of the text. We investigated whether normalizing these scores by sentence length would improve rankings, but our evaluations here are based on unnormalized probability scores.

After selecting the most-probable variant for each sentence, we assembled a final narrative for each of the 100 causal graphs. For example, the graph in Figure 1 produces the following output:

> *The circle creeps up on the big triangle because she does not want him to see her. He flinches because he sees her.*

6 Evaluation

We evaluated the quality of our narrative NLG approach by soliciting ratings of writing quality from crowdsourced annotators, comparing the output of our system, our baseline NLG system, and original human-authored narratives for each of the 100 questions in the Triangle-COPA question set. In each annotation task, the annotator watched the short movie associated with a given question, read the text associated with the question randomly selected from our three conditions, then rated the writing quality of the text on a 5-point Likert scale - from (1) *Horrible gibberish* to (5) *Excellent, professional quality*. In addition, we asked raters to answer a factual multiple-choice question about each movie to validate their effort on this crowdsourced task. After filtering annotators who failed this validation task, we analyzed 717 ratings evenly distributed across the three conditions and 100 questions, shown in Table 1. Significant gains in quality ratings were observed for our approach over the Baseline NLG system. The differences observed between human-authored narratives and our system were not significant.

Condition	Ratings	Mean score (1-5)
Human authored	233	3.69
Our system	236	3.59 *
Baseline NLG	248	3.11

Table 1: Ratings of writing quality. (*) significant at p<0.05

7 Conclusions

This research demonstrates that high-quality textual narratives can be generated from causal graph representations of stories. The use of hand-authored grammatical transformation rules helps ensure that all textual variations retain the semantics of the original input, while probabilistic parsing helps identify the variation that corresponds best to the structures produced by native speakers.

In our study, the input causal graphs were also automatically generated, identified as the most-probable explanations of series of observable events using logical abduction. Having combined automated *interpretation* with automated *narrative generation*, we now wonder if automated *perception* algorithms could serve as the input to similar pipelines to enable future systems to generate human-like narratives of the events in real-world situations.

Acknowledgments

This research was supported by the Office of Naval Research, grant N00014-13-1-0286. This material is based upon work supported by the National Science Foundation under Grant No. 1263386.

References

Byung-Chul Bae and R Michael Young. 2008. A use of flashback and foreshadowing for surprise arousal in narrative using a plan-based approach. In *International Conference on Interactive Digital Storytelling*.

Eugene Charniak and Mark Johnson. 2005. Coarse-to-fine n-best parsing and maxent discriminative reranking. In *43rd Annual Meeting on Association for Computational Linguistics*.

Yun-Gyung Cheong and R Michael Young. 2014. Suspenser: A story generation system for suspense. *Transactions on Computational Intelligence and Artificial Intelligence in Games*.

David Elson. 2012. *Modeling Narrative Discourse*. Ph.D. thesis, Columbia University.

Juri Ganitkevitch, Benjamin Van Durme, and Chris Callison-Burch. 2013. PPDB: The paraphrase database. In *2013 Meeting of the North American Association for Computational Linguistics*.

Albert Gatt and Ehud Reiter. 2009. SimpleNLG: A realisation engine for practical applications. In *12th European Workshop on Natural Language Generation*.

Andrew S. Gordon. 2016. Commonsense interpretation of triangle behavior. In *30th AAAI Conference on Artificial Intelligence*.

Fritz Heider and Marianne Simmel. 1944. An experimental study of apparent behavior. *The American Journal of Psychology*, 57(2):243–259.

Stephanie Lukin and Marilyn Walker. 2015. Generating sentence planning variations for story telling. In *16th Annual SIGdial meeting on Discourse and Dialogue*.

Nicole Maslan, Melissa Roemmele, and Andrew S. Gordon. 2015. One hundred challenge problems for logical formalizations of commonsense psychology. In *12th International Symposium on Logical Formalizations of Commonsense Reasoning*.

Tom Trabasso and Paul Van Den Broek. 1985. Causal thinking and the representation of narrative events. *Journal of memory and language*, 24(5):612–630.

Stephen Ware and R Michael Young. 2011. Cpocl: A narrative planner supporting conflict. In *7th International Conference on Artificial Intelligence and Interactive Digital Entertainment*.

The Multilingual Affective Soccer Corpus (MASC): Compiling a biased parallel corpus on soccer reportage in English, German and Dutch

Nadine Braun (n.braun@uvt.nl)
Martijn Goudbeek (m.b.goudbeek@uvt.nl)
Emiel Krahmer (e.j.krahmer@uvt.nl)

Tilburg center for Cognition and Communication (TiCC), Faculty of Humanities, Tilburg University, PO Box 90153, 5000 LE Tilburg, The Netherlands

Abstract

The emergence of the internet has led to a whole range of possibilities to not only collect large, but also highly specified text corpora for linguistic research. This paper introduces the Multilingual Affective Soccer Corpus. MASC is a collection of soccer match reports in English, German and Dutch. Parallel texts are collected manually from the involved soccer clubs' homepages with the aim of investigating the role of affect in sports reportage in different languages and cultures, taking into account the different perspectives of the teams and possible outcomes of a match. The analyzed aspects of emotional language will open up new approaches for biased automatic generation of texts.

1 Introduction

Sports reportage provided by sports clubs themselves is one of the most interesting registers available for linguistic analyses of emotionally charged language. It opens up a lot of room for creative language use, starting with the headlines of the match reports (Smith and Montgomery, 1989). Another reason is that the point of view of the author of a match report is clearly definable from the beginning, as it is either a reaction to a tie (that might still be perceived as a net loss or win by the team) or, depending on the perspective, a loss or a win for the soccer club. So, it is easy to assume that the different possible outcomes of such a match would also produce different match reports in terms of language and communicated emotion. Take for example the following introductory sentences:

(1) "Peterborough United suffered a 2-1 defeat at Burton Albion in Sky Bet League One action and lost defender Gabi Zakuani to a straight red card during a nightmare spell at the Pirelli Stadium, but what angered all connected with the club happened in the final moments of the encounter." (PB220815, MASC, 2016)

Compared to:

(2) "If all League One games at the Pirelli Stadium this season are going to be like this it is going to be an entertaining if nerve jangling season." (BA220815, MASC, 2016)

Both describe the exact same match and happenings, but the emotional nuances are completely different. While the match resulted in a loss for the British club Peterborough United, as evident in quote (1), it turned out to be a win for Burton Albion, see quote (2). This results in very different emotions shining through in the corresponding texts: while all the frustration for Peterborough seems to be piled up in a long first sentence already ("suffer... a defeat", "nightmare spell", "anger"), the winners' text is shorter and much more positive ("entertaining").

Knowing about these and other differences that occur in biased sports reporting would be especially valuable for automatic generation of natural language. NLG can be and is currently applied in many different ways, ranging from photo captions (Feng and Lapata, 2010) to neonatal intensive care reports (Portet et al., 2009) and narrative prose (Callaway and Lester, 2001). Bateman and Paris (1989) stress the importance of tailoring machine generated language to the needs of the intended audience. Taking this one step further, Hovy (1990) describes how considering different perspectives on the same event, by taking into account the speaker's emotional state, rhetorical, and communicative goals, is crucial for generating suitable texts for different hearers. Several companies worldwide already offer automatically generated narratives based on databases, e.g. Automated Insights (USA) or Arria NLG (UK). However, the reality of automatic text generation is that not many NLG systems are able to adapt to the mood of the recipients of the produced text (Mahamood and Reiter, 2009) and to convey the mood of the author. While this may not be a problem if simple data-to-text output is the aim of the system, Portet et al.'s (2009) study shows that there are indeed situations that call for a more emotionally informed approach.

To find out more about the emotional language in texts that are produced in negative and positive emotional states, the Multilingual Affective Soccer Corpus (MASC) was compiled and will be analyzed for several aspects of the relation between emotion and written language production in three different languages. To our knowledge, nothing similar to MASC exists at the moment. There is a variety of studies concerned with emotional language (e.g. Stirman and Pennebaker, 2001) and studies that mainly deal with sports reportage (e.g. Müller, 2007), but none of the existing ones includes a complete corpus of parallel texts of the same event from two different perspectives over a whole season in three different languages. This paper introduces this new corpus and highlights possible uses and advantages. MASC is available to interested researchers on request.

2   Building MASC

The corpus includes match reports in (British) English, German and Dutch and was compiled manually, with the texts being copied directly from the individual participating clubs' homepages. This means that the texts are the official reports endorsed by the clubs which are published shortly after the matches have taken place. The overall corpus comprises the 121 different clubs (See Tab. 1) which participate in the first and second league in their respective countries. This includes the British Sky Bet League 1 and 2 (UK 1/2), the German Bundesliga 1 and 2 (GER 1/2) as well as the Eredivisie and the Jupiler League (NL 1/2) in the Netherlands (Tab. 1).

2.1   Data Collection

Depending on the websites, the match reports are either linked by the clubs themselves as such in the "fixtures and results" tables, in which case those texts were chosen and saved, or the individual reports have to be located in the respective news archives.

In some instances, reports were missing for individual matches. Those cases are marked as "not available (n.a.)" in the metadata files. As the perspectives on those unavailable matches cannot be compared later on, they might be disregarded in the actual analysis. In the affected matches, the counterparts to the missing texts are still included in the dataset.

League	Time Frame 2015/16
Bundesliga 1 (GER 1)	14.08.2015 – 14.05.2016 34 game days 18 clubs
Bundesliga 2 (GER 2)	14.08.2015 – 14.05.2016 34 game days 18 clubs
Sky Bet League 1 (UK 1)	08.08.2015 – 08.05.2016 46 game days 24 clubs
Sky Bet League 2 (UK 2)	08.08.2015 – 07.05.2016 46 game days 24 clubs
Eredivisie (NL 1)	07.08.2015 – 08.05.2016 34 game days 18 clubs
Jupiler (NL 2)	07.08.2015 – 29.04.2016 38 game days 19 clubs

Table 1: Overview: soccer season 2015/16 (UK, GER, NL)

The reports are saved as plain text files in UTF-8 coding in separate folders according to which subcorpus and category (WIN, LOSS, TIE) they belong to. The metadata for the three main subcorpora is split into three separate files. These tables contain the names of the text files, the clubs' and the opponents' names, the dates the matches actually took place, the outcomes from the respective clubs' perspectives and the date the club homepages were accessed. They also include basic information about the subcorpus, like average lengths or number of texts in the conditions.

As of now, MASC includes the written reports themselves, meaning that (elementary) statistics on the match, match photos etc. are not part of the corpus.

3 Descriptive Statistics

This description will present observations about the completed corpus, including the whole season 2015/16 in the three aforementioned countries. It contains an overall of 2,916,265 tokens (Tab.2). MASC can be divided into different subcorpora, either according to language, league or outcome. Differentiating between the three languages, 1,515,442 tokens are part of the British subcorpus, while 803,793 belong to the German and 597,030 to the Dutch part (Tab.3).

	UK 1	UK 2	GER 1	GER 2	NL 1	NL 2
WIN	410	414	233	221	231	257
LOSS	409	413	232	221	232	253
TIE	272	284	143	171	145	145
Texts	4,686					
Tokens	2,916,265					

Table 2: Number of texts and tokens

In general, the corpus includes 4,686 reports (Tab. 2). The difference in numbers between WINs and LOSSes as well as the uneven number of TIEs is caused by not available texts, which could not be collected and are therefore left aside in the final calculations. The substantially greater numbers of participating clubs and game days result in almost twice as many texts in the British leagues compared to the Dutch or German ones (Tab.2). This is also one reason for the significantly higher number of tokens in the English subcorpus.

Table 3 provides a first impression of the average lengths of the match reports, which might be an interesting factor for NLG. There are clear differences (or preferences) not only between the three languages, but also the competitions themselves and the outcomes. The shortest texts throughout all languages and leagues by far are the Dutch match reports, which fall short of the English and German ones by about 200 tokens on average. The shortest Dutch report comprises only 24 tokens (Tab.3, *NL 1*) in total. Compared to this, the shortest texts in the other first leagues of the other countries are at least about four times as long. Furthermore, reports describing WINs are, on average, longer than reports describing LOSSes or TIEs throughout all languages and leagues. The length of the reportage on tied or lost matches, on the other hand, varies slightly across leagues and languages (Tab.3).

Besides text length and emotion words, which have already been mentioned in examples (1) and (2) in the introductory part of this paper, shift of focus is another interesting aspect that we observe in the texts in the different conditions. For example, consider the following excerpts that have been selected from several possible alternatives in the corpus:

(3) "Pijnlijke nederlaag Ajax bij FC Utrecht (…) Ajax kreeg de bal niet uit het eigen strafschopgebied, waarop de middenvelder venijnig uithaalde: 1-0." (AX131215, MASC, 2016)

(4) "FC Utrecht wint van Ajax (…) Het is dat ene balletje waarvan je 86 minuten lang hoopt dat-ie valt. En drie minuten voor tijd gebeurt dat." (FCU131215, MASC, 2016)

The texts again describe the same match, but they stress different details. While the loss is an "embarrassing defeat" for league leader Ajax ("pijnlijke nederlaag"), the win for Utrecht triggers pride and happiness ("the one thing you've been hoping for all 86 minutes long"). Following example (4), we can find a detailed account of the winning goal. For Ajax, on the other hand, the short mention of the deciding goal in example (3) is preceded by a detailed account of the teams' (unsuccessful) defense. So, the focus shifts according to the author's affiliation. However, emotions and focus shift do not only show in reports of decided

	UK 1	UK 2	GER 1	GER 2	NL 1	NL 2
Shortest	290	87	294	201	24	39
Longest	1,798	1,634	1,261	1,350	986	1208
TOTAL	1,516,876		803,793		597,035	
WIN	757.87	674.31	723.48	658.21	473.03	509.08
LOSS	708.19	632.50	704.85	568.85	443.68	456.30
TIE	717.85	631.77	689.66	599.69	483.52	477.78
MEAN	688.21		658.31		472.71	

Table 3: (Average) text lengths in the MASC subcorpora and conditions

matches. Examples (5) and (6) are taken from texts about an, again, randomly selected tied match.

> (5) "Der 1. FC Nürnberg verliert in der Nachspielzeit zwei wichtige Punkte." (FCN171015, MASC, 2016)

> (6) "Der FSV Frankfurt sichert sich einen Punkt in Mittelfranken" (FSV171015, MASC, 2016)

As we can see, both clubs perceive the tie differently – for the FCN in example (5), it is a lost match because the club "loses points ("verliert… Punkte"), while the FSV in (6) thinks of the outcome as a WIN ("sichert sich einen Punkt") as they "secure a point". This means that TIEs are usually also perceived as lost or won matches and might even trigger the same emotional response in both teams (LOSS/LOSS or WIN/WIN). So far, the mentioned aspects of match reportage seem to appear in all three languages.

4   Discussion

In this paper, we introduced MASC as a new text collection for linguistic research aimed at improving biased output of NLG systems across different languages. English, German and Dutch might be similar and from the same language family, but the realization of emotions in a text is not only a matter of linguistic preferences, but also rooted in the respective soccer culture. This is why – even though close in geographic and linguistic proximity – the way emotions are expressed and the emotions themselves (e.g. excitement, disappointment, shame, happiness etc.) in the conditions may vary more than the similarity in languages would imply.

As a first step towards analyzing the corpus for emotional language, we will use the text analysis program LIWC (Pennebaker et al., 2001). For example, LIWC can help to determine the proportions of negative and positive emotion words, such as "defeat" in example (1) or "entertaining" in example (2). It can even be expected that the soccer culture differences in the three countries in question are significant enough to also shine through in the language of the match reports. The corpus will help to contribute to the understanding of how different emotional states influence and change written language production. After MASC has been completed, we are planning a detailed descriptive analysis on surface features, such as already indicated text lengths and emotion words, as well as a more

in-depth analysis of, for example, referential expressions and pronouns. Further, an analysis of the preferred pronouns or referential items in general can be carried out. By analyzing the pronouns, it is possible to ascertain the focus of the author in the respective outcome of the game. If the match results in a WIN, does the report focus on the own team's great performance or on the opponent's failure ("us vs. them")? Does even the perspective on one's own team change ("we vs. they")? Or, in case of a LOSS, are the positive aspects of the game for the own team highlighted or rather the superiority of the other team? Additionally, we plan to investigate whether there are linguistic features that are related to the affect present in the texts – for example, whether certain grammatical constructions occur more in positive or negative contexts. For instance, Beukeboom and Semin (2006) suggest that abstract language correlates with positive affect.

Besides looking at potential effects of emotional state on language production, we also want to investigate how authors select game events for their reportage. For this purpose, we plan to collect game statistics for all games in MASC, to see which events are realized in the respective reports, and whether there is any bias in this selection procedure. This could also provide useful information about how game events are generally expressed in language, which is helpful for the development of new NLG applications.

These are some of the research questions that we seek to answer with MASC. As indicated before, the corpus is available on request.

Acknowledgements

We received financial support for this work from The Netherlands Organization for Scientific Research (NWO), via Grant PR-14-87 (Producing Affective Language: Content Selection, Message Formulation and Computational Modelling), which is gratefully acknowledged. We benefitted from discussions with the members of the Tilburg Language Production group, and with Charlotte Out in particular.

References

Bateman, J. A., & Paris, C. (1989, August). Phrasing a text in terms the user can understand. In *IJCAI* (pp. 1511-1517).

Beukeboom, C. J., & Semin, G. R. (2006). How mood turns on language. *Journal of experimental social psychology*, *42*(5), 553-566.

Callaway, C. B., & Lester, J. C. (2002). Narrative prose generation. *Artificial Intelligence*, *139*(2), 213-252.

Feng, Y., & Lapata, M. (2010, July). How many words is a picture worth? Automatic caption generation for news images. In *Proceedings of the 48th annual meeting of the Association for Computational Linguistics* (pp. 1239-1249). Association for Computational Linguistics.

Hovy, E. H. (1990). Pragmatics and natural language generation. *Artificial Intelligence*, *43*(2), 153-197.

Mahamood, S., & Reiter, E. (2011, September). Generating affective natural language for parents of neonatal infants. In *Proceedings of the 13th European Workshop on Natural Language Generation* (pp. 12-21). Association for Computational Linguistics.

Müller, T. (2007). *Football, language and linguistics: time-critical utterances in unplanned spoken language, their structures and their relation to non-linguistic situations and events* (Doctoral dissertation, The University of Sheffield).

Pennebaker, J. W., Francis, M. E., & Booth, R. J. (2001). Linguistic inquiry and word count: LIWC 2001. *Mahway: Lawrence Erlbaum Associates*, *71*, 2001.

Portet, F., Reiter, E., Gatt, A., Hunter, J., Sripada, S., Freer, Y., & Sykes, C. (2009). Automatic generation of textual summaries from neonatal intensive care data. *Artificial Intelligence*, *173*(7), 789-816.

Smith, M. K., & Montgomery, M. B. (1989). The semantics of winning and losing. *Language in Society*, *18*(01), 31-57.

Stirman, S. W., & Pennebaker, J. W. (2001). Word use in the poetry of suicidal and nonsuicidal poets. *Psychosomatic Medicine*, *63*(4), 517-522.

MASC. (2016). AX131215.
BA220815.
FCU131215.
FCN171015.
FSV171015.
PB220815.

Challenges of Argument Mining: Generating an Argument Synthesis based on the Qualia Structure

Patrick Saint-Dizier

IRIT-CNRS, 118 route de Narbonne

31062 Toulouse France

stdizier@irit.fr

Abstract

Given a controversial issue, argument mining from texts in natural language is extremely challenging: besides linguistic aspects, domain knowledge is often required together with appropriate forms of inferences to identify arguments. A major challenge is then to organize the arguments which have been mined to generate a synthesis that is relevant and usable. We show that the Generative Lexicon (GL) Qualia structure, enhanced in different manners and associated with inferences and language patterns, allows to capture the typical concepts found in arguments and to organize a relevant synthesis.

1 Introduction to Argument Mining

One of the main goals of argument mining is, given a controversial issue, to identify in a set of texts the arguments for or against that issue. These arguments act as supports or attacks of the issue. Arguments may also attack or support the arguments which support or attack that controversial issue in order to reinforce or cancel out their impact. Arguments are difficult to identify, in particular when they are not adjacent to the controversial issue, possibly not in the same text, because their linguistic, conceptual or referential links to that issue are rarely explicit.

For example, given the controversial issue: *Vaccine against Ebola is necessary*, the link with statements such as *Ebola adjuvant is toxic*, *Ebola vaccine production is costly*, or *7 people died during Ebola vaccine tests* is not straightforward without domain knowledge, including finding the polarity of these statements. For example, a knowledge-based analysis of the third statement shows that it is irrelevant or neutral w.r.t. the issue (Saint-Dizier 2016).

Argument mining is an emerging research area which introduces new challenges in natural language processing and generation. Argument mining research applies to written texts, e.g. (Mochales Palau et ali.., 2009), (Kirschner et ali., 2015), for example for opinion analysis, e.g. (Villalba et al., 2012), mediation analysis (Janier et al. 2015) or transcribed argumentative dialog analysis, e.g. (Budzynska et ali., 2014), (Swanson et ali., 2015). The analysis of the NLP techniques relevant for argument mining from annotated structures is analyzed in e.g. (Peldszus et al. 2016). Annotated corpora are now available, e.g. the AIFDB dialog corpora or (Walker et al., 2012). These corpora are very useful to understand how argumentation is realized in texts, e.g. to identify argumentative discourse units (ADUs), linguistic cues (Nguyen et al., 2015), and argumentation strategies, in a concrete way, possibly in association with abstract argumentation schemes, as shown in e.g. (Feng et al., 2011). In natural language generation, argument generation started as early as (Zuckerman et ali. 2000). Finally, reasoning aspects related to argumentation analysis are developed in e.g. (Fiedler et al., 2007) and (Winterstein, 2012) from a formal semantics perspective. Abstracting over arguments allows to construct summaries and to induce customer preferences or value systems.

In (Saint-Dizier 2016), a corpus analysis identifies the type of knowledge that is required to develop argument mining. It is briefly reported in this paper. Then, the Generative Lexicon (GL) is shown to be an appropriate model, sufficiently expressive, to characterize the types of knowledge, inferences and lexical data that are required to accurately identify arguments related to an issue. The present contribution focuses on the next stage: given a set of arguments for or against an issue that have been mined in various texts, how to generate a synthesis that is consistent, well-structured and usable?

2 Mining Arguments: the need of knowledge

To explore and characterize the forms of knowledge that are required to develop argument mining in texts, we constructed and annotated four corpora based on four independent controversial issues. The texts considered are extracts from various sources, e.g.: newspaper articles and blogs from associations. Issues deal with (1) Ebola vaccination, (2) women's situation in India, (3) nuclear plants and (4) organic agriculture. The total corpus includes 51 texts, a total of 24500 words for 122 different arguments. From our manual analysis, the following argument polarities are observed: attacks: 51 occurrences, supports: 32, argumentative concessions: 17, argumentative contrasts: 18 and undetermined: 4.

Our analysis shows that for 95 arguments (78%), some form of knowledge is involved to establish an argumentative relation with an issue. An important result is that the number of concepts involved is not very large: 121 concepts for 95 arguments over 4 domains. These concepts are mainly related to purposes, functions, parts, properties, creation and development of the concepts in the issues. These are relatively well defined and implemented in the Qualia structure of the Generative Lexicon, which is the framework adopted in our modeling.

The Generative Lexicon (GL) (Pustejovsky, 1995) is an attempt to structure lexical semantics knowledge in conjunction with domain knowledge. In the GL, the Qualia structure of an entity is a kind of lexical and knowledge repository composed of four fields called roles:

- **the constitutive role** describes the various parts of the entity and its physical properties, it may include subfields such as material, parts, shape, etc.
- **the formal role** describes what distinguishes the entity from other objects,

- **the telic role** describes the entity functions, uses, roles and purposes,
- **the agentive role** describes the origin of the entity, how it was created or produced.

Let us consider the controversial issue (1): *The vaccine against Ebola is necessary.* The Qualia structure of the head term of (1), vaccine(X), is:

$$\left[\begin{array}{l} \text{CONSTITUTIVE: } \left[\text{ACTIVE\_PRINCIPLE, ADJUVANT} \right], \\[4pt] \text{TELIC: } \left[\begin{array}{l} \text{MAIN: PROTECT\_FROM(X,Y,D),} \\ \text{AVOID(X,DISSEMINATION(D)),} \\ \text{MEANS: INJECT(Z,X,Y)} \end{array} \right], \\[4pt] \text{FORMAL: } \left[\text{MEDICINE, ARTEFACT} \right], \\[4pt] \text{AGENTIVE : } \left[\begin{array}{l} \text{DEVELOP(T,X), TEST(T,X),} \\ \text{SELL(T,X)} \end{array} \right] \end{array} \right]$$

The Qualia structure of Ebola is:

$$\left[\begin{array}{l} \text{FORMAL: } \left[\text{VIRUS, DISEASE} \right], \\[4pt] \text{TELIC: } \left[\begin{array}{l} \text{INFECT(E1,EBOLA,P)} \Rightarrow \text{GET\_SICK(E2,P)} \\ \Rightarrow \Diamond \text{DIE(E3,P)} \wedge \text{E1} \leq \text{E2} \leq \text{E3} \end{array} \right] \end{array} \right]$$

Then, via formula expansion, the formal representation of the controversial issue is:

$\Box$ *(protect_from(X,Y, (infect(E1,ebola, Y)* $\Rightarrow$ *get_sick(E2,Y)* $\Rightarrow \Diamond$ *die(E3,Y)))*
$\wedge$ *avoid(X,dissemination(ebola)).*

3 Generation of an argument synthesis related to a controversial issue

3.1 A Network of Qualias to Characterize the Generative Expansion of Arguments

Our observations show that arguments attack or support (1) specific concepts found in the Qualia of the head terms in the controversial issue (called **root concepts**) or (2) concepts derived from these root concepts, via their Qualia. For example, arguments can attack properties or purposes of the adjuvant or of the protocols used to test the vaccine. Then, a network of Qualias must be defined to develop the argument synthesis. This network is limited to three levels because derived concepts must remain functionally close to the root concepts.

A Qualia Q_i describes major features of a concept such as vaccine(X), it can be formally defined as follows:

$Q_i : [\, R_X : T_j^{i,X} \,]$, where:

- R_X denotes the four roles: $X \in \{formal, constitutive, agentive, telic\}$ and possibly subroles,
- $T_j^{i,X}$ is a term which is a formula, a predicate or a constant T_j in the role X of Q_i.

A network of Qualias is then defined as follows:
- nodes are of two types: [terminal concept] (no associated Qualia) or [non terminal concept, associated Qualia],
- the root is the semantic representation of the controversial issue and the related Qualias Q_i,
- Step 1: the first level of the network is composed of the nodes which correspond to the terms $T_j^{i,X}$ in the roles of the Qualias Q_i The result of this step is the set T of terminal nodes $\{ T_j^{i,X} \}$ and non terminal nodes $\{ T_j^{i,X}, Q'_{i'} : [R_X : T'^{i',X}_{j'}]\}$.
- Step 2: similarly, the terms $T'^{i',X}_{j'}$ from the $Q'_{i'}$ of step 1 introduce new nodes into the network together with their own Qualia when they are non-terminal concepts. They form the set T', derived from T.
- Step 3: the same operation is carried out on T' to produce T''.
- Final step: production of T'''. The set of concepts involved is: $\{T \cup T' \cup T'' \cup T'''\}$.

This network of Qualias forms the backbone of the argument mining system. This network develops the **argumentative generative expansion of the controversial issue**. This network is the organization principle, expressed in terms of relatedness, that guides the generation of a synthesis where the different facets of the Qualias it contains are the structuring principles.

3.2 Synthesis Generation Input Data

Arguments which have been mined are automatically tagged with the following attributes:
- the argument identifier (an integer),
- the **identifier of what the argument attacks or supports** (issue or another argument),
- the **text span involved** that delimits the argument compound and its kernel,
- the **polarity of the argument** w.r.t. the issue with one of the following values: support, attack, argumentative concession or contrast.
- the **concepts involved**, to identify the argument: list of the main concepts from the Qualias used in the mining process,

- the **strength of the argument**, based on linguistic marks found in the argument,
- the **discourse structures** in the compound, associated with the argument kernel, as processed by our discourse analysis platform TextCoop.

Argument 11 is tagged as follows:

<argument Id= 11, polarity= attack with concession, relationWith=issue, conceptsInvolved= efficiency measure, safety measure, test, evaluation method, strength= moderate >

<concession> Even if the vaccine seems 100% efficient and without any side effects on the tested population, < /concession>

<main arg> it is necessary to wait for more conclusive data before making large vaccination campaigns. < /main arg>

<elaboration> The national authority of Guinea has approved the continuation of the tests on targeted populations. </elaboration> < /argument>.

At this stage no metadata is considered such as date of argument or author status. This notation was defined independently of any ongoing task such as ConLL15.

Argument kernels are expressed in various ways:
- **evaluative expressions:** *Vaccine development is very costly, adjuvant is toxic,*
- **comparatives:** *number of sick people much smaller than for Malaria.*
- **facts related to properties of the main concept(s) of the issue:** *Vaccine is not yet available. There is no risk of dissemination.*
- **facts related to the consequences, functions, purposes, uses or goals** of the issue: *vaccine prevents bio-terrorism, 3 vaccinated people died.*

An indicative evaluation provides an accuracy of about 82% of the mining and tagging processes compared to our manual annotation.

3.3 A Multi-facet Argument Synthesis Generation

The network of Qualias together with the attributes 'relationWith', 'Polarity' and 'ConceptsInvolved' are the most crucial elements to generate a structured argument synthesis that corresponds to the domain conceptual organization. Each node of the Qualia network defines a cluster to which mined arguments are associated. Clusters are organized hierarchically by decreasing relatedness to the issue.

Redundant arguments characterized by lexical duplicates are eliminated.

The generation of a synthesis proceeds informally as follows:

(1) The concepts of the network of Qualias are organized hierarchically and by role. Level 0 of the synthesis contains the concepts $T_j^{i,X}$ of the set T, since they are the most relevant. They are organized by role: constitutive, agentive and telic (which is the main role for argument mining). Each concept in a role is considered separately. In the telic role, the list starts by the 'Main' category and then the other types are considered, such as 'Means'.

(2) Each of these concepts defines a cluster that contains the mined arguments that have this concept in their 'conceptsInvolved' attribute, with the constraint that the argument concerns the issue (relationWith=issue), the other arguments are treated as presented in (6). For example, the concept `sell(T,X)` includes the mined argument with the value *production costs* its its attribute 'conceptsInvolved'.

(3) This process goes on with the lower levels of the network of Qualias: the concepts $T'^{i',X}_{j'}$ associated with the Qualias $Q_{i'}$ are considered and then, the sets T'' and T''' defined in 3.1.

(4) When an argument involves several concepts, it is included into the concept cluster that is the highest in the network of concepts.

(5) For each concept, related arguments are structured by polarity: first supports and then attacks, for each of polarity, arguments are listed, with an indication of their number of occurrences found while mining to give an estimate of their recurrence.

(6) To deal with the generation of a more comprehensive graph of attacks and supports, a further stage of the generation process consists in considering that each argument that has been mined can also be an issue which can be attacked or supported. This is specified in the attribute 'relationWith'. Therefore, the same process as for the controversial issue is applied, while keeping the same network of Qualias.

Let us consider our example on vaccination, then:
(a) the root concepts (Level 0) in the Qualia hierarchy are those of vaccine and ebola, e.g.: constitutive: *active principle, adjuvant*; agentive: *develop, test, sell*; telic: *protect-from, dissemination, infect, get-sick, die, inject.*
(b) Level 1 concepts are those associated with the Qualias of the root concepts given in (a), e.g. those in the Qualias of: adjuvant (e.g. *dilute*), tests (e.g. *efficiency measure, evaluation methods*), develop (e.g. *production costs, availability, ethics*), etc.

For example, a synthesis would be composed of the following clusters:

Level 0: e.g.:

Cluster 1: Adjuvant: attack: *adjuvant is toxic* (3 occurrences) ...

Cluster 2: Dissemination: support: *reduces dissemination (5)*..

Cluster 3: Get-sick: concessive support: *limited number of cases and deaths compared to other diseases (2)*, ...

Level 1:, e.g.:

Cluster 4: Production costs: attack: *high production and development costs (6)* ...

Cluster 5: Availability: concessive attack: *vaccine not yet available (4)*, etc.

Finally, in order to make the synthesis based on Qualia network structure more clear, each of the concepts is associated with a simple and direct definition, directly generated via language patterns from the Qualia structure network, e.g.:
- *Side-effect* and *toxicity* are related to the use of a medicine,
- *Contamination* entails *disease dissemination*.
- *Population isolation* avoids *disease dissemination*.
- *Production costs* are related to the creation and development of any product,
- *Efficiency* must be measured during the *test* phase.

These definitions are defined for each cluster. The result is a hierarchically organized and well articulated set of clusters that account for the various arguments for or against an issue found in various texts, where each level is made clear to the reader. No evaluation of the relevance of this type of clustering technique has been carried out so far. This evaluation should involve the analysis of the adequacy of this clustering technique by real users, its granularity and its adequacy to the problem to investigate. It may also depend on the type of issue and arguments that have been mined. Deeper forms of argument synthesis could be desirable, but these involve complex conceptual planning issues. To the best of our knowledge, such a task has never been undertaken.

References

K., Budzynska, M., Janier, C., Reed, P. Saint-Dizier, M., Stede, and O. Yakorska. 2014. A model for processing illocutionary structures and argumentation in debates. In proc. LREC, 2014.

V. W., Feng and G, Hirst. 2011. Classifying arguments by scheme. In Proceedings of the 49th ACL: Human Language Technologies, Portland, USA.

A., Fiedler and H., Horacek. 2007. Argumentation within deductive reasoning. International Journal of Intelligent Systems, 22(1):49-70.

M., Janier, C. and Reed, C. 2015. Towards a Theory of Close Analysis for Dispute Mediation Discourse, Journal of Argumentation.

C., Kirschner, J., Eckle-Kohler and I., Gurevych. 2015. Linking the Thoughts: Analysis of Argumentation Structures in Scientific Publications. In: Proceedings of the 2nd Workshop on Argumentation Mining, Denver.

R., Mochales Palau and M.F., Moens. 2009. Argumentation mining: the detection, classification and structure of arguments in text. Twelfth international ICAIL'09, Barcelona.

H., Nguyen and D. Litman. 2015. Extracting Argument and Domain Words for Identifying Argument Components in Texts. In: Proc of the 2nd Workshop on Argumentation Mining, Denver.

A., Peldszus and M., Stede. 2016. From argument diagrams to argumentation mining in texts: a survey. International Journal of Cognitive Informatics and Natural Intelligence (IJCINI).

J., Pustejovsky. 1995. The Generative Lexicon, MIT Press.

P. Saint-Dizier. 2016. Argument Mining: the bottleneck of knowledge and lexical ressources, LREC, Portoroz.

R., Swanson, B., Ecker and M., Walker. 2015. Argument Mining: Extracting Arguments from Online Dialogue, in proc. SIGDIAL.

M.G., Villalba and P., Saint-Dizier. 2012. Some Facets of Argument Mining for Opinion Analysis, COMMA, Vienna, IOS Publishing.

M., Walker, P., Anand, J.E., Fox Tree, R., Abbott and J., King. 2012. A Corpus for Research on Deliberation and Debate. Proc. of LREC, Istanbul.

G., Winterstein. 2012. What but-sentences argue for: An argumentative analysis of 'but', in Lingua 122.

I., Zuckerman, R., McConachy and K. Korb. 2000. Using Argumentation Strategies in Automatic Argument Generation, INLG.

Tense and Aspect in Runyankore using a Context-Free Grammar

Joan Byamugisha and **C. Maria Keet** and **Brian DeRenzi**
Department of Computer Science, University of Cape Town, South Africa,
{jbyamugisha,mkeet,bderenzi}@cs.uct.ac.za

Abstract

The provision of personalized patient information has been encouraged as a means of complementing information provided during patient-doctor consultations, and linked to better health outcomes through patient compliance with prescribed treatments. The generation of such texts as a controlled fragment of Runyankore, a Bantu language indigenous to Uganda, requires the appropriate tense and aspect, as well as a method for verb conjugation. We present how an analysis of corpora of explanations of prescribed medications was used to identify the simple present tense and progressive aspect as appropriate for our selected domain. A CFG is defined to conjugate and generate the correct form of the verb.

1 Introduction

In Uganda, patients receive medical information verbally during the patient-doctor consultation. However, DiMarco et al., (2005; 2006) and Wilcox et al., (2011) noted that patients consistently retain a rather small fraction of the verbal information after the consultation, possibly resulting in improper compliance to medical instructions. Further, it was found that personalized information increases the likelihood for a patient to be more engaged and likely to read, comprehend, and act upon such information better (Cawsey et al., 2000; Wilcox et al., 2011).

The fundamental complexity in the customization of patient information is the number of different combinations of characteristics, which can easily be in the tens or hundreds of thousands (DiMarco et al., 2005). Natural Language Generation (NLG) has successfully been applied to generate personalized patient information (DiMarco et al., 2005; DiMarco et al., 2006; De Carolis et al., 1996; de Rosis and Grasso, 2000).

Localized patient information is encouraged because the use of English exacerbates literacy difficulties already prevalent in situations of health (DiMarco et al., 2009). Our broader programme of NLG for Bantu languages aims to apply NLG to generate drug explanations in Runyankore—a Bantu language indigenous to Uganda, where English is the official language, but indigenous languages are predominantly spoken in rural areas. Runyankore sentences generated through ontology verbalization (Byamugisha et al., 2016) exposed two crucial issues: (1) *What tense and aspect is used in explanations of prescribed medication?* and (2) *Is a context-free grammar (CFG) sufficient to conjugate verbs in Runyankore?* Through the analysis of two relevant corpora, we identify that the simple present (universal) tense with the progressive aspect would be best for generating explanations of prescribed medications. We demonstrate that this can be done for Runyankore using a CFG for verb conjugation.

In the rest of the paper, we first summarize the Runyankore verbal morphology (Section 2) and related work (Section 3). Section 4 presents the corpus analysis. The relevant CFGs for the Runyankore verb are presented in Section 5. We discuss in Section 6 and conclude in Section 7.

2 Verbal Morphology of Runyankore

Runyankore is a Bantu language spoken in the south western part of Uganda by over two million people, which makes it one of the top five most populous languages in Uganda (Asiimwe, 2014; Tayebwa, 2014; Turamyomwe, 2011). Like other Bantu languages, it is highly agglutinative to the extent that a word can be composed of over five constituents (Asiimwe, 2014; Tayebwa, 2014). Runyankore has twenty noun classes, (NC), and each noun belongs to a specific class.

Our discussion of tense and aspect in Runyankore throughout this paper is based on work done by Turamyomwe (2011). The standard classification of tense by dividing time into past, present, and future is further subdivided, resulting in fourteen tenses. Aspect focuses on the internal nature of events, instead of their grounding in time. There are two major aspects: the perfective and imperfective the latter subdivided into persistive, habitual, and continuous, with the progressive as a subtype of the continuous). Runyankore expresses tense as prefixes and aspect as affixes to the right of the verb stem. Table 2 shows the different 'slots' in Runyankore's verbal morphology. We illustrate the general structure of the Runyankore verbal morphology, where neg is negation, RM is remote past, VS is verb stem, App is applicative, FV is final vowel, Loc is locative, Emp is emphatic, and Dec is declarative.

- titukakimureeterahoganu
  'We have never ever brought it to him'
- ti tu ka ki mu reet er a ho ga nu
- neg-(NC2 SC)-RM-(NC7 SC)-(NC1 SC)-VS-App-FV-Loc-Emp-Dec

The compulsory slots are the *initial*, *formative* (except in the case of the universal and near past tense), *verb-stem*, and *final*.

3   Related work

We center our discussion here around the existing methods of verb conjugation for tense and aspect in agglutinated languages like Tamil (Rajan et al., 2014) and Turkish (Fokkens et al., 2009). The placement of morphemes in a word, and rules governing the combinations of morphemes to form semantic categories are important in agglutinated languages (Jayan and Bhadran, 2015). Similar to Runyankore, the sequence of morphemes can express mood, tense, and aspect (Rajan et al., 2014; Fokkens et al., 2009; Turamyomwe, 2011).

There are several approaches for text generation in agglutinated languages, being corpus-based, paradigm-based, Finite-State Transducer (FST)-based, rule-based, and algorithm-based (Antony, 2012). Some of these are currently inapplicable to Runyankore because it is structurally different or too under-resourced. We thus decided to implement tense and aspect in Runyankore using a rule-based approach, derived from a set of grammar rules and a dictionary of roots and morphemes. A CFG is powerful enough to depict complex relations among words in a sentence, yet computationally tractable enough to enable efficient algorithms to be developed (Jurafsky and Martin, 2007). Because the verb conjugation work presented here is intended to be one of the components in a Runyankore grammar engine, the use of a CFG is justified.

Slot	Grammatical Category	Morpheme
pre-initial	1. primary negative 2. cont. marker	1. ti- 2. ni-
initial	subject marker	depends on the NC
post-initial	secondary negative	-ta-
formative	tense	all tenses except near past
limitative	persistive aspect	-ki-
infix	object marker	depends on NC
extensions	App; Cs; Ps; Rec; Rev; Stv; Itv; Red; Ism	-er-, -erer-, -ir-; zi-, -is-; -w-; -n-; -ur-, -uur-; -gur-; repeat the stem; -is+ pre-initial
final	1. final vowel (a) indicative, (b) subjunctive 2. near past tense	1. (a) -a (b) -e 2. -ire
post-final	1. locatives 2. emphatic 3. declarative	1. -ho, -mu-yo 2. -ga 3. -nu

Table 1: Verbal Morphology of Runyankore (Turamyomwe, 2011); App: applicative, Cs: causative, Ps: passive, Rec: reciprocal, Rev: reversive, Stv: stative, Itv: intensive, Red: reduplicative, Ism: instrumental

4 Tense and Aspect in Prescription Explanations

To the best of our knowledge, there is no prior work specifically discussing tense and aspect for explanations of prescribed medications. We instead analyze text describing drug prescriptions from empirical studies (Berry et al., 1995; Berry et al., 1997).

We limited our analysis here to the corpora from Berry et al., (1995; 1997), compiled from a series of empirical studies done to ascertain the kind of information patients and doctors considered important about prescribed medication. We further only considered the tense in the main clause of the sentences in the corpus in order to simplify our initial scope.

We analyzed 27 sentences, 18 from (Berry et al., 1997) and 9 from (Berry et al., 1995), describing medication prescriptions. We were interested in the form of the verb, in order to identify the tense and aspect used. Table 2 shows how often each verb form occurred in each unique sentence in the corpus.

Example	Tense, Aspect	|Occ.|
have	simple pres. ind.	2
reduce	simple pres. ind.	1
is	simple pres. ind.	5
should take	pres. imp.	3
contains	simple pres. ind.	1
are	simple pres. ind.	3
if it does not relieve	pres. cond.	3
may be taken	past perf. subj.	1
may cause	simple pres. subj.	2
should be avoided	past perf. imp.	2
do not contain	simple pres. ind.	1
to store	infinitive	1
are produced	pres. perf. ind.	2

Table 2: Tense and Aspect used in Prescription Explanations; pres.=present, perf.=perfect, ind.=indicative, subj=subjunctive, imp.=imperative, cond.=conditional, occ.=occurence

The simple present tense is used in 55.5% of the corpus, in 48.2% with the indicative aspect, and in 7.7% with the subjunctive. The simple present tense and indicative aspect is used in those sentences which are informational in nature, but the present tense and imperative aspect for those which are instructional (for example 'should take Fennodil ...' and 'should adopt a more suitable ...').

5 Verb Conjugation using a CFG

We devise a CFG for verb conjugation in the simple present tense (Runyankore's 'universal' tense), and the auxiliary 'has' and copulative 'is' (from 'to be') as special cases that do not conform to the standard grammatical structure.

5.1 Universal Tense in Runyankore

The universal tense has no special tense marker, and as such is sometimes called the null tense (Turamyomwe, 2011). We apply the progressive aspect, which marks a situation which is ongoing at the time of use. This is appropriate for informational sentences such as those listed in Section 4, because this information will always be true as long as one is on that medication. We introduce a new non-terminal, *initial group*, which, depending on the tense and aspect applied, has productions for one or more of the three 'initial' slots (cf. Table 2). We only consider five slots here: the *pre-initial*, as well as the four compulsory 'slots' discussed in Section 2. We assign all six nonterminals the symbols: IG for initial group, PN for pre-initial, IT for initial, FM for formative, VS for verb-stem, and FV for final vowel. Finally, since this tense has no tense morpheme, we will use the production $FM \rightarrow \emptyset$ to illustrate it. The example shows productions with verb stems *kyendez* 'reduce,' *gw* 'fall,' *vug* 'drive,' and *gend* 'go':

$$S \rightarrow IG\ FM\ VS\ FV$$
$$IG \rightarrow PN\ IT$$
$$PN \rightarrow \text{ti} \mid \text{ni}$$
$$IT \rightarrow \text{a} \mid \text{o} \mid \text{n} \mid \text{tu} \mid \text{mu} \mid \text{ba} \mid \text{gu} \mid \text{gi} \mid \text{ri} \mid \text{ga} \mid \text{ki} \mid$$
$$\text{bi} \mid \text{e} \mid \text{zi} \mid \text{ru} \mid \text{tu} \mid \text{ka} \mid \text{bu} \mid \text{ku} \mid \text{gu} \mid \text{ga}$$
$$FM \rightarrow \emptyset$$
$$VS \rightarrow \text{kyendez} \mid \text{gw} \mid \text{vug} \mid \text{gend}$$
$$FV \rightarrow \text{a} \mid \text{e} \mid \text{ire}$$

The production of IT has several possible values, depending on the noun class of the subject of the sentence. For all verbs, except 'has' and 'to be,' FV will always be the indicative final vowel 'a'.

5.2 Deviations from Standard Grammar

There are two verbs which deviate from the standard Runyankore grammar: the auxiliary 'has' (verb stem *in*) and the copulative 'to be' (verb stem *ri*). The auxiliary deviates in two main ways: first, the continuous marker is dropped, and second, the subjunctive final vowel 'e' is used instead. The copulative deviates even further because it both drops the pre-initial and has no final vowel. It is thus our design decision to use separate CFGs for these special cases, for two main reasons: firstly, to prevent the generation of sentences like *nibaina, niguine* or *nibaria, nigurie* which do not exist in the language. Secondly, there is no way to limit the inclusion of $\emptyset$ as a terminal for PN and FV to only these special cases, instead of having it applied to all verbs. The CFG for 'has' (verb-stem *-in-*):

$$S \rightarrow IG\ FM\ VS\ FV$$
$$IG \rightarrow PN\ IT$$
$$PN \rightarrow \emptyset$$
$$IT \rightarrow \text{a} \mid \text{o} \mid \text{n} \mid \text{tu} \mid \text{mu} \mid \text{ba} \mid \text{gu} \mid \text{gi} \mid \text{ri} \mid \text{ga} \mid \text{ki} \mid$$
$$\text{bi} \mid \text{e} \mid \text{zi} \mid \text{ru} \mid \text{tu} \mid \text{ka} \mid \text{bu} \mid \text{ku} \mid \text{gu} \mid \text{ga}$$
$$FM \rightarrow \emptyset$$
$$VS \rightarrow \text{in}$$
$$FV \rightarrow \text{e}$$

The CFG for the case of 'to be' (verb-stem *-ri*) is almost the same as for 'have', except for the following two production rules:

$$VS \rightarrow \text{ri}$$
$$FV \rightarrow \emptyset$$

The CFGs show that verb conjugation can be achieved following the grammar rules on the verbal morphology. We have limited our non-terminals to six, only those necessary to generate text in our selected tense and aspect. However, by including more of the grammatical categories presented in Table 2, it would be possible to create the rules to generate many more tenses and aspects.

The patterns for generating Runyankore sentences from ontologies required a method for verb conjugation in order to generate correct text. We thus illustrate the use of the CFG in this context, using a sentence taken from the corpus by (Berry et al., 1997), which we modify and represent as a side effect in the example *Fennodil $\sqsubseteq$ $\exists hasSideEffect.Diarrhea$*: *Buri Fennodil eine hakiri ekirikurugamu kitagyendereirwe kimwe ekya okwirukana* 'Each Fennodil has at least one side effect of diarrhea'. According to Byamugisha et al., (2016), *Buri* is the translation of 'each' for subsumption ($\sqsubseteq$), *eine* for 'has', *hakiri* for 'at least', and *kimwe* for 'one'; *ekirikurugamu kitagyendereirwe* is 'side effect', and *okwirukana* is 'diarrhea'. The *eine* 'has' has *e* as the subject prefix because Fennodil is placed in NC 9. With the CFG, one can thus gener-

ate several variations for 'has' that occur whenever a noun in a different NC is to the left of $\sqsubseteq$ in the axiom; for example *aine, baine, giine, riine* for NC 1, 2, 4, and 5 respectively.

6 Discussion

The identification of the tense and aspect relevant to our domain of interest—explanations of prescribed medications—through the analysis of corpora on medicine prescription enabled us to narrow down the scope of the text to be generated, in terms of tense and aspect, to only the simple present (universal) tense and continuous aspect. It is interesting that the present tense is appropriate for our target domain, because an ontology will be the input of our NLG system. Therefore, the consideration of generation of sentences, for example with the verb 'has,' mirrors axioms which either have 'has' as a role or the 'hasX' role naming, such as $hasSymptom$. In this way, our work here builds upon (Byamugisha et al., 2016) to verbalize ontologies in Runyankore, by solving two crucial issues: which tense and aspect to use, and how to achieve verb conjugation.

The use of CFGs allows for easy extensibility both to more tenses, and perhaps even other Bantu languages. For the case of tenses, we would only need to add new rules. The near past tense, for example, can be generated by changing the rule on FM from $FM \rightarrow \emptyset$ to $FM \rightarrow$ ka. CFGs for other Bantu languages can be produced by stating language-specific rules and terminals.

7 Conclusion

Through the analysis of corpora of prescription explanations, we identified that the simple present tense and progressive aspect were most suitable when generating informational drug explanations. Therefore, a CFG for universal tense, the auxiliary verb 'has', and the copulative was developed. Future work will include the implementation of these CFGs, inclusion of the imperative aspect, and evaluating the generated messages.

Acknowledgements

This work is based on the research supported by the Hasso Plattner Institute (HPI) Research School in CS4A at UCT and the National Research Foundation of South Africa (Grant Number 93397).

References

K P Antony, P J an Samon. 2012. Computational morphology and natural language parsing for indian languages: A literature survey. *International Journal of Scientific and Engineering Research*, 3.

Allen Asiimwe. 2014. *Definiteness and Specificity in Runyankore-Rukiga*. Ph.D. thesis, Stallenbosch University, Cape Town, South Africa.

C. Dianne Berry, Tony Gillie, and Simon Banbury. 1995. What do patients want to know: An empirical approach to explanation generation and validation. *Expert Systems with Applications*, 8:419 — 428.

C. Dianne Berry, C. Irene Michas, Tony Gillie, and Melanie Forster. 1997. What do patients want to know about their medicines and what do doctors want to tell them: A comparative study. *Psychology and Health*, 12:467–480.

Joan Byamugisha, C. Maria Keet, and Brian DeRenzi. 2016. Bootstrapping a runyankore CNL from an isizulu CNL. In *5th Workshop on Controlled Natural Language*, Aberdeen, Scotland. Springer.

J. Alison Cawsey, B. Ray Jones, and Janne Pearson. 2000. The evaluation of a personalized health information system for patients with cancer. *User Modeling and User-Adapted Interaction*, 10(1):47–72.

Berardina De Carolis, Fiorella de Rosis, Floriana Grasso, Anna Rossiello, C. Dianne Berry, and Tony Gillie. 1996. Generating recipient-centered explanations about drug prescription. *Artificial Intelligence in Medicine*.

Fiorella de Rosis and Floriana Grasso. 2000. Affective natural language generation. In *Affective Interactions, LANI*, pages 204 – 218.

Chrysanne DiMarco, Peter Bray, Dominic Covvey, Don Cowan, Vic DiCiccio, Eduard Hovy, Joan Lipa, and Cathy Yang. 2005. Authoring and generation of tailored preoperative patient education materials. In *Workshop on Personalization in e-Health, User Modeling, Conference*, Edinburgh, Scotland.

Chrysanne DiMarco, Don Cowan, Peter Bray, Dominic Covvey, Vic DiCiccio, Eduard Hovy, Joan Lipa, and Doug Mulholland. 2006. A physician's authoring tool for generation of personalized health education in reconstructive surgery. In *American Association for Artificial Intelligence (AAAI) Spring Symposium on Argumentation for Consumers of Healthcare*, Stanford University.

Chrysanne DiMarco, David Wiljer, and Eduard Hovy. 2009. Self-managed access to personalized healthcare through automated generation of tailored health educational materials from electronic health records. In *American Association for Artificial Intelligence (AAAI) Fall Symposium on Virtual Health Interaction*, Washington D. C.

Antske Fokkens, Laurie Paulson, and M. Emily Bender. 2009. Inflectional morphology in turkish VP coordination. In *The HPSG09*, Germany.

V. Jayan and V. K. Bhadran. 2015. Difficulties in processing malayalam verbs for statistical machine translation. *International Journal of Artificial Intelligence and Applications (IJAIA)*, 6.

Daniel Jurafsky and H. James Martin. 2007. *Speech and Language Processing: An Introduction to Natural Language Processing, Computational Linguistics, and Speech Recognition*. Prentice Hall, Inc., USA.

K. Rajan, V. Ramalingam, and M. Ganesan. 2014. Machine learning of phonologically conditioned noun declensions for tamil morphological generators. *International Journal of Computer Engineering and Applications*, 4.

Doreen Daphine Tayebwa. 2014. Demonstrative determiners in runyankore-rukiga. Master's thesis, Norwegian University of Science and Technology, Norway.

Justus Turamyomwe. 2011. Tense and aspect in runyankore-rukiga: Linguistic resources and analysis. Master's thesis, Norwegian University of Science and Technology, Norway.

Lauren Wilcox, Dan Morris, Desney Tan, Justin Gatewood, and Eric Horvitz. 2011. Characterising patient-friendly micro-explanations of medical events. In *The SIGCHI Conference on Human Factors in Computing Systems (CHI'11)*, pages 29–32, New York. ACM.

Task demands and individual variation in referring expressions

Adriana Baltaretu and **Thiago Castro Ferreira**
Tilburg center for Cognition and Communication (TiCC)
Tilburg University
The Netherlands
`{a.a.baltaretu,tcastrof}@tilburguniversity.edu`

Abstract

Aiming to improve the human-likeness of natural language generation systems, this study investigates different sources of variation that might influence the production of referring expressions (REs), namely the effect of task demands and inter- intra- individual variation. We collected REs using a discrimination game and varied the instructions, telling speakers that they would get points for being fast, creative, clear, or no incentive would be mentioned. Our results show that task-demands affected REs production (number of words, number of attributes), and we observe a considerable amount of variation among the length of REs produced by single speakers, as well as among the REs of different speakers referring to the same targets.

1 Introduction

In Natural Language Generation, Referring Expression Generation (REG) is the task of generating references to discourse entities (Krahmer and Van Deemter, 2012). One of the most explored problems in REG is content selection, namely deciding what properties of the referent to include in a definite description, which is the focus of this work.

In general, REG algorithms have been developed on corpora collected with subtly different instructions. These nuanced instructions might have led to biases (e.g., influencing the types and frequency of attributes), which in turn could have led to biases in how REG algorithms operate, when trained on these corpora; or perhaps not. We propose a study investigating the effect of task demands on reference production. Moreover, REG typically focuses on generating unique descriptions by selecting content to distinguish the referent (target) from the other objects in the context (distractors). As result, computational models had been developed deterministically, always generating the same referring expression for a particular situation (Frank and Goodman, 2012; Van Gompel et al., 2012, for probabilistic models). This raises the question to what extent REs vary as a function of task demands and individual differences.

A number of studies have collected dedicated corpora of referring expressions, typically asking participants to produce distinguishable descriptions. However, these studies had nuanced instructions, and most of them relied on simple, schematic stimuli (grids of objects). For example, instructions emphasize accuracy and briefness (Viethen and Dale, 2010; van Deemter et al., 2006), introduce time pressure (Kazemzadeh et al., 2014) or use open ended formulations, asking participants to describe marked objects in such a way that they can be distinguished from other objects (Koolen et al., 2011). Task demands could influence the level of specification of the REs and the selection of (specific) attributes (Arts et al., 2011).

Another source of variation arises from speaker differences. Humans show individual style differences during language production, and speaker-dependent variation has been argued to be an important factor shaping the content of references (Viethen and Dale, 2010). Variation among individuals and across tasks has been proposed to arise from limitations of cognitive capacities of speakers and listeners (Hendriks, 2016). That individual variation exists is beyond doubt, however, we do not know of any studies to look at the amount of intra-individual variation (variation among the references of a same speaker) and inter-individual variation (variation among the references of different speakers in a same situation) in content selection using complex naturalistic scenes.

This paper focuses on human REs production in natural scenes, and we propose analysing whether RE production is influenced by task demands and speaker variation. We take a subset of stimuli and the instructions of an already existing reference game (Kazemzadeh et al., 2014) and ask participants to describe the object as best as possible (baseline condition), add time pressure, ask for creative and for clear REs. Compared to the baseline condition, we expect time pressure to trigger minimal short references with few adjectives; creativity to bring up novel and unusual ways of expressing attributes; clear REs to be longer and more detailed (more attributes). Regarding individual variation, we would like to measure to what extent REs of a speaker vary from each other, as well as the REs of different speakers for a same situation.

2   Methods

Participants   Ninety native English speakers were paid to take part in the experiment via Crowd-Flower, a crowdsourcing service similar to Amazon Mechanical Turk. We removed data from 17 respondents, as they declared not being native English speakers, not finishing, or misunderstanding the task. The final sample included 73 participants (31 males, mean age 38 years). The study followed APA guidelines for conducting experiments.

Materials   Experimental materials consisted of 40 target objects, each presented in a different scene. These scenes have been semi-randomly selected from the larger set of images, illustrating aspects of everyday life, used to elicit REs in the ReferIt game (Kazemzadeh et al., 2014) . Our selection contains scenes that have at least one other object of the same type as the target, so as to elicit more than one word descriptions. To present participants with a wide range of objects, 20 scenes had animate targets and 20 scenes had inanimate ones. In each scene, the target was highlighted with a red bounding box, see

Figure 1: Experimental scenes depicting an animate target (above) and an inanimate one (below)

Figure 1.

Procedure   Participants were randomly assigned to one of the conditions. We used and adapted the instructions of the ReferIt Game [1]. Participants' task was to produce distinguishable descriptions. For all conditions the instructions were identical except for the last sentence, that emphasized that participants should play fast (Fast condition, FA), be creative (creative condition, CR), clear and thorough (Clear and Thorough condition, CT) or no emphasis was be added (none condition, NO). Participants had to write down the description in a blank space provided under the scene. The scene remained on the screen until the participant introduced his description and pressed a button to continue. For each description participants received points, and were shown the score after submitting each description. The stimuli were presented in random order.

Analysis   This study had a single independent variable Instruction type (levels: FA, CR, CT, NO) as between participants factor. The dependent variables were the length of the references (number of words), number of adjectives in a RE, type and frequency of adjectives (e.g., color, location), and number of unique words (words that occur only

---

[1]For the exact wording of the instructions see Annex 1

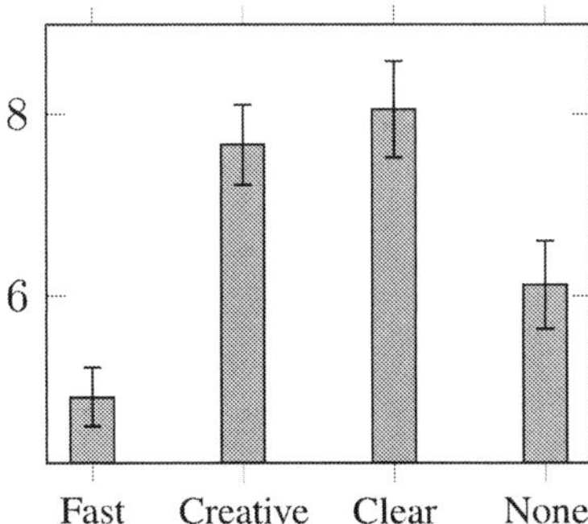

Figure 2: Average length of REs, split by condition. Error bars represent the 95% confidence intervals, y-axes represents mean number of words.

Table 1: Type of attributes, examples and frequency split by task

Type	Examples	Frequency			
		Fast	Creative	Clear	None
location	man on the left	21%	32%	27 %	20%
color	white building	21%	30%	30%	19%
part	with balconies / with red nose	4%	37%	36%	23%
action	man holding a paper / bicycle being ridden	8%	35%	31%	26%
size	small monkey	18%	30%	34%	18%
emotion	smiling man	17%	33%	30%	20%
other		12%	35%	30%	23%

in a given condition). In order to test the observed differences, we conducted separate ANOVA tests. Individual variation was measured by computing the standard deviation of the REs' length. For intra-individual variation, standard deviation was measured for the group of REs produced by each speaker. For inter-variation, standard deviation was measured for the group of REs produced for each stimuli. Values close to zero indicate no intra- and inter- individual variation.

3 Results

In total 2920 references were produced (73 speakers * 40 scenes, FA, NO and CT conditions 18 participants each; CR condition 19 participants). The referring expressions consisted of a noun denoting the target object and all the phrases attached to it. Below, we report only significant effects.

Length of expressions There was a significant main effect of Instruction Type on the number of words, $F(3, 70) = 6.666$, $p = .01$, $\eta^2 = .222$ (see Figure 2). The FA condition had the shortest references ($M = 3.95$, $SE = .59$), followed by the NO condition ($M = 4.68$, $SE = .59$), the CT condition ($M = 6.36$, $SE = .59$) and the CR condition ($M = 7.19$, $SE = .56$). A post–hoc Tukey test showed that, compared to NO, only the CR and the CT conditions were significantly different ($p = .05$). The FA condition was significantly different from the CR ($p = .001$) and the CT conditions ($p = .006$).

Number of adjectives There was a significant main effect of Instruction Type on the number of adjectives, $F(3, 70) = 4.362$, $p = .007$, $\eta^2 = .159$. The FA condition had the smallest number of adjectives ($M = .55$, $SE = .10$), followed by the NO condition ($M = .66$, $SE = .11$), the CT condition ($M = .88$, $SE = .10$) and the CR condition ($M = 1.03$, $SE = .99$). A post–hoc Tukey test showed that compared to the NO condition, there were no significant differences. The only significant difference was between the FA and the CR condition ($p = .008$) and there was an emerging trend suggesting a difference between the CR and the NO condition ($p = .065$).

Type and frequency of adjectives Speakers referred to the target objects using several types of attributes (see Table 1). In all conditions, the same types of attributes were present. The conditions with highest frequencies were CR and CL. The *other* category contains references with various attributes such as orientation (*dog facing left*), age (*the old building*), clothing (*the man wearing a white hat*), body descriptions (*the man holding his face in his hand*) and geographical origin (*the Indian man*).

Unique words Out of the total number of different words present in the corpus, the NO condition had 5% unique words, the FA condition 3% unique words, the CT condition 28% unique words and the CR condition 30% unique words.

Individual Variation Figure 3 depicts the intra- and inter- individual variation in the data. These results reveal, as one would expect, that there is indeed variation between participants in the amount of words they use for the same stimulus (($M = 6.09$,

$SD = 1.69$, $t(1, 39) = 22.406$, $p < 0.001$) and also variation between the stimuli (intra-individual variation, $M = 3.18$, $SD = 2.7$, $t(1, 72) = 14.80$, $p < 0.001$).

4   Conclusion and Discussion

Generally, content selection algorithms for definite descriptions generation behave deterministically by not taking into account factors like task demands or individual variation. The current paper investigated these two possible factors in the generation of definite descriptions, aiming to improve the *human-likeness* of NLG systems.

In particular, results showed that task demands (such as asking speakers to be fast, clear or creative) influences REs. Speakers who had to describe fast produced shorter references with less adjectives than the baseline condition. We assume that speakers in the fast condition may have lacked time and cognitive capacity to produce detailed references. Contrastively, speakers who had to be creative or clear produced longer and more detailed references. For example, the monkey in Figure 1 would be described as: *jumping monkey, FA*; *a primate showing off his business end, CR*; *small monkey with a very long tail, CT*; *a monkey on a persons' head, NO*. An interesting point for future research would be to investigate speaker's strategies across the four conditions, and to assess the accuracy with which listeners would be able to find the correct targets. Moreover, an open question remains how would the same REG algorithm perform when trained on datasets collected with different instructions.

Surprisingly, we did not observe any difference between the creative and clear references. Participants produced similar long and detailed references and the same types of attributes could be found in all conditions. Yet, the number of unique words for each of these conditions does hint there might be some other type of differences. Less creativity can also be due to the expectations workers have from MechanicalTurk tasks, which usually do not involve a 'creative' component. Participants might have interpreted our request for creativity as a request for explicit and detailed REs.

Our results also suggest a considerable amount of variation among the REs of a single speaker as well

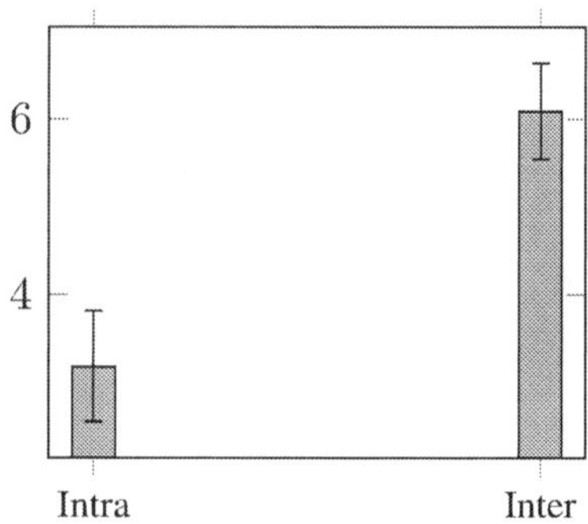

Figure 3: Average SDs of the length of REs per participant (intra-individual variation) and stimuli (inter-individual variation). Error bars represent 95% confidence intervals.

as among the REs of different speakers for a same situation. This result is in agreement with studies like (Viethen and Dale, 2010). An interesting observation for future research is that the level of intra-individual variation is lower than the level of inter-individual variation. As far as we know there are no computational REG models that take both inter- and intra- individual variation into account, and we wonder to what extent this could improve the *human-likeness* of the generated REs.

Annex 1. Instructions to the participants

Welcome to this game! In moments you will be shown a picture. In each picture there is an item bounded in red. Your goal is to describe the object as best as possible for another player, who has to select the object you describe. For each description you will earn points.

- *FA condition* The faster you play, the more points you win.
- *CT condition* The more clearly and thoroughly you describe, the more points you win.
- *CR condition* The more creative you are, the more points you win.
- *NO condition* Nothing

Acknowledgments

This work has been supported by the National Council of Scientific and Technological Development from Brazil (CNPq).

References

Anja Arts, Alfons Maes, Leo Noordman, and Carel Jansen. 2011. Overspecification facilitates object identification. *Journal of Pragmatics*, 43(1):361–374.

Michael Frank and Noah Goodman. 2012. Predicting pragmatic reasoning in language games. *Science*, 336(6084):998–998.

Petra Hendriks. 2016. Cognitive modeling of individual variation in reference production and comprehension. *Frontiers in Psychology*, 7(506).

Sahar Kazemzadeh, Vicente Ordonez, Mark Matten, and Tamara Berg. 2014. Referitgame: Referring to objects in photographs of natural scenes. In *Proceedings of the EMNLP*, pages 787–798, Stroudsburg, PA, USA. Association for Computational Linguistics.

Ruud Koolen, Albert Gatt, Martijn Goudbeek, and Emiel Krahmer. 2011. Factors causing overspecification in definite descriptions. *Journal of Pragmatics*, 43(13):3231–3250.

Emiel Krahmer and Kees Van Deemter. 2012. Computational generation of referring expressions: A survey. *Computational Linguistics*, 38(1):173–218.

Kees van Deemter, Ielka van der Sluis, and Albert Gatt. 2006. Building a semantically transparent corpus for the generation of referring expressions. In *Proceedings of the Fourth INLG Conference*, pages 130–132. Association for Computational Linguistics.

Roger Van Gompel, Albert Gatt, Emiel Krahmer, and Kees Deemter. 2012. Pro: A computational model of referential overspecification. In *Proceedings of AMLAP*.

Jette Viethen and Robert Dale. 2010. Speaker-dependent variation in content selection for referring expression generation. In *Proceedings of the 8th Australasian Language Technology Workshop*.

Category-Driven Content Selection

Rania Mohamed Sayed
Université de Lorraine
Nancy (France)
rania.mohamed.sayed@gmail.com

Laura Perez-Beltrachini
CNRS/LORIA
Nancy (France)
laura.perez@loria.fr

Claire Gardent
CNRS/LORIA
Nancy (France)
claire.gardent@loria.fr

Abstract

In this paper, we introduce a content selection method where the communicative goal is to describe entities of different categories (e.g., astronauts, universities or monuments). We argue that this method provides an interesting basis both for generating descriptions of entities and for semi-automatically constructing a benchmark on which to train, test and compare data-to-text generation systems.

1   Introduction

With the development of the Linked Open Data framework (LOD[1]), a considerable amount of RDF(S) data is now available on the Web. While this data contains a wide range of interesting factual and encyclopedic knowledge, the RDF(S) format in which it is encoded makes it difficult to access by lay users. Natural Language Generation (NLG) would provide a natural means of addressing this shortcoming. It would permit, for instance, enriching existing texts with encyclopaedic information drawn from linked data sources such as DBPedia; or automatically creating a wikipedia stub for an instance of an ontology from the associated linked data. Conversely, because of its well-defined syntax and semantics, the RDF(S) format in which linked data is encoded provides a natural ground on which to develop, test and compare Natural Language Generation (NLG) systems.

In this paper, we focus on content selection from RDF data where the communicative goal is to describe entities of various categories (e.g., astronauts

or monuments). We introduce a content selection method which, given an entity, retrieves from DBPedia an RDF subgraph that encodes relevant and coherent knowledge about this entity. Our approach differs from previous work in that it leverages the categorial information provided by large scale knowledge bases about entities of a given type. Using n-gram models of the RDF(S) properties occurring in the RDF(S) graphs associated with entities of the same category , we select for a given entity of category C, a subgraph with maximal n-gram probability that is, a subgraph which contains properties that are true of that entity, that are typical of that category and that support the generation of a coherent text.

2   Method

Given an entity e of category C and its associated DBPedia *entity graph* G_e, our task is to select a (target) subgraph T_e of G_e such that:

- T_e is *relevant*: the DBPedia properties contained in T_e are commonly (directly or indirectly) associated with entities of type C

- T_e maximises *global coherence*: DBPedia entries that often co-occur in type C are selected together

- T_e supports *local coherence*: the set of DBPedia triples contained in T_e capture a sequence of entity-based transitions which supports the generation of locally coherent texts i.e., texts such that the propositions they contain are related through shared entities.

---

[1] http://lod-cloud.net/

Category	Nb.Entities	Nb.Triples	Nb.Properties
Astronaut	110	1664033	4167
Monument	500	818145	6521
University	500	969541	7441

Table 1: Category Graphs

	Entity	Depth1	Depth2
Astronaut	e1	14	24
	e2	21	32
	e3	16	28
	e4	12	24
	e5	15	22
Monument	e1	13	18
	e2	20	21
	e3	7	14
	e4	6	14
	e5	4	11
University	e1	6	20
	e2	13	21
	e3	6	10
	e4	9	16
	e5	27	34

Table 2: Entity Graphs

To provide a content selection process which implements these constraints, we proceeds in three main steps.

First, we build n-gram models of properties for DBPedia categories. That is, we define the probability of 1-, 2- and 3-grams of DBPedia properties for a given category.

Second, we extract from DBPedia, entity graphs of depth four.

Third, we use the n-gram models of DBPedia properties and Integer Linear Programming (ILP) to identify subtrees of entity graphs with maximal probability. Intuitively, we select subtrees of the entity graph which are relevant (the properties they contain are frequent for that category), which are locally coherent (the tree constraints ensure that the selected triples are related by entity sharing) and that are globally coherent (the use of bi- and tri-gram probabilities supports the selection of properties that frequently co-occur in the graphs of entities of that category).

2.1 Building n-gram models of DBPedia properties.

To build the n-gram models, we extract from DBPedia the graphs associated with all entities of those categories up to depth 4. Table 1 shows some statistics for these graphs. We build the n-gram models using the SRILM toolkit. To experiment with various versions of n-gram information, we create for each category, 1-, 2- and 3-grams of DBPedia properties.

2.2 Building Entity Graphs.

For each of the three categories, we then extract from DBPedia the graphs associated with 5 entities considering RDF triples up to depth two. Table 2 shows the statistics for each entity depending on the depth of the graph.

2.3 Selecting DBPedia Subgraphs

To retrieve subtrees of DBPedia subgraphs which are maximally coherent, we use an the following ILP model.

Representing tuples Given an entity graph G_e for the DBPedia entity e of category C (e.g. Astronaut), for each triple $t = (s, p, o)$ in G_e, we introduce a binary variable $x_{s,o}^p$ such that:

$$x_t = x_{s,o}^p = \begin{cases} 1 & \text{if the tuple is preserved} \\ 0 & \text{otherwise} \end{cases}$$

Because we use 2- and 3-grams to capture global coherence (properties that often co-occur together), we also have variables for bi-grams and trigrams of tuples. For bigrams, these variables capture triples which share an entity (either the object of one is the subject of the other or they share the same subject). So for each bigram of triples $t_1 = (s1, p1, o1)$ and $t2 = (s2, p2, o2)$ in G_e such that $o1 = s2, o2 = s1$ or $s1 = s2$, we introduce a binary variable y_{t_1,t_2} such that:

$$y_{t_1,t_2} = \begin{cases} 1 & \text{if the pair of triples is preserved} \\ 0 & \text{otherwise} \end{cases}$$

Similarly, there is a trigram binary variable z_{t_1,t_2,t_3} for each connected set of triples t_1, t_2, t_3 in G_e such that:

$$z_{t_1,t_2,t_3} = \begin{cases} 1 & \text{if the trigram of triples is preserved} \\ 0 & \text{otherwise} \end{cases}$$

Maximising Relevance and Coherence To maximise relevance and coherence, we seek to find a subtree of the input graph G_e which maximises the following objective function:

$$S(X) = \sum_x x_t \cdot P(p) \\ + \sum_y Y_{t_i,t_j} \cdot B(t_i,t_j) \qquad (1) \\ + \sum_z Z_{t_i,t_j,t_k} \cdot T(t_i,t_j,t_k)$$

where $P(p)$, the unigram probability of p in entities of category C, is defined as follows, let T_c be the set of triples occurring in the entity graphs (depth 2) of all DBPedia entities of category C. Let P_c be the set of properties occurring in T_c and let $count(p,C)$ be the number of time p occurs in T_c, then:

$$P(p) = \frac{count(p,C)}{\sum_i count(p_i,C)}$$

Similarly, $B(t_i,t_j)$ and $T(t_i,t_j,t_k)$ are the 2- and 3-gram probability $P(t_2|t_1)$ and $P(t_3|t_1t_2)$.

Consistency Constraints We ensure consistency between the unary and the binary variables so that if a bigram is selected then so are the corresponding triples:

$$\forall i,j, y_{i,j} \leq x_i$$

$$\forall i,j, y_{i,j} \leq x_j$$

$$y_{i,j} + (1 - x_i) + (1 - x_j) \geq 1$$

Ensuring Local Coherence (Tree Shape) Solutions are constrained to be trees by requiring that each object has at most one subject (eq. 2) and all tuples are connected (eq. 3).

$$\forall o \in X, \sum_{s,p} x^p_{s,o} \leq 1 \qquad (2)$$

$$\forall o \in X, \sum_{s,p} x^p_{s,o} - \frac{1}{|X|} \sum_{u,p} x^p_{o,u} \geq 0 \qquad (3)$$

Model	Selected Triples
Baseline	Elliot_See birthDate "1927-07-23"
	Elliot_See birthPlace Dallas
	Elliot_See almaMater University_of_Texas_at_Austin
	Elliot_See source "See's feelings about ..."
	Elliot_See status "Deceased"
	Elliot_See deathPlace St._Louis
1-Gram	Elliot_See birthPlace Dallas
	Elliot_See nationality United_States
	Elliot_See almaMater University_of_Texas_at_Austin
	Elliot_See rank United_States_Navy_Reserve
	Elliot_See mission "None"
	Elliot_See deathPlace St._Louis
2-Gram	Elliot_See birthDate "1927-07-23"
	Elliot_See birthPlace Dallas
	Elliot_See nationality United_States
	Elliot_See almaMater University_of_Texas_at_Austin
	Elliot_See status "Deceased"
	Elliot_See deathPlace St._Louis
3-Gram	Elliot_See birthDate "1927-07-23"
	Elliot_See birthPlace Dallas
	Elliot_See almaMater University_of_Texas_at_Austin
	Elliot_See deathDate "1966-02-28"
	Elliot_See status "Deceased"
	Elliot_See deathPlace St._Louis

Table 3: Example content selections

where X is the set of words that occur in the solution (except the root node). This constraint makes sure that if o has a child then it also has a head. The first part of Eq 3 counts the number of head properties. The second part counts the children of p which could be greater than 0. It is therefore normalised with X to make it less than 1. And then the difference should be greater than 0.

Restricting the size of the resulting tree Solutions are constrained to contain α tuples.

$$\sum_x x^p_{s,o} = \alpha \qquad (4)$$

3 Discussion

Table 3 shows content selections which illustrate the main differences between four models, a baseline model with uniform n-gram probability versus a unigram, a bigram and a 3-gram model.

The baseline model tends to generate solutions with little cohesion between triples. Facts are enumerated which each range over distinct topics (e.g., birth date and place, place of study, status and deathplace). It may also include properties such as

Dead_Man's_Plack location England
England capital London
England establishedEvent Acts_of_Union_1707
England religion Church_of_England
Dead_Man's_Plack dedicatedTo Athelwald
Dead_Man's_Plack monumentName "Dead Man's Plack"
Dead_Man's_Plack material Rock

Table 4: Output of Depth 2

"source" which are generic rather than specific to the type of entity being described.

The 1-gram model is similar to the baseline in that it often generates solutions which are simple enumerations of facts belonging to various topics (birth place, nationality, place of study, rank in the army, space mission, death place). Contrary to the baseline solutions however, each selected fact is strongly characteristic of the entity type.

The 2- and 3-gram models tend to yield more coherent solutions in that they often contain sets of topically related properties (e.g., birth date and birth place; death date and date place).

4 Conclusion

We have presented a method for content selection from DBPedia data which supports the selection of semantically varied content units of different sizes. While the approach yields good results, one shortcoming is that most of the selected subtrees are trees of depth 1 and that moreover, trees of depth 2 have limited coherence. For instance, the 1-gram model generates the solution shown in Table 4 where the triples about England are not particularly relevant to the description of the Deam Man's Plack's monument. More generally, bi- and 3-grams mostly seem to trigger the selection of 2- and 3-grams that are directly related to the target entity rather than chains of triples. We are currently investigating whether the use of interpolated models could help resolve this issue.

Another important point we are currently investigating concerns the creation of a benchmark for Natural Language Generation. Most existing work on data-to-text generation rely on a parallel or comparable data-to-text corpus.

To generate from the frames produced by a dialog system, (DeVault et al., 2008) describes an approach in which a probabilistic Tree Adjoining Grammar is induced from a training set aligning frames and sentences and used to generate using a beam search that uses weighted features learned from the training data to rank alternative expansions at each step.

More recently, data-to-text generators (Angeli et al., 2010; Chen and Mooney, 2008; Wong and Mooney, 2007; Konstas and Lapata, 2012b; Konstas and Lapata, 2012a) were trained and developed on data-to-text corpora from various domains including the air travel domain (Dahl et al., 1994), weather forecasts (Liang et al., 2009; Belz, 2008) and sportscasting (Chen and Mooney, 2008).

Creating such data-to-text corpora is however difficult, time consuming and non generic. Contrary to parsing where resources such as the Penn Treebank succeeded in boosting research, natural language generation still suffers from a lack of common reference on which to train and evaluate parsers. Using crowdsourcing and the content selection method presented here, we plan to construct a large benchmark on which data-to-text generators can be trained and tested.

5 Acknowledgments

We thank the French National Research Agency for funding the research presented in this paper in the context of the WebNLG project.

References

Gabor Angeli, Percy Liang, and Dan Klein. 2010. A simple domain-independent probabilistic approach to generation. In *Proceedings of the 2010 Conference on Empirical Methods in Natural Language Processing*, pages 502–512. Association for Computational Linguistics.

Anja Belz. 2008. Automatic generation of weather forecast texts using comprehensive probabilistic generation-space models. *Natural Language Engineering*, 14(4):431–455.

David L Chen and Raymond J Mooney. 2008. Learning to sportscast: a test of grounded language acquisition. In *Proceedings of the 25th international conference on Machine learning*, pages 128–135. ACM.

Deborah A Dahl, Madeleine Bates, Michael Brown, William Fisher, Kate Hunicke-Smith, David Pallett, Christine Pao, Alexander Rudnicky, and Elizabeth Shriberg. 1994. Expanding the scope of the atis task: The atis-3 corpus. In *Proceedings of the workshop on*

Human Language Technology, pages 43–48. Association for Computational Linguistics.

David DeVault, David Traum, and Ron Artstein. 2008. Making grammar-based generation easier to deploy in dialogue systems. In *Proceedings of the 9th SIGdial Workshop on Discourse and Dialogue*, pages 198–207. Association for Computational Linguistics.

Ioannis Konstas and Mirella Lapata. 2012a. Concept-to-text generation via discriminative reranking. In *Proceedings of the 50th Annual Meeting of the Association for Computational Linguistics: Long Papers-Volume 1*, pages 369–378. Association for Computational Linguistics.

Ioannis Konstas and Mirella Lapata. 2012b. Unsupervised concept-to-text generation with hypergraphs. In *Proceedings of the 2012 Conference of the North American Chapter of the Association for Computational Linguistics: Human Language Technologies*, pages 752–761. Association for Computational Linguistics.

Percy Liang, Michael I Jordan, and Dan Klein. 2009. Learning semantic correspondences with less supervision. In *Proceedings of the Joint Conference of the 47th Annual Meeting of the ACL and the 4th International Joint Conference on Natural Language Processing of the AFNLP: Volume 1-Volume 1*, pages 91–99. Association for Computational Linguistics.

Yuk Wah Wong and Raymond J Mooney. 2007. Generation by inverting a semantic parser that uses statistical machine translation. In *HLT-NAACL*, pages 172–179.

Evaluative Pattern Extraction for Automated Text Generation

Chia-Chen Lee and **Shu-Kai Hsieh**

Graduate Institute of Linguistics, National Taiwan University

she767219@gmail.com, shukai@gmail.com

Abstract

Getting travel tips from the experienced bloggers and online forums has been one of the important supplements to the travel guidebook in the web society. In this paper we present a novel approach by identifying and extracting evaluative patterns, providing a different linguistically-motivated framework for automated evaluative text generation. We target at domain-specific observation in online travel blogs in Chinese. Results suggest that the semantic prosody accompanying the patterns demonstrates that online travel bloggers prefer to employ tacit pragmatic strategy in presenting their sentiment polarity in comments. The extracted patterns and their differentiation can be beneficial to identifying and characterizing evaluative language for further automated opinion summarization and macro/micro planning in natural language generation (NLG) as well.

1 Introduction

With the rapidly growing use of the Internet, text mining, sentiment analysis, and evaluative language analysis of online resources are becoming essential issues. Online travel blogs serve as main opinions and comments providers sharing their traveling experiences where the texts are constructed with authors' evaluation about the traveling. The automation of text planning in this domain has become highly demanded. This paper aims to propose a linguistic framework of working with evaluative expressions by examining domain-restricted specialized discourse of traveling articles. Identifying the particular linguistic behaviors and patterns of evaluative language agglomerative structure would facilitate both the macro/ micro planning in NLG in this domain.

In online travel blog articles, evaluative language is expressed in several kinds. lexical level terms such as 'recommend', 'delicious', and 'surprise', are explicit evaluations. Other than this, patterns are found and can be generalized into a certain fixed meanings in traveling domain. For instance, 有 N 味 'has the flavor/feeling of N' is a common pattern used as in 有 家鄉 味 'has the feeling of home', 有 台灣 味 'has the feeling of Taiwan' as positive evaluation in the data. We propose to adopt pattern grammar (Hunston, 1999) in approaching the evaluative prosody widely occurred in the travel blogs. Pattern grammar focuses on the concept that meaning belongs to patterns, targeting on the recurring co-occurrences and the particularly shared meanings of lexical item nodes. There is specialized domain-specific grammar not applying to general grammar, resulting a fixed meaning of patterns in that specific domain. As Sinclair (1991) said: "It seems that there is a strong tendency for sense and syntax to be associated", suggesting that meaning and its patterns are highly related. Francis (1993) used the pattern *v it adj* as an example, which limits the choices of its lexical items on either verbs or adjectives, indicating that the meaning of a pattern is also limited and patterns will occur with words through semantic restriction. Therefore, patterns extracted from the texts should be the primary consideration and observation for natural language processing, particularly for semantic and sentiment analysis, whether as for annotation, summarization or text generation.

2 Literature Review

In NLG, content determination is an essential process to decide what is the communicated information in texts (Reiter, 1995). In order to generate natural-language text, a system must be able to determine what to include and how to organize the information to achieve its communicative goal most effectively. McKeown (1985) based on discourse strategies as a guide for natural-language text generation, which generated paragraph-length responses. In domain-specific texts such as weather forecast (Adeyanju, 2012), automated text generation is expected to have similar weather conditions where its language pattern is observable. In traveling blog articles, the evaluative language is its dominant feature. Evaluative language has been researched since 1970s, starting from Halliday (1976), with others making further developments or moving on to new approaches such as Chafe (1986), Biber and Finegan (1989), Hunston (1994), Francis (1995), and Martin and White (2000). Hunston (1994, 2000, 2004) defined evaluative language as which is "expressed through language which indexes the act of evaluation or the act of stance-taking. It expresses an attitude towards a person, situation, or other entity and is both subjective and located within a societal value system". It is the driving force behind virtually all communications. (Thompson and Hunston, 2000). Patterns of a word are defined as "all the words and structures which are regularly associated with the word and which contribute to its meaning". The relationship between patterns and lexis is mutually dependent, in that each pattern appears with a limited set of lexical items, and each lexical item occurs with a restricted set of patterns. As patterns are highly associated with meaning, words sharing a given pattern will also tend to share an aspect of meaning (Hunston, 1999).

With the concepts combination of evaluative language and pattern grammar, we can discover that how evaluation is spread across texts with fixed meanings. The necessity of examining evaluation language is obvious in that online travel blog articles serve as the purpose for sharing comments and opinions to readers, and to find out if there are certain structures or patterns in the texts are utilizable for generating opinion summaries.

3 Patterns and Evaluative Meanings in Content Determination

The categorization of evaluation languages is diverse for different research purposes. To fit the communicative goal in the traveling context, where *recommendation* instead of neutral descriptions is needed, the following relevant attributes are targeted: attraction, hotel, restaurant, food, and event. Among these targets, evaluative expressions are realized in different aspects. For instance, main

evaluated aspects for attraction are its environment, transportation, popularity, culture, and so on. While in food, its price, taste, quality, or quantity are main discussed issues. **Table 1** shows the attributes and their evaluated aspects.

Attributes	Evaluated Aspects
Attraction	Environment (space, design, atmosphere, weather), transportation, popularity
Hotel	Environment (space, design, atmosphere), transportation, popularity, price, service
Restaurant	Environment (space, design, atmosphere), transportation, popularity, price, service
Food	Popularity, price, taste, quality, quantity
Event	Environment (space, design, atmosphere, weather), popularity, product(price, package, quality)

Table 1: Lightweight ontology in traveling domain

In this study, data are crawled from ten online travel blogs nominated as the ten most popular online travel blogs in GOLDDOT Award 2015[1], held by Pixnet in Taiwan, with 540 articles in total. A corpus-based approach is taken for exploring the data and extracting the patterns. As evaluated patterns are embodied within sentences and flexible in its unit, there is no straightforward way to observe them in the corpus. Annotation is based on the attributes mentioned earlier for categorization, using LOPOTATOR, an online linguistic annotation tool designed by LOPE lab[2]. One annotator is involved in annotation process. Chunks are considered as units for patterns detection, mostly restricted in phrasal units, where the evaluator and the evaluation are included so as to know the relationship between the property of evaluated entity and the evaluation expression. For instance, chunk like 值得一探的美景 'a beautiful view that is worth visiting' will be annotated as with the evaluator 美景 'beautiful view' and its expression 值得一探的 'something which is worth visiting'. The processing pipeline is shown in **Figure 1**.

---

[1] http://2015golddot.events.pixnet.net/

[2] http://lopen.linguistics.ntu.edu.tw:8001/lope.anno

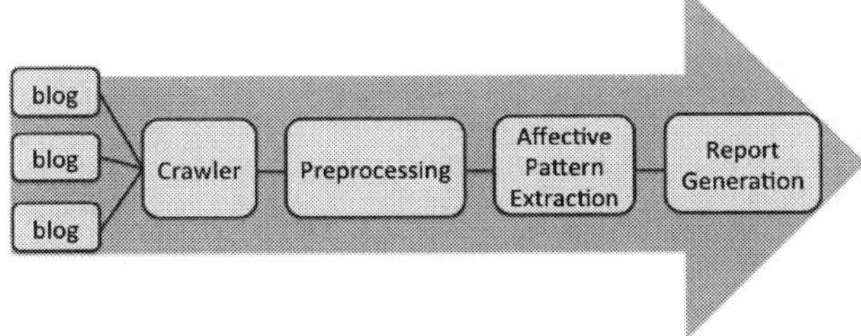

Figure 1: Processing pipeline.

4 Data Annotation and Analysis

Different from previous linguistic formalisms (such as Rhetorical Structure Theory) used in document structuring, where the main focus is hierarchical construct of messages, the *evaluative pattern grammar* as proposed in this paper explores the linear interaction of lexis and configuration at the evaluative level. In our corpus, lexical items are explicitly observable evaluation, such as 大 'big', 新 'new', 好 'good', 分享 'share', 推薦 'recommend', 喜歡 'like', and 享受 'enjoy' are frequently occurred in the data. Our primary attention here is to extract the fixed patterns denoting fossilized polarity in evaluation co-occurring with a variety of word choices.

Manual annotation for patterns extraction in online travel blog articles provides an exhaustive result of all possible evaluative use.

In all annotated units, expressions with similar meanings and structures can be generalized into patterns, generating a fixed basic meaning, where they seem to be neutral but denote a polarity when used in a context. **Table 2** summaries the patterns listed by different aspects, with a symbol '+' and '-' representing the polarity being positive or negative the pattern implies. Due to limit of pages a few patterns are listed as instances. Whenever a pattern occurs, it brings out a value merging with the meaning of its variant noun, verb, or adjectives. 非常有 N 味 'so full of N's flavor or feeling' is taken as an example. In this pattern, it's the comment on the food evaluator that it is 'full of the flavor or feeling' of the noun phrase, with implicit neutral evaluation until noun phrase is filled in, such as 非常有 家鄉 味 and realized as the meaning of 'full of home's feeling; the food makes you feel or think of home', gaining positive evaluation.

Patterns	Instances	Polarity
[N 直逼 N] 'N can nearly compete with N'	設計感 直逼 W Hotel 'its design can compete with W Hotel'	+
[N 有梗] 'N is interesting'	空間 有梗 'the space is interesting'	+
[N 破表] 'it's quite over of the degree of N'	浪漫指數 破表 'it 's quite over of the degree of the romance'	+
[讓你有種 N 的感覺] 'make you have the feeling of N'	讓你有種 家 的感覺 'make you have the feeling to be home'	+
[絕對是 N 的 N] 'it's definite N's N'	絕對是 飯店 的 基本配備 'it's definite the basic equipment of a hotel'	+
[N 對我來說已是 N] 'N is already N to me'	甜度 對我來說已是 極限 'the sweetness is already way too enough to me'	-
[非常有 N 味] 'so full of N's feeling'	非常有 家鄉 味 'so full of home's feeling'	+
[N 十足] 'a lot of N; high degree of N'	咬勁 十足 'high degree of texture'	+
[光是 V 就知它的 N] 'knowing its N just by V'	光是 看顏色 就知它的 粉嫩程度 **'knowing its freshness just by looking at the color'**	+

Table 2: Evaluative patterns and data instances.

Patterns shown in **Table 2** are case-specific to the traveling domain, and they can be taken as self-embedded evaluative meaning carriers which are useful cues in content determination in that a pattern can simply be a comment unit shown a positive or negative evaluation toward the evaluated targets.

Figure 2: User interface snapshots of traveling recommendation searching and searching results.

Figure 2 is a temporary template of user interface where users can search for traveling comments or opinions, and the comments can be either using the evaluative patterns generated from our work or the origin sentences from the author.

Comments from several authors' comments and scores of the traveling targets are useful when only searching for a single and specific target, such as Taipei 101 or W Hotel. However, common occasions are that people want to know all possible comments on one target, such as recommendation for traveling in Tokyo, with all things might be experienced in Tokyo. Therefore, we create a simplified plan (exemplified in English version) as in **Figure 3** for generating the evaluative summary from a single author's traveling article. Parenthesis units such as '(name of the author)' in **Figure 3** are information to be extracted from the article, including author's name, places or things experienced by the author with comments. Evaluators are comment units extracting from our pattern generation work. Both opinions are informative generation results.

> The blogger _(author's name)_ came to _(traveling places)_ for traveling, where he/ she experienced __(place1)_, _(place2)_, _(place3)_, and _(place4)_. About _(evaluator 1)_, _(name of the author)_ like because he/she thinks that it is _(evaluative pattern 1)_, particularly _(part of evaluator 1)_ is worth trying. In addition, he/ she also went to _(evaluator 2)_, and he/she recommended it because of_(evaluative pattern 2)_. Among

that, _(part of evaluator 2)_ is the most recommended one. ...

Figure 3. Simplified document plan.

In short, the identification of evaluative patterns in texts, as inspired by usage-based linguistic pattern grammar theory, can be utilized as a key feature for domain-specialized research on opinion mining and generation in evaluative texts.

5 Conclusion and Future Work

Due to the socio-pragmatic reasons, the evaluative patterns found in online travel blogs have their own characteristics and therefore call for more attention. On one hand, the recurrent linguistic means of evaluation as performed in texts of this genre are mostly beyond the word level; on the other hand, bloggers often tacitly organize their discourse of feelings or assessments in a relatively polite manner. It constitutes a challenge for content selection and text planning, more linguistic framework should be involved in properly tailoring the data for potential users.

The approach proposed in this paper can handle with affective contents as seen crucial in the opinionated text mining and generation, has encountered its limitation mainly related to the annotation process. Manual annotation can achieve higher accuracy in extracting possible patterns, however subjective annotation with only one annotator causes time-consuming and inefficiency problems. There are few studies relating to the evaluative language in online traveling blog domain, this paper serves as a point of departure in discovering the evaluative patterns, and as a reference for probing into other domain-specific evaluative language. Patterns extraction can be applied to other domains and the annotated data can be used for automatic pattern extraction algorithms and for text summarization in the process of document planning in NLG. For text generation, pattern is a significant feature as a representation of the sentiment or polarity toward the evaluation. Automated patterns extraction will be a valuable progress in generating evaluative text summary.

References

Adeyanju, I. 2012. *Generating weather forecast texts with case based reasoning.* International Journal of Computer Applications, 45.

Biber, D., and E. Finegan. 1989. *Styles of stance in English: Lexical and grammatical marking of evidentiality and affect.* Text 9.93-124. Special issue on *The pragmatics of affect*, ed. by Elinor Ochs).

Chafe, Wallace and Nichols, Johanna. 1986. *Evidentiality: the Linguistic Coding of Epistemology.* Norwood, New Jersey: Ablex

Francis, G. 1993. *A corpus-driven approach to grammar — principles, methods and examples.* In Baker et al. (eds), 137–156.

Francis, G. 1995. *Corpus-driven grammar and its relevance to the learning of English in a cross-cultural situation.* In English in Education: Multicultural perspectives, A. Pakir (ed). Singapore: Unipress.

Hunston, S. and Francis, G. 1999 *Pattern Grammar: a corpus-driven approach to the lexical grammar of English.* Amsterdam: Benjamins.

Hunston, S. and Sinclair, J. 2000 'A local grammar of evaluation' in Hunston and Thompson (eds.) *Evaluation in Text: authorial stance and the construction of discourse.* Oxford: Oxford University Press.

Martin, J. R. & White, P. R. R. 2005. *The language of evaluation: appraisal in English.* Basingstoke : Palgrave Macmillan.

Sinclair, J.M. 1991. *Corpus, Concordance, Collocation.* Oxford: OUP.

McKeown, K. R. 1985. *Discourse strategies for generating natural-language text.* Artificial Intelligence, 27(1), 1-41.

Reiter E. and Dale R. 1997. *Building applied natural language generation systems. Natural Language Engineering*, 3, pp 57-87.

Statistics-Based Lexical Choice for NLG from Quantitative Information

Xiao Li and **Kees van Deemter** and **Chenghua Lin**
Computing Science department
University of Aberdeen
King's College
Aberdeen, AB24 3FX, UK
{xiao.li, k.vdeemter, chenghua.lin}@abdn.ac.uk

Abstract

We discuss a fully statistical approach to the expression of quantitative information in English. We outline the approach, focussing on the problem of Lexical Choice. An initial evaluation experiment suggests that it is worth investigating the method further.

1 Introduction

NLG systems express information in human language. To do this well, these systems need to "know"what expressions are most suitable for expressing a given piece of information. The most direct way to define words in NLG systems is manual coding, as it was done in systems such as FoG (Golberg et al., 1994) and SumTime-Mousam (Sripada et al., 2003). However, manual coding is time consuming, it can be argued to be theoretically unsatisfactory, and it is error prone even when performed by domain experts. The process is complicated in the fact that words like *pink* (Roy, 2002) and *evening* (Reiter et al., 2005) have different meanings for individual speakers.

Recent NLG approaches learn the use of words through statistical analysis of data-text corpora. For example, Belz's semi-automatic system for weather forecasting automatically learns a grammar based on a pre-existing (i.e., manually coded) set of grammar rules (Belz, 2008). Liang et al. (2009) developed a fully statistical alignment-based algorithm that automatically acquires a mapping from quantitative information to English words by adopting a hierarchical hidden semi-Markov model trained by Expectation Maximization. Konstas and Lapata (2013) introduced a generation model based on Liang's algorithm . However, these existing approaches have difficulty handling situations in which a word expresses a *combination* of data dimensions, for example as when the word "mildëxpresses a combination of warm temperatures and low wind speed.

In this paper, we discuss a new approach to the problem; the approach is fully statistical and it is able to handle situations in which a word or phrase maps to a combination of data dimensions. We focus on Lexical Choice but are investigating applications to other areas of NLG.

2 Methodology

In many areas of perception research, a method called "contour stylizationïs employed to mimic a complex signal (i.e., a complex graph) by means of a limited number of straight lines (Johan t Hart and Cohen, 1990). Our method uses the similar idea and applies it to two dimensions (i.e., weather data and language) at the same time. Our approach builds a bridge between quantitative information and words by discretising the data.

2.1 Representing Data in Vector

A continuous dimension can be represented by a set of discrete parameters, so called **key-points**. For example, wind speed (ws) is a continuous dimension with its value between 0 knot to 36 knots. A group of key-points can then be used to represent any value of wind speed. For instance, a possible key-point group is $\{ws = 0, ws = 12, ws = 24, ws = 36\}$, in which key-points are evenly spaced. The aim of using key-points is to transform the original quantitative dimension into probability dimensions. This process is similar to Signal Analysis (Reiter 2007) in which each key-point plays a role as a Signal Sensor. In the above example, 5 key-points are used to represent wind speed collectively, where each key-point specifies a specific range of wind speed. In this way, if a word describes wind speed within a certain range, we will find the connection of the word to the relative key-points.

Based on this formulation, any wind speed can be represented by weighted key-points through linear interpolation. Suppose one would like to represent an arbitrary wind speed, say $ws = 5$. Note that $ws = 5$ falls between the range of key-points $ws = 0$ and $ws = 12$ as described above. Using linear interpolation, one can derive the weights of key-points $ws = 0$ and $ws = 12$ for representing $ws = 5$, which are 0.58 and 0.42 respectively. Because the remaining key points does not contribute to represent wind speed $ws = 5$, their weights are set to 0. Finally, the wind speed $ws = 5$ can be represented as a vector $\langle 0.58, 0.42, 0, 0 \rangle$, which encodes the weights for the key-point group.

Although in the above example key-points $\{ws = 0, ws = 12, ws = 24, ws = 36\}$ are set evenly spaced, it should be noted that the setting of key-points (e.g., the choice of key-point values) has relatively little impact on predicting the use of words. This is because the our method can be regarded as fitting the occurrence function of words by a straight line in the contour stylization angle (in addition to the Signal Analysis), and the key-points present the inflection points' abscissa of the straight line. Although carefully selecting key-points can possibly enhance the model's performance, our model adopt the evenly spaced key-points, which empirically works well enough in general.

2.2 Representing Words in Vector

Expressions such as words can be represented by key-points weight vectors as well. For example, in English the expression *calm* is only used to describe wind speed close to 0. So, *calm* can also be represented using the same key-point group as before, i.e., represented with a high weight for $ws = 0$ (such as 0.9, for instance), and a low weight for $ws = 12$ (e.g., 0.01). For the moment, the weights of *calm* are estimated by hand. In section 2.4 we will see how the weights can be estimated from a data-text corpus.

2.3 Lexical Choice

This section introduces how our proposed approcah handles the lexical choice in the NLG process through Cosine similarity. Suppose both quantitative information and lexical expressions have been converted into vectors (i.e., $\vec{q}$ and $\vec{e}$) in the same vector space parameterised by the key-points. The problem of finding the most likely expression ($\vec{e}$) for the given quantitative information ($\vec{q}$) can be transformed to the process of finding the most similar lexical expression vector $\vec{e}$ to $\vec{q}$. We exemplify the lexical choice process below, using wind speed as quantitative dimension.

Suppose the key-points are still $\{ws = 0, ws = 12, ws = 24, ws = 36\}$. The candidate expression words are *calm* and *breeze*, which can be represented in a form of key-point weight vectors as below:

$$\vec{e}_{calm} = \langle 0.9, 0.01, -0.9, -1 \rangle \qquad (1)$$
$$\vec{e}_{breeze} = \langle 0.7, 0.9, -0.8, -1 \rangle \qquad (2)$$

Now our goal is to choose the most suitable word to describe wind speed $ws = 5$ from the available candidate word expressions (i.e., *calm* and *breeze*). As discussed in Section 2.1, $ws = 5$ can also be represented by a key-point weight vector

$$\vec{q}_{ws=5} = \langle 0.58, 0.42, 0, 0 \rangle \qquad (3)$$

Based on the same key-point vector space, we calculate the Cosine similarities between each candidate word and the target wind speed $ws = 5$, and the most suitable word is naturally the one with the highest similarity to $ws = 5$.

$$\text{Sim}(\vec{e}_{calm}, \vec{q}_{ws=5}) = \frac{\vec{e}_{calm} \cdot \vec{q}_{ws=5}}{\|\vec{e}_{calm}\| \, \|\vec{q}_{ws=5}\|} = 0.45 \qquad (4)$$

$$\text{Sim}(\vec{e}_{breeze}, \vec{q}_{ws=5}) = \frac{\vec{e}_{breeze} \cdot \vec{q}_{ws=5}}{\|\vec{e}_{breeze}\| \, \|\vec{q}_{ws=5}\|} = 0.64 \qquad (5)$$

As can be seen above, the similarity between $\vec{q}_{ws=5}$ and $\vec{e}_{breeze}$ is higher than that of $\vec{e}_{clam}$. Therefore, *breeze* is a better choice for expressing $ws = 5$.

2.4 Estimating Weight Vector for Word Expressions

One key challenge in applying our approach for learning the relationship between quantitative information and words is to find the optimal vector $\vec{e}$ for each possible expression word. Suppose we have r data to text pairs denoted as $< data_i, text_i >_{i=1}^{r}$, where $data_i$ in the pairs consists of quantitative dimensions and $text_i$ refers to the expression words as shown in Eq. 6.

$$< data, text > \Rightarrow \{dim_{1,...,m}, exp_{1,...,n}\} \qquad (6)$$

Following section 2.1, for each data to text pair, we firstly discretise the data dimensions $(dim_{1,...,m})$ into a key-point group $\{\vec{d}_1, \vec{d}_2, ..., \vec{d}_m\} \equiv \vec{d}$. Next, we can find the optimal values for weight vector $\vec{e}_i$ by solving Eq. 7 constructed based on the training data $< data_i, text_i >_{i=1}^{r}$.

$$\begin{bmatrix} \vec{d}_1 \\ \vec{d}_2 \\ \vdots \\ \vec{d}_r \end{bmatrix} \vec{e}_i^{\,T} = \begin{bmatrix} \mathrm{isOccur}(exp_i|text_1) \\ \mathrm{isOccur}(exp_i|text_2) \\ \vdots \\ \mathrm{isOccur}(exp_i|text_r) \end{bmatrix} \qquad (7)$$

The function $\mathrm{isOccur}(exp_i|text_i)$ returns 1 if exp_i occurs in the corresponding $text_i$, and returns 0 otherwise.

Generally, there are fewer free parameters than the number of equations, so we can always find the optimised solution for estimating $\vec{e}_i$ using Least Square. If there are more than one solution, we adopt the solution with the least norm. In the same way, we can obtain weight vectors for all the candidate expressions.

So far we have described how to estimate the key-point weight vector for every candidate expression from training data, i.e., data-text pairs. In the test phase, to predict the most likely words for unseen data, we firstly represent data as a weight vector, and then compare its cosine similarity against every candidate expression. Since the weight vectors for expressions $\vec{e}_i$ are trained through the occurrence function $\mathrm{isOccur}()$, the similarity between unseen data and a candidate expression reflects the suitability of an expression in expressing the data.

2.5 Discussion: Handling multiple dimensions

One of the important features of our approach is the ability of choosing expressions for data with multiple dimensions. We stress that both the training process and lexical choice process are applicable to multiple data dimensions. First, in the training process, information of different quantitative dimensions is converted into key-point weights, so the boundaries between different dimensions have disappeared. The training process could even calculate the implicit relationship between expressions and quantitative data. Second, the lexical choice process selects expressions based on a set of dimensions rather than each single dimension. This is why this approach can handle the multiple dimension information.

3   Evaluating the proposed approach to Lexical Choice

To perform an initial sanity check on our approach, we built a small corpus from SumTime-Meteo Corpus (Sripada et al., 2002), which contains human writing weather forecasts with meteorological data. We selected 144 wind speed forecasts with data whose wind speeds do not change a lot during a forecast period, and summarize these data into three dimensions, as shown in Table 1.

We randomly selected 96 records of the total 114 data records to train the model, and adopt the rest of data records to evaluate. We evaluated 10 words[1]: *LESS, N, S, OR, SE, NE, VARIABLE, GUSTS, WS, MAINLY*, which are the words occurring more than 5 times in the small corpus. For each candidate word w_i, we separate the testing data into two groups. Forecast texts in group 1 contain word w_i but not in group 2. When we use our model (trained with the SumTime-Meteo Corpus) to predict the occurring probability of w_i in group 1 and group 2 respectively, we expect to obtain higher occurring probability $p(w_i|G_1)$ from group 1 than $p(w_i|G_2)$ from group 2. The results are shown in Figure 1.

As shown in Figure 2, it is clear that experimental results are inline with our expectation: our approach does produce higher occurring probabilities in group 1 than in group 2. Recall that one key feature of our approach is its capability to model multiple dimensional features. To show the benefit of this feature, we have also applied our approach modelling taking into account each single dimension separately. By comparing Table 1 and Table 2, we can see that the

---

[1]"Words in the SumTime-Meteo Corpus include abbreviations such as SW (South-West) etc., see Table 1 for examples of text fragments and data.

Tabel 1: Some sample records of our corpus.

	Wind Speed	Wind Direction	Wind Variance
MAINLY W-NW 10 OR LESS	4.2	282	7
VARIABLE 8 OR LESS	7.5	319	12
...	...	...	...

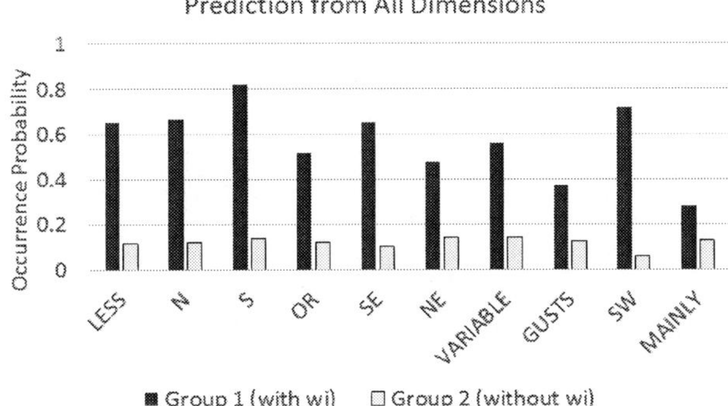

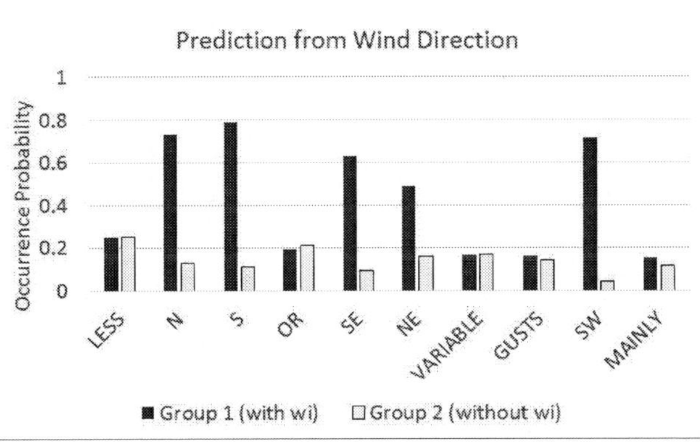

Figuur 1: The predicted occurring probabilities based on data of all dimensions.

prediction performance of words based on multiple dimension outperforms all the models considering a single dimension only, especially when predicting words *variable* and *mainly*.

4   Conclusion

We have sketched an approach to choosing lexical expressions according to multiple quantitative information. To have this ability, this approach learns the relationship between quantitative information and words by the following steps: a) resolving quantitative information and the occurrence of expressions into the same linear space; b) building equations of expressions' weight vector; c) finding the best solution of the equations. Initial evaluation suggest that this approach may be on the right track.

The possibility of applications to Lexical Choice in Natural Language Generation is perhaps most obvious, but the mapping that we learn is applicable to interpretation as well. In other words, our proposal aims to solve the age-old problem in Linguistics and Fuzzy Logic of how to specify the meaning of vague words (Van Deemter, 2012), which resists traditional approaches to semantics, because these words admit borderline cases.

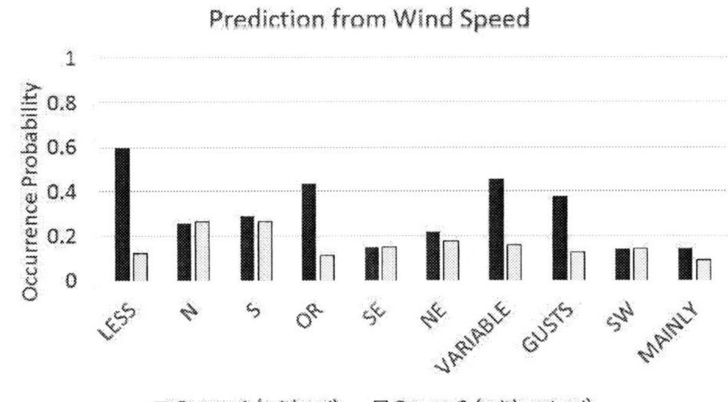

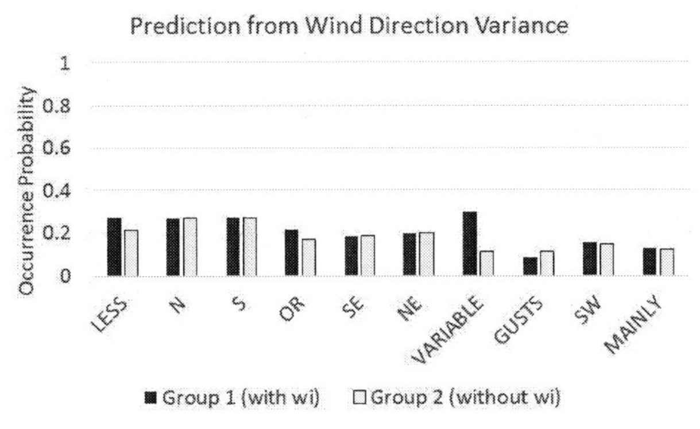

Figuur 2: The predicted occurring probabilities based on data of single dimension: *wind direction, wind speed, and wind direction variation.*

Acknowledgments

This work is supported by the award made by UK Economic & Social Research Council (ESRC); award reference ES/M001628/1.

References

Anja Belz. 2008. Automatic generation of weather forecast texts using comprehensive probabilistic generation-space models. *Natural Language Engineering*, 14(04):431–455.

Eli Golberg, Richard Kittredge, and Norbert Driedger. 1994. A new approach to the synthesis of weather forecast text. *IEEE Expert*.

Rene Collier Johan t Hart and Antonie Cohen. 1990. A perceptual study of intonation.

Ioannis Konstas and Mirella Lapata. 2013. A global model for concept-to-text generation. *J. Artif. Intell. Res.(JAIR)*, 48:305–346.

Percy Liang, Michael I Jordan, and Dan Klein. 2009. Learning semantic correspondences with less supervision. In *Proceedings of ACL-47*, pages 91–99.

Ehud Reiter, Somayajulu Sripada, Jim Hunter, Jin Yu, and Ian Davy. 2005. Choosing words in computer-generated weather forecasts. *Artificial Intelligence*, 167(1):137–169.

Deb K Roy. 2002. Learning visually grounded words and syntax for a scene description task. *Computer Speech & Language*, 16(3):353–385.

Somayajulu Sripada, Ehud Reiter, Jim Hunter, and Jin Yu. 2002. Sumtime-meteo: Parallel corpus of naturally occurring forecast texts and weather data. *Computing Science Department, University of Aberdeen, Aberdeen, Scotland, Tech. Rep. AUCS/TR0201*.

Somayajulu Sripada, Ehud Reiter, and Ian Davy. 2003. Sumtime-mousam: Configurable marine weather forecast generator. *Expert Update*, 6(3):4–10.

Kees Van Deemter. 2012. *Not exactly: In praise of vagueness*. Oxford University Press.

Incremental Generation of Visually Grounded Language in Dialogue (demonstration system)

Arash Eshghi
Interaction Lab
Heriot-Watt University
a.eshghi@hw.ac.uk

Yanchao Yu
Interaction Lab
Heriot-Watt University
y.yu@hw.ac.uk

Oliver Lemon
Interaction Lab
Heriot-Watt University
o.lemon@hw.ac.uk

We present a multi-modal dialogue system for interactive learning of perceptually grounded word meanings from a human tutor (Yu et al.,). The system integrates an incremental, semantic, and bi-directional grammar framework – Dynamic Syntax and Type Theory with Records (DS-TTR[1], (Eshghi et al., 2012; Kempson et al., 2001)) – with a set of visual classifiers that are learned throughout the interaction and which ground the semantic/contextual representations that it produces (c.f. Kennington & Schlangen (2015) where words, rather than semantic atoms, are grounded in visual classifiers). Our approach extends Dobnik et al. (2012) in integrating perception (vision in this case) and language within a single formal system: Type Theory with Records (TTR (Cooper, 2005)). The combination of deep semantic representations in TTR with an incremental grammar (Dynamic Syntax) allows for complex multi-turn dialogues to be parsed and generated (Eshghi et al., 2015). These include clarification interaction, corrections, ellipsis and utterance continuations (see e.g. the dialogue in Fig. 1).

Architecture: the system is made up of two key components – a **Vision system** and the **DS-TTR parser/generator**. The Vision system classifies a (visual) situation, i.e. deems it to be of a particular type, expressed as a TTR Record Type (RT) (see Fig. 1). This is done by deploying a set of binary attribute classifiers (Logistic Regression SVMs with Stochastic Gradient Descent, see Yu et al. (2015)) which ground the simple types (atoms) in the system (e.g. 'red', 'square'), and composing their output to construct the more complex, total type of the visual scene. This representation then acts not only as (1) the non-linguistic context of the dialogue for DS-TTR, for the resolution of e.g. definite references and indexicals (see Hough & Purver (2014)); but also (2) the logical database from which answers to questions about the objects' attributes are generated. Questions are parsed and their logical representation acts directly as a query on the non-linguistic/visual context to retrieve an answer (via *type checking* in TTR, itself done via *unification*, see Fig. 1 for a simple example). Conversely, the system can generate questions to the tutor about the attributes of objects based on the entropy of the classifiers that ground the semantic concepts, e.g. those for colour and shape. The tutor's answer then acts as a training instance for the classifiers (basic, atomic types) involved - see Fig. 1 for a snapshot of the current system.

Incremental Generation in Context: Generation (surface realisation) in DS-TTR follows exactly the same dynamics as parsing except for an additional *subsumption check* after every word against some *goal concept/context* (Purver et al., 2014). Generation is therefore just as incremental and contextual as parsing (Eshghi et al., 2015). This allows for the *generation of acceptances, elliptical utterances, short answers, and corrections, as well as continuations.* Here, it is the dialogue manager that constructs the goal concept from the semantic analysis of the visual scene, and sends it the the grammar for surface realisation – whether this is the semantics of a question, an answer, or an object description (see the system responses in Fig. 1).

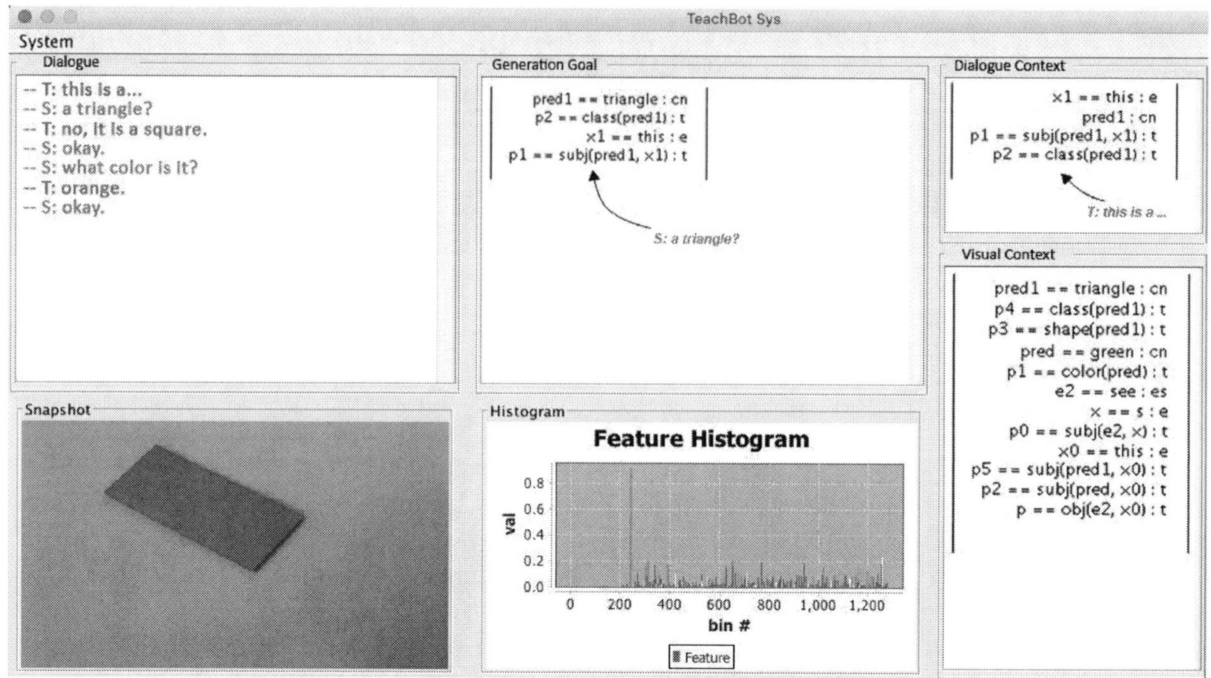

Figure 1: Incremental, visually grounded NLG in the Concept Learning System. T= tutor, S=system (screenshot)

We will show an interactive demonstration of this system at the conference, illustrating how questions, answers and object descriptions are derived and generated incrementally in real-time (Yu et al.,). Work in progress addresses: (1) more complex dialogues; (2) data-driven, incremental dialogue management at the lexical level; (3) integrating the existing DS-TTR model of incremental definite reference generation within the implemented system.

References

Robin Cooper. 2005. Records and record types in semantic theory. *Journal of Logic and Computation*, 15(2):99–112.

Simon Dobnik, Robin Cooper, and Staffan Larsson. 2012. Modelling language, action, and perception in type theory with records. In *Proceedings of the 7th International Workshop on Constraint Solving and Language Processing (CSLPÄô12)*, pages 51–63.

Arash Eshghi, Julian Hough, Matthew Purver, Ruth Kempson, and Eleni Gregoromichelaki. 2012. Conversational interactions: Capturing dialogue dynamics. In S. Larsson and L. Borin, editors, *From Quantification to Conversation*, volume 19, pages 325–349.

A. Eshghi, C. Howes, E. Gregoromichelaki, J. Hough, and M. Purver. 2015. Feedback in conversation as incremental semantic update. In *Proceedings of the 11th International Conference on Computational Semantics (IWCS 2015)*, London, UK. Association for Computational Linguisitics.

Julian Hough and Matthew Purver. 2014. Probabilistic type theory for incremental dialogue processing. In *Proceedings of the EACL 2014 Workshop on Type Theory and Natural Language Semantics (TTNLS)*, pages 80–88, Gothenburg, Sweden, April. Association for Computational Linguistics.

Ruth Kempson, Wilfried Meyer-Viol, and Dov Gabbay. 2001. *Dynamic Syntax: The Flow of Language Understanding*. Blackwell.

Casey Kennington and David Schlangen. 2015. Simple learning and compositional application of perceptually grounded word meanings for incremental reference resolution. In *Proc. ACL-IJCNLP*.

Matthew Purver, Julian Hough, and Eleni Gregoromichelaki. 2014. Dialogue and compound contributions. In S. Bangalore and A. Stent, editors, *Natural Language Generation in Interactive Systems*, pages 63–92. Cambridge University Press, June.

Yanchao Yu, Arash Eshghi, and Oliver Lemon. Training an adaptive dialogue policy for interactive learning of visually grounded word meanings. In *Proc. SIGDIAL 2016*.

Yanchao Yu, Arash Eshghi, and Oliver Lemon. 2015. Comparing attribute classifiers for interactive language grounding. In *Proceedings of ENMLP workshop on Vision and Language*.

Unsupervised Sentence Simplification Using Deep Semantics

Shashi Narayan
School of Informatics
The University of Edinburgh
Edinburgh, EH8 9AB, UK
shashi.narayan@ed.ac.uk

Claire Gardent
CNRS, LORIA, UMR 7503
Vandoeuvre-lès-Nancy, F-54500, France
claire.gardent@loria.fr

Abstract

We present a novel approach to sentence simplification which departs from previous work in two main ways. First, it requires neither hand written rules nor a training corpus of aligned standard and simplified sentences. Second, sentence splitting operates on deep semantic structure. We show (i) that the unsupervised framework we propose is competitive with four state-of-the-art supervised systems and (ii) that our semantic based approach allows for a principled and effective handling of sentence splitting.

1 Introduction

Sentence simplification maps a sentence to a simpler, more readable one approximating its content. As has been argued in (Shardlow, 2014), sentence simplification has many potential applications. It is useful as a preprocessing step for a variety of NLP systems as parsers and machine translation systems (Chandrasekar et al., 1996), summarisation (Knight and Marcu, 2000), sentence fusion (Filippova and Strube, 2008) and semantic role labelling (Vickrey and Koller, 2008). It also has wide ranging potential societal applications as a reading aid for people with aphasia (Carroll et al., 1999), for low literacy readers (Watanabe et al., 2009) and for non native speakers (Siddharthan, 2002).

In this paper, we present a novel approach to sentence simplification which departs from previous work in two main ways. First, it requires neither hand written rules nor a training corpus of aligned standard and simplified sentences. Instead, we exploit non aligned Simple and English Wikipedia to learn the probability of lexical simplifications, of the semantics of simple sentences and of optional phrases i.e., phrase which may be deleted when simplifying. Second, sentence splitting is semantic based. We show (i) that our unsupervised framework is competitive with four state-of-the-art systems and (ii) that our semantic based approach allows for a principled and effective handling of sentence splitting.

2 Related Work

Earlier work on sentence simplification relied on handcrafted rules to capture syntactic simplification e.g., to split coordinated and subordinated sentences into several, simpler clauses or to model e.g., active/passive transformations (Siddharthan, 2002; Chandrasekar and Srinivas, 1997; Canning, 2002; Siddharthan, 2011; Siddharthan, 2010). While these hand-crafted approaches can encode precise and linguistically well-informed syntactic transformations, they do not account for lexical simplifications and their interaction with the sentential context. Siddharthan and Mandya (2014) therefore propose an approach where hand-crafted syntactic simplification rules are combined with lexical simplification rules extracted from aligned English and simple English sentences, and revision histories of Simple Wikipedia.

Using the parallel dataset formed by Simple English Wikipedia (SWKP)[1] and traditional English Wikipedia (EWKP)[2], further work has focused on developing machine learning approaches to sentence simplification.

Zhu et al. (2010) constructed a parallel Wikipedia corpus (PWKP) of 108,016/114,924 complex/simple sentences by aligning sentences from EWKP and SWKP and used the resulting bitext to train a simplification model inspired by *syntax-based* machine translation (Yamada and Knight, 2001). Their simplification model encodes the probabilities for four rewriting operations on the parse tree of an input sen-

---

[1] http://simple.wikipedia.org
[2] http://en.wikipedia.org

tences namely, substitution, reordering, splitting and deletion. It is combined with a language model to improve grammaticality and the decoder translates sentences into simpler ones by greedily selecting the output sentence with highest probability.

Using both the PWKP corpus developed by Zhu et al. (2010) and the edit history of simple Wikipedia, Woodsend and Lapata (2011) learn a quasi synchronous grammar (Smith and Eisner, 2006) describing a loose alignment between parse trees of complex and of simple sentences. Following Dras (1999), they then generate all possible rewrites for a source tree and use integer linear programming to select the most appropriate simplification. They evaluate their model on the same dataset used by Zhu et al. (2010) namely, an aligned corpus of 100/131 EWKP/SWKP sentences.

Wubben et al. (2012), Coster and Kauchak (2011) and Xu et al. (2016) saw simplification as a monolingual translation task where the complex sentence is the source and the simpler one is the target. To account for deletions, reordering and substitution, Coster and Kauchak (2011) trained a phrase based machine translation system on the PWKP corpus while modifying the word alignment output by GIZA++ in Moses to allow for null phrasal alignments. In this way, they allow for phrases to be deleted during translation. Similarly, Wubben et al. (2012) used Moses and the PWKP data to train a phrase based machine translation system augmented with a post-hoc reranking procedure designed to rank the output based on their dissimilarity from the source sentence. Unlinke Wubben et al. (2012) and Coster and Kauchak (2011) who used machine translation as a black box, Xu et al. (2016) proposed to modify the optimization function of SMT systems by tuning them for the sentence simplification task. However, in their work they primarily focus on lexical simplification.

Finally, Narayan and Gardent (2014) present a hybrid approach combining a probabilistic model for sentence splitting and deletion with a statistical machine translation system trained on PWKP for substitution and reordering.

Our proposal differs from all these approaches in that it does not use the parallel PWKP corpus for training. Nor do we use hand-written rules. Another difference is that we use a deep semantic representation as input for simplification. While a similar approach was proposed in (Narayan and Gardent, 2014), the probabilistic models differ in that we determine splitting points based on the maximum likelihood of sequences of thematic role sets present in SWKP whereas Narayan and Gardent (2014) derive the probability of a split from the aligned EWKP/SWKP corpus using expectation maximisation. As we shall see in Section 4, because their data is more sparse, Narayan and Gardent (2014) predicts less and lower quality simplifications by sentence splitting.

3 Simplification Framework

Our simplification framework pipelines three dedicated modules inspired from previous work on lexical simplification, syntactic simplification and sentence compression. All three modules are unsupervised.

3.1 Example Simplification

Before describing the three main modules of our simplification framework, we illustrate its working with an example. Figure 1 shows the input semantic representation associated with sentence (1C) and illustrates the successive simplification steps yielding the intermediate and final simplified sentences shown in ($1S_1$-S).

(1) **C.** In 1964 Peter Higgs published his second paper in *Physical Review Letters* describing Higgs mechanism which predicted a new massive spin-zero boson for the first time.
S_1 **(Lex Simp).** In 1964 Peter Higgs wrote his second paper in *Physical Review Letters* explaining Higgs mechanism which predicted a new massive elementary particle for the first time.
S_2 **(Split).** In 1964 Peter Higgs wrote his second paper in *Physical Review Letters* explaining Higgs mechanism. Higgs mechanism predicted a new massive elementary particle for the first time.
S (Deletion). In 1964 Peter Higgs wrote his paper explaining Higgs mechanism. Higgs mechanism predicted a new elementary particle.

First, the input (1C) is rewritten as ($1S_1$) by replacing standard words with simpler ones using the context aware lexical simplification method proposed in (Biran et al., 2011).

Splitting is then applied to the semantic representation of ($1S_1$). Following Narayan and Gardent (2014), we use Boxer [3] (Curran et al., 2007) to map the output sentence from the lexical simplification step (here S_1) to a Discourse Representation Structure (DRS, (Kamp, 1981)). The DRS for

---

[3] http://svn.ask.it.usyd.edu.au/trac/candc, Version 1.00

In 1964 Peter Higgs published his second paper in Physical Review Letters describing Higgs mechanism which predicted a new massive spin-zero boson for the first time .

Lex Simpl.

In 1964 Peter Higgs wrote his second paper in Physical Review Letters explaining Higgs mechanism which predicted a new massive elementary particle for the first time .

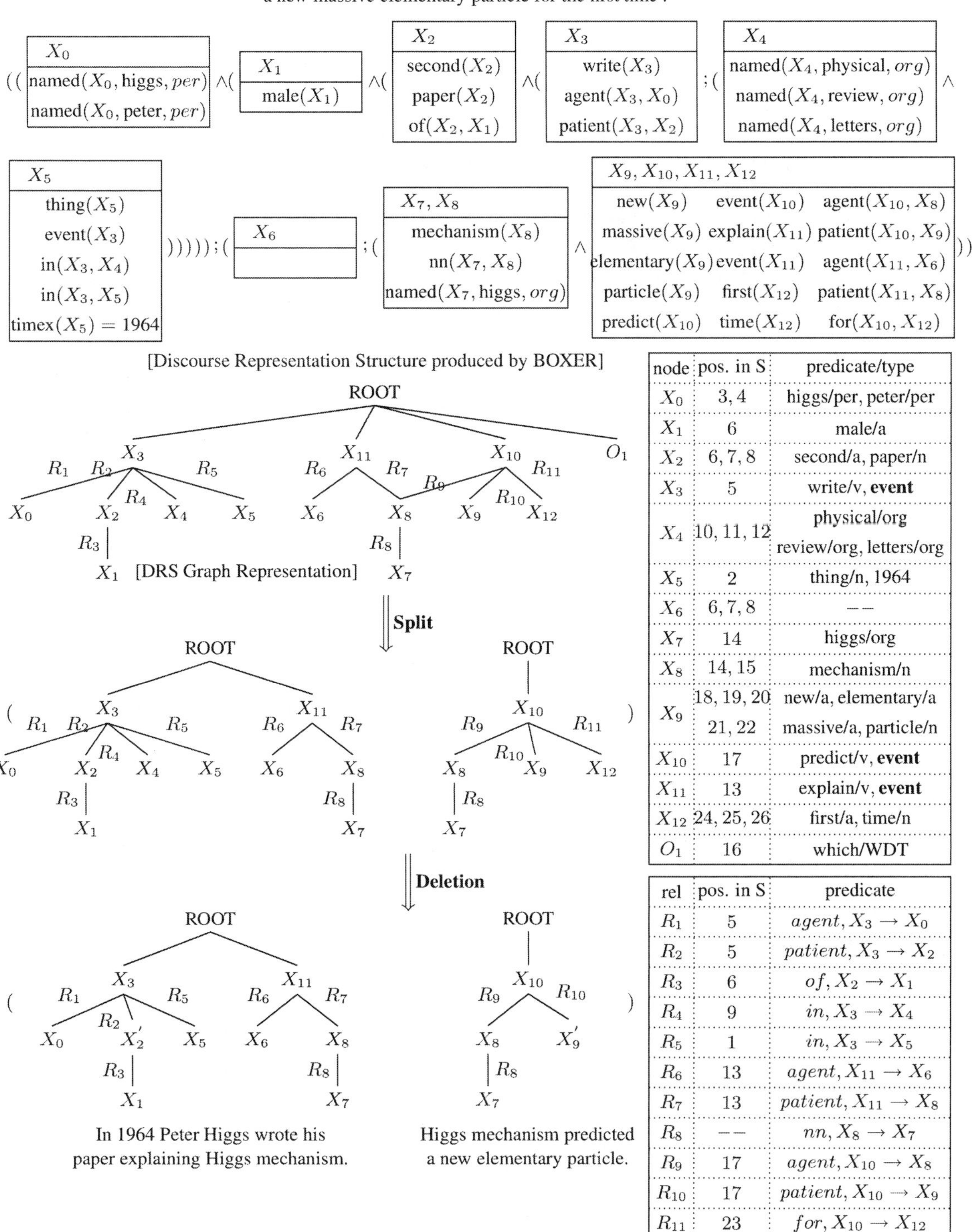

Figure 1: Simplification of *"In 1964 Peter Higgs published his second paper in Physical Review Letters describing Higgs mechanism which predicted a new massive spin-zero boson for the first time."*

113

S_1 is shown at the top of Figure 1 and a graph representation[4] of the dependencies between its variables is shown immediately below. In this graph, each DRS variable labels a node in the graph and each edge is labelled with the relation holding between the variables labelling its end vertices. The two tables to the right of the picture show the predicates (top table) associated with each variable and the relation label (bottom table) associated with each edge. Boxer also outputs the associated positions in the complex sentence for each predicate (not shown in the DRS but shown in the graph tables). Orphan words i.e., words which have no corresponding material in the DRS (e.g., *which* at position 16), are added to the graph (node O_1) thus ensuring that the position set associated with the graph exactly generates the input sentence.

Using probabilities over sequences of thematic role sets acquired from the DRS representations of SWKP, the split module determines where and how to split the input DRS. In this case, one split is applied between X_{11} (*explain*) and X_{10} (*predict*). The simpler sentences resulting from the split are then derived from the DRS using the word order information associated with the predicates, duplicating or pronominalising any shared element (e.g., *Higgs mechanism* in Figure 1) and deleting any Orphan words (e.g., *which*) which occurs at the split boundary. Splitting thus derives S_2 from S_1.

Finally, deletion or sentence compression applies transforming S_2 into S_3.

3.2 Context-Aware Lexical Simplification

We extract context-aware lexical simplification rules from EWKP and SWKP[5] using the approach described by Biran et al. (2011). The underlying intuition behind these rules is that the word C from EWKP can be replaced with a word S from SWKP if C and S share similar contexts (ten token window) in EWKP and SWKP respectively. Given an input sentence and the set of simplification rules extracted from EWKP and SWKP, we

then consider all possible (C, S) substitutions licensed by the extracted rules and we identify the best combination of lexical simplifications using dynamic programming and rule scores which capture the adequacy, in context, of each possible substitution[6].

3.3 Sentence Splitting

A distinguishing feature of our approach is that splitting is based on deep semantic representations rather than phrase structure trees – as in (Zhu et al., 2010; Woodsend and Lapata, 2011) – or dependency trees – as in (Siddharthan and Mandya, 2014).

While Woodsend and Lapata (2011) report learning 438 splitting rules for their simplification approach operating on phrase structure trees Siddharthan and Mandya (2014) defines 26 handcrafted rules for simplifying apposition and/or relative clauses in dependency structures and 85 rules to handle subordination and coordination.

In contrast, we do not need to specify or to learn complex rewrite rules for splitting a complex sentence into several simpler sentences. Instead, we simply learn the probability of sequences of thematic role sets likely to cooccur in a simplified sentence.

The intuition underlying our approach is that:

> Semantic representations give a clear handle on events, on their associated roles sets and on shared elements thereby facilitating both the identification of possible splitting points and the reconstruction of shared elements in the sentences resulting from a split.

For instance, the DRS in Figure 1 makes clear that sentence ($1S_1$) contains 3 main events and that *Higgs mechanism* is shared between two propositions.

To determine whether and where to split the input sentence, we use a probabilistic model trained on the DRSs of the Simple Wikipedia sentences and a language model also trained on Simple Wikipedia. Given the event variables contained in the DRS of the input sentence, we consider all possible splits between subsequences of events and choose the split(s) with maximum split score. For instance, in the sentence shown in Figure 1, there are three event variables X_3, X_{10} and X_{11}

---

[4]The DRS to graph conversion goes through several pre-processing steps: the relation *nn* is inverted making modifier noun (*higgs*) dependent of modified noun (*mechanism*), *named* and *timex* are converted to unary predicates, e.g., $named(x, peter)$ is mapped to $peter(x)$ and $timex(x) = 1964$ is mapped to $1964(x)$; and nodes are introduced for orphan words (e.g., *which*).

[5]We downloaded the snapshots of English Wikipedia dated 2013-12-31 and of Simple English Wikipedia dated 2014-01-01 available at `http://dumps.wikimedia.org`.

[6]For more details on the lexical simplification process, we refer the reader to Biran et al. (2011).

in the DRS. So we will consider 5 split possibilities namely, no split ($\{X_3, X_{10}, X_{11}\}$), two splits resulting in three sentences describing an event each ($\{X_3\}, \{X_{10}\}, \{X_{11}\}$) and one split resulting in two sentences describing one and two events respectively (i.e., ($\{X_3\}, \{X_{10}, X_{11}\}$), ($\{X_3, X_{10}\}, \{X_{11}\}$) and $\{X_{10}\}, \{X_3, X_{11}\}$). The split $\{X_{10}\}, \{X_3, X_{11}\}$ gets the maximum split score and is chosen to split the sentence (1S$_1$) producing the sentences (1S$_2$).

Semantic Pattern	prob.
$\langle\,(agent, patient)\,\rangle$	0.059
$\langle\,(agent, in, in, patient)\,\rangle$	0.002
$\langle\,(agent, patient), (agent, in, in, patient)\,\rangle$	0.023

Table 1: Split Feature Table (SFT) showing some of the semantic patterns from Figure 1.

Formally, the split score P_{split} associated with the splitting of a sentence S into a sequence of sentences $s_1...s_n$ is defined as:

$$P_{split} = \frac{1}{n} \sum_{s_i} \frac{L_{split}}{L_{split} + \mid L_{split} - L_{s_i} \mid} \times lm_{s_i} \times SFT_{s_i}$$

where n is the number of sentences produced after splitting; L_{split} is the average length of the split sentences ($L_{split} = \frac{L_S}{n}$ where L_S is the length of the sentence S); L_{s_i} is the length of the sentence s_i; lm_{s_i} is the probability of s_i given by the language model and SFT_{s_i} is the likelihood of the semantic pattern associated with s_i. The Split Feature Table (SFT, Table 1) is derived from the corpus of DRSs associated with the SWKP sentences and the counts of sequences of thematic role sets licenced by the DRSs of SWKP sentences. Intuitively, P_{split} favors splits involving frequent semantic patterns (frequent sequences of thematic role sets) and sub-sentences of roughly equal length. This way of semantic pattern based splitting also avoids over-splitting of a complex sentence.

3.4 Phrasal Deletion

Following Filippova and Strube (2008), we formulate phrase deletion as an optimization problem which is solved using integer linear programming[7]. Given the DRS K associated with a sentence to be simplified, for each relation $r \in K$, the deletion module determines whether r and its associated DRS subgraphs should be deleted by maximising the following objective function:

$$\sum_x x_{h,w}^r \times P(r|h) \times P(w) \quad r \notin \{agent, patient, theme, eq\}$$

where for each relation $r \in K$, $x_{h,w}^r = 1$ if r is preserved and $x_{h,w}^r = 0$ otherwise; $P(r|h)$ is the conditional probability (estimated on the DRS corpus derived from SWKP) of r given the head label h; and $P(w)$ is the relative frequency of w in SWKP[8].

Intuitively, this objective function will favor obligatory dependencies over optional ones and simple words (i.e., words that are frequent in SWKP). In addition, the objective function is subjected to constraints which ensure (i) that some deletion takes place and (ii) that the resulting DRS is a well-formed graph.

4 Evaluation

We evaluate our approach both globally and by module focusing in particular on the splitting component of our simplification approach.

4.1 Global evaluation

The testset provided by Zhu et al. (2010) was used by four supervised systems for automatic evaluation using metrics such as BLEU, sentence length and number of edits. In addition, most recent simplification approaches carry out a human evaluation on a small set of randomly selected complex/simple sentence pairs. Thus Wubben et al. (2012), Narayan and Gardent (2014) and Siddharthan and Mandya (2014) carry out a human evaluation on 20, 20 and 25 sentences respectively.

Accordingly, we perform an automatic comparative evaluation using (Zhu et al., 2010)'s testset namely, an aligned corpus of 100/131 EWKP/SWKP sentences; and we carry out a human-based evaluation.

Automatic Evaluation Following Wubben et al. (2012), Zhu et al. (2010) and Woodsend and Lapata (2011), we use metrics that are directly related to the simplification task namely, the number of splits in the overall data, the number of output sentences with no edits (i.e., sentences which have not

---

[7]In our implementation, we use *lp_solve*, `http://sourceforge.net/projects/lpsolve`.

[8]To account for modifiers which are represented as predicates on nodes rather than relations, we preprocess the DRSs and transform each of these predicates into a single node subtree of the node it modifies. For example in Figure 1, the node X_2 labeled with the modifier predicate *second* is updated to a new node X_2' dominating a child labeled with that predicate and related to X_2' by a modifier relation.

System	Levenshtein Edit distance				BLEU w.r.t simple	Sentences with splits	Average sentence length	Average token length
	Complex to System		System to Simple					
	LD	No edit	LD	No edit				
GOLD	12.24	3	0	100	100	28	27.80	4.40
Zhu	7.87	2	14.64	0	37.4	80	24.21	4.38
Woodsend	8.63	24	16.03	2	42	63	28.10	4.50
Wubben	3.33	6	13.57	2	41.4	1	28.25	4.41
Narayan	6.32	4	11.53	3	53.6	10	26.24	4.36
UNSUP	6.75	3	14.29	0	38.47	49	26.22	4.40

Table 2: Automatic evaluation results. Zhu, Woodsend, Wubben, Narayan are the best output of the models of Zhu et al. (2010), Woodsend and Lapata (2011), Wubben et al. (2012) and Narayan and Gardent (2014) respectively. UNSUP is our model.

System	Levenshtein Edit distance				BLEU Scores with respect to		Average sentence length	Average token length
	Complex to System		System to Simple					
	LD	No edit	LD	No edit	complex	simple		
complex	0	100	12.24	3	100	49.85	27.80	4.62
LexSimpl	2.07	22	13.00	1	82.05	44.29	27.80	4.46
Split	2.27	51	13.62	1	89.70	46.15	29.10	4.63
Deletion	2.39	4	12.34	0	85.15	47.33	25.41	4.54
LexSimpl-Split	4.43	11	14.39	0	73.20	41.18	29.15	4.48
LexSimpl-Deletion	4.29	3	13.09	0	69.84	41.91	25.42	4.38
Split-Deletion	4.63	4	13.42	0	77.82	43.44	26.19	4.55
LexSimpl-Split-Deletion	6.75	3	14.29	0	63.41	38.47	26.22	4.40
GOLD (simple)	12.24	3	0	100	49.85	100	23.38	4.40

Table 3: Automated Metrics for Simplification: Modular evaluation. LexSimpl-Split-Deletion is our final system UNSUP.

been simplified) and the average Levenshtein distance (LD) between the system output and both the complex and the simple reference sentences. We use BLEU[9] as a means to evaluate how close the systems output are to the reference corpus.

Table 2 shows the results of the automatic evaluation. The most noticeable result is that our unsupervised system yields results that are similar to those of the supervised approaches.

The results also show that, in contrast to Woodsend system which often leaves the input unsimplified (24% of the input), our system almost always modifies the input sentence (only 3% of the input are not simplified); and that the number of simplifications including a split is relatively high (49% of the cases) suggesting a good ability to split complex sentences into simpler ones.

Human Evaluation Human judges were asked to rate input/output pairs w.r.t. to adequacy (How much does the simplified sentence(s) preserve the meaning of the input?), to simplification (How much does the generated sentence(s) simplify the complex input?) and to fluency (how grammatical and fluent are the sentences?).

We randomly selected 18 complex sentences from Zhu's test corpus and included in the evaluation corpus: the corresponding simple (Gold)

sentence from Zhu's test corpus, the output of our system (UNSUP) and the output of the other four systems (Zhu, Woodsend, Narayan and Wubben) which were provided to us by the system authors[10]. We collected ratings from 18 participants. All were either native speakers or proficient in English, having taken part in a Master taught in English or lived in an English speaking country for an extended period of time. The evaluation was done online using the LG-Eval toolkit (Kow and Belz, 2012)[11] and a Latin Square Experimental Design (LSED) was used to ensure a fair distribution of the systems and the data across raters.

Systems	Simplicity	Fluency	Adequacy
GOLD	3.62	4.69	3.80
Zhu	2.62	2.56	2.47
Woodsend	1.69	3.15	3.15
Wubben	1.52	3.05	3.38
Narayan	2.30	3.03	3.35
UNSUP	2.83	3.56	2.83

Table 4: Average Human Ratings for simplicity, fluency and adequacy.

Table 4 shows the average ratings of the human evaluation on a scale from 0 to 5. Pairwise comparisons between all models and their statistical significance were carried out using a one-way ANOVA with post-hoc Tukey HSD tests.

[9]Moses support tools: multi-bleu http://www.statmt.org/moses/?n=Moses.SupportTools.

[10]We upload the outputs from all the systems as supplementary material with this paper.

[11]http://www.nltg.brighton.ac.uk/research/lg-eval/

System pairs		Average Score (number of split sentences)					
A	B	ALL-A	ALL-B	ONLY-A	BOTH-AB		ONLY-B
					A	B	
UNSUP	GOLD	2.37(49)	3.85(28)	2.15(32)	2.80(17)	3.70(17)	4.05(11)
	Zhu		2.25(80)	1.53(4)	2.45(45)	2.42(45)	2.02(35)
	Woodsend		2.08(63)	2.42(11)	2.36(38)	2.29(38)	1.78(25)
	Wubben		2.73(1)	2.32(48)	4.75(1)	2.73(1)	0(0)
	Narayan		2.09(10)	2.29(41)	2.78(8)	1.79(8)	3.81(2)

Table 5: Pairwise split evaluation: Each row shows the pairwise comparison of the quality of splits in UNSUP and some other system. Last six columns show the average scores and number of associated split sentences. The second column (ALL-A) and the third column (ALL-B) present the quality of all splits by systems A and B respectively. The fourth column (ONLY-A) represents sentences where A splits but not B. The fifth and sixth columns represents sentences where both A and B split. The seventh column (ONLY-B) represents sentences where B splits but not A.

If we group together systems for which there is no significant difference (significance level: $p < 0.05$), our system is in the first group together with Narayan and Zhu for simplicity; in the first group for fluency; and in the second group for adequacy (together with Woodsend and Zhu). A manual examination of the results indicates that UNSUP achieves good simplicity rates through both deletion and sentence splitting. Indeed, the average word length of simplified sentences is smaller for UNSUP (26.22) than for Wubben (28.25) and Woodsend (28.10); comparable with Narayan (26.19) and higher only than Zhu (24.21).

4.2 Modular Evaluation

To assess the relative impact of each module (lexical simplification, deletion and sentence splitting), we also conduct an automated evaluation on each module separately. The results are shown in Table 3.

One first observation is that each module has an impact on simplification. Thus the average Levenshtein Edit distance (LD) to the source clause (complex) is never null for any module while the number of "No edit" indicates that lexical simplification modifies the input sentence in 78%, sentence splitting 49% and deletion 96% of the cases.

In terms of output quality and in particular, similarity with respect to the target clause, deletion is the most effective (smallest LD, best BLEU score w.r.t. target). Further, the results for average token length indicate that lexical simplification is effective in producing shorter words (smaller average length for this module compared to the other two modules).

Predictably, combining modules yields systems that have stronger impact on the source clause (higher LD to complex, lower number of No Edits) with the full system (i.e., the system combining the 3 modules) showing the largest LD to the

sources (LD to complex) and the smallest number of source sentences without simplification (3 No Edits).

4.3 Sentence Splitting Using Deep Semantics

To compare our sentence splitting approach with existing systems, we collected in a second human evaluation, all the outputs for which at least one system applied sentence splitting. The raters were then asked to compare pairs of split sentences produced by two distinct systems and to evaluate the quality (0:very bad to 5:very good) of these split sentences taking into account boundary choice, sentence completion and sentence reordering.

Table 5 shows the results of this second evaluation. For each system pair comparing UNSUP (A) with another system (B), the Table gives the scores and the number of splits of both systems: for the inputs on which both systems split (BOTH-AB), on which only UNSUP splits (ONLY-A) and on which only the compared system split (ONLY-B).

UNSUP achieves a better average score (ALL-A = 2.37) than all other systems (ALL-B column) except Wubben (2.73). However Wubben only achieves one split and on that sentence, UNSUP score is 4.75 while Wubben has a score of 2.73 and produces an incorrect split (cf. S_3 in Figure 6). UNSUP

In terms of numbers of splits, three systems often simplify by splitting namely Zhu (80 splits), Woodsend (63) and UNSUP (49). Interestingly, Narayan, trained on the parallel corpus of Wikipedia and Simplified Wikipedia splits less often (10 splits vs 49 for UNSUP) and less well (2.09 average score versus 2.37 for UNSUP). This is unsurprising as the proportion of splits in SWKP was reported in (Narayan and Gardent, 2014) to be a low 6%. In contrast, the set of observations we use to learn the splitting probability is the set of all sequences of thematic role sets derived from the DRSs of the SWKP corpus.

S1	**Complex.** This array distributes data across multiple disks, but the array is seen by the computer user and operating system as one single disk. **Zhu.** This array sells data across multiple disks but the array is seen. The computer user and operating as one disk. [0] **Woodsend.** This array distributes data across several disks. The array is seen by the computer user and operating system as one single disk. [4.85] **UNSUP.** This array moves data across disks. The array is seen by the computer user and operating system as one disk. [4.83]
S2	**Complex.** Here, simulations of evolution using evolutionary algorithms and artificial life started with the work of Nils Aall Barricelli in the 1960s, and was extended by Alex Fraser, who published a series of papers on simulation of artificial selection. **Zhu.** Here, simulations of evolution using evolutionary algorithms and artificial life started with the work of nils aall barricelli in the 1960s, and was extended by alex fraser. Alex fraser published a series of papers on feeling of artificial selection. [3.6] **Woodsend.** It has Genetic algorithms. Evolution is using artificial life. This is Nils Aall Barricelli in the 1960s. Here, simulations started with the work. He was extended by Alex Fraser. He published a group of papers on simulation of artificial selection. [0.33] **UNSUP.** Here, models of evolution using evolutionary algorithms and artificial life started with the work in the 1960s, and was led by Alex Fraser. Alex Fraser wrote a series of papers on model of selection. [5]
S3	**Complex.** By 1928, the regional government was moved from the old Cossack capital Novocherkassk to Rostov, which also engulfed the nearby Armenian town of Nor Nakhijevan. **Zhu.** By 1928, the government was moved from the old cossack capital novocherkassk to rostov. Rostov also of the city the nearby armenian town of nor nakhijevan. [2.8] **Woodsend.** By 1928, the regional government was moved from the old Cossack capital Novocherkassk to Rostov. Both also engulfed the nearby Armenian town of Nor Nakhijevan. [3] **Wubben.** by 1928 , the regional government was moved from the old cossack capital novocherkassk to rostov. the nearby armenian town of nor nakhichevan. [2.7] **Narayan.** by 1928, the regional government was moved from the old cossack capital novocherkassk to rostov. rostov that engulfed the nearby armenian town of nor nakhichevan. [2.7] **UNSUP.** The regional government was moved from the old Cossack capital Novocherkassk to Rostov. Rostov also absorbed the nearby town of Nor Nakhijevan. [4.75]

Table 6: Example Outputs for Sentence splitting with their average human annotation scores.

In sum, the unsupervised, semantic-based splitting strategy allows for a high number (49%) of good quality (2.37 score) sentence splits . Because there are less possible patterns of thematic role sets in simple sentences than possible configurations of parse/dependency trees for complex sentences, it is less prone to data sparsity than the syntax based approach. Because the probabilities learned are not tied to specific syntactic structures but to more abstract semantic patterns, it is also perhaps less sensitive to parse errors.

4.4 Examples from the Test Set

Table 6 shows some examples from the evaluation dataset which were selected to illustrate the workings of our approach and to help interpret the results in Table 2, 4 and 5.

S1 and S2 and S3 show examples of context-aware unsupervised lexical substitutions which are nicely performed by our system. In S1, *The array distributes data* is correctly simplified to *The array moves data* whereas Zhu's system incorrectly simplifies this clause to *The array sells data*. Similarly, in S2, our system correctly simplifies *Papers on simulation of artificial selection* to *Papers on models of selection* while the other systems either do not simplify or simplify to *Papers on feeling*.

For splitting, the examples show two types of splitting performed by our approach namely, splitting of coordinated sentences (S1) and splitting between a main and a relative clause (S2,S3). S2 illustrates how the Woodsend system over-splits, an issue already noticed in (Siddharthan and Mandya, 2014); and how Zhu's system predicts an incorrect split between a verb (*seen*) and its agent argument (*by the user*). Barring a parse error, such incorrect splits will not be predicted by our approach since, in our cases, splits only occur between (verbalisations of) events. S1, S2 and S3 also illustrates how our semantic based approach allows for an adequate reconstruction of shared elements.

5 Conclusion

A major limitation for supervised simplification systems is the limited amount of available parallel standard/simplified data. In this paper, we have shown that it is possible to take an unsupervised approach to sentence simplification which requires a large corpus of standard and simplified language but no alignment between the two. This allowed for the implementation of contextually aware substitution module; and for a simple, linguistically principled account of sentence splitting and shared element reconstruction.

6 Acknowledgements

We are grateful to Zhemin Zhu, Kristian Woodsend and Sander Wubben for sharing their data. We would like to thank our annotators for participating in our human evaluation experiments and to anonymous reviewers for their insightful comments. This research was supported by an EPSRC grant (EP/L02411X/1) and an EU H2020 grant (688139/H2020-ICT-2015; SUMMA). We also thank the French National Research Agency for funding the research presented in this paper in the context of the WebNLG project.

References

Or Biran, Samuel Brody, and Noémie Elhadad. 2011. Putting it simply: a context-aware approach to lexical simplification. In *Proceedings of the 49th Annual Meeting of the Association for Computational Linguistics: Human Language Technologies: short papers-Volume 2*, pages 496–501. Association for Computational Linguistics.

Yvonne Margaret Canning. 2002. *Syntactic simplification of Text*. Ph.D. thesis, University of Sunderland.

John Carroll, Guido Minnen, Darren Pearce, Yvonne Canning, Siobhan Devlin, and John Tait. 1999. Simplifying text for language-impaired readers. In *Proceedings of 9th Conference of the European Chapter of the Association for Computational Linguistics (EACL)*, volume 99, pages 269–270. Citeseer.

Raman Chandrasekar and Bangalore Srinivas. 1997. Automatic induction of rules for text simplification. *Knowledge-Based Systems*, 10(3):183–190.

Raman Chandrasekar, Christine Doran, and Bangalore Srinivas. 1996. Motivations and methods for text simplification. In *Proceedings of the 16th International conference on Computational linguistics (COLING)*, pages 1041–1044. Association for Computational Linguistics.

William Coster and David Kauchak. 2011. Learning to simplify sentences using wikipedia. In *Proceedings of the Workshop on Monolingual Text-To-Text Generation*, pages 1–9. Association for Computational Linguistics.

James R Curran, Stephen Clark, and Johan Bos. 2007. Linguistically motivated large-scale NLP with C&C and Boxer. In *Proceedings of the 45th Annual Meeting of the Association for Computational Linguistics (ACL) on Interactive Poster and Demonstration Sessions*, pages 33–36. Association for Computational Linguistics.

Mark Dras. 1999. *Tree adjoining grammar and the reluctant paraphrasing of text*. Ph.D. thesis, Macquarie University NSW 2109 Australia.

Katja Filippova and Michael Strube. 2008. Dependency tree based sentence compression. In *Proceedings of the Fifth International Natural Language Generation Conference (INLG)*, pages 25–32. Association for Computational Linguistics.

Hans Kamp. 1981. A theory of truth and semantic representation. In J.A.G. Groenendijk, T.M.V. Janssen, B.J. Stokhof, and M.J.B. Stokhof, editors, *Formal methods in the study of language*, number pt. 1 in Mathematical Centre tracts. Mathematisch Centrum.

Kevin Knight and Daniel Marcu. 2000. Statistics-based summarization-step one: Sentence compression. In *Proceedings of the Seventeenth National Conference on Artificial Intelligence (AAAI) and Twelfth Conference on Innovative Applications of Artificial Intelligence (IAAI)*, pages 703–710. AAAI Press.

Eric Kow and Anja Belz. 2012. LG-Eval: A Toolkit for Creating Online Language Evaluation Experiments. In *Proceedings of the 8th International Conference on Language Resources and Evaluation (LREC)*, pages 4033–4037.

Shashi Narayan and Claire Gardent. 2014. Hybrid simplification using deep semantics and machine translation. In *Proceedings of the 52nd Annual Meeting of the Association for Computational Linguistics*. Association for Computational Linguistics.

Matthew Shardlow. 2014. A survey of automated text simplification. *International Journal of Advanced Computer Science and Applications (IJACSA), Special Issue on Natural Language Processing*.

Advaith Siddharthan and Angrosh Mandya. 2014. Hybrid text simplification using synchronous dependency grammars with hand-written and automatically harvested rules. In *Proceedings of the 14th Conference of the European Chapter of the Association for Computational Linguistics*, pages 722–731, Gothenburg, Sweden, April. Association for Computational Linguistics.

Advaith Siddharthan. 2002. An architecture for a text simplification system. In *Proceedings of the Language Engineering Conference (LEC)*, pages 64–71. IEEE Computer Society.

Advaith Siddharthan. 2010. Complex lexico-syntactic reformulation of sentences using typed dependency representations. In *Proceedings of the 6th International Natural Language Generation Conference (INLG)*, pages 125–133. Association for Computational Linguistics.

Advaith Siddharthan. 2011. Text simplification using typed dependencies: a comparison of the robustness of different generation strategies. In *Proceedings of the 13th European Workshop on Natural Language Generation (ENLG)*, pages 2–11. Association for Computational Linguistics.

David A Smith and Jason Eisner. 2006. Quasi-synchronous grammars: Alignment by soft projection of syntactic dependencies. In *Proceedings of the HLT-NAACL Workshop on Statistical Machine Translation*, pages 23–30. Association for Computational Linguistics.

David Vickrey and Daphne Koller. 2008. Sentence simplification for semantic role labeling. In *Proceedings of the 46th Annual Meeting of the Association for Computational Linguistics (ACL) and the Human Language Technology Conference (HLT)*, pages 344–352.

Willian Massami Watanabe, Arnaldo Candido Junior, Vinícius Rodriguez Uzêda, Renata Pontin de Mattos Fortes, Thiago Alexandre Salgueiro Pardo, and Sandra Maria Aluísio. 2009. Facilita: reading assistance for low-literacy readers. In *Proceedings of the 27th ACM international conference on Design of communication*, pages 29–36. ACM.

Kristian Woodsend and Mirella Lapata. 2011. Learning to simplify sentences with quasi-synchronous grammar and integer programming. In *Proceedings of the Conference on Empirical Methods in Natural Language Processing (EMNLP)*, pages 409–420. Association for Computational Linguistics.

Sander Wubben, Antal van den Bosch, and Emiel Krahmer. 2012. Sentence simplification by monolingual machine translation. In *Proceedings of the 50th Annual Meeting of the Association for Computational Linguistics (ACL): Long Papers-Volume 1*, pages 1015–1024. Association for Computational Linguistics.

Wei Xu, Courtney Napoles, Ellie Pavlick, Quanze Chen, and Chris Callison-Burch. 2016. Optimizing statistical machine translation for text simplification. *Transactions of the Association for Computational Linguistics*.

Kenji Yamada and Kevin Knight. 2001. A syntax-based statistical translation model. In *Proceedings of the 39th Annual Meeting on Association for Computational Linguistics (ACL)*, pages 523–530. Association for Computational Linguistics.

Zhemin Zhu, Delphine Bernhard, and Iryna Gurevych. 2010. A monolingual tree-based translation model for sentence simplification. In *Proceedings of the 23rd International Conference on Computational Linguistics (COLING)*, pages 1353–1361, Stroudsburg, PA, USA. Association for Computational Linguistics.

Enabling text readability awareness during the micro planning phase of NLG applications[1]

Priscilla Moraes, Kathleen McCoy, Sandra Carberry
Computer and Information Sciences Department
University of Delaware, Newark, DE
pmoraes | mccoy | carberry@udel.edu

Abstract

Currently, there is a lack of text complexity awareness in NLG systems. Much attention has been given to text simplification. However, based upon results of an experiment, we unveiled that sophisticated readers in fact would rather read more sophisticated text, instead of the simplest text they could get. Therefore, we propose a technique that considers different readability levels during the micro planning phase of an NLG system. Our technique considers grammatical and syntactic choices, as well as lexical items, when generating text. The application uses the domain of descriptive summaries of line graphs as its use case. The technique proposed uses learning for identifying features of text complexity; a graph search algorithm for efficient aggregation given a target reading level, and a combination of language modeling and word vectors for the creation of a domain-aware *synset* which allows the creation of disambiguated lexicon that is appropriate to different reading levels. We found that generating text at different target reading levels is indeed preferred by readers with varying reading abilities. To the best of our knowledge, this is the first time readability awareness is considered in the micro planning phase of NLG systems.

1 Introduction

Prior work has concentrated on simplifying text in order to make it accessible to people with cognitive disabilities or low literacy levels. On the other hand, as stated by (Williams & Reiter, 2005b), most NLG systems generate text for readers with good reading ability. Our contention, however, is that NLG systems will be much more effective if they can target their output to the preferences of the reader. This not only enables easy comprehension, but it also makes the experience more enjoyable for them. Based on that claim, we propose an approach that considers a target reading level in order to decide on the syntactic and grammatical structure of the generated text and to select appropriate lexical items.

Our overall goal is to generate text at a target reading level. The process of generating text takes in a number of propositions and outputs a set of English sentences which are realizations of these propositions. Each proposition can be realized in several different ways, e.g., as a single sentence, aggregated with another proposition as an adjective attached to a noun, as a relative clause, or as another noun phrase in a coordination. In addition, different lexical items can be used to describe a term, and these might also vary in complexity and grade level appropriateness. The devised approach is applied to the domain of line graph description. Information graphics (non-pictorial images such as line graphs, bar and pie charts) are commonly used by authors in

---

[1] This document has been adapted from the instructions for earlier ACL and NAACL proceedings, including those for NAACL-HLT-15 by Matt Post and Adam Lopez, NAACL-HLT-12 by Nizar Habash and William Schuler, NAACL-HLT-10 by Claudia Leacock and Richard Wicen- towski, NAACL-HLT-09 by Joakim Nivre and Noah Smith, for ACL-05 by Hwee Tou Ng and Kemal Oflazer, for ACL-02 by Eugene Charniak and Dekang Lin, and earlier ACL and EACL formats. Those versions were written by several people, including John Chen, Henry S. Thompson and Donald Walker. Additional elements were taken from the formatting instructions of the *International Joint Conference on Artificial Intelligence*. Microsoft Word formatting was added by Alexander Mamishev (Mamishev, 2013).

order to convey a message or to make a point regarding the topic being discussed in the document or article.

To efficiently select realizations at a particular reading level, we devised an approach that uses a graph search algorithm guided by a heuristic. To construct the heuristic, the features of text complexity were identified through machine learning. The lexical choice implements a concept expansion phase followed by an approach which combines language modeling and word vectors to disambiguate domain-relevant concepts. In the last step a grade level appropriate lexicon is applied. To the best of our knowledge, this is the first effort made during the micro planning phase of an NLG system that both **considers different reading abilities when generating text** and **presents automated approaches in order to do it**.

The next section describes related work on text readability and text simplification. Sections 3 to 5 discuss the graph search algorithm for the aggregation phase, the learning of feature measurements and the identification of grade level appropriate and domain aware lexicons. Section 6 shows some examples of summaries generated by the system. Section 7 presents the evaluations of the system and Sections 8 and 9 provide conclusions and thoughts on future work, respectively.

2   Related Work

The approach proposed by (Wilkinson, 1995) presents the aggregation process divided into two major steps: semantic grouping and sentence structuring. Although they are interdependent, both are needed in order to achieve aggregation in a text. (Barzilay & Lapata, 2006), (Bayyarapu, 2011), (Walker, Rambow, & Rogati, 2001) are some examples of learning aggregation rules and grouping constraints in order to aggregate text. It differs from our approach in that we are considering readability constraints when making such decisions.

(Elhadad, Robin, & McKeown, 1997) present work on lexical choice considering constraints regarding syntax, semantics, pragmatics, the lexicon, and the underlying domain that float from one phase to the next in the generation of text. Our work differs in that lexical items are restrained by their appropriateness to the level of the reader and the creation of the lexicon is guided by defining a domain-aware *synset* for description of line graphs.

Other NLG systems decide on text complexity based on available scales such as the D-level sentence complexity (Covington, He, Brown, Naci, & Brown, 2006). One example is presented in (Demir, Carberry, & McCoy, 2012), where tree structures are built representing all the possible ways sentences can be aggregated and the choice of the tree attempts to balance the number of sentences, their D-level complexity, and the types of relative clauses. The work presented in (P. Moraes, McCoy, & Carberry, 2014) describe a template-based approach for creating summaries at different reading levels. It does not, however, present an adaptive approach that can be applied to the micro planning phase of any NLG system.

Another area, text simplification, aims to target low-skilled readers and users with language disabilities. SkillSum (Williams & Reiter, 2004, 2005a; Williams, Reiter, & Osman, 2003) is a system which adapts its output for readers with poor literacy after assessing their reading and numeracy skills. Their results show that, for these target readers, the micro planning choices made by SkillSum enhanced readability. (Carroll et al., 1999) presents a text simplification methodology to help language-impaired users; (Rello, Baeza-Yates, Bott, & Saggion, 2013) propose a system that uses lexical simplification to enhance readability and understandability of text for people with dyslexia; while (Siddharthan, 2003) aims to make the text easier to read for some target group (like aphasics and people with low reading ages) or easier to process by some program (like a parser or machine translation system). One of our evaluation experiments (citation suppressed for anonymity) performed with college students showed that the simplest text was rather unpleasant for them to read. We therefore propose a technique that focuses on adjusting the generated text to the reading level of the surrounding text.

The closest work to the one proposed in this paper is presented in (Bateman & Paris, 1989). It presents an approach to tailoring phrasing during the generation of natural text to different types of users. It employs a technique that leverages a knowledge base in order to make decisions during text planning in a rule based fashion. This work, in contrast, generates natural text aimed at a specific reading level by applying a graph search that allows the automation of the aggregation of propositions.

3 Aggregation of Propositions

The goal of the micro planning phase in NLG systems is to realize the set of selected propositions as sentences. The NLG system developed in the context of this work generates summaries of the high-level message conveyed by line graphs present in popular media. In the context of describing line graphs, there are many ways these propositions can be realized. They can each constitute a sentence; some of them can be realized as an adjective attached to a noun phrase, as a noun phrase added to a conjunction with a preexisting noun phrase, or as a subordinating conjunction. The last three realization options require what we call aggregation of propositions, where multiple propositions are composed to form a complete sentence. Consider how the proposition **graph_type**, for example, can be realized: A sentence: "There is a line graph." / An adjective (or compound noun): "…line graph…" – where "graph" is the head noun / A relative clause: "…which is lined…" – where the head noun is "graph".

The other propositions in the context of line graphs can also have their realizations made in different ways (based on grammatical restrictions on how each concept can be described) and the realizations constrain each other. A hard decision, therefore, is to choose which realization to apply to each proposition. We decided to implement the aggregation phase by employing a graph search algorithm. Since there is a large number of options and we do not know which combination will give us a final summary at the desired reading level, a graph search allows us to explore the whole search space and, through the use of a heuristic, to efficiently get to a goal node.

3.1 The Graph Search Problem

The search space for the aggregation of propositions problem is defined as:

States: A state consists of two parts: a list of unrealized propositions and the realizations performed so far (which can consist of full sentences or sentence fragments). **Initial state**: The initial state contains the set of all unrealized propositions. **Goal state**: It checks if all the propositions have been realized and if all of them are aggregated into full sentences. **Actions**: The actions in a given state take the next unrealized proposition and realize it (generating a new state for each realization the proposition allows). For most propositions, the possible actions are: *realize_as_active_sentence, realize_as_passive_sentence, realize_as_adjective, realize_as_relative_clause and realize_as_conjunction*. Each proposition contains a set of its allowed actions. When realizing a proposition as a fragment, if the needed head noun is not present in any of the realizations, then the proposition will be realized as the respective fragment (adjective, relative clause, conjunction) and will wait until such a head noun is generated to be added to a full sentence. If the required head noun is already realized in a full sentence, the fragment is then attached to the existing realization.

In order to find a goal node efficiently, we developed a heuristic that takes into account three factors. The first factor considers the realizations performed so far in a node. It measures the values of the different features of text complexity (explained in the next section) in the summary realized so far. The second factor estimates how likely a node is to stay within a range of allowed values for the different features that define text complexity. This estimation is done by looking at the propositions that still need to be realized and the probability of them increasing or decreasing the values of the features. The third factor favors nodes that are deeper in the tree. Since all goal nodes are at the same level (defined by the number of unrealized propositions), this aspect favors the nodes that are closer to a goal.

To be able to build the heuristic, the set of features of text complexity that could be explicitly measured and used during generation had to be identified. For that, we use a learning approach that classifies text into different target reading levels and that provides the values that the features had in the different classifications. The next section explains the learning approach.

4 Learning Text Complexity Features

The features to be used in the heuristic needed to be chosen based on both their effect on text complexity and their usability. The choice of features for constructing the model was made based on the work presented by (Vajjala & Meurers, 2012) which uses features that are based on Second Language Acquisition (SLA) research combined with traditional readability features, such as word length and sentence length, in order to classify text into different grades. Their work results in classifiers that outperform previous approaches on readability classification, reaching higher classification accuracy. However, since we still need to map features back to the NLG aggregation phase, the set of features used here represents a subset of the features presented in their work. The final set of features, motivated by (Vajjala & Meurers, 2012), consisted of 15 features. Examples of features are: *Percentage of passive sentences (percPassiveSent); Percentage of conjunctions (percConjunction); Percentage of prepositions (percPreposition); Percentage of adjectives (percAdjective); Percentage of adverbs (percAdverb); Percentage of relative clauses (percRelativeClauses); Average noun phrase length (avgNounPhraseLength); Average sentence length (avgSentLengthWord)*;

For the learning algorithm a decision tree is used. The goal of the learning algorithm was to provide the system with concrete measures of the chosen features that can be mapped to the graph search heuristic during the aggregation phase.

4.1 Corpus of Grade Level Annotated Text

Data was obtained from text exemplars classified at different grade bands available in Appendix B of the Common Core State Standards (Common Core State Standards Initiative, 2010) and various articles written and annotated at different reading levels. Magazine articles collected from the Austin Public Library electronic catalog (Library, 2015) were annotated using the Lexile measure ("Lexile Framework for Reading," 2015). Classes for the learning algorithm were grouped as **4th - 5th grades, 6th - 8th, 9th - 10th**, and **11th - College**. One hundred articles, varying in size, were collected for each one of the grade level groups. These articles were in HTML format and they were preprocessed to remove tags and special characters. After preprocessing the files, they were split into smaller passages, of at least 150 words, which is equivalent to the average size of the summaries the system generates. Because the passages needed to have complete sentences in order to obtain more accurate

measurement of the features during learning, the splitting step counted words sentence by sentence and, after reaching 150 words, it stopped adding sentences to the current passage. Splitting the articles resulted in 1874 passages, which were used as instances in the learning algorithm.

After splitting the articles into similar passage sizes, the values of the features were calculated using the Style & Diction tool (FSF, 2005) for assessing some of the syntactic features and NLTK (Loper & Bird, 2002) for grammatical features. After all the features were assessed, a tab file (appropriate input file type for use with the Orange toolbox (Demsar et al., 2013) is generated and ready for training.

4.2 Classification Task

Before choosing decision trees as the learning algorithm to be used for this classification task, other algorithms were analyzed using the data described in the previous section and their results were compared. Random forests, Bayesian networks, Classification (or decision) trees and Neural Networks were applied to the classification task. Using leave-one-out cross validation, the system achieved a classification accuracy of 85.38% and F1 measure of 87.97% using decision trees. The Neural Network outperformed the classification accuracy of the decision tree by 1.39%, but had a smaller F1 measure. The neural network used 20 hidden layers, which would probably complicate reading the features weights due to the combination functions within the hidden layers. Since the goal is to be able to map the weights of the features to a heuristic in a graph search algorithm, the best option turned out to be the decision tree since it can be interpreted as rules, which allow the values of the features to be captured.

The paths from the root to the leaves (or classes, in this case) provide logical rules that represent the values of the different features that led to that classification. The logic rules can be read as *path1 OR path2 OR ... pathN* for a given grade level group (grade level groups are the target classes of the leaf nodes). Only nodes with a classification confidence above 70 percent were used to construct the set of logic rules that is used by the system. A set of rules for a 9th − 10th grade level band is shown here as an example of what the decision tree produces:

(avgParagLengthSent <= 10 AND
  (13 < avgSentLengthWord <= 15 AND
  percPassiveSent <= 0.4 AND
  percRelativeClauses<=0.6AND
  0.2 < percBegSentPronoun <= 0.5)
OR
(avgParagLengthSent <= 9 AND
  (14 < avgSentLengthWord <= 16) AND
  percPassiveSent <= 0.1 AND
  percRelativeClauses <= 0.8)

We use rules such as this to build the heuristic to help guide the search to a realization that satisfies the target reading level. When using these rules within our heuristic, the function will be estimating the cost based on how well the to-be-realized propositions, combined with the realizations performed so far, fall within those ranges in order to be inside the grade level constraints.

4.3 Mapping the Rules to a Heuristic Function

In calculating the heuristic, for the propositions that have not been realized yet, the features are divided into two groups. The first group contains features that only increase as new propositions are realized. One example is the number of relative clauses in a paragraph. As the number of sentences in the paragraph increases, the value of this feature can never go down. The second group contains features whose values can fluctuate (either up or down) as new propositions are realized. The average sentence length in words, for example, can go up or down as new propositions are realized since they can become new sentences (making it go down) or be aggregated with existing sentences (making it go up). For this reason, the heuristic calculates the estimated cost that is added to h(n) differently for these two groups.

Estimating the Cost Added by Feature Values

To illustrate, suppose that the decision tree learned that, for paragraphs that contain around 150 words, the range of values for the *numberAdjectives* feature is 2 <= *numberAdjectives* <= 5 for a 4th grade level text. The sequence of rules to calculate the cost for this type of feature is:

1. If the measured value of the feature in what has already been realized is above the upper limit of its range (if it is equal to 6 for the example above), add an infinite cost to the estimation. Since these

feature's values can never go down, this node cannot satisfy the requirements for the grade level.

2. If the measured feature is within the predefined range (if it is equal to 3 for the example above), add to the estimation the probability of increasing the value of the feature based on the unrealized propositions. In this case, the probability of increasing the feature is the ratio of possible realizations that increase the feature's value (e.g. a proposition that has a possible realization as an adjective will increase the *numberAdjectives*) over all possible realizations amongst the set of unrealized propositions. In the example above, if there were 6 unrealized propositions from which 2 could be realized as active and passive voice sentence (4 possible realizations), 1 could be realized as active voice, passive voice sentence and relative clause (3 possible realizations), and 3 could be realized as active voice sentence, passive voice sentence, adjective, and relative clause (12 possible realizations), the number of possible realizations would be 19. Since only 3 could be realized as an adjective, the probability of increasing the value of this feature is 3/19 ($\sim$ 0.16). This value would be added to the cost, versus 0.31 (6/19) if there were 6 possible realizations as adjectives in the set of all possible realizations.

3. If the measured value is less than the lower limit (if it is equal to 1 for the example above), multiply the probability of increasing the value of the feature given the unrealized propositions (as explained above) by the inverse of the value that the feature can increase by (feature upper limit – feature value = 2 for the example above), then multiply the result by the number of possible realizations that use the feature. In this case, the more chances to realize a proposition as an adjective the better since the value is currently lower than desired.

Following the same logic, the calculation of features that fluctuate is performed by also taking into account the fact that the feature values can also fall under the lower limit provided by the rules (a case which the cost estimation also needs to address).

The final value for *h(n)* is the sum of all estimated costs when going through the set of features defined by the rules. The node with lowest value is expanded next.

5 Lexical Choice for Generating Summaries at Different Grade Levels

The lexicalization phase of this work is composed of three main sub phases. The first is a concept expansion phase achieved by the collection of synonyms starting from a set of seed words used to describe the different concepts of line graphs. The second step is concerned with narrowing the set of synonyms to the ones that are relevant to the domain of line graphs. This disambiguation step is performed by using language modeling (5-grams from Google Books) (Michel et al., 2011) and word vectors (word2vec) (Mikolov, Chen, Corrado, & Dean, 2013). The last step builds lexicons, based on the final set of synonyms for a concept, which are appropriate to the different target reading levels.

The seed words (base lexical item for each one of the concepts) were gathered from an experiment performed by (Greenbacker, Carberry, & McCoy, 2011) in which participants were asked to describe the important aspects they noticed were present in line graphs. From these passages, the most common words used to describe concepts such as volatility and steepness were used as the starting point for lexical building.

For expanding these concepts, Thesaurus.com (Dictionary.com, 2015) was used. Thesaurus.com was selected because it has a better coverage with respect to synonyms of nouns, verbs, adjectives and adverbs than WordNet (Fellbaum, 1998) and VerbNet (Kipper, Dang, & Palmer, 2000). Thesaurus.com provides synonyms for concepts in a varied number of senses and parts of speech by grouping synonyms within part_of_speech + *synsets*.

Choosing the most appropriate concept *synsets* for the domain of line graphs did not appear to be the best approach, as the *synsets* were not always comprehensive and precise. In other words, all *synsets* individually contained some synonyms which were not appropriate and appropriate synonyms were found across multiple *synsets*. Besides, choosing a single best *synset* would not lead to a technique that could perform the synonym expansion without human supervision. For this reason, the decision was therefore to use all *synsets* with a given part of speech and to further filter the resulting set.

This provided the system with an extensive (and noisy) list of synonyms. The set of synonyms was too broad; it included synonyms that would not apply to the domain of line graph description, so disambiguating the synonyms and filtering only the domain relevant ones was needed.

5.1 Using Language Modeling and Word Vectors for Filtering Synonyms

The intuition here is that we want to keep only synonyms that the language model indicates appear in a context containing key words indicative of the line graph context.

The language model used is the 5-gram corpus from Google Books (Michel et al., 2011). The system selects all the 5-gram instances that were found to contain a synonym of the concept being expanded which co-occurs with one of the words from the "concept context". The concept context is the set of head nouns that can appear in a sentence with the concept being expanded; in the example above, the concept context for "show" would be the terms "image", "graph", and "trend", since the possible contexts are the sentences: "The image shows a graph" and "The graph shows a trend". This set of lexical contexts is the same one used to seed the lexical expansion of concepts described earlier and originated from the most common terms used to express concepts in the experiment presented in (Greenbacker et al., 2011).

However, the set still contained terms that were inappropriate for the graph summarization domain. Thus, we devised a vector space model approach trained on Wikipedia (Wikipedia, 2004) data, which is available as a default corpus for training the word2vec tool available at (Mikolov et al., 2013). Word representation in vector spaces has shown to be a promising tool for acquiring terms' semantic knowledge. This technique builds vectors that represent the context of a term. The vector for the term "house", for example, has a higher count for the terms "big", "white", "spacious", than for the terms "hungry", "bag", and "sky". The vector is built by assigning co-occurrence counts to all the words in the language in question, and two terms can be compared on how similar they are in their contexts by measuring the similarity of their vectors. The idea is that two synonyms ought to occur in the same linguistic context; therefore, their word2vec scores should be very close.

By using the word2vec tool, the system was able to filter the set of synonyms collected from the language model step and further customize it to the line graph domain context. The reader might ask why both steps are needed in order to come up with the set of appropriate synonyms. It was noticed that the language model alone was not sufficient since no threshold could be set in the system in order to consider a synonym for inclusion in the set, the reason being that any threshold eliminated the chances of good synonyms for the context of line graphs (volatility, for example), that were not as commonly used in the literature, from being added to the set. Using word vector representations alone, on the other hand, poses another challenge. The approach used by vector representation does not allow differentiation of a synonym from an antonym. The words "pretty" and "ugly" would have a very similar vector representation since they can be used within the same context. By collecting synonyms from a dictionary and starting the set of possible replacements from them, the antonyms were already filtered. By filtering co-occurrence present in Google N-grams (generated from digitized books), the noise is significantly decreased. One can then perform additional filtering by looking at the vector space models of the senses being disambiguated, which has good results for the line graph use case. This combined approach proved to be a way of allowing a system to create a customized *synset* of a domain by starting from a set of context words.

5.2 Creation of Lexicons for Different Reading Levels

These disambiguation steps enabled the system to come up with a set of terms that were appropriate lexical items for the line graph concepts needed for our summaries. Since the focus of the system is to generate text at different grade levels, a step to bin those terms based on their grade level appropriateness was also necessary. For any given concept, some of the lexical items may be rather simple and others might be considered more advanced.

In order to build grade level appropriate lexicons, the final set of synonyms disambiguated for the line graph domain was further divided into grade levels by checking for their lemma forms in the data previously used to learn text complexity feature measurements (the annotated corpus of different grade levels). From this step, each group of grade levels

ended up with one or more terms that could describe the concepts used to generate descriptive summaries of line graphs. Since lexical choice can affect the final readability measurement of the generated text, the system randomly selects terms at the target reading level that will represent concepts before starting the graph search explained earlier in the previous section. Evaluation results for the micro planning phase are presented in Section 7.

6 Summaries at Different Reading Levels

The following summaries illustrate the different output from the system given different target reading levels. These summaries were generated for the graph shown in Figure 1. The propositions used in the generated summaries were provided by the content selection module of the system, which employs a centrality-based algorithm in order to select propositions (P. S. Moraes, Carberry, & McCoy, 2013).

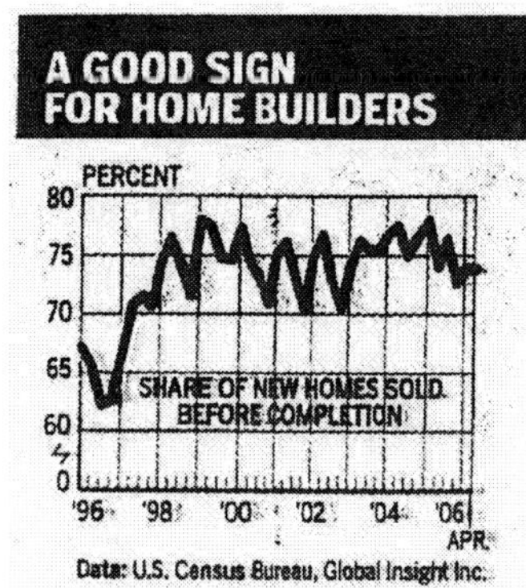

Figure 1: Example of graph extracted from online popular media.

4th – 5th summary: *There is an image. The image shows a line graph. The share of new homes sold before completion in percent is given by the graph. The graph consists of a changing trend composed of a rising trend from 1996 to 1999 followed by a stable trend through 2006. The graph is variable. The graph has the top value of 78.09 percent. The graph has the lowest value of 62.65 percent.*

11th – College summary: *A volatile line diagram, which presents the share of new homes sold before completion in percent and consists of a changing trend composed of a rising trend from 1996 to 1999 followed by a stable trend through 2006, is revealed by the image. The maximum value of 78.09 percent is reached by the graph, which has the minimal value of 62.65 percent.*

7   Evaluation of the Microplanning Phase

Four different evaluations were performed to assess the effectives of the system on generating summaries at different target reading levels. These evaluations intended to assess:

1) **The ability of the system, given a target reading level, to generate a summary that is as close as possible to that target**. For this experiment we used a set of 11 line graphs. We ran the system five times, generating five slightly different summaries at the reading level identified for the article in which the graphs appeared. These five summaries differ since, on each iteration of the system, the lexical choice randomly selects lexical items from the pool of appropriate options. The average grade level was used as the final reading level. 63.6% of the graphs had their summaries produced by the system matching their target reading level exactly. 27.3% of the graphs had their summaries generated by the system really close to the target reading level, having 1 summary produced at grade level 8.8 with a target $9^{th} - 10^{th}$ and 2 summaries produced at grade levels 10.7 and 10.9 with a target 11th - College. And only one of the graphs had the summary generated at 2 grade levels lower than the target reading level (7.2 with a target of $9^{th} - 10^{th}$).

2) **The ability of the system to generate different summaries appropriate for different grade levels for any given graph in the experiment set**. The system was able to successfully generate summaries for all 11 graphs with increasing complexity as the target reading level increased (this also used the average of five runs). It generated 11% of the summaries at a reading level that did not change, having generated summaries at 9th - 10th grade level that targeted the 11th – college grade group. This was due to the lack of enough propositions to perform grammatical combinations that would lead to a higher reading level.

3) **The ability of the system on varying the text complexity as perceived by human readers**. For this experiment, 90 Human Intelligent Tasks (HITs) were undertaken through Amazon Mechanical Turk (10 graphs, 9 *turkers* per graph). Each HIT produced an ordering which corresponded to the grade level the *turkers* believed the summaries belonged to. Each summary could be associated to only one grade level. Since choosing one wrong grade level

to a summary would lead to another misclassification, a pair-wise relationship approach was applied to analyze the results. From 348 valid pairwise relationship results, 252 had a correct ordering, yielding a similarity between human readers and the system's perception of text complexity of 72%. Another evaluation made on the results provided by the *turkers* was through calculating the average of the nDCGs obtained on the orderings. Using the formula presented in Figure 2, the results obtained were the ones presented in Table 1.

$$\mathrm{DCG_p} = rel_1 + \sum_{i=2}^{p} \frac{rel_i}{\log_2(i)}$$

Figure 2: nDCG formula used to assess the goodness of the ordering.

Graph	nDCG
L3	0.9598
L6	0.9860
L18	0.8975
L21	0.8893
L23	0.9451
L26	0.9752
L28	0.9888
L42	0.9365
L89	0.9851
L95	0.9798

Table 1: Results of applying nDCG to orderings provided by the *turkers*.

The results of applying nDCG are higher than the ones gotten from the pairwise relationship approach. Although the nDCG score is a useful metric for evaluating relevance ranking, it might not be the most appropriate metric for evaluating the results of the task performed with the *turkers* since it penalizes top ranked results more and we would like to penalize misplaced assigned summary grades according to their distance from the target reading level.

4) **The usability of summaries generated at different reading levels for users with different reading skills**. For this evaluation 16 students at the 5th grade and 34 freshmen college students were recruited. They received two summaries for each of nine different graphs: one at the $4^{th} - 5^{th}$ and the other at the 11th - college reading level. They were asked to choose which summary they preferred and why. Results per grade and per graph are presented

in Table 2 for the 5th graders and in Table 3 for college students. Additionally, they were asked to circle things they did not like in either summary. From 73 responses collected from the 5th graders, 57 chose the summaries at their reading level and from the 163 responses collected from the college students, 115 chose the summaries at their reading level. Table 4 shows that the results are statistically significant given p = 3.67816E-12 calculated using the chi-squared test.

Line graph	Chose 4th-5th	Chose 11th - cc
L6	9	3
L17	10	1
L18	1	0
L21	6	3
L26	5	2
L28	8	2
L42	7	0
L89	7	1
L95	4	4
Total	**57**	**16**

Table 2: Results from reading level experiment with 5th graders.

Line graph	Chose 4th-5th	Chose 11th - cc
L6	5	13
L17	6	14
L18	4	15
L21	6	16
L26	5	14
L28	5	15
L42	5	10
L89	6	10
L95	6	8
Total	**48**	**115**

Table 3: Results from reading level experiment with freshmen College students.

	5th graders	College students	Total	Prob
5th grader text	57	48	105	0.44
College text	16	115	131	0.56
Total	73	163	236	

Table 4: Statistical significance data.

From these results we conclude that the system is able to successfully generate summaries that match the reading level of the articles on which the line graphs appear and that its perception of text complexity matches that of human readers at a rate of 72%. In order to assess how good this result is, another possible experiment could contain the same tasks, but compare the results of our system with those obtained from a baseline. Such baseline currently does not exist. One possibility could be to provide them with summaries generated using Benetech (Benetech, 2016) guidelines for line graph description as they are made available, for example. We also confirmed our initial contention that readers with different reading abilities prefer text that matches their reading skills, instead of always reading the simplest text they can get.

8   Conclusion

This work presents novel approaches applied to the microplanning phase to enable NLG system to tailor the generated text to match different target reading levels. After identifying through an experiment that more sophisticated readers prefer more sophisticated text and that readers at lower reading levels would prefer text that was simpler, we developed and successfully evaluated a system that uses learning, a graph search algorithm with the help of a heuristic for aggregation and a lexicalization phase that chooses domain relevant and grade level appropriate lexical items when generating summaries of line graphs. This contributes to the NLG research area by describing and evaluating automated aggregation and lexicalization approaches that consider different reading abilities.

9   Future Work

For the microplanning phase of the system we envision future work on the pronominalization phase and coordination of lexical items. For the latter, we want to enable to use of different lexical items to describe the same concept in the summary by using a different referring expression. Additionally, we want to enable the system to coordinate contrasting concepts when choosing lexical items. One example is to coordinate *top* vs *bottom*, *maximum* vs *minimum*, *first* vs *last*, *higher* vs *lower*, instead of randomly selecting lexical items.

References

Barzilay, R., & Lapata, M. (2006). *Aggregation via set partitioning for natural language generation.* Paper presented at the the the Proceedings of the Human Language Technology Conference of the North American Chapter of the Association of Computational Linguistics.

Bateman, J. A., & Paris, C. L. (1989). *Phrasing a Text in Terms the User Can Understand.* Paper presented at the Proceedings of the 11th International Joint Conference on Artificial Intelligence - Volume 2, San Francisco, CA, USA.

Bayyarapu, H. S. (2011). *Efficient algorithm for Context Sensitive Aggregation in Natural Language generation.* Paper presented at the RANLP.

Benetech. (2016). Benetech.

Carroll, J., Minnen, G., Pearce, D., Canning, Y., Devlin, S., & Tait, J. (1999). *Simplifying Text for Language-Impaired Readers.* Paper presented at the In Proceedings of the 9th Conference of the European Chapter of the Association for Computational Linguistics (EACL.

Common Core State Standards Initiative, C. (2010). Common Core State Standards for English language arts and literacy in history/social studies, science and technical subjects. Retrieved from http://www.corestandards.org/

Covington, M., He, C., Brown, C., Naci, L., & Brown, J. (2006). *How Complex is that Sentence? A Proposed Revision of the Rosenberg and Abbeduto D-Level Scale.* Paper presented at the Research Report, Artificial Intelligence Center, University of Georgia.

Demir, S., Carberry, S., & McCoy, K. F. (2012). Summarizing Information Graphics Textually. *Computational Linguistics, 38*(3), 527-574.

Demsar, J., Curk, T. v., Erjavec, A. v., Gorup, v. r., Ho\vc, e. T. v., Milutinovi\vc, M., . . . Zupan, B. v. (2013). Orange: Data Mining Toolbox in Python. *J. Mach. Learn. Res., 14*(1), 2349-2353.

Dictionary.com, L. L. C. (2015). Thesaurus.com.

Elhadad, M., Robin, J., & McKeown, K. (1997). Floating Constraints in Lexical Choice. *Comput. Linguist., 23*(2), 195-239.

Fellbaum, C. (1998). *WordNet: An electronic Lexical Database*: The MIT Press.

FSF. (2005). Style and Diction GNU project. Retrieved from www.gnu.org/software/diction

Greenbacker, C., Carberry, S., & McCoy, K. (2011, July). *A Corpus of Human-written Summaries of Line Graphs.* Paper presented at the Proceedings of the UCNLG+Eval: Language Generation and Evaluation Workshop, Edinburgh, Scotland.

Kipper, K., Dang, H. T., & Palmer, M. (2000). *Class-Based Construction of a Verb Lexicon.* Paper presented at the Proceedings of the Seventeenth National Conference on Artificial Intelligence and Twelfth Conference on Innovative Applications of Artificial Intelligence.

Lexile Framework for Reading. (2015).

Library, A. (2015, August). Austin Public Library Electronic Catalog. Retrieved from http://library.austintexas.gov/

Loper, E., & Bird, S. (2002). *NLTK: The Natural Language Toolkit.* Paper presented at the Proceedings of the ACL-02 Workshop on Effective Tools and Methodologies for Teaching Natural Language Processing and Computational Linguistics - Volume 1, Stroudsburg, PA, USA.

Michel, J. B., Shen, Y. K., Aiden, A. P., Veres, A., Gray, M. K., Pickett, J. P., . . . Aiden, E. L. (2011). Quantitative analysis of culture using millions of digitized books. *Science, 331*(6014), 176-182.

Mikolov, T., Chen, K., Corrado, G., & Dean, J. (2013). Efficient Estimation of Word Representations in Vector Space. *CoRR, abs/1301.3781*.

Moraes, P., McCoy, K., & Carberry, S. (2014). *Adapting Graph Summaries to the Users'' Reading Levels.* Paper presented at the Proceedings of the 8th International Natural Language Generation Conference.

Moraes, P. S., Carberry, S., & McCoy, K. (2013). *Providing access to the high-level content of line graphs from online popular media.* Paper presented at the Proceedings of the 10th International Cross-Disciplinary Conference on Web Accessibility, Rio de Janeiro, Brazil.

Rello, L., Baeza-Yates, R., Bott, S., & Saggion, H. (2013). *Simplify or Help?: Text Simplification Strategies for People with Dyslexia.* Paper presented at the Proceedings of the 10th International Cross-Disciplinary Conference on Web Accessibility, New York, NY, USA.

Siddharthan, A. (2003). *Preserving Discourse Structure when Simplifying Text.* Paper presented at the In Proceedings of the 2003 European Natural Language Generation Workshop.

Vajjala, S., & Meurers, D. (2012). *On Improving the Accuracy of Readability Classification Using Insights from Second Language Acquisition.* Paper presented at the Proceedings of the Seventh Workshop on Building Educational Applications Using NLP, Stroudsburg, PA, USA.

Walker, M. A., Rambow, O., & Rogati, M. (2001). *SPoT: a trainable sentence planner.* Paper presented at the Proceedings of the second meeting of the North American Chapter of the Association for Computational Linguistics on Language technologies, Stroudsburg, PA, USA.

Wikipedia. (2004). Wikipedia, The Free Encyclopedia.

Wilkinson, J. (1995). *Aggregation in Natural Language Generation: Another Look*. Retrieved from

Williams, S., & Reiter, E. (2004, August). *Reading errors made by skilled and unskilled readers: evaluating a system that generates reports for people with poor literacy*. Paper presented at the Fourteenth Annual Meeting of the Society for Text and Discourse, Chicago.

Williams, S., & Reiter, E. (2005a). *Appropriate Microplanning Choices for Low-Skilled Readers*. Paper presented at the IJCAI.

Williams, S., & Reiter, E. (2005b). *Generating readable texts for readers with low basic skills*. Paper presented at the Proceedings of the 10th European Workshop on Natural Language Generation (EWNLG 2005).

Williams, S., Reiter, E., & Osman, L. (2003, August). *Experiments with discourse-level choices and readability*. Paper presented at the Proceedings of the 9th European Workshop on Natural Language Generation (ENLG-2003), Budapest.

Invited Speaker

Vera Demberg
Saarland University

How can we adapt generation to the users cognitive load?

Abstract

As language-based interaction becomes more ubiquitous and is used by in a larger and larger variety of different situations, the challenge for NLG systems is to not only convey a certain message correctly, but also do so in a way that is appropriate to the situation and the user. From various studies, we know that humans adapt the way they formulate their utterances to their conversational partners and may also change the way they say things as a function of the situation that the conversational partner is in (e.g. while talking to someone who is driving a car). Approaches from psycholinguistics (using information-theoretic measures as well as other complexity metrics) provide a way to formulate and quantify the demands that a certain formulation places on a hearer. In this talk, I will briefly survey ways of assessing human cognitive load in realistic settings, present current models of information density at the content level, and discuss the extent to which these measures have been found to drive choice of formulation in humans.

Selecting Domain-Specific Concepts for Question Generation
With Lightly-Supervised Methods

Yiping Jin and **Phu T. V. Le**
Knorex Pte. Ltd.
1003 Bukit Merah Central
Singapore 159836
{jinyiping, le_phu}@knorex.com

Abstract

In this paper we propose content selection methods for question generation (QG) which exploit domain knowledge. Traditionally, QG systems apply syntactical transformation on individual sentences to generate open domain questions. We hypothesize that a QG system informed by domain knowledge can ask more important questions. To this end, we propose two lightly-supervised methods to select salient target concepts for QG based on domain knowledge collected from a corpus. One method selects important semantic roles with bootstrapping and the other selects important semantic relations with Open Information Extraction (OpenIE). We demonstrate the effectiveness of the two proposed methods on heterogeneous corpora in the business domain. This work exploits domain knowledge in QG task and provides a promising paradigm to generate domain-specific questions.

1   Introduction

Automatic question generation (QG) has been successfully applied in various applications. QG was used to generate reading comprehension questions from text (Heilman and Smith, 2009; Becker et al., 2012), to aid academic writing (Liu et al., 2010; Liu et al., 2012) and to build conversational characters (Yao et al., 2012; Nouri et al., 2011).

In this work, we focus on generating a set of question and answer (Q&A) pairs for a given input document. Possible applications of this task are to automatically generate a Q&A section for company profiles or product descriptions. It can also help the reader to recapitulate the main ideas of a document in a lively manner.

We can coarsely divide QG into two steps: "what to ask" (*target concept selection* and *question type determination*), and "how to ask" (*question realisation*) (Nielsen, 2008).

It is important to view question generation not merely as realising a question from a declarative sentence. When the input is a document, the sentences (and candidate concepts) are of different importance. It is therefore critical for a QG system to identify a set of salient concepts as target concepts before it attempts to generate questions. In this work, we propose two novel target concept selection methods that lead to QG systems which can ask more important questions.

Our approaches are motivated by the conditions for a human reader to ask good questions. In order to ask good questions, he needs to satisfy three prerequisites: 1) good command of the language, 2) good reasoning and analytical skills and 3) sufficient domain knowledge. Some may argue prior knowledge is not necessary because we ask about things we do not know. However, it is no surprise that a professor in computational linguistics may not ask as important and relevant questions in the field of organic chemistry as a second-year chemistry student. What makes the difference is the domain knowledge.

Correspondingly, we hypothesize that a successful QG system needs to satisfy the following requirements: 1) able to generate questions that are grammatical and understandable by humans, 2) able to analyse the input document (e.g. keyword identification, discourse parsing or summarization), and 3) able to exploit domain knowledge.

Previous works mainly focused on addressing the first two requirements. Researchers tend to prefer systems that ask open domain questions because the dependency on domain knowledge is usually regarded as an disadvantage. Several NLG applications successfully utilized domain knowledge, such as virtual shopping assistant (Chai et al., 2001) and sport event summarization (Bouayad-Agha et al., 2011). However, the domain knowledge that they used are manually constructed by human experts. To the best of our knowledge, this paper is the first work in QG that attempts to utilize domain knowledge obtained in a lightly-supervised manner.

Although we choose QG as the application in this work, the lightly-supervised content selection methods that we propose could also be applied to augment other NLG tasks such as summarization.

In section 2, we present previous works of QG and how we position this work into the full storyline. In section 3, we briefly describe the dataset we use. Section 4 introduces two target concept selection methods based on automatically constructed domain knowledge. Section 5 describes methods to generate Q&A pairs from target concepts. In section 6, we present our experimental results. Lastly, we present conclusions and suggest future directions. The contributions of this paper are:

1. Propose to select target concepts for question generation with lightly-supervised approaches.

2. Demonstrate that the use of domain knowledge helps to ask more important questions.

3. Quantitatively evaluate the impact of different ways to represent and select target concepts on question generation task.

2 Connections with Prior Work

Olney et al. (2012) classified question generation (QG) approaches into two categories: knowledge-poor and knowledge-rich.

The knowledge-poor approaches (Ali et al., 2010; Heilman and Smith, 2009; Kalady et al., 2010; Varga, 2010; Wyse and Piwek, 2009) focus mainly on question realisation. A representative approach was proposed by Heilman et. al (2009). Their system took an "overgenerate-and-rank" strategy.

Firstly, they applied manual transformation rules to simplify declarative sentences and to transform them into questions. The system generated different types of questions by applying different transformation rules. Secondly, they utilized a question ranker to rank all the questions generated from a input document based on features such as length, language model and the presence of WH words.

The knowledge-poor approaches suffer mainly from two problems. Firstly, they have difficulty determining the question type (Olney et al., 2012). Secondly, it is difficult to evaluate the importance of the questions with respect to the input document.

In contrast, the knowledge-rich approaches build intermediate semantic representations before generating questions. Knowledge-rich approaches not only address "how to ask" but also propose promising methods to select target concepts to generate questions. Knowledge-rich approaches have the advantage of asking more important questions with the help of specific linguistic phenomena, discourse connectors or topic modelling.

Chen (2009) made use of discourse relations (conditions and temporal contexts) as well as modality verbs to generate questions. His work acknowledged that language understanding is tightly related to question asking (Graesser and Franklin, 1990; Olson et al., 1985). After knowing the discourse relation in the sentence, the system could ask questions like "what-would-happen-if" or "when-would-x-happen" using a handful of question templates. However, the system is limited to asking only condition, temporal and modality questions.

Olney et al. (2012) continued the progress made by Chen (2009). They semi-automatically built a concept graph using 30 abstract and domain-independent relations[1]. To extract the relation triples, they firstly applied semantic role labelling and then labeled the argument A0, A1 or A2 to the desired argument of the relations with a manual mapping created for every frequent predicate in the corpus. To generate questions from conceptual graph, they firstly rendered the relation triple as a declarative sentence. Then they substituted one of the relation nodes with "what" to form the question.

---

[1]Examples of relations are "after", "enables", "has-consequence", "requires", "implies".

Becker et al. (2010) utilized summarization to select key sentences for QG. Internally, the summariser identifies key concepts, links the concepts and selects the important ones through concept graph analysis.

Chali and Hasan (2015) employed similar sentence simplification and transformation pipeline as the knowledge-poor system proposed in Heilman (2009). However, the system performed topic modelling to identify subtopics of the document. It then ranked the questions based on how well they align towards the subtopics.

Our approach belongs to knowledge-rich category and is most similar to Becker et al. (2010) and Chali and Hasan (2015). However, these two systems do not take domain knowledge into consideration when selecting the target concepts. When the input document contains multiple topics, the underlying summarization and topic modeling methods may not select a balanced list of concepts (Gupta and Lehal, 2010; Lu et al., 2011). Instead of relying on the input document alone, we also exploit automatically constructed domain knowledge to select concepts that are important not only to the input document, but also to the underlying domain.

3 Datasets

We make use of two datasets obtained from the Internet. One is 200k company profiles from Crunch-Base. Another is 57k common crawl business news articles. We refer to these two corpora as "Company Profile Corpus" and "News Corpus". Each article in News Corpus is also assigned a subcategory by editors (e.g. credit-debt-loan, financial planning, hedge fund, insurance.). There are altogether 12 subcategories.

We randomly selected 30 company profiles and 30 news articles for manual evaluation. The rest of the datasets are used for development.

4 Target Concept Selection

We propose two target concept selection methods based on the following intuitions:

1. Target concepts shall contain important semantic roles (e.g. company name, product name).

2. Target concepts shall contain important semantic relations (e.g. merger, acquisition).

Whether a target concept is important depends not only on itself, but also on the input document and the domain. Hence, we choose to rely primarily on contextual statistics calculated in a corpus instead of human-crafted knowledge in the form of annotated data, lexicons or rules.

4.1 Role-Based Target Concept Selection

Our role-based concept selection method identifies different semantic roles and ask questions about them. This method is inspired by Wikipedia Infobox. Wikipedia Infobox contains key facts (concepts) of the entities. Extracting infobox-like information prior to generating questions solves the two problems of knowledge-poor QG systems. Firstly, we can easily determine the correct question type by knowing the semantic class. For example, for "customer" and "competitor", it is natural to ask a "Who" question while for "product" we will ask a "What" question. Secondly, because we extract concepts defined in Wikipedia Infobox, they are by nature important. Therefore the system is less likely to generate trivial or unrelated questions.

We could have chosen to manually define extraction rules to perform information extraction. However, such method is not portable to other domains. Suppose we build a rule-based QG system for company profiles, if we want to port it to product descriptions, we need to rewrite almost all the rules. We prefer a system that takes as little manual supervision as possible, yet able to capture the important semantic roles in a domain.

We employed bootstrapping to mine semantic roles. Bootstrapping is not limited to a predefined set of roles, but can adapt itself based on the seed words the user provides. We used Basilisk (Thelen and Riloff, 2002) to perform bootstrapping. Basilisk was originally designed to mine semantic lexicons. As shown in figure 1, Basilisk takes a small set of seed nouns for each semantic class, learns the patterns that extract these nouns and uses the patterns to extract more nouns playing the same semantic role. The authors applied this system on MUC-4 corpus and demonstrated it was able to learn high-quality semantic lexicons for multiple categories.

We used Basilisk to learn extraction patterns for different semantic categories. We chose the categories based on the frequency and whether we felt

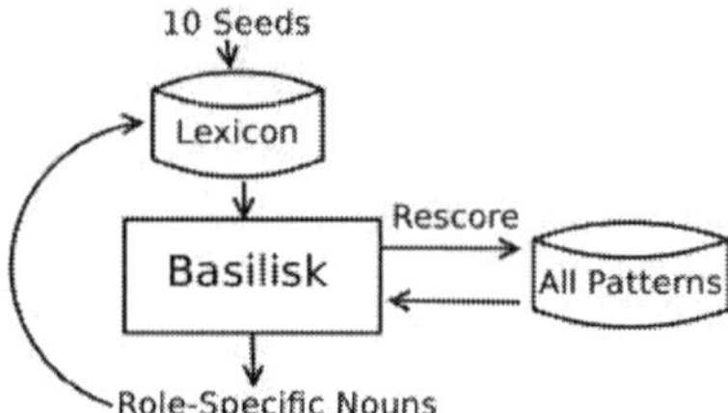

Figure 1: Basilisk algorithm.

the category is important. For this work, we used the following categories: company, location, product/service, customer, partner and date. Following Phillips and Riloff (2007), we only used patterns whose anchor is a verb. We empirically tuned the number of iterations for bootstrapping to avoid domain drifting. The number of iterations in our experiment ranged from 50 to 500.

Note that some of the categories (company, location and date) can also be identified using named entity recognisers (NER) trained on annotated corpora. The difference between bootstrapping and NER is bootstrapping determines the semantic class of a word not by the surrounding window, but by the semantic role it plays. Since it is not the focus of this work, we neither use information from NER, nor compare the accuracy of our bootstrapping method with NER systems.

Basilisk tends to prefer low frequency terms that occur only with patterns in the pattern dictionary. In our experiment, the highest ranked locations were "Rijsenhout", "Dunston" and "Endicott". All of them are little-known towns. The low frequency terms did not provide robust statistics and easily caused domain drift. We modified the original formula (formula 1) to boost more frequent candidate words (formula 2). [2] We do not add 1 to F_j, so all the infrequent patterns that co-occur with only one candidate word will be ignored. We take square root to the denominator P_i to encourage words that co-occur with more patterns. Table 1 shows example words learned for each semantic category along with the top patterns in the corresponding category.

$$AvgLog(word_i) = \frac{\sum_{P_i}^{j=1} log_2(F_j + 1))}{P_i} \quad (1)$$

Company:	*Communications, Electronics, Networks, Energy, Media, Packaging* <SUBJ>_passive_verb(base) <SUBJ>_active_verb(offer) noun(subsidiary)_prep_of_<POBJ>
Location:	*East, Africa, Republic, Asia, Zealand, Kingdom, America, Europe* passive_verb(base)_prep_in_<POBJ> passive_verb(headquarter)_prep_in_<POBJ> noun(office)_prep_in_<POBJ>
Product:	*equipment, devices, food, material, electronics, infrastructure, vehicles* active_verb(provide)_<DOBJ> noun(manufacture)_prep_of_<POBJ> active_verb(sell)_<DOBJ>
Customer:	*consumers, manufacturers, professionals, organizations, retailers, agencies* active_verb(serve)_<DOBJ> active_verb(provide)_prep_to_<POBJ> active_verb(enable)_<DOBJ>
Partner:	*alliance, partnership, agreement, relationship, shareholding, royalty* active_verb(sign)_<DOBJ> noun(alliances)_have_<DOBJ>
Date:	*March, August, 2009, 2010* passive_verb(found)_prep_in_<POBJ> active_verb(announce)_prep_on_<POBJ> active_verb(introduce)_prep_during_<POBJ>

Table 1: Example semantic lexicon entries and extraction patterns.

$$AvgLog^*(word_i) = \frac{\sum_{P_i}^{j=1} log_2(F_j))}{\sqrt{P_i}} \quad (2)$$

We used the bootstrapped patterns to extract semantic roles. The system first identifies all the noun phrases in the input document. A noun phrase will be tagged if it triggers one of the patterns in the pattern dictionary. [3] We noted that a few general patterns also appeared in the pattern dictionary (e.g. <PRODUCT>_active_verb(include). Subsequently all the subject of the trigger "include" will be regarded as "product"). This may cause problem when we determine the question word based on the semantic type. However, we did not manually edit the bootstrapped pattern dictionary, trying to adhere to our lightly-supervised paradigm.

---

[2] P_i is the number of patterns that extract $word_i$, and F_j is the number of distinct category members extracted by pattern j.

[3] We also tried to restrict the head word of the noun phrase to appear in the bootstrapped lexicon. However, it will reduce the recall significantly.

4.2 Relation-Based Target Concept Selection

Our second approach selects salient relations as target concepts. Traditionally, relation extraction systems worked only for predefined relation types and required sizeable training data for each type of relation (GuoDong et al., 2005). Open Information Extraction (OpenIE) becomes the right choice because we neither want to limit the types of relations, nor want to spend many hours annotating training data.

OpenIE systems extract <subject, relation, object> triples using surface, part-of-speech or dependency patterns (Fader et al., 2011; Angeli et al., 2015). Some OpenIE implementations also provide confidence measure for the extracted triples. However, this measure only evaluates the validity of the triples, but not the importance. Balasubramanian et al. (2013) observed that one of the major error sources of OpenIE systems was generating trivial and not informative triples.

We borrowed idea from an early work in semi-supervised information extraction to rank the relation triples based on domain relevance. Riloff (1996) proposed to rank patterns based on unlabelled relevant and irrelevant corpora. A pattern is regarded important if it occurs relatively frequently in the relevant corpus and much less frequently in the irrelevant corpus. She used the $RlogF$ score (formula 3) to rank all the patterns.

$$RlogF_i = log_2(relfreq_i) * P(relevant|pattern_i) \quad (3)$$

We first ran OpenIE [4] on News Corpus and extracted roughly 1.7 million relation triples. Extending the idea of Riloff (1996), we ran one-versus-all experiments for each subcategory. In each run, we treated the documents in one subcategory as the relevant corpus and the rest as irrelevant corpus. Every relation phrase would receive a $RlogF$ score for each subcategory (it received 0 score for subcategories where it did not appear in). If a relation phrase appeared in multiple subcategories, we simply took the highest $RlogF$ score it received as the final score. More formally, we used formula 4 to calculate the salience for each relation phrase. Where $count_{i,j}$ is the number of times relation phrase i appears in documents in subcategory j while $count_i$ is

---

[4] We used the implementation of Angeli et al. (2015).

Hedge Fund	Investing
lose value in	have trade between
be underwriter for	cross below
pend against	represent premium to
Stocks	**Retirement Planning**
be pay on	retire at
trade dividend on	be underfund by
release earnings on	contribute at_time
Credit Debt Loans	**Financial News**
contribute from	arrest in
be cut at_time	outraise
downgrade	have donate

Table 2: Top relation phrases for selected subcategories.

the number of times relation phrase i appears in the whole News Corpus.

$$RlogF_i^* = \arg\max_j(log_2(count_{i,j}) * \frac{count_{i,j}}{count_i}) \quad (4)$$

Table 2 shows the top relation phrases for selected subcategories.

We measured the salience of each triple based on information collected on sentence, triple and word level. The $RlogF$ score measures the relevance of a *triple* to a domain. We denote this score as S_{triple}. We also used LexRank (Erkan and Radev, 2004), a summarization algorithm to calculate the salience of the source *sentence* where the question is generated. We denote this score as S_{sent}. Lastly, we used $TF\text{-}IDF$ scores of the triple's subject head *word* to estimate the importance of the subject. We denote this score as S_{subj}.

We also incorporated trigram language model score S_{lm} of the triple [5] to ensure the fluency of the generated QA pairs. The final score of a triple is calculated as linear combination of the individual scores. We empirically tuned the weights of the terms and obtained the final equation: [6]

$$S = 2 \cdot S_{triple} + 1 \cdot S_{sent} + 0.3 \cdot S_{subj} + 10 \cdot S_{lm} \quad (5)$$

5 Question Generation From Concepts

We used SimpleNLG (Gatt and Reiter, 2009) to realise questions for both role-based and relation-

---

[5] We did not calculate language model scores based on generated questions because our language model is trained on a large News Corpus, where questions are relatively rare.

[6] Scores are not normalized to [0,1], so the weights cannot be directly interpreted as the contribution of each component.

active_verb(offer) dobj(PRODUCT)
What does Zoho offer?
Zoho offer Office Suite.
passive_verb(acquire) prep_in(DATE)
Q: When was StumbleUpon acquired in?
A: StumbleUpon was acquired in May 2007.
passive_verb(acquire) agent(COMPANY)
Q: StumbleUpon was acquired by whom?
A: Ebay.

Table 3: Sample output of role-based QG.

based systems. SimpleNLG is a natural language generation framework which has been widely used for summarization, sentence simplification and data-to-text generation (Gatt et al., 2009; Genest and Lapalme, 2010). SimpleNLG can also transform declarative sentences to questions simply by declaring the interrogative type.

For role-based QG, we proceed to generate question if at least one semantic role is extracted from the sentence. We also identify from the sentence the subject, direct and indirect object and open clausal complement. We choose one of the noun phrases as answer phrase [7] and determine the question word (Who, What, When, Where, How many, How much) based on the semantic type of the answer phrase. Table 3 shows examples of Q&A pairs role-based QG generated together with the patterns that extracted the answer phrase.

For relation-based QG, we proceed to generate questions from a triple if the triple's final score is above 1.0. We set the maximum number of questions for an input document to 15.

The triples are in <subject, relation, object> format. However, the "object" of the triple is not always the direct object or indirect object of the sentence. It can be an object of a preposition or even a verb compliment. As observed by Genest and Lapalme (2010), the syntactical roles known to SimpleNLG are not the same as those known to a dependency parser. There is a need to treat the arguments differently based on their syntactic roles. We followed Genest and Lapalme (2010)'s approach to build noun phrase, prepositional phrase, verb compliment and verb phrase using SimpleNLG.

---

[7]The term "answer phrase" refers to phrases which may serve as targets for questions, and therefore as possible answers to generated questions.

<Mr. Gibbs, consulting with, White House chief of staff>
Who is consulting with the White House chief of staff?
Mr. Gibbs.
<estimated cost, is, $6.65 billion>
How much is the estimated cost?
$6.65 billion for the 43 banks.
<finance minister, post, link to satirists video>
What did the finance minister post?
A link to satirists video on affair on Twitter.

Table 4: Sample output of relation-based QG.

We followed algorithm 1 to select the answer phrase (subject, object or none if it is a Yes/No question). If the answer phrase is a named entity, we choose the question word according to the entity type. Table 4 shows example relation triples and the Q&A pairs generated from the triples.

Algorithm 1 Algorithm to select the answer phrase

if relation is a single frequent verb (e.g. do, go) **then**
    generate Yes/No question
else if object is a named entity **then**
    select object as answer phrase
else if subject is a named entity **then**
    select subject as answer phrase
else if object is longer than subject **then**
    select object as answer phrase
else
    select subject as answer phrase
end if

---

6 Evaluation

We benchmarked our two systems with Heilman and Smith(2009), which is often used as a baseline for later QG systems [8]. Heilman's system took an overgeneration approach which relied on a question ranker to rank the Q&A pairs. We noted that many top questions the system generated are near duplicates of each other [9]. Hence, we manually removed the near duplicate Q&A pairs before the evaluation and kept only the ones with the highest score.

---

[8]The source code is available at *www.ark.cs.cmu.edu/mheilman/questions/*.

[9]Generated by applying different question templates on the same source sentence. E.g. "Q: Is Windows Microsoft's product? A: Yes." and "Q: Whose product is Windows? A: Microsoft".

We generated questions with the three systems (Heilman, role-based QG and relation-based QG) on the evaluation set, which consists of 30 company profiles and 30 news articles.

6.1 Method

Following 2010 Question Generation Shared Task Evaluation Challenge (QG-STEC) (Boyer and Piwek, 2010) Task A[10], we assigned individual scores for different aspects to assess the quality of the generated question and answer pairs.

Besides the five criteria used in QG-STEC[11], we added another measure "importance" as we prefer questions that ask about the main idea of the document. We also modified the "specificity" criterion to require the question to be sufficiently specific. A question like "Tell me about IBM." is not specific enough and "What system does IBM provide?" is preferred in our evaluation.

The "specificity", "syntax", "semantics", "importance" and "question type correctness" scores are assigned for each question. They receive a binary score (0 for unacceptable and 1 for acceptable/good).

The "overall" and "diversity" scores are assigned for the set of questions a system generated for an input document. They receive a score between 0 (worst) to 3 (best). 0 means "unacceptable", 1 means "slightly unacceptable", 2 means "acceptable" and 3 means "good". The "overall" score is not an average of the individual scores. It is the subjective judgement on whether the set of Q&A pairs resembles the Q&A pairs a human would construct after reading the same document. We assign high "overall" score if the individual questions are of good quality and the set of questions covers the main ideas of the input document.

We invited two human judges to rate all the Q&A pairs independently. Both of the judges are native English speaker and are not involved in the development of this work. The judges were asked to read the input document before rating the Q&A pairs. They blindly rated the system output without being told which system generated the Q&A pairs.

---

[10]Task A is "Question Generation from Paragraph", while task B is "Question Generation from Sentence".

[11]The five criteria are for "specificity", "syntax", "semantics", "question type correctness" and "diversity"

Measure	κ	% Agreement
Overall	0.51	(0.82)
Specificity	0.18	(0.77)
Syntactic	0.11	(0.85)
Semantic	0.18	(0.79)
QType	0.27	(0.87)
Importance	0.10	(0.50)
Diversity	0.80	(0.91)

Table 5: Inter-Rater reliability.

Corpus	Heilman Prf.	Heilman News	Role-Based Prf.	Role-Based News	Relation-Based Prf.	Relation-Based News
Overall	1.65	<u>1.9</u>	1.67	1.7	**1.85**	<u>1.88</u>
Diversity	**2.15**	<u>2.27</u>	1.68	1.98	2.1	<u>2.28</u>
Specificity	0.84	<u>0.88</u>	0.83	0.76	**0.93**	<u>0.87</u>
Syntactic	0.86	0.89	0.88	0.92	**0.93**	**0.95**
Semantic	0.82	<u>0.87</u>	0.83	0.83	**0.90**	<u>0.86</u>
QType	0.86	0.9	0.9	0.84	**0.93**	**0.94**
Importance	0.87	0.85	0.87	0.86	**0.92**	**0.92**

Table 6: Mean ratings across different systems and genre. "Prf." denotes results on the 30 company profiles in the evaluation dataset and "News" denotes results on the 30 news articles in the evaluation dataset. The best score for each measure is bolded. If there is a tie for the best score (difference <1%), both scores are underlined.

We used weighted Cohen's κ to measure inter-rater reliability between the two judges. For "overall" and "diversity" scores, we penalized only when the scores assigned by the two annotators differed for more than 1. Table 5 show both κ and percentage of agreement between them.

Although κ is consistently low, the judges assigned the same score about 80% of the times (except for the importance measurement). There are two main reasons for the low κ score. Firstly, both the annotators assigned 1 (acceptable) for most questions, making the probability of random agreement very high. Secondly, we observe annotator 1 is consistently more generous than annotator 2 when assigning scores. Most of the disagreement cases consist of annotator 1 assigning 1 (acceptable) and annotator 2 assigning 0 (unacceptable).

6.2 Results

Table 6 presents the mean ratings of the three systems assigned by the two human judges.

We can observe that relation-based QG outperformed the other two systems by large margin on Company Profile Corpus. For News Corpus, relation-based QG and Heilman's system performed roughly equally well. Relation-based QG outperformed Heilman's system in terms of "question type" and "importance" on both corpora, confirming that exploiting domain knowledge helped QG systems to ask more important questions.

Our two systems also generated more grammatical Q&A pairs. Heilman's system relied heavily on manual transformation rules on the parse tree to simplify sentences. Instead of trying to remove unimportant constituents (e.g.: relative clauses, temporal modifiers), our systems focused on important concepts and generated questions about them. As a result, the questions our systems generated are often more concise compared to the questions generated by Heilman's system. The average length of questions generated by role-based and relation-based QG were 7.4 and 9.1 words. Heilman's system generated questions with average length of 14.4 words, 95% and 58% longer.

The performance of role-based QG was lackluster. It managed to obtain similar scores as the baseline on Company Profile Corpus, yet still lagging behind relation-based QG. On News Corpus, it performed noticeably worse than the other two systems.

Why relation-based QG performs better than role-based QG? OpenIE triples have been widely used in different tasks, including question answering, information retrieval and inference (Angeli et al., 2015). Their advantage is that they are concise and yet are able capture either a static relation or an event. It is relatively simple to realise sentences from relation triples and we do not need to refer to the original sentence to realise the questions.

We identified two major problems with the role-based approach. Firstly, not all sentences containing an important semantic role should be considered for QG. Some sentences only mention the semantic role briefly, making it difficult to generate self-contained questions. That is why relation triples might be a more preferable unit than single semantic roles to represent target concepts. Secondly, although we used lightly-supervised method, we still need to handpick the semantic categories. For company profiles, it is acceptable because the number of candidate concepts are fewer. For news articles, the categories we predefined may fail to cover the variety of topics (E.g. semantic types like stock name, funding rounds are not covered in our list).

While individual questions received relatively high scores ($>80\%$) across different measures, none of the three systems managed to obtain comparable overall score (the highest being 63%). This suggests possible directions for future work to select, organize and present a set of questions generated from a text document in a meaningful manner to replace manually compiled FAQs.

7 Conclusions and Future Works

Motivated by the prerequisites for humans to ask good questions, we proposed two target concept selection methods for question generation (QG) that acquire and exploit domain knowledge.

We divided QG into two steps: firstly to extract target concepts in the form of semantic roles or relation triples, secondly to ask questions about the extracted concepts. Aiming to make the approach general and easily adaptable, both target concept selection approaches are lightly-supervised and do not require manually written rules or lexicons.

One of our proposed systems, relation-based QG, was able to generate more important questions on heterogeneous corpora, showing the feasibility of building a domain-specific question generation system without heavy human supervision. By focusing on the most important concepts, our systems could also to ask more concise and grammatical questions.

In future work, we plan to benchmark our systems with other knowledge-rich QG systems such as Olney et al.(2012), Becker et al.(2010) and Chali and Hasan.(2015). We want to quantitatively evaluate the advantage of using domain knowledge over relying on content analysis of the input document alone. We also aim to generate high-level questions that are beyond single sentence and to learn paraphrases of questions from community-based Q&A websites.

Acknowledgments

We would like to thank Tang Wei Ren and Hoe Xiu Ming for helping to evaluate the questions; as well as Dr. Justin Choo and the anonymous reviewers for their helpful feedback. This work was supported by Capabilities Development Grant – Technology Innovation (CDG-TI) offered by SPRING Singapore.

References

Husam Ali, Yllias Chali, and Sadid A Hasan. 2010. Automation of question generation from sentences. In *Proceedings of QG2010: The Third Workshop on Question Generation*, pages 58–67.

Gabor Angeli, Melvin Johnson Premkumar, and Christopher D Manning. 2015. Leveraging linguistic structure for open domain information extraction. In *Proceedings of the 53rd Annual Meeting of the Association for Computational Linguistics and the 7th International Joint Conference on Natural Language Processing of the Asian Federation of Natural Language Processing, ACL*, pages 26–31.

Niranjan Balasubramanian, Stephen Soderland, Oren Etzioni Mausam, and Robert Bart. 2013. out of the box information extraction: a case study using bio-medical texts.

Lee Becker, Rodney D Nielsen, Ifeyinwa Okoye, Tamara Sumner, and Wayne H Ward. 2010. Whats next? target concept identification and sequencing. In *Proceedings of QG2010: The Third Workshop on Ques-tion Generation*, page 35.

Lee Becker, Sumit Basu, and Lucy Vanderwende. 2012. Mind the gap: learning to choose gaps for question generation. In *Proceedings of the 2012 Conference of the North American Chapter of the Association for Computational Linguistics: Human Language Technologies*, pages 742–751. Association for Computational Linguistics.

Nadjet Bouayad-Agha, Gerard Casamayor, and Leo Wanner. 2011. Content selection from an ontology-based knowledge base for the generation of football summaries. In *Proceedings of the 13th European Workshop on Natural Language Generation*, pages 72–81, Nancy, France, September. Association for Computational Linguistics.

Kristy Elizabeth Boyer and Paul Piwek. 2010. Proceedings of qg2010: The third workshop on question generation.

Joyce Yue Chai, Malgorzata Budzikowska, Veronika Horvath, Nicolas Nicolov, Nanda Kambhatla, and Wlodek Zadrozny. 2001. Natural language sales assistant-a web-based dialog system for online sales. In *IAAI*, pages 19–26.

Yllias Chali and Sadid A Hasan. 2015. Towards topic-to-question generation. *Computational Linguistics*.

Wei Chen, Gregory Aist, and Jack Mostow. 2009. Generating questions automatically from informational text. In *Proceedings of the 2nd Workshop on Question Generation (AIED 2009)*, pages 17–24.

Günes Erkan and Dragomir R Radev. 2004. Lexrank: Graph-based lexical centrality as salience in text summarization. *Journal of Artificial Intelligence Research*, 22:457–479.

Anthony Fader, Stephen Soderland, and Oren Etzioni. 2011. Identifying relations for open information extraction. In *Proceedings of the Conference on Empirical Methods in Natural Language Processing*, pages 1535–1545. Association for Computational Linguistics.

Albert Gatt and Ehud Reiter. 2009. Simplenlg: A realisation engine for practical applications. In *Proceedings of the 12th European Workshop on Natural Language Generation*, pages 90–93. Association for Computational Linguistics.

Albert Gatt, Francois Portet, Ehud Reiter, Jim Hunter, Saad Mahamood, Wendy Moncur, and Somayajulu Sripada. 2009. From data to text in the neonatal intensive care unit: Using nlg technology for decision support and information management. *Ai Communications*, 22(3):153–186.

Pierre-Etienne Genest and Guy Lapalme. 2010. Text generation for abstractive summarization. In *Proceedings of the Third Text Analysis Conference, Gaithersburg, Maryland, USA. National Institute of Standards and Technology*.

Arthur C Graesser and Stanley P Franklin. 1990. Quest: A cognitive model of question answering. *Discourse processes*, 13(3):279–303.

Zhou GuoDong, Su Jian, Zhang Jie, and Zhang Min. 2005. Exploring various knowledge in relation extraction. In *Proceedings of the 43rd annual meeting on association for computational linguistics*, pages 427–434. Association for Computational Linguistics.

Vishal Gupta and Gurpreet Singh Lehal. 2010. A survey of text summarization extractive techniques. *Journal of Emerging Technologies in Web Intelligence*, 2(3):258–268.

Michael Heilman and Noah A Smith. 2009. Question generation via overgenerating transformations and ranking. Technical report, DTIC Document.

Saidalavi Kalady, Ajeesh Elikkottil, and Rajarshi Das. 2010. Natural language question generation using syntax and keywords. In *Proceedings of QG2010: The Third Workshop on Question Generation*, pages 1–10. questiongeneration. org.

Ming Liu, Rafael A Calvo, and Vasile Rus. 2010. Automatic question generation for literature review writing support. In *Intelligent Tutoring Systems*, pages 45–54. Springer.

Ming Liu, Rafael A Calvo, and Vasile Rus. 2012. G-asks: An intelligent automatic question generation system for academic writing support. *Dialogue and Discourse: Special Issue on Question Generation*, 3(2):101–124.

Yue Lu, Qiaozhu Mei, and ChengXiang Zhai. 2011. Investigating task performance of probabilistic topic models: an empirical study of plsa and lda. *Information Retrieval*, 14(2):178–203.

Rodney D Nielsen. 2008. Question generation: Proposed challenge tasks and their evaluation. In *In Proceedings of the Workshop on the Question Generation Shared Task and Evaluation Challenge. Arlington, VA*.

Elnaz Nouri, Ron Artstein, Anton Leuski, and David R Traum. 2011. Augmenting conversational characters with generated question-answer pairs. In *AAAI Fall Symposium: Question Generation*.

Andrew M Olney, Arthur C Graesser, and Natalie K Person. 2012. Question generation from concept maps. *Dialogue and Discourse*, 3(2):75–99.

Gary M Olson, Susan A Duffy, and Robert L Mack. 1985. Question-asking as a component of text comprehension. *The psychology of questions*, pages 219–226.

William Phillips and Ellen Riloff. 2007. Exploiting role-identifying nouns and expressions for information extraction. In *Proceedings of International Conference on Recent Advances in Natural Language Processing*, pages 165–172. Citeseer.

Ellen Riloff. 1996. Automatically generating extraction patterns from untagged text. In *Proceedings of the national conference on artificial intelligence*, pages 1044–1049.

Michael Thelen and Ellen Riloff. 2002. A bootstrapping method for learning semantic lexicons using extraction pattern contexts. In *Proceedings of the ACL-02 conference on Empirical methods in natural language processing-Volume 10*, pages 214–221. Association for Computational Linguistics.

Andrea Varga. 2010. Le an ha 2010 wlv: A question generation system for the qgstec 2010 task b. In *Proceedings of QG2010: The Third Workshop on Question Generation*, pages 80–83.

Brendan Wyse and Paul Piwek. 2009. Generating questions from openlearn study units.

Xuchen Yao, Emma Tosch, Grace Chen, Elnaz Nouri, Ron Artstein, Anton Leuski, Kenji Sagae, and David Traum. 2012. Creating conversational characters using question generation tools. *Dialogue and Discourse*, 3(2):125–146.

Statistical Natural Language Generation from Tabular Non-textual Data

Joy Mahapatra and **Sudip Kumar Naskar** and **Sivaji Bandyopadhyay**
Jadavpur University, India
joymahapatra90@gmail.com, sudip.naskar@cse.jdvu.ac.in,
sbandyopadhyay@cse.jdvu.ac.in

Abstract

Most of the existing natural language generation (NLG) techniques employing statistical methods are typically resource and time intensive. On the other hand, handcrafted rule-based and template-based NLG systems typically require significant human/designer efforts. In this paper, we proposed a statistical NLG technique which does not require any semantic relational knowledge and takes much less time to generate output text. The system can be used in those cases where source non-textual data are in the form of tuple in some tabular dataset. We carried out our experiments on the Prodigy-METEO wind forecasting dataset. For the evaluation purpose, we used both human evaluation and automatic evaluation. From the evaluation results we found that the linguistic quality and correctness of the texts generated by the system are better than many existing NLG systems.

1 Introduction

The aim of a natural language generation (NLG) system is to produce apprehensible natural language text from non-textual data source which could be a table, an image, numerical data or graphical data (Reiter and Dale, 1997). NLG is just the reverse process of the natural language understanding task.

Although many NLG systems have been proposed so far, there are mainly two types of language generation systems: knowledge-intensive systems and knowledge-light systems (Adeyanju, 2012). Knowledge-intensive NLG systems can be categorized mainly into two categories: template-based systems and handcrafted rule-based systems.

Knowledge-intensive generation approaches take significant human effort or expert advise for building an NLG system. Some examples of this type of NLG systems are SumTime system (Reiter et al., 2005), FoG system (Goldberg et al., 1994), PLANDOC system (McKeown et al., 1994), etc. On the other hand, knowledge-light NLG systems mostly use statistical methods to generate output text and take less human effort. Being automatic systems, knowledge-light systems mostly employ machine learning and data mining techniques. There are many types of knowledge-light systems; n-gram based NLG (Langkilde and Knight, 1998), neural network based NLG (Sutskever et al., 2011), case based NLG (Pan and Shaw, 2004), etc. However, it has been observed that knowledge-intensive systems typically perform better than knowledge-light systems as per human evaluation (Adeyanju, 2012).

Beside knowledge-intensive and knowledge-light NLG systems, there are also some NLG systems which can be built through semi-automatic techniques. Probabilistic synchronous context free grammar (PSCFG) based NLG system (Belz, 2008) falls into this category of NLG systems.

In this paper we propose a novel, knowledge-light approach based NLG system which converts a tuple of tabular-formed non-textual data into its corresponding natural language text data. Unlike most of the existing NLG systems, our system does not require any human effort or domain expert help. Moreover, the system does not require much time and computer resources (i.e., hardware equipments) for training and generation purpose. Most of the neural network (especially Recurrent Neural Net-

"

work) based knowledge-light NLG systems demand advanced computer resources and processing time for training. Contrastingly, without taking much human effort and resources, our system is able to generate intelligible and readable text output.

The remainder of the paper is organized as follows. Section 2 briefly presents relevant related work. The proposed NLG system is described in Section 3. Section 4 elaborates the experimental settings, dataset and the corresponding results. Section 5 concludes the paper.

2 Related works

Till date, a number of knowledge-light approach based language generator systems have been proposed and some of them achieved quite good results in the generation task. Two such successful statistical NLG systems are Nitrogen (Knight and Hatzivassiloglou, 1995; Langkilde and Knight, 1998) and Oxygen (Habash, 2000). These two NLG systems are based on statistical sentence realizer. Similarly Halogen (Langkilde and Knight, 1998) represents another statistical language generator which is based on statistical n-gram language model. Oh and Rudnicky (2000) also proposed an NLG system based on statistical language model.

Since its inception, statistical machine translation (Brown et al., 1993; Koehn, 2010) has gained immense popularity and it is the most prominent approach and represents the state-of-the-art in automatic machine translation. The task of NLG can be thought as a machine translation task because of the similarity between their end objectives - converting from one language to another. Langner and Black (2009) proposed an NLG system, Mountain, which modelled the task of NLG as statistical machine translation (SMT). They used the MOSES[1] toolkit (Koehn et al., 2007) for this purpose. Belz and Kow (2009) proposed another SMT based NLG system which made use of the phrase-based SMT (PB-SMT) model (Koehn et al., 2003). The MOSES toolkit offers an efficient implementation of the PB-SMT model. However, the linguistic quality and readability of PB-SMT based NLG systems were not as good as compared to other statistical NLG systems like Nitrogen, Oxygen, etc. (Belz and Kow,

___
[1] http://www.statmt.org/moses

2009).

Some semi-automatic NLG systems had also been proposed. The Probabilistic synchronous context-free grammar (PSCFG) generator (Belz, 2008) represents this category of NLG systems which can be created mostly automatically but requires manual help to certain extent. In synchronous context-free grammar (SCFG) a pair of CFGs are considered, where one CFG of CFG pair is responsible for the meaning representation and the other CFG of the pair is responsible for generating the natural language text output.

Another type of automatic NLG systems makes use of case-based reasoning (CBR) or instance based learning. This type of CBR based NLG systems are based on the concept that similar set of problems will appear in future and the same set of solutions will compensate or solve those problems. SEGUE NLG system (Pan and Shaw, 2004) was partly a CBR based NLG system; SEGUE was built with a mix of CBR approach and rule based policy. Adeyanju (2012) designed a CBR approach based weather forecasting text generation tool CBR-METEO. The advantage of CBR based system is that it takes very little manual help and if the given prior dataset covers almost all types of input instances then CBR based systems perform better.

Recently, some neural network based NLG systems have been proposed. With the advent of recurrent neural network (RNN) based language models (RNNLM) (Mikolov et al., 2010), some RNN based NLG systems have been proposed. An idea of generating text through recurrent neural network based approach with Hessian-free optimization was proposed by (Sutskever et al., 2011). However, this method takes a long training time. An RNN based NLG technique was proposed by (Wen et al., 2015) based on a joint recurrent and convolutional neural network structure. This system was able to train on dialogue act-utterance pairs without any semantic alignments or predefined grammar trees.

Although rule based knowledge-intensive NLG systems take long time and expert knowledge and feedback to be developed, this type of systems most of the times are able to generate high quality natural language text output. For example, SumTime (Reiter et al., 2005) weather forecasting system is essentially a rule based NLG system, however, its output text quality was found to be quite better compared to other automatic NLG systems. Another rule based system, probabilistic context free grammar based generator (Belz, 2008) is also able to generate high quality sentences which mostly correlate well with the given corpus text. In PCFG based system, all possible generation grammars are first discovered manually and then probabilities are assigned to those grammars automatically by observing the corpus.

3 System Description

This section describes our knowledge-light, statistical NLG system. Like any other computer software system, the system goes through similar development stages. We describe those stages in the following subsections.

3.1 Task definition

The primary objective of the system is to generate natural language text output from tuple record of a non-textual table structure dataset. The table contains a set of different attributes (qualitative or quantitative). Each row or tuple of the table represents a single unit of non-textual data which represents a vector of that particular tuple's attribute values.

Figure 1 visualizes this task for a typical weather forecasting application. According to that figure, the task is to generate textual data t_{tx} from a tuple-formed non-textual data t_{ntx} of the T_{ntx} dataset (table). The T_{ntx} dataset (table) has four attributes, a_x, where $x = 1....4$.

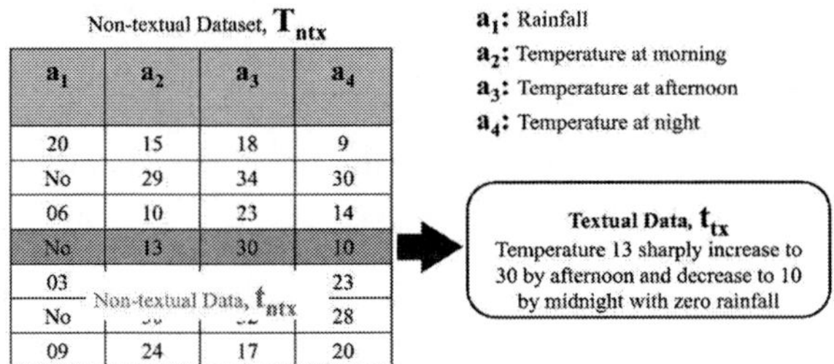

$\mathbf{a_1}$	$\mathbf{a_2}$	$\mathbf{a_3}$	$\mathbf{a_4}$
20	15	18	9
No	29	34	30
06	10	23	14
No	13	30	10
03			23
No			28
09	24	17	20

Figure 1: Basic input-output structure of our system

3.2 Requirement analysis

Being a supervised statistical model, the system needs a parallel corpus for training purpose which should be a collection of non-textual tuple data and the corresponding textual data. We make an assumption here, that most of the attribute values present in any non-textual data will also appear in the corresponding textual data for that non-textual data. For our experiments we used the Prodigy-METEO (Belz, 2009) parallel corpus on wind-speed forecast data.

3.3 Design and development

To generate human readable and easily understandable textual data from non-textual data, an NLG system must ensure two criteria. Firstly, natural language text output should be related to the corresponding non-textual data's topic, i.e., output text must contain appropriate information. Secondly, the output text must be fluent, i.e., the output text must ensure its linguistic quality.

In the design step, we divide our system into two modules; one module holds the responsibility of ensuring informativeness and the other module maintains linguistic quality of the generated output text.

3.3.1 Informativeness Management Module

We define informative quality of a generated output text by considering how many attribute values of its corresponding non-textual data are present in the generated output text and in which order. It can be noted that if a given parallel corpus holds our requirement analysis criteria (cf. Section 3.2) then we can represent each textual data as a sequence of attribute-names (which should later be replaced with attribute-values) of its corresponding non-textual data with interlinked word-groups between two adjacent attribute values present in the sequence. This concept is illustrated in figure 2. Figure 2 shows the steps which are necessary for maintaining informativeness of the output textual data. The example shown in Figure 2 is taken from a non-textual tuple formed data from a temperature and rainfall weather dataset which is not our actual experimental dataset; it is presented only for illustration purpose.

We subdivide the informativeness module into two submodules. First submodule predicts the appropriate sequence of attribute names while the second submodule's job is to select all the interlinked word-groups that should be present in the sequence predicted by the first submodule.

Step 1:   Non-textual data t_{ntx}

rainfall	temp (morning)	temp (afternoon)	temp (night)
no	13	30	10

Step 2(iterative):

I.   Attributes' name sequence $s_{t_{ntx}}$ for t_{ntx} (note: no match in found on 'rainfall' attribute value)

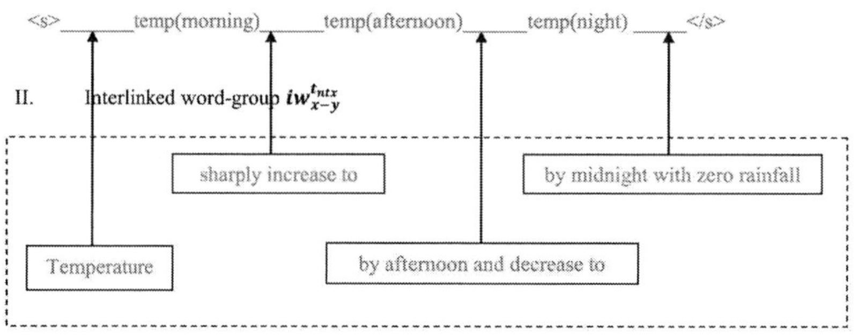

Step 3:   Result of step 1 and step 2, t_{tx}

<s> Temperature 13 sharply increase to 30 by afternoon and decrease to 10 by midnight with zero rainfall </s>

Figure 2: Steps for maintaining informativeness in the system

Let us consider generating text t_{tx} from a given non-textual data t_{ntx}. To achieve this we first need to find out the attributes' name sequence $s_{t_{ntx}}$ and thereafter identify all interlinked word-groups $iw^{t_{ntx}}_{*-*}$. Mathematically we can express this as in Equation 1 since t_{tx} is made up of $s_{t_{ntx}}$ and $iw^{t_{ntx}}_{*-*}$.

$$P(t_{tx}|t_{ntx}) = P(s_{t_{ntx}}, iw^{t_{ntx}}_{*-*}|t_{ntx}) \qquad (1)$$

$$P(t_{tx}|t_{ntx}) = P(s_{t_{ntx}}|t_{ntx}) * P(iw^{t_{ntx}}_{*-*}|t_{ntx}, s_{t_{ntx}}) \qquad (2)$$

Equation 2 rewrites Equation 1 as the product of two individual models where the first model, $P(s_{t_{ntx}}|t_{ntx})$, denotes prediction of attribute name sequence $s_{t_{ntx}}$ for the non-textual data t_{ntx}, while the second model, $P(iw^{t_{ntx}}_{*-*}|t_{ntx}, s_{t_{ntx}})$, denotes prediction of all the interlinked word-groups $iw^{t_{ntx}}_{*-*}$ for t_{ntx} in the attribute name sequence $s_{t_{ntx}}$ predicted by the first model.

i. Predicting Attribute Name Sequence

This model predicts the probable attribute name sequence for a given tuple-formed non-textual data. For this prediction, firstly each attribute value of a non-textual data needs to be identified in the corresponding textual data. It may so happen that some of the attribute values of the non-textual data might not be present in the corresponding textual data. However, we must add those attribute values (as features) in predicting attribute name sequence since they can play a crucial role in that prediction. After identification of all the attribute values present in each training textual data, we can train a model on this dataset which can take a new non-textual data and identify the corresponding textual data's attribute sequence. After predicting the attribute name sequence for a test non-textual data, we replace the attributes' names with their corresponding values.

Let us consider that we want to find the attribute name sequence $s_{t_{ntx}}$ corresponding to some non-textual data t_{ntx}. Let the non-textual dataset T_{ntx} ($t_{ntx} \in T_{ntx}$) contain $a_1, a_2, ...a_n$ attributes and the corresponding attribute values in t_{ntx} are $a_1^{t_{ntx}}, a_2^{t_{ntx}}, ...a_n^{t_{ntx}}$. Then we can express the attribute name sequence prediction for t_{ntx} as given in Equation 3.

$$P(s_{t_{ntx}}|t_{ntx}) =$$

$$P(s_{t_{ntx}}|a_1^{t_{ntx}}, a_2^{t_{ntx}}, ..., a_n^{t_{ntx}}) \qquad (3)$$

ii. **Predicting interlinked word-groups**

For a sequence containing n possible attribute names/values corresponding to a textual data, there will be $n + 1$ number of interlinked word(s) (or word-groups) as we introduce two default pseudo-attributes, one at the start and the other at the end of the text.

We predict the interlinking word-group between two attribute names along the attribute name sequence predicted in the earlier step for a test textual data from a context window of six attribute names around the two attribute names currently being considered. Therefore, predicting the interlinked word-groups for a textual data are considered to be independent of each other. We also consider the attribute names of the non-textual data which do not appear in the attribute name sequence. Let us consider that we want to predict the interlinking word-groups $iw_{*-*}^{t_{ntx}}$ for an attribute name sequence $s_{t_{ntx}}$ of a non-textual data t_{ntx}. Let this $s_{t_{ntx}}$ sequence be $[...a_l\text{--}a_m\text{--}a_n\text{--}a_o\text{--}a_r\text{--}a_s\text{--}a_t\text{--}a_u...]$ and we want to determine the intermediate word-group between a_o and a_r. Let us also assume that some of the attributes' (a_e, a_f, a_g) values of t_{ntx} are not present in $s_{t_{ntx}}$, which are $a_e^{t_{ntx}}$, $a_f^{t_{ntx}}$ and $a_g^{t_{ntx}}$. We model this task of predicting interlinking word-group between a_o and a_r for t_{ntx} and $s_{t_{ntx}}$ as in Equation 4.

$$P(iw_{o-r}^{t_{ntx}}|t_{ntx}, s_{t_{ntx}}) =$$

$$P(iw_{o-r}^{t_{ntx}}|a_m^{t_{ntx}}, a_n^{t_{ntx}}, a_o^{t_{ntx}}, a_r^{t_{ntx}}, a_s^{t_{ntx}},$$
$$a_t^{t_{ntx}}, a_e^{t_{ntx}}, a_f^{t_{ntx}}, a_g^{t_{ntx}}) \qquad (4)$$

More precisely we can write the $P(iw_{*-*}^{t_{ntx}}|t_{ntx}, s_{t_{ntx}})$ term as the product of independent interlinking word-group prediction tasks as in Equation 5, where $prev$ (previous) and $next$ (next) are any of two adjacent attribute names in $s_{t_{ntx}}$.

$$P(iw_{*-*}^{t_{ntx}}|t_{ntx}, s_{t_{ntx}}) =$$

$$\prod P(iw_{(prev)-(next)}^{t_{ntx}}|t_{ntx}, s_{t_{ntx}}) \qquad (5)$$

Therefore, Equation 2 can be rewritten as in Equation 6.

$$P(t_{tx}|t_{ntx}) = P(s_{t_{ntx}}, iw_{*-*}^{t_{ntx}}|t_{ntx})$$

$$= P(s_{t_{ntx}}|t_{ntx}) * P(iw_{*-*}^{t_{ntx}}|t_{ntx}, s_{t_{ntx}})$$

$$= P(s_{t_{ntx}}|t_{ntx}) * \prod P(iw_{(prev)-(next)}^{t_{ntx}}|t_{ntx}, s_{t_{ntx}})$$
$$(6)$$

3.3.2 Linguistic Quality Management Module

The informativeness management module tries to answer "what will be content within the output textual data ", but it does not concern the linguistic quality of the generated text, e.g., fluency, readability, etc. In the linguistic quality management module we try to deal with the deficiency of linguistic quality in the generated textual data. Statistical language modelling is a well established technique for ensuring fluency and readability in natural language text. Therefore, as a final component, we incorporate a language model in our system. Hence, to maintain both informativeness and linguistic quality of the generated textual data, we model the task of NLG as given in Equation 7, where $PP(x)$ stands for the perplexity of string x.

$$P(t_{tx}|t_{ntx}) = P(s_{t_{ntx}}|t_{ntx})$$

$$* \prod P(iw_{(prev)-(next)}^{t_{ntx}}|t_{ntx}, s_{t_{ntx}}) * PP^{-1}(t_{tx})$$
$$(7)$$

For our experiments, we trained a trigram language model on the training set textual data with a minor modification by replacing the attribute values with their attribute names.

3.3.3 Decoding

The search space of the NLG problem as modelled by Equation 7 is enormous. For example, if we consider top ten attribute name sequences, and for each attribute name sequence there are overall fifteen interlinked word-groups and for selecting each of these interlinked word-group we consider only top five candidates, then the search space for the generation task will contain $10 * 5^{15}$ candidates. To reduce the size of the search space and keep the computation problem tractable, we implemented the task of text generation as modelled in Equation 7 using *stack decoding* (Jelinek, 1969) with histogram pruning which limits the number of most promosing hypotheses to be explored by the size of the stack. In stack decoding with histogram pruning, the stack at any point of time contains only N (size of the stack) most promising partial hypotheses and during hypothesis expansion, a partial hypothesis is placed on the stack provided there is space in the stack, or, it is more promising than at least one of the partial hypotheses already stored in the stack. In case of stack overflow, the least promising hypothesis is discarded.

4 Experiments

This section presents the dataset used in our experiments and the evaluation results of our system compared to some other NLG systems.

4.1 Dataset

As mentioned in Section 3.2, a non-textual–textual parallel dataset is required to train our system. The parallelism should be in such a form that each non-textual data can be represented as a tuple of attribute value instances and most of those attribute values should be present in its corresponding textual data.

We used the Prodigy-METEO[2] corpus (Belz, 2009), a wind forecast dataset, for our experiment. In the Prodigy-METEO corpus a single pair of non-textual–textual data stands for a particular day's wind forecast report. A non-textual data in that dataset is represented by a seven-component vector, where each component expresses a particular feature of wind data measurement at a moment of time. The seven components belong to a vector represented by [*id, direction, speed_min, speed_max, gust-speed_min, gust-speed_max, time*]. In that vector representation *id* stands for identification of the vector, *direction* mentions the wind speed direction, *speed_max and speed_min* denote the maximum and mnimum wind speed respectively, *gust_max and gust_min* represent the maximum and minimum wind gust speed respectively, and the last component *time* denotes the specific time instance

---

[2]http://www.nltg.brighton.ac.uk/home/Anja.Belz/Prodigy

when rest of components' readings were measured. For example, 1st April, 2001 wind forecast data is represented in this dataset as [[1,_SW,28,32,42,-,0600],[2,-,20,25,-,-,0000]] , where '-' represents a missing reading value.

As mentioned earlier our proposed model can process only a single tuple formed non-textual data at a time. However, the Prodigy-METEO corpus represents each non-textual data (wind forecast data for a particular day) by a sequence of multi-component vectors. For this reason, we merge all the vectors of a particular day's wind forecast data into a single tuple formed data. The merging of a particular day's wind forecast data vectors is illustrated in Figure 3. The Prodigy-METEO corpus comes with five pre-

Corpus Non-Textual Data

Id	Dir	Speed_max	Speed_min	Gust_max	Gust_min	Ts
1	_S	20	24	-	-	0600
2	-	34	38	46	-	1800

Corresponding Textual Data
S'LY 20-24 INCREASING 34-38 GUSTS 46 BY EVENING

Our format of the Non-Textual data

Id(1)	Dir(1)	Spee	Spee	Gust	Gust	Ts(1)	Id(2)	Dir(2)	Spee	Spee	Gust	Gust	Ts(2)
1	S	20	24	-	-	0600	2	-	34	38	46	-	1800

Figure 3: Transformation of Prodigy-METEO corpus non-textual data representation for the system's input

defined splits each of which has on an average 490 pairs of non-textual tuple data and the corresponding textual data.

4.2 Evaluation

We evaluated our system using both automatic evaluation metrics and human evaluation. For both human and automatic evaluation, we compared our system with ten existing NLG systems whose outputs on the Prodigy-METEO testset are also available in the Prodigy-METEO corpus. These ten NLG systems are PCFG-Greedy, PSCFG-Semantic, PSCFG-Unstructured, PCFG-Viterbii, PCFG-2gram, PCFG-Roulette, PBSMT-Unstructured,

148

Non-Textual Data	[[1,_SW-WSW,08,12,-,-,0600],[2,_VAR,02,06,-,-,1800]]
Corpus	SW-WSW 08-12 FALLING VARIABLE 02-06 BY LATE AFTERNOON
SumTime	SW-WSW 10 OR LESS BECOMING VARIABLE BY LATE AFTERNOON
PSCFG-Semantic	SW-WSW 08-12 FALLING VARIABLE 02-06 BY EVENING
PSCFG-Unstructured	SW-WSW 08-12 FALLING VARIABLE 02-06 BY EVENING
Our Proposed System	**SW-WSW 08-12 FALLING VARIABLE 02-06 BY EVENING**
PCFG-Greedy	SW-WSW 8-12 THEN FALLING VARIABLE 2-6 BY EVENING
PCFG-Viterbi	SW-WSW 8-12 THEN FALLING VARIABLE 2-6
PCFG-Roulette	SW-WSW 8-12 FALLING VARIABLE 2-6
PCFG-2gram	SW-WSW 8-12 THEN VARIABLE 2-6
PCFG-Random	SOON SW-WSW 8-12 THEN STEADILY EASING TO VARIABLE'LY 2-6 AHEAD OF THE FRONT FOR A TIME THIS AFTERNOON
PBSMT-Unstructured	LESS SW-WSW 08-12 GRADUALLY FALLING VARIABLE 02-06 BY EVENING
PBSMT-Structured	GUSTS SW-WSW 08-12 BY IN TO AND FALLING TO UNKNOWN VARIABLE 02-06 BY EVENING

Figure 4: An sample of input and outputs of different NLG system

SumTime-Hybrid, PBSMT-Structured and PCFG-Random (Belz and Kow, 2009). Figure 4 shows a sample input and outputs of all the above mentioned systems including our system.

4.2.1 Automatic Evaluation

For automatic evaluation, we used two automatic evaluation metrics; BLEU (Papineni et al., 2002) and METEOR (Banerjee and Lavie, 2005). Both BLEU and METEOR were originally proposed for evaluation of machine translation (MT) systems However, due to the similarity between the two tasks (i.e., MT and NLG) from the point of view of their working principles, most of the NLG systems are also evaluated using these two automatic MT evaluation metrics.

Because of the relatively small size of the dataset, we took a five-fold cross validation policy which was predefined in the Prodigy-METEO corpus. Table 1 presents the evaluation results obtained with BLEU and METEOR on our system along with the ten other NLG systems.

System	BLEU score	Meteor score
Corpus	1	1
PCFG-Greedy	0.65	0.85
PSCFG-Semantic	0.64	0.83
PSCFG-Unstructured	0.62	0.81
Proposed System	**0.61**	**0.82**
PCFG-Viterbii	0.57	0.76
PCFG-2gram	0.56	0.76
PCFG-Roulette	0.52	0.76
PBSMT-Unstructured	0.51	0.81
SumTime-Hybrid	0.46	0.67
PBSMT-Structure	0.34	0.59
PCFG-Random	0.28	0.52

Table 1: Comparison using automatic metric evaluation

4.2.2 Human-based Evaluation

Evaluation using automatic evaluation metrics is very popular among researchers and developers since automatic evaluation is very fast and cheap. Automatic evaluation metrics are good indicators of system performance and they greatly help day-to-day system development. However, despite being very time intensive and costly, human evaluation still serves as the de-facto evaluation standard and the worth of automatic evaluation metrics are typically judged based on how well they correlate with human evaluation.

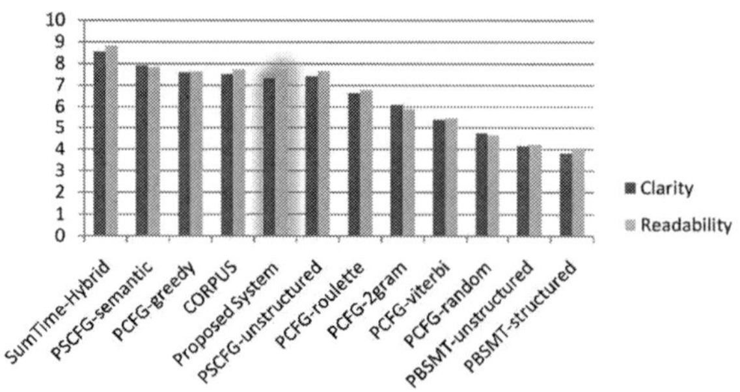

Figure 5: Comparison using human evaluation

We also evaluated the systems using human evaluation on a part of the test dataset. We carried out human evaluation to measure the clarity and readability of the texts generated by the NLG systems. Clarity measures truthfulness and correctness of a textual data whereas readability concerns fluency of the textual data. 30 instances (out of total 232) were randomly chosen from the testset for the pilot human evaluation and the output from 11 different systems along with the corresponding non-textual data were presented to the human evaluators. Five students from different backgrounds who acted as human evaluators were asked to rate 72 outputs each in a 10 point scale. The output of human evaluation is presented in Figure 5.

4.3   Result Analysis

As per the outcomes of automatic evaluation, our system provided the third and fourth best results in METEOR and BLEU, respectively. According to METEOR, our system is only behind the PCGF-Greedy and PSCFG-Semantic systems while according to BLEU, PCFG-greedy, PSCFG-Semantic and PSCFG-Unstructured systems perform better than our proposed model. However, these systems which are ahead of our system in performance as per automatic evaluation are not fully automatic, whereas our system does not require any human effort or additional knowledge other than a non-textual–textual parallel corpus.

Human evaluation preferred rule based systems over automatic knowledge-light systems. The Sum-Time system, which is a rule based system and is placed in the ninth position according to both BLEU and METEOR, is adjudged the best system in human evaluation. Our system ranks fourth among the 11 systems according to human evaluation. The gold standard reference set was also provided to the human evaluators for evaluation without their knowledge and, surprisingly, the reference set was ranked fourth.

We calculated Pearson correlation coefficient between scores produced by automatic evaluation metrics (BLEU and METEOR) and human evaluation. For human evaluation we considered the average of clarity and readability. The correlation coefficients are r(Human, Bleu)=0.61 and r(Human, METEOR)=0.57 .

5   Conclusions

The statistical NLG system presented in this paper does not require any external agents' involvement. It is a domain independent system and can easily be shifted from one application domain to another without any change.

To avail good quality output text from the system, one must conform to the requirement specified in Section 3.2. The NLG system will perform accurately if all attributes present in the training tuple-formed non-textual data contain distinct values. If this criterion can be assured, then it will be trivial to match each of those attribute values present in the non-textual data to their appearance in the corresponding textual data. However, if this constraint is not possible to be satisfied the system will still work. It is worth to be mentioned here that in cases when not a single attribute value of non-textual data can be found in the corresponding textual data, then our system will behave like an instance based NLG system.

Acknowledgments

This work is partially supported by Media Lab Asia, Department of Electronics and Information Technology (DeitY), Government of India, under the Young Faculty Research Fellowship of the Visvesvaraya PhD Scheme for Electronics & IT and through the project "CLIA System Phase II".

References

Ibrahim Adeyanju. 2012. Article: Generating weather forecast texts with case based reasoning. *International Journal of Computer Applications*, 45(10):35–40, May. Full text available.

Satanjeev Banerjee and Alon Lavie. 2005. Meteor: An automatic metric for mt evaluation with improved correlation with human judgments. pages 65–72.

Anja Belz and Eric Kow. 2009. System building cost vs. output quality in data-to-text generation. In *Proceedings of the 12th European Workshop on Natural Language Generation*, ENLG '09, pages 16–24, Stroudsburg, PA, USA. Association for Computational Linguistics.

Anja Belz. 2008. Automatic generation of weather forecast texts using comprehensive probabilistic generation-space models. *Nat. Lang. Eng.*, 14(4):431–455, October.

Anja Belz. 2009. Prodigy-meteo: Pre-alpha release notes (nov 2009).

Peter F. Brown, Vincent J. Della Pietra, Stephen A. Della Pietra, and Robert L. Mercer. 1993. The mathematics of statistical machine translation: Parameter estimation. *Comput. Linguist.*, 19(2):263–311, June.

Eli Goldberg, Norbert Driedger, and Richard I. Kittredge. 1994. Using natural-language processing to produce weather forecasts. *IEEE Expert: Intelligent Systems and Their Applications*, 9(2):45–53, April.

Nizar Habash, 2000. *Envisioning Machine Translation in the Information Future: 4th Conference of the Association for Machine Translation in the Americas, AMTA 2000 Cuernavaca, Mexico, October 10–14, 2000 Proceedings*, chapter Oxygen: A Language Independent Linearization Engine, pages 68–79. Springer Berlin Heidelberg, Berlin, Heidelberg.

F. Jelinek. 1969. Fast sequential decoding algorithm using a stack. *IBM J. Res. Dev.*, 13(6):675–685, November.

Kevin Knight and Vasileios Hatzivassiloglou. 1995. Two-level, many-paths generation. In *Proceedings of the 33rd Annual Meeting on Association for Computational Linguistics*, ACL '95, pages 252–260, Stroudsburg, PA, USA. Association for Computational Linguistics.

Philipp Koehn, Franz Josef Och, and Daniel Marcu. 2003. Statistical phrase-based translation. In *Proceedings of the 2003 Conference of the North American Chapter of the Association for Computational Linguistics on Human Language Technology - Volume 1*, NAACL '03, pages 48–54, Stroudsburg, PA, USA. Association for Computational Linguistics.

Philipp Koehn, Hieu Hoang, Alexandra Birch, Chris Callison-Burch, Marcello Federico, Nicola Bertoldi, Brooke Cowan, Wade Shen, Christine Moran, Richard Zens, Chris Dyer, Ondřej Bojar, Alexandra Constantin, and Evan Herbst. 2007. Moses: Open source toolkit for statistical machine translation. In *Proceedings of the 45th Annual Meeting of the ACL on Interactive Poster and Demonstration Sessions*, ACL '07, pages 177–180, Stroudsburg, PA, USA. Association for Computational Linguistics.

Philipp Koehn. 2010. *Statistical Machine Translation*. Cambridge University Press, New York, NY, USA, 1st edition.

Irene Langkilde and Kevin Knight. 1998. Generation that exploits corpus-based statistical knowledge. In *Proceedings of the 36th Annual Meeting of the Association for Computational Linguistics and 17th International Conference on Computational Linguistics, Volume 1*, pages 704–710, Montreal, Quebec, Canada, August. Association for Computational Linguistics.

Brian Langner and Alan W Black. 2009. Mountain: a translation-based approach to natural language generation for dialog systems.

Kathleen McKeown, Karen Kukich, and James Shaw. 1994. Practical issues in automatic documentation generation. In *Proceedings of the Fourth Conference on Applied Natural Language Processing*, pages 7–14, Stuttgart, Germany, October. Association for Computational Linguistics.

Tomas Mikolov, Martin Karafiát, Lukás Burget, Jan Cernocký, and Sanjeev Khudanpur. 2010. Recurrent neural network based language model. In *INTERSPEECH 2010, 11th Annual Conference of the International Speech Communication Association, Makuhari, Chiba, Japan, September 26-30, 2010*, pages 1045–1048.

Alice H. Oh and Alexander I. Rudnicky. 2000. Stochastic language generation for spoken dialogue systems. In *Proceedings of the 2000 ANLP/NAACL Workshop on Conversational Systems - Volume 3*, ANLP/NAACL-ConvSyst '00, pages 27–32, Stroudsburg, PA, USA. Association for Computational Linguistics.

Shimei Pan and James Shaw. 2004. Segue: A hybrid case-based surface natural language generator. In *In Proceedings of INLG 2004*, pages 130–140.

Kishore Papineni, Salim Roukos, Todd Ward, and Wei-Jing Zhu. 2002. Bleu: A method for automatic evaluation of machine translation. In *Proceedings of the 40th Annual Meeting on Association for Computational Linguistics*, ACL '02, pages 311–318, Stroudsburg, PA, USA. Association for Computational Linguistics.

Ehud Reiter and Robert Dale. 1997. Building applied natural language generation systems. *Nat. Lang. Eng.*, 3(1):57–87, March.

Ehud Reiter, Somayajulu Sripada, Jim Hunter, Jin Yu, and Ian Davy. 2005. Choosing words in computer-generated weather forecasts. *Artif. Intell.*, 167(1-2):137–169, September.

Ilya Sutskever, James Martens, and Geoffrey E. Hinton. 2011. Generating text with recurrent neural networks. In Lise Getoor and Tobias Scheffer, editors, *Proceedings of the 28th International Conference on Machine Learning (ICML-11)*, pages 1017–1024, New York, NY, USA. ACM.

Tsung-Hsien Wen, Milica Gasic, Dongho Kim, Nikola Mrksic, Pei-hao Su, David Vandyke, and Steve J. Young. 2015. Stochastic language generation in dialogue using recurrent neural networks with convolutional sentence reranking. *CoRR*, abs/1508.01755.

Paraphrase Generation from Latent-Variable PCFGs for Semantic Parsing

Shashi Narayan, Siva Reddy and Shay B. Cohen
School of Informatics, University of Edinburgh
10 Crichton Street, Edinburgh, EH8 9LE, UK
shashi.narayan@ed.ac.uk, siva.reddy@ed.ac.uk, scohen@inf.ed.ac.uk

Abstract

One of the limitations of semantic parsing approaches to open-domain question answering is the lexicosyntactic gap between natural language questions and knowledge base entries – there are many ways to ask a question, all with the same answer. In this paper we propose to bridge this gap by generating paraphrases of the input question with the goal that at least one of them will be correctly mapped to a knowledge-base query. We introduce a novel grammar model for paraphrase generation that does not require any sentence-aligned paraphrase corpus. Our key idea is to leverage the flexibility and scalability of latent-variable probabilistic context-free grammars to sample paraphrases. We do an extrinsic evaluation of our paraphrases by plugging them into a semantic parser for Freebase. Our evaluation experiments on the WebQuestions benchmark dataset show that the performance of the semantic parser improves over strong baselines.

1 Introduction

Semantic parsers map sentences onto logical forms that can be used to query databases (Zettlemoyer and Collins, 2005; Wong and Mooney, 2006), instruct robots (Chen and Mooney, 2011), extract information (Krishnamurthy and Mitchell, 2012), or describe visual scenes (Matuszek et al., 2012). In this paper we consider the problem of semantically parsing questions into Freebase logical forms for the goal of question answering. Current systems accomplish this by learning task-specific grammars (Berant et al., 2013), strongly-typed CCG grammars (Kwiatkowski et al., 2013; Reddy et al., 2014),

or neural networks without requiring any grammar (Yih et al., 2015). These methods are sensitive to the words used in a question and their word order, making them vulnerable to unseen words and phrases. Furthermore, mismatch between natural language and Freebase makes the problem even harder. For example, Freebase expresses the fact that *"Czech is the official language of Czech Republic"* (encoded as a graph), whereas to answer a question like *"What do people in Czech Republic speak?"* one should infer *people in Czech Republic* refers to *Czech Republic* and *What* refers to the *language* and *speak* refers to the predicate *official language*.

We address the above problems by using paraphrases of the original question. Paraphrasing has shown to be promising for semantic parsing (Fader et al., 2013; Berant and Liang, 2014; Wang et al., 2015). We propose a novel framework for paraphrasing using latent-variable PCFGs (L-PCFGs). Earlier approaches to paraphrasing used phrase-based machine translation for text-based QA (Duboue and Chu-Carroll, 2006; Riezler et al., 2007), or hand annotated grammars for KB-based QA (Berant and Liang, 2014). We find that phrase-based statistical machine translation (MT) approaches mainly produce lexical paraphrases without much syntactic diversity, whereas our grammar-based approach is capable of producing both lexically and syntactically diverse paraphrases. Unlike MT based approaches, our system does not require aligned parallel paraphrase corpora. In addition we do not require hand annotated grammars for paraphrase generation but instead learn the grammar directly from a large scale question corpus.

The main contributions of this paper are two fold. First, we present an algorithm (§2) to generate paraphrases using latent-variable PCFGs. We use the spectral method of Narayan and Cohen (2015) to estimate L-PCFGs on a large scale question treebank. Our grammar model leads to a robust and an efficient system for paraphrase generation in open-domain question answering. While CFGs have been explored for paraphrasing using bilingual parallel corpus (Ganitkevitch et al., 2013), ours is the first implementation of CFG that uses only monolingual data. Second, we show that generated paraphrases can be used to improve semantic parsing of questions into Freebase logical forms (§3). We build on a strong baseline of Reddy et al. (2014) and show that our grammar model competes with MT baseline even without using any parallel paraphrase resources.

2 Paraphrase Generation Using Grammars

Our paraphrase generation algorithm is based on a model in the form of an L-PCFG. L-PCFGs are PCFGs where the nonterminals are refined with latent states that provide some contextual information about each node in a given derivation. L-PCFGs have been used in various ways, most commonly for syntactic parsing (Prescher, 2005; Matsuzaki et al., 2005; Petrov et al., 2006; Cohen et al., 2013; Narayan and Cohen, 2015; Narayan and Cohen, 2016).

In our estimation of L-PCFGs, we use the spectral method of Narayan and Cohen (2015), instead of using EM, as has been used in the past by Matsuzaki et al. (2005) and Petrov et al. (2006). The spectral method we use enables the choice of a set of feature functions that indicate the latent states, which proves to be useful in our case. It also leads to sparse grammar estimates and compact models.

The spectral method works by identifying feature functions for "inside" and "outside" trees, and then clusters them into latent states. Then it follows with a maximum likelihood estimation step, that assumes the latent states are represented by clusters obtained through the feature function clustering. For more details about these constructions, we refer the reader to Cohen et al. (2013) and Narayan and Cohen (2015).

The rest of this section describes our paraphrase generation algorithm.

2.1 Paraphrases Generation Algorithm

We define our paraphrase generation task as a sampling problem from an L-PCFG G_{syn}, which is estimated from a large corpus of parsed questions. Once this grammar is estimated, our algorithm follows a pipeline with two major steps.

We first build a word lattice W_q for the input question q.[1] We use the lattice to constrain our paraphrases to a specific choice of words and phrases that can be used. Once this lattice is created, a grammar G'_{syn} is then extracted from G_{syn}. This grammar is constrained to the lattice.

We experiment with three ways of constructing word lattices: naïve word lattices representing the words from the input question only, word lattices constructed with the Paraphrase Database (Ganitkevitch et al., 2013) and word lattices constructed with a bi-layered L-PCFG, described in §2.2. For example, Figure 1 shows an example word lattice for the question *What language do people in Czech Republic speak?* using the lexical and phrasal rules from the PPDB.[2]

Once G'_{syn} is generated, we sample paraphrases of the input question q. These paraphrases are further filtered with a classifier to improve the precision of the generated paraphrases.

L-PCFG Estimation We train the L-PCFG G_{syn} on the Paralex corpus (Fader et al., 2013). Paralex is a large monolingual parallel corpus, containing 18 million pairs of question paraphrases with 2.4M distinct questions in the corpus. It is suitable for our task of generating paraphrases since its large scale makes our model robust for open-domain questions. We construct a treebank by parsing 2.4M distinct questions from Paralex using the BLLIP parser (Charniak and Johnson, 2005).[3]

Given the treebank, we use the spectral algorithm of Narayan and Cohen (2015) to learn an L-PCFG

---

[1] Word lattices, formally weighted finite state automata, have been used in previous works for paraphrase generation (Langkilde and Knight, 1998; Barzilay and Lee, 2003; Pang et al., 2003; Quirk et al., 2004). We use an unweighted variant of word lattices in our algorithm.

[2] For our experiments, we extract rules from the PPDB-Small to maintain the high precision (Ganitkevitch et al., 2013).

[3] We ignore the Paralex alignments for training G_{syn}.

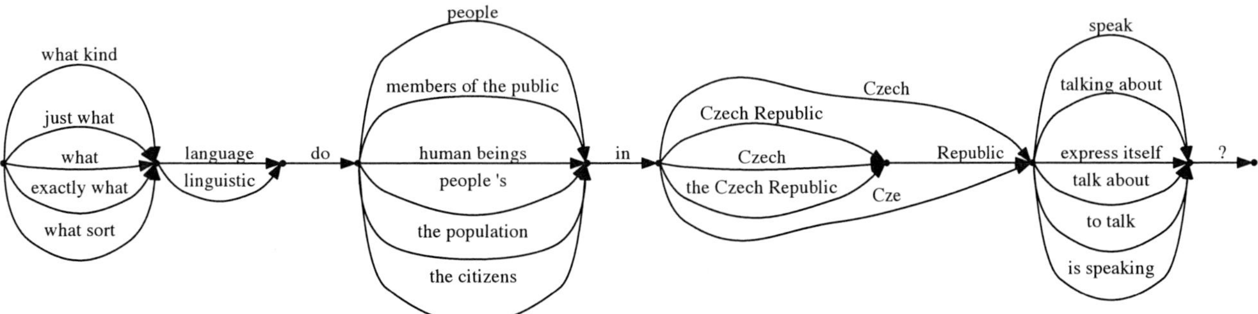

Figure 1: An example word lattice for the question *What language do people in Czech Republic speak?* using the lexical and phrasal rules from the PPDB.

for constituency parsing to learn G_{syn}. We follow Narayan and Cohen (2015) and use the same feature functions for the inside and outside trees as they use, capturing contextual syntactic information about nonterminals. We refer the reader to Narayan and Cohen (2015) for more detailed description of these features. In our experiments, we set the number of latent states to 24.

Once we estimate G_{syn} from the Paralex corpus, we restrict it for each question to a grammar G'_{syn} by keeping only the rules that could lead to a derivation over the lattice. This step is similar to lexical pruning in standard grammar-based generation process to avoid an intermediate derivation which can never lead to a successful derivation (Koller and Striegnitz, 2002; Narayan and Gardent, 2012).

Paraphrase Sampling   Sampling a question from the grammar G'_{syn} is done by recursively sampling nodes in the derivation tree, together with their latent states, in a top-down breadth-first fashion. Sampling from the pruned grammar G'_{syn} raises an issue of oversampling words that are more frequent in the training data. To lessen this problem, we follow a *controlled sampling* approach where sampling is guided by the word lattice W_q. Once a word w from a path e in W_q is sampled, all other parallel or conflicting paths to e are removed from W_q. For example, generating for the word lattice in Figure 1, when we sample the word *citizens*, we drop out the paths *"human beings"*, *"people's"*, *"the population"*, *"people"* and *"members of the public"* from W_q and accordingly update the grammar. The controlled sampling ensures that each sampled question uses words from a single start-to-end path in W_q. For example, we could sample a question *what*

is Czech Republic 's language? by sampling words from the path *(what, language, do, people 's, in, Czech, Republic, is speaking, ?)* in Figure 1. We repeat this sampling process to generate multiple potential paraphrases.

The resulting generation algorithm has multiple advantages over existing grammar generation methods. First, the sampling from an L-PCFG grammar lessens the lexical ambiguity problem evident in lexicalized grammars such as tree adjoining grammars (Narayan and Gardent, 2012) and combinatory categorial grammars (White, 2004). Our grammar is not lexicalized, only unary context-free rules are lexicalized. Second, the top-down sampling restricts the combinatorics inherent to bottom-up search (Shieber et al., 1990). Third, we do not restrict the generation by the order information in the input. The lack of order information in the input often raises the high combinatorics in lexicalist approaches (Kay, 1996). In our case, however, we use sampling to reduce this problem, and it allows us to produce syntactically diverse questions. And fourth, we impose no constraints on the grammar thereby making it easier to maintain bi-directional (recursive) grammars that can be used both for parsing and for generation (Shieber, 1988).

2.2   Bi-Layered L-PCFGs

As mentioned earlier, one of our lattice types is based on bi-layered PCFGs introduced here.

In their traditional use, the latent states in L-PCFGs aim to capture syntactic information. We introduce here the use of an L-PCFG with two layers of latent states: one layer is intended to capture the usual syntactic information, and the other aims to capture semantic and topical information by using a

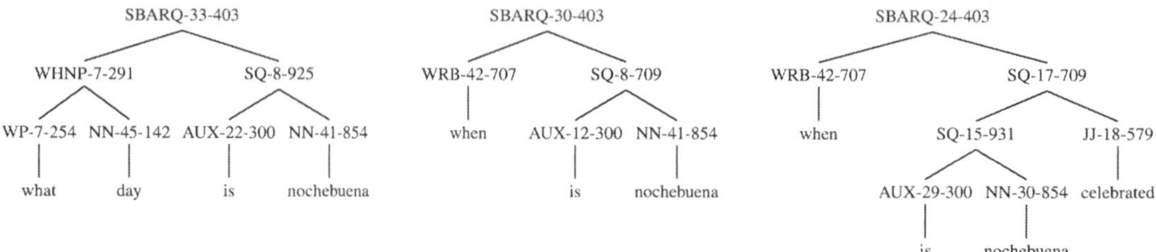

Figure 2: Trees used for bi-layered L-PCFG training. The questions *what day is nochebuena, when is nochebuena* and *when is nochebuena celebrated* are paraphrases from the Paralex corpus. Each nonterminal is decorated with a syntactic label and two identifiers, e.g., for WP-7-254, WP is the syntactic label assigned by the BLLIP parser, 7 is the syntactic latent state, and 254 is the semantic latent state.

large set of states with specific feature functions.[4]

To create the bi-layered L-PCFG, we again use the spectral algorithm of Narayan and Cohen (2015) to estimate a grammar G_{par} from the Paralex corpus. We use the word alignment of paraphrase question pairs in Paralex to map inside and outside trees of each nonterminals in the treebank to bag of word features. The number of latent states we use is 1,000.

Once the two feature functions (syntactic in G_{syn} and semantic in G_{par}) are created, each nonterminal in the training treebank is assigned two latent states (cluster identifiers). Figure 2 shows an example annotation of trees for three paraphrase questions from the Paralex corpus. We compute the parameters of the bi-layered L-PCFG G_{layered} with a simple frequency count maximum likelihood estimate over this annotated treebank. As such, G_{layered} is a combination of G_{syn} and G_{par}, resulting in 24,000 latent states (24 syntactic x 1000 semantic).

Consider an example where we want to generate paraphrases for the question *what day is nochebuena*. Parsing it with G_{layered} will lead to the leftmost hybrid structure as shown in Figure 2. The assignment of the first latent states for each nonterminals ensures that we retrieve the correct syntactic representation of the sentence. Here, however, we are more interested in the second latent states assigned to each nonterminals which capture the paraphrase information of the sentence at various levels. For example, we have a unary lexical rule (NN-*-142 day) indicating that we observe *day* with NN of the paraphrase type 142. We could use this information to extract unary rules of the form (NN-*-142 w) in the treebank that will generate

words w which are paraphrases to *day*. Similarly, any node WHNP-*-291 in the treebank will generate paraphrases for *what day*, SBARQ-*-403, for *what day is nochebuena*. This way we will be able to generate paraphrases *when is nochebuena* and *when is nochebuena celebrated* as they both have SBARQ-*-403 as their roots.[5]

To generate a word lattice W_q for a given question q, we parse q with the bi-layered grammar G_{layered}. For each rule of the form $X\text{-}m_1\text{-}m_2 \rightarrow w$ in the bi-layered tree with $X \in \mathcal{P}$, $m_1 \in \{1, \ldots, 24\}$, $m_2 \in \{1, \ldots, 1000\}$ and w a word in q, we extract rules of the form $X\text{-}*\text{-}m_2 \rightarrow w'$ from G_{layered} such that $w' \neq w$. For each such (w, w'), we add a path w' parallel to w in the word lattice.

2.3 Paraphrase Classification

Our sampling algorithm overgenerates paraphrases which are incorrect. To improve its precision, we build a binary classifier to filter the generated paraphrases. We randomly select 100 distinct questions from the Paralex corpus and generate paraphrases using our generation algorithm with various lattice settings. We randomly select 1,000 pairs of input-sampled sentences and manually annotate them as "correct" or "incorrect" paraphrases.[6] We train our classifier on this manually created training data.[7] We

---

[4]For other cases of separating syntax from semantics in a similar way, see Mitchell and Steedman (2015).

[5]We found out that our G_{par} grammar is not fine-grained enough and often merges different paraphrase information into the same latent state. This problem is often severe for nonterminals at the top level of the bilayered tree. Hence, we rely only on unary lexical rules (the rules that produce terminal nodes) to extract paraphrase patterns in our experiments.

[6]We have 154 positive and 846 negative paraphrase pairs.

[7]We do not use the paraphrase pairs from the Paralex corpus to train our classifier, as they do not represent the distribution of our sampled paraphrases and the classifier trained on them performs poorly.

follow Madnani et al. (2012), who used MT metrics for paraphrase identification, and experiment with 8 MT metrics as features for our binary classifier. In addition, we experiment with a binary feature which checks if the sampled paraphrase preserves named entities from the input sentence. We use WEKA (Hall et al., 2009) to replicate the classifier of Madnani et al. (2012) with our new feature. We tune the feature set for our classifier on the development data.

3 Semantic Parsing using Paraphrasing

In this section we describe how the paraphrase algorithm is used for converting natural language to Freebase queries. Following Reddy et al. (2014), we formalize the semantic parsing problem as a graph matching problem, i.e., finding the Freebase subgraph (grounded graph) that is isomorphic to the input question semantic structure (ungrounded graph).

This formulation has a major limitation that can be alleviated by using our paraphrase generation algorithm. Consider the question *What language do people in Czech Republic speak?*. The ungrounded graph corresponding to this question is shown in Figure 3(a). The Freebase grounded graph which results in correct answer is shown in Figure 3(d). Note that these two graphs are non-isomorphic making it impossible to derive the correct grounding from the ungrounded graph. In fact, at least 15% of the examples in our development set fail to satisfy isomorphic assumption. In order to address this problem, we use paraphrases of the input question to generate additional ungrounded graphs, with the aim that one of those paraphrases will have a structure isomorphic to the correct grounding. Figure 3(b) and Figure 3(c) are two such paraphrases which can be converted to Figure 3(d) as described in §3.2.

For a given input question, first we build ungrounded graphs from its paraphrases. We convert these graphs to Freebase graphs. To learn this mapping, we rely on manually assembled question-answer pairs. For each training question, we first find the set of *oracle* grounded graphs—Freebase subgraphs which when executed yield the correct answer—derivable from the question's ungrounded graphs. These oracle graphs are then used to train a structured perceptron model. These steps are discussed in detail below.

3.1 Ungrounded Graphs from Paraphrases

We use GRAPHPARSER (Reddy et al., 2014) to convert paraphrases to ungrounded graphs. This conversion involves three steps: 1) parsing the paraphrase using a CCG parser to extract syntactic derivations (Lewis and Steedman, 2014), 2) extracting logical forms from the CCG derivations (Bos et al., 2004), and 3) converting the logical forms to an ungrounded graph.[8] The ungrounded graph for the example question and its paraphrases are shown in Figure 3(a), Figure 3(b) and Figure 3(c), respectively.

3.2 Grounded Graphs from Ungrounded Graphs

The ungrounded graphs are grounded to Freebase subgraphs by mapping entity nodes, entity-entity edges and entity type nodes in the ungrounded graph to Freebase entities, relations and types, respectively. For example, the graph in Figure 3(b) can be converted to a Freebase graph in Figure 3(d) by replacing the entity node *Czech Republic* with the Freebase entity CZECHRE-PUBLIC, the edge *(speak.arg$_2$, speak.in)* between x and *Czech Republic* with the Freebase relation *(location.country.official_language.2, location.country.official_language.1)*, the type node *language* with the Freebase type *language.human_language*, and the TARGET node remains intact. The rest of the nodes, edges and types are grounded to *null*. In a similar fashion, Figure 3(c) can be grounded to Figure 3(d), but not Figure 3(a) to Figure 3(d). If no paraphrase is isomorphic to the target grounded grounded graph, our grounding fails.

3.3 Learning

We use a linear model to map ungrounded graphs to grounded ones. The parameters of the model are learned from question-answer pairs. For example, the question *What language do people in Czech Republic speak?* paired with its answer {CZECHLANGUAGE}. In line with most work on question answering against Freebase, we do not rely on annotated logical forms associated with the question for training and treat the mapping of a question to its grounded graph as latent.

---

[8]Please see Reddy et al. (2014) for more details.

157

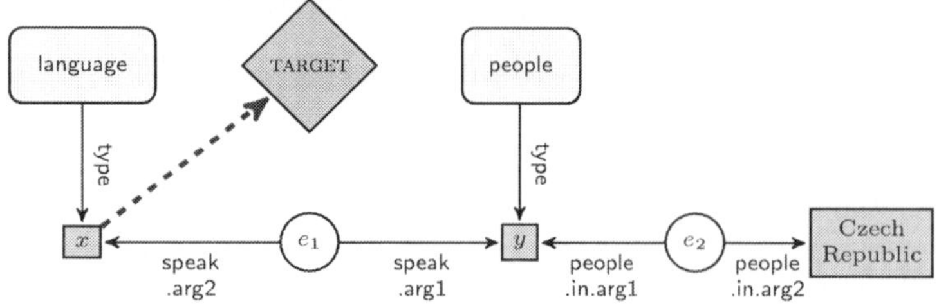
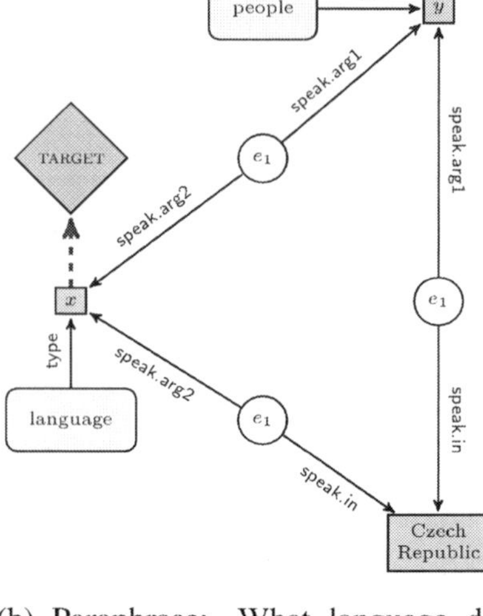

(a) Input sentence: What language do people in Czech Republic speak?

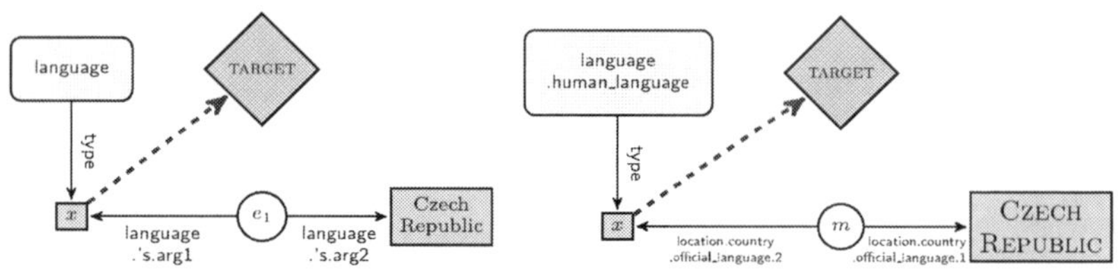
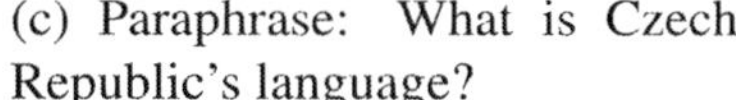

(c) Paraphrase: What is Czech Republic's language?

(d) Freebase grounded graph

(b) Paraphrase: What language do people speak in Czech Republic?

Figure 3: Ungrounded graphs for an input question and its paraphrases along with its correct grounded graph. The green squares indicate NL or Freebase entities, the yellow rectangles indicate unary NL predicates or Freebase types, the circles indicate NL or Freebase events, the edge labels indicate binary NL predicates or Freebase relations, and the red diamonds attach to the entity of interest (the answer to the question).

Let q be a question, let p be a paraphrase, let u be an ungrounded graph for p, and let g be a grounded graph formed by grounding the nodes and edges of u to the knowledge base $\mathcal{K}$ (throughout we use Freebase as the knowledge base). Following Reddy et al. (2014), we use beam search to find the highest scoring tuple of paraphrase, ungrounded and grounded graphs $(\hat{p}, \hat{u}, \hat{g})$ under the model $\theta \in \mathbb{R}^n$:

$$(\hat{p}, \hat{u}, \hat{g}) = \arg\max_{(p,u,g)} \theta \cdot \Phi(p, u, g, q, \mathcal{K}),$$

where $\Phi(p, u, g, q, \mathcal{K}) \in \mathbb{R}^n$ denotes the features for the tuple of paraphrase, ungrounded and grounded graphs. The feature function has access to the paraphrase, ungrounded and grounded graphs, the original question, as well as to the content of the knowledge base and the denotation $|g|_\mathcal{K}$ (the denotation of a grounded graph is defined as the set of entities or attributes reachable at its TARGET node). See §4.3 for the features employed. The model parameters are estimated with the averaged structured perceptron (Collins, 2002). Given a training question-answer pair $(q, \mathcal{A})$, the update is:

$$\theta^{t+1} \leftarrow \theta^t + \Phi(p^+, u^+, g^+, q, \mathcal{K}) - \Phi(\hat{p}, \hat{u}, \hat{g}, q, \mathcal{K}),$$

where (p^+, u^+, g^+) denotes the tuple of gold paraphrase, gold ungrounded and grounded graphs for

q. Since we do not have direct access to the gold paraphrase and graphs, we instead rely on the set of *oracle tuples*, $\mathcal{O}_{\mathcal{K},\mathcal{A}}(q)$, as a proxy:

$$(p^+, u^+, g^+) = \arg\max_{(p,u,g) \in \mathcal{O}_{\mathcal{K},\mathcal{A}}(q)} \theta \cdot \Phi(p, u, g, q, \mathcal{K}),$$

where $\mathcal{O}_{\mathcal{K},\mathcal{A}}(q)$ is defined as the set of tuples (p, u, g) derivable from the question q, whose denotation $|g|_\mathcal{K}$ has minimal F_1-loss against the gold answer $\mathcal{A}$. We find the oracle graphs for each question a priori by performing beam-search with a very large beam.

4 Experimental Setup

Below, we give details on the evaluation dataset and baselines used for comparison. We also describe the model features and provide implementation details.

4.1 Evaluation Data and Metric

We evaluate our approach on the WebQuestions dataset (Berant et al., 2013). WebQuestions consists of 5,810 question-answer pairs where questions represents real Google search queries. We use the standard train/test splits, with 3,778 train and 2,032 test questions. For our development experiments we tune the models on held-out data consisting of 30% training questions, while for final testing we use the complete training data. We use average precision (avg P.), average recall (avg R.) and average F_1 (avg F_1) proposed by Berant et al. (2013) as evaluation metrics.[9]

4.2 Baselines

ORIGINAL We use GRAPHPARSER without paraphrases as our baseline. This gives an idea about the impact of using paraphrases.

MT We compare our paraphrasing models with monolingual machine translation based model for paraphrase generation (Quirk et al., 2004; Wubben et al., 2010). In particular, we use Moses (Koehn et al., 2007) to train a monolingual phrase-based MT system on the Paralex corpus. Finally, we use Moses decoder to generate 10-best distinct paraphrases for the test questions.

4.3 Implementation Details

Entity Resolution For WebQuestions, we use 8 handcrafted part-of-speech patterns (e.g., the pattern `(DT)?(JJ.?|NN.?){0,2}NN.?` matches the noun phrase *the big lebowski*) to identify candidate named entity mention spans. We use the Stanford CoreNLP caseless tagger for part-of-speech tagging (Manning et al., 2014). For each candidate mention span, we retrieve the top 10 entities according to the Freebase API.[10] We then create a lattice in which the nodes correspond to mention-entity pairs, scored by their Freebase API scores, and the edges encode the fact that no joint assignment of entities to mentions can contain overlapping spans. We take the top 10 paths through the lattice as possible entity disambiguations. For each possibility, we generate n-best paraphrases that contains the entity mention spans. In the end, this process creates a total of $10n$ paraphrases. We generate ungrounded graphs for these paraphrases and treat the final entity disambiguation and paraphrase selection as part of the semantic parsing problem.[11]

GRAPHPARSER Features. We use the features from Reddy et al. (2014). These include edge alignments and stem overlaps between ungrounded and grounded graphs, and contextual features such as word and grounded relation pairs. In addition to these features, we add two new real-valued features – the paraphrase classifier's score and the entity disambiguation lattice score.

Beam Search We use beam search to infer the highest scoring graph pair for a question. The search operates over entity-entity edges and entity type nodes of each ungrounded graph. For an entity-entity edge, there are two operations: ground the edge to a Freebase relation, or skip the edge. Similarly, for an entity type node, there are two operations: ground the node to a Freebase type, or skip the node. We use a beam size of 100 in all our experiments.

5 Results and Discussion

In this section, we present results from five different systems for our question-answering experiments: ORIGINAL, MT, NAIVE, PPDB and BILAYERED. First two are baseline systems. Other three systems use paraphrases generated from an L-PCFG grammar. NAIVE uses a word lattice with a single start-to-end path representing the input question itself, PPDB uses a word lattice constructed using the PPDB rules, and BILAYERED uses bi-layered L-PCFG to build word lattices. Note that NAIVE does not require any parallel resource to train, PPDB requires an external paraphrase database, and BILAYERED, like MT, needs a parallel corpus with paraphrase pairs. We tune our classifier features and GRAPHPARSER features on the development data. We use the best setting from tuning for evaluation on the test data.

Results on the Development Set Table 1 shows the results with our best settings on the development data. We found that oracle scores improve significantly with paraphrases. ORIGINAL achieves an oracle score of 65.1 whereas with paraphrases we achieve an F_1 greater than 70 across all the models. This shows that with paraphrases we eliminate substantial mismatch between Freebase and ungrounded graphs. This trend continues for the final prediction with the paraphrasing models performing better than the ORIGINAL.

---

[9] `https://github.com/percyliang/sempre/blob/master/scripts/evaluation.py`

[10] `http://developers.google.com/freebase/`

[11] To generate ungrounded graphs for a paraphrase, we treat each entity mention as a single word.

All our proposed paraphrasing models beat the MT baseline. Even the NAIVE model which does not use any parallel or external resource surpass the MT baseline in the final prediction. Upon error analysis, we found that the MT model produce too similar paraphrases, mostly with only inflectional variations. For the question *What language do people in Czech Republic speak*, the top ten paraphrases produced by MT are mostly formed by replacing words *language* with *languages*, do with *does*, *people* with *person* and *speak* with *speaks*. These paraphrases do not address the structural mismatch problem. In contrast, our grammar based models generate syntactically diverse paraphrases.

Our PPDB model performs best across the paraphrase models (avg F_1 = 47.9). We attribute its success to the high quality paraphrase rules from the external paraphrase database. For the BILAYERD model we found 1,000 latent semantic states is not sufficient for modeling topical differences. Though MT competes with NAIVE and BILAYERED, the performance of NAIVE is highly encouraging since it does not require any parallel corpus. Furthermore, we observe that the MT model has larger search space. The number of oracle graphs – the number of ways in which one can produce the correct Freebase grounding from the ungrounded graphs of the given question and its paraphrases – is higher for MT (77.2) than the grammar-based models (50–60).

Results on the Test Set Table 2 shows our final results on the test data. We get similar results on the test data as we reported on the development data. Again, the PPDB model performs best with an F_1 score of 47.7. The baselines, ORIGINAL and MT, lag with scores of 45.0 and 47.1, respectively. We also present the results of existing literature on this dataset. Among these, Berant and Liang (2014) also uses paraphrasing but unlike ours it is based on a template grammar (containing 8 grammar rules) and requires logical forms beforehand to generate paraphrases. Our PPDB outperforms Berant and Liang's model by 7.8 F_1 points. Yih et al. (2015) and Xu et al. (2016) use neural network models for semantic parsing, in addition to using sophisticated entity resolution (Yang and Chang, 2015) and a very large unsupervised corpus as additional training data. Note that we use GRAPHPARSER as our semantic parsing

Method	avg oracle F_1	# oracle graphs	avg F_1
ORIGINAL	65.1	11.0	44.7
MT	71.5	77.2	47.0
NAIVE	71.2	53.6	47.5
PPDB	71.8	59.8	47.9
BILAYERED	71.6	55.0	47.1

Table 1: Oracle statistics and results on the WebQuestions development set.

Method	avg P.	avg R.	avg F_1
Berant and Liang '14	40.5	46.6	39.9
Bast and Haussmann '15	49.8	60.4	49.4
Berant and Liang '15	50.4	55.7	49.7
Reddy et al. '16	49.0	61.1	50.3
Yih et al. '15	52.8	60.7	52.5
Xu et al. '16	53.1	65.5	53.3
This paper			
ORIGINAL	53.2	54.2	45.0
MT	48.0	56.9	47.1
NAIVE	48.1	57.7	47.2
PPDB	48.4	58.1	47.7
BILAYERED	47.0	57.6	47.2

Table 2: Results on WebQuestions test dataset.

framework for evaluating our paraphrases extrinsically. We leave plugging our paraphrases to other existing methods and other tasks for future work.

Error Analysis The upper bound of our paraphrasing methods is in the range of 71.2–71.8. We examine the reason where we lose the rest. For the PPDB model, the majority (78.4%) of the errors are partially correct answers occurring due to incomplete gold answer annotations or partially correct groundings. Note that the partially correct groundings may include incorrect paraphrases. 13.5% are due to mismatch between Freebase and the paraphrases produced, and the rest (8.1%) are due to wrong entity annotations.

6 Conclusion

We described a grammar method to generate paraphrases for questions, and applied it to a question answering system based on semantic parsing. We showed that using paraphrases for a question answering system is a useful way to improve its performance. Our method is rather generic and can be applied to any question answering system.

Acknowledgements

The authors would like to thank Nitin Madnani for his help with the implementation of the paraphrase classifier. We would like to thank our anonymous reviewers for their insightful comments. This research was supported by an EPSRC grant (EP/L02411X/1), the H2020 project SUMMA (under grant agreement 688139), and a Google PhD Fellowship for the second author.

References

Regina Barzilay and Lillian Lee. 2003. Learning to paraphrase: An unsupervised approach using multiple-sequence alignment. In *Proceedings of NAACL-HLT*.

Hannah Bast and Elmar Haussmann. 2015. More accurate question answering on Freebase. In *Proceedings of CIKM*.

Jonathan Berant and Percy Liang. 2014. Semantic parsing via paraphrasing. In *Proceedings of ACL*.

Jonathan Berant and Percy Liang. 2015. Imitation learning of agenda-based semantic parsers. *Transactions of the Association for Computational Linguistics*, 3:545–558.

Jonathan Berant, Andrew Chou, Roy Frostig, and Percy Liang. 2013. Semantic parsing on Freebase from question-answer pairs. In *Proceedings of EMNLP*.

Johan Bos, Stephen Clark, Mark Steedman, James R. Curran, and Julia Hockenmaier. 2004. Wide-coverage semantic representations from a CCG parser. In *Proceedings of COLING*.

Eugene Charniak and Mark Johnson. 2005. Coarse-to-fine n-best parsing and maxent discriminative reranking. In *Proceedings of ACL*.

David L. Chen and Raymond J. Mooney. 2011. Learning to interpret natural language navigation instructions from observations. In *Proceedings of AAAI*.

Shay B. Cohen, Karl Stratos, Michael Collins, Dean P. Foster, and Lyle Ungar. 2013. Experiments with spectral learning of latent-variable PCFGs. In *Proceedings of NAACL*.

Michael Collins. 2002. Discriminative training methods for hidden markov models: Theory and experiments with perceptron algorithms. In *Proceedings of EMNLP*.

Pablo Ariel Duboue and Jennifer Chu-Carroll. 2006. Answering the question you wish they had asked: The impact of paraphrasing for question answering. In *Proceedings of NAACL-HLT*.

Anthony Fader, Luke Zettlemoyer, and Oren Etzioni. 2013. Paraphrase-driven learning for open question answering. In *Proceedings of ACL*.

Juri Ganitkevitch, Benjamin Van Durme, and Chris Callison-Burch. 2013. PPDB: The Paraphrase Database. In *Proceedings of NAACL-HLT*.

Mark Hall, Eibe Frank, Geoffrey Holmes, Bernhard Pfahringer, Peter Reutemann, and Ian H Witten. 2009. The WEKA data mining software: An update. *ACM SIGKDD Explorations Newsletter*, 11(1):10–18.

Martin Kay. 1996. Chart generation. In *Proceedings of ACL*.

Philipp Koehn, Hieu Hoang, Alexandra Birch, Chris Callison-Burch, Marcello Federico, Nicola Bertoldi, Brooke Cowan, Wade Shen, Christine Moran, Richard Zens, Chris Dyer, Ondřej Bojar, Alexandra Constantin, and Evan Herbst. 2007. Moses: Open source toolkit for statistical machine translation. In *Proceedings of ACL*.

Alexander Koller and Kristina Striegnitz. 2002. Generation as dependency parsing. In *Proceedings of ACL*.

Jayant Krishnamurthy and Tom Mitchell. 2012. Weakly supervised training of semantic parsers. In *Proceedings of EMNLP*.

Tom Kwiatkowski, Eunsol Choi, Yoav Artzi, and Luke Zettlemoyer. 2013. Scaling semantic parsers with on-the-fly ontology matching. In *Proceedings of EMNLP*.

Irene Langkilde and Kevin Knight. 1998. Generation that exploits corpus-based statistical knowledge. In *Proceedings of ACL-COLING*.

Mike Lewis and Mark Steedman. 2014. A* CCG parsing with a supertag-factored model. In *Proceedings of EMNLP*.

Nitin Madnani, Joel Tetreault, and Martin Chodorow. 2012. Re-examining machine translation metrics for paraphrase identification. In *Proceedings of NAACL-HLT*.

Christopher D. Manning, Mihai Surdeanu, John Bauer, Jenny Finkel, Steven J. Bethard, and David McClosky. 2014. The Stanford CoreNLP natural language processing toolkit. In *Proceedings of ACL*.

Takuya Matsuzaki, Yusuke Miyao, and Jun'ichi Tsujii. 2005. Probabilistic CFG with latent annotations. In *Proceedings of ACL*.

Cynthia Matuszek, Nicholas FitzGerald, Luke Zettlemoyer, Liefeng Bo, and Dieter Fox. 2012. A joint model of language and perception for grounded attribute learning. In *Proceedings of ICML*.

Jeff Mitchell and Mark Steedman. 2015. Orthogonality of syntax and semantics within distributional spaces. In *Proceedings of ACL*.

Shashi Narayan and Shay B. Cohen. 2015. Diversity in spectral learning for natural language parsing. In *Proceedings of EMNLP*.

Shashi Narayan and Shay B. Cohen. 2016. Optimizing spectral learning for parsing. In *Proceedings of ACL*.

Shashi Narayan and Claire Gardent. 2012. Structure-driven lexicalist generation. In *Proceedings of COLING*.

Bo Pang, Kevin Knight, and Daniel Marcu. 2003. Syntax-based alignment of multiple translations: Extracting paraphrases and generating new sentences. In *Proceedings of NAACL-HLT*.

Slav Petrov, Leon Barrett, Romain Thibaux, and Dan Klein. 2006. Learning accurate, compact, and interpretable tree annotation. In *Proceedings of COLING-ACL*.

Detlef Prescher. 2005. Head-driven pcfgs with latent-head statistics. In *Proceedings of IWPT*.

Chris Quirk, Chris Brockett, and William B. Dolan. 2004. Monolingual machine translation for paraphrase generation. In *Proceedings of EMNLP*.

Siva Reddy, Mirella Lapata, and Mark Steedman. 2014. Large-scale semantic parsing without question-answer pairs. *Transactions of the Association for Computational Linguistics*, 2:377–392.

Siva Reddy, Oscar Täckström, Michael Collins, Tom Kwiatkowski, Dipanjan Das, Mark Steedman, and Mirella Lapata. 2016. Transforming Dependency Structures to Logical Forms for Semantic Parsing. *Transactions of the Association for Computational Linguistics*, 4:127–140.

Stefan Riezler, Alexander Vasserman, Ioannis Tsochantaridis, Vibhu Mittal, and Yi Liu. 2007. Statistical machine translation for query expansion in answer retrieval. In *Proceedings of ACL*.

Stuart M. Shieber, Gertjan van Noord, Fernando C. N. Pereira, and Robert C. Moore. 1990. Semantic head-driven generation. *Computational Linguistics*, 16(1):30–42.

Stuart M. Shieber. 1988. A uniform architecture for parsing and generation. In *Proceedings of COLING*.

Yushi Wang, Jonathan Berant, and Percy Liang. 2015. Building a semantic parser overnight. In *Proceedings of ACL*.

Michael White. 2004. Reining in ccg chart realization. In Anja Belz, Roger Evans, and Paul Piwek, editors, *Natural Language Generation*, volume 3123 of *Lecture Notes in Computer Science*, pages 182–191. Springer Berlin Heidelberg.

Yuk Wah Wong and Raymond J. Mooney. 2006. Learning for semantic parsing with statistical machine translation. In *Proceedings of NAACL*.

Sander Wubben, Antal van den Bosch, and Emiel Krahmer. 2010. Paraphrase generation as monolingual translation: Data and evaluation. In *Proceedings of INLG*.

Kun Xu, Siva Reddy, Yansong Feng, Songfang Huang, and Dongyan Zhao. 2016. Question Answering on Freebase via Relation Extraction and Textual Evidence. In *Proceedings of ACL*.

Yi Yang and Ming-Wei Chang. 2015. S-MART: Novel tree-based structured learning algorithms applied to tweet entity linking. In *Proceedings of ACL*.

Wen-tau Yih, Ming-Wei Chang, Xiaodong He, and Jianfeng Gao. 2015. Semantic parsing via staged query graph generation: Question answering with knowledge base. In *Proceedings of ACL*.

Luke S. Zettlemoyer and Michael Collins. 2005. Learning to map sentences to logical form: Structured classification with probabilistic categorial grammars. In *Proceedings of UAI*.

The WebNLG Challenge: Generating Text from DBPedia Data

Emilie Colin[1] **Claire Gardent**[1] **Yassine M'rabet**[2] **Shashi Narayan**[3] **Laura Perez-Beltrachini**[1]
[1] CNRS/LORIA and Université de Lorraine, Nancy, France
`{emilie.colin,claire.gardent,laura.perez}@loria.fr`
[2] National Library of Medicine, Bethesda, USA
`yassine.m'rabet@nih.gov`
[3] School of Informatics, University of Edinburgh, UK
`snaraya2@inf.ed.ac.uk`

1 Introduction

With the emergence of the linked data initiative and the rapid development of RDF (Resource Description Format) datasets, several approaches have recently been proposed for generating text from RDF data (Sun and Mellish, 2006; Duma and Klein, 2013; Bontcheva and Wilks, 2004; Cimiano et al., 2013; Lebret et al., 2016). To support the evaluation and comparison of such systems, we propose a shared task on generating text from DBPedia data. The training data will consist of Data/Text pairs where the data is a set of triples extracted from DBPedia and the text is a verbalisation of these triples. In essence, the task consists in mapping data to text. Specific subtasks include sentence segmentation (how to chunk the input data into sentences), lexicalisation (of the DBPedia properties), aggregation (how to avoid repetitions) and surface realisation (how to build a syntactically correct and natural sounding text).

2 Context and Motivation

DBPedia is a multilingual knowledge base that was built from various kinds of structured information contained in Wikipedia (Mendes et al., 2012). This data is stored as RDF triples of the form (SUBJECT, PROPERTY, OBJECT) where the subject is a URI (Uniform Resource Identifier), the property is a binary relation and the object is either a URI or a literal value such as a string, a date or a number. The English version of the DBpedia knowledge base currently encompasses 6.2M entities, 739 classes, 1,099 properties with reference values and 1,596 properties with typed literal values.[1]

There are several motivations for generating text from DBPedia.

First, the RDF language in which DBPedia is encoded is widely used within the Linked Data framework. Many large scale datasets are encoded in this language (e.g., MusicBrainz[2], FOAF[3], LinkedGeoData[4]) and official institutions[5] increasingly publish their data in this format. Being able to generate good quality text from RDF data would permit e.g., making this data more accessible to lay users, enriching existing text with information drawn from knowledge bases such as DBPedia or describing, comparing and relating entities present in these knowledge bases.

Second, RDF data, and in particular, DBPedia, provide a framework that is both limited and arbitrarily extensible from a linguistic point of view. In the simplest case, the goal would be to verbalise a single triple. In that case, the task mainly consists in finding an appropriate *"lexicalisation"* for the property. The complexity of the generation task can be closely monitored however by increasing the number of input triples, using input with different shapes[6], working with different semantic domains and/or enriching the RDF graphs with additional

---

[1] `http://wiki.dbpedia.org/`
`dbpedia-dataset-version-2015-10`

[2] `https://musicbrainz.org/`

[3] `http://www.foaf-project.org/`

[4] `http://linkedgeodata.org/`

[5] See `http://museum-api.pbworks.com` for examples.

[6] DBPedia data forms a graph. Different graph shapes induce different verbalisation structures.

(e.g., discourse) information. We plan to produce a dataset which varies along at least some of these dimensions so as to provide a benchmark for generation that will test systems on input of various complexity.

Third, there has been much work recently on applying deep learning (in particular, sequence to sequence) models to generation. The training data used by these approaches however often have limited variability. For instance, (Wen et al., 2015)'s data is restricted to restaurant descriptions and (Lebret et al., 2016)'s to WikiData frames. Typically the number of attributes (property) considered by these approaches is very low (between 15 and 40) and the text to be produced have a stereotyped structure (restaurant description, biographic abstracts). By providing a more varied dataset, the WebNLG data-text corpus will permit investigating how such deep learning models perform on more varied and more linguistically complex data.

3   Task Description

In essence, the task consists in mapping data to text. Specific subtasks include sentence segmentation (how to chunk the input data into sentences), lexicalisation (of the DBPedia properties), aggregation (how to avoid repetitions) and surface realisation (how to build a syntactically correct and natural sounding text). The following example illustrates this.

(1)   a. Data: (JOHN_E_BLAHA BIRTHDATE 1942_08_26)
          (JOHN_E_BLAHA BIRTHPLACE SAN_ANTONIO)
          (JOHN_E_BLAHA OCCUPATION FIGHTER_PILOT)

      b. Text: *John E Blaha, born in San Antonio on 1942-08-26, worked as a fighter pilot*

Given the input shown in (1a), generating (1b) involves lexicalising the OCCUPATION property as the phrase *worked as*, using PP coordination (*born in San Antonio on 1942-08-26*) to avoid repeating the word *born* (aggregation) and verbalising the 3 triples by a single complex sentence including an apposition, a PP coordination and a transitive verb construction (sentence segmentation and surface realisation).

Relation to Previous Shared Tasks   Other NLG shared task evaluation challenges have been organised in the past. These have focused on different generation subtasks overlapping with the task we

propose but our task differs from them in various ways.

KBGen generation challenge. The recent KBGen (Banik et al., 2013) task focused on sentence generation from Knowledge Bases (KB). In particular, the task was organised around the AURA (Gunning et al., 2010) KB on the biological domain which models n-ary relations. The input data selection process targets the extraction of KB fragments which could be verbalised as a single sentence. The content selection approach was semi-automatic, starting with the manual selection of a set of KB fragments. Then, using patterns derived from those fragments, a new set of candidate KB fragments was generated which was finally manually revised. The verbalisation of the sentence sized KB fragments was generated by human subjects.

Although our task also concerns text generation from KBs the definition of the task is different. Our proposal aims at the generation of text beyond sentences and thus involves an additional subtask that is sentence segmentation. The tasks also differ on the KBs used, we propose using DBPedia which facilitates changing the domain by focusing on different categories. Moreover, the set of relations on both KBs pose different challenges for generation, while the AURA KB contains n-ary relations DBPedia contains relations names challenging for the lexicalisation subtask. A last difference with our task is the content selection method. Our method is completely automatic and thus permits the inexpensive generation of a large benchmark. Moreover, it can be used to select content ranging from a single triple to several triples and with different shapes.

The Surface Realisation Shared Task (SR'11). The major goal of the SR'11 task (Belz et al., 2011) was to provide a common ground for the comparison of surface realisers on the task of regenerating sentences in a treebank. Two different tracks are considered with different input representations. The 'shallow' input provides a dependency tree of the sentence to be generated and the 'deep' input provides a graph representation where syntactic dependencies have been replaced by semantic roles and some function words have been removed.

The focus of the SR'11 task was on the linguistic realisation subtask and the broad coverage of linguistic phenomena. The task we propose here starts from non-linguistic KB data and puts forward other NLG subtasks.

Generating Referring Expressions (GRE). The GRE shared tasks pioneered the proposed NLG challenges. The first shared task has only focused on the selection of distinguishing attributes (Belz and Gatt, 2007) while subsequent tasks have considered the referring expression realisation subtask proposing a complete referring expression generation task (Gatt et al., 2008; Gatt et al., 2009). This tasks aimed at the unique identification of the referent and brevity of the referring expression. Slightly different, the GREC challenges (Belz et al., 2008; Belz et al., 2009; Belz et al., 2010) propose the generation of referring expressions in a discourse context. The GREC tasks use a corpus created from Wikipedia abstracts on geographic entities and people and with two referring expression annotation schemes, reference type and word strings. Rather than generating from data input these tasks consist in labelling underspecified referring expressions in a given text.

Our task concerns the generation of entity descriptions and requires the production of referring expressions, specially in the cases where multiple sentences will be generated. However, it does not foresee the selection of additional content (e.g. attributes). In contrast, our proposal targets all generation subtasks involved in content realisation.

4   Data

As illustrated in Example 1 above, the training corpus consists of (D, T) pairs such that D is a set of DBPedia triples and T is an English text (possibly consisting of a single sentence). This corpus will be constructed in two steps by first, extracting from DBPedia content units that are both coherent and diverse and second, associating these content units with English text verbalising their content.

Data   To extract content units from DBPedia, we will use the content selection procedure sketched in (Mohammed et al., 2016). This procedure consists of two steps. First, bigram models of DBPedia properties specific to a given DBPedia category (e.g., Astronaut) are learned from the DBPedia graphs associated with entities of that category. Second, an ILP program is used to extract from DBPedia, subtrees that maximise bigram probability. In effect, the extracted DBPedia trees are coherent entity descriptions in that the property bigram they contain often cooccur together in the DBPedia graphs associated with entities of a given DBPedia category. The method can be parameterised to produce content units for different DBPedia categories, different DBPedia entities and various numbers of DBPedia triples. It is fully automatic and permit producing DBPedia graphs that are both coherent, diverse and that bear on different domains (e.g., Astronauts, Universities, Musical work).

Text   To associate the DBPedia trees extracted in the first phase with text, we will combine automatic techniques with crowdsourcing in two ways.

First, we will lexicalise DBPedia properties by using the lexicalisations contained in the Lemon English Lexicon for DBPedia[7](Walter et al., 2013; Walter et al., 2014a; Walter et al., 2014b) and by manually filtering the lexicalisations produced by the lexicalisation method described in (Perez-Beltrachini and Gardent, 2016) and by the relation extraction and clustering method described in (c.f. (Nakashole et al., 2012))[8]. We will then ask crowdsourcers to verbalise sets of DBPEdia triples in which properties have already been lexicalised (e.g., CREW1UP will be lexicalised as *commander of*).

Second, we will exploit the data-to-text alignment method presented in (Mrabet et al., 2016) to semi-automatically align Wikipedia text with sets of DBPedia triples. The method consists in (i) automatically annotating phrases with DBPedia entities, (ii) associating sentences with DBPedia triples relating entities annotating these sentences and (iii) using crowdsourcing to align sentences with triples. In the third step, annotators are asked to "align" triples and sentences that is, to remove from the sentence all material that is irrelevant to express the associated triples and vice versa, to remove any triples that is not expressed by the sentence.

Statistics, Schedule and Funding   The WebNLG shared task will be funded by the WebNLG ANR

---

[7]http://lemon-model.net/lexica/dbpedia_en/

[8]https://d5gate.ag5.mpi-sb.mpg.de/pattyweb/

Project[9]. We aim to produce a data-text corpus of medium size (between 10K and 50K data-text pairs) bearing on at least 5 different domains and consisting of input data containing between 2 and 5 RDF triples. Ideally, training data will be made available early in 2017 and testing will be carried out in early summer (May-June 2017).

5 Evaluation

Evaluation of the generated texts will be done both with automatic evaluation metrics (BLEU, TER or/and METEOR) and using human judgements obtained through crowdsourcing. The human evaluation will seek to assess such criteria as fluency, grammaticality and appropriateness (does the text correctly verbalise the input data?).

Acknowledgments

We thank the French National Research Agency for funding the research presented in this paper in the context of the WebNLG project[10].

References

Eva Banik, Claire Gardent, and Eric Kow. 2013. The kbgen challenge. In *the 14th European Workshop on Natural Language Generation (ENLG)*, pages 94–97.

Anja Belz and Albert Gatt. 2007. The attribute selection for gre challenge: Overview and evaluation results. *Proceedings of UCNLG+ MT: Language Generation and Machine Translation*, pages 75–83.

Anja Belz, Eric Kow, Jette Viethen, and Albert Gatt. 2008. The grec challenge: Overview and evaluation results.

Anja Belz, Eric Kow, and Jette Viethen. 2009. The grec named entity generation challenge 2009: overview and evaluation results. In *Proceedings of the 2009 Workshop on Language Generation and Summarisation*, pages 88–98. Association for Computational Linguistics.

Anja Belz, Eric Kow, Jette Viethen, and Albert Gatt. 2010. Generating referring expressions in context: The grec task evaluation challenges. In *Empirical methods in natural language generation*, pages 294–327. Springer.

Anja Belz, Michael White, Dominic Espinosa, Eric Kow, Deirdre Hogan, and Amanda Stent. 2011. The first surface realisation shared task: Overview and evaluation results. In *Proceedings of the 13th European Workshop on Natural Language Generation*, ENLG '11, pages 217–226, Stroudsburg, PA, USA. Association for Computational Linguistics.

Kalina Bontcheva and Yorick Wilks. 2004. Automatic report generation from ontologies: the miakt approach. In *International Conference on Application of Natural Language to Information Systems*, pages 324–335. Springer.

Philipp Cimiano, Janna Lüker, David Nagel, and Christina Unger. 2013. Exploiting ontology lexica for generating natural language texts from rdf data. In *Proceedings of the 14th European Workshop on Natural Language Generation*, pages 10–19.

Daniel Duma and Ewan Klein. 2013. Generating natural language from linked data: Unsupervised template extraction. *Association for Computational Linguistics, Potsdam, Germany*, pages 83–94.

Albert Gatt, Anja Belz, and Eric Kow. 2008. The tuna challenge 2008: Overview and evaluation results. In *Proceedings of the Fifth International Natural Language Generation Conference*, pages 198–206. Association for Computational Linguistics.

Albert Gatt, Anja Belz, and Eric Kow. 2009. The tunareg challenge 2009: Overview and evaluation results. In *Proceedings of the 12th European Workshop on Natural Language Generation*, pages 174–182. Association for Computational Linguistics.

David Gunning, Vinay K. Chaudhri, Peter Clark, Ken Barker, Shaw-Yi Chaw, Mark Greaves, Benjamin Grosof, Alice Leung, David McDonald, Sunil Mishra, John Pacheco, Bruce Porter, Aaron Spaulding, Dan Tecuci, and Jing Tien. 2010. Project Halo Update – Progress toward digital aristotle. *AI Magazine*, Fall.

Rémi Lebret, David Grangier, and Michael Auli. 2016. Generating text from structured data with application to the biography domain. *CoRR*, abs/1603.07771.

Pablo N Mendes, Max Jakob, and Christian Bizer. 2012. Dbpedia: A multilingual cross-domain knowledge base. In *LREC*, pages 1813–1817. Citeseer.

Rania Mohammed, Laura Perez-Beltrachini, and Claire Gardent. 2016. Category-driven content selection. In *Proceedings of the nintth International Natural Language Generation Conference*, INLG 2016.

Yassine Mrabet, Pavlos Vougiouklis, Halil Kilicoglu, Claire Gardent, Dina DemnerFushman, Jonathon Hare, and Elena Simperl. 2016. Aligning texts and knowledge bases with semantic sentence simplification. In *Proceedings of the 2nd International Workshop on Natural Language Generation and the Semantic Web*.

---

[9] http://talc1.loria.fr/webnlg/stories/about.html

[10] http://talc1.loria.fr/webnlg/stories/about.html

Ndapandula Nakashole, Gerhard Weikum, and Fabian Suchanek. 2012. Discovering and exploring relations on the web. *Proceedings of the VLDB Endowment*, 5(12):1982–1985.

Laura Perez-Beltrachini and Claire Gardent. 2016. Learning embeddings to lexicalise rdf properties. In *Proceedings of the Fifth Joint Conference on Lexical and Computational Semantics*.

Xiantang Sun and Chris Mellish. 2006. Domain independent sentence generation from rdf representations for the semantic web. In *Combined Workshop on Language-Enabled Educational Technology and Development and Evaluation of Robust Spoken Dialogue Systems, European Conference on AI, Riva del Garda, Italy*.

Sebastian Walter, Christina Unger, and Philipp Cimiano. 2013. A corpus-based approach for the induction of ontology lexica. In *Natural Language Processing and Information Systems*, pages 102–113. Springer.

Sebastian Walter, Christina Unger, and Philipp Cimiano. 2014a. Atolla framework for the automatic induction of ontology lexica. *Data & Knowledge Engineering*, 94:148–162.

Sebastian Walter, Christina Unger, and Philipp Cimiano. 2014b. M-atoll: a framework for the lexicalization of ontologies in multiple languages. In *The Semantic Web–ISWC 2014*, pages 472–486. Springer.

Tsung-Hsien Wen, Milica Gasic, Nikola Mrkšić, Pei-Hao Su, David Vandyke, and Steve Young. 2015. Semantically conditioned lstm-based natural language generation for spoken dialogue systems. In *Proceedings of the 2015 Conference on Empirical Methods in Natural Language Processing*, pages 1711–1721, Lisbon, Portugal, September. Association for Computational Linguistics.

The aNALoGuE Challenge: Non Aligned Language GEneration

Jekaterina Novikova and **Verena Rieser**
The Interaction Lab, Heriot-Watt University, Edinburgh, UK
`j.novikova,v.t.rieser@hw.ac.uk`

Abstract

We propose a shared task based on recent advances in learning to generate natural language from meaning representations using semantically unaligned data. The aNALoGuE challenge aims to evaluate and compare recent corpus-based methods with respect to their scalability to data size and target complexity, as well as to assess predictive quality of automatic evaluation metrics.

1 Relevance

Natural language generation plays a critical role for Conversational Agents (CAs) as it has a significant impact on a users impression of the system. Most CAs utilise domain-dependent methods including hand-written grammars or domain-specific language templates for surface realisation, both of which are costly to develop and maintain. Recent corpus-based methods hold the promise of being easily portable across domains, e.g. (Angeli et al., 2010; Konstas and Lapata, 2012; Mairesse and Young, 2014), but require high quality training data consisting of meaning representations (MR) paired with natural language (NL) utterances, augmented by alignments between elements of meaning representation and natural language words. Creating aligned data is a non-trivial task in its own right, see e.g. (Liang et al., 2009). This shared task aims to strengthen recent research on corpus-based NLG from unaligned data, e.g. (Dušek and Jurcicek, 2015; Wen et al., 2015; Mei et al., 2015; Sharma et al., 2016). These approaches do not require costly semantic alignment, but are based on parallel data sets, which can

be collected in sufficient quality and quantity using effective crowd-sourcing techniques (Novikova and Rieser, 2016), and as such open the door for rapid development of NLG components for CAs in new domains.

In addition, we hope to attract interest from related disciplines, such as semantic parsing or statistical machine translation, which face similar challenges when learning from parallel non-aligned data sets.

Flat MR	NL reference
name[The Eagle], eatType[coffee shop], food[French], priceRange[moderate], customerRating[3/5], area[riverside], kidsFriendly[yes], near[Burger King]	1. There is a riverside coffee shop called The Eagle that has French food at an average price range. It is child friendly, located near Burger King, and has a 3 star customer rating. 2. The three star coffee shop, The Eagle, gives families a mid-priced dining experience featuring a variety of wines and cheeses. Find The Eagle near Burger King. 3. The Eagle coffee shop is based in the riverside area near Burger King. It serves food at mid range prices. It has a three star rating and is family friendly.

Table 1: An example of a data instance.

2 Data Description

The data provided for this shared challenge was collected by using the CrowdFlower platform and quality controlled as described in (Novikova and

"

Rieser, 2016). The dataset provides information about restaurants and consists of more than 50k combinations of a dialogue act-based meaning representation and up to 5 references in natural language, as shown in Table 1. Each MR consists of 3 - 8 attributes (labels), such as name, food or area. The detailed ontology of all attributes and values is provided in Table 2. The dataset will be split into training, validation and testing sets (70/15/15). The training and validation sets will be provided to the participants, while the testing set is used for the final evaluation of the systems. The sets are constructed to ensure a similar distribution of single-sentenced and multi-sentenced references in each set, as well as a similar distribution of MRs of different length.

Attribute	Data Type	Example value
name	verbatim string	The Eagle, ...
eatType	dictionary	restaurant, pub, ...
familyFriendly	boolean	Yes / No
priceRange	dictionary	cheap, expensive, ...
food	dictionary	French, Italian, ...
near	verbatim string	market square, ...
area	dictionary	riverside, city center, ...
customerRating	enumerable	1 of 5 (low), 4 of 5 (high), ...

Table 2: Domain ontology.

3 Evaluation

We will provide two types of baseline systems, which are frequently used by previous corpus-based methods, e.g. (Wen et al., 2015; Mairesse and Young, 2014): a challenging hand-crafted generator and n-gram Language Models, following early work by (Oh and Rudnicky, 2002). To evaluate the results, both objective and subjective metrics will be used. We will explore automatic measures, such as BLEU-4 (Papineni et al., 2002) and NIST (Doddington, 2002) scores, which are widely used in a machine translation and NLG research, and will allow comparing the results of this challenge with previous work. Since automatic metrics may not consistently agree with human perception, human evaluation will be used to assess subjective quality of generated utterances. Human judges will be recruited using CrowdFlower. Judges will be asked to compare utterance generated by different systems and score them in terms of informativeness (*"Does the utterance contains all the information specified in the MR?"*), naturalness (*"Could the utterance have been produced by a native speaker?"*) and phrasing (*"Do you like the way the utterance has been expressed?"*). Here, we will explore different experimental setups for evaluation following previous shared tasks, e.g. (Belz and Kow, 2011). The challenge will also benefit from a national research grant on Domain Independent NLG (EP/M005429/1) which will provide funds for crowd-based evaluation.

4 Research Questions

The task is set up to answer the following research questions with respect to corpus-driven methods:

• *"How much data is enough?"* So far, corpus-based methods have been trained on limited data sets, such as BAGEL (404 target utterances), Cambridge SF (5193) or RoboCup (1919). We release a data set which is almost 10-times times bigger in size than previous corpora. This allows us to test the upper quality boundary of corpus-driven NLG, as well as to determine the optimal/minimal data size per algorithm.

• *"Can they model more complex targets?"* So far, corpus-driven methods are restricted to single sentences. Our corpus contains 37% examples with multiple (2-6) sentences. We predict that longer target outputs are challenging for, e.g. neural networks due to the vanishing gradient problem. Furthermore, our crowd-sourced utterances were elicited using pictures, which makes them more varied in sentence structure and vocabulary than previously used corpora (Novikova and Rieser, 2016).

• *"How good is BLEU?"* Previous research has shown that automatic metrics like BLEU do not consistently agree with human perception (Stent et al., 2004; Belz and Gatt, 2008). We will therefore explore how well they correlate with human judgement. We will also explore how well these metrics are able to capture desired variation given a set of possible reference sentences, following similar shared tasks in machine translation, e.g. (Stanojević et al., 2015).

Acknowledgments

This research received funding from the EPSRC projects GUI (EP/L026775/1), DILiGENt (EP/M005429/1) and MaDrIgAL (EP/N017536/1).

References

Gabor Angeli, Percy Liang, and Dan Klein. 2010. A simple domain-independent probabilistic approach to generation. In *Conference on Empirical Methods in Natural Language Processing (EMNLP)*.

Anja Belz and Albert Gatt. 2008. Intrinsic vs. extrinsic evaluation measures for referring expression generation. In *Proceedings of ACL-08: HLT, Short Papers*, pages 197–200, Columbus, Ohio, June. Association for Computational Linguistics.

Anja Belz and Eric Kow. 2011. Discrete vs. continuous rating scales for language evaluation in nlp. In *Proceedings of the 49th Annual Meeting of the Association for Computational Linguistics: Human Language Technologies: Short Papers - Volume 2*, HLT '11, pages 230–235, Stroudsburg, PA, USA. Association for Computational Linguistics.

George Doddington. 2002. Automatic evaluation of machine translation quality using n-gram co-occurrence statistics. In *Proceedings of the second international conference on Human Language Technology Research*, pages 138–145. Morgan Kaufmann Publishers Inc.

Ondřej Dušek and Filip Jurcicek. 2015. Training a natural language generator from unaligned data. In *Proceedings of the 53rd Annual Meeting of the Association for Computational Linguistics and the 7th International Joint Conference on Natural Language Processing (Volume 1: Long Papers)*, pages 451–461, Beijing, China, July. Association for Computational Linguistics.

Ioannis Konstas and Mirella Lapata. 2012. Unsupervised concept-to-text generation with hypergraphs. In *Conference of the North American Chapter of the Association for Computational Linguistics (NAACL)*.

Percy Liang, Michael I. Jordan, and Dan Klein. 2009. Learning semantic correspondences with less supervision. In *Proc. of ACL-IJCNLP*.

François Mairesse and Steve Young. 2014. Stochastic language generation in dialogue using factored language models. *Comput. Linguist.*, 40(4):763–799, December.

Hongyuan Mei, Mohit Bansal, and Matthew R. Walter. 2015. What to talk about and how? selective generation using lstms with coarse-to-fine alignment. *CoRR*, abs/1509.00838.

Jekaterina Novikova and Verena Rieser. 2016. Crowdsourcing NLG data: Pictures elicit better data. In *Proc. of the 9th International Natural Language Generation conference (INLG)*.

Alice H. Oh and Alexander I. Rudnicky. 2002. Stochastic natural language generation for spoken dialog systems. *Computer Speech and Language*, 16:387–407.

Kishore Papineni, Salim Roukos, Todd Ward, and Wei-Jing Zhu. 2002. Bleu: a method for automatic evaluation of machine translation. In *Proceedings of the 40th annual meeting on association for computational linguistics*, pages 311–318. Association for Computational Linguistics.

Shikhar Sharma, Jing He, Kaheer Suleman, Hannes Schulz, and Philip Bachman. 2016. Natural language generation in dialogue using lexicalized and delexicalized data. *CoRR*, abs/1606.03632.

Miloš Stanojević, Amir Kamran, Philipp Koehn, and Ondřej Bojar. 2015. Results of the wmt15 metrics shared task. In *Proceedings of the Tenth Workshop on Statistical Machine Translation*, pages 256–273, Lisbon, Portugal, September. Association for Computational Linguistics.

Amanda Stent, Rashmi Prasad, and Marilyn Walker. 2004. Trainable sentence planning for complex information presentation in spoken dialog systems. In *Proceedings of the 42nd annual meeting on association for computational linguistics*, page 79. Association for Computational Linguistics.

Tsung-Hsien Wen, Milica Gasic, Nikola Mrkšić, Pei-Hao Su, David Vandyke, and Steve Young. 2015. Semantically Conditioned LSTM-based Natural Language Generation for Spoken Dialogue Systems. In *Proceedings of the 2015 Conference on Empirical Methods in Natural Language Processing*, pages 1711–1721, Lisbon, Portugal, September. Association for Computational Linguistics.

A Challenge Proposal for Narrative Generation Using CNLs

Eugenio Concepción and **Gonzalo Méndez** and **Pablo Gervás** and **Carlos León**
Facultad de Informática
Instituto de Tecnología del Conocimiento
Universidad Complutense de Madrid
`{econcepc,gmendez,pgervas,cleon}@ucm.es`

Abstract

We propose a competitive shared evaluation task for Narrative Generation. It would involve the generation of new stories for a given domain from common ground knowledge shared by all systems. A set of source materials will be provided for development, represented in Controlled Natural Language (CNL), which should also be used to phrase the text outputs of participating systems. By having all participating systems operate from the same sources for knowledge and generate in a compatible output format, comparability of the results will be enhanced. Submitted results will be subject to both automatic and human evaluation.

1   Introduction

A story generator algorithm (SGA) refers to a computational procedure resulting in an artefact that can be considered a story (Gervás, 2012). The term `story generation system` can be considered as a system that applies a SGA to construct stories. There is a growing population of such story generation systems that share two significant characteristics: one, they operate from a set of knowledge resources that act as input to the story generation process; two, they rely on elementary text building solutions – usually based on template filling – for producing human-readable versions of their outputs. Comparative evaluations of any kind between these story generation systems are very difficult because: different systems start from different (unrelated) knowledge resources, and text outputs of the different systems are heavily influenced by the (different) sets of templates employed to render them. A common approach to acquiring knowledge resources is to mine a set of reference stories, to obtain from them the required knowledge. These resources usually make explicit two types of information that is implicit in the stories: relation between events in the story and latent variables relevant to it – such as causality, emotion, affinities between characters, narratological concepts... –, and/or information about typical/acceptable sequencing between events – depending on the degree of refinement of the system, sometimes based on the latent variables.

The present proposal revolves around the idea of developing a Controlled Natural Language (CNL) that can be used to specify the *source material* for a story generation task. A CNL is an engineered subset of natural languages whose grammar and vocabulary have been restricted in order to reduce both ambiguity and complexity of full natural languages (Schwitter, 2010). If such a CNL could be used to represent a set of reference stories, while ensuring that any latent variables are made explicit in the representation, it should be possible to automatically extract the relevant knowledge resources from such source material. To make this possible, the type of source material required should include a set of example stories either enriched with explicit mentions of latent variables or accompanied by explicit declaration of the relation between elements in the stories and the latent variables. If textual outputs of story generation systems could be phrased in such a CNL, it should be feasible to compare outputs of different systems on a shared common footing.

2   Conceptual Basis

In (Gervás and León, 2014) the authors provided a list of the most relevant classifications of the story generation systems according to the type of knowledge resources that they rely on, and the way these knowledge resources are implemented as specific data structures. That paper proposed a list of aspects of a narrative relevant to story telling systems in this sense: including the discourse produced for the story, the representation of the activity of agents – in terms of actions, interactions, mental states, and movement between locations –, the causal relations between elements in the story, the motivations of agents, the theme of parts of the story, the emotions involved in or produced by the story, the intentions of the author, and the narratological concepts involved in the story structure. These various aspects constitute sources of candidate features for the role of latent features relevant for story telling.

CNLs can be considered as a tradeoff between the expressivity of natural languages and the need for a formal representation that can be handled by computers. The requirements for the definition of a CNL grammar (Kuhn, 2010) relevant for the present purpose are: that it should be fully formalized and interpretable by computers, it should not depend on a concrete algorithm or implementation, it should be easy to implement in different programming languages, and it should be sufficiently expressive (for the task at hand).

3   A Proposal for a Story Generation Shared Task

The feasibility of the shared task relies on the development of two basic resources: a grammar for a CNL capable of representing the various aspects relevant to story telling and the resources required by story generation systems, and a set of source materials that encode the necessary knowledge for generating stories in a specific domain covering a selected set of the relevant aspects.

The challenge as proposed is addressed to existing story generation systems.[1] The task would involve: extracting task-specific instances of the knowledge

---

[1]It may be undertaken by researchers willing to develop a system from scratch if they consider it feasible, but the effort involved would be much higher.

resources required for the candidate system from the source materials provided, adapting the text rendering modules of the story generation system to generate stories as close as possible to the the CNL developed for the task, and submitting the resulting stories for evaluation.

3.1   Development of Resources

The proponents of the challenge intend to enlist the collaboration of authors of existing story generation systems with a two-fold purpose: to ensure that the developed resources provide coverage of as many aspects of narrative deemed relevant from a computational perspective, and to raise interest in the challenge and build a community of candidate participants. The collaboration envisaged would take the form of providing sample instances of the knowledge resources employed by their system for generation in a domain of their choice.

3.1.1   The CNL

Such resources will be used to inform the iterative development of the grammar for the CNL. An initial grammar will be built covering aspects common to all systems and all resources. This grammar will be progressively enriched with any additional aspects covered by some systems and not by others, until all selected aspects are covered. Depending on what aspects are covered by the compiled resources and how easy they are to embed into a story, decisions will need to be made on how to represent the relevant latent variables, either as explicit enrichment of stories or as separate declaration of their relation to story elements. Some progress has already been made along these lines (Concepción et al., 2016).

A parser will be developed for the CNL, capable of building actual data structures for the various aspects represented. Both the grammar for the CNL and the code for the parser will be made available to participants. The parser will be designed so that it has a specific module for saving the data structures to disk. Such module may be reinstantiated by participants to select which part of the knowledge in the data structure is saved onto what particular representation format for a particular system.

3.1.2 The Source Materials

The CNL will be used to develop source materials for a particular domain chosen as focus for the challenge. Source materials may consist of a set of enriched stories and/or a set of definitions of relations between story elements and latent variables. Additional knowledge relevant to the domain may also need to be encoded – using the CNL – in the source materials. The basic scope and structure of such additional material will be based on the concept of a *story bible* or *show bible* as considered by screenwriters for information on a television series' characters, settings, and other elements.

3.1.3 Evaluation Procedures

Textual outputs produced by participating systems will be processed using the parser described in 3.1.1. Outputs will be rated automatically on the following parameters: grammaticality – based on conformance to the grammar –, novelty with respect to reference stories in the source materials – data structures built by the parser from the outputs will be compared with those arising from the reference stories according to existing metrics for narrative similarity (Peinado et al., 2010; Hervás et al., 2015) – , and additional rating schemes developed for any relevant features – as the data structures generated by the parser will include explicit representation of these aspects, development for specif metrics is possible for features like degree of causal connectivity, rise and fall of emotion or affinity between characters over a story, or any others explicitly represented.

For the parameters chosen, judgements from human evaluators will also be compiled.

3.1.4 Expected Timeline

A tentative timeline is proposed which would involve: requesting contributions – as samples of knowledge resources – from interested researchers by the end of September 2016, publish source materials in March 2017, outputs to be submitted by participants by July 2017, final results presented at INLG 2017. However, in view of the various uncertainties existing in the proposal, it may be necessary to comtemplate the need to postpone the submission deadline to 2018, in which case the tentative timeline may be re-distributed accordingly over the intervening period.

4 Expected Benefits

The development of agreed versions of source materials from which story generation resources can be extracted, a grammar for outputs of story systems, and procedures for quantitative measurement of relevant features would constitute significant benefits.

Acknowledgments

This proposal has been partially supported by projects WHIM (611560) and PROSECCO (600653) funded by the European Commission, Framework Program 7, the ICT theme, and the Future Emerging Technologies FET program, and by project IDiLyCo (MINECO/FEDER TIN2015-66655-R), funded by the Spanish Ministry of Economy and the European Regional Development Fund.

References

E. Concepción, P. Gervás, G. Méndez, and C. León. 2016. Using CNL for knowledge elicitation and exchange across story generation systems. In *5th Workshop on Controlled Natural Language (CNL 2016)*, Aberdeen, Scotland, 07/2016. Springer, Springer.

P. Gervás and C. León. 2014. The need for multi-aspectual representation of narratives in modelling their creative process. In *5th Workshop on Computational Models of Narrative*, OASIcs-OpenAccess Series in Informatics.

P. Gervás. 2012. Story generator algorithms. In *The Living Handbook of Narratology*. Hamburg University Press.

R. Hervás, A. Sánchez-Ruiz, P. Gervás, and C. León. 2015. Calibrating a metric for similarity of stories against human judgment. In *Creativity and Experience Workshop, International Conference on Case-Based Reasoning*, Bad Homburg, Frankfurt, Germany, 09/2015.

T. Kuhn. 2010. Codeco: A practical notation for controlled english grammars in predictive editors. In *Controlled Natural Language*, pages 95–114. Springer.

F. Peinado, V. Francisco, R. Hervás, and P. Gervás. 2010. Assessing the novelty of computer-generated narratives using empirical metrics. *MINDS AND MACHINES*, 20(4):588, 10/2010.

R. Schwitter. 2010. Controlled natural languages for knowledge representation. In *Proc. of the 23rd International Conference on Computational Linguistics: Posters*, COLING '10, pages 1113–1121, Stroudsburg, PA, USA. Association for Computational Linguistics.

On the verbalization patterns of part-whole relations in isiZulu

C. Maria Keet[1] and **Langa Khumalo**[2]
[1] Department of Computer Science, University of Cape Town,
South Africa, mkeet@cs.uct.ac.za
[2] Linguistics Program, University of KwaZulu-Natal,
South Africa, khumalol@ukzn.ac.za

Abstract

In the highly multilingual setting in South Africa, developing computational tools to support the 11 official languages will facilitate effective communication. The exigency to develop these tools for healthcare applications and doctor-patient interaction is there. An important component in this set-up is generating sentences in the language isiZulu, which involves part-whole relations to communicate, for instance, which part of one's body hurts. From a NLG viewpoint, the main challenge is the fluid use of terminology and the consequent complex agreement system inherent in the language, which is further complicated by phonological conditioning in the linguistic realisation stage. Through using a combined approach of examples and various literature, we devised verbalisation patterns for both meronymic and mereological relations, being structural/general parthood, involvement, containment, membership, subquantities, participation, and constitution. All patterns were then converted into algorithms and have been implemented as a proof-of-concept.

1 Introduction

Hitherto text-based human language technologies in South Africa have been developed by CTexT through the Autshumato project, whereas speech technologies have been developed by the Meraka Institute, which include Automatic Speech Recognition (ASR), pronunciation dictionaries and text-to-speech (TTS) technologies under the auspices of the Lwazi project. However, there is no computational technology in all indigenous official languages (including isiZulu), and the HLT audit (Sharma Grover et al., 2011) indicated a huge gap in information and knowledge processing in particular. This is important to address for application areas such as doctor-patient interactions, for which now only a small app with canned bilingual text exist[1]. The app was well-received for being a very small step toward meeting a well-known need of personalised health communication (Mettler and Kemper, 2003; Wilcox et al., 2011). However, due to the entirely manual efforts, the mobilezulu app with its canned text is obviously not scalable to cover all areas of medicine, like captured in standards such as SNOMED CT[2] and for which terminology in isiZulu is being developed (Engelbrecht et al., 2010) and standardised following PANSALB terminology development processes (Khumalo, 2016). SNOMED CT has a logic-based foundation by having the terms, relations, and the constraints that hold among them represented in the Description Logics-based OWL 2 EL ontology language (Motik et al., 2009a). OWL is also becoming popular as structured input for NLG (Bouayad-Agha et al., 2014) and CNLs (Safwat and Davis, 2016). Some results have been obtained in generating grammatically correct natural language sentences in isiZulu for the OWL 2 EL constructors (Keet and Khumalo, 2016), which makes it look promising to use. Exploratory experiments revealed several issues with verbalising axioms involving the pervasive part-whole relations (OWL object properties), however. The part-whole relation is compli-

---

[1] mobilezulu.org.za and mobilexhosa.org.za
[2] http://www.ihtsdo.org/snomed-ct/

cated by the fluid use in speech and terminology. For instance, structural parts (e.g., the jawbone of the head), involvement (swallowing as part of eating), and membership is generalised as *ingxenye* in isiZulu, yet participation is divided into individual (e.g., the patient) and collective (e.g., the operating team) participation, using different terms. The isiZulu-English dictionary lists 19 translations for 'part' alone (Dent and Nyembezi, 2009). It also introduces the need to process prepositions, which are present only in the deep structure in isiZulu (Mathonsi, 2001), rather than as identifiable isolated words in the better-resourced languages (such as 'of', *von* [DE], *van* [NL], *de* [SP]) that generally do have to be considered in NLG (Baldwin et al., 2009).

Linguistic and cognitive analyses of part-whole relations have resulted in part-whole relation taxonomies, notably the seminal first one by (Winston et al., 1987) and the most recent update in (Keet and Artale, 2008), which have been used successfully in NLP (e.g., (Tandon et al., 2016)). Such analyses start from the underspecified 'part' in natural language to examine what it really is ontologically. For NLG in isiZulu, we face a 'double direction' of analyses for non-English languages: *which parts are there, which terms are used for that, and how?* The general task at hand, thus, is to figure out how the lexicalisation and linguistic realisation of part-whole relations work in isiZulu.

We solve this problem by starting from an established taxonomy of part-whole relations and adjust where needed to cater for differences in conceptualisation as expressed in grammatically correct natural language. Unlike in English, where the same string—like 'has part', 'is part of', and 'contains'— can be plugged in a template unaltered[3], the lexicalisation and linguistic realisation in isiZulu depend on other constituents in the sentence. These include the noun class of the noun that plays the part or whole role in the sentence, the agreement system between a noun and a verb, phonological conditioning, and processing a preposition. In total, there are 13 such constituents for the part-whole relations covered. Instead of templates, this demands for *verbalisation patterns* such that a complete sentence can be generated during runtime. The results presented

here thus also provide a first account of how to construct a full—albeit still highly structured—sentence in isiZulu that has more dependent components (so-called 'concordial agreement') than just verb conjugation with the subject concord and quantification with the quantitative concord. These patterns have been converted into algorithms and have been implemented as a proof-of-concept, substantially extending algorithms for verbalising OWL 2 EL axioms with 'simple' relations (verbs) and for pluralising nouns (Keet and Khumalo, 2016; Byamugisha et al., 2016), notably regarding locatives, concords, a preposition, and more comprehensive phonological conditioning.

The remainder of the paper is structured as follows. In Section 2 we outline the preliminaries on part-whole relations and CNLs for isiZulu. We spell out the patterns for the parts and wholes in isiZulu in Section 3. We describe the tool design considerations and implementation in Section 4. We discuss in Section 5 and conclude in Section 6.

2 Preliminaries

Part-whole relations in the context of natural language commenced seriously with (Winston et al., 1987), with various modifications to its latest instalment by (Keet and Artale, 2008) as to which part-whole relations there are. These part-whole relations are also used in NLP (e.g., (Tandon et al., 2016)), and in ontologies and controlled vocabularies in medicine, such as openGalen and SNOMED CT. There is a principal distinction between mereology (parthood) and meronymy (parts in natural language), where the latter includes the former. They are summarised with an example in Table 1.

CNLs are gaining popularity as a version of NLG in the scope of data(base/RDF)-to-text and knowledge(/logic/OWL)-to-text. It has been shown that straightforward templates do not suffice for Bantu languages such as isiZulu, because (almost) *all words* in *any* sentence *need* some processing (Keet and Khumalo, 2016), cf. an occasional rule for flexibility or beautification that one may still rather classify as a template-based approach (van Deemter et al., 2005). This is due mainly to the system of noun classes, the agreement system among the various constituents in a sentence, and the agglutinative characteristics (Keet and Khumalo, 2016). The noun

---

[3]check, e.g., SWAT NL (Third et al., 2011) or ACE online (Fuchs et al., 2010).

Table 1: Main part-whole relations.

Relation	Example
structural parthood	wall is part of a house, human has part a heart (physical objects)
involvement	eating involves swallowing (processes)
location	city is located in a country (2D region with occupant)
containment	nucleus contained in cell, bolus of food is contained in the stomach (3D region with occupant)
membership	player is member of a team (role & collective)
participation	enzyme participates in a catalytic reaction (object & process)
subquantities	sugar is a subquantity of lemonade, blood sample is a sub quantity of blood (stuffs/masses)
constitution	a vase is constituted of clay (object & stuff)

classes for isiZulu with relevant concords affecting other words in a sentence is shown in Table 2. The noun class system is one of the salient features of the isiZulu language. Every noun belongs to a noun class (NC). The noun is made up of two formatives, the prefix and the stem (e.g., for NC2: *aba-* + *fana* = *abafana* 'boys'). Crucially, the NC governs the agreement of all words that modify the noun. Most NCs are set off into pairs in isiZulu such that most nouns have a singular form in one class and a plural form in another as summarised in Table 2. It must also be pointed out that for the most part the semantics of a noun determines its class (cf. (Twala, 1992)).

So-called 'verbalisation patterns' and algorithms have been developed by (Byamugisha et al., 2016; Keet and Khumalo, 2016), which cover knowledge representation language features from the Description Logic (DL) $\mathcal{ALC}$ (Baader et al., 2008)—hence, OWL 2 EL (Motik et al., 2009a)—such as existential and universal quantification, subsumption, and negation, which have been implemented by the authors in the meantime. The relevant aspects are summarised here to keep the paper self-contained:

- Conjunction 'and' ($\sqcap$ in DL notation), enumerative: *na-* is added to the second noun, using phonological conditioning (see below).
- Subsumption: The copulative is either *y-* or *ng-*

, depending on the first letter of the name of the superclass, and added to the name of the superclass; e.g., *inja yisilwane* 'dog is an animal'.

- Quantification, restricted to usage in simple inclusions of the form $C \sqsubseteq \exists R.D$, i.e., 'all Cs R at least one D'. The $\forall$ 'all' is determined by the noun class of the plural of C's name, R is a present tense verb conjugated in concordance with the head noun (C, in plural), and the 'at least one' is made up of the relative concord and quantitative concord of the noun class of D's name and ends with *-dwa*. For instance, uSolwazi $\sqsubseteq$ -fundisa.isifundo becomes *bonke oSolwazi bafundisa isifundo esisodwa* 'all professors teach at least one course': First, *uSolwazi*, in NC3, is pluralised to *oSolwazi*, in NC4. Second, the word for $\forall$ for NC4 is *bonke* and, third, the subject concord for it is *ba-*, making *bafundisa*. Fourth, the noun class of *isifundo* is 7, so the relative concord is *esi-* and quantitative concord is *-so-*, forming *esisodwa* for the verbalisation of $\exists$.

Phonological conditioning occurs in multiple occasions (Miti, 2006), but the one relevant here concerns adding a concord to the noun, because isiZulu does not have two successive vowels in a word. This is known as *vowel coalescence*, and the basic rules are: *-a + a- = -a-, -a + e- = -e-, -a + i- = -e-, -a + o- = -o-*, and *-a + u- = -o-*. For instance, *ubisi na+ibhotela* becomes *ubisi nebhotela* ('milk and butter'), *ibhotela na+ubisi* becomes *ibhotela nobisi*, and *nga+ubumba* becomes *ngobumba* 'of clay'. Further, the locative suffix *-ini* is phonologically conditioned by the final vowel: *-a+-ini=-eni, -e+-ini=-eni, -o+ini=-weni, u+ini=-wini, -phu + -wini = -shini*, and the few loanwords that end in *-phu* become *-phini*.

3 Patterns for Parts and Wholes

To describe the patterns, we systematically take the axioms for 'has part' (wp), $W \sqsubseteq \exists hasPart.P$, and 'is part of' (pw), $P \sqsubseteq \exists isPartOf.W$ to demonstrate what is going on linguistically. Ontologically, in a majority of cases, only one of the two reading directions is applicable despite the pervasive informal use of the inappropriate one[4]; such ontological

---

[4]e.g., it is true that all humans have some heart ($Human \sqsubseteq \exists hasPart.Heart$), but not that all hearts are part of some hu-

Table 2: Zulu noun classes with examples and a selection of concords. NC: Noun class; PRE: prefix; QC: quantitative concord; RC: relative concord; PC: possessive concord.

NC	Full PRE	QC ($\forall$)	RC	QC ($\exists$)	SC	PC
1	um(u)-	wonke	o-	ye-	u-	wa-
2	aba-	bonke	aba-	bo-	ba-	ba-
1a	u-	wonke	o-	ye-	u-	wa-
2a	o-	bonke	aba-	bo-	ba-	ba-
3a	u-	wonke	o-	ye-	u-	wa-
2a	o-	bonke	aba-	bo-	ba-	ba-
3	um(u)-	wonke	o-	wo-	u-	wa-
4	imi-	yonke	e-	yo-	i-	ya-
5	i(li)-	lonke	eli-	lo-	li-	la-
6	ama-	onke	a-	wo-	a-	a-
7	isi-	sonke	esi-	so-	si-	sa-
8	izi-	zonke	ezi	zo-	zi-	za-
9a	i-	yonke	e-	yo-	i-	ya-
6	ama-	onke	a-	wo-	a-	a-
9	i(n)-	yonke	e-	yo-	i-	ya-
10	izi(n)-	zonke	ezi-	zo-	zi-	za-
11	u(lu)-	lonke	olu-	lo-	lu-	lwa-
10	izi(n)-	zonke	ezi-	zo-	zi-	za-
14	ubu-	bonke	obu-	bo-	bu-	ba-
15	uku-	konke	oku-	ko-	ku-	kwa-
17	ku-	lonke	olu-	lo-	lu-	kwa-

Table 3: Abbreviations (Var.) used in the verbalisation patterns.

Var.	Full name	Comment
W	entity playing whole	our abbreviation
P	entity that plays the part	our abbreviation
CONJ	Conjunction	enumerative-and (not a connective-and); *na-*
COP	Copulative	*y-* or *ng-*
LOC	Locative	locative prefix; *ku-* for NC 1a, 2a, 3a, and 17, *e-* otherwise
LOC-SUF	Locative	here used for the locative suffix; *-ini*
PRE	Preposition	only *nga-* is used here
EP	Epenthetic	*-s-*
PASS	Passive tense	*-iw-*
FV	Final Vowel	in this case just *-e* to go with PASS
SC	Subject Concord	$\sim$ conjugation; depends on NC: see Table 2
PC	Possessive Concord	depends on NC: see Table 2
RC	Relative Concord	depends on NC: see Table 2
QCall	quantitative concord	universal quantification; depends on NC: see Table 2
QC	quantitative concord	existential quantification; depends on NC: see Table 2

aspects are beyond the scope of this paper.

Regarding notation, ultimately what is needed is a detailed grammar for the verbalisation patterns. At this stage, however, there is insufficient linguistic knowledge to pursue this. Therefore, we use variables in the patterns, as listed in Table 3, where each variable is to be substituted with the appropriate string (terminal, if it were a CFG), and subscripts, omitting the orthogonal phonological conditioning that is included in the explanation instead. A dash between variables indicates they are part of one word. Subscripts indicate 'agreement' of the various elements. So, for instance, a "$W_{nc_{x,pl}}$" is the entity (its name assumed to be given in the singular) that plays the role of the whole, which is of noun class ("nc") x that is to be pluralised, and its preceding "$QCall_{nc_{x,pl}}$" is the term for the universal quantification for the noun class that is the plural of noun class x; e.g., if W is inja, in NC9, then $W_{nc_{x,pl}}$ is

izinja in NC10, and its $QCall_{nc_{x,pl}}$ is zonke.

structural/general parts and wholes   Let us commence with a parthood relation between objects. The verbalisation patterns in isiZulu (for any noun class) in the 'has part' (*wp*) and 'part of' (*pw*) reading directions are as follows:

wp: $QCall_{nc_{x,pl}}$ $W_{nc_{x,pl}}$ $SC_{nc_{x,pl}}$-CONJ-P_{nc_y} RC_{nc_y}-QC_{nc_y}-*dwa*

pw: $QCall_{nc_{x,pl}}$ $P_{nc_{x,pl}}$ $SC_{nc_{x,pl}}$-COP-*ingxenye* $PC_{ingxenye}$-W_{nc_y} RC_{nc_y}-QC_{nc_y}-*dwa*

Note that the whole-part relation does not have one single string like a 'has part', but it is composed of SC+CONJ, and is thus dependent on both the noun class of the whole (as the SC is) and on the first letter of the name of the part (as the string for CONJ, *na-*, depends on that). The 'is part of' reading direction is made up of the 'part' *ingxenye*, which is a noun that is preceded with the COP *y-* and together amounts to 'is part'. The 'of' is accounted for by the possessive concord (PC) of *ingxenye* (NC9), be-

---

man ($^{*}Heart \sqsubseteq \exists isPartOf.Human$), as there are hearts that are part of another, non-human, animal.

ing *ya-*, taking into account vowel coalescence. The SC for concordance with the P has been included because, while in multiple examples, either SC-COP-*ingxenye* or COP-*ingxenye* suffices, in some cases it really does not. The patterns are illustrated in the following two examples for heart (*inhliziyo*, NC9) standing in a part-whole relation to human (*umuntu*, NC1), with the 'has part' and 'is part of' underlined:

wp-ex: bonke abantu <u>bane</u>nhliziyo eyodwa

pw-ex: zonke izinhliziyo <u>ziyingxenye</u> yomuntu oyedwa

involved in   is the same as for general parts. The salient difference is that both P and W belong to nominals that are in NC15. An example is that eating (*ukudla*) involves swallowing (*ukugwinya*):

wp-ex: konke ukudla <u>kuno</u>kugwinya okukodwa

pw-ex: konke ukugwinya <u>kuyingxenye</u> yokudla okukodwa

Observe that "bane-" in the previous example is different from the "kuno-" here, due to the different SCs (*abantu* is in NC2 (ba-) and *ukudla* in NC15 (ku-), and vowel coalescence: *na+i* = -ne- in the former example and *na+u* = -no- here, yet the pattern is exactly the same.

containment   has a spatial component to it, which is indicated with the locative affixes (LOC) in the pw direction of verbalisation. Because isiZulu proscribes vowel sequencing, the epenthetic *-s-* is required between the SC and the LOC *e-*. Patterns, for any noun class:

wp: QCall$_{nc_x,pl}$ W$_{nc_x,pl}$ SC$_{nc_x,pl}$-CONJ-P$_{nc_y}$ RC$_{nc_y}$-QC$_{nc_y}$-*dwa*

pw: QCall$_{nc_x,pl}$ P$_{nc_x,pl}$ SC$_{nc_x,pl}$-EP-LOC-W$_{nc_y}$-LOCSUF RC$_{nc_y}$-QC$_{nc_y}$-*dwa*

This is illustrated for the usual example (Donnelly et al., 2006) of a bolus of food (*indilinga yokudla*, NC9) that is contained in the stomach (*isisu*, NC7):

wp-ex: Zonke izisu <u>zine</u>ndilinga yokudla eyodwa

pw-ex: Zonke izindilinga zokudla <u>zisesiswini</u> esisodwa

The zine- comes from the SC of NC10 of *izisu* 'stomachs', which is followed by the *na+i*=-ne- for CONJ. The zise- is the result of NC10's SC, zi- (see Table 2), the EP -s-, and LOC e-, and then *-u+-ini=-*wini as LOCSUF.

membership   The patterns are as for general parthood; e.g., a doctor (*udokotela*, NC1a) is a member of an operating team (*iqembu labahlinzi*, NC5):

wp-ex: onke amaqembu abahlinzi <u>ano</u>dokotela oyedwa

pw-ex: bonke odokotela <u>bayingxenye</u> yeqembu labahlinzi elilodwa

subquantities   Ontology has so far recognised two core different usages of subquantities. First, as parts, like alcohol is a subquantity of wine, flour of bread and so on. While many of the mass nouns are in NC5 or NC6 in isiZulu, this is not always the case and if in the singular it stays singular and in some cases, the term can be both a count noun and a mass noun, as is the case in English (e.g., 'stone'). Therefore, we change the pattern for part-subquantities so that it omits the pluralisation. Also, one does not count stuffs, so the 'at least one' is omitted as well.

wp: QCall$_{nc_x}$ W$_{nc_x}$ SC$_{nc_x}$-CONJ-P$_{nc_y}$

pw: QCall$_{nc_x}$ P$_{nc_x}$ SC$_{nc_x}$-COP-*ingxenye* PC$_{ingxenye}$-W$_{nc_y}$

For instance, water (*amanzi*, NC6) as a subquantity of urine (*umshobingo*, NC3):

wp-ex: wonke umshobingo <u>unamanzi</u>

pw-ex: onke amanzi <u>ayingxenye</u> yomshobingo

The second reading of subquantities is portions, i.e., parts of the whole amount of stuff that are made of the same stuff, be this a tissue sample under the microscope glass that came from a patient's tissue, or the left-half of someone's brain. In isiZulu, there are two types: *umunxa* (NC3) as a kind of 'spatial' portion as in 'the portion of the kitchen where the kitchen utensils are', and *isiqephu* (NC7) as a portion for solid objects, like the tissue. For the 'spatial' portion, we obtain:

wp: QCall$_{nc_x,pl}$ W$_{nc_x,pl}$ SC$_{nc_x,pl}$-CONJ-P$_{nc_y}$

pw: QCall$_{nc_x,pl}$ P$_{nc_x,pl}$ SC$_{nc_x,pl}$-COP-*umunxa* PC$_{umunxa}$-W$_{nc_y}$

Observe that the COP is *ng-*, not *y-*, because of the *u*-commencing *umunxa*; e.g., a hospital (*isibhedlela*, NC7) has a portion that is an operating theatre (*ithiyetha yokuhlinzela*, NC9a):

wp-ex: zonke izibhedlela <u>zine</u>thiyetha yokuhlinzela

pw-ex: onke amathiyetha okuhlinzela <u>angumunxa</u> wesibhedlela

For the solid objects type of portion, the whole is an amount of matter (mass noun), thus remains in the noun class it is rather than being pluralised:

wp: QCall$_{nc_x}$ W$_{nc_x}$ SC$_{nc_x}$-CONJ-P$_{nc_y}$ RC$_{nc_y}$-QC$_{nc_y}$-*dwa*

pw: QCall$_{nc_x,pl}$ P$_{nc_x,pl}$ SC$_{nc_x,pl}$-COP-*isiqephu*
PC$_{isiqephu}$-W$_{nc_y}$ RC$_{nc_y}$-QC$_{nc_y}$-*dwa*

with as example a blood sample as a portion of blood
wp-ex: Lonke igazi <u>line</u>sampula legazi elilodwa
pw-ex: Onke amasampula egazi <u>ayisiqephu</u> segazi
elilodwa

For the W in the *pw*, there is again vowel coalescence: *sa-+igazi* = segazi, with *sa-* the PC for *isiqephu*'s NC7. The part P is computationally complicated. It may be a noun phrase, like 'slice of bread', where the 'of' is again catered for by a PC, being the one for the noun class of the noun that is the quantity (slice, piece, bowl, etc). So, e.g., *ucezu* (NC11) has PC *lwa-*, resulting in *lwa-+isinkwa* = lwesinkwa 'of bread'. Yet, a 'sample of blood', *isampula legazi*, is considered a compound noun, not a noun phrase.

participation can be divided into two typologies in isiZulu. There is individual type of participation and a group type of participation, like a citizen vs the electorate participating (taking part) in an election. For individual objects, one can include an optional ASP between the SC and COP, restricted to *-be-* in this case. This is not used here so as to match with the rest, assuming that it will suffice. As example, a doctor (*udokotela*, NC1a) participates in an operation (*ukuhlinza*, NC15):

wp-ex: Konke ukuhlinza <u>kuno</u>dokotela oyedwa
pw-ex: bonke odokotela <u>bayingxenye</u> yokuhlinza
okukodwa

For the collective/group participation, a different 'part' is used, *-hlanganyele*, which is part in the sense of participating by combining to do something, acting in unison (perfect tense). This is verbalised in the singular only:

wp: QCall$_{nc_x}$ W$_{nc_x}$ SC$_{nc_x}$-CONJ-P$_{nc_y}$ RC$_{nc_y}$-
QC$_{nc_y}$-*dwa*

pw: QCall$_{nc_x}$ P$_{nc_x}$ SC$_{nc_x}$-*hlanganyele* LOC-W$_{nc_y}$-
LOCSUF RC$_{nc_y}$-QC$_{nc_y}$-*dwa*.

Either a LOC as prefix only is allowed, or a locative circumfix can be used, i.e., LOC-W-LOCSUF with vowel elision for the W on both sides. Here, the latter is chosen. For instance, the operating team, (*iqembu labahlinzi*, NC5) participating in an operation (*ukuhlinza*, NC15):

wp-ex: Konke ukuhlinza <u>kuneqembu</u> labahlinzi
elilodwa
pw-ex: Lonke iqembu labahlinzi <u>lihlanganyele</u>
okuhlinzeni okukodwa

Decomposing the locative aspects that result in okuhlinzeni: the o- is the outcome of the vowel coalescence of LOC *e-+u-* and -weni is the outcome of the phonological conditioning *-o+-ini*'s LOCSUF.

constitution Also in this case of meronymic part-whole relation, it partially diverges in that there is no variation of 'part' as a noun, but a verb is used, as in the previous case: it is either *-akha* 'build' for objects that are made/constituted of some matter in some structural sense or *-enza* otherwise. As this is verbalised only as wholes being constituted of something, only that one is included:

wp: QCall$_{nc_x,pl}$ W$_{nc_x,pl}$ SC$_{nc_x,pl}$-*akh*-PASS-FV
PRE-P$_{nc_y}$.

wp: QCall$_{nc_x,pl}$ W$_{nc_x,pl}$ SC$_{nc_x,pl}$-*enz*-PASS-FV
PRE-P$_{nc_y}$.

The PRE here is restricted to *nga-*, with phonological conditioning. Relatively, this construction is similar to the notion of preposition contraction in Romance languages (de Oliveira and Sripada, 2014). For instance, in 'all houses (*izindlu* 'house') are constituted of stone (*itshe*, NC5)', the passive and final vowel causes the -iwe end, and likewise for 'all pills (*amaphilisi*, NC6) are made of starch (*isitashi*, NC7)':

wp-ex: zonke izindlu <u>zakhiwe</u> ngetshe
wp-ex: onke amaphilisi <u>enziwe</u> ngesitashi

The SC is modified because the stem starts with a vowel: if the vowel of the SC is a high vowel (i-; u-) and precedes the vowel of the stem which is low (a-), there is hiatus resolution (Mudzingwa and Kadenge, 2011). The pattern is as follows: *i-* + *a-* = *y* and *u-* + *a-* = *w*. Hiatus resolution is followed by the elision of the initial vowel with the semi-vowel attaching to the initial vowel of the stem (*u-* + *akhiwe* = *yakhiwe*).

This concludes the list of patterns.

4   Design and Implementation

We describe the transformation from the patterns to the algorithms, some tool design considerations, and the architecture of the implementation.

4.1   From verbalisation patterns to algorithms

The variables used in the verbalisation patterns belie what needs to be done in the background, which differs by variable in three principal ways. First, there are the variables that algorithmically amount to straight-forward *look-up functions* to retrieve something using the noun class, such as the SC, RC, and QC as listed in Table 2. Second, there are *functions that change a word*, notably the pluraliser, which is not simply a case of list look-up (Byamugisha et al., 2016). Third, there are the *functions for phonological conditioning* that are needed for CONJ, LOC, LOCSUF, PC, and PRE. Most of the algorithms to verbalise part-whole relations need all three groups of functions. For instance, Algorithm 1 for the verbalisation of the basic whole-part has the straightforward look-up ones ("*get...*"), the call to another algorithm for pluralisation (line 7), and one call to the rules for vowel coalescence (phonological conditioning) in line 11. The algorithm for the 'is part of' direction is similar except that instead of line 11, the phonological conditioning is *phonoCondition('ya', c_2)* and sc_1 stringed together with yingxenye.

4.2 Design considerations

As the patterns demonstrate, the actual string for 'has part' depends on the noun of the entity that plays the role of the whole and noun of the entity that plays the role of the part, which means that it is not feasible to store all possible strings, but this has to be computed on-the-fly. Yet, OWL requires a single, fixed, string of text for its 'object property' (relationship), i.e., a single IRI (Motik et al., 2009b). Integrating this with OWL means handling object properties differently and full integration with a linguistic model, yet the *lemon* model (McCrae et al., 2012) already needs an extension to deal with the noun classes (Chavula and Keet, 2014), or: that structured representation does not suffice for isiZulu at present. As solving that diverts away from a proof-of-concept implementation of the algorithms for part-whole relations to evaluate whether they and the patterns they implement are correct, we chose an incremental approach with Python instead. Also, the patterns and algorithms presented in (Keet and Khumalo, 2016; Byamugisha et al., 2016) have been implemented in Python, so we extended that with the algorithms for the novel part-whole patterns.

The architecture of the components of the verbaliser are straightforward (see Fig. 1): nouns are stored with their noun class, whereas verb stems

---

Algorithm 1: Determine the verbalisation of basic whole-part in an axiom

1: $\mathcal{C}$ set of classes, language $\mathcal{L}$, $\sqsubseteq$ for subsumption, $\exists$ for existential quantification; variables: A axiom, NC_i noun class, $c_1, c_2 \in \mathcal{C}$, $o \in \mathcal{R}$, a_1 a term; r_2, q_2 concords;

Require: axiom of the form $W \sqsubseteq \exists wp.P$ has been retrieved for verbalisation

2: $c_1 \leftarrow getFirstClass(A)$ {get whole}

3: $c_2 \leftarrow getSecondClass(A)$ {get part}

4: $wp \leftarrow getObjProp(A)$
    {get wp type ('default' parthood here)}

5: $NC_1 \leftarrow getNC(c_1)$ {obtain noun class whole}

6: $NC_2 \leftarrow getNC(c_2)$ {obtain noun class part}

7: $c_{pl} \leftarrow pluralise(c_1, NC_1)$
    {generate plural, using the pluraliser algorithm}

8: $NC_1' \leftarrow getPlNC(NC_1)$
    {obtain plural NC, from known list}

9: $a_1 \leftarrow getQCAll(NC_1')$
    {obtain quantitative concord (QC(all))}

10: $sc_1 \leftarrow getSC(NC_1')$ {obtain subject concord}

11: $conjp \leftarrow phonoCondition('na', c_2)$
    {prefix P with the CONJ, phonologically conditioned}

12: $r_2 \leftarrow getRC(NC_2)$ {obtain relative conc. for c_2}

13: $q_2 \leftarrow getQC(NC_2)$
    {obtain quant. concord for c_2 from the QC (exists)-list}

14: RESULT $\leftarrow$ ' a_1 c_{pl} $sc_1 conjp$ $r_2 q_2$dwa. '
    {verbalise the simple axiom}

15: **return** RESULT

---

are stored to facilitate processing of tense, for automatically determining this has only partial solutions thus far (Pretorius and Bosch, 2003; Spiegler et al., 2010). Each axiom type and each type of part-whole relation relates to a Python function (which calls others). The script is yet to be connected to the SNOMED CT's owl file to fetch the data, so the code emulates that output such that the user adds the terms in the input (see Fig. 2, "->" lines). The code and other examples can be downloaded from http://www.meteck.org/files/geni/ and a few examples are shown in Fig. 2. It worked for 38 of the 42 test cases (90.5%). The four errors were mainly due to the incomplete pluraliser of (Byamugisha et al., 2016) (e.g., *ucezi* $\mapsto$ *izincezi*, not *izicezi*) and one due to ambiguity of *-akh* vs. *-enz* for constitution.

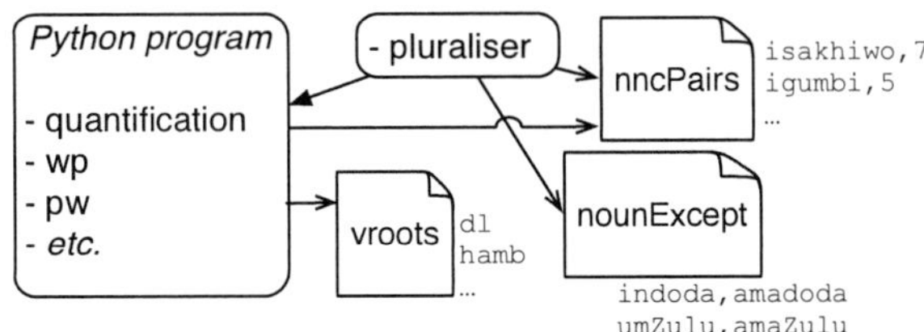

Figure 1: Components of the proof-of-concept implementation of the isiZulu verbaliser. The three txt files were created manually (examples of their contents are shown in `courier` font).

```
> wp('umuntu','inhliziyo')
  'Bonke abantu banenhliziyo eyodwa'
> wp_cp('ukhetho','umphakathi')
  'Lonke ukhetho lunomphakathi owodwa'
> wp_s('umshobingo','amanzi')
  'Wonke umshobingo unamanzi'
> pw('ukugwinya','ukudla')
  'Konke ukugwinya kuyingxenye yokudla okukodwa'
> pw_ci('indilinga yokudla','isisu')
  'Zonke izindilinga zokudla zisesiswini esisodwa'
> constitution('ivazi','ubumba')
  'Onke amavazi akhiwe ngobumba'
```

Figure 2: Screenshot of working code; wp/pw: general wholes/ parts; wp_cp: collective participation; wp_s: subquantity; pw_ci: containment.

5 Discussion

The patterns showed that, like in English, isiZulu has several more specific terms for 'part'—*ingxenye*, *indawo*, *isiqephu*, *umunxa*, and *hlanganyele*— although they do not match 1:1 with the established part-whole relation categorisations as in Table 1. Such ontological analyses are left for future work. It does illustrate that in this case sentence planning was a major hurdle compared to just linguistic realisation.

The patterns reconfirm results by (Keet and Khumalo, 2016) that the template-based approach is not feasible for isiZulu, and, by extension, Bantu languages that all share the features of noun classes and concordance. This, however, also makes it an imperative to develop a grammar. While this exercise broadened the scope on understanding what linguistic elements are needed for an NLG, and a quasi pattern language was still sufficient to specify the patterns, with the increased number of elements to keep track of compared to (Keet and Khumalo, 2016), soon this limit will be reached. In addition, rules need to be found so as to process *groups* of tokens so as to know which one is a compound noun and which one is a noun phrase, in order to process them correctly. Hopefully then also sufficient insight is gained to construct a set of requirements for the grammar and either practical ones might be extended, such as the CFG of Ukwabelana (Spiegler et al., 2010), explorations of (Zeller, 2005) worked out in detail, or a natural language-independent approach like in (Kuhn, 2013) may be adjusted, or a new one devised to handle the syntactic elements to generate sentences with the intended semantics.

Finally, although the patterns have been specified for isiZulu only, bootstrapping resources for related Bantu languages—Xhosa, Swati, and Ndebele— based on isiZulu resources have yielded good results (Bosch et al., 2008), and thus solving it for isiZulu will open up HLT prospects for even lesser resourced languages.

6 Conclusions

We devised verbalisation patterns for both meronymic and mereological relations. New constituents in the patterns with respect to related works are, notably, the possessive concord, locative affixes, and a basic treatment of prepositions and the passive tense. The verbalisation patterns were implemented successfully using a proof-of-concept implementation of the algorithms, and tested with 42 examples, resulting in a 90.5% success rate. The patterns reaffirm the infeasibility of the template-based approach for isiZulu and Bantu languages because of the complex morphosyntax.

The patterns also indicated that it is becoming a pressing matter to commence with formally defining a generative grammar for isiZulu. Another avenue will be to take the latest medical terminology terms in isiZulu and create a fully functional medical app.

Acknowledgments

This work is based on the research supported in part by the National Research Foundation of South Africa (CMK: Grant Number 93397).

References

F. Baader, D. Calvanese, D. L. McGuinness, D. Nardi, and P. F. Patel-Schneider, editors. 2008. *The Description Logics Handbook – Theory and Applications*. Cambridge University Press, 2 edition.

Timothy Baldwin, Valia Kordoni, and Aline Villavicencio. 2009. Prepositions in applications: A survey and introduction to the special issue. *Computational Linguistics*, 35(2):119–149.

Sonja Bosch, Laurette Pretorius, and Axel Fleisch. 2008. Experimental bootstrapping of morphological analysers for nguni languages. *Nordic Journal of African Studies*, 17(2):66–88.

N. Bouayad-Agha, G. Casamayor, and L. Wanner. 2014. Natural language generation in the context of the semantic web. *Semantic Web Journal*, 5(6):493–513.

Joan Byamugisha, C. Maria Keet, and Langa Khumalo. 2016. Pluralising nouns in isiZulu and similar languages. In A. Gelbkuh, editor, *Proceedings of CICLing'16*, page in print. Springer.

Catherine Chavula and C. Maria Keet. 2014. Is lemon sufficient for building multilingual ontologies for Bantu languages? In C. Maria Keet and Valentina Tamma, editors, *Proceedings of the 11th OWL: Experiences and Directions Workshop (OWLED'14)*, volume 1265 of *CEUR-WS*, pages 61–72. Riva del Garda, Italy, Oct 17-18, 2014.

Rodrigo de Oliveira and Somayajulu Sripada. 2014. Adapting simplenlg for brazilian portuguese realisation. In *Proceedings of the 8th International Natural Language Generation Conference (INLG)*, pages 93–94, Philadelphia, Pennsylvania, U.S.A., June. Association for Computational Linguistics.

G. R. Dent and C. L. S. Nyembezi. 2009. *Scholar's Zulu Dictionary*. Shuter & Shooter Publishers, 4 edition.

M. Donnelly, T. Bittner, and C. Rosse. 2006. A formal theory for spatial representation and reasoning in biomedical ontologies. *Artif Intell Med*, 36(1):1–27.

C. Engelbrecht, N.C. Shangase, S.J. Majeke, S.Z. Mthembu, and Z.M. Zondi. 2010. Isizulu terminology development in nursing and midwifery. *Alternation*, 17(1):249–272.

Norbert E. Fuchs, Kaarel Kaljurand, and Tobias Kuhn. 2010. Discourse Representation Structures for ACE 6.6. Technical Report ifi-2010.0010, Dept of Informatics, University of Zurich, Switzerland.

C. Maria Keet and Alessandro Artale. 2008. Representing and reasoning over a taxonomy of part-whole relations. *Applied Ontology*, 3(1-2):91–110.

C. M. Keet and L. Khumalo. 2016. Toward a knowledge-to-text controlled natural language of isiZulu. *Language Resources and Evaluation*, in print:DOI: 10.1007/s10579–016–9340–0.

L. Khumalo. 2016. Disrupting language hegemony: Intellectualizing African languages. In M. Samuel, R. Dunpath, and N. Amin, editors, *Towards a posthumanist higher education curriculum: Undoing cognitive damage*, page (accepted). SENSE Publishers, Rotterdam.

Tobias Kuhn. 2013. A principled approach to grammars for controlled natural languages and predictive editors. *Journal of Logic, Language and Information*, 22(1):33–70.

N. N. Mathonsi. 2001. Prepositional and adverb phrases in Zulu: a linguistic and lexicographic problem. *South African Journal of African Languages*, 2:163–175.

John McCrae, Guadalupe Aguado de Cea, Paul Buitelaar, Philipp Cimiano, Thierry Declerck, Asunción Gómez-Pérez, Jorge Gracia, Laura Hollink, Elena Montiel-Ponsoda, Dennis Spohr, and Tobias Wunner. 2012. The Lemon cookbook. Technical report, Monnet Project.

M. Mettler and D.W. Kemper. 2003. Information therapy: Health education one person at a time. *Health Prom. Prac.*, 4(3):214–217.

L. Miti. 2006. *Comparative Bantu phonology and morphology*. Cape Town: The Center for Advanced Studies of African Societies (CASAS).

Boris Motik, Bernardo Cuenca Grau, Ian Horrocks, Zhe Wu, Achille Fokoue, and Carsten Lutz. 2009a. OWL 2 Web Ontology Language Profiles. W3C recommendation, W3C, 27 Oct.

Boris Motik, Peter F. Patel-Schneider, and Bijan Parsia. 2009b. OWL 2 web ontology language structural specification and functional-style syntax. W3c recommendation, W3C, 27 Oct. http://www.w3.org/TR/owl2-syntax/.

C. Mudzingwa and M. Kadenge. 2011. Comparing hiatus resolution in karanga and nambya: An optimality theory account. *Nordic Journal of African Studies*, 20(3):203–240.

L. Pretorius and E. S. Bosch. 2003. Finite-state computational morphology: An analyzer prototype for Zulu. *Machine Translation*, 18(3):195–216.

Hazem Safwat and Brian Davis. 2016. CNLs for the semantic web: a state of the art. *Language Resources & Evaluation*, in print:DOI: 10.1007/s10579–016–9351–x.

A. Sharma Grover, G.B. Van Huyssteen, and M.W. Pretorius. 2011. The South African human language technology audit. *Language Resources & Evaluation*, 45:271–288.

Sebastian Spiegler, Andrew van der Spuy, and Peter A. Flach. 2010. Ukwabelana – an open-source morphological Zulu corpus. In *Proceedings of the 23rd International Conference on Computational Linguistics (COLING'10)*, pages 1020–1028. Association for Computational Linguistics. Beijing.

Niket Tandon, Charles Hariman, Jacopo Urbani, Anna Rohrbach, Marcus Rohrbach, and Gerhard Weikum. 2016. Commonsense in parts: Mining part-whole relations from the web and image tags. In *Proceedings of the Thirtieth AAAI Conference on Artificial Intelligence (AAAI'16)*, pages 243–250. AAAI Press.

Allan Third, Sandra Williams, and Richard Power. 2011. OWL to English: a tool for generating organised easily-navigated hypertexts from ontologies. poster/demo paper, Open Unversity UK. 10th International Semantic Web Conference (ISWC'11), 23-27 Oct 2011, Bonn, Germany.

E. K. Twala. 1992. The noun class system of isizulu. M.A. dissertation. University of Johannesburg.

Kees van Deemter, Emiel Krahmer, and Mariët Theune. 2005. Real versus tempalte-based natural language generation: a false opposition? *Computational Linguistics*, 31(1):15–23.

L. Wilcox, D. Morris, D. Tan, J. Gatewood, and E. Horvitz. 2011. Characterising patient-friendly micro-explanations of medical events. In *SIGCHI Conference on Human Factors in Computing Systems (CHI'11)*, pages 29–32. ACM.

M.E. Winston, R. Chaffin, and D. Herrmann. 1987. A taxonomy of partwhole relations. *Cognitive Science*, 11(4):417–444.

Jochen Zeller. 2005. Universal principles and parametric variation: remarks on formal linguistics and the grammar of zulu. *Ingede Journal of African Scholarship*, 1(3):20p.

SimpleNLG-IT: adapting SimpleNLG to Italian

Alessandro Mazzei and **Cristina Battaglino** and **Cristina Bosco**
Dipartimento di Informatica
Università degli Studi di Torino
Corso Svizzera 185, 10149 Torino
`[mazzei,battagli,bosco]@di.unito.it`

Abstract

This paper describes the SimpleNLG-IT realiser, i.e. the main features of the porting of the SimpleNLG API system (Gatt and Reiter, 2009) to Italian. The paper gives some details about the grammar and the lexicon employed by the system and reports some results about a first evaluation based on a dependency treebank for Italian. A comparison is developed with the previous projects developed for this task for English and French, which is based on the morpho-syntactical differences and similarities between Italian and these languages.

1 Introduction

Natural Language Generation (NLG) involves a number of elementary tasks that can be addressed by using different approaches and architectures. A well defined standard architecture is the pipeline proposed by Reiter and Dale (Reiter and Dale, 2000).

In this approach, three steps transform raw data into natural language text, that are: document planning, sentence-planning and surface realization. Each one of these modules triggers the next one addressing a distinct issue as follows. In document planning the user decides the information content of the text to be generated (*what to say*). In sentence-planning, the focus is instead on the design of a number of features that are related to the information contents as well as to the specific language, as the choice of the words. Finally, in surface realisation, sentences are generated according to the decisions taken in the previous stages and by fulfilling the morpho-syntactic constraints related to the language specific features, like word order, inflection and selection of functional words.

Surface realisers can be classified on the basis of their input. Fully fledged realisers accept as input an unordered and uninflected proto-syntactic structure enriched with semantic and pragmatic features that are used to produce the most plausible output string. OpenCCG is a member of this category of realisers (White, 2006). Indeed, OpenCCG accepts as input a semantic graph representing a set of hybrid logic formulas. The hybrid logic elements are indeed the semantic specification of syntactic CCG structures defined in the grammar realiser. The semantic graph under-specifies morpho-syntactic information and delegates to the realiser many lexical and syntactic choices (e.g. function words). Chart based algorithms and statistical models are used to resolve the ambiguity arising from under-specification.

In contrast, *realisation engines* are simpler systems which perform just linearisation and morphological inflections of the proto-syntactic input. As a consequence, realization engine presumes a more detailed morpho-syntactic information as input. A member of this category is SimpleNLG (Gatt and Reiter, 2009). It assumes a complete syntactic specification, but unordered and uninflected, of the sentence in the form of a mixed constituency/dependency structure. Content and function words are chosen in input as well as modifiers order. The greatest advantage of this system is its simplicity, which allows to pay more efforts in the previous stages of the NLG pipeline.

SimpleNLG was originally designed for English but it has been successively adapted to German,

French, Brazilian-Portuguese and Telugu (Bollmann, 2011; Vaudry and Lapalme, 2013; de Oliveira and Sripada, 2014; Dokkara et al., 2015). The first contribution of this paper is the adaptation of SimpleNLG for Italian[1]. The most challenging issues under this respect of this project (see Sections 2 and 3) are: (1) the Italian verb conjugation system, that cannot be easily mapped to the English system and shows many idiosyncrasies; (2) the high complexity of the Italian morphological inflections; (3) the lack of a publicly available computational lexicon suitable for generation. Nevertheless, the contribution of this paper goes beyond the adaptation of the existing implementation to a novel language. We applied indeed a treebank-based methodology (see the monolingual and multilingual resources cited below) for both evaluating our results (see sec. 4), and describing in a comparative perspective the features of the implemented grammar, referring to the differences between Italian, French and English. This makes the work more linguistically sound and data-driven. We started our work from SimpleNLG-EnFr1.1, that is an adaptation to French (Vaudry and Lapalme, 2013) of the model developed for English in (Gatt and Reiter, 2009). A property of our project is multilingualism: by using the same architecture of SimpleNLG-EnFr1.1 we are able to multilingual documents with sentences in English, French and Italian.

In porting SimpleNLG-EnFr1.1 to SimpleNLG-IT, we created 10 new packages and modified 28 existing classes. The morphology and morphonology processors needed to be written from scratch because of the features that differentiate Italian with respect to French and English. The Syntax processor needed to be adapted, especially for the management of noun and verb phrases and for clauses. However, at this stage, we used the same orthography processor of French. We needed to extend the system with 33 new lexical features, necessary for accounting verb irregularities (subjunctive, conditional, remote past, etc.) and for processing the superlative irregular form of the adjectives.

In the next Sections we survey the main features of SimpleNLG-IT, in particular: in Section 2 we describe the grammar defined by the system, that has been developed starting from the SimpleNLG-EnFr1.1. grammar; in Section 3 we describe the lexicon adopted, that has been built starting from three lexical resources available for Italian; Section 4 describes the evaluation of the system, which is based on examples from both grammar books (Patota, 2006) and an Italian treebank (Nivre et al., 2016); finally, Section 5 closes the paper with some final considerations and pointing to future works.

2 From French to Italian grammar

In this Section we will focus on the generation of constituents and on their order within the sentence in Italian. In this achievement, the main reference for Italian grammar is (Patota, 2006). In general, it must be observed that Italian, like French, is featured by a rich inflection that is clearly attested by Verbs, but also by the behavior of other grammatical categories whose *morphosyntactic* features (e.g. gender, number and case) are crucial for determining their syntactical order in the phrases to be generated. As stated above, our approach is based on that adopted for French in (Vaudry and Lapalme, 2013), which has been in turn inspired by that used for English (Gatt and Reiter, 2009). First of all, we developed therefore a comparison among Italian and these other two languages in order to detect the main novel features to be taken into account in the development of SimpleNLG-IT. The parallel treebank ParTUT[2] developed for Italian/French/English helped us in this comparison.

In the rest of this Section we organize these features in the main classes which did drive the processes we implemented: morphology and syntax, which are strictly interrelated because of the concordance phenomena, and morphonology.

2.1 Morphology and syntax

2.1.1 Verb conjugation

Italian is featured by a complexity of inflection which is typical of morphologically rich languages and its richness, in this perspective, positively compares with that of French. Nevertheless, in order to

---

[1]SimpleNLG-IT: https://github.com/alexmazzei/SimpleNLG-IT

[2]http://www.di.unito.it/~tutreeb/treebanks.html

develop a suitable model for Italian verbs, we differentiate the implementation of SimpleNLG-IT under this respect with that exploited in SimpleNLG-FrEn1.1.

The main traits that we have assumed in this phase of the project for modeling verbs are tense, progressive and perfect, as can it be seen in the Table 1. The opposition between the different features, i.e. perfect and imperfect, can be expressed by using different means in different languages. While in English aspect is especially relevant and strictly interrelated with mood and tense, in Italian and other Romance languages derived from Latin several means are available for expressing it, which vary from inflection, to lexical selection, to syntactic choice of periphrastic forms and a system of moods richer than that of English. On the one hand, the imperfect forms for present (I'm writing) and past (I was writing) and the perfect forms for present (I have written) and past (I had written) exploited in English cannot always find a unique correspondence in Italian forms. On the other hand, while the progressive form *Io sto scrivendo* surely corresponds to *I'm writing*, the form *Io scrivo* can be translated with *I write* or *I'm writing*, and the second selection is preferred in particular when a modifier is associated with the verb, like in *Io scrivo in questo momento* (I'm writing in this moment).

In order to reproduce the complete Italian verb conjugation system, we used the features TENSE[3], PERFECT, PROGRESSIVE (Table 1). Moreover we used the feature FORM to set the tenses gerund, infinitive, subjunctive.

2.1.2 Noun phrase construction

The noun phrase may include, beyond the noun, also specifiers (i.e. determiners) and modifiers (i.e. adjectives and adverbs). For specifiers the main issue to be dealt with consists in setting their morphosyntactic features according to those of the noun, assuming that their position within the noun phrase is before the noun and the premodifiers. It can be observed that Italian is more similar to French than to English for what concerns specifiers, since in most of cases nouns are mandatorily associated with spec-

---

[3]We add the values simple_past, remote_past, plus_past, plus_remote_past as possible values of the feature TENSE.

Italian conjugation	Tense	PE	PR
indicativo presente	present	F	F
imperfetto	past	F	F
futuro semplice	future	F	F
futuro anteriore	future	T	F
passato prossimo	past	T	F
passato remoto	remote-past	T	F
trapassato prossimo	plus-past	T	F
trapassato remoto	plus-remote-past	T	F
passato remoto	remote-past	T	F
presente progressivo	present	F	T
passato progressivo	past	F	T
futuro progressivo	future	F	T
condizionale presente	present	F	F
condizionale passato	past	F	F
congiuntivo presente	present	F	F
congiuntivo imperfetto	past	F	F
congiuntivo passato	past	T	F
congiuntivo trapassato	plus-past	T	F

Table 1: Relation between verb tenses and traits in Italian: **TENSE** is a multi-value feature; **PE**rfect and **PR**ogressive are two boolean features.

ifiers, while English nouns often occur without determiners.

The canonical NP word order is spec > preMod > noun > complements > postMod, but we need to introduce a number of new lexical features to account for the peculiar adjective word order with adjective types. The position that an adjective assumes with respect to the noun varies indeed accordingly with its type: ordinal, possessive and qualitative adjectives usually precede the associated noun, while colour, geografic and relation adjectives behave as noun's postmodifiers. See, e.g., *la grande casa gialla* (the big yellow house) where the adjective *big* is a qualitative adjective while *yellow* is a colour adjective. Moreover, when more than one adjective occurs, like a pre or postmodifier, a specific order must be respected, e.g. possessive > ordinal > qualitative is the canonical order for premodifiers. See e.g. *il mio primo grande viaggio* (my first big travel).

Finally, similar to SimpleNLG-EnFr1.1 we treated interrogative and demonstrative adjectives as specifiers, in contrast to the reference grammar book, which considers them as modifiers.

2.1.3 Verb phrase and sentence construction

Among the main features to be taken into account in generating a sentence there is the order of constituents, which can also strongly vary according to language and typology of sentence. For what concerns Italian, the word order in declarative sentences, as reported in the study based on the parallel treebank ParTUT developed for Italian/French/English (Sanguinetti et al., 2013), is featured by a larger variability with respect to the other two languages, since the SVO order is detected in 74.5% of Italian sentences, in 82.4% of French sentences and in 88.5% of the English ones. Nevertheless, observing that SVO is usually tolerated in Italian in most of cases, at least for the purpose of practical NLG applications, the SVO order can be exploited. The conventional word order adopted by SimpleNLG-IT in the construction of the verbal phrase is `auxiliarie(s) > premod > verb > premod > complements > postmod` where the order of the complements is `direct-object > indirect-object > other-complements`. See e.g. *ho spesso dato libri a Mario in regalo* ([I] often gave books to Mario as present).

2.1.4 Negative sentences

In French, negative sentences are featured by the canonical presence of the adverb *pas* after the verb negated by the adverb *ne* (not). For instance in *Je ne mange pas les pommes* (I don't eat apples). In Italian the negation adverb *non* (not) precedes the verb and only in particular context a second negation adverb can occur, but in order to express a particular form of topicalization on the negation. See e.g. *Io non mangio mele* (I don't eat apples) and *Io non ho nemmeno mangiato la mela* (I have not even eaten the apple). In the implementation of SimpleNLG-IT we modified therefore that made for French, by considering *non* instead of *ne* and by allowing the presence of a *negation_auxiliary* when the user want (instead of the adverb *pas*).

2.2 Morphonology

In this section we present the issues addressed for making the generated linguistic expression compliant with the morphonological tenets of Italian, like e.g. elision, preposition-article contraction and the fusion of clitics with other words.

2.2.1 Article elision

Elision affects all the Italian articles that precede nouns and adjectives beginning with a vowel. Two simple examples are: (1) *l'uomo* (the man) = *lo* [Definite Article Masculine Singular] + *uomo* [Common Noun Masculine Singular] (2) *un'interessante proposta* (an interesting proposal) = *una* [Undefined Article Feminine Singular] + *interessante* [Qualitative Adjective Feminine Singular] + *proposta* [Common Noun Feminine Singular]. We adapted with specific rules the morphonological processor introduced in SimpleNLG-EnFr1.1 to manage these cases.

2.2.2 Preposition contraction

Similar to French and Brazilian Portuguese (de Oliveira and Sripada, 2014), Italian provides a morphophonological mechanism to contract the articles and the prepositions which are associated with them in prepositional articles. Among the ten Italian proper prepositions (*di* (of), *a* (to), *da* (from), *in* (in), *con* (with), *su* (on), *per* (for), *tra* (among), *fra* (among)) only three do not contract with the article (i.e. per, tra and fra). For instance, *la casa **della** zia* (the house of-the aunt) = *la* [Definite Article Feminine Singular] + *casa* [common noun feminine singular] + ***della*** [*di* [preposition] + *la* [definite article feminine singular]] + *zia* [common noun feminine Singular]. Also for this morphophonological phenomenon we added some specific rules in the processor.

2.2.3 Clitics

Clitics are pronouns that in particular cases in Italian can be included in the verb form, like in the following example: *Dam**mi** la mela* (Give-**me** the apple). More complex forms of clitic-fusion are possible, e.g. *Dam**mela*** (Give-**me**-**it**). However, considering that in most of cases the form with the clitic separated from the verb is tolerated[4], in this phase of the project we decided to simplify clitic morphology management by applying fusion with the verb only to the pronoun that play direct-object role: if there are other pronouns they are managed by us-

---

[4]See the distinction between *strong* and *weak pronouns* in (Patota, 2006).

ing prepositions. So, SimpleNLG-IT will generate for the first example above the form *Dai a me la mela* (Give me the apple), where the prepositional phrase *a me* (to me) semantically and pragmatically corresponds to the clitic *-mi*, while the second example will be *Dalla a me* (Give-it to me) where the direct objet clitic pronoun *la* (it [feminine singular]) is fused with the verb but the indirect object (*a me*) is separated.

3 The SimpleNLG-IT lexicon

Each lexicon can be split in two major classes: open and closed classes. The closed class, that is usually composed by function words (i.e. prepositions, determiners, conjunctions, pronouns, etc.) is one to which new words are very rarely added. In contrast, the open class, that is usually composed by lexical words (i.e. nouns, verbs, adjectives, adverbs), is one that accepts the addition of new words. We adopted the same strategy of (Vaudry and Lapalme, 2013): we built by hand the closed part of the Italian lexicon and we built automatically the open part by using available resources.

Additionally, even though, if several lexical corpora are available for Italian, as the detailed map of the Italian NLP resources produces within the PARLI project shows[5], unfortunately most of them are designed to represent lexical semantics rather than morphosyntactic relations. This makes them not adequate for the sake of our task. In order to build the open class of the Italian lexicon, which is suitable for SimpleNLG-IT, we need both a large coverage and a detailed account of morphological irregularities, also considering their high frequency in Italian. Moreover, in order to have good time execution performance in the realiser (cf. (de Oliveira and Sripada, 2014)), a trade-off between the size of the lexicon and its usability for our task must be achieved, which consists in assuming a form of word classification where fundamental Italian words are distinguished from the less-fundamental ones. In order to build a so designed lexicon, we decided to merge the information represented in three existing resources for Italian, namely *Morph-it!* (Zanchetta and Baroni, 2005), the *Vocabolario di base della lin-*

gua italiana (De Mauro, 1985) and, for a specific issue, Wikipedia[6]. The difference between them can be referred to both the reasons for which the authors developed them and the adopted methodology and approach. This makes these resources especially useful for us, since they provide information relevant for SimpleNLG-IT which are the same as observed in different perspective, or complementing each other.

The dataset of the Morph-it! project consists of a lexicon organized according to the inflected word forms, with associated lemmas and morphological features (Zanchetta and Baroni, 2005). The lexicon is provided by the authors as a text file where the values of the information about each lexical entry are simply separated by a tab key. It is in practice an alphabetically ordered list of triples form-lemma-features. An example of the annotation for the form *corsi (ran)* is:

```
corsi correre-VER:ind past+1+s
```

where the features are PoS (VERb), mood of the verb (indicative), tense (past), person (1), and the number (singular). The last released version of Morph-it! (v.48, 2009-02-23) contains $505,074$ different forms corresponding to $35,056$ lemmas. It has been realized starting from a large newspaper corpus, nevertheless it is not balanced and a small number of also very common Italian words are not included in the lexicon, e.g. *sposa* (bride), *ovest* (west) or *aceto* (vinegar). Morph-IT! represents extensionally the Italian language by listing all the morphological inflections, i.e. adjective, verbs, nouns inflections are represented as a list rather than by using morphological rules. As a consequence the lexicon is huge and using the whole Morph-IT! in SimpleNLG-IT would cause time complexity problem.

The second main resource we exploited for populating the SimpleNLG-IT lexicon is the "Vocabolario di base della lingua italiana" (VdB-IT henceforth), a collection of $7,000$ words created by the linguist Tullio De Mauro and his team (De Mauro, 1985)[7]. The development of this vocabulary has been mainly driven by the distinction between the

---

[5]http://parli.di.unito.it/resources_en.html

[6]https://it.wikipedia.org

[7]The second edition of the vocabulary has been announced (Chiari and De Mauro, 2014) and it is going to be released (p.c.).

```
foreach adverb ∈ Morph-IT! ∩ VdB-IT do
│   Add the adverb in normal form into L
end
foreach adjective ∈ Morph-IT! ∩ VdB-IT do
│   Add the adjective in normal form (masculine-singular) and
│   in feminine-singular, masculine-plural, feminine-plural
│   forms, into L
end
foreach noun ∈ Morph-IT! ∩ VdB-IT do
│   Add the noun in normal form (singular), the plural form, and
│   the gender into L
end
foreach verb ∈ Morph-IT! ∩ VdB-IT do
│   if the verb is irregular then
│   │   Add into L all the inflections for the indicativo
│   │   presente, congiuntivo presente, futuro semplice,
│   │   condizionale, imperfetto, participio passato, passato
│   │   remoto
│   else
│   │   if the verb is reflexive then
│   │   │   Set active the reflexive feature in the lexicon
│   │   end
│   │   if the verb is incoativo then
│   │   │   Set active the incoativo feature in the lexicon
│   │   end
│   │   Add the verb in normal form into L
│   end
end
```

Algorithm 1: The algorithm for building the lexicon L

most frequent words (around $5,000$) and the most *familiar* words (around $2,000$). VdB-IT is therefore organized in the following three sections:

- the *vocabolario fondamentale* (fundamental vocabulary), which contains $2,000$ words featured by the highest frequency into a balanced corpus of Italian texts (composed of novels, movie and theater scripts, newspapers, basic scholastic books); *amore* (love), *lavoro* (work), *pane* (bread) are in this section.

- the *vocabolario di alto uso* (vocabulary of high usage), which includes other $2,937$ words with high frequency; *ala* (wing), *seta* (silk), *toro* (bull) are in this section

- the *vocabolario di alta disponibilità* (vocabulary of high availability), is composed of $1,753$ words not often used in written language, but featured by a high frequency in spoken language, which are indeed perceived as especially familiar by native speakers; *aglio* (garlic), *cascata* (waterfall), *passeggero* (passenger) are in this section.

This resource helps us in addressing the issues related to the comprehensibility and readability of the

PoS	Number	%
Adverb	146	2
Adjective	1333	19
Noun	4092	58
Verb	1451	21
(Irregular)	(283)	(4)
Total	7022	100

Table 2: Number of elements for the open categories in the SimpleNLG-IT lexicon.

generated texts in the SimpleNLG-IT project: indeed by using only words from the *vocabolario fondamentale* we can be confident that we are generating outputs that will be considered as comprehensible for at least 66% of the Italian speakers (De Mauro, 1985).

VdB-IT helped us to limit the size of the lexicon but does not provide information about verb behavior. We need instead to distinguish regular verbs, that are inflected by using rules extracted from the reference grammar, from the irregular ones. The reference grammar reports a partial list of the principal Italian irregular verbs, but we decided to use the larger list of verbs reported in Wikipedia[8]. Another linguistic distinction for Italian verbs reported in Wikipedia[9] has been exploited in the lexicon: the *incoativi* verbs have a special behavior in the present time and need to be marked in the lexicon. In Algorithm 1 we reported the algorithm for the creation of the SimpleNLG-IT lexicon and in Table 2 we reported some statistics about its composition.

4   SimpleNLG-IT Evaluation

NLG systems can be evaluated by using controlled as well as real world examples: the former examples can be exploited in evaluating specific features of the system, while the latter ones for testing the usability of the system in an application context. In order to provide a first but accurate evaluation of SimpleNLG-IT, we decided to apply both strategies. First, we test the system in the generation of a number of sentences obtained from

---

[8] https://it.wikipedia.org/wiki/Verbi_irregolari_italiani
[9] https://it.wikipedia.org/wiki/Verbi_incoativi

SimpleNLG-ENFr1.1. Second, we considered 20 sentences from the Italian section of the Universal Dependency Treebank (Nivre et al., 2016).

We first tested SimpleNLG-IT by running a set of Junit Tests on 96 sentences extracted and adapted from the reference grammar book and from SimpleNLG-EnFr1.1 JUnit Tests. The tests cover different sections of the Italian grammar: adjectives order, different types of sentences (relative, interrogative, coordinated, passive), verbs conjugation, clitics, etc. are analyzed. For this test, the loading into the memory of the lexicon took $1,433$ ms and the test bundle run finished in $3,145$ ms on a computer equipped with 8GB and i7 processor: all the test are passed by SimpleNLG-IT.

In the second evaluation, we wanted to test if SimpleNLG-IT is able to realize sentences from real world. The Universal Dependency Treebank (UD) is a recent project that aims to "create cross-linguistically consistent treebank annotation for many languages within a dependency-based lexicalist framework" (Nivre et al., 2016). UD released freely available treebanks for 33 languages (in this work, version 1.2). Each UD treebank is split in three sections, *train*, *dev* and *test*, which can be exploited in the evaluation of NLP/NLG systems. Indeed, for the evaluation of the SimpleNLG-it we used the test section of the Italian UD treebank (UD-IT-test). We chose 10 declarative sentences and 10 interrogative sentences, which have length up to ten words, from UD-IT-test. In Table 3 we report the sentences employed. We tried to generate each one of these sentences in SimpleNLG-IT but, since the system can generate canned text, we need to specify a number of *rules* that we respect in order to convert the dependency structure of the sentences into the SimpleNLG input structure: (i) We build a SimpleNLG input *isomorphic* to the gold dependency tree. So, we use the corresponding functions for subject, object, complement, passive verbs etc. (ii) We do not use canned texts and we do not provide information about word order. So we do not use the `insertPreModifier` and `insertPostModifier` functions. (iii) We do not provide information about genre and number for words in the lexicon. (iiii) We do not account for the punctuation inside the sentence.

We obtained very different results for declara-

tive sentences and for interrogative sentences[10]. For declarative sentences we have: two realized sentences are identical to the gold (6, 7); four realized sentences are different only in the word order respect to the gold (1, 3, 8, 10); two realized sentences are different only for clitics respect to the gold (2, 4); one realized sentence is different respect to the gold since the verb is not present in the lexicon (9); one realized sentence is different respect to the gold since the a verb is not treated as irregular (5). In contrast, in interrogative sentences we have more problematic cases: one realized sentence is identical to the gold (19); two realized sentences are different only in the word order respect to the gold (14, 16); one realized sentence is different respect to the gold since the verb is not present in the lexicon (11); six realized sentences are different respect to the gold since the SimpleNLG is not able to apply a WH-question to the specific argument (12, 13, 15, 17, 18, 20), i.e. the realiser is not able to produce HOW-MANY, WHAT, WHICH questions on the object or complements. Finally, we note that most word order errors are caused by the SVO order that is adopted in SimpleNLG-IT. Indeed, the sentences 1, 3, 8, 10, 14, 16 are grammatical but the gold sentences have a different topic-focus information structure represented with a different word order.

5   Conclusions and future work

In this paper we presented the first version of SimpleNLG-IT, a realisation engine for Italian. We introduced with respect to previous implementations a number of new features to account for the morphological and syntactical peculiarities of Italian. We developed a new schema for encoding the Italian verb tense system and a new lexicon by merging two different lexical resources. We performed a first evaluation of the system based on both controlled and real word sentences.

In future work we intend to expand SimpleNLG-IT by using information from UD-IT treebank. In particular, we want to exploit the syntactic information contained in the treebank in order: (1) to decide the correct auxiliary verb to use in order to form complex verb tense, (2) the word order of some adjectives. Indeed, both such notions cannot be ac-

---

[10]Henceforth the numbers in parentheses refer to Table 3

ID	Gold sentence	Realized sentence
1	*Chiedi al computer il tuo menù.* (Ask to the computer your menu.)	Chiedi il tuo menù al computer.
2	*Dimmi dove si trova la compagnia DuPont.* (Tell me where the DuPont company is.)	Dici a me dove la compagnia Du Pont si trova.
3	*È stato concordato un pacchetto di riforme.* (It was arranged a reform package.)	Un pacchetto di riforme è stato concordato.
4	*Lui le regalò un porcellino salvadanaio.* He gave her a piggy bank.	Egli regalò a lei un porcellino salvadanaio.
5	*È successo un quarto d'ora fa.* (It happened fifteen minutes ago.)	Ha successo un quarto d'ora fa.
6	*Mai nessuna azzurra aveva conquistato un titolo iridato.* (Never any Italian athletes had won a world title.)	Mai nessuna azzurra aveva conquistato un titolo iridato.
7	*L'espropriazione è realizzata attraverso un atto amministrativo;* (The expropriation is carried out through an administrative act;)	L'espropriazione è realizzata attraverso un atto amministrativo;
8	*Non ho preclusioni ideologiche, spiega.* (I have no ideological barriers, he explains.)	Spiega non ho preclusioni ideologice.
9	*Ogni fosso interposto tra due fondi si presume comune.* (Each ditch interposed between two funds is assumed to be shared.)	Ogni fosso interporre tra due fondi si presume comune.
10	*L'insieme di tutte queste operazioni viene chiamato stigliatura.* (The set of all these operations is called decortication.)	L'insieme di queste operazioni tutte è chiamato stigliatura.
11	*In che modo le Hawaii divennero uno stato?* (How did Hawaii become a state?)	Come le Hawai divenirono uno stato?
12	*Quante fossette ha una pallina regolamentare da golf?* (How many dimples does a regular golf ball have?)	-
13	*Da quante repubbliche era composta l'Unione Sovietica?* (How many republics did compose the USSR?)	-
14	*E i soldi delle piramidi dove sono finiti?* (And where did the money of the pyramids go?)	Dove i soldi delle piramidi sono finiti?
15	*Che cosa ha influenzato l'effetto Tequila?* (What did influence the Tequila effect?)	-
16	*Quanto si stima che costeranno le stazioni spaziali internazionali?* (How much is estimated that will cost the international space stations?)	Quanto si stima che le stazioni spaziali internazionali costeranno?
17	*Quali paesi ha visitato la first lady Hillary Clinton?* (Which countries did the first lady Hillary Clinton visit?)	-
18	*In quale giorno avvenne l'attacco a Pearl Harbor?* (Which is the date when Pearl Harbor was attacked?)	-
19	*Quando Panama si vide restituire il Canale di Panama?* (When did Panama see to return back the Panama Canal?)	Quando Panama si vide restituire il Canale di Panama?
20	*Da quale animale si ricava il veal?* (From which animal do you get the veal?)	-

Table 3: Ten sentences from the UD-IT-TEST: 1-10 are declarative sentences and 11-20 are interrogative sentences.

counted by using rules from grammar books but they need an empirical approach. Finally, in order to have a larger set of tests, we want to develop an algorithm for automatically convert dependency tree of UD-IT in SimpleNLG-IT input. In this way, we can use the whole test section of the treebank as benchmark.

References

Marcel Bollmann. 2011. Adapting SimpleNLG to German. In *Proceedings of the 13th European Workshop on Natural Language Generation*, pages 133–138, Nancy, France, September. Association for Computational Linguistics.

Isabella Chiari and Tullio De Mauro. 2014. The New Basic Vocabulary of Italian as a linguistic resource. In Roberto Basili, Alessandro Lenci, and Bernardo Magnini, editors, *1th Italian Conference on Computational Linguistics (CLiC-it)*, volume 1, pages 93–97. Pisa University Press, December.

Tullio De Mauro. 1985. *Guida all'uso delle parole.* Libri di base. Editori Riuniti.

Rodrigo de Oliveira and Somayajulu Sripada. 2014. Adapting SimpleNLG for Brazilian Portuguese reali-sation. In *Proceedings of the 8th International Natural Language Generation Conference (INLG)*, pages 93–94, Philadelphia, Pennsylvania, U.S.A., June. Association for Computational Linguistics.

Sasi Raja Sekhar Dokkara, Suresh Verma Penumathsa, and Somayajulu Gowri Sripada. 2015. A Simple Surface Realization Engine for Telugu. In *Proceedings of the 15th European Workshop on Natural Language Generation (ENLG)*, pages 1–8, Brighton, UK, September. Association for Computational Linguistics.

Albert Gatt and Ehud Reiter. 2009. SimpleNLG: A Realisation Engine for Practical Applications. In *Proceedings of the 12th European Workshop on Natural Language Generation (ENLG 2009)*, pages 90–93, Athens, Greece, March. Association for Computational Linguistics.

Joakim Nivre, Marie-Catherine de Marneffe, Filip Ginter, Yoav Goldberg, Jan Hajic, Christopher D. Manning, Ryan McDonald, Slav Petrov, Sampo Pyysalo, Natalia Silveira, Reut Tsarfaty, and Daniel Zeman. 2016. Universal dependencies v1: A multilingual treebank collection. In *Proceedings of the Tenth International Conference on Language Resources and Evaluation*

(LREC 2016), Paris, France, may. European Language Resources Association (ELRA).

Giuseppe Patota. 2006. *Grammatica di riferimento dell'italiano contemporaneo.* Guide linguistiche. Garzanti Linguistica.

Ehud Reiter and Robert Dale. 2000. *Building Natural Language Generation Systems*. Cambridge University Press, New York, NY, USA.

Manuela Sanguinetti, Cristina Bosco, and Leonardo Lesmo. 2013. Dependency and constituency in translation shift analysis. In *Proceedings of the 2nd Conference on Dependency Linguistics (DepLing)*, pages 282–291, Prague (Czech Republic). Charles University in Prague, Matfyzpress.

Pierre-Luc Vaudry and Guy Lapalme. 2013. Adapting SimpleNLG for Bilingual English-French Realisation. In *Proceedings of the 14th European Workshop on Natural Language Generation*, pages 183–187, Sofia, Bulgaria, August. Association for Computational Linguistics.

Micheal White. 2006. Efficient realization of coordinate structures in combinatory categorial grammar. *Research on Language and Computation*, 2006(4(1)):39—75.

Eros Zanchetta and Marco Baroni. 2005. Morph-it! a free corpus-based morphological resource for the italian language. *Corpus Linguistics 2005*, 1(1).

Don't Mention the Shoe! A Learning to Rank Approach to Content Selection for Image Description Generation

Josiah Wang
Department of Computer Science
University of Sheffield
United Kingdom
j.k.wang@sheffield.ac.uk

Robert Gaizauskas
Department of Computer Science
University of Sheffield
United Kingdom
r.gaizauskas@sheffield.ac.uk

Abstract

We tackle the sub-task of content selection as part of the broader challenge of automatically generating image descriptions. More specifically, we explore how decisions can be made to select what object instances should be mentioned in an image description, given an image and labelled bounding boxes. We propose casting the content selection problem as a learning to rank problem, where object instances that are most likely to be mentioned by humans when describing an image are ranked higher than those that are less likely to be mentioned. Several features are explored: those derived from bounding box localisations, from concept labels, and from image regions. Object instances are then selected based on the ranked list, where we investigate several methods for choosing a stopping criterion as the 'cut-off' point for objects in the ranked list. Our best-performing method achieves state-of-the-art performance on the ImageCLEF2015 sentence generation challenge.

1 Introduction

In recent years, there has been significant interest in developing systems capable of generating literal, sentential descriptions of images (*a boy playing with a frisbee in the park*). The task poses an interesting and difficult challenge for natural language generation, and is important for improved text and image retrieval. The image description task could potentially advance research and provide insights into multimodal natural language generation, e.g. building language models of how humans naturally describe the visual world.

A standard paradigm for approaching this task is to first detect instances of pre-defined concepts in the image to be described, and then to reason about the detected concepts to generate image descriptions. Thus, such approaches may involve various components of a standard Natural Language Generation pipeline (Reiter and Dale, 2000), such as document planning (including content determination), microplanning (lexicalisation/referring expression generation) and realisation.

In this paper, we concentrate on a specific sub-problem in such an image description generation pipeline. More specifically, we explore the *content selection* problem proposed by Wang and Gaizauskas (2015). In this setting, object instances are assumed to have already been localised in an image. Thus, given gold standard labelled bounding boxes of object instances in an image, the task is to select the appropriate bounding box instances to be mentioned in the eventual image description that is to be generated (see Figure 1 for an example). To our knowledge, there has been minimal work specifically tackling the content selection problem. However, the task is important to image description generation as not all entities depicted in an image will be mentioned by humans. For example, a fork lying on a table probably will not be mentioned in a picture of a family having dinner in the kitchen. Determining which entity will be described thus poses an interesting research question, and may provide insights into how humans decide what is important enough to be described in an image description.

Thus, the main objective of this paper is to propose methods for learning to predict the object entities depicted in an image that will be mentioned in a human-authored description of the image. Our main contribution is to develop a ranking-based content selection system that exploits stronger tex-

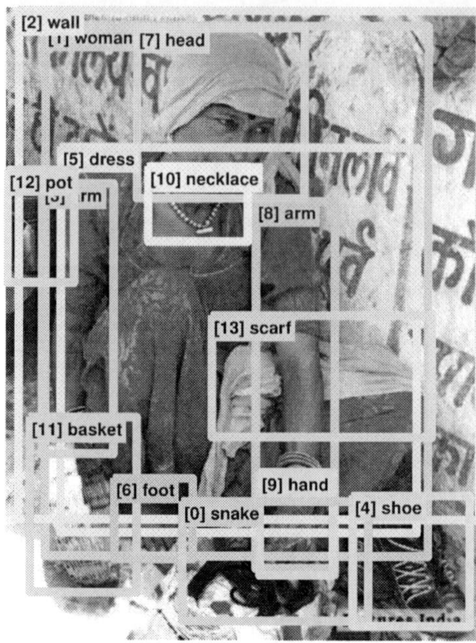

Figure 1: Given labelled bounding boxes as input, we tackle the *content selection* task, i.e. deciding which bounding box instances should be selected to be mentioned in the corresponding image description. This is an important task as humans do not mention everything that is depicted in an image. We propose casting the content selection problem as a ranking task, that is to order the bounding box instances by how likely they are to be mentioned in a human-authored image description.

tual and image features from data for the content selection problem, than those used in the baselines proposed in Wang and Gaizauskas (2015). We propose casting the content selection problem as a learning to rank problem. More specifically, given a set of labelled bounding boxes in an image, bounding boxes instances are ranked by how likely they are to be mentioned in a corresponding human description. However, as we are interested in both precision and recall, we do not require all labelled bounding boxes to be ranked; for example object instances that are unlikely to be mentioned in the description need not be ranked. Thus, we also propose various 'stopping criterion' to automatically select only relevant instances based on the rankings. Our hypothesis is that humans inherently prioritise important entities to be selected based on background knowledge and other cues, and we will thus be able to exploit this to tackle the content selection problem.

1.1 Overview

We discuss related work on the content selection problem in Section 2. In Section 3, we present our proposed approach to treat content selection as a learning to rank problem, discussing the formulation of the task (Section 3.1), features derived from bounding box localisations, concept labels and visual appearances (Section 3.2), and the various ranking algorithms explored (Section 3.3). In Section 3.4, we also propose some automatic stopping criteria to select important objects to be described from the ranking list. Experimental results are presented in Section 4, with regards to concatenating all features (Section 4.2) as well as treating individual features independently (Section 4.3). We also provide a summary of our feature ablation study in Section 4.4, and present conclusions in Section 5.

2 Related work

Image description generation. Various approaches have been proposed in the literature for the task of generation image descriptions, for example (Yao et al., 2010; Kulkarni et al., 2011; Yang et al., 2011; Mitchell et al., 2012; Karpathy and Fei-Fei, 2015; Donahue et al., 2015; Vinyals et al., 2015), among others. Most previous work concentrates on solving the problem 'end-to-end', that is to generate a description given an image as input. Such systems are also evaluated in an extrinsic manner, that is by comparing output image descriptions to multiply-annotated gold standard descriptions of the same image using global measures such as BLEU (Papineni et al., 2002), ROUGE (Lin, 2004), Meteor (Denkowski and Lavie, 2014) or CIDEr (Vedantam et al., 2015). Whilst such evaluation methodologies are useful to evaluate image description generation systems as a whole (how similar is the generated description to human-authored descriptions?), they make it hard to identify which components of the generation process contribute to any performance gains or losses. Wang and Gaizauskas (2015) propose evaluating image description generation systems in a fine grained manner, i.e. evaluating each component of the image description generation pipeline independently. To demonstrate this, they proposed the task of content selection as a precursor to generating image descriptions and performed fine-grained evaluation on this specific task.

Content selection. There has been some work on selecting objects that are important or interesting in an image. Elazary and Itti (2008) propose learning to predict object *interestingness* by the order in which objects are labelled by annotators in LabelMe. Spain and Perona (2010) propose learning to predict object importance, by asking multiple annotators (25 per image) to name 10 objects they see in each image. The annotations are then aggregated: important objects are those that are mentioned by many annotators.

Most related to our work is Berg et al. (2012), who explore factors (compositional, semantic, and contextual) that can be used to predict what is being described in an image. For prediction, they focus on a binary prediction problem – is this object described? yes or no? – and treat bounding boxes as independent of each other. In our case, we treat other bounding boxes as context, as a frequently occurring object may not be mentioned when co-occurring with some other object. Dodge et al. (2012) tackle an inverse problem: learning to predict segments of Flickr captions (noun phrases) that are 'visual', i.e. predicting whether a noun phrase in the caption is depicted in the image.

There has also been some work on measuring image memorability (what makes an image memorable to humans?), for example, Isola et al. (2011), among others. However, most work deals with memorability at image-level, rather than object level. Dubey et al. (2015) tackle image memorability at object level, that is, what objects are memorable (worth remembering) to a person in an image. This acts as a precursor to the content selection problem of choosing what to describe in an image description.

Ortiz et al. (2015) treat image description generation as a Statistical Machine Translation (SMT) task, and concentrate on describing abstract, clipart scenes. Part of their pipeline involves a content selection module where rankings of object *pairs* are optimised as an integer linear programming (ILP) problem, allowing object pairs that frequently co-occur and are close to each other to be ranked higher than those that are not. Our approach is not constrained to pairwise features, and automatically learns to optimise rankings across all *instances* directly from a training set, using arbitrary feature vectors.

Directly related to our work is Wang and Gaizauskas (2015), who propose some baselines for content selection assuming 'clean' visual input is provided in the form of bounding boxes labelled with concepts. The baselines are based on various textual and visual cues. We aim to move beyond these baselines and attempt to improve the performance of content selection on the same dataset used in their paper.

Learning to rank. Learning to rank is a problem common in the field of Information Retrieval. Many approaches have been proposed to learn to rank instances in a document in order of their relevance to a query. The approaches can generally be divided into three main groups:

- **Pointwise** ranking: Each instance in a document are treated independently of each other.

- **Pairwise** ranking: The relative rank of pairs of instances are optimized in the objective function.

- **Listwise** ranking: The rankings are optimised directly on the evaluation metric (e.g. normalied discounted cumulative gain (NDCG)).

We refer readers to Li (2011) for a summary of different techniques for learning to rank.

3 Learning to rank object instances

In this paper, we use the dataset from the Image-CLEF 2015 Scalable Image Annotation, Localization and Sentence Generation challenge (Villegas et al., 2015; Gilbert et al., 2015). More specifically, we tackle the 'clean track' of the sentence generation task. In this track, participants are provided with images with bounding box instances labelled with a WordNet sysnet (from 251 possible synset categories). Each image also contains 5-51 corresponding descriptions per image. Each description has been annotated with the correspondence between a bounding box instance and a textual term in the description (e.g. "man" in description refers to bounding box instance 1 in the image). There are 500 development images and 450 test images. At test time, participants are provided labelled bounding boxes as input, and are asked to produce systems capable of selecting the bounding boxes that are mentioned in the human-authored descriptions.

3.1 Problem definition

Let $B^i = \{b_1^i, b_2^i, ..., b_k^i\}$ be the set of labelled bounding boxes for an image $i \in I$, where $b_j^i = (l_j^i, c_j^i)$, and l_j^i is the bounding box localisation (position and size), and $c_j^i \in C$ is the concept label for the bounding box j, and $|C| = 251$ is the number of pre-defined categories. Given the set of input bounding boxes B^i for each image i, the eventual task is to predict the set of bounding box instances that are most likely to be mentioned in the gold standard descriptions. Casting this as a ranking task, we aim to predict the relevance of the bounding boxes, i.e. most likely to be mentioned in the gold standard, and then rank the bounding box instances by their relevance.

As a learning to rank problem, our objective is to learn, from some training data, to predict the relevance of an unseen bounding box instance for a test image, given other bounding box instances of the same image as well as features x_j^i derived from each bounding box instance b_j^i.

3.2 Features

We explore different features, derived from (i) the bounding box localisation, l_j^i; (ii) the concept label, c_j^i; or (iii) the visual appearance of the region in image i bounded by l_j^i. The features we explore are:

- **bboxsize**: the area of the object bounding box relative to the image.

- **bboxdist**: distance of the centre of the object bounding box from the image centre. For this paper, we negate the distance to accommodate classifiers that assume positive linear relations.

- **textiv**: a 251 dimensional one-hot vector with 1 for the matching concept label and 0 for the others.

- **textemb**: a 300 dimensional synset embedding derived from word2vec pretrained on the Google News Dataset (Mikolov et al., 2013). As each concept label is a WordNet synset, we further fine-tuned the embeddings to obtain *synset embeddings* in the original word2vec embedding space with AutoExtend (Rothe and Schütze, 2015), where an autoencoder is learnt based on WordNet terms, lexemes and hypernym relations.

- **imgemb**: a 4,096 dimensional image embedding for the object region enclosed by the bounding box. For this paper we used the penultimate layer (FC7) of the 16-layer variant of VGGNet (VGG-16) (Simonyan and Zisserman, 2014). Intuitively, this feature represents the visual appearance of the region enclosed by the bounding box.

In early experiments, we experimented with using the absolute bounding box positions (x and y coordinates) as a features. However, these features yielded poor performance, and were thus discarded in subsequent experiments.

We also explore combining the features to examine the contribution of each feature, to determine which features play a role in the content selection task.

3.3 Ranking algorithms

For ranking, we consider several commonly used algorithms in the literature for Learning to Rank. We select one example from each of the group of approaches (pointwise, pairwise, listwise):

- **rforest**: Random forests (Breiman, 2001), an algorithm using *pointwise* ranking. We use the implementation of random forests in RankLib[1] in this paper.

- **svmrank**: Ranking SVM (Joachims, 2002), an algorithm using *pairwise* ranking. We use the SVM^{rank} implementation (Joachims, 2006) of Ranking SVM in this paper. A linear kernel is used for this paper. [2]

- **cascent**: Coordinate ascent (Metzler and Croft, 2007), an algorithm using *listwise* ranking. In our paper, we optimise the rankings using NDCG@10 as a metric. Again, we use the implementation of coordinate ascent in RankLib.

For these algorithms, we compute the relevance score for each bounding box instance as the proportion of human-authored, gold standard descriptions that mention the concept. The task is to learn to predict the relevance score given the features in Section 3.2, and subsequently rank the bounding box instances for each image by this score. As

---

[1] http://www.lemurproject.org/ranklib.php
[2] We have experimented with an RBF kernel, but found the results comparable to a linear kernel.

such, this task is treated as a continuous regression problem.[3]

Our intuition is that pairwise and listwise ranking algorithms would suit our task better than pointwise algorithms, as pairwise/listwise ranking implicitly considers all other object instances as context rather than treating each instance independently as in pointwise ranking. For example, a *table* might be important and frequently mentioned, but might not be mentioned when co-occurring with *kitchen*.

3.4 Stopping criteria

While the ranking process will result in a ranked list of *all* input object instances per images, there is a need to provide a cut-off point in the rankings for the eventual task of content selection.

From our initial experiments, we found that the number of selected object instances greatly affects the F-scores (see Section 4.1 for evaluation measure). Selecting fewer good object instances per image will raise precision at the expense of lower recall, while selecting more objects will increase recall at the expense of lower precision. Wang and Gaizauskas (2015) propose a fixed threshold for the maximum number of object instances to be selected, and found that selecting 3 to 4 object instances yields an optimal balance between precision and recall (the mean number of unique bounding box instances per description is 2.89 in the development dataset). However, it may be more beneficial to have a variable threshold across images depending on the number of input object instances. For example, the bigram-based feature proposed in Wang and Gaizauskas (2015) has an internal stopping criterion, resulting in higher overall precision when compared to other fixed length features.

Motivated by the high precision scores of the aforementioned system, in this paper we propose two variable stopping criteria:

- **absolute**: Retaining only object instances with a predicted relevance score above a certain threshold.

- **relative**: Setting the cut-off point at the largest *difference* in relevance scores.

In the former case (**absolute**), we first normalise the predicted score across bounding boxes per image, where the highest-ranked bounding box is assigned a score of 1 and the lowest-ranked a score of 0. We retain only bounding box instances where the normalised predicted score is above a threshold (0.5 in our experiments).

The motivation for the latter case (**relative**) stems from our observation that the relevance scores in the development set reduces dramatically once the most important object instances are selected. For example, the most relevant object instances may have a relevance score of 0.9 and 0.8 followed by 0.2. Thus, a suitable cut-off point would be between 0.8 and 0.2. Cutting off at the point that immediately precedes the biggest difference in scores (after 0.8 in the example above) we refer to as **relative1** in our experiments. We also found that cutting off the ranked list after the point that *follows* the largest difference in score (after 0.2 in the example above) produces a marginally higher F-score (increased recall at the expense of precision). We therefore also report the results for this as a variant, which we refer to as **relative2**.

4 Experimental results

4.1 Evaluation measure

Following the convention of the ImageCLEF2015 Sentence Generation challenge, we evaluate content selection using the fine-grained evaluation metric proposed in Wang and Gaizauskas (2015) and Gilbert et al. (2015). More specifically, we measure the F-score (including $Precision$ and $Recall$) when comparing the object instances selected by our system to the object instances mentioned in the gold standard human-authored image descriptions. The human upper-bound is estimated by evaluating one description against the other descriptions of the image and repeating the process for all descriptions.

We compare our results to the winning participants of past ImageCLEF challenges. **RUC 2015** (Li et al., 2015) achieved the best performance in the 2015 edition (Villegas et al., 2015; Gilbert et al., 2015) with high precision, but used an external image description dataset to train their joint CNN-LSTM image captioning system, and performed content selection in a retrospective manner. **DUTh 2016** (Barlas et al., 2016) achieved the best performance (high recall) in the 2016 edition (Villegas et al., 2016; Gilbert et al., 2016),

---

[3]We also experimented with ordinal regression, where regression scores are partitioned into a set of integers {0,1,2,3,4} based on the relevance score (with 4 being the most relevant). We found performance to be lower, in general. Thus, we only report results for continuous regression.

	Stopping Criterion	P	R	F
	RUC 2015	0.68 ± 0.30	0.48 ± 0.24	0.53 ± 0.23
	DUTh 2016	0.45 ± 0.17	0.79 ± 0.20	0.55 ± 0.15
	W&G 2015	0.59 ± 0.19	0.58 ± 0.22	0.56 ± 0.18
cascent	**$k = 3$**	0.59 ± 0.22	0.56 ± 0.23	0.55 ± 0.20
	$k = 4$	0.50 ± 0.20	0.63 ± 0.22	0.54 ± 0.17
	absolute	0.42 ± 0.22	0.72 ± 0.22	0.49 ± 0.17
	relative1	0.72 ± 0.33	0.57 ± 0.29	0.53 ± 0.22
	relative2	0.56 ± 0.25	0.66 ± 0.26	0.54 ± 0.20
svmrank	**$k = 3$**	0.60 ± 0.20	0.59 ± 0.22	0.57 ± 0.18
	$k = 4$	0.53 ± 0.18	0.68 ± 0.21	0.58 ± 0.16
	absolute	0.43 ± 0.20	0.80 ± 0.19	0.52 ± 0.15
	relative1	0.67 ± 0.31	0.61 ± 0.29	0.53 ± 0.19
	relative2	0.55 ± 0.25	0.70 ± 0.25	0.55 ± 0.18
rforest	**$k = 3$**	0.69 ± 0.18	0.68 ± 0.21	0.66 ± 0.16
	$k = 4$	0.60 ± 0.17	0.76 ± 0.19	0.65 ± 0.14
	absolute	0.84 ± 0.19	0.64 ± 0.21	**0.70 ± 0.16**
	relative1	0.89 ± 0.18	0.57 ± 0.23	0.66 ± 0.18
	relative2	0.71 ± 0.18	0.69 ± 0.21	0.68 ± 0.17
	Human	0.77 ± 0.11	0.77 ± 0.11	0.74 ± 0.12

Table 1: Results of combining all features: Mean Precision, Recall and F-score (with standard deviations) for different algorithms and stopping criteria, compared to the winning ImageCLEF participants (**RUC 2015** and **DUTh 2016**), the best reported results of Wang and Gaizauskas (2015) (**W&G 2015**) and a human upper-bound.

using a binary SVM classifier with bounding box localisation and visual features. We also compare our performance to the best reported results in Wang and Gaizauskas (2015) (**W&G 2015**), namely by combining bigram and bounding box size priors with a stopping criterion of $k = 3$.

4.2 Combining features

We first report the results of concatenating all features (Section 3.2) as a single vector, and compare the performance of the various ranking algorithms (Section 3.3) and stopping criteria (Section 3.4). The intuition is that the ranking algorithm will perform automatic feature selection to select the most discriminative features useful for predicting the relevance score.

Table 1 shows the results of using a combination of all features. The pointwise ranking based Random Forests classifier performs best overall, achieving an F-score of 0.70, close to the human upper-bound of 0.74. This significantly exceeds the previous state-of-the-art result on the same training and test data of $F = 0.56$, as reported in Wang and Gaizauskas (2015). The coordinate ascent ranker and Ranking SVM achieved comparable scores, the latter perhaps having a slight edge.

	Stopping Criterion	P	R	F
cascent	**$k = 3$**	0.63 ± 0.21	0.62 ± 0.21	0.60 ± 0.17
	$k = 4$	0.55 ± 0.19	0.69 ± 0.21	0.59 ± 0.16
	absolute	0.54 ± 0.22	0.71 ± 0.20	0.58 ± 0.15
	relative1	0.84 ± 0.25	0.57 ± 0.24	0.61 ± 0.18
	relative2	0.63 ± 0.22	0.66 ± 0.23	0.61 ± 0.17
svmrank	**$k = 3$**	0.65 ± 0.19	0.64 ± 0.22	0.62 ± 0.17
	$k = 4$	0.57 ± 0.18	0.72 ± 0.21	0.61 ± 0.15
	absolute	0.81 ± 0.24	0.55 ± 0.23	0.62 ± 0.18
	relative1	0.85 ± 0.24	0.51 ± 0.23	0.59 ± 0.17
	relative2	0.69 ± 0.21	0.65 ± 0.22	0.64 ± 0.18
rforest	**$k = 3$**	0.69 ± 0.18	0.68 ± 0.20	0.66 ± 0.16
	$k = 4$	0.60 ± 0.17	0.75 ± 0.19	0.64 ± 0.14
	absolute	0.83 ± 0.19	0.66 ± 0.21	**0.71 ± 0.16**
	relative1	0.88 ± 0.18	0.59 ± 0.23	0.67 ± 0.18
	relative2	0.70 ± 0.17	0.70 ± 0.21	0.68 ± 0.15

Table 2: Results of combining features derived from bounding box localisation and concept labels (excluding image region features). In contrast to Table 1, excluding image region features improves the performance of both **cascent** and **svmrank**.

The performance of the various stopping criteria seems to be dependent on the ranking algorithm. The **absolute** stopping criterion seems to be sensitive to the type of ranking algorithm. As expected, **relative1** achieved higher precision than **relative2**, whereas **relative2** achieved better recall with the additional object instance being selected.

In an earlier experiment, we have explored combining only features derived from bounding box localisation and concept labels, excluding image region features (**imgemb**). Interestingly, we found better performance by excluding image region features for **cascent** and **svmrank**, but not much difference for **rforest** (compare Table 1 and Table 2). This is very likely because the high dimensional image features (4,096D) dominated the ranking decisions for these rankers, compared to **rforest** which seemed less affected by the imbalance. The performance of **cascent** and **svmrank** in Table 1 is similar to that of using only image region features (c.f. Table 5, to be discussed later), further confirming our suspicion.

4.3 Individual features

We now explore each feature individually to investigate the contributions of each. Table 3 shows the results for the features derived from bounding box localisation (**bboxsize** and **bboxdist**). The same scores are obtained from both **cascent** and **svmrank**, possibly because both these features are single dimensional vectors. **rforest** requires higher dimensionality to operate, and as such is unable

	Stopping Criterion	P	R	F
bboxsize	k = 3	0.53 ± 0.20	0.55 ± 0.26	0.53 ± 0.21
	k = 4	0.50 ± 0.16	0.66 ± 0.24	0.55 ± 0.17
	absolute	0.56 ± 0.28	0.44 ± 0.28	0.46 ± 0.25
	relative1	0.56 ± 0.34	0.36 ± 0.29	0.40 ± 0.27
	relative2	0.54 ± 0.22	0.51 ± 0.28	0.49 ± 0.22
bboxdist	k = 3	0.39 ± 0.22	0.40 ± 0.27	0.38 ± 0.23
	k = 4	0.36 ± 0.18	0.48 ± 0.28	0.39 ± 0.21
	absolute	0.32 ± 0.19	0.71 ± 0.20	0.41 ± 0.16
	relative1	0.40 ± 0.30	0.64 ± 0.32	0.40 ± 0.21
	relative2	0.34 ± 0.21	0.69 ± 0.31	0.39 ± 0.19

Table 3: Mean $Precision$, $Recall$ and F-score for features derived from bounding box localisation. Both **cascent** and **svmrank** return the same scores (shown). **rforest** is unable to handle single dimensional vectors. The results for **k=3** and **k=4** are comparable to Wang and Gaizauskas (2015).

	Stopping Criterion	P	R	F
cascent textiv	k = 3	0.61 ± 0.22	0.59 ± 0.22	0.58 ± 0.19
	k = 4	0.53 ± 0.20	0.66 ± 0.22	0.57 ± 0.17
	absolute	0.54 ± 0.30	0.76 ± 0.20	0.55 ± 0.19
	relative1	0.58 ± 0.36	0.69 ± 0.28	0.48 ± 0.18
	relative2	0.48 ± 0.29	0.78 ± 0.23	0.51 ± 0.20
cascent textemb	k = 3	0.60 ± 0.21	0.59 ± 0.21	0.57 ± 0.18
	k = 4	0.52 ± 0.19	0.65 ± 0.21	0.56 ± 0.17
	absolute	0.36 ± 0.19	0.79 ± 0.19	0.46 ± 0.15
	relative1	0.59 ± 0.37	0.71 ± 0.27	0.50 ± 0.21
	relative2	0.45 ± 0.26	0.76 ± 0.25	0.49 ± 0.20
svmrank textiv	k = 3	0.60 ± 0.22	0.58 ± 0.22	0.57 ± 0.19
	k = 4	0.53 ± 0.19	0.68 ± 0.21	0.57 ± 0.16
	absolute	0.70 ± 0.32	0.60 ± 0.27	0.54 ± 0.16
	relative1	0.71 ± 0.33	0.59 ± 0.27	0.53 ± 0.17
	relative2	0.57 ± 0.26	0.69 ± 0.25	0.55 ± 0.18
svmrank textemb	k = 3	0.60 ± 0.21	0.58 ± 0.22	0.57 ± 0.18
	k = 4	0.51 ± 0.20	0.64 ± 0.21	0.55 ± 0.17
	absolute	0.77 ± 0.28	0.56 ± 0.23	0.59 ± 0.18
	relative1	0.82 ± 0.26	0.52 ± 0.23	0.58 ± 0.18
	relative2	0.63 ± 0.22	0.62 ± 0.23	0.60 ± 0.18
rforest textiv	k = 3	0.64 ± 0.21	0.63 ± 0.22	0.61 ± 0.18
	k = 4	0.56 ± 0.19	0.70 ± 0.21	0.60 ± 0.16
	absolute	0.79 ± 0.23	0.62 ± 0.22	0.66 ± 0.19
	relative1	0.84 ± 0.23	0.57 ± 0.23	0.64 ± 0.20
	relative2	0.66 ± 0.19	0.67 ± 0.21	0.64 ± 0.17
rforest textemb	k = 3	0.65 ± 0.20	0.64 ± 0.22	0.62 ± 0.18
	k = 4	0.57 ± 0.19	0.71 ± 0.21	0.61 ± 0.16
	absolute	0.78 ± 0.23	0.64 ± 0.21	0.67 ± 0.18
	relative1	0.84 ± 0.22	0.58 ± 0.23	0.65 ± 0.19
	relative2	0.67 ± 0.19	0.68 ± 0.21	0.65 ± 0.17

Table 4: Mean $Precision$, $Recall$ and F-score for features derived from concept labels (one-hot indicator vectors and text embeddings).

to handle these one-dimensional features. The results are consistent with what was reported by Wang and Gaizauskas (2015) – that whilst both **bboxdist** and **bboxsize** show that content selection is dependent on these features, **bboxsize** is a better predictor for an object being selected compared to **bboxdist**.[4]

Table 4 shows the results for features derived from concept labels (**textiv** and **textemb**). For these three rankers, **textemb** seems to outperform **textiv**. The only exception is for **cascent** when the stopping criterion is **absolute**, where **textiv** seemed to give better precision than **textemb**. Comparing Table 3 and Table 4, we can see that features derived from concept labels are stronger predictors for content selection.

Table 5 shows the results of using only image region features (**imgemb**). Here, **cascent** does not perform as well as **svmrank** and **rforest**, due to the high dimensionality of the CNN embeddings. The performance of image region features seem to be on par with features derived from concept labels (Table 4), and better than bounding box features (Table 3). Noteworthy is how image region features yield higher recall than other features in general, at the expense of lower precision.

4.4 Feature ablation

We also performed a feature ablation study to gain insights into which features are important to content selection and the interaction between the features. This is done by testing different combinations of features to investigate which features contribute better to the overall performance and thus play a bigger role for content selection.

Because of space constraints, we only provide a summary of interesting observations. Table 6 shows the F-scores for the **rforest** ranker with the **absolute** stopping criterion. We found that the features based on concept labels are dominant and influential in our experiments compared to those based on bounding box localisation or visual appearances. Combining **textiv** and **textemb** alone already yielded an F-score of 0.67. This demonstrates that semantic concept labels are the best predictors for content selection. Adding **bboxsize** to **imgemb** improves the F-scores marginally, suggesting that the object size does play some role on top of visual appearances in selecting important objects. We also found that for **rforest** rankers, **textemb** plays a larger role in predicting content selection compared to **textiv**, as evidenced by a greater drop in F-scores when omitting **textemb** compared to **textiv**.

---

[4]This was demonstrated in the errata provided by Wang and Gaizauskas (2015) after the paper was published.

	Stopping Criterion	P	R	F
cascent imgemb	k = 3	0.50 ± 0.23	0.47 ± 0.24	0.47 ± 0.21
	k = 4	0.45 ± 0.19	0.55 ± 0.24	0.48 ± 0.19
	absolute	0.29 ± 0.14	0.80 ± 0.22	0.40 ± 0.14
	relative1	0.39 ± 0.30	0.73 ± 0.32	0.39 ± 0.18
	relative2	0.34 ± 0.22	0.79 ± 0.29	0.40 ± 0.17
symrank imgemb	k = 3	0.60 ± 0.20	0.59 ± 0.22	0.57 ± 0.18
	k = 4	0.53 ± 0.18	0.67 ± 0.21	0.57 ± 0.16
	absolute	0.43 ± 0.20	0.80 ± 0.19	0.52 ± 0.15
	relative1	0.66 ± 0.31	0.61 ± 0.29	0.53 ± 0.20
	relative2	0.54 ± 0.25	0.69 ± 0.26	0.54 ± 0.19
rforest imgemb	k = 3	0.60 ± 0.20	0.59 ± 0.22	0.58 ± 0.18
	k = 4	0.53 ± 0.18	0.67 ± 0.22	0.57 ± 0.16
	absolute	0.47 ± 0.19	0.76 ± 0.20	0.55 ± 0.15
	relative1	0.64 ± 0.29	0.62 ± 0.28	0.55 ± 0.19
	relative2	0.52 ± 0.22	0.69 ± 0.26	0.55 ± 0.17

Table 5: Mean Precision, Recall and F-score for features derived from image region features (image embeddings).

4.5 Discussion

We observed that the pointwise-based random forests ranker performs better than the pairwise and listwise-based rankers. This is surprising as we expected either pairwise- or listwise-based rankers to perform better than pointwise-based rankers, which treat each instance in a document as independent without considering other instances within the same document. It still remains unclear whether this is due to the random forests classifier itself being strong or that context plays a lesser role in content selection for this particular dataset. Further work is required to ascertain this.

5 Conclusion

We explored the content selection problem of deciding what needs to be mentioned in the description of an image, given labelled bounding boxes as input. We proposed casting the problem as a learning to rank task, where object instances that are more likely to be mentioned in human-authored descriptions are ranked higher than those less likely to be mentioned. Several features are explored: those derived from bounding box localisations, concept labels and visual appearances for each object instance. We also proposed methods to automatically estimate a cut-off point in each ranked list, to select only object instances that are likely to be mentioned in the image description.

Our method showed excellent results, achieving the state-of-the-art F-score of 0.70 on the Image-CLEF2015 content selection dataset, substantially out-performing the highest figures previously re-

	Feature				rforest
bboxdist	bboxsize	textiv	textemb	imgemb	F
✓					-
	✓				-
		✓			0.66 ± 0.19
			✓		0.67 ± 0.18
				✓	0.55 ± 0.15
✓	✓				-
✓		✓			0.66 ± 0.17
✓			✓		0.69 ± 0.16
✓				✓	0.55 ± 0.15
	✓	✓			0.67 ± 0.18
	✓		✓		0.70 ± 0.16
	✓			✓	0.57 ± 0.16
		✓	✓		0.67 ± 0.18
		✓		✓	0.62 ± 0.16
			✓	✓	0.70 ± 0.16
✓	✓	✓			0.67 ± 0.17
✓	✓		✓		0.70 ± 0.16
✓	✓			✓	0.57 ± 0.15
✓		✓	✓		0.69 ± 0.16
✓		✓		✓	0.63 ± 0.16
✓			✓	✓	0.69 ± 0.16
	✓	✓	✓		0.70 ± 0.16
	✓	✓		✓	0.64 ± 0.16
	✓		✓	✓	0.70 ± 0.17
		✓	✓	✓	0.69 ± 0.16
✓	✓	✓	✓		0.71 ± 0.16
✓	✓	✓		✓	0.64 ± 0.17
✓	✓		✓	✓	0.70 ± 0.17
✓		✓	✓	✓	0.69 ± 0.16
	✓	✓	✓	✓	0.70 ± 0.16
✓	✓	✓	✓	✓	0.70 ± 0.16

Table 6: Results of the feature ablation test: mean F-scores for **rforest** with the **absolute** stopping criterion, for various combinations of features. Some results are omitted because **rforest** does not work well with single or two dimensional features.

ported on this test set. We also found that for the proposed features, those that are derived from the concept labels are better predictors for the content selection task than those derived from bounding box localisations or visual appearance of regions.

The proposed learning to rank approach is general enough and may also be relevant to content selection tasks in other areas of natural language generation. Future work could include exploring even stronger features. There is also scope to automatically gather a larger noisy dataset to enable more robust learning and reduce reliance on annotating training data. We hope that these additions will further improve the content selection capabilities of the proposed system.

6 Acknowledgements

The authors acknowledge funding from the ERA-NET CHIST-ERA Visual Sense (ViSen) project – UK EPSRC grant reference: EP/K019082/1.

References

Georgios Barlas, Maria Ntonti, and Avi Arampatzis. 2016. DUTh at the ImageCLEF 2016 Image Annotation Task: Content Selection. In *CLEF2016 Working Notes*, CEUR Workshop Proceedings, Évora, Portugal, September. CEUR-WS.org.

Alexander C. Berg, Tamara L. Berg, Hall Daumé III, Jesse Dodge, Amit Goyal, Xufeng Han, Alyssa Mensch, Margaret Mitchell, Aneesh Sood, Karl Stratos, and Kota Yamaguchi. 2012. Understanding and predicting importance in images. In *Proceedings of the IEEE Conference on Computer Vision & Pattern Recognition*.

Leo Breiman. 2001. Random forests. *Machine Learning*, 45(1):5–32, October.

Michael Denkowski and Alon Lavie. 2014. Meteor universal: Language specific translation evaluation for any target language. In *Proceedings of the EACL 2014 Workshop on Statistical Machine Translation*.

Jesse Dodge, Amit Goyal, Xufeng Han, Alyssa Mensch, Margaret Mitchell, Karl Stratos, Kota Yamaguchi, Yejin Choi, Hal Daumé III, Alexander C. Berg, and Tamara L. Berg. 2012. Detecting visual text. In *Proceedings of the North American Chapter of the Association for Computational Linguistics (NAACL)*.

Jeffrey Donahue, Lisa Anne Hendricks, Sergio Guadarrama, Marcus Rohrbach, Subhashini Venugopalan, Kate Saenko, and Trevor Darrell. 2015. Long-term recurrent convolutional networks for visual recognition and description. In *Proceedings of the IEEE Conference on Computer Vision & Pattern Recognition*.

Rachit Dubey, Joshua Peterson, Aditya Khosla, Ming-Hsuan Yang, and Bernard Ghanem. 2015. What makes an object memorable? In *Proceedings of the IEEE International Conference on Computer Vision*.

Lior Elazary and Laurent Itti. 2008. Interesting objects are visually salient. *Journal of Vision*, 8(3:3):1–15, Mar.

Andrew Gilbert, Luca Piras, Josiah Wang, Fei Yan, Emmanuel Dellandrea, Robert Gaizauskas, Mauricio Villegas, and Krystian Mikolajczyk. 2015. Overview of the ImageCLEF 2015 Scalable Image Annotation, Localization and Sentence Generation task. In *CLEF2015 Working Notes*, CEUR Workshop Proceedings, Toulouse, France, September 8-11. CEUR-WS.org.

Andrew Gilbert, Luca Piras, Josiah Wang, Fei Yan, Arnau Ramisa, Emmanuel Dellandrea, Robert Gaizauskas, Mauricio Villegas, and Krystian Mikolajczyk. 2016. Overview of the ImageCLEF 2016 Scalable Concept Image Annotation Task. In *CLEF2016 Working Notes*, CEUR Workshop Proceedings, Évora, Portugal, September 5-8. CEUR-WS.org.

Phillip Isola, Jianxiong Xiao, Antonio Torralba, and Aude Oliva. 2011. What makes an image memorable? In *Proceedings of the IEEE Conference on Computer Vision & Pattern Recognition*, pages 145–152.

Thorsten Joachims. 2002. Optimizing search engines using clickthrough data. In *Proceedings of the Eighth ACM SIGKDD International Conference on Knowledge Discovery and Data Mining*, KDD '02, pages 133–142, New York, NY, USA. ACM.

Thorsten Joachims. 2006. Training linear SVMs in linear time. In *Proceedings of the 12th ACM SIGKDD International Conference on Knowledge Discovery and Data Mining*, KDD '06, pages 217–226, New York, NY, USA. ACM.

Andrej Karpathy and Li Fei-Fei. 2015. Deep visual-semantic alignments for generating image descriptions. In *Proceedings of the IEEE Conference on Computer Vision & Pattern Recognition*.

Girish Kulkarni, Visruth Premraj, Sagnik Dhar, Siming Li, Yejin Choi, Alexander C. Berg, and Tamara L. Berg. 2011. Baby talk: Understanding and generating image descriptions. In *Proceedings of the IEEE Conference on Computer Vision & Pattern Recognition*.

Xirong Li, Qin Jin, Shuai Liao, Junwei Liang, Xixi He, Yu-Jia Huo, Weiyu Lan, Bin Xiao, Yanxiong Lu, and Jieping Xu. 2015. RUC-Tencent at ImageCLEF 2015: Concept Detection, Localization and Sentence Generation. In *CLEF2015 Working Notes*, CEUR Workshop Proceedings, Toulouse, France, September 8-11. CEUR-WS.org.

Hang Li. 2011. A short introduction to learning to rank. *IEICE Transactions*, 94-D(10):1854–1862.

Chin-Yew Lin. 2004. ROUGE: A package for automatic evaluation of summaries. In *Proc. ACL workshop on Text Summarization Branches Out*, page 10.

Donald Metzler and W. Bruce Croft. 2007. Linear feature-based models for information retrieval. *Information Retrieval*, 10(3):257–274.

Tomas Mikolov, Ilya Sutskever, Kai Chen, Greg Corrado, and Jeffrey Dean. 2013. Distributed representations of words and phrases and their compositionality. In *Advances in Neural Information Processing Systems*.

Margaret Mitchell, Jesse Dodge, Amit Goyal, Kota Yamaguchi, Karl Stratos, Xufeng Han, Alyssa Mensch, Alex Berg, Tamara Berg, and Hal Daume III. 2012. Midge: Generating image descriptions from computer vision detections. In *Proceedings of the 13th Conference of the European Chapter of the Association for Computational Linguistics*, pages 747–756, Avignon, France, April. Association for Computational Linguistics.

Luis Gilberto Mateos Ortiz, Clemens Wolff, and Mirella Lapata. 2015. Learning to interpret and describe abstract scenes. In *Proceedings of the 2015 Conference of the North American Chapter of the Association for Computational Linguistics: Human Language Technologies*, pages 1505–1515, Denver, Colorado, May–June. Association for Computational Linguistics.

Kishore Papineni, Salim Roukos, Todd Ward, and Wei-Jing Zhu. 2002. Bleu: a method for automatic evaluation of machine translation. In *Proceedings of 40th Annual Meeting of the Association for Computational Linguistics*, pages 311–318, Philadelphia, Pennsylvania, USA, July. Association for Computational Linguistics.

Ehud Reiter and Robert Dale. 2000. *Building Natural Language Generation Systems*. Cambridge University Press, New York, NY, USA.

Sascha Rothe and Hinrich Schütze. 2015. Autoextend: Extending word embeddings to embeddings for synsets and lexemes. In *the 53rd Annual Meeting of the Association for Computational Linguistics and the 7th International Joint Conference on Natural Language Processing (ACL)*.

Karen Simonyan and Andrew Zisserman. 2014. Very deep convolutional networks for large-scale image recognition. *CoRR*, abs/1409.1556.

Merrielle Spain and Pietro Perona. 2010. Measuring and predicting object importance. *International Journal of Computer Vision*.

Ramakrishna Vedantam, C. Lawrence Zitnick, and Devi Parikh. 2015. Cider: Consensus-based image description evaluation. In *Proceedings of the IEEE Conference on Computer Vision & Pattern Recognition*, June.

Mauricio Villegas, Henning Müller, Andrew Gilbert, Luca Piras, Josiah Wang, Krystian Mikolajczyk, Alba García Seco de Herrera, Stefano Bromuri, M. Ashraful Amin, Mahmood Kazi Mohammed, Burak Acar, Suzan Uskudarli, Neda B. Marvasti, José F. Aldana, and María del Mar Roldán García. 2015. General Overview of ImageCLEF at the CLEF 2015 Labs. In Josiane Mothe, Jacques Savoy, Jaap Kamps, Karen Pinel-Sauvagnat, Gareth J. F. Jones, Eric San Juan, Linda Cappellato, and Nicola Ferro, editors, *Experimental IR Meets Multilinguality, Multimodality, and Interaction*, volume 9283 of *Lecture Notes in Computer Science*, pages 444–461. Springer International Publishing.

Mauricio Villegas, Henning Müller, Alba García Seco de Herrera, Roger Schaer, Stefano Bromuri, Andrew Gilbert, Luca Piras, Josiah Wang, Fei Yan, Arnau Ramisa, Emmanuel Dellandrea, Robert Gaizauskas, Krystian Mikolajczyk, Joan Puigcerver, Alejandro H. Toselli, Joan-Andreu Sánchez, and Enrique Vidal. 2016. General Overview of Image-CLEF at the CLEF 2016 Labs. In Norbert Fuhr,

Paulo Quaresma, Teresa Gonçalves, Birger Larsen, Krisztian Balog, Craig Macdonald, Linda Cappellato, and Nicola Ferro, editors, *Experimental IR Meets Multilinguality, Multimodality, and Interaction*, volume 9822 of *Lecture Notes in Computer Science*. Springer International Publishing.

Oriol Vinyals, Alexander Toshev, Samy Bengio, and Dumitru Erhan. 2015. Show and tell: A neural image caption generator. In *Proceedings of the IEEE Conference on Computer Vision & Pattern Recognition*.

Josiah Wang and Robert Gaizauskas. 2015. Generating image descriptions with gold standard visual inputs: Motivation, evaluation and baselines. In *Proceedings of the 15th European Workshop on Natural Language Generation (ENLG)*, pages 117–126, Brighton, UK, September. Association for Computational Linguistics.

Yezhou Yang, Ching Teo, Hal Daumé III, and Yiannis Aloimonos. 2011. Corpus-guided sentence generation of natural images. In *Proceedings of the Conference on Empirical Methods in Natural Language Processing (EMNLP)*, pages 444–454. Association for Computational Linguistics.

Benjamin Z. Yao, Xiong Yang, Liang Lin, Mun Wai Lee, and Song Chun Zhu. 2010. I2T: Image parsing to text description. *Proceedings of the IEEE*, 98(8):1485–1508.

Good Automatic Authentication Question Generation

Simon S. Woo
Univ. of Southern California
Information Sciences Institute
Marina del Rey, CA
simonwoo@usc.edu

Zuyao Li
Univ. of Southern California
Los Angeles, CA
zuyaoli@usc.edu

Jelena Mirkovic
Univ. of Southern California
Information Sciences Institute
Marina del Rey, CA
mirkovic@isi.edu

Abstract

We explore a novel application of Question Generation (QG) for authentication use, where questions are widely used to verify user identity for online accounts. In our approach, we prompt users to provide a few sentences about their personal life events. We transform user-provided input sentences into a set of simple fact-based authentication questions. We compared our approach with previous QG systems, and evaluation results show that our approach yielded better performance and the promise of future personalized authentication question generation.

1   Introduction

An authentication question (also known as a security question), such as "What is your mother's maiden name?" is widely used for verifying user identity for many online accounts — such as email, banking, e-commerce and social networking. However, past numerous breaches on security questions identify the weakness of the current fixed set of authentication questions. Answers to some of those authentication questions are easy to guess based on simple common sense, with little or no prior knowledge about the individual. Since current security questions are not personalized, users can choose from a finite set of questions whose answers are easily guessed. Also, not all questions are applicable to all users.

Motivated by the research of Woo et al. (2014), in our study we automatically generate security questions from user-provided short texts from personal life events. Given user-provided text such as, *"I visited Beijing in 2001 with John,"* we generate more meaningful authentication questions, such as: *"What city did you visit?" "What year did you visit?" "Who were you with?"* These are more

difficult to guess than the maiden name of a user's mother. The contribution of this work is to automatically generate rule-based, concise, simple, fact-based shallow *WH** questions, where we explore 1) dependency parsing based, and 2) semantic role labeling (SRL) based approaches to generating questions.

2   Related Work

Previous Question Generation (QG) research (Heilman and Smith, 2010a; Yao et al., 2012; Heilman and Smith, 2010b; Heilman, 2011) focused on syntactic transformation to construct questions at the sentence level. Also, recent research by Mazidi and Nielsen (2014) improved the QG performance over that of Heilman and Smith (2010a) using semantic role labeling at the paragraph level to construct deeper questions. However, most QG research, including the results presented in the *2010 Question Generation Shared Task Evaluation Challenge*, has primarily focused on generating grammatical, deep, and complete questions for educational purposes. No prior QG research has considered an application for generating personalized authentication questions, which require different Q&A usability characteristics than those needed for education applications.

3   Approach

In our QG system we prompt users to provide a few sentences in a free-form format regarding personal life events (as shown in Woo et al. (2014)). Research has demonstrated that compared to current security questions, the answers to questions which are generated from unique personal memories/events are less likely to be guessed by others, but are far easier for users to remember. While past QG research focused on generating long and grammatically fluent questions, authentication questions impose unique challenges due to security and usability concerns:

- **One concrete fact per question**: If a question is vague, deep, or ambiguous, it can potentially lead to multiple answers, making it difficult to validate user responses. If multiple or similar answers are accepted, then security can be drastically impacted. Hence, it is crucial to ask a *specific* question to reduce the variability in user response and maintain security.

- **Simplicity and brevity**: It is important for a question to be *simple*, *short* and *concise* so that users can interact and enter their authentication responses quickly in real time.

- **Difficult to guess answers:** Answers cannot be easily inferred from the given contexts or questions.

With these design goals, we automatically generate authentication questions from user-provided texts. We take a rule-based, two-phase approach to generate questions: 1) sentence simplification and 2) question generation.

3.1   Phase1: Sentence Simplifications

We break a complex source sentence into shorter sentences. Although other research (Heilman and Smith, 2010a) considered sentence simplification before question generation, we focused on each derived short sentence having one concrete fact. In order to generate a simple one-fact based question, it is crucial to simplify a source sentence as much as possible. To identify a subject, we use clause-, phrase-, and word-level POS tags to break a sentence iteratively, as well as dependency parsing (Collobert et al., 2011) and semantic role labeling (Björkelund et al., 2010) to identify a subject. For example, if the input sentence is *"Caitlin was our flower girl, and got tips, and danced at the dinner,"* then we produce the following three shorter sentences *"Caitlin was our flower girl." "Caitlin got tips."* and *"Caitlin danced at the dinner."* These are the input sentences to the next QG phase. Our iterative sentence break approach works as follows: we first process each word from left to right sequentially for a potential sentence breakpoint, and identify subjects and main verbs in an input source sentence. Then, we take the following steps to break a sentence:

Step 1. Iteratively read word tokens from left to right, and break a sentence before the next subject (Subj), or verb (VB*), or modal (MD) or coordinating conjunction (CC), or subordinating conjunction (IN) occurs; these are potential breakpoints.

Step 2. Clean unnecessary words from the obtained sentences such as CC, IN and ADV.

Step 3. Determine if two consecutive outputs can be combined.

Step 4. Assign a subject using SRL.

However, sentence breaking at Step 1 overbreaks and generates over-simplified output in some cases. Hence, in Step 3, we attempt to combine any two consecutive outputs from Step 1.

The outputs can be combined to produce a better sentence for the following cases by 1) connecting sentences split by "to"; 2) handling gerunds in a subject; and 3) using phrasal verbs (i.e., do, let). After Step 3, the final subject of the combined sentence is assigned to each shorter sentence. The proposed simple sentence breaking-combining approach is capable of handling most of the following input sentence patterns:

$$(WDT/WRB/WP/WP\$)+Subj1+(MD1)+VB1$$
$$+(CC1)+(Subj2)+(MD2)+VB2+...,$$

where POS tags inside parentheses are optional in a sentence. For more complex sentences that include subordinate clauses, in which the left-to-right iterative approach does not apply, we adopt the tree-based transformation in Heilman and Smith (2010a). However, in most cases, their approach does not simplify the process enough for us to directly generate short questions. Hence, we apply the iterative rules in Step 1 to further break generated sentences after applying Heilman and Smith's tree-based transformation (Heilman and Smith, 2010a) to achieve the one-fact rule for a simplified sentence.

3.2   Phase 2: Question Generation

After breaking sentences, we identify possible answers from simplified sentences. Generally, difficult-to-guess answers are related with location, time, and person, as well as subject, object, and semantic roles in a sentence. We use dependency parsing, semantic role labeling, and a named entity recognizer (NER) to identify the answer phrases and construct questions.

3.2.1   Dependency parsing based approach

Since dependency parsing can capture the relationship among verb, subject, and object, we use the dependency parser (Björkelund et al., 2010). Once we identify the subject and object, we construct the *who* and *what* question types (QType). If an input sentence has LOC (location) and TMP (time), we can construct *where* and *when* questions. Next, we replace a question type with an answer and shift the question type to the left in a simplified sentence. Then, verb tense and subject position are adjusted while preserving the rest of the words in the sentence. Finally, we produce a question. For example, given the input sentence, *"Alice lived in Shenyang in 2007,"* we can construct the following questions:

Q1. We extract the subject *Alice* and replace it with a *Who* QType, and then generate a question: *"Who lived in Shenyang in 2007?"*

Q2. We extract the location *"in Shenyang"* and replace it with a *Where* QType. Then, we shift the QType to the left and adjust the verb tense and produce a question: *"Where did Alice live in 2007?"*

Q3. Similarly, we can produce *"When did Alice live in Shenyang?"* after replacing *in 2007* with *When*, shifting QType to the left, and adjusting the verb form.

We remove generated questions with pronoun answers such as *I*, *We*, *She*, *He*, and *They* as those are very easy to guess. Furthermore, we can refine this to more a specific question word such as *What year* instead of *When*, or *What city* instead of *Where*. This can help users provide more specific information.

3.2.2 Semantic Role Labeling (SRL) based approach

In this approach we focus on verb (action) and *semantic roles* (arguments of a predicate) for question generation; *who* did *what* to *whom?* is important information for QG. We employ a SRL to utilize the several semantic parts with respect to the verb. For each verb, we extract its arguments and identify different semantic roles. They are all potential answers. We mainly focus on four semantic roles in Table 1, where these roles can produce more concrete and specific information. A0 is agent or experiencer, and A1 is usually theme or result. Location and time are specified by AM-LOC and AM-TMP.

We construct a question by replacing a question type with an argument. Then we move a QType to the left and adjust the verb tense and subject position, and keep the rest of the words in a sentence to generate a question. For instance, given a short

Role	Question Type (QType)
A0, A1	who (a person), what (not a person)
AM-LOC	where
AM-TMP	when

Table 1: Question type mapping from a semantic role

input sentence *"Bob liked eating hamburgers and drinking Coke"*:

Q1. We extract *liked* and its argument (A0: Bob), and generate a question, *"Who liked eating hamburgers and drinking Coke?"*

Q2. Similarly, for another argument (A1: eating hamburgers and drinking Coke), we can generate the question, *"What did Bob like?"*

4 Data Collection

We obtained approval from our Institutional Review Board (IRB) to conduct user studies, and collected data from 28 students and 12 Amazon Mechanical Turk workers. We manually created authentication question and answer pairs from user input, extracting factoids about locations, people, time, and activities as baseline results for a comparison. Instructions were given to generate questions similar to current online security question sets that we collected. For consistency, one person from our team generated 519 security question and answer pairs from 358 source sentences from user-provided personal experience over various topics. On average, per each source input sentence, 1.54 security questions were generated. We used these sentences as inputs to the QG system for performance comparison.

5 Evaluation

We compared our systems to two other QG systems developed by Yao et al. (2012) and Heilman and Smith (2010b). Both of those approaches over-generate questions and rank them to provide the best QA pairs. We calculated the average precision, recall, and F1 score based on an exact word match for each question and answer pair. The evaluation results are shown in Table 2, where the dependency parsing system is denoted as *DepPar*, the SRL-based approach is denoted as *SRL*, the system by Yao et al. (2012) is denoted as *OA*, and the system by Heilman and Smith (2010b) is denoted as *H&S*.

The precision is measured by comparing the question type, and the sequence of words between

System	Precision	Recall	F1
SRL	0.407	0.805	0.541
DepPar	0.477	0.927	0.630
OA	0.399	0.807	0.534
H&S	0.325	0.699	0.444

Table 2: Precision, recall, and F1 score for Generated Questions based on an exact word match

System	Precision	Recall	F1
SRL	0.492	0.805	0.611
DepPar	0.524	0.927	0.670
OA	0.439	0.807	0.568
H&S	0.236	0.699	0.352

Table 3: Precision, recall, and F1 score for Generated Answers based on an exact word match

manually generated Q&A pairs and Q&A pairs generated from each approach. From Table 2, we observe that the *DepPar* system performs better than *OA* and *H&S*. The dependency parser approach is better in capturing objects, time, and locations from simplified sentences, constructing better what, when and where questions, covering all the QTypes from manually generated data. The SRL-based system has the second-best performance. On the other hand, *H&S* has the lowest recall and performed poorly since it only generated 70% of the required QA set. The reason that *OA* performed poorly is that it generates the longest questions with an average of 9.8 words per question, while the average number of words in the manual dataset, *H&S*, *DepPar*, and *SRL* is 7.3, 7.2, 7.5, and 8.8 words per question, respectively. Hence, extra words in *OA* are penalized for precision, where the length of generated sentences is critical for the calculation of these evaluation metrics. Also, we evaluated the generated answers from each approach in Table 3, with manually generated answers based on an exact word match. Both dependency and SRL-based approaches were better at capturing the candidate answers for date, location, people, subject, and object. Hence, those approaches constructed better authentication questions. On the other hand, other approaches missed required answers, and their F1 scores were lower as a result.

6   Conclusion

Our research explores the novel applications of Question Generation. Although our approach is simple, we generate more suitable authentications than prior QG systems. In the future, we plan to perform a human evaluation of generated questions and answers, as well as leverage machine learning approaches to improve QG.

7   Acknowledgements

We would like to thank the anonymous reviewers for their helpful comments, as well as Ron Artstein, Elsi Kaiser, and Janice Wheeler for their advice.

References

Anders Björkelund, Bernd Bohnet, Love Hafdell, and Pierre Nugues. 2010. A high-performance syntactic and semantic dependency parser. In *Proceedings of the 23rd International Conference on Computational Linguistics: Demonstrations*, pages 33–36. Association for Computational Linguistics.

Ronan Collobert, Jason Weston, Léon Bottou, Michael Karlen, Koray Kavukcuoglu, and Pavel Kuksa. 2011. Natural language processing (almost) from scratch. *The Journal of Machine Learning Research*, 12:2493–2537.

Michael Heilman and Noah A Smith. 2010a. Extracting simplified statements for factual question generation. In *Proceedings of QG2010: The Third Workshop on Ques-tion Generation*, page 11.

Michael Heilman and Noah A Smith. 2010b. Good question! statistical ranking for question generation. In *Human Language Technologies: The 2010 Annual Conference of the North American Chapter of the Association for Computational Linguistics*, pages 609–617. Association for Computational Linguistics.

Michael Heilman. 2011. *Automatic factual question generation from text*. Ph.D. thesis, Carnegie Mellon University.

Karen Mazidi and Rodney D Nielsen. 2014. Linguistic considerations in automatic question generation. In *ACL (2)*, pages 321–326.

Simon S Woo, Jelena Mirkovic, Ron Artstein, and Elsi Kaiser. 2014. Life-experience passwords (leps). In *Symposium on Usable Privacy and Security (SOUPS)*.

Xuchen Yao, Emma Tosch, Grace Chen, Elnaz Nouri, Ron Artstein, Anton Leuski, Kenji Sagae, and David Traum. 2012. Creating conversational characters using question generation tools. *Dialogue & Discourse*, 3(2):125–146.

Automatic Generation of Student Report Cards

Amy Isard
School of Informatics
University of Edinburgh
Scotland, U.K.
amy.isard@ed.ac.uk

Jeremy Knox
School of Education
University of Edinburgh
Scotland, U.K.
jeremy.knox@ed.ac.uk

Abstract

The Learning Analytics Report Card (LARC) is a pilot system which takes time-series data from a student's course-related activity in a Virtual Learning Environment and generates automatic textual summaries in real time. Students are able to generate reports as often as they like, and to choose which aspects of their behaviour are included in each report. As well as rating a student's scores against set standards, the generated texts make comparisons with the individual student's previous behaviour from the same course, and with the average scores of their student cohort. In addition, we carry out sentiment analysis on the student's forum posts, and generate a summary using quantifiers. We report some student reactions to initial trials of the system.

1 Introduction

The Learning Analytics Report Card (LARC) project was an interdisciplinary pilot project at the University of Edinburgh involving researchers in Education and Computational Linguistics, as well as Information Services. Its overall aim was to raise students' critical awareness of the ways in which learning analytics (Ferguson, 2012) can intervene in and mediate educational activity. The project explored the analysis and presentation through Natural Language Generation (NLG) of data from the Moodle Virtual Learning Environment[1], which students were using as part of a Distance Learning course.

Student involvement was incorporated at all stages of the project. The design, development, and testing phases of LARC were informed by formal student representation, motivated by a general concern for ethical practices in data collection. Students can experience learning analytics applied to them as individuals as "snooping" (Parr, 2014), and the LARC project aimed to avoid this by giving students a chance to interact with their data. The students taking part in the pilot project were studying either "Understanding Learning in the Online Environment" or "Digital Futures for Learning" and were asked to provide feedback about the LARC system. We intended that some of the generated texts would be controversial, and would provoke strong reactions from students, to cause them to consider aspects of data interpretation and ownership.

2 Related Work

Previous research has investigated the use of NLG techniques to generate reports from time-series data in a number of different domains (Sripada et al., 2003b). These include medical data summarization in the BabyTalk Project, providing decision support in a Neonatal Intensive Care Unit (Gatt et al., 2009; Hunter et al., 2011), and weather forecasts in SUMTIME-MOUSAM (Sripada et al., 2003a).

There are also a number of systems which have analysed data from Virtual Learning Environments, presenting it to the students themselves or to their institutions (Gašević et al., 2015), and global companies such as Civitas[2] and Knewton[3] offer large-scale data analytics solutions to educational institutions and publishers. However, there are only a few

---

[1] https://moodle.org

[2] https://www.civitaslearning.com/

[3] https://www.knewton.com/approach/platform

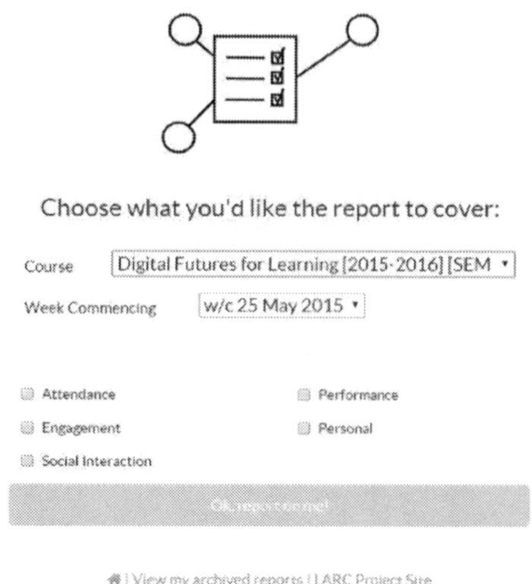

Choose what you'd like the report to cover:

Course   Digital Futures for Learning [2015-2016] [SEM ▾]

Week Commencing   w/c 25 May 2015 ▾

☐ Attendance   ☐ Performance
☐ Engagement   ☐ Personal
☐ Social Interaction

Ok, report it for me!

🏠 | View my archived reports | LARC Project Site

Figure 1: LARC user interface

systems which have made use of NLG in presenting their data.

The SkillSum project generated reports for adult students taking a basic skills test designed to check their basic numeracy and literary skills (Reiter et al., 2006; Williams and Reiter, 2008). It generated reports which used language tailored to the reading ability of the students, informing them whether or not their skill levels were suited to adult education courses in which they were interested. Our system deals with different sorts of data, and provides a more general report, rather than giving tailored advice on course choice.

The research of Gkatzia et al (2013) relates most closely to the LARC project - they generated reports based on time-series data from student lecture attendance and weekly questionnaires, and used reinforcement learning informed by the lecturers' method of providing feedback to choose the content to be contained in the report. They also compared students to their own past behaviours and to the student cohort. Our work differs from theirs in the nature of the data – the LARC data was all automatically gathered from the Moodle platform – and in the fact that we allow the students rather than the software to choose what should be presented. In addition, our pilot system was entirely rule-based. We also performed sentiment analysis on student forum posts, and to our knowledge are the first to have presented the results of this analysis using NLG.

The following is a reproduction of the LARC generated report shown in Figure 2:

Your attendance has in general been excellent but this week you logged on less often than usual.
You have mostly been very engaged with the course content and this week you seemed more interested in the topic than usual.
You have usually been extremely social during the course but this week you interacted less with others than usual. Most of your forum posts were neutral in tone, some were positive, and none were negative.
You are fairly concerned what others in the class think about you. You are in the middle third of students for social interaction and engagement, but the highest third of students for attendance.

Figure 2: LARC generated report with all 5 themes selected

3 User Interface

The LARC interface consists of a web form, accessible to students when they log in through a secure system. The interface is shown in Figure 1. The students used check boxes to select one or more of the five themes presented (described in Section 4), and the week for which they would like their report to be generated. They could generate a report as often as they wanted, and if they wished, they could at any time generate a report for a previous week. The data used to generate the LARC reports was automatically downloaded once a day from the Moodle server into an SQL database, which was then accessed and analysed by the NLG software in order to construct a report.

4 Report Themes

We chose five report themes, and values were set by the course lecturer in order to quantify the student's performance. For *attendance* (weekly login frequency), *engagement* (clicks on course pages) and *social* (accesses of the course discussion forum), (Table 1). For *personal*, we counted a student's posts to the course's "Introductions" forum and clicks by others on their profile. For *performance* we compared the student's performance to the average of the student cohort (Section 5.2). In addition, we generated a summary of sentiment analysis carried out on the student's posts to the discussion forum (Section 5.3).

5 Report Generation and Contents

The report consisted of a short paragraph on each of the selected themes, generated in real-time by a

Theme \ Rating	poor	adequate	good	excellent
attendance	<5	<10	<15	>=15
engagement	<10	<25	<100	>=100
social	<4	<8	<12	>=12

Table 1: Report Theme Values

Rating \ This Week vs Previous	higher (+)	lower (-)
poor (-)	contrast	similarity
adequate (-)	contrast	similarity
good (+)	similarity	contrast
excellent (+)	similarity	contrast

Table 2: Individual Comparisons

Java-based system with custom templates. Figure 2 shows a sample report.

5.1 Individual Comparisons

For the *attendance*, *engagement* and *social* themes, the student's scores for the week selected were compared to their average scores up to that point, and a sentence containing a comparison between the two was generated. The clause describing the student's general performance expresses the value judgments as described in Section 4, and in the generated texts the weekly score is compared to the previous average using Rhetorical Structure Theory similarity and contrast relations (Mann and Thompson, 1998) (Table 2). If the scores are identical, no comparison is included. A contrast relation is expressed by the conjunction "but" and a similarity relation by "and". For example, if the student's average attendance was 12 (good, +), and the current week 18 (higher, +), the generated sentence would be "Your attendance has in general been *good*, **and** this week you logged on *more* than usual" whereas if the average engagement was 120 (excellent +) and the current week 80 (lower, -) we would generate "You have mostly been *very engaged* with the course content **but** this week you seemed *less* interested in the topic than usual".

5.2 Cohort Comparisons

If a student selected the *performance* theme, we generated a sentence comparing their average performance to their course cohort. We included comparisons on *attendance*, *engagement* and *social* if any had been selected, or an average of all three if not.

We calculated the student's position within the cohort, and assigned them to the bottom, middle, or top third for each chosen theme. If more than one theme was chosen, we aggregated all of the matching positions, and combined the dissimilar ones with similarity or contrast relations, as in the following example "You are in the *highest* third of students for attendance **and** engagement, **but** the *lowest* third for social interaction."

5.3 Sentiment Analysis

To enable us to include a summary of the sentiments expressed in the students' forum posts, we experimented with two sentiment analysis packages. The first, part of the Stanford CoreNLP tools (Manning et al., 2014), comes with a model trained on movie review texts, which did not transfer well to our domain. Since we did not have any annotated data with which to train our own model, we used the rule-based Pattern system, (De Smedt and Daelemans, 2012) which generalized more successfully. We obtained sentiment subjectivity and polarity ratings for each blog post, which ranged between 1 and 0. For each post, we considered the sentiment to be neutral unless the subjectivity and polarity were both greater than .2. These levels were set after initial testing and are an aspect which we would hope to refine in future versions of the system (Section 7).

5.4 Quantifiers

There is a large body of research on the theory and use of quantifiers (Moxey and Sanford, 1986; Bos and Nissim, 2006; Lappin, 2000), and Varges and van Deemter (2005) give a theoretical handling of generation, but we are not aware of existing systems which actually generate quantifiers. We based our algorithm on recent research which investigated which quantifiers human subjects found acceptable when presented with an image of a bowl containing different numbers of blue and green candies (Yildirim et al., 2013; Yildirim et al., 2016). They found a high degree of individual variation and overlap but general consensus on some areas, having analysed human subjects' classification of "naturalness" for five quantifiers, and based on their results, we used the quantifiers shown in Table 3 to describe the results of our sentiment analysis (Section 5.3). For example, if a student made 20 blog posts, of which 13 (65%) were positive, 5 (25%) neutral and 2 (10%) negative the output would be "**Many** of your blog posts were positive, **some** were neutral and **few**

all	most	many	some	few	none
total	>60%	>40%	>20%	>1	0

Table 3: Generated Quantifiers

were negative".

5.5 Filler Sentences

If the student did not select all of the themes, filler sentences were added so that all reports would be of similar length. Each theme has a set of four sentences for each level of performance, so that if a single theme is selected, there will still be five sentences in the report. These sentences give general guidance, for example "attendance is key to achieving your aims on the course, and this an area you could improve upon" and "engaging with course content demonstrates your participation in the course, and you are showing yourself to be highly active".

6 Initial Student Reactions

Student feedback was given throughout the duration of the course, and as a result some changes were made before the trial ended, while others will be considered in future. This feedback is anecdotal and cannot be considered an evaluation, but we were informed by some comments and changed the structure of the output accordingly. Some feedback was positive, but we have concentrated here on comments which raised issues for us.

The initial version of the system presented only the average behaviour of the students over all of the preceding weeks, and therefore there was often no change in a student's report from one week to the next if their behaviour had remained consistent. We therefore introduced comparisons with the current week, to make it clear that the data was being analysed on a weekly basis.

Some students wanted to see the numbers underlying the generated sentences, so at the end of the pilot we introduced a data summary at the bottom of the report We intend to present this in a more user-friendly format, and integrate it with potential future graphical representations

One student commented that "As a student, I like friendly feedback" and wanted to see more "human language" for example encouraging comments such as "well done". Several students mentioned their worries about the ethics of learning analytics, with comments such as "We should adopt an ethical approach when extracting conclusions from analytical reports: they should be reviewed with caution" and one quotes EDUCAUSE[4] (a non-profit association whose stated mission is to "advance higher education through the use of information technology"), saying "Even then the best evaluative algorithms can result in misclassifications and misleading patterns, in part because such programs are based on inferences about what different sorts of data might mean relative to student success".

7 Future Work

As LARC was a pilot project, we did not have the time or resources for all of the development that we would have liked to carry out. We would like to add several functionalities to the system:

- Allow the students to choose from multiple report styles or personalities, which could be more encouraging, or more critical.

- Investigate more alternative sentiment analysis packages, and potentially allow the students to compare the outputs on their forum posts.

- Add graphical elements to the report. We would like to accompany the texts with visualizations such as circle graphs or heat maps in order to give a different view over the data.

We would also like to carry out formal user evaluations on various aspects of the generated texts:

- How the students rate the generated texts compared to a fixed baseline, and hand-written reports

- The use of the various quantifiers in describing the sentiment of forum posts

- The use of the contrast/similarity comparisons and the ordering of the various types of data within them

Finally and most importantly, we would like to continue our work to ensure that students understand how their data are used, and are happy with the resulting analyses.

---

[4]http://www.educause.edu

References

Johan Bos and Malvina Nissim. 2006. An Empirical Approach to the Interpretation of Superlatives. In *Proceedings of the 2006 Conference on Empirical Methods in Natural Language Processing*, EMNLP '06, pages 9–17, Stroudsburg, PA, USA. Association for Computational Linguistics.

Tom De Smedt and Walter Daelemans. 2012. Pattern for python. *The Journal of Machine Learning Research*, 13(1):2063–2067.

Rebecca Ferguson. 2012. Learning analytics: drivers, developments and challenges. *International Journal of Technology Enhanced Learning*, 4(5/6):304.

Dragan Gašević, Shane Dawson, and George Siemens. 2015. Let's not forget: Learning analytics are about learning. *TechTrends*, 59(1):64–71.

Albert Gatt, Francois Portet, Ehud Reiter, Jim Hunter, Saad Mahamood, Wendy Moncur, and Somayajulu Sripada. 2009. From data to text in the neonatal intensive care unit: Using NLG technology for decision support and information management. *Ai Communications*, 22(3):153–186.

Dimitra Gkatzia, Helen Hastie, Srinivasan Janarthanam, and Oliver Lemon. 2013. Generating student feedback from time-series data using Reinforcement Learning. *Proceedings of the 14th European Workshop on Natural Language Generation*.

James Hunter, Yvonne Freer, Albert Gatt, Ehud Reiter, Somayajulu Sripada, Cindy Sykes, and Dave Westwater. 2011. Bt-nurse: computer generation of natural language shift summaries from complex heterogeneous medical data. *Journal of the American Medical Informatics Association*, 18(5):621–624.

Shalom Lappin. 2000. An intensional parametric semantics for vague quantifiers. *Linguistics and philosophy*, 23(6):599–620.

William Mann, C. and Sandra Thompson, A. 1998. Rhetorical Structure Theory: Toward a functional theory of text organization. *Text*, 3:243–281.

Christopher D. Manning, Mihai Surdeanu, John Bauer, Jenny Finkel, Steven J. Bethard, and David McClosky. 2014. The Stanford CoreNLP natural language processing toolkit. In *Association for Computational Linguistics (ACL) System Demonstrations*, pages 55–60.

Linda M. Moxey and Anthony J. Sanford. 1986. Quantifiers and Focus. *Journal of Semantics*, 5(3):189–206, January.

Chris Parr. 2014. Lecturer calls for clarity in use of learning analytics. *Times Higher Education Supplement*, 6 Novebmer. https://www.timeshighereducation.com/news/lecturer-calls-for-clarity-in-use-of-learning-analytics/2016776.article.

Ehud Reiter, Sandra Williams, and Lesley Crichton. 2006. Generating feedback reports for adults taking basic skills tests. In *Applications and Innovations in Intelligent Systems XIII*. Springer.

Somayajulu Sripada, Ehud Reiter, and Ian Davy. 2003a. Sumtime-mousam: Configurable marine weather forecast generator. *Expert Update*, 6(3):4–10.

Somayajulu G. Sripada, Ehud Reiter, Jim Hunter, and Jin Yu. 2003b. Generating English summaries of time series data using the Gricean maxims. In *Proceedings of the ninth ACM SIGKDD international conference on Knowledge discovery and data mining*, pages 187–196. ACM.

Sebastian Varges and Kees Van Deemter. 2005. Generating referring expressions containing quantifiers. *Proceedings of the 6th International Worskhop on Computational Semantics*.

Sandra Williams and Ehud Reiter. 2008. Generating basic skills reports for low-skilled readers. *Natural Language Engineering*, 14(04).

Ilker Yildirim, Judith Degen, Michael K. Tanenhaus, and T. Florian Jaeger. 2013. Linguistic variability and adaptation in quantifier meanings. In *Proceedings of the Thirty-Fifth Annual Conference of the Cognitive Science Society*, pages 3835–3840.

Ilker Yildirim, Judith Degen, Michael K. Tanenhaus, and T. Florian Jaeger. 2016. Talker-specificity and adaptation in quantifier interpretation. *Journal of Memory and Language*, 87:128–143.

Collecting Reliable Human Judgements on Machine-Generated Language: The Case of the QG-STEC Data [*]

Keith Godwin[†] and **Paul Piwek**[‡]

The Open University, UK

Abstract

Question generation (QG) is the problem of automatically generating questions from inputs such as declarative sentences. The Shared Evaluation Task Challenge (QG-STEC) Task B that took place in 2010 evaluated several state-of-the-art QG systems. However, analysis of the evaluation results was affected by low inter-rater reliability. We adapted Nonaka & Takeuchi's knowledge creation cycle to the task of improving the evaluation annotation guidelines with a preliminary test showing clearly improved inter-rater reliability.

1 Introduction

Since 2008, researchers from Discourse Analysis, Dialogue Modelling, Formal Semantics, Intelligent Tutoring Systems, NLG, NLU and Psycholinguistics have met at a series of QG workshops (Piwek and Boyer, 2012). These workshops bring together different researchers working on QG activities and collectively are of great value to the QG community.

One such activity was the Shared Task Evaluation Challenge Task B that took place in 2010 (Rus et al., 2012). The challenge was to generate specific questions from single sentences. These questions were evaluated independently by human judges. The average scores of the annotations were used to rank participating QG-STEC systems on these criteria. Of particular interest were the criteria relating to relevance of the generated questions and their grammaticality and fluency. Ideally, when a system generates a question from a sentence, the question should be about the information in that sentence (i.e., be relevant) and it should be fluent and grammatical. Our assumption is that ordinary speakers of English are reasonably in agreement with each other when they make such judgements.

However, in practice, we found low inter-rater reliability (IRR) for the task results. We established this using Krippendorff's α, see Table 6. For four evaluation criteria, α was well below 0.4, with only one criterion achieving an α of 0.409. This does not meet Krippendorff's requirement of an α of at least 0.8, if one wants to draw any conclusions from the results. Nor does it meet the requirement that tentative conclusions are only permitted for $0.67 < \alpha < 0.8$.

It is common practice when evaluating statistical NLP to create an annotation manual. The manual must systematise the annotation process, making it as unambiguous as possible. It should contain a scheme and a set of guidelines. The scheme represents the theoretical backbone of the evaluation process. The guidelines that supplement the scheme provide additional information, often with examples, making clear the scheme usage (Palmer and Xue, 2010). In the original evaluation, the guidelines were minimal.

As the QG-STEC IRR reliability scores show, it seems that judges interpret an annotation scheme for these criteria very differently, when they use the scheme independently, with minimal guidelines.

---

[*]We would like to thank Alistair Willis and Brian Plüss for helpful feedback on the work reported in this paper.

[†] keith.godwin@open.ac.uk

[‡] paul.piwek@open.ac.uk

Rank	Description
1	The question is completely relevant to the input sentence.
2	The question relates mostly to the input sentence.
3	The question is only slightly related to the input sentence.
4	The question is totally unrelated to the input sentence.

Table 1: Relevance. Questions should be relevant to the input sentence. This criterion measures how well the question can be answered based on what the input sentence says.

Rank	Description
1	The question is grammatically correct and idiomatic/natural.
2	The question is grammatically correct but does not read as fluently as we would like.
3	There are some grammatical errors in the question.
4	The question is grammatically unacceptable.

Table 2: Syntactic correctness and fluency. The syntactic correctness is rated to ensure systems can generate sensible output. In addition, those questions which read fluently are ranked higher.

Rank	Description
1	The question is unambiguous.
2	The question could provide more information.
3	The question is clearly ambiguous when asked out of the blue.

Table 3: Ambiguity. The question should make sense when asked more or less out of the blue. Typically, an unambiguous question will have one very clear answer.

Rank	Description
1	The question is of the target question type.
2	The type of the generated question and the target question type are different.

Table 4: Question Type. Questions should be of the specified target question type. E.g. who, what, where, when etc..

Rank	Description
1	The two questions are different in content.
2	Both ask the same question, but there are grammatical and/or lexical differences.
3	The two questions are identical.

Table 5: Variety. Pairs of questions in answer to a single input are evaluated on how different they are from each other. This rewards those systems which are capable of generating a range of different questions for the same input.

Typically when the IRR is low this can be attributed to the complexity of the phenomena being annotated. Capturing complex phenomena requires complex theory which in turn requires complex instructions (Hovy and Lavid, 2010). Either the scheme does not accurately represent the theory behind identifying the phenomena, or the guidelines to the scheme were insufficient to explain it to the breadth of audience using the scheme, or the the annotators did not receive appropriate training. For this research we assumed the scheme was sound and our goal was to improve the guidelines without modifying the scheme. Training length and intensity would be addressed once we had an appropriate set of guidelines.

The scheme criteria used by evaluators in the QG-STEC are described in Tables 1-5. The criteria defined by these tables were applied to each of the generated questions independently during evaluation. The ranges of Rank vary, but 1 is always the highest score.

As a first step towards remedying guidelines, we used a set of judges to iteratively and collaboratively train using the guidelines accompanying the scheme, until we were satisfied that they had reached a common understanding of the scheme. This allowed us to 'debug' the guidelines whilst the judges produced improved guidelines (see Section 2).

Our next step would be to use the scheme with the revised guidelines and a new set of judges to annotate the QG-STEC data. This would allow us to find out whether the new guidelines facilitate IRR. However, this is work in progress and in advance of that, we decided to find out a possible upper-bound on IRR that could be achieved with these new guidelines. To do so, we got our current judges to independently annotate the QG-STEC data. The results, see Table 6, are very encouraging.

2 Annotation Method

The problem we identified in Section 1 is that if the judges disagree significantly (and thus have internalised their own version of the annotation scheme, which isn't documented, and therefore isn't repeatable or open for critical analysis) then the analysis will suffer. We defined a significant difference as a disagreement greater than one rank, therefore we

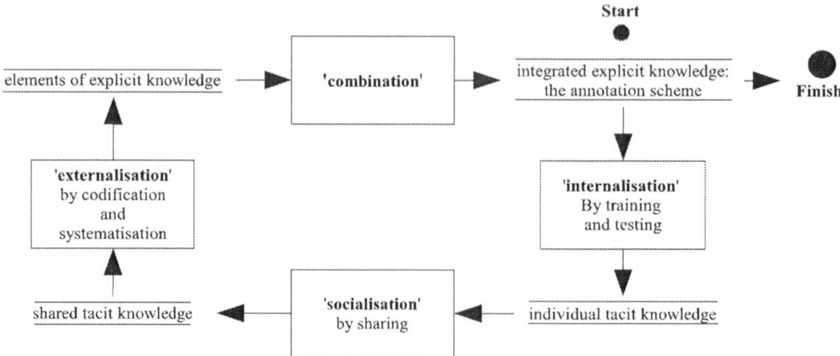

Figure 1: The knowledge creation cycle of collaborative training.

kept training until the judges mostly agreed to within one rank.

This process is shown in Figure 1 where we describe it using a modified version of the Knowledge Creation Cycle of Nonaka and Takeuchi (1995). The main difference being the much shorter time between iterations of the cycle in our method. The training began at the start position with the existing annotation scheme and minimal guidelines. This was the initial version of the integrated explicit knowledge that existed at the start of training. The four stages of the cycle are detailed as follows:

i) INTERNALISATION: The judges read through the annotation scheme and guidelines. Each judge was given a training set of nine input sentences with a series of generated questions (approximately 40) to annotate, simulating the evaluation activity. The input sentences used for training were disjoint from the QG-STEC data, but similar in nature: selected at random from The Guardian Newspaper in an attempt to interest the annotators and keep them motivated. The generated questions were mostly created using the question generator developed by Heilman (2011), to provide realistic examples. For each iteration through this stage a new training set was provided. Upon completion each judge would have internalised the annotation scheme and guidelines to the best of their ability and would have developed additional tacit knowledge based on their experience with the simulated evaluation process. The results were compared and any differences greater than one rank apart were marked for discussion during the Socialisation stage.

ii) SOCIALISATION: Motivated by the marked results above, the judges discussed how they reached their individual evaluation, sharing and discussing their tacit knowledge.

iii) EXTERNALISATION: The judges were encouraged to think about a way to generalise describing this process by codification and systematisation. When the judges reached a consensus, they moved onto the next stage.

iv) COMBINATION: The annotation guidelines were updated to reflect the changes developed in this iteration of the training cycle, ready for the next iteration. This cycle repeated until a sufficient degree of agreement was reached, as described above.

The actual training activity consisted of three iterations. The first iteration, which had 48 significant differences (evaluations different by more than one rank), was dominated by a discussion on the administration of the evaluation. Changes to the guidelines included correcting simple mistakes such as inappropriate wording in the guidelines or getting the rank order the wrong way round. E.g. general advise: 'Each criteria, defined below, is assigned a rank, with 1 being the greatest.'

The second iteration had 17 significant differences. The judges began to identify a number of key conceptual questions which should be answered during the process of making an evaluation. E.g. for ambiguity: 'One consideration when assessing this criterion is to ask the following question: Can more information be added from the input sentence to make the question more specific?'

The last iteration had three significant differences. At this point the training was deemed complete and our criterion for internalising the scheme had been

Criteria	QG-STEC	QG-STEC+
Relevance	0.25	0.806
Question Type	0.323	0.859
Correctness	0.409	0.838
Ambiguity	0.334	0.688
Variety	0.348	0.904

Table 6: Krippendorff's alpha IRR measure for original and re-evaluated data.

met. The judges were now having discussions that were constructed using the language and evaluation skill that had been collaboratively produced and recorded in the evaluation guidelines document.

3 Results

Table 6 compares the current results QG-STEC+[1] and those of the original QG-STEC. The IRR results of the QG-STEC are mostly rated Fair, using the Koch and Landis Scale. By contrast QG-STEC+ data are mostly rated Perfect.

4 Conclusion and Further Work

The purpose of the QG-STEC was to measure the quality of the automatically generated questions. We think of this quality in terms of the judgements of ordinary speakers of English. There isn't necessarily a gold standard: if most speakers of English deem a question fluent and relevant, the system has achieved its goal – even if an expert judges it to be flawed relative to some gold standard. For this reason, our main concern regarding the annotation scheme is reproducibility rather than accuracy. Following Artstein and Poesio (2008) we consider reproducibility 'the degree to which different coders achieve the same coding when working independently.'

If a question is given a particular rating by our judges, this should predict reliably how a new independent judge is going rate the question. Our current study has only revealed the upper-bound achievable, when using the judges that arrived at the revised guidelines. Future studies will need to prove the efficacy of these revised guidelines.

For now, one further check that can give us some confidence in the preliminary results, is to look at the distribution of judgements by our judges. See Figures 2 and 3. This allows us to rule out certain

---

[1]https://github.com/Keith-Godwin/QG-STEC-plus

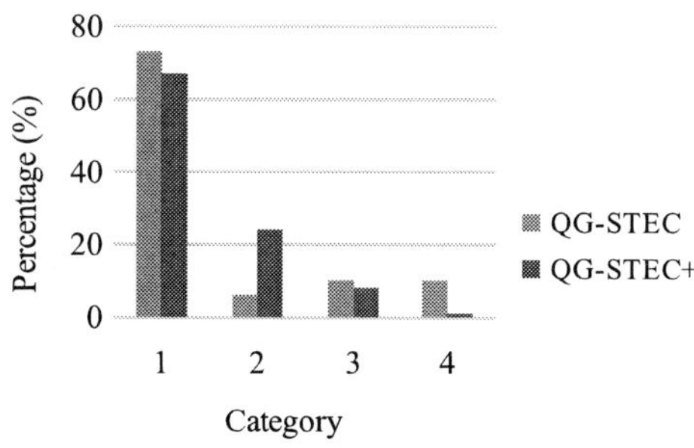

Figure 2: Distribution across categories for relevance

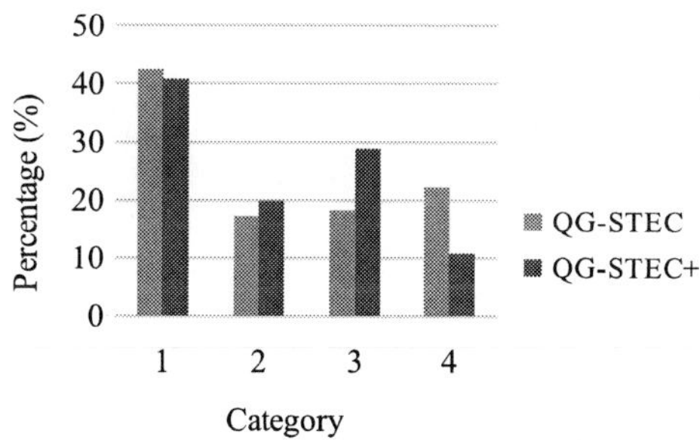

Figure 3: Distribution across categories for correctness

types of bias (e.g., the judges always agreeing to rate at a certain point on the scale).

References

Ron Artstein and Massimo Poesio. 2008. Survey Article Inter-Coder Agreement for Computational Linguistics. *Association for Computational Linguistics*, 34(4):555 – 596.

Michael Heilman. 2011. *Automatic factual question generation from text*. Ph.D. thesis, Carnegie Mellon University.

Eduard Hovy and Julia Lavid. 2010. Towards a "Science" of Corpus Annotation : A New Methodological Challenge for Corpus Linguistics. *International Journal of Translation*, 22(1):1–25.

Ikujir Nonaka and Hirotaka Takeuchi. 1995. *The knowledge-creating company*. Oxford University Press.

Martha Palmer and Nianwen Xue. 2010. Linguistic Annotation. In Alexander Clark, Chris Fox, and Shalom Lappin, editors, *The handbook of computational linguistics and natural language processing*, chapter 10, pages 238–270. John Wiley & Sons.

Paul Piwek and KE Boyer. 2012. Varieties of question generation: introduction to this special issue. *Dialogue & Discourse*, 3(2):1–9.

Vasile Rus, Brendan Wyse, Paul Piwek, Mihai Lintean, Svetlana Stoyanchev, and Cristian Moldovan. 2012. A detailed account of the First Question Generation Shared Task Evaluation challenge. *Dialogue & Discourse*, 3(2):177–204.

Ranking Automatically Generated Questions Using Common Human Queries

Yllias Chali and **Sina Golestanirad**
University of Lethbridge
Alberta Canada

Abstract

In this paper, we challenge a form of paragraph-to-question generation task. We propose a question generation system which can generate a set of comprehensive questions from a body of text. Besides the tree kernel functions to assess the grammatically of the generated questions, our goal is to rank them by using community-based question answering systems to calculate the importance of the generated questions. The main assumption behind our work is that each body of text is related to a topic of interest and it has a comprehensive information about the topic.

1 Introduction

Human beings are not very good at asking questions about topics. They are often forgetful, which causes difficulties in expressing what is in their minds (Hasan, 2013). Also sometimes, Humans, in front of a search engine, have difficulties to express their needs and intents as query terms. Imagine that you want to find out what was the first logo for Apple Inc. You may use a search engine such as *Google* and the search query *Apple Logos*, the result might have the exact information that you need. However, they may also include other information, such as who designed the logo or where it was designed or any other information that you are not interested in. We believe if before showing the list of websites the search engine had shown some suggested queries you would benefit from this question generation (QG) system. This way search engines' users will be able to use right queries to gain what they

are looking for. Suggestions could be questions like: *What is the logo of Apple Inc.? What was the first logo designed for Apple Inc.? Do we have any information about where Apple's logo was designed?* etc. In this paper, we address the challenge of generating questions from topics, which is motivated by the fact that people do not always obtain the desired results from search engines. In this task, we assume that for each search-engine user's query there is a body of text having useful information about it. Our goal is to generate and show a few questions to the user in order to help her/him to find exactly what she/he is looking for. We need to rank the questions because the number of generated questions could be many to be shown and we may have to show only top-ranked ones.

We generate the questions for a given topic in two steps. First, we tag the name entities in the topic and its associated body. Then, we apply some general rules and generate the basic questions. At this level, the answers for the basic questions may not be in the body of the text, but the reason of generating them is to have more variety. Second, we use predicates and their arguments from the sentences in the given body of text to generate specific questions, which answers can be generated from the text. As the number of generated questions may be too large we rank them and show the top ones to the users. The ranking of question consists of two steps. First, we investigate other questions being asked by people in community-based question answering (CQA) systems such as Yahoo! Answers to see how common our questions are. Second, we apply the tree kernel functions in order to compute the syntactic similarity between each question and the text from which the question is generated. This way we can determine the correctness of the grammatically of the generated questions. Then, the questions are ranked by their importance and grammatical correctness.

2   Related Work

An automated question generation system can also be used for educational purposes, and some works address the task of automatically generating questions from reading materials in order to advance educational assessment and practice (Mitkov and Ha, 2003; Wang et al., 2008; Xu et al., 2009; Rus and Graesser, 2009; Heilman and Smith, 2010a; Agarwal and Mannem, 2011; Agarwal et al., 2011). Heilman and Smith (2010b) proposed a system that over-generates some questions and then uses a model, which has been trained on a dataset in order to rank the generated questions. Liu et al. (2010) proposed an automatic question generation system which helps students to write literature reviews. Gate (2008) developed a question generation system that generates questions in order to help students while reading an article rather than afterwards. Lindberg et al. (2013) introduced a sophisticated template based system which merges semantic role labels into a system that automatically generates natural language questions to support online learning. Mazidi and Nielsen (2014) proposed an automatic question generator which benefits from semantic pattern recognition to generate questions which have different depth and type for tutoring or self-study purposes. Rokhlenko and Szpektor (2013) challenged the task of automatically generating questions which are relevant to a given text but do not exist in the text. Labutov et al. (2015) developed an approach for generating deep (i.e, high-level) comprehension questions from novel text. Chali and Hasan (2015) addressed the problem of automatically generating questions from topics.

3   Question Generation

Our question generation approach is built in five steps. In the first step, we tag named entities from a text which is related to the query. In the next step, we use question templates to generate basic questions, based on the tags from the previous step. In the third step, we apply a text simplifier to all of the sentences in the text and then we use a semantic role tagger to tag all of the arguments and predicates in these sentences. Fourth step is about applying another set of question rules to the extracted arguments and predicates in order to generate specific questions. In the final step, we use our proposed algorithm to rank all of the generated questions.

3.1   Generating Basic Questions

The named entities, which are in the topic and its relevant text are tagged using the Illinois Named Entity Tagger. Then, we apply our general rules to generate the basic questions. At this level, the answers to these questions may not be in the text and the reason for generating these questions is to have more diversity in our question pool. We designed 265 question templates and an algorithm that generates the basic questions with regard to the tagged named entities.

3.2   Generating Specific Questions

The grammar of the sentences in the body of the text may be complicated, that is why the sentences have to be simplified before we can generate more accurate questions. To do the task of simplification, we use the simplified factual statement extraction toolkit (Heilman and Smith, 2010a). This model simplifies sentences by changing semantic and syntactic structures, eliminating phrase types, etc.

For the next step, we need to parse sentences in the text semantically. To this end, we use Automatic Statistical SEmantic Role Tagger (ASSERT)[1]. When a sentence is given to ASSERT, it applies a full syntactic analysis of that sentence, identifies all of the verb predicates, then extracts features for constituents within the parse tree relative to the predicate, and eventually identifies and tags the constituents with the appropriate semantic arguments. The outputs contain verbs (predicates) with their arguments (semantic roles). Those arguments can be used to generate specific questions.

In order to generate the specific questions, we used 350 rules to transform the tagged sentences into questions. These rules are designed in a way that the answer words in a sentence could be discovered and replaced by question words.

---

[1]Available at http://www.cemantix.org/.

4　Ranking of the Questions

As the number of generated questions is usually too large, we have to rank and show the top N ones. We score the questions regarding to their importance and syntactic correctness. We give equal weight to both importance and correctness.

4.1　Importance of the Generated Questions

In Chali and Hasan (2015), the importance of the generated questions was estimated by their similarities to the text. We believe that there is another source to use in order to do the task of ranking the importance of the generated questions. Nowadays, it is becoming a common habit for people to ask their questions in online forums, which are called community-based question answering (CQA) systems, such as Yahoo! Answers' web site. We believe that there are many common questions being asked by people that can be used to study what people need and what they are mostly curious about. The key point is that people using CQA systems use more informative sentences to ask and so if these sentences are similar to the search engines' queries then we can extract additional information about the users' probable interests. Our algorithm predicts what the user might be looking for by investigating other questions asked by other people, then this knowledge can be used to rank the importance of the generated questions.

4.1.1　Database

Our algorithm needs a CQA system, we use then Yahoo! Answers dataset. Yahoo! Answers is growing quickly, it is suggested that researchers increasingly use Yahoo! Answers dataset and it is becoming a popular source of information, such as advice or opinion (Liu and Agichtein, 2008). The data that we use in our experiments is Yahoo! Answers corpus as of 10/25/2007. In Yahoo! Answers people usually ask their questions in two steps. First, they ask a short and informative question which is called *subject*. Then, they try to explain the question in a few sentences, which is called *content*. The content part does not often provide more information.

4.1.2　Ranking Algorithm

1. To begin, we extract all subjects from Yahoo! Answers database.

2. When a user performs a Search Engine Query (SEQ), we calculate the semantic similarity between the SEQ and each extracted subject.

3. Then we store the top scored subjects in an array, named Top-Subjects and also the scores of these Top-Subjects in another array called Top-Subjects-Scores.

4. At this step, we find the similarity scores of the first generated question with all Top-Subjects.

5. We store these scores in an array called Generated-Question-Similarities-to-Top-Subjects.

6. To obtain an overall score we take the average of all scores in both vectors Top-Subjects-Scores & Generated-Question-Similarities-to-Top-Subjects.

At this point, we have one score showing us how similar the generated question is to the questions that people have asked in Yahoo! Answers. The same steps will be taken for each generated question resulting in one similarity score per generated question. Then we sort the generated questions by these scores and show the user as many top ones as required.

In our experiments, we use the semantic similarity toolkit SEMILAR[2]. It has different methods for calculating the semantic similarity scores (Rus et al., 2013a; Rus et al., 2013b). We use LDA-Optimal method as its accuracy is quite acceptable.

4.2　Judging Syntactic Correctness

It is strongly believed that a question has a similar syntactic structure to the sentences from where it is generated (Chali and Hasan, 2015). Therefore, to judge the syntactic correctness of each generated question, we apply tree kernel functions (Collins and Duffy, 2001) in order to compute the syntactic similarity between each question and its associated body of text. To measure the syntactic similarity between two sentences, we first parse them syntactically which results in a parse tree for each sentence, then we apply tree kernel functions to these trees.

---

[2]Available at http://www.semanticsimilarity.org/.

The tree kernel function produces the syntactic similarity score between each sentence in the given body of text and the generated question. Each sentence contributes a score to the questions and then the questions are ranked by considering the average of their similarity scores.

5   Experiments

5.1   Corpus

In our experiments, we use the dataset from the Question Generation Shared Task and Evaluation Challenge (Rus and Graesser, 2009; Rus et al., 2010) to tackle the task of automatically generating questions. The dataset consists of 60 paragraphs, each related to 60 topics. They are originally selected from several articles such as OpenLearn, Wikipedia and Yahoo!Answers. The paragraphs are constructed from approximately 57 sentences, a total number of 100,200 tokens including punctuations. As mentioned before, to do our task, we assume that there exists a text related to each query containing useful information about it, so we consider the topics as queries and treat paragraphs as the associated body of the texts.

5.2   Evaluation Setup

Our methodology to evaluate the performance of our automated question generation system is inspired by Hasan (2013). Three unknown native English speakers were chosen to judge the result of our system. They were asked to score the generated questions according to two criteria: syntactic correctness and topic relevance. Judges give scores between 1 (very poor) and 5 (very good). There were four scores for each generated question. To evaluate the topic relevance criterion, judges were given three aspects, and they score each question according to each aspect. Aspects were: 1) questions' semantic correctness 2) question type correctness and 3) clarity of referential. For syntactic correctness, they score the generated questions considering if they are grammatically correct or not. Then the average of the judges' scores is calculated for each question.

To evaluate our system, we compare it with the state-of-the-art question generation system proposed by Chali and Hasan (2015). To do so, we use a publicly available question generation system by Heilman and Smith (2010a) as a benchmark. In our evaluation, we generated the questions from 20 randomly chosen texts and then select the top 10 ranked questions. We also generate the questions for the same texts by Heilman and Smith (2010a) question generation toolkit and again select top 10 ranked ones. The human judges were presented with 20 questions per text, top 10 from our system and top 10 from the system proposed by Heilman and Smith (2010a). We have 20 texts for the total number of 400 questions for each judge. After comparing our system with Heilman and Smith (2010a) system, we calculate our system advancement in comparison with the one created by Chali and Hasan (2015).

5.3   Results and Discussion

Table 2 lists the average of syntactic correctness and topic relevance scores for each system. These results confirm that our proposed automated question generation system outperforms the Heilman and Smith system (2010a) by 29.39%, and 18.71%, and over the Chali and Hasan system (2015) by 25.38%, and 14.04%, respectively. In this paper, we have shown that by using semantic similarity between a topic of interest and a group of pre-asked questions we can extract related ones to the concept of the topic and then we can use them to find the importance of a new generated question.

Systems	Syntactic Correctness	Topic Relevance
Heilman and Smith	3.13	3.42
State-of-the-art	3.23	3.56
Proposed QG System	4.05	4.06

Table 1: Syntactic correctness and topic relevance scores

6   Conclusion

We presented a novel system for automatically generating questions for topics of interests. The main assumption is that each topic is associated with an informative text. We have designed 265 templates to generate basic questions, and 350 rules to generate specific questions. The main aspect of this proposed method is the use of CQA systems to improve ranking of the generated questions. We used CQA to investigate the importance of questions and tree kernel functions to gauge how grammatically they are correct. We believe that there might be some ways in which this research could be continued, for example, our proposed system is rule-based, however, one of the ways to scale up these rules is learning them using learning techniques, in other words, the templates may be learned / acquired from a corpus of CQA data.

References

M. Agarwal and P. Mannem. 2011. Automatic gap-fill question generation from text books. In *Proceedings of the 6th Workshop on Innovative Use of NLP for Building Educational Applications*, pages 56–64.

M. Agarwal, R. Shah, and P. Mannem. 2011. Automatic question generation using discourse cues. In *Proceedings of the 6th Workshop on Innovative Use of NLP for Building Educational Applications*, pages 1–9.

Y. Chali and S. Hasan. 2015. Towards topic-to-question generation. *Computational Linguistics*.

M. Collins and N. Duffy. 2001. Convolution kernels for natural language. In *Advances in neural information processing systems*, pages 625–632.

D. M. Gates. 2008. Automatically generating reading comprehension look-back strategy: Questions from expository texts. Technical report, DTIC Document.

S. Hasan. 2013. *Complex question answering: minimizing the gaps and beyond*. Ph.D. thesis, University of Lethbridge, Alberta, Canada.

M. Heilman and N. A. Smith. 2010a. Extracting simplified statements for factual question generation. In *Proceedings of QG2010: The Third Workshop on Question Generation*.

M. Heilman and N. A. Smith. 2010b. Good question! statistical ranking for question generation. In *Human Language Technologies: The 2010 Annual Conference of the North American Chapter of the Association for Computational Linguistics*, pages 609–617.

I. Labutov, S. Basu, and L. Vanderwende. 2015. Deep questions without deep understanding. In *Proceedings of the 53rd Annual Meeting of the Association for Computational Linguistics and the 7th International Joint Conference on Natural Language Processing*, pages 889–898.

D. Lindberg, F. Popowich, J. Nesbit, and P. Winne. 2013. Generating natural language questions to support learning on-line. In *Proceedings of the 14th European Workshop on Natural Language Generation*, pages 105–114, Sofia, Bulgaria.

Y. Liu and E. Agichtein. 2008. On the evolution of the yahoo! answers qa community. In *Proceedings of the 31st annual international ACM SIGIR conference on Research and development in information retrieval*, pages 737–738.

M. Liu, R. A. Calvo, and V. Rus. 2010. Automatic question generation for literature review writing support. In *Intelligent Tutoring Systems*, pages 45–54.

K. Mazidi and R. D. Nielsen. 2014. Linguistic considerations in automatic question generation. In *Proceedings of the 52nd Annual Meeting of the Association for Computational Linguistics*, pages 321–326.

R. Mitkov and L. A. Ha. 2003. Computer-aided generation of multiple-choice tests. In *Proceedings of the HLT-NAACL 03 workshop on Building educational applications using natural language processing-Volume 2*, pages 17–22.

O. Rokhlenko and I. Szpektor. 2013. Generating synthetic comparable questions for news articles. In *Proceedings of the 51st Annual Meeting of the Association for Computational Linguistics*, pages 742–751.

V. Rus and A. C. Graesser. 2009. *The question generation shared task and evaluation challenge*. The University of Memphis. National Science Foundation.

V. Rus, B. Wyse, P. Piwek, M. Lintean, S. Stoyanchev, and C. Moldovan. 2010. The first question generation shared task evaluation challenge. In *Proceedings of the 6th International Natural Language Generation Conference*, pages 251–257.

V. Rus, M. C. Lintean, R. Banjade, N. B. Niraula, and D. Stefanescu. 2013a. Semilar: The semantic similarity toolkit. In *Proceedings of the 51st Annual Meeting of the Association for Computational Linguistics*, pages 163–168.

V. Rus, N. Niraula, and R. Banjade. 2013b. Similarity measures based on latent dirichlet allocation. In *Proceedings of the Computational Linguistics and Intelligent Text Processing*, pages 459–470.

W. Wang, T. Hao, and W. Liu. 2008. Automatic question generation for learning evaluation in medicine. In *Advances in Web Based Learning – ICWL*, pages 242–251.

Y. Xu, A. Goldie, and S. Seneff. 2009. Automatic question generation and answer judging: a q&a game for language learning. In *Proceedings of the SIGSLaTE*.

Towards proper name generation: A corpus analysis

Thiago Castro Ferreira and **Sander Wubben** and **Emiel Krahmer**
Tilburg center for Cognition and Communication (TiCC)
Tilburg University
The Netherlands
{tcastrof,s.wubben,e.j.krahmer}@tilburguniversity.edu

Abstract

We introduce a corpus for the study of proper name generation. The corpus consists of proper name references to people in webpages, extracted from the Wikilinks corpus. In our analyses, we aim to identify the different ways, in terms of length and form, in which a proper names are produced throughout a text.

1 Introduction

In natural language generation systems, referring expression generation (REG) is the process of producing references to discourse entities. Among the referential forms which can be used to distinguish an entity, proper names are an important and commonly used one. For instance, Ferreira et al. (2016) showed that writers produce a proper name as a first mention to an entity in 91% of the analysed texts.

In generation systems, not only the choice of whether a proper name should be generated is important, but also which *form* the proper name should take. For instance, *Barack Hussein Obama II* is the birth name of the 44th president of United States of America. However, he is also commonly referred to as *Barack Obama*, *Obama*, *President Obama*, etc. How to automatically decide which form to use?

In this paper, we introduce a new corpus of 53,102 proper names referring to people in 15,241 texts[1]. We analyse the corpus in terms of distribution of proper name lengths, intuitively expecting an inversely proportional relation between length of a

---

[1] https://ilk.uvt.nl/~tcastrof/regnames

name and sentence number in a text. We also analyse these references in terms of the presence of the first, middle and last name of the entity; and whether the reference is accompanied by a title or an appositive.

2 Related Studies

Unlike the generation of descriptions (Krahmer and van Deemter, 2012), only a few studies have focussed on the automatic generation of proper names. Reiter and Dale (2000) suggests the use of a full proper name for initial reference, optionally followed by an appositive to indicate properties of the entity important for the discourse. However, their approach does not account for variation in proper name references.

Van Deemter (2014) argues that proper name variants can be generated using standard algorithms for the generation of descriptions. In other words, van Deemter (2014) proposes describing proper names based on a knowledge base of attribute-value pairs. Just like a set of attribute-value pairs $\{(type, cube), (color, blue)\}$ is generated when the target needs to be singled out from differently coloured objects, a proper name like *Frida Kahlo* can be seen to single out one person from a context set. When the set is smaller, generally a shorter name will suffice. Van Deemter, however, does not apply this model in the context of text generation.

Siddharthan et al. (2011) presented a model to (re)generate referring expressions to people in extractive summaries. When generating a proper name, the model chooses between a full name or only a surname. Moreover, it also decides whether to use pre- (role, affiliation and temporal modifiers) or post-modifiers (appositives and relative clauses). As far as we know, this is the only study that introduced a corpus analysis of how humans produce proper names in a discourse. However, it only distinguished proper names among full names and surnames in a small set of 876 news texts.

3 Data Gathering

3.1 Materials

To analyse how proper names are used in text, we analysed webpages from the Wikilinks corpus (Singh et al., 2012). This corpus was originally created to study cross-document coreference and comprises around 40 million mentions to 3 million entities. All the mentions were extracted automatically by finding hyperlinks to Wikipedia pages related to the entities.

To collect our data, we identified the 1,000 most frequently mentioned people in the corpus. To determine which entities are persons, we used DBpedia, a database that provides structured information from Wikipedia (Bizer et al., 2009). From the Wikilinks corpus, we then randomly chose a subset of webpages that contain at least one mention to one of the most frequently mentioned persons. In total, our corpus contains texts from 15,241 webpages.

3.2 Annotation

To annotate the proper name references, we created a knowledge base which describes all variations of a proper name for the studied persons. We also parsed the webpages to identify in which part of the discourse the different proper name references were used. The annotation procedure is explained in more detail below.

Proper Names Knowledge Base We used two ontologies present on DBpedia to extract different proper names for the studied entities. The FOAF (*Friend-of-a-Friend*) ontology was used to extract the name (foaf:name), the given name (foaf:givenName) and the surname (foaf:surname) of a person. From the DBpedia ontology, we extracted the birth name of the entities (dbo:birthName).

Based on the proper names collected in DBpedia, we created a knowledge base by identifying 3 proper name attributes: **first name**, **middle name** and **last name**. First names consist of the first token from the name, given name and birth name, whereas last names consist of the token from the surname and the last tokens from the name and birth name. Middle names are all the tokens which are not the first token in the given and birth names and last token in the name and birth name. For instance, *Charles Bukowski* has *Charles*, *Bukowski*, *Charles Bukowski* and *Heinrich Karl Bukowski* as his given name, surname, name and birth name in DBpedia, respectively. Based on this information, the knowledge base for this entity would consist of *Charles* and *Heinrich* as first names; *Karl* as middle name; and *Bukowski* as last name.

Discourse Annotation The webpages were parsed using the Stanford CoreNLP software (Manning et al., 2014). Using this tool, we performed part-of-speech tagging, lemmatization, named entity recognition, dependency parsing, syntactic parsing, sentiment analysis and coreference resolution.

To improve the coreference resolution we performed a post hoc sanity check, to see whether references which were labelled as being to the same entity were correct. For each entity distinguished by the software, we checked the proper nouns of each proper name reference. If at least the proper nouns of one proper name were values present in the knowledge base of the target entity, all the references of the entity distinguished by the software were considered references to the target entity.

Once the references to the target entity were distinguished, we annotated their syntactic positions based on the output of the dependency parser and their referential statuses in the text and in the sentence - whether a reference is a first or an old mention to an entity. We also checked for the presence of a title or an appositive in the proper name references. These features were extracted based on the named entity recognition and dependency parser, respectively. In total, 53,102 proper name references were annotated in this way (an average of 3 per text).

3.3 Analyses

To analyse how proper names referring to people are distributed over a text, we checked the length of these references in terms of tokens. We also anal-

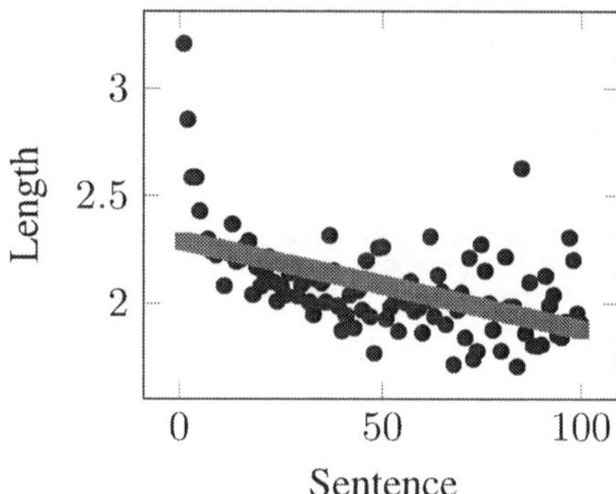

Figure 1: Average length of the proper names in tokens by sentence.

Title	2.4%
First Name	59.3%
Middle Name	7.1%
Last Name	89%
Appositive	1.7%

Table 1: Percentage of the proper name attributes

ysed the possible variations of a proper name by checking the presence of the first, middle and last name of the entity, and whether the proper name was accompanied by a title or an appositive.

4   Results

Figure 1 depicts the average length of proper name references in the first 100 sentences of the texts. A linear regression clearly shows that the length of a proper name decreases along the text, as predicted. Table 1 summarized the percentage of proper name attributes. It reveals that the last name is the most used one, followed by first name. The others occur less frequently.

Figure 2 shows the average length of proper name references as a function of syntactic position and referential status. Proper names in the object role of a sentence are generally longer than those in subject position (a); proper names that are new in the text are longer than those that have been mentioned in the text before, and vice versa when looking at new/old references per sentence (b).

Table 2 depicts frequency of various attribute sets, as a function of syntactic position and referential status in the text and sentence. Proper names consisting of both first and last name are the most common in the corpus. This proper name form is the most common one in the subject role of a sentence and as a mention to a new entity in the discourse. On the other hand, in the object role of a sentence and as mention to an old entity in the text, the use of only the last name is most common.

In general, proper names described by the first and last names, and by the first, middle and last names occur more often in the subject role of a sentence as a mention to a new entity in the text. The combination of first and last names is also more likely as a mention to old entities in the sentence. Proper names described by just one proper name attribute reveal the opposite behaviour, occurring more in the object role of a sentence as a mention to an old entity in the text or new in the sentence.

5   Discussion

This study introduced a corpus for the study of proper name generation. We analysed the different forms in which proper name references occur in text by checking their length as well as the occurrence of different proper name attributes including the first, middle, last names of the mentioned entity, as well as possible modifiers, such as titles or appositives.

Analyses revealed that longer proper names - in terms of number of tokens and proper name attributes - are more likely to be generated early in the text, in the object role of a sentence, and as the reference to a new entity in the text or an old in the sentence. Concerning referential status in text, our results are broadly in line with Siddharthan et al. (2011), which shows that a new entity in the text is more likely to be referred to the full name, whereas only the surname is used for an old entity. Concerning referential status in the sentence, the fact that a proper name reference to an old entity in the text is more likely to be longer than one to a new entity was somewhat unexpected, since some referential theories argue that a reference to previously mentioned entities tend to be shorter (Chafe, 1994). A possible explanation could be the presence of cataphora, as in *Unlike **his** peers, **Harold Camping** does not pack a positive punch.*

As future work, we aim to develop a computational model for proper name generation based on the reported findings. Besides the variation between proper name forms in different parts of

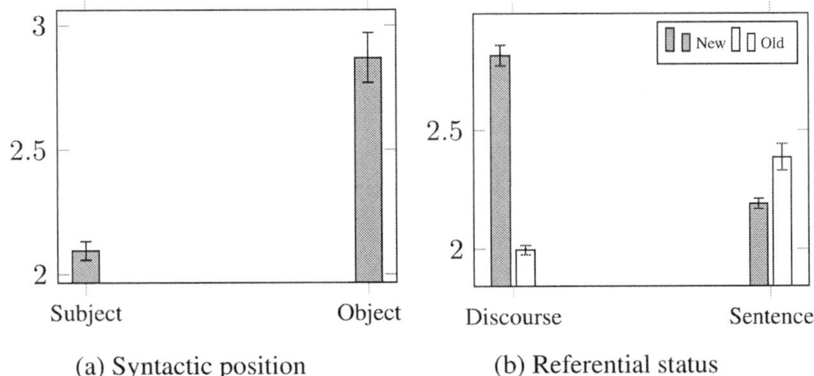

(a) Syntactic position   (b) Referential status

Figure 2: Average length of the proper names as a function of: (2a) syntactic position and (2b) referential status. Error bars represent 95% confidence intervals.

	Syntax		Text		Sentence		General
	Subject	Object	New	Old	New	Old	
First+Last	57.41%	38.74%	69.52%	36.53%	44.19%	57.16%	46.2%
Last	24.45%	37.17%	10.60%	44.26%	35.93%	26.61%	34.9%
First	6.15%	11.98%	4.33%	10.12%	8.58%	7.78%	8.5%
Middle+Last	3.39%	3.38%	4.62%	2.02%	2.91%	1.76%	2.8%
First+Middle+Last	2.92%	2.79%	4.72%	1.36%	2.44%	1.53%	2.3%
Middle	1.06%	1.88%	0.78%	1.74%	1.57%	0.80%	1.5%
Others	4.62%	4.06%	5.43%	3.97%	4.38%	4.36%	3.8%

Table 2: Percentage of the attribute sets in the proper name references

a text, this model should be able to address the proper name preferences for each entity. For instance, it should account that *Winston Churchill* is typically mentioned by his surname (*Churchill*), whereas *Napoleon Bonaparte* is by his first name (*Napoleon*). We will address this by training individual models combining the a priori probability of a particular proper name for a particular individual with contextual factors. Additionally, we plan to annotate the proper name references to all the entities present in the texts of our corpus, and not only the references to the 1,000 people studied here. We think this expansion will give a broader view of the generation of proper names, since we will be able to study the process as a function of other discourse conditions, as topicality.

Acknowledgments

This work has been supported by the National Council of Scientific and Technological Development from Brazil (CNPq).

References

Christian Bizer, Jens Lehmann, Georgi Kobilarov, Sren Auer, Christian Becker, Richard Cyganiak, and Sebastian Hellmann. 2009. Dbpedia - a crystallization point for the web of data. *Web Semantics: Science, Services and Agents on the World Wide Web*, 7(3):154 – 165. The Web of Data.

Wallace L. Chafe. 1994. *Discourse, Consciousness, and Time: The Flow and Displacement of Conscious Experience in Speaking and Writing*. University of Chicago Press.

Thiago Castro Ferreira, Emiel Krahmer, and Sander Wubben. 2016. Individual variation in the choice of referential form. In *Proceedings of the 2016 Conference of the North American Chapter of the Association for Computational Linguistics: Human Language Technologies*, San Diego, California. Association for Computational Linguistics.

Emiel Krahmer and Kees van Deemter. 2012. Computational generation of referring expressions: A survey. *Comput. Linguist.*, 38(1):173–218, March.

Christopher D. Manning, Mihai Surdeanu, John Bauer, Jenny Finkel, Steven J. Bethard, and David McClosky. 2014. The Stanford CoreNLP natural language processing toolkit. In *Association for Computational Linguistics (ACL) System Demonstrations*, pages 55–60.

Ehud Reiter and Robert Dale. 2000. *Building natural language generation systems*. Cambridge University Press, New York, NY, USA.

Advaith Siddharthan, Ani Nenkova, and Kathleen McKeown. 2011. Information status distinctions and referring expressions: An empirical study of references to people in news summaries. *Computational Linguistics*, 37(4):811–842.

Sameer Singh, Amarnag Subramanya, Fernando Pereira, and Andrew McCallum. 2012. Wikilinks: A large-scale cross-document coreference corpus labeled via links to Wikipedia. Technical Report UM-CS-2012-015.

Kees van Deemter. 2014. Referability. In Amanda Stent and Srinivas Bangalore, editors, *Natural Language Generation in Interactive Systems*, chapter 5, pages 101–103. Cambridge University Press, New York, NY, USA.

An Analysis of the Ability of Statistical Language Models to Capture the Structural Properties of Language

Aneiss Ghodsi and **John DeNero**
Computer Science Division
University of California, Berkeley
{aneiss, denero}@berkeley.edu

Abstract

We investigate the characteristics and quantifiable predispositions of both n-gram and recurrent neural language models in the framework of language generation. In modern applications, neural models have been widely adopted, as they have empirically provided better results. However, there is a lack of deep analysis of the models and how they relate to real language and its structural properties. We attempt to perform such an investigation by analyzing corpora generated by sampling from the models. The results are compared to each other and to the results of the same analysis applied to the training corpus. We carried out these experiments on varieties of Kneser-Ney smoothed n-gram models and basic recurrent neural language models. Our results reveal a number of distinctive characteristics of each model, and offer insights into their behavior. Our general approach also provides a framework in which to perform further analysis of language models.

1 Introduction

Statistical language modelling is critical to natural language processing and many generation systems. In recent years use has shifted from the previously prevalent n-gram model to the recurrent neural network paradigm that now dominates in most applications. Researchers have long sought to find the best language modeling solutions for particular applications, but it is important to understand the behavior of language models in a more generalizable way. This is advantageous both in developing language models and in applying them practically. Whether in tasks where statistical models are used to directly generate language or in cases where the model is used for ranking for surface realization, the statistical predispositions of the language model will be reflected in the results. In this paper we compare the behavior of n-gram models and Recurrent Neural Network Language Models (RNNLMs) with regard to properties of their generated language.

We use the SRILM toolkit for training and generating from n-gram models (Stolcke and others, 2002). Our n-gram model is a modified Kneser-Ney back-off interpolative model, unless otherwise stated (Chen and Goodman, 1999). We use Tomas Mikolov's implementation of an RNNLM, available at *rnnlm.org* (Mikolov et al., 2010). This model has a single hidden recurrent layer, and three defining parameters: class size, hidden layer size, and backpropagation through time (BPTT) steps. Classes are used to factor the vocabulary mappings to improve performance, by predicting a distribution over classes of words and then over words in a class (Mikolov et al., 2011). BPTT steps determine how many times the recurrent layer of the network is unwrapped for training. Unless otherwise mentioned all neural models have class of 100 and use four BPTT steps. We use the Penn Tree Bank (PTB), constructed from articles from the Wall Street Journal, as our primary training corpus, with the standard training split of 42068 sentences (Marcus et al., 1993). Correspondingly, our generated language corpora also contain 42068 sentences. Novel sentences are easily sampled from trained language models by prompting with a start of sentence token,

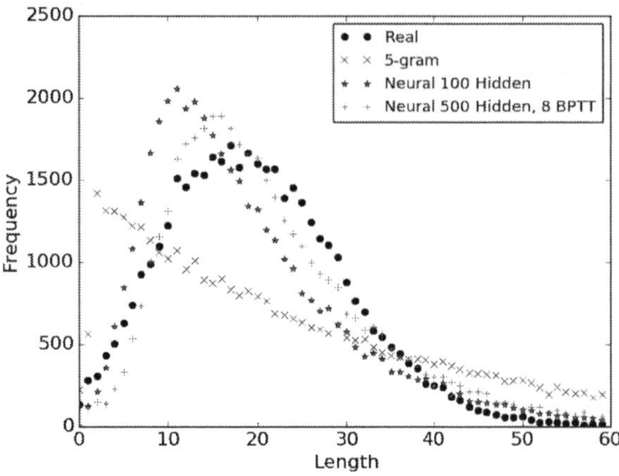

Figure 1: Sentence Length Distributions

Corpus	Sum of Error
Trigram	27736
5-gram	29694
Neural Hidden 100	19237
Neural Hidden 500	14132

Table 1: Sum of errors for sentence lengths, including normalized over total sentences.

sampling from the predicted distribution, using the result as context, and repeating until an end of sentence token is encountered.

We select three primary metrics with which to evaluate the various resulting corpora. The first is the distribution of sentence lengths. Sentence length is compared visually and through the sum of error as compared to the length distribution from the training corpus. The second metric is word frequency. Word frequency is analyzed by fitting a Zipfian distribution (Kingsley, 1932), and comparing between the distributions for each model. Third is pronoun frequency relative to distance from the start of a sentence. This was selected as a metric due to the fact that one-word pronouns are a small class fairly easily identifiable regardless of context (though there are a few that can be other parts of speech), partly avoiding the ambiguities and challenges that follow from part of speech taggers. This is especially useful in a corpus with a restricted vocabulary resulting in the replacement of uncommon tokens with a single token, such as the PTB, and with generated language that is not always semantically sound. These experiments were repeated multiple times with small variations, ensuring the key patterns in the results were not a product of chance.

Through these three metrics we seek to develop some insights into the behavior of standard stochastic models in language generation.

2   Sentence Lengths

The natural expectation is that a recurrent neural model, with its superior ability to 'remember' com-

plex context, would vastly outperform even fairly high order n-gram models in modeling sentence length. While in training errors are only propagated as far back as truncated backpropagation is executed (the BPTT steps hyperparameter), the power of the recurrent layer seems to exceed its apparent depth during training, taking advantage of the ability of recurrent memory to retain subtle contextual information. As seen in Figure 1, even the four BPTT step model performs fairly well. Contrastingly, n-gram models perform very poorly. Table 1 notes the sum of the absolute errors across the full range of models. N-gram models exhibit no improvement with increasing order. In neural production, however, we see substantial improvements with increasing network complexity; specifically, with an increase in the size of the hidden layer and the number of BPTT steps. However, the neural models tested here are unable to replicate the precise shape of the distribution. All models overestimate the incidence of very long sentences.

3   Vocabulary Distribution

Zipf's Law states that, for N unique words and s as the defining parameter, the frequency of a word with rank k is given by the following (Kingsley, 1932):

$$f(k; s, N) = \frac{1/k^s}{\sum_{n=1}^{N}(1/n^s)}$$

There are two aspects of evaluation for word frequencies: First, the difference between the Zipf parameters of distributions fitted to various text sources; second, the error on the data set to which a Zipfian distribution is fitted, indicating how closely the data follows a distribution known to match natural language production.

As shown in table 2, n-gram smoothing techniques have a significant effect on the accuracy of the generated Zipf distribution. As an n-gram model approaches being a simple unigram model, it should

Corpus	s	LL
Real	0.99193	-104598
Unigram 0-Discount	0.99293	-104416
Trigram 0-Discounts	0.98348	-103967
Trigram Discounts	0.97921	-104049
Trigram Back-Off Only	0.93515	-102532
Neural Hidden 100	0.98707	-104332
Neural Hidden 500	0.99735	-104655

Table 2: Zipf fit parameters s with Log-Likelihood.

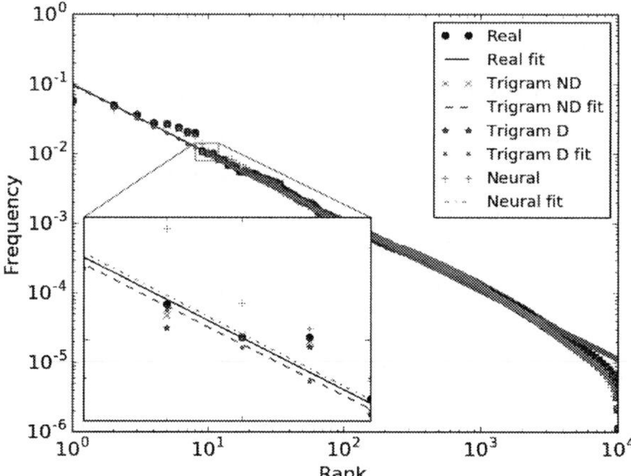

Figure 2: Zipf Distributions

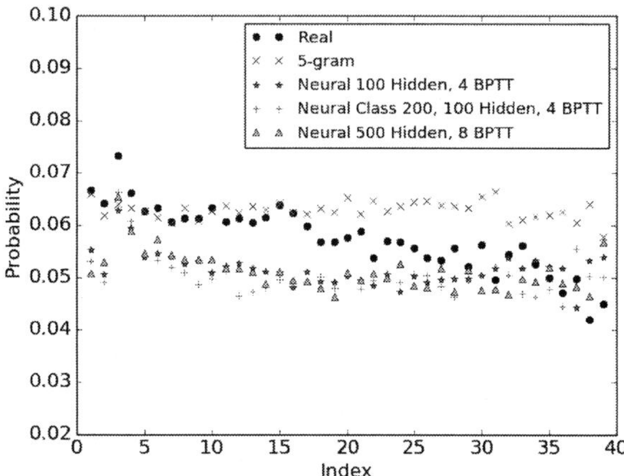

Figure 3: Pronoun Probability with Position

approach the same distribution as real language, due to the fact that a unigram model behaves like direct sampling of words from the training corpus. Thus it is intuitive that the interpolated models, in which unigram information always influences generation, performs better than a simple Kneser-Ney back-off model. Critically, on any configuration, non-zero discounting seems to worsen the distribution. As discounting is a method by which probability is held out to distribute amongst less likely or unseen sequences or tokens, it is reasonable that it would affect the distribution. Figure 2 shows the distributions from a selection of models on a log-log scale, with the trigram model with non-zero discounts (D) and with zero discounts (ND).

4 Pronoun Frequency with Depth

Finally, we observe the probability of encountering a pronoun at an index according to the following expression:

$$\frac{\sum_{s \in sentences} s[i] \in pronouns}{\sum_{s \in sentences} len(s) \geq i + 1}$$

We find that there is a spike in the probability of encountering a pronoun as the first word in a sentence, to approximately 0.15, an intuitive result given the prevalence of pronouns as sentence subjects. All models captured this fairly well. More interestingly, the probability of generating or observing a pronoun decreases with depth into a sentence. This phenomenon is clearly observable in the training set, with a fairly linear slope, which we calculate to be approximately -6.9×10^{-4} when restricted to the first twenty indices, excluding zero, due to the low number of samples at further positions in the sentence causing noise to dominate. In order to verify this result, the slope was calculated by sampling 20 subsets of sentences and averaging the slope across subsets. A comparable slope exists even when the domain is restricted to a set of sentences all of the same length (for example fourteen word sentences). This means the phenomenon is not an artifact resulting from the distribution of sentence lengths and a relationship between pronoun occurrences and sentence endings.

Neither class of model does particularly well at capturing this property, as can been seen in Figure 3. N-gram models were able to effectively capture the pronoun probability at the first word, as expected given the model should more or less reproduce the first-word distribution of the training data. They also appear to reflect the probabilities at the next several indices, but as with sentence length, they fail at any significant sentence depth regardless of n-gram order. The distribution in the n-gram generated language becomes approximately uniform. Neural models seem to capture some negative slope in the first ten to twenty words, but with depressed overall probabilities, and a loss of the pattern after a certain depth. Figure 3 also shows that increasing RNNLM complexity, whether in class, hidden size, or number of BPTT steps, does little to change the performance of the model in this metric.

This is concerning regarding the ability of this form of RNNLM to capture certain complex structural patterns, and indicates that the structure is inherently limited. It may be that a model with a Long-Short Term Memory unit (LSTM) as the recurrent component could perform better, with its superior ability to capture longer term contextual dependencies (Hochreiter and Schmidhuber, 1997). Indeed, LSTMs have become highly popular in many sequential learning tasks. However, given that these same basic RNNLMs performed well in the position-dependent sentence length metric, this result is disappointing.

5   Future Work

There are a number of clear steps to expand on this line of research, including experimenting with a greater variety of language models. In particular, a recurrent model with a Long Short-Term Memory unit (LSTM) might improve on the weaknesses of the simple RNNLM demonstrated here.

Additionally, further diversification of data sets is important to learning about patterns as they differ or remain consistent across sources. For example, preliminary analysis of the more stylistically diverse Brown corpus (Francis, 1964) indicates that the pronoun trend observed in the PTB may not be present in other domains, at least not as clearly. Additionally to profiling models on specific text genres, the experiments must be recreated on a far more sizeable dataset, such as the Wikipedia text corpus.

Finally, the introduction of new metrics to the language model analysis could add further value. Automatic tagging and parsing systems are likely to suffer from significant inaccuracy on the often flawed text produced by stochastic models; however, the results from applying such systems could prove informative about language model quality, as a model is not effectively capturing structural and semantic properties of language if parsing and tagging results statistics are not comparable to those of real language. Statistical analysis of parsing results would help expand the quantitative portrait of a language model.

6   Conclusion

Our work characterizes some key structural properties of language generated from two common statistical models. The results presented here verify many of the expectations regarding the behavior of n-gram and RNN techniques, and also introduce some new observations. RNNs have a structural capacity largely missing from n-gram models, which is particularly apparent in sentence length distributions. The recurrent model used here, however, struggled in reproducing the more complex pattern represented by the pronoun distribution over position. The results of the Zipfian distribution analysis indicate that neural networks with reasonable complexity are capable of approaching the correct vocabulary distribution, and competing favorably with the most vocabulary-optimized n-gram models. We found some interesting phenomena where smoothing, especially with high order n-gram models, flattened the Zipf distribution. At the very least we see that basic RNNLMs exhibit no real weaknesses next to n-gram models, beyond training time.

Overall, the methods we present here comprise an approach to language model analysis that is more independent from specific applications than previous reviews of language model performance. By selecting structural properties of language that are measurable and ideally equally valid on real and sampled language, it is possible to characterize language models and examine their learning capacities and predispositions in generation and ranking. Future avenues of investigation in line with this paradigm can provide more detailed portraits and serve as guidance both in the selection of models for applications and for further developments in statistical language modeling.

Acknowledgments

We would like to thank the members of the NLP group at the University of California, Berkeley for their contributions to discussions, as well as the two anonymous reviewers of this paper for their suggestions.

References

Stanley F Chen and Joshua Goodman. 1999. An empirical study of smoothing techniques for language modeling. *Computer Speech & Language*, 13(4):359–393.

Winthrop Nelson Francis. 1964. A standard sample of present-day english for use with digital computers.

Sepp Hochreiter and Jürgen Schmidhuber. 1997. Long short-term memory. *Neural computation*, 9(8):1735–1780.

Zipf George Kingsley. 1932. Selective studies and the principle of relative frequency in language.

Mitchell P Marcus, Mary Ann Marcinkiewicz, and Beatrice Santorini. 1993. Building a large annotated corpus of english: The penn treebank. *Computational linguistics*, 19(2):313–330.

Tomas Mikolov, Martin Karafiát, Lukas Burget, Jan Cernockỳ, and Sanjeev Khudanpur. 2010. Recurrent neural network based language model. In *INTERSPEECH*, volume 2, page 3.

Tomáš Mikolov, Stefan Kombrink, Lukáš Burget, Jan Černockỳ, and Sanjeev Khudanpur. 2011. Extensions of recurrent neural network language model. In *2011 IEEE International Conference on Acoustics, Speech and Signal Processing (ICASSP)*, pages 5528–5531. IEEE.

Andreas Stolcke et al. 2002. Srilm-an extensible language modeling toolkit. In *INTERSPEECH*, volume 2002, page 2002.

Enhancing PTB Universal Dependencies for Grammar-Based Surface Realization

David King and **Michael White**
Department of Linguistics
The Ohio State University
Columbus, OH 43210, USA
`king.2138@osu.edu,mwhite@ling.osu.edu`

Abstract

Grammar-based surface realizers require inputs compatible with their reversible, constraint-based grammars, including a proper representation of unbounded dependencies and coordination. In this paper, we report on progress towards creating realizer inputs along the lines of those used in the first surface realization shared task that satisfy this requirement. To do so, we augment the Universal Dependencies that result from running the Stanford Dependency Converter on the Penn Treebank with the unbounded and coordination dependencies in the CCGbank, since only the latter takes the Penn Treebank's trace information into account. An evaluation against gold standard dependencies shows that the enhanced dependencies have greatly enhanced recall with moderate precision. We conclude with a discussion of the implications of the work for a second realization shared task.

1 Introduction

Surface realization systems employing reversible, broad coverage constraint-based grammars together with statistical ranking models have achieved impressive results in multiple languages, using a variety of formalisms (HPSG, TAG, LFG, CCG). However, these systems all require somewhat different inputs, making comparative evaluation difficult. In the first surface realization shared task (Belz et al., 2011, henceforth SR-11), which aimed to ameliorate these difficulties, attempts to use grammar-based realizers were unsuccessful, as converting shared task inputs to system-native inputs turned out to be more difficult than anticipated. Subsequently, Narayan & Gardent (2012) demonstrated that grammar-based systems can be substantially improved with error mining techniques, and Gardent and Narayan (2013) showed that augmenting the (shallow) SR-11 representation of coordination to include shared dependencies can benefit grammar-based realizers. White (2014) then showed that even better results can be achieved by inducing a grammar (Kwiatkowski et al., 2011; Artzi and Zettlemoyer, 2013) that is directly compatible with (an enhanced version of) the SR-11 inputs. However, as explained below, subsequent analysis revealed substantial remaining issues with the data, which this paper takes a step towards addressing.

">

A common thread in work on reversible, constraint-based grammars is emphasis on properly representing unbounded dependencies and coordination. For parsing, this emphasis has been shown to pay off in improved recall of unbounded dependencies (Rimell et al., 2009; Nguyen et al., 2012; Oepen et al., 2014). For realization, however, it remains an open question as to whether approaches based on constraint-based grammars can likewise yield an empirical payoff, given the continuing lack of a common input representation that adequately treats unbounded dependencies and coordination, as these grammars require.

With this issue in mind, White (2014) experimented with a version of the shallow SR-11 inputs (created by Richard Johansson) which included extra dependencies for unbounded dependencies and coordination, yielding dependency graphs extending core dependency trees. Unlike the rewrite rules employed by Gardent and Narayan (2013), the extra dependencies were derived from the gold traces in the Penn Treebank (Marcus et al., 1993, PTB), which is necessary to adequately handle right node raising and relativization. However, this version was still found to be incomplete, in particular because it was missing cases where the extra dependencies are encoded structurally in the PTB.

Since then, Universal Dependencies (Nivre et al., 2016, UDs), which aim to represent syntactic dependencies similarly across languages, have become increasingly prominent. Building on the enhanced Stanford dependencies for English (de Marneffe et al., 2013)—which were designed to properly represent unbounded dependencies in dependency graphs—enhanced UDs for English have been partially implemented in the Stanford Dependency Converter (Schuster and Manning, 2016, SDC). The SDC transforms automatic or gold PTB-style trees into UDs; unfortunately, however, it was not designed to take traces into account, and thus the treatment of unbounded dependencies and coordination is only heuristic. To address this impasse, in this paper we report on progress towards creating SR-11–style realizer inputs that are both based on enhanced UDs and which accurately represent unbounded dependencies and coordination. To do so, we augment the UDs that result from running the SDC on the PTB with the dependencies in the CCG-bank (Hockenmaier and Steedman, 2007), since the latter includes lexicalized dependencies derived from gold PTB traces.

2   Background

Figures 1–2 show an example where the CCG-bank preserves the information provided by the trace in a free relative clause along with a crucial structurally encoded dependency. In Figure 1 (left), the unbounded dependency between *what* and *achieve* is annotated via a trace in the PTB. Figure 1 (right) shows the SDC output for the sentence. While the SDC manages to capture the unbounded dependency in this case, *what* is not recognized as the head of the free relative clause and there is no direct dependency from the copula to *what*, contrary to de Marneffe et al.'s (2013) specifications. The inadequacy of the representation here—which is essentially the same as the SR-11 representation for the sentence—has serious implications for realization, as it will be difficult for any realizer to determine that *what* should appear at the start of the free relative clause rather than following *achieve*, where direct objects would normally appear (or perhaps sentence initially). By contrast, Figure 2 shows how the Combinatory Categorial Grammar (Steedman, 2000; Steedman and Baldridge, 2011, CCG) derivation yields

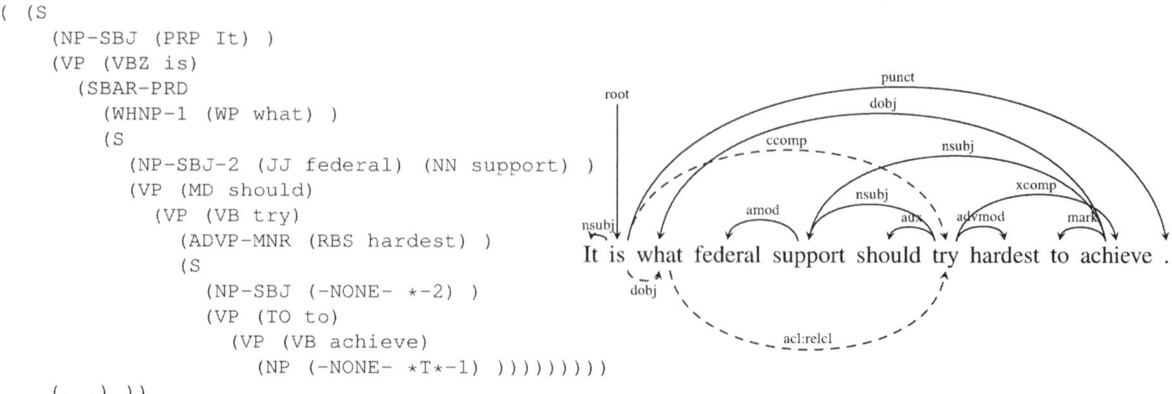

Figure 1: Left: An example of PTB annotation of a free relative clause (*wsj_2412.80*); note the co-indexation between the trace **T*-1* and *WHNP-1*. Right: Automatic SDC output of the gold annotated PTB structure treats *try* as the head of the copula's complement and has no direct dependency from the copula to *what*, contrary to de Marneffe et al.'s (2013) specifications. Dashed lines show new (below) and deleted (above) dependencies in this work.

Figure 2: Abbreviated CCGbank derivation showing how PTB trace information is preserved via NP co-indexation; composition operations enable the missing object of *achieve* to be passed up to where its role can be filled by *what*.

a structural dependency between *what* and *is* along with the unbounded dependency between *what* and *achieve*. (More commonly, the SDC captures the structural dependency but not the unbounded one, especially in right node raising and object relatives.)

3 Using the CCGbank to Augment PTB Universal Dependencies

Unlike UDs, CCGbank dependencies are numeric and depend on the lexical category of the functor (e.g. *what* fills the second argument of the category for *achieve* in Figure 2). To determine UD labels, we employ a maxent classifier taking information from CCGbank as input. Comparing the CCGbank and SDC output, the classifier is trained where their dependencies overlap and predicts both a label and head-dependent direction. Features used are functor and argument categories; functor and argument tokens; functor and argument POS tags; and functor and argument relative directionality.

Our system for augmenting the SDC's PTB output begins by combining the SDC basic and enhanced output, since the basic representation does not skip words while the enhanced representation already includes many correct extra dependencies. The system then scans the SDC output and CCGbank for 3 triggers: (i) shared arguments in coordination (e.g. shared objects

		All items	Without CCG gaps
exact	SDC	51	51
	System	**82****	**86****
unlabeled	SDC	57	57
	System	**86****	**91****

Table 1: Results from Rimell et al's (2009) dev set (Wall Street Journal portion). ** – p < 0.01

		All items	Without CCG gaps
exact	SDC	42	44
	System	**68*****	**70*****
unlabeled	SDC	50	52
	System	**75*****	**78*****

Table 2: Results from Rimell et al's (2009) test set (Wall Street Journal portion). *** – p ≤ 0.0001

in right node raising), (ii) CCGbank unbounded dependency annotations, and (iii) underspecified SDC *dep* relations (i.e. instances where the SDC cannot determine the appropriate dependency relation). In each case, the maxent classifier is used to predict UD labels for the CCGbank dependencies in question. Predictions are only added to the corpus if there is no (non-*dep*) SDC dependency already present. In addition, *ccomp* and *csubj* relations that co-occur with free relatives are remapped to make the relative the head of the clause. Finally, structural changes for coordination and compounding along SR-11 lines are carried out.

4 Evaluation

The system's recall was evaluated on Rimell et al.'s (2009) unbounded dependency corpus, a hand-curated corpus with gold annotations for constructions including object free relatives, right node raising, subject extraction, and object extraction. During the creation of CCGbank, some problematic sentences involving gapping were left out of the CCGbank. As a result, we evaluate the system using four different criteria: with and without the skipped CCG sentences,

and with both exact and unlabeled matches. Tables 1 and 2 show significant improvements across the board over the SDC.

Precision was evaluated by manually examining 401 predictions from the system's output to see whether the proposed edits adhered to UD specifications. Precision from the converter is 70% for exact label matches and 91% for unlabeled matches.

5 Discussion and Future Work

We have adapted and extended White's (2014) CCG induction algorithm to work with the augmented UDs that our system produces. White's algorithm assumed CCG phrases are only rarely projected from a dependent rather than a head— e.g., where an NP is projected from a determiner, which is a dependent of the head noun— and thus could be easily handled by handcrafted lexical entries. Since such cases are very common in UDs, the algorithm needed to be extended to induce such categories automatically. Once this was done, the algorithm yielded complete derivations in most cases (approx. 94%). In particular, derivations were induced that captured all but one of the extra dependencies in Table 1 that appear in the CCGbank dev section, and realization experiments with the UD-based representations are underway.

With the augmented UD reported in this paper, we expect the resulting dependency graphs to serve as a promising basis for a second surface realization challenge (with using just the basic dependency trees as an option). A remaining obstacle, however, are the dependent cluster and gapping cases in the PTB, for which the SDC produces rather degenerate output. A promising avenue here would be to adapt Gardent and Narayan's (2013) method of enhancing the SR-11 representations for these cases.

Acknowledgments

We thank Marie-Catherine de Marneffe, Micha Elsner, the OSU Clippers group and the anonymous reviewers for helpful feedback. This work was supported in part by NSF grant 1319318.

References

Yoav Artzi and Luke Zettlemoyer. 2013. Weakly supervised learning of semantic parsers for mapping instructions to actions. *TACL*, 1:49–62.

Anja Belz, Michael White, Dominic Espinosa, Eric Kow, Deirdre Hogan, and Amanda Stent. 2011. The first surface realisation shared task: Overview and evaluation results. In *Proc. ENLG*.

Marie-Catherine de Marneffe, Miriam Connor, Natalia Silveira, Samuel R Bowman, Timothy Dozat, and Christopher D Manning. 2013. More Constructions, More Genres: Extending Stanford Dependencies. In *Proc. DepLing 2013*.

Claire Gardent and Shashi Narayan. 2013. Generating elliptic coordination. In *Proceedings of the 14th European Workshop on Natural Language Generation*, pages 40–50.

Julia Hockenmaier and Mark Steedman. 2007. CCGbank: A Corpus of CCG Derivations and Dependency Structures Extracted from the Penn Treebank. *Computational Linguistics*, 33(3):355–396.

Tom Kwiatkowski, Luke Zettlemoyer, Sharon Goldwater, and Mark Steedman. 2011. Lexical generalization in CCG grammar induction for semantic parsing. In *Proceedings of the Conference on Empirical Methods in Natural Language Processing*, pages 1512–1523.

Mitchell P. Marcus, Mary Ann Marcinkiewicz, and Beatrice Santorini. 1993. Building a large annotated corpus of English: The Penn Treebank. *Computational linguistics*, 19(2):313–330.

Shashi Narayan and Claire Gardent. 2012. Error mining with suspicion trees: Seeing the forest for the trees. In *Proc. COLING*.

Luan Nguyen, Marten Van Schijndel, and William Schuler. 2012. Accurate unbounded dependency recovery using generalized categorial grammars. In *Proceedings of COLING 2012*, pages 2125–2140.

Joakim Nivre, Marie-Catherine de Marneffe, Filip Ginter, Yoav Goldberg, Jan Hajič, Christopher Manning, Ryan McDonald, Slav Petrov, Sampo Pyysalo, Natalia Silveira, et al. 2016. Universal dependencies v1: A multilingual treebank collection. In *Proceedings of the 10th International Conference on Language Resources and Evaluation (LREC 2016)*.

Stephan Oepen, Marco Kuhlmann, Yusuke Miyao, Daniel Zeman, Dan Flickinger, Jan Hajic, Angelina Ivanova, and Yi Zhang. 2014. Semeval 2014 task 8: Broad-coverage semantic dependency parsing. In *Proceedings of the 8th International Workshop on Semantic Evaluation (SemEval 2014)*, pages 63–72.

Laura Rimell, Stephen Clark, and Mark Steedman. 2009. Unbounded Dependency Recovery for Parser Evaluation. In *Proceedings of the 2009 Conference on Empirical Methods in Natural Language Processing: Volume 2-Volume 2*, pages 813–821.

Sebastian Schuster and Christopher D. Manning. 2016. Enhanced english universal dependencies: An improved representation for natural language understanding tasks. In *Proceedings of the Tenth International Conference on Language Resources and Evaluation (LREC 2016)*.

Mark Steedman and Jason Baldridge. 2011. Combinatory Categorial Grammar. *Non-Transformational Syntax: Formal and Explicit Models of Grammar. Wiley-Blackwell.*

Mark Steedman. 2000. *The syntactic process.* MIT Press, Cambridge, MA, USA.

Michael White. 2014. Towards surface realization with CCGs induced from dependencies. In *Proceedings of the 8th International Natural Language Generation Conference (INLG)*, pages 147–151.

Effect of Data Annotation, Feature Selection and Model Choice on Spatial Description Generation in French

Anja Belz
Computing, Engineering and Maths
University of Brighton
Lewes Road, Brighton BN2 4GJ, UK
a.s.belz@brighton.ac.uk

Adrian Muscat   **Brandon Birmingham**
Communications & Computer Engineering
University of Malta
Msida MSD 2080, Malta
adrian.muscat@um.edu.mt

Jessie Levacher   **Julie Pain**   **Adam Quinquenel**
INSA Rouen
Avenue de l'Université
76801 Saint-Étienne-du-Rouvray Cedex, France
{firstname.lastname}@insa-rouen.fr

Abstract

In this paper, we look at automatic generation of spatial descriptions in French, more particularly, selecting a spatial preposition for a pair of objects in an image. Our focus is on assessing the effect on accuracy of (i) increasing data set size, (ii) removing synonyms from the set of prepositions used for annotation, (iii) optimising feature sets, and (iv) training on best prepositions only vs. training on all acceptable prepositions. We describe a new data set where each object pair in each image is annotated with the best and all acceptable prepositions that describe the spatial relationship between the two objects. We report results for three new methods for this task, and find that the best, 75% Accuracy, is 25 points higher than our previous best result for this task.

1 Introduction

The research in this paper addresses the area of image description generation with applications in automatic image captioning and assistive technologies. An important aspect, and long-standing research topic, is to identify the entities, or objects, in images. However, a good image description will also say something about how entities relate to each other, not just list them. Spatial relations, and prepositions to express them, are particularly important in this context, but until very recently there had been no research directly aimed at this subtask, although

some research came close (Mitchell et al., 2012; Kulkarni et al., 2013; Yang et al., 2011). Elliott & Keller (Elliott and Keller, 2013) did address the subtask, but with hardwired rules for just eight preposition. The work reported by Ramisa et al. (2015) is closely related to our work and also uses geometric and label features to predict prepositions.

2 Data

The new data set we have created for the experiments in this paper is a set of photographs in which objects in 20 classes are annotated with bounding boxes and class labels, and each object pair with prepositions that describe the spatial relationship between the objects. The data was derived from the VOC'08 data (Everingham et al., 2010) by selecting images with 2 or 3 bounding boxes, and adding the preposition annotations. The data has twice as many images as in our previous work (Belz et al., 2015), and a smaller set of prepositions (see below).

2.1 Annotation

For each object pair in each image, and for both orderings of the object labels, L_s, L_o and L_o, L_s, three French native speakers selected (i) the best preposition for the given pair (free text entry), and (ii) the possible prepositions for the given pair (from a given list) that accurately described the spatial relationship between the two objects in the pair. As a result, we have a total of 4,140 object pair annotations which fold out into 9,278 training instances.

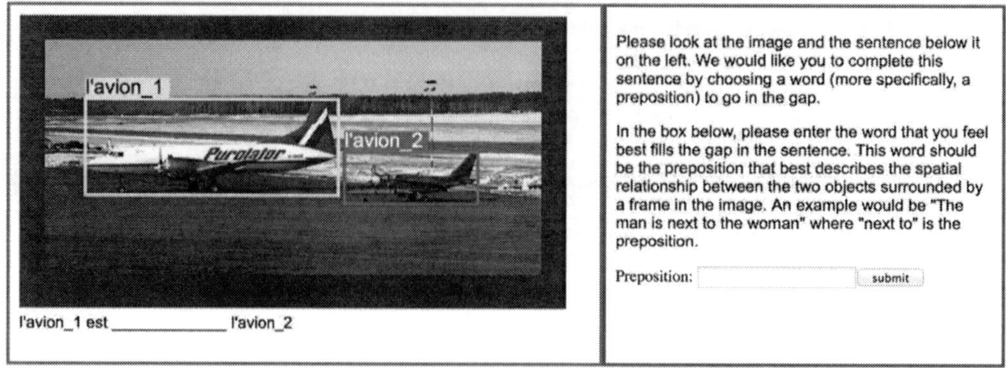

Figure 1: Screen grab of annotation tool, showing first task (free-text entry of single best preposition).

Figure 1 is a screen grab from our annotation tool showing the first annotation task (free-text entry of single best preposition). In the second task, annotators chose from the following set of 17 prepositions:

à côté de, a l'éxterieur de, au dessus de, au niveau de, autour de, contre, dans, derrière, devant, en face de, en travers de, le long de, loin de, par delà, près de, sous, sur.

In our previous work with French data (Belz et al., 2015) we additionally had *en dessous de, en haut de, parmi* and *à l'interieur de*. We removed *parmi*, because it was never used in our previous annotation efforts, and the other three because the preposition set also contains near synonyms for them. Below, we refer to the data annotated with the smaller set as **DS-17** and that with the larger **DS-21**.

We previously used only images with exactly 2 object bounding boxes; these images are also included (newly annotated) in our new data set. In some of our experiments below we report results for just this subset and refer to it as **DS-17-2o**. The remaining half of the data (containing only images with 3 bounding boxes) is referred to as **DS-17-3o**.

We replaced the VC'08 object class labels with their French equivalents in the annotations, yielding the following set of words (used for the language features, see Section 3.1 below):

la personne, le chien, la voiture, la chaise, le cheval, le chat, l'oiseau, le vélo, la moto, l'écran, l'avion, la bouteille, le bateau, le canapé, le train, la plante, le mouton, la vache, la table, le bus.

We used pairwise kappa to assess inter-annotator and intra-annotator agreement for our three annotators (who annotated one third of the data each). For

selection of best prepositions this is straightforward; for all prepositions it is less straightforward, because the sets of selected prepositions differ in set size and overlap size. Our approach was to align the preposition sets and to pad out the aligned sets with blank labels if an annotator did not select a preposition selected by another annotator. Calculated in this way on a batch of 40 images, for *best* prepositions, average inter-annotator agreement was 0.67, and average intra-annotator agreement was 0.81. For *all* prepositions, average inter-annotator agreement was 0.63, and average intra-annotator agreement was 0.77.[1]

2.2 Object Class Label and Preposition Counts

The following table shows occurrence counts for the 12 most frequent object class labels in DS-17:

la personne	la voiture	le chien	la chaise	le cheval	le chat	l'oiseau	le bateau	l'écran	la plante	la bouteille	l'avion
3946	606	518	419	349	347	345	321	285	278	273	259

Some prepositions were selected far more frequently than others; the top 12 are:

près de	à côté de	devant	derrière	au niveau de	contre	sous	sur	loin de	en face de	au dessus de	le long de
2183	1483	1084	1031	926	704	434	380	372	271	123	78

3 Methods

The training data contains a separate training instance (L_s, L_o, p) for each preposition p selected

---

[1]These would have been even higher had it not been for one of the annotators who had much lower kappas than the others.

by human annotators for the template 'L_s est p L_o' (e.g. *le chien est devant la personne*), given an image in which (just) Obj_s and Obj_o are surrounded by bounding boxes labelled with object class labels L_s and L_o. All models are trained and tested with leave-one-out cross-validation.

3.1 Learning Methods

Naive Bayes Model (NB): We use a Naive Bayes model as in our previous work (Belz et al., 2015) which maps our set of language and visual features to prepositions (for details of all features see Section 3.1). The model uses the language features for defining the prior model and the visual features for defining the likelihood model.

SVM Model: Using the same features, we trained a multi-class SVM model employing one-versus-one classification.[2] This involves training $k(k-1)/2$ pairs of binary preposition classifiers for a multi-class prediction task involving k prepositions. The SVM model was trained with an RBF kernel, characterised by a coefficient of $1/(|features|)$.

Decision-Tree Model (DT): Again using the same features, we created a multi-class probabilistic decision-tree model[2] with a maximum tree depth of 4 for the DS-17 data set, and 5 for the DS-21 data set (from training and validation error plots).

Logistic Regression Model (LR): Using the same features, we trained a multi-class logistic regression model employing one-versus-rest classification[1]. The model makes use of L1-norm regularisation with an inverse regularisation strength of 0.9.

3.2 Evaluation methods

To compare results in this paper, we use variants of Accuracy from our previous work (Belz et al., 2015). The dimension along which the variants we use here differ is output rank. Different variants, denoted $Acc(n)$, where $n = 1...4$, return Accuracy rates for the top n outputs produced by systems, such that a system output is considered correct if a target (human-selected) output is among the top n outputs produced by the system (so for $s = 1$ the measure is just standard Accuracy).

	DS-21	DS-17-2o
	$Acc(1)$	$Acc(1)$
NB	50.2	67.0
DT	50.4	66.2
SVM	46.1	59.4
LR	**53.4**	**72.7**

Table 1: $Acc(1)$ results for the data with the larger (DS-21) and smaller (DS-17-2o) preposition sets, for all 4 models.

3.3 Features

The four methods described in the following section all use the following feature set (described in more detail in Belz et al., 2015):

$F0$: Object label L_s.
$F1$: Object label L_o.
$F2$: Area of bounding box of Obj_s normalised by image size.
$F3$: Area of bounding box of Obj_o normalised by image size.
$F4$: Ratio of Obj_s bounding box area to that of Obj_o.
$F5$: Distance between bounding box centroids.
$F6$: Area of overlap of bounding boxes normalised by the smaller bounding box.
$F7$: Distance between centroids divided by approximated average width of bounding boxes.
$F8$: Position of Obj_s relative to Obj_o (N, E, S, W).

Note that to make the categorial features (F0, F1, F8) work for the logistic regression model we map them to 1-hot encodings (n bits for n feature values).

4 Experiments and Results

4.1 Preposition Set

In this set of experiments, we wanted to see what the effect on learning is of removing synonyms from the set of prepositions and re-annotating the data with the reduced set. We compared results for our previous French data (DS-21) with the corresponding subset of our new data (DS-17-2o), both with similar numbers of training instances. Note that because the annotations differ, we are testing on slightly different sets of target outputs. Table 1 shows the Accuracy results for the four models from Section 3.1.

Numbers clearly demonstrate a very substantial benefit from removing synonyms for all tested methods, improvement ranging from 13.3 points to 19.3. The benefit is biggest for LR, smallest for SVM.

---

[2]Implemented using scikit-learn (http://scikit-learn.org).

	DS-17-2o		DS-17	
	$Acc(1)$	$Acc(2)$	$Acc(1)$	$Acc(2)$
NB	67.0	82.0	64.7	80.9
DT	66.2	80.5	67.7	81.4
SVM	59.4	78.5	-	-
LR	**72.7**	**86.8**	**74.9**	**89.2**

Table 2: $Acc(1)$ and $Acc(2)$ results for the smaller (DS-17-2o) and larger (DS-17) data sets with 17 prepositions.

4.2 Data Set Size

Here we look at the effect of adding more data to the training set, comparing results for DS-17-2o (1,020 images; 4,426 training instances) with results for the whole of DS-17 (2,070 images; 9,278 training instances). Table 2 shows the results: there are some improvements from the size increase for all methods except NB, but the only sizeable one is for LR.

4.3 Different Models

Tables 1 and 2 provide an overview of results for the four models above on DS-21, DS-17-2o and DS-17. Of the new methods (SVM, DT, LR), SVM does much worse than the others (we therefore leave it out of the remaining experiments below). The LR model achieves the best results across all data sets.

Looking at Acc(1) vs. Acc(2) results (Table 2), differences are very similar (around 14-15 points) for all methods except for SVM for which it is much bigger, implying that SVM more often has a target preposition in second place.

4.4 Feature Optimisation

We start with the results on DS-17 for the three best models as a baseline and try to improve over them using greedy lasso as a simple feature optimisation method which starts by selecting the single best feature and then keeps adding the next feature that achieves the best result in combination with previously selected feature(s). Table 3 shows $Acc(1)$, $Acc(2)$ and $Acc(3)$ results for DS-17, before and after feature optimisation. Feature optimisation does not make a difference to LR, but improves the results for DT slightly, and for NB substantially, by leaving out features 5, 6 and 8, and 6 and 7, respectively.

4.5 Best vs. All Annotations

Unlike in our previous work, our new data contains information about which preposition annotators thought was best out of the ones they considered possible (see Section 2), so we can now compare results for training on best prepositions only vs. all possible prepositions for object pairs.

There are more than twice the number of training instances for all possible prepositions (9,278) than for best prepositions only (4,140), so it is not a like-for-like comparison. We therefore also report (under the heading 'all-sub' in Table 4) results for a randomly selected subset of the all-prepositions data of the same size as the best-prepositions-only data (averaged over 4 different runs).

The results in Table 4 show very clearly the benefit of training on all possible prepositions compared to best only, although the benefit is less marked for the NB method. While results for 'all-sub' are lower than for 'all', and some of the improvement in the 'all' results is likely due to larger data set size, the 'all-sub' results nevertheless show clearly that the largest part of the improvement is due to training on all possible prepositions (that being the only difference between the 'best' and 'all-sub' data).

5 Discussion

It is worth recalling that the task we are trying to solve is to guess the actual 3D spatial relationship between two objects in a photograph, from just the object types and various geometric properties of the objects' bounding boxes which give just a rough idea even of the object's size and 2D dimensions in the image. Nevertheless this rudimentary information is enough to predict a correct 3D preposition 75% of the time in the case of our best method, LR, moreover across a variety of large and small, animate and inanimate objects, in indoors and outdoors scenes. The most closely related existing work (Ramisa et al., 2015) reported slightly higher accuracy rates, but for different data sets. Our own previous results (Belz et al., 2015) were considerably worse at around 50%.

The Acc(n) results for $n > 1$ are interesting. E.g. LR places a target preposition in the top two almost 90% of the time. At the same time, our annotators chose on average 2.2 prepositions per (ordered) object pair, with a kappa agreement of 0.63, indicating that there may be more than two good prepositions for an object pair. In future work we will evaluate

	DS-17			DS-17, optimised			
	$Acc(1)$	$Acc(2)$	$Acc(3)$	$Acc(1)$	$Acc(2)$	$Acc(3)$	Best feature set
DT	67.7	81.4	91.0	68.4	82.3	90.7	{0,1,2,3,4,7}
NB	64.7	80.9	90.4	71.6	86.3	93.1	{0,1,2,3,4,5,8}
LR	**74.9**	89.2	94.2	**74.9**	89.2	94.2	{0,1,2,3,4,5,6,7,8}

Table 3: $Acc(1)$, $Acc(2)$ and $Acc(3)$ results for DS-17, before and after feature optimisation, for the three best models.

	DS-17								
	best			all			all-sub		
	$Acc(1)$	$Acc(2)$	$Acc(3)$	$Acc(1)$	$Acc(2)$	$Acc(3)$	$Acc(1)$	$Acc(2)$	$Acc(3)$
DT	51.6	71.8	83.1	67.7	81.4	91.0	64.7	80.9	88.8
NB	57.6	74.8	84.0	64.7	80.9	90.4	61.2	78.8	88.3
LR	**59.3**	78.8	88.8	**74.9**	89.2	94.2	**73.6**	88.4	93.9

Table 4: $Acc(1)$ and $Acc(2)$ results for DS-17, using only best prepositions ('best'), using all prepositions ('all'), and using all prepositions but only a randomly selected subset ('all-sub') of instances from 'all' of size equal to that of the best preposition data.

the acceptability by human evaluators of the top n results. If it turns out, as seems likely, that the top two prepositions are acceptable to human evaluators, then the real accuracy would be closer to 90%.

6 Conclusion

In this paper, we have reported new results for automatic generation of spatial descriptions in French. We described a new data set where object pairs in images are annotated with the best preposition, as well as all possible prepositions, that describe the spatial relationship between the objects. We reported results for three new methods for this task, and found that (i) increasing the size of the data set on its own only has a small beneficial effect on results; (ii) removing synonyms from the annotations results in dramatically improved results for all methods tested, and (iii) training on all possible prepositions for an object pair instead of training on the single best preposition only is of substantial benefit for all methods tested. The best result for our task was achieved with the LR classifier, on the preposition set without synonyms, using all possible prepositions for object pairs. That result, 75% Accuracy, is an entire 25 points higher than our previous best result for this task.

Acknowledgments

This work originated during a Short-term Scientific Mission under European COST Action IC1307 (European Network on Integrating Vision & Language).

We are indebted to the INLG'06 reviewers for comprehensive and helpful comments; we have implemented as many as we could in the available time.

References

A. Belz, A. Muscat, M. Aberton, and S. Benjelloun. 2015. Describing spatial relationships between objects in images in English and French. In *Proceedings of VL'15*.

D. Elliott and F. Keller. 2013. Image description using visual dependency representations. In *Proceedings of EMNLP'13*, pages 1292–1302.

M. Everingham, L. Van Gool, C. Williams, J. Winn, and A. Zisserman. 2010. The PASCAL Visual Object Classes (VOC) Challenge. *International Journal of Computer Vision*, 88(2):303–338.

G. Kulkarni, V. Premraj, V. Ordonez, S. Dhar, S. Li, Y. Choi, A. Berg, and T. Berg. 2013. Babytalk: Understanding and generating simple image descriptions. *Pattern Analysis and Machine Intelligence, IEEE Transactions on*, 35(12):2891–2903.

M. Mitchell, X. Han, J. Dodge, A. Mensch, A. Goyal, A. Berg, K. Yamaguchi, T. Berg, K. Stratos, and H. Daumé III. 2012. Midge: Generating image descriptions from computer vision detections. In *Proceedings of EACL'12*.

A. Ramisa, J. Wang, Y. Lu, E. Dellandrea, F. Moreno-Noguer, and R. Gaizauskas. 2015. Combining geometric, textual and visual features for predicting prepositions in image descriptions. In *Proceedings of EMNLP'15*, pages 214–220.

Y. Yang, C. Teo, H. Daumé III, and Y. Aloimonos. 2011. Corpus-guided sentence generation of natural images. In *Proceedings of EMNLP'11*, pages 444–454.

QGASP: a Framework for Question Generation Based on Different Levels of Linguistic Information

Hugo Rodrigues
INESC-ID
IST - Universidade de Lisboa
Lisboa, Portugal
Carnegie Mellon University
Pittsburgh, PA, USA
hpr@l2f.inesc-id.pt

Luísa Coheur
INESC-ID
IST - Universidade de Lisboa
Lisboa, Portugal
luisa.coheur@inesc-id.pt

Eric Nyberg
Language Technologies Institute
Carnegie Mellon University
Pittsburgh, PA, USA
ehn@cs.cmu.edu

Abstract

We introduce QGASP, a system that performs question generation by using lexical, syntactic and semantic information. QGASP uses this information both to learn patterns and to generate questions. In this paper, we briefly describe its architecture.

1 Introduction

As in the TheMentor system (Curto et al., 2012), QGASP (**Q**uestion **G**eneration with **S**emantic **P**atterns) creates patterns based on a set of seeds. However, contrary to TheMentor that relies on lexicon-syntactic patterns, QGASP tries to take advantage of semantic information. The use of semantic information is not new (see, for instance, Mannem et al. (2010)), but to the best of our knowledge QGASP is the first system that relies on the lexical, syntactic and semantic information in both the Pattern Acquisition (PA) and the Question Generation (QG) steps.

2 QGASP overview

Figure 1 illustrates QGASP architecture.

2.1 Pattern Acquisition

Our seeds are triples constituted by a question, its answer (optional), and a snippet that could answer that question. The question and the snippet from each seed are processed by the Stanford syntactic and dependency parsers (de Marneffe et al., 2006), and MatePlus Semantic Role Labeler (SRL) (Roth and Woodsend, 2014). A pattern is a bidirectional

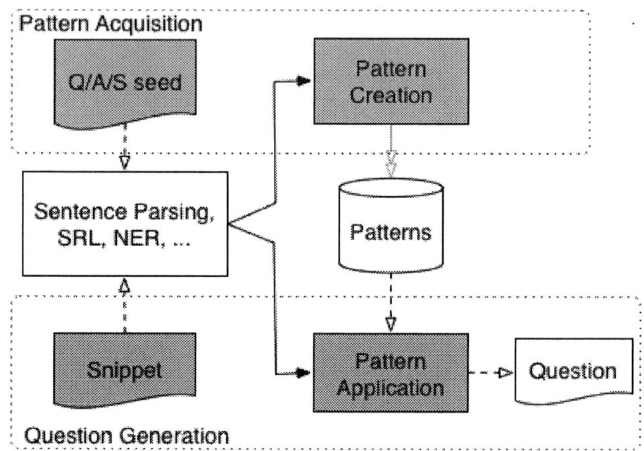

Figure 1: QGASP overview

mapping between subtrees of the question and the correspondent snippet.

2.2 Question Generation

Given a sentence, QGASP starts by parsing it, exactly as before; then it matches the previously learned patterns with the obtained structures.

2.3 The Matching Step

The matching step is the same, both in the PA and QG stage. Considering that a loose matching strategy will result in many patterns and questions, thus introducing noise, whereas a too restrict approach will end up in too specific patterns and low variability of questions, QGASP allows the matches to be done at lexical, syntactic and semantic level. First, it compares both subtrees by checking if their structure is the same, that is, if the subtrees' labels are syntactically equivalent and the number of children is the same (as suggested by Wang and Neumann

(2007)). Then, QGASP checks, for each token pair, if they match. For the lexical match, lemmas are obtained from WordNet. The semantic match is based on the SRL predicted verb and a verb dictionary. This dictionary is the mapping between PropBank (Palmer et al., 2005), VerbNet (Kipper et al., 2000) and FrameNet (Baker et al., 2003), gathered from SemLink[1]. If two verbs belong to the same set in any of the resources, they are considered to match. It is also considered a semantic match if two non-verb tokens belong to the same synset, from WordNet (Miller, 1995), or if two Named Entitiess (NEs) have the same type, according to Stanford Named Entity Recognition (NER).

3   Evaluation

We tested QGASP on the Engarte corpus[2]. We used Engarte's 32 revised triples labeled as true. These triples were then used both for PA and QG, and tested in a leave one out approach (that is, if a pattern is learned from a specific sentence during the PA step, that pattern is not applied to that same sentence during the QG phase).

In the PA step we obtained 23 Semantic patterns. The generated questions with those patterns were manually evaluated by two annotators according to a simplification of Curto et al. (2012) guidelines: plausible, with exception of minor edits such as verb agreement (y), plausible needing context (c), and implausible (n). There are 201 questions generated, from which 92% are considered plausible of any sort – a total of 184, from which only 32 were labeled as plausible needing context. The Cohen's Kappa agreement was calculated on a subset of 115 random questions. The obtained value was 0.67, considered as a substantial agreement.

4   Conclusions and Future Work

This paper briefly describes QGASP, a framework for question generation. Although several points can be improved in QGASP, it is possible to demonstrate how seeds are learned, and how semantic features can improve the QG process.

---

[1]http://verbs.colorado.edu/semlink
[2]http://nlp.uned.es/clef-qa/repository/ave.php

Acknowledgement

This work was partially supported by national funds through FCT (Fundação para a Ciência e a Tecnologia) under project UID/CEC/50021/2013 and through the project LAW-TRAIN with reference H2020-EU.3.7.653587. Hugo Rodrigues is supported by a PhD fellowship from FCT (SFRH/BD/51916/2012).

References

Collin F. Baker, Charles J. Fillmore, and Beau Cronin. 2003. The structure of the FrameNet database. 16(3):281–296.

Sérgio Curto, Ana Cristina Mendes, and Luísa Coheur. 2012. Question generation based on lexico-syntactic patterns learned from the web. *Dialogue & Discourse*, 3(2):147–175, March.

Marie-Catherine de Marneffe, Bill MacCartney, and Christopher D. Manning. 2006. Generating typed dependency parses from phrase structure parses. In *Proceedings of the International Conference on Language, Resources and Evaluation (LREC)*, pages 449–454.

Karin Kipper, Hoa Trang Dang, and Martha Palmer. 2000. Class-based construction of a verb lexicon. In *Proceedings of the Seventeenth National Conference on Artificial Intelligence and Twelfth Conference on Innovative Applications of Artificial Intelligence*, pages 691–696. AAAI Press.

Prashanth Mannem, Rashmi Prasad, and Aravind Joshi. 2010. Question generation from paragraphs at upenn: Qgstec system description. In *Proceedings of QG2010: The Third Workshop on Question Generation*, pages 84–91.

George A. Miller. 1995. Wordnet: a lexical database for english. *Commun. ACM*, 38:39–41, November.

Martha Palmer, Daniel Gildea, and Paul Kingsbury. 2005. The proposition bank: An annotated corpus of semantic roles. *Comput. Linguist.*, 31(1):71–106, March.

Michael Roth and Kristian Woodsend. 2014. Composition of word representations improves semantic role labelling. In *Empirical Methods for Natural Language Processing*, pages 407–413.

Rui Wang and Günter Neumann. 2007. Recognizing textual entailment using sentence similarity based on dependency tree skeletons. In *Proceedings of the ACL-PASCAL Workshop on Textual Entailment and Paraphrasing*, RTE '07, pages 36–41, Stroudsburg, PA, USA. Association for Computational Linguistics.

Automatic Reports from Spreadsheets: Data Analysis for the Rest of Us

Pablo Ariel Duboue
Textualization.com
White Plains, New York, USA

Abstract

The current interest in data acquisition and analysis has resulted in a large number of solutions available to the public. However, anyone other than professionals in the field can find it difficult to make sense of this sea of data. This demo showcases a tool that produces general static reports (as opposed to query or intention based systems of past NLG interest) of combined text and graphics given any spreadsheet sent by email.

1 Introduction

The current interest in data acquisition and analysis has resulted in a large number of solutions available to the public (Microsoft Power BI,[1] Pentaho,[2] etc.). However, anyone other than professionals in the field can find it difficult to make sense of this sea of data. Report generation from tabular data has a long tradition in NLG (Fasciano and Lapalme, 1996; Kerpedjiev et al., 1997; Yu et al., 2007; Hunter et al., 2012). However, these systems assume that a knowledgeable user can guide the system with explicit communicative intentions in the form of queries or emphasis in particular columns or relations (Fasciano, 1996; Labbé et al., 2015). How to fulfill those expectations when confronted with a novice user can span whole research projects in smart User Interfaces. Instead, in this demo we present a tool that produces general static reports of combined text and graphics given any spreadsheet. Our tool incorporates concepts of *surprise,* popularized from the

KDD community (Guillet and Hamilton, 2007) and employed lateraly in other NLG systems (Molina et al., 2011).

Our system is based on the ANA architecture (Kukich, 1983): fact generation, message generation, content planning and tactical generation. It takes any spreadsheet in Excel, CSV and OpenDocument format sent by email[3] and produces a OpenDocument text document with a textual description of the data and embedded graphs, a form of multimedia generation (André, 2000).

It addresses two traditional conditions in report generation (Kittredge and Polguere, 2000): a primary interest in objective or fixed type data and a conceptual summarization over said data. Two other conditions are approximated (a temporal dimension in the data, which is attempted using a number of heuristics) or left for potential follow up consulting engagements (recurrent situation of communication).

Similar to (Molina et al., 2011), we seek to summarize relevant facts with explanatory descriptions and graphical information. However, we have a different main goal which is to provide an overview of any tabular data without extra domain knowledge provided by the user. We also share the secondary goal of producing reports that are informative and persuasive, useful for non-expert users and have a uniform style.

2 Structure of the Demo

Our demo shows a number of spreadsheets (Figure 1 (a), adapted from Foreman (2013)) from which

---

[1] http://powerbi.microsoft.com/
[2] http://pentaho.com

[3] To the address get@thedatareport.com

"""

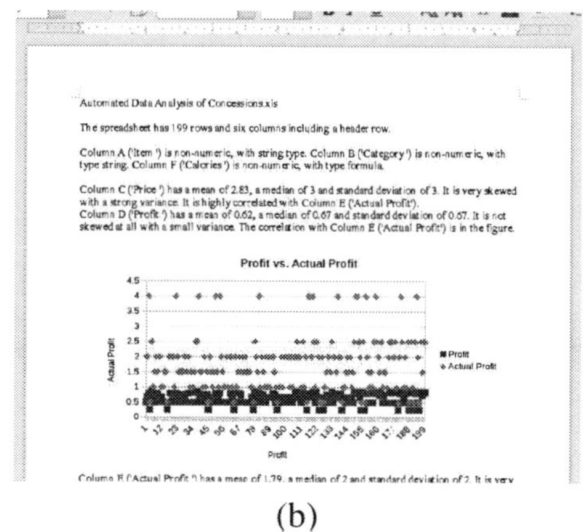

(a)

(b)

Figure 1: (a) Input data, adapted from Foreman (2013); (b) Example output.

the audience can change the data with a provided OpenCalc instance running in the machine. Then the spreadsheet will be submitted to the system and the resulting multi-page report will be shown and discussed (Figure 1 (b)).

Acknowledgements

The author would like to thank the reviewers and Annie Ying for comments and references.

References

Elisabeth André. 2000. The generation of multimedia presentations. *Handbook of natural language processing*, pages 305–327.

Massimo Fasciano and Guy Lapalme. 1996. Postgraphe: a system for the generation of statistical graphics and text. In *Proceedings of the Eighth International Workshop on Natural Language Generation*, pages 51–60.

Massimo Fasciano. 1996. *Génération intégrée de textes et de graphiques statistiques*. Université de Montréal.

John W Foreman. 2013. *Data smart: using data science to transform information into insight*. John Wiley & Sons.

Fabrice Guillet and Howard J Hamilton. 2007. *Quality measures in data mining*, volume 43. Springer.

James Hunter, Yvonne Freer, Albert Gatt, Ehud Reiter, Somayajulu Sripada, and Cindy Sykes. 2012. Automatic generation of natural language nursing shift summaries in neonatal intensive care: Bt-nurse. *Artificial intelligence in medicine*, 56(3):157–172.

Stephan Kerpedjiev, Giuseppe Carenini, Steven F Roth, and Johanna D Moore. 1997. Autobrief: a multimedia presentation system for assisting data analysis. *Computer Standards & Interfaces*, 18(6):583–593.

Robert I Kittredge and Alain Polguere. 2000. The generation of reports from databases. *Handbook of natural language processing*, pages 261–304.

Karen Kukich. 1983. Design of a knowledge-based report generator. In *Proc. of ACL*.

Cyril Labbé, Claudia Roncancio, and Damien Bras. 2015. A personal storytelling about your favorite data. In *Proc. of ENLG 2015*, September.

Martin Molina, Amanda Stent, and Enrique Parodi. 2011. Generating automated news to explain the meaning of sensor data. In *International Symposium on Intelligent Data Analysis*, pages 282–293. Springer.

Jin Yu, Ehud Reiter, Jim Hunter, and Chris Mellish. 2007. Choosing the content of textual summaries of large time-series data sets. *Natural Language Engineering*, 13(01):25–49.

Towards Generating Colour Terms for Referents in Photographs: Prefer the Expected or the Unexpected?

Sina Zarrieß and **David Schlangen**
Dialogue Systems Group // CITEC // Faculty of Linguistics and Literary Studies
Bielefeld University, Germany
first.last@uni-bielefeld.de

Abstract

Colour terms have been a prime phenomenon for studying language grounding, though previous work focussed mostly on descriptions of simple objects or colour swatches. This paper investigates whether colour terms can be learned from more realistic and potentially noisy visual inputs, using a corpus of referring expressions to objects represented as regions in real-world images. We obtain promising results from combining a classifier that grounds colour terms in visual input with a recalibration model that adjusts probability distributions over colour terms according to contextual and object-specific preferences.

1 Introduction

Pioneering work on natural language generation from perceptual inputs has developed approaches that learn to describe visual scenes from multimodal corpus data and model the connection between words and non-symbolic perceptual features (Roy, 2002; Roy and Reiter, 2005). In this paradigm, colour terms have received special attention. Intuitively, a model of perceptually grounded meaning should associate words for colour with particular points or regions in a colour space, e.g. (Mojsilovic, 2005). On the other hand, their visual association seems to vary with the linguistic context such as 'red' in the context of 'hair', 'car' or 'wine' (Roy and Reiter, 2005).

Recently, large-scale data sets of real-world images and image descriptions, e.g. (Young et al., 2014), or referring expressions (Kazemzadeh et al.,

2014; Gkatzia et al., 2015) have become available and can now serve as a realistic test bed for models of language grounding. In this paper, we use the ReferIt corpus (Kazemzadeh et al., 2014) to assess the performance of classifiers that predict colour terms from low-level visual representations of their corresponding image regions.

A number of studies on colour naming have looked at experimental settings where speakers referred to simple objects or colour swatches instantiating a single value in a colour space. Even in these controlled settings, speakers use colour terms in flexible, context-dependent ways (Baumgaertner et al., 2012; Meo et al., 2014). Therefore, probabilistic models and classifiers, allowing for variable thresholds and boundaries between regions in a colour space, have been proposed to capture their grounded meaning (Roy, 2002; Steels and Belpaeme, 2005; Meo et al., 2014; Larsson, 2015).

Can we learn to predict colour terms for more complex and potentially noisy visual inputs? In contrast to simple colour swatches, real-world objects often have internal structure, their visual colour values are hardly ever uniform and the colour terms can refer to a specific segment of the referent (see image a) and b) in Figure 1). Moreover, the low-level visual representation of objects in real-world images can vary tremendously with illumination conditions, whereas human colour perception seems to be robust to illumination, which is known as the "colour constancy" problem (Brainard and Freeman, 1997). Research on colour perception suggests that speakers use "top-down" world knowledge about the prototypical colours of an object to *recalibrate* their per-

(a)"small red car on right"   (b"yellow building"

(c)"green"   (d)"first set of green on right"

(e)"red plants in the middle"   (f)"red rock bluff center"

Figure 1: Example images and REs from the ReferIt corpus

ception of an object to its expected colours (Mitterer and De Ruiter, 2008; Kubat et al., 2009). For instance, the use 'green' for the two, rather different hues in Figure 1 (c-d) might be attributed to the fact that both objects are plants and expected to be green.

However, recalibration to expected colours is not the only possible effect of context. Despite or because of special illumination conditions, the mountain in Figure 1 (f) and the plants in Figure 1 (e) are described as 'red', a rather atypical, unexpected colour that is, therefore, contextually salient and informative. This relates to research on referential over-specification showing that speakers are more likely to (redundantly) name a colour if it is atypical (Westerbeek et al., 2014; Tarenskeen et al., 2015).

In our corpus study, we find that these various contextual effects pose a considerable challenge for accurate colour term classification. We explore two ways to make perceptually grounded classifiers sensitive to context: grounded classifiers that are restricted to particular object types and "recalibration" classifiers that learn to adjust predictions by a general visual classifier to the preferences of an object and its context. Whereas object-

specific colour classifiers perform poorly, we find that the latter recalibration approach yields promising results. This seems to be in line with a model by Gärdenfors (2004) that assumes context-independent colour prototypes which can be projected into the space of known colours for an object.

2 Grounding colour Terms: Visual Classifiers

In this Section, we present "visual classifiers" for colour terms that predict the colour term of an object given its low-level visual properties. We assess to what extent the visual classifiers can cope with the real-world challenges discussed above.

2.1 Corpus and Data Extraction

We train and evaluate on the ReferIt data set collected by Kazemzadeh et al. (2014). The basis of the corpus is a collection of "20,000 still natural images taken from locations around the world" (Grubinger et al., 2006), which was manually augmented by Escalante et al. (2010) with segmentation masks identifying objects in the images (see Figure 4). This dataset also provides manual annotations of region labels, with the labels being organised in an ontology (Escalante et al., 2010). Kazemzadeh et al. (2014) collected a large number of expressions referring to objects (for which segmentations exist) from these images (130k REs for 96k objects), using a game-based crowd-sourcing approach.

We extract all pairs of REs containing a colour word and their image region from the corpus. We consider REs with at least one of the 11 basic colour words *'blue'*, *'red'*, *'green'*, *'yellow'*, *'white'*, *'black'*, *'grey'*, *'pink'*, *'purple'*, *'orange'*, *'brown'*. We remove relational REs, containing one of the following prepositions: *'below'*, *'above'*, *'not'*, *'behind'*, *'under'*, *'underneath'*, *'right of'*, *'left of'*, *'ontop of'*, *'next to'*,*'middle of'* in order to filter instances where the colour term describes a landmark object. We split the remaining pairs into 11207 instances for training and 1328 for testing. Table 1 shows the frequencies of the colour adjectives in the training set.

2.2 Visual Input

Research in image processing has tried to define colour spaces and colour descriptors which are to

colour term	%	colour term	%
white	26.7	black	8.7
blue	20.5	brown	6.2
green	16.7	pink,orange	2.8
red	14.6	grey,purple	1.4
yellow	9.9		

Table 1: Distribution of colour words in training data

some extent invariant to illumination and closer to human perception, cf. (Manjunath et al., 2001; Van De Sande et al., 2010). As we are more interested in the linguistic aspects of the problem, we have focussed on the standard, available feature representations. We extracted RGB and HSV colour histograms for region segments with `opencv` (Bradski, 2000). As the region segments are sized differently, we normalised the histograms to represent relative instead of absolute frequencies.

Ideally, we would like to use a feature representation that could be generalised to other words contained in referring expressions. Therefore, we have extracted features that have been automatically learned with a high-performance convolutional neural network (Szegedy et al., 2015). We computed the smallest rectangular bounding box for our image regions, applied the ConvNet and extracted the final fully-connected layer before the classification layer. As bounding boxes are less precise than segmentation masks, it is expected that this representation will perform worse – but it gives us an interesting estimate as to how much the performance of our model degrades on visual input that is less tailored to colour terms. To summarise, we have extracted the following representations of our visual inputs:

- mean RGB values for region segment (3 features)
- RGB histograms with 512 bins (8 bins per channel) for region segment (512 features)
- HSV histograms with 512 bins (8 bins per channel) for region segment (512 features)
- ConvNet features for bounding box (1027 features)

2.3 Experimental Set-up

The task We define our classification problem as follows: input is a feature vector x, a visual representation of a referent in an image, and output is a label y, a colour term for the referent. For the sake of simplicity, we only consider training and testing instances that contain colour terms and do not

model the decision whether a colour term should be generated at all. In standard NLG terminology, we are only interested in realisation, and not in content selection. A lot of research on REG has actually focussed on content selection, assuming perfect knowledge about appropriate colour terms for referents in a scene, cf. (Pechmann, 1989; Viethen and Dale, 2011; Viethen et al., 2012; Krahmer and Van Deemter, 2012; Koolen et al., 2013).

The classifiers We used a multilayer perceptron that learns a function from colour histograms (or ConvNet features) to colour terms, i.e. defining an input layer corresponding to the dimensions of the colour histogram and an output layer of 11 nodes. We did not extensively tune the hyper parameters for our different visual inputs, but tested some parameter settings of the perceptron trained on RGB histograms, singling out a development set of 500 instances from the training set described above. We report results for training on the entire training set with two hidden layers (240 nodes and 24 nodes), a drop out set to 0.2 and 25 epochs. When training on the mean RGB values as input, we use simple logistic regression as we only have 3 features.

We also tested a Knn (nearest neighbour) classifier which simply stores all instances of x in the training data, and during testing, retrieves the k instances that are most similar to the testing example based on some distance metric. We used the default implementation of Knn in `scikit-learn` (Pedregosa et al., 2011) which is based on Minkowski distance. Testing on the development set, we obtained best results with setting k to 10 and uniform weights (all neighbours of a testing instance treated equally).

Evaluation We report accuracy scores. When there are multiple colour terms for the same region, we use the top n predictions of the visual classifier.

2.4 Results

Table 2 reports the performance of the visual classifiers for the different visual inputs and the two classification methods. We see that Knn performs consistently worse than Perceptron. The ConvNet features perform dramatically worse than the colour histograms and do not even come close to a simple logistic regression trained on mean RGB values of

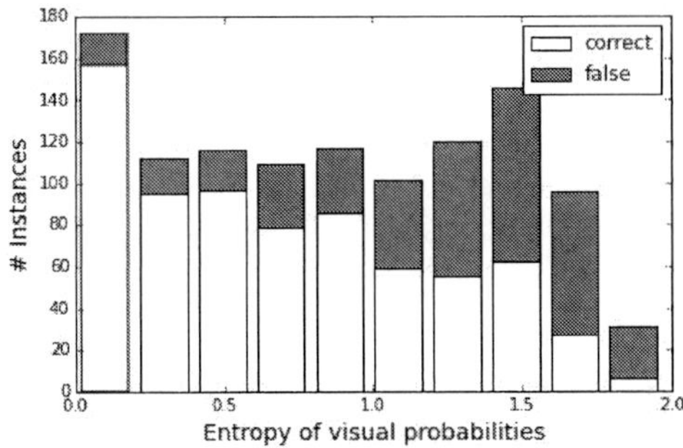

Figure 2: Proportion of correct vs. false predictions depending on the visual probability of the top-ranked colour term

the image regions. Surprisingly, we obtain better results with RGB histograms than with HSV.

	Perceptron	Knn
Mean RGB	57.29	55.65
RGB histogram (3d)	63.7	59.32
HSV histogram (3d)	62.84	55.73
ConvNet features	47.77	38.79

Table 2: Accuracies for general visual colour classifiers

Figure 2(a) shows the accuracy of the visual classifier depending on the (binned) entropy of the predicted probability distribution over colour terms. The accuracy (shown as the proportion of white and grey parts of a bar) is systematically higher in cases when the entropy is low, i.e. when the top colour has a clearly higher probability than the remaining colour candidates. This pattern suggests that the predicted probability distributions reflect the confidence of the visual classifier somewhat reliably. We consider this as evidence that the visual classifier learns to identify the prototypical instances of colour terms, whereas other, more ambiguous hues are associated with distributions of higher entropy.

2.5 Lexical vs. visual colour probabilities

Additionally, we assess the visual classifiers for different types of objects, based on the label annotations included in the corpus. We average the predicted visual probabilities for colour over all instances of an object label and compute the lexical probabilities of a colour term conditioned on the object label. These lexical probabilities tell us how often a colour co-occurs with a particular object label. Figure 3 shows the lexical and predicted visual probabilities (striped bars) for the labels 'flower',

'horse', 'hill', and 'car', illustrating some object-specific variation. For instance, flowers occur with many different colours, except "black", "brown" and "green". Horses, on the other hand, only occur with "white", "brown" and "black".

Depending on the object, the visual probabilities come more or less close to the lexical probabilities. The classifier predicts that flowers are more likely to be "green" than "blue", which reflects that flowers are likely to have certain green parts. The lexical probabilities, however, show a clear preference for "blue" over "green" since speaker mostly describe the salient, non-green parts of flowers. A more drastic case is "horse" where "brown" is frequent, but the classifier seems to systematically mis-represent this colour, predicting much more black horses than expected. For "hill", speakers almost exclusively use the colour "green" whereas the visual classifier predicts a flatter distribution among "blue", "green" and "white". As hills are often located in the background of images, the high probability for 'blue' certainly reflects a systematic, contextual illumination problem (see Figure 1(d) for a 'blueish' mountain).

Generally, the lexical colour probabilities in Figure 3 clearly show object-specific tendencies. In the following, we investigate how we can leverage that knowledge to adjust colour probabilities predicted on visual input to lexical preferences.

3 Object-specific Visual Classifiers

A simple way to make visual classifiers aware of object-specific colour preferences is to train separate classifiers for particular object types. This may not be a theoretically pleasing model for the meaning of colour terms, but in the following, we test whether this model improves the empirical performance for of colour term classification.

3.1 Object Types and Classes

Obviously, an object-specific model of colour terms crucially depends on the types of objects that we assume. How fine-grained does our object classification need to be? Intuitively, there are clear expectations about prototypical colours of certain objects (e.g. bananas vs. carrots), whereas other objects are more neutral (e.g. buildings, cars).

Fortunately, the ReferIt corpus comes with de-

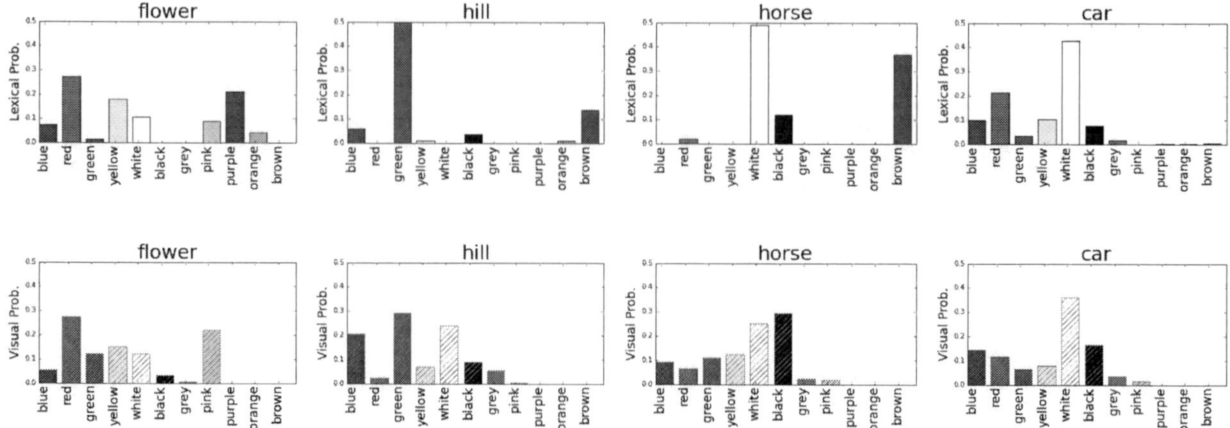

Figure 3: Lexical probabilities for colour terms conditioned on different types of objects (top row) and average visual probabilities predicted by the classifier trained on RGB histograms (bottom row)

tailed label annotations of the image regions (e.g. several types humans like 'child-boy', 'child-girl', 'face-of-person'). These object types are organised in an ontology, such that we can map relatively specific object type labels (e.g. 'car') to their general class (e.g. 'vehicle').[1] Table 3 shows the most frequent type labels and their classes in our training data. One very frequent type actually encodes colour information ('sky-blue' as opposed to 'sky-white' and 'sky-night' – leaves of the class 'sky').

object labels (classes)	# instances	top colour
man (humans)	1244	blue (22%)
woman (humans)	869	red (21%)
sky-blue (sky)	503	blue (98%)
group-of-persons (humans)	425	red (22%)
wall (construction)	421	white (42%)
car (vehicle)	418	white (42%)

Table 3: Most frequent object labels, their classes and most frequently mentioned colour (in the training instances of the visual classifier for colour)

3.2 Experimental Set-up

The Classifiers We use the same training data as in our previous experiment (Section 2.3). But now, we separate the training instances according to their labels (Section 3.1) and train several visual colour classifiers, i.e. one multi-class multi-layer perceptron per object label. In order to assess the impact of the underlying object classification, we used la-

bels corresponding to (i) to the annotated, specific object types, (ii) the more general object classes. In each case, we only trained visual classifiers for labels with more than 50 instances in the training data. This leaves us with 52 visual classifiers for object types, and 33 visual classifiers for object classes.

Evaluation During testing, we assume that the object labels are known and we retrieve the corresponding visual classifiers. For objects with unknown labels (not contained in the training set) or an infrequent label (with less than 50 instances in the training set) we use the general visual classifier from Section 2.3 (the perceptron trained on RGB histograms). In Table 4, we report the colour prediction accuracy on the overall test set and on the subset of testing instances where the object-specific classifiers predicted a different colour term than the general visual classifier. This way, we assess how often the object-specific classifiers actually 'recalibrate' the decision of the general classifier and whether this calibration leads to an improvement.

3.3 Results

Table 4 shows that the classifiers trained for object types ($visual_{object}$) revise the decisions of the general classifier ($visual_{general}$) relatively often (for 619 out of 1328 testing instances), but rarely make a prediction that is different from the general classifier *and* correct (19% of the cases). Thus, overall, they severely decrease the performance of the colour term prediction. Similarly, the visual classifiers for object classes lead to a considerable decrease in performance. Interestingly, the predictions

---

[1] We map all object types below the node 'humans to 'humans'. Other categories on the same level are too general, e.g. 'man-made objects', 'landscape-nature' – here, we use the immediate mother node of the object label in the ontology.

Classifiers	# recalibrated colour terms	Accuracy on recalibrated subset		Overall Accuracy	
		$\text{visual}_{general}$	visual_{object}	$\text{visual}_{general}$	$\text{visual}_{general/object}$
Object types	619	57.9	19.	63.7	45.19
Object classes	357	72.54	8	63.7	45.58

Table 4: colour term prediction for general ($\text{visual}_{general}$) and object-specific (visual_{object}) visual classifiers, accuracies reported on the recalibrated subset where predictions differ between the general and the object-specific classifiers, and for the whole testset

of this model seem to often differ from the general visual classifier when the latter is relatively confident: the general visual accuracy on this subset is much higher (72%) than on the overall test set. This suggests that the object-specific visual classifiers do not learn prototypical meanings of colour terms and are much more sensitive to noise whereas the general colour classifier has an advantage rather than a disadvantage from seeing a lot of different instances of a particular colour.

4 Recalibrating Colour Terms

A model that generally adjusts its predictions to the expected colour terms for specific objects is clearly not successful. In this Section, we present an alternative approach that separates the grounding of colour terms on low-level visual from object-specific and contextual effects. Thus, instead of training object-specific colours directly on low-level visual inputs, we now learn to predict systematic adjustments or recalibration of the probability distributions that a robust general visual classifier produces.

4.1 Data preparation

In order to learn recalibrations of visual probability distributions over colour terms, we need training instances annotated with "realistic" output of the visual classifier (where the colour term with the highest probability does not necessarily correspond to the gold label). Therefore, we split our training data into 10 folds and apply 10-fold cross-validation (or so-called "jackknifing") on the training data, i.e. we have 10 folds that we annotate with a respective visual classifier trained on the remaining 9 folds.

4.2 Context-based Recalibration

So far, we have looked at the prediction of colour terms as a purely local problem. However, we expect other objects surrounding the target referent to have an effect on the selected colour terms, especially in cases where the visual classifier is less confident.

For each target region, we extract all the remaining distractor regions from the same image and apply the visual classifier. We compute a context vector by averaging over these regions and use the mean probability of each colour term. Based on the contextual colour probabilities, we can learn a function that adjusts the local probabilities for colour terms given additional evidence from the context.

The Classifiers We train logistic regression models for each colour term, where e.g. objects described as 'blue' are positive instances and objects described with a different colour are negative instances for the blue classifier. Instead of low-level visual input (colour histograms) we use the distributions over colour terms predicted by the $\text{visual}_{general}$ classifier as features and train the context-based recalibration on 22 features (11 probabilities for the region and 11 probabilities for the context).

4.3 Object-specific Recalibration

We can also model recalibration separately for each type of object. For instance, a recalibration classifier for 'horse' could learn that many horses classified as 'black' are actually referred to as 'brown' (see Section 2.5). Thus, we want to test whether object-specific recalibration classifiers learn to recover from systematic errors made by the general visual classifier for certain types of objects.

Combining object-specific and context-based recalibration could help to distinguish colours that are unusual and salient from unexpected colours that are due to e.g. specific illumination conditions. For instance, this classifier could learn that a 'blueish' hill is very unlikely to be blue, if there are a lot of other blue objects in the image.

The Classifiers For each object label, we train 11 regressions that adjust the probabilities of a colour terms predicted by the general visual classifier and whose training samples are restricted to instances of that object. We compare a simple object-specific

Recalibration	# recalibrated colour terms	Accuracy on recalibrated subset		Overall Acurracy	
		visual$_{general}$	recalibrated	visual$_{general}$	recalibrated
Context	135	43.7	40	63.7	63.3
Object types	193	38.3	42	63.7	64.5
Object classes	185	36.75	46.48	63.7	65.1
Object classes + context	201	34.32	46.26	63.7	65.57

Table 5: Colour term prediction with context-based, object-specific and combined recalibration of the visual classifier, accuracies are reported on the recalibrated subset where predictions differ between the general visual classifiers and recalibrated colour terms, and for the whole testset

SUCCESSFUL OBJECT-SPECIFIC RECALIBRATIONS   INCORRECT OBJECT-SPECIFIC RECALIBRATIONS

(a) brown, visual: black   recalibrated: brown   (b) black, visual: black   recalibrated: green

(c) green, visual: blue   recalibrated: green   (d) blue, visual: blue   recalibrated: white

SUCCESSFUL CONTEXT-BASED RECALIBRATION   INCORRECT CONTEXT-BASED RECALIBRATION

(e) red, visual: green   recalibrated: red   (f) red, visual: pink   recalibrated: white

SUCCESSFUL COMBINED RECALIBRATION   INCORRECT COMBINED RECALIBRATION

(g): black, visual: red   recalibrated: black   (h) yellow, visual: yellow   recalibrated: white

Figure 4: Examples for successfully and mistakenly recalibrated colour term predictions, target regions on the left, full image on the right

recalibration that only takes the distribution over colour terms as input (11 features), and a combined recalibration based on a vector of 22 features (11 probabilities for the region and 11 probabilities for the context). Moreover, we train recalibration classifiers on object types (52×11 regressions) and object classes (33×11 regressions).

4.4 Results and Discussion

Evaluation We only recalibrate the visual probabilities for an object, if we have observed more than 50 training instances (same as in Section 3). For the remaining instances, we simply use the colour terms predicted by the general visual classifier. Thus, we will again be particularly interested in the subset of testing instances where the recalibration classifiers change the predictions of the visual classifier, which is the set of "recalibrated colour terms".

Table 5 shows the accuracies for the entire test set and the recalibrated subset. Except for the context-based recalibration which slightly degrades the accuracy compared to using only the visual probabilities (63.7%), the recalibration now improves the general visual classifier. The accuracies on the recalibrated subset reveal why recalibration is more successful than the object-specific visual classifiers discussed in Section 3: it is much more conservative in changing the predictions of the visual classifier. Moreover, the accuracy of the general visual classifier on the recalibrated test sets is substantially lower than on the overall test set. This shows that the recalibration classifiers learn to adjust those cases where the visual classifier is not very confident.

The accuracy of the visual classifier is not zero on the recalibrated subsets, meaning that some originally correct predictions are mistakenly recalibrated. Examples for correct and incorrect recalibration are shown in Figure 4, illustrating that the model has to strike a balance between expected and unexpected colour terms in context. There are several examples where the object-specific recalibration gives a higher probability to the more prototypical colour of the object (e.g. 'green' for trees and 'white' for houses in (a) and (c)), but this can lead to less salient, non-distinguishing or misleading colour terms being selected (Figure 4 (b,d)). The general context-based recalibration, on the other hand, often gives more weight to colours that are salient in the im-

age (Figure 4(e)) , but sometimes calibrates the distribution in the wrong direction (Figure 4(f)). The combination of context-based and object-specific recalibration adjusts colour probabilities most reliably, and also seems to capture some cases of colour segments (Figure 4(g)). But there are still cases where the preference for expected or visually salient, unexpected colour is hard to predict, e.g. the "yellow cloud" in Figure 4(h).

These examples also suggest that an evaluation of the colour term prediction in terms of their interactive effectiveness might reveal different effects. The recalibration-based model lends itself for dynamic, interactive systems that adjust or correct their usage of colour terms based on interactive feedback.

Related Work Our notion of "recalibration" is related to a geometrical approach by (Gärdenfors, 2004) that separates colour naming conventions and prototypical, context-independent colour term meaning. Similarly, in distributional semantics, adjectives have been modeled as matrixes that map distributional vectors for nouns to composed vectors for adjective-noun pairs (Baroni and Zamparelli, 2010). Our recalibration classifiers can also be seen as first step towards modeling a compositional effect, but in our model, the noun (object label) adjusts the predictions of the adjective (colour). Finally, this works relates to research on vagueness of colour terms. But, instead of adjusting single thresholds between colour categories (Meo et al., 2014), the recalibration adjusts distributions over colour terms.

5 Conclusions

When speakers refer to an object in a scene, they often use colour terms to distinguish the target referent from its distractors. Accurate colour term prediction is thus an important step for a system that automatically generates referring expressions from visual representations of objects, cf. (Kazemzadeh et al., 2014; Gkatzia et al., 2015). This study has presented perceptually grounded classifiers for colour terms trained on instances of their corresponding referents in real-world images. We showed that this approach needs to balance various contextual effects (due to illumination, salience, world knowledge) and obtained promising results from a recalibration model that adjust predictions of a general visual classifier.

Acknowledgments

We acknowledge support by the Cluster of Excellence "Cognitive Interaction Technology" (CITEC; EXC 277) at Bielefeld University, which is funded by the German Research Foundation (DFG).

References

Marco Baroni and Roberto Zamparelli. 2010. Nouns are vectors, adjectives are matrices: Representing adjective-noun constructions in semantic space. In *Proceedings of the 2010 Conference on Empirical Methods in Natural Language Processing*, pages 1183–1193. Association for Computational Linguistics.

Bert Baumgaertner, Raquel Fernández, and Matthew Stone. 2012. Towards a flexible semantics: colour terms in collaborative reference tasks. In *Proceedings of the First Joint Conference on Lexical and Computational Semantics*, pages 80–84. Association for Computational Linguistics.

G. Bradski. 2000. OpenCV. *Dr. Dobb's Journal of Software Tools*.

David H Brainard and William T Freeman. 1997. Bayesian color constancy. *JOSA A*, 14(7):1393–1411.

Hugo Jair Escalante, Carlos a. Hernández, Jesus a. Gonzalez, a. López-López, Manuel Montes, Eduardo F. Morales, L. Enrique Sucar, Luis Villaseñor, and Michael Grubinger. 2010. The segmented and annotated IAPR TC-12 benchmark. *Computer Vision and Image Understanding*, 114(4):419–428.

Peter Gärdenfors. 2004. *Conceptual spaces: The geometry of thought*. MIT press.

Dimitra Gkatzia, Verena Rieser, Phil Bartie, and William Mackaness. 2015. From the virtual to the real world: Referring to objects in real-world spatial scenes. In *Proceedings of EMNLP 2015*. Association for Computational Linguistics.

Michael Grubinger, Paul Clough, Henning Müller, and Thomas Deselaers. 2006. The IAPR TC-12 benchmark: a new evaluation resource for visual information systems. In *Proceedings of the International Conference on Language Resources and Evaluation (LREC 2006)*, pages 13–23, Genoa, Italy.

Sahar Kazemzadeh, Vicente Ordonez, Mark Matten, and Tamara L Berg. 2014. ReferItGame: Referring to Objects in Photographs of Natural Scenes. In *Proceedings of the Conference on Empirical Methods in Natural Language Processing (EMNLP 2014)*, pages 787–798, Doha, Qatar.

Ruud Koolen, Emiel Krahmer, and Marc Swerts. 2013. The impact of bottom-up and top-down saliency cues on reference production. In *Proceedings of the 35th annual meeting of the Cognitive Science Society (CogSci)*, pages 817–822.

Emiel Krahmer and Kees Van Deemter. 2012. Computational generation of referring expressions: A survey. *Computational Linguistics*, 38(1):173–218.

Rony Kubat, Daniel Mirman, and Deb Roy. 2009. Semantic context effects on color categorization. In *Proceedings of the 31st Annual Cognitive Science Society Meeting*.

Staffan Larsson. 2015. Formal semantics for perceptual classification. *Journal of logic and computation*, 25(2):335–369.

Bangalore S Manjunath, Jens-Rainer Ohm, Vinod V Vasudevan, and Akio Yamada. 2001. Color and texture descriptors. *IEEE Transactions on Circuits and Systems for Video Technology*, 11(6):703–715.

Timothy Meo, Brian McMahan, and Matthew Stone. 2014. Generating and resolving vague color references. In *Proceedings of the 18th Workshop Semantics and Pragmatics of Dialogue (SemDial)*.

Holger Mitterer and Jan Peter De Ruiter. 2008. Recalibrating color categories using world knowledge. *Psychological Science*, 19(7):629–634.

A. Mojsilovic. 2005. A computational model for color naming and describing color composition of images. *IEEE Transactions on Image Processing*, 14(5):690–699, May.

Thomas Pechmann. 1989. Incremental speech production and referential overspecification. *Linguistics*, 27(1):89–110.

F. Pedregosa, G. Varoquaux, A. Gramfort, V. Michel, B. Thirion, O. Grisel, M. Blondel, P. Prettenhofer, R. Weiss, V. Dubourg, J. Vanderplas, A. Passos, D. Cournapeau, M. Brucher, M. Perrot, and E. Duchesnay. 2011. Scikit-learn: Machine learning in Python. *Journal of Machine Learning Research*, 12:2825–2830.

Deb Roy and Ehud Reiter. 2005. Connecting language to the world. *Artificial Intelligence*, 167(12):1 – 12. Connecting Language to the World.

Deb K Roy. 2002. Learning visually grounded words and syntax for a scene description task. *Computer Speech & Language*, 16(3):353–385.

Luc Steels and Tony Belpaeme. 2005. Coordinating perceptually grounded categories through language: a case study for colour. *Behavioral and Brain Sciences*, 28:469–489, 8.

Christian Szegedy, Wei Liu, Yangqing Jia, Pierre Sermanet, Scott Reed, Dragomir Anguelov, Dumitru Erhan, Vincent Vanhoucke, and Andrew Rabinovich. 2015. Going deeper with convolutions. In *CVPR 2015*, Boston, MA, USA, June.

Sammie Tarenskeen, Mirjam Broersma, and Bart Geurts. 2015. Hand me the yellow stapler or Hand me the yellow dress: Colour overspecification depends on object category. page 140.

Koen EA Van De Sande, Theo Gevers, and Cees GM Snoek. 2010. Evaluating color descriptors for object and scene recognition. *IEEE Transactions on Pattern Analysis and Machine Intelligence*, 32(9):1582–1596.

Jette Viethen and Robert Dale. 2011. Gre3d7: A corpus of distinguishing descriptions for objects in visual scenes. In *Proceedings of the UCNLG+ Eval: Language generation and evaluation workshop*, pages 12–22. Association for Computational Linguistics.

Jette Viethen, Martijn Goudbeek, and Emiel Krahmer. 2012. The impact of colour difference and colour codability on reference production. In *Proceedings of the 34th annual meeting of the Cognitive Science Society (CogSci 2012)*.

Hans Westerbeek, Ruud Koolen, and Alfons Maes. 2014. On the role of object knowledge in reference production: Effects of color typicality on content determination. In *CogSci 2014: Cognitive Science Meets Artificial Intelligence: Human and Artificial Agents in Interactive Contexts*, pages 1772–1777.

Peter Young, Alice Lai, Micah Hodosh, and Julia Hockenmaier. 2014. From Image Descriptions to Visual Denotations: New Similarity Metrics for Semantic Inference over Event Descriptions. *Transactions of the Association for Computational Linguistics (TACL)*, 2(April):67–78.

Absolute and Relative Properties in Geographic Referring Expressions

Rodrigo de Oliveira, Somayajulu Sripada and **Ehud Reiter**
University of Aberdeen
{rodrigodeoliveira, yaji.sripada, e.reiter}@abdn.ac.uk

Abstract

This paper discusses the importance of computing relative properties and not just retrieving absolute properties when generating geographic referring expressions such as "northern France". We describe an algorithm that computes spatial properties at run-time by means of spatial operations such as intersecting and analyzing parts of wholes. The evaluation of the algorithm suggests that part-whole relations are key in geographic expressions.

1   Introduction

This paper discusses the role of spatial operations in 'creating' properties to be used for generating geographic expressions. For example, we generate the expression "northern France" by retrieving the property FRANCE from our knowledge base, and subsequently computing (or creating) the property NORTH at run-time. The algorithm we describe in this article is meant to be used by Natural Language Generation (NLG) systems (Reiter and Dale, 2000), especially those in the Data-to-Text family (Reiter, 2007), which automatically write reports in natural language such as English, given structured data such as those we typically store in databases. Our domain is weather forecast and our input data conforms with that typically found in Geographic Information Systems (Worboys and Duckham, 2004).

The many algorithms for doing Referring Expression Generation (REG) as outlined in Krahmer and Van Deemter (2012) assume that Knowledge Bases (KBs) exhaustively specify all properties that are inherent (i.e. absolute) to entities. The REG style we

propose here is inspired in alternative work (Kelleher and Kruijff, 2006; Viethen and Dale, 2008) that computes relational properties, rather than storing them in KBs. We base our approach on evidence observed in human-authored texts, as it shall be explained in Section 4. The underlying philosophy is that some properties are absolute, i.e. inherent to entities, while some properties are relative to other properties. An example of the relative type of properties in the spatial domain is the part-whole relation, henceforth *mereology* (Cohn and Renz, 2008, 577). For example, a given city will absolutely be a part of a country (or continent) or not, so the properties COUNTRY and CONTINENT are absolute. On the other hand, whether a city lies in the North depends on the area that is chosen as the whole, so the property DIRECTION is relative to another property. Paris is in the North of France, but lies in the centre of Europe. NORTH and CENTRAL are in a mereological relation to FRANCE and EUROPE, respectively.

Our approach is very much in line with that proposed by Van Deemter (2002), since we process sets (not individuals) by computing intersection, a typical set-theoretic operation. The key difference from a fully set-theoretic approach is that we also compute mereological relations. As described in Sections 2 and 3, our algorithm takes point-based data and outputs sets of semantic labels such as (COASTAL ⊓ (NORTH, FRANCE)). Such sets can be further converted into a natural language expression such as "northern coast of France" or "coast in northern France" in a full NLG system. The performance of our approach is evaluated and discussed in Section 5.

2 Concepts Underlying the Algorithm

Before explaining the procedure the algorithm follows, we first need to look at some background concepts that were implemented in the algorithm.

Descriptors are qualitative labels such as NORTH, ABERDEEN, HIGH or COASTAL. When constructing objects representing descriptions, we transform primitive values from the dataset (e.g. elevation=800m) into descriptor labels (e.g. HIGH).

Frames of Reference assign descriptors to particular subsets of the data. Frames are relations between data points and some other spatial entity, using some measurement. Our model ended up with two types of frames, depending on how much the number of relative spatial entities varied:

Absolute Frames are those whose relative spatial entities are few or only one. For instance, whether a point lies on high or low ground always depends (in our domain) on the spatial entity called 'sea' and some arbitrary metric, such as the distance on the z-axis to that entity. This allows descriptors to be labelled as HIGH or LOW, by simply retrieving absolute values of data points. For example, if all points in a subset of points have values above 200 for the property *height*, a descriptor with label HIGH is created to describe that subset. To mimic expressions in our corpus, 3 absolute frames were implemented: COASTALPROXIMITY ≡ (COASTAL ∧ INLAND), ELEVATION ≡ (HIGH ∧ LOW) and NAMEDAREAS ≡ (ABERDEEN ∧ ABERDEENSHIRE ∧ MORAY).

Relative Frames are those whose relative spatial entities are too many, which makes it inappropriate to list all possible relations as potential descriptors of that frame. For example, the 3 regions of NAMEDAREAS (see above) can still be split into compass directions. Assigning a single direction value such as NORTH to a descriptor is ambiguous, since that will depend on the area used as reference. Because the direction of a point in our corpus depends on different spatial entities, we modelled DIRECTIONS as the only relative frame, which contains the 4 cardinal directions (e.g. NORTH) and the 4 inter-cardinal directions (e.g. NORTHEAST)[1].

Geocharacterization is the process of mapping points to descriptors. Geocharacterization creates a finite set of Frames of Reference such as COASTALPROXIMITY and ELEVATION.

Descriptions are sets of descriptors such as (NORTH ⊓ COASTAL)[2] that identify a particular subset of the data. A description never contains more than one descriptor of the same Frame of Reference.

Intersection is the relation between descriptors of a description in which only those points that are common between the descriptors are considered. For example, the description (NORTH ⊓ COASTAL) means that the subset of points being referred to are only those that belong to both NORTH and COASTAL.

Mereology is the relation between descriptors of a description in which a part-whole relation is created, where a named descriptor becomes the whole and a direction descriptor the part. For example, the description (NORTH, ABERDEENSHIRE) implies only the subset of ABERDEENSHIRE we can also label as NORTH. In our approach, we implemented a 4-tile half-panes model (Frank, 1992, 361), where a bounding box is created around a named area. Each half of the box becomes a cardinal direction – the upper half becomes NORTH, the left half WEST, etc., and the intersections between halves become the inter-cardinal directions, e.g. NORTHEAST ≡ NORTH ⊓ EAST.

The concept of Descriptions is particularly important to our approach: they are the representation of geographic referring expressions and are the output of the algorithm. A Description such as (NORTH, COASTAL) can be used by a realiser in an NLG system to generate surface expressions such as "north-

---

[1]Our dichotomy *absolute vs. relative* does not align with Levinson's relative and absolute frames. We implement frames as functions and call *absolute* those functions that take only the data point as argument (e.g. coastal-proximity(oxford) = inland), and we call *relative* those that take a second argument (e.g. directions(oxford, uk) = south, but directions(oxford, europe) = northwest).

[2]For the sake of readability, when a direction is relative to the entire region, we omit the relation. The description ((NORTH, WHOLE_REGION) ⊓ COASTAL) is simplified to (NORTH ⊓ COASTAL).

(a) Yellow = NORTH, green = EAST, red = COASTAL   (b) the North, the West and the coast   (c) the northern coast and the West   (d) the northern and western coast

Figure 1: Some interpretations of a description (NORTH ? EAST ? COASTAL). To generate expression 1c, our approach needs to output 2 descriptions and unify them: (NORTH ⊓ COASTAL) ⊔ WEST.

ern coasts", "coasts in the North", "N coast", etc. In our work, we assume such expressions to be surface variations of the same semantic structure. Our algorithm thus outputs a semantic structure (a Description), not a surface form (an expression).

Slightly different forms of the above concepts were used in the work of Turner et al. (2010). However Turner and colleagues limit Frames of Reference (and the set of Descriptors they are made of) to be only absolute, i.e. there is only one specific set of points for each descriptor. Our research, as we explain in more detail below, has shown that this is not true for mereological relations. There is also the danger of selecting content for a referring expression that is not ideal for surface forms as Horacek (2004) and Khan et al. (2008) alert. In the work of Turner and colleagues, descriptions could contain many direction descriptors and the relation between descriptors was not defined (represented as ?). This is harmless for expressions such as "the North and the West", where the description is (NORTH ? EAST). The approach becomes problematic when the final description is (NORTH ? EAST ? COASTAL), as seen in Figure 1. Possible realizations of this description are "the North, the West and the coast", or "the northern coast and the West", "the northern and western coast", among others. Not knowing the relation between the directions and COASTAL enables the system to admit any of these realizations as possible, which could be misleading for a reader. In this paper, we describe mereology as a key spatial relation, but surely others exist. The spatial extension of the Generalized Upper Model (Bateman et al., 2010) lists *internal* and *external* directions, so NORTH could be internal or external to a named area.

For example, NORTH is internal in "northern London" (so a mereological relation exists) but it can be either internal or external in "North of London".

It is important to note too that constructing Frames of Reference (i.e. doing geocharacterization) can be influenced by many factors, as suggested by Ramos-Soto et al. (2016), and thus the number of geocharacterization models could be infinite. For instance, the north of regions cannot always be viewed as the absolute upper half of a region. What one calls "North" may depend on many features pertinent to the region. The existence of a mountain range in the middle of an area could become the boundary between north and south. The same applies for coastal proximity. The width of a coastal area may vary depending on the scale with which one looks at a map. We cannot exclude the possibility of geocharacterization variation between individuals either. Therefore we do not claim our specific geocharacterization to be universal; it simply enables us to run an algorithm that should reflect human behaviour when employing spatial operations to generate geographic referring expressions, while leaving geocharacterization models as an open and intriguing question. In other words, our geocharacterization is an *assumption*, and what we carefully investigate is the role of spatial operations in generating geographic expressions.

3 The Algorithm

In this section we explain how our algorithm goes from point-based data to semantic representations of geographic referring expressions. The entire procedure occurs in 2 steps: overgeneration and scoring. The overgeneration step starts with the entire

A1	B1	C1	D1	E1	F1
A2	B2	C2	D2	E2	F2
A3	B3	C3	D3	E3	F3
A4	B4	C4	D4	E4	F4
A5	B5	C5	D5	E5	F5
A6	B6	C6	D6	E6	F6

(a) Raw data.   (b) COASTALPROXIMITY.   (c) NAMEDAREAS.   (d) DIRECTIONS.

Figure 2: Hypothetical geocharacterization models for a region. Model A is the raw data representing the entire region, where the subset {C1, D1, E1, F1, E2, F2} is the target. B represents the COASTALPROXIMITY frame, where blue denotes COASTAL and yellow INLAND. C represents the NAMEDAREAS frame, where blue denotes MORAY, yellow ABERDEENSHIRE and green ABERDEEN. D represents the DIRECTIONS frame for ABERDEENSHIRE. Blue denotes *northwest*, green *northeast*, orange *southwest* and yellow *southeast*. NORTH is the union of *northwest* and *northeast*, EAST the union of *northeast* and *southeast*, and so on.

dataset, which is already tagged with absolute properties (such as named area and altitude). Its goal is to produce all possible descriptions for a subset of the dataset, the target set (e.g. all points where precipitation is observed). At any point, descriptions that do not overlap with the target subset are rejected. The overgeneration algorithm functions as follows:

1. Start a list of candidate descriptions by building single-descriptor descriptions from all absolute frames.

2. Increment the list of candidates with mereological descriptions, i.e. for each NAMEDAREAS descriptor combine it with each relative descriptor (currently only DIRECTIONS descriptors).

3. Increment the list of candidates with all valid intersections[3] among the current candidate descriptions.

4. Compute description scores and select the highest scoring description.

In order to score descriptions in our domain (weather), we followed two intuitions. First that there is a minimum ratio of true positives a description can capture in order to be accepted as candidate. For example, if a description A overlaps with only 70% of the target points and description B with 90%, and we require at least 80% of true positives, description B is a candidate and A should be ignored. The second intuition states that, of all candidate descriptions, the description with the highest balance of true positives and true negatives should win. We used recall as the metrics for minimum threshold of true positives and F-measure as the metrics to balance out true positives and negatives. These are computed as (precision is also provided, since F-measure requires it):

$$precision = \frac{description \cap target}{description}$$

$$recall = \frac{description \cap target}{target}$$

$$Fmeasure = 2 \cdot \frac{precision \cdot recall}{precision + recall}$$

Where *description* is the set of points associated with a description (e.g. (NORTH ⊓ COASTAL)) and *target* is the set of points associated with the target subset (e.g. those that represent rain).

Below is an example of the procedure with a hypothetical data set and target. Let us assume Figure 2a is the entire data set and represents the entire region, where the subset {C1, D1, E1, F1, E2, F2} is the target subset for which a description needs to

---

[3]The algorithm rejects intersections that are semantically redundant (e.g. ((NORTH, MORAY) ⊓ (MORAY)) ≡ (NORTH, MORAY)) or linguistically awkward (e.g. ((NORTH, MORAY) ⊓ (NORTH) → "the area of intersection between the North of Moray and the North of the whole region").

be generated. The preparatory step before the algorithm starts is to do geocharacterization with the absolute Frames of Reference. Let us assume our full geocharacterized model should contain 3 frames: NAMEDAREAS, COASTAL and DIRECTIONS. DIRECTIONS is a relative frame and needs the descriptors of NAMEDAREAS to exist, so initially we can only construct the frames COASTALPROXIMITY and NAMEDAREAS (Figures 2b and 2c).

At any given point, a description is only considered as candidate if it scores higher than 0 recall, i.e. if it intersects at least once with the target set. This results in the following initial list of candidate descriptions (where R=recall and F-M=F-measure):

Absolute Descriptions	R	F-M
COASTAL	0.83	0.59
ABERDEENSHIRE	1.00	0.40

Now the algorithm creates mereological descriptions with the DIRECTIONS frame (Figure 2d), as explained in Section 2. Once this interim geocharacterization step is done, mereological descriptions are added to the list of candidates:

Mereological Descriptions	R	F-M
NORTHEAST, ABERDEENSHIRE	0.83	0.67
NORTH, ABERDEENSHIRE	1.00	0.67
EAST, ABERDEENSHIRE	0.83	0.45
NORTHWEST, ABERDEENSHIRE	0.17	0.22
EAST, ABERDEENSHIRE	0.17	0.13

The next step is to generate intersections between all current candidate descriptions, as long as they are valid (see above), and add them to the list of candidates:

Intersected Descriptions	R	F-M
COASTAL ⊓ (NORTH, ABERDEENSHIRE)	0.83	0.83
COASTAL ⊓ (EAST, ABERDEENSHIRE)	0.83	0.77
COASTAL ⊓ (NORTHEAST, ABERDEENSHIRE)	0.67	0.73
COASTAL ⊓ ABERDEENSHIRE	0.83	0.71
COASTAL ⊓ (NORTHEAST, ABERDEENSHIRE)	0.17	0.29

Once the overgeneration algorithm is done, the scoring algorithm chooses the description with highest F-measure score, after filtering by recall. Assuming a recall threshold of 0.80, the description (COASTAL ⊓ (NORTH, ABERDEENSHIRE)) is the winner, as it has the highest F-Measure score of all remaining candidates. However if there is a need to raise the recall threshold to 1.00, i.e. no target point must be ignored, then the winning description is (NORTH, ABERDEENSHIRE). The choice for a particular recall threshold may vary from domain to domain. In the studies we have carried out, we achieve best performance at a threshold of 0.60 for one testbed, and 0.80 for another, as explained in Section 5.

4   Knowledge Acquisition

In this section we explain how we created a corpus of aligned data and text, which had a two-fold use: (a) inform us about the spatial operations employed by humans when producing geographic expression, and (b) serve as a testbed to evaluate the development of the algorithm.

From the work of de Oliveira et al. (2015) it became evident that named areas played an important role in geographic referring expressions, especially by allowing a mereological relation between certain unnamed descriptors and named descriptors. However that study provided only a high-level understanding of how often each Frame of Reference is used by humans when producing geographic referring expressions. In this study we conducted an experiment to produce an aligned data-and-text corpus, where each expression is associated with a particular subset of points (similar to the SUMTIME-METEO corpus (Sripada et al., 2002)). This enables the use of corpus entries as test cases, by running the algorithm with the subset of points of each entry, and comparing the output of the algorithm with the description in the entry.

Another interesting aspect of the corpus is its source. The texts were written by human experts (2 meteorologists), which guarantees that the geographic expressions in the corpus are similar to those in published weather forecasts. We could not guarantee this if the same texts were written by non-experts, for example using crowd-sourcing platforms. Nonetheless it is important to remember that our corpus – as strongly advised by the experiment participants – does not reflect the nature of real-life weather reports, with all the complexity that is involved in describing the weather. The corpus we present here is a collection of geographic expressions written by people with a life-time experience in producing geographic expressions; it is not a collection of real-life-like weather reports.

Using a web-based tool[4], the experts were exposed to 20 data sets. Each data set hypothetically represented a simplified weather forecast for the Scottish Grampian Region. When plotted onto the map, data points that represented some form of precipitation were highlighted in red, as shown in Figure 3. The experts were asked to write a pseudo weather forecast, describing where precipitation and/or dry weather was expected.

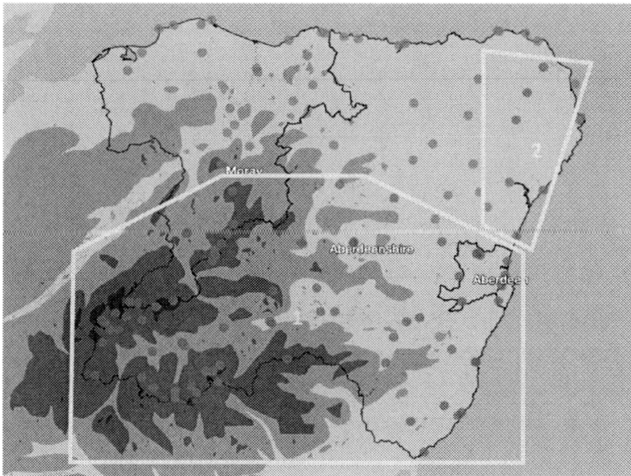

Figure 3: A map the meteorologists saw to write a weather forecast. Red points denote precipitation and green points dry weather. The numbered boxes were added for the alignment step, after texts had been written. Numbers on texts and boxes mark the alignment between points and expressions.

The above was only the first task of the experiment. The outcome of the the first task was a set of free-text paragraphs describing the location of wet and/or dry weather for the entire data set seen. The first observation we made from the raw responses is that some data clustering was taking place, because paragraphs contained many expressions (effectively noun phrases) to describe a single data set. This meant an alignment between parts of the texts and subsets (or clusters) of points had to be made. We

prepared a document by hand where we provided the authors with screenshots of the maps they saw, along with the texts they wrote for each map. We numbered each expression on the texts and placed numbered boxes on the subset of points we judged to be referred to by each expression, as shown in Figure 3. The authors' task was to review our suggested alignment and fix it where applicable.

The last task to effectively build a corpus of data-and-text alignments was to annotate each referring expression with semantic labels. This task was carried out by one group of 3 human annotators per meteorologist – henceforth M1 and M2 – whereby 1 annotator participated in both annotations. The annotation task (for both M1 and M2) consisted of tagging expressions with labels of various categories. The following categories and labels were available:

Main direction Included the cardinal and intercardinal directions.

Direction modifier For words such as *far* and *central*, as well as the cardinal directions of complex direction expressions such as "NNW", where we assume the main direction to be NORTHEAST and the modifier to be NORTH-. This category is mainly for completeness, since we did not implement any of them.

Area The 3 Authority Areas of the Scottish Grampian region: ABERDEEN, ABERDEEN-SHIRE and MORAY.

Coastness Whether COASTAL or INLAND.

Altitude Whether HIGH or LOW.

Each category relates to a frame of reference in our system, and labels relate to descriptors. For each category, a null annotation was also available, in case the frame of reference was not mentioned. Annotators were instructed to annotate expressions entirely based on the linguistic material provided, not using their world knowledge. For example, if they were familiar with Aberdeen City and recognized it as a coastal city, but the expression was simply "Aberdeen", they should provide only { ABERDEEN } as annotation and not { ABERDEEN, COASTAL }.

Overall agreement between annotators was high – 92% for M1 and 98% for M2 – whereby the category Coastness had the highest disagreement (63%)

for M1, as shown in Table 1. This was probably due to bad instructions as we suspect one annotator was using his world knowledge to judge whether a referred area was close to or far from the Grampian coast. All annotators live in Aberdeen City, but they saw only the expressions and no images. We improved instructions before annotating M2.

M1 sub-corpus	AB	AC	BC	ABC
Main direction	1.00	0.98	0.98	0.97
Direction modifier	1.00	0.96	0.96	0.97
Area	1.00	1.00	1.00	1.00
Coastness	0.92	0.52	0.46	0.63
Altitude	1.00	1.00	1.00	1.00
All categories	**0.98**	**0.89**	**0.88**	**0.92**
M2 sub-corpus	**AD**	**AE**	**DE**	**ADE**
Main direction	1.00	0.97	0.97	0.98
Direction modifier	0.96	0.87	0.91	0.92
Area	1.00	1.00	1.00	1.00
Coastness	1.00	1.00	1.00	1.00
Altitude	1.00	1.00	1.00	1.00
All categories	**0.99**	**0.97**	**0.98**	**0.98**

Table 1: The Kappa agreement scores when labelling expressions produced by both meteorologist (M1 and M2). Columns 2-4 show the pair-wise agreement, and the column 5 the averages of pair-wise agreements per category. Figures at the bottom of each sub-corpus are the averages of each column.

After annotation, there were no cases where all three annotations were different, so there was a most frequent annotation for each data set. We kept those as the final set of labels for each entry in the corpus. After annotation, the M1 sub-corpus contained a total of 57 data-and-text aligned entries, while M2 contained 41. In the next section we explain how we used both M1 and M2 to evaluate the progress when developing the algorithm.

5   Evaluation and Discussion

Our algorithm development was carried out in two phases. First, we used a Gold Standard from M1 to develop the logic of the algorithm, and subsequently used a Gold Standard from M2 to test its performance. For each phase, we ran the algorithm with 3 distinct combinations of spatial operations: a) no operation, so only absolute descriptions such as (COASTAL) and non-specific directions such as (NORTH) were generated; b) mereology only, where

mereological descriptions such as (NORTH, MORAY) were generated in addition to the ones above; c) both mereology and intersection, where the most complex descriptions such as (COASTAL ⊓ (NORTH ⊓ MORAY)) were also generated. The evaluation method was intrinsic, as described by Belz and Gatt (2008), whereby we computed the similarity between corpus descriptions and the output of the algorithm using the DICE coefficient of similarity. The Gold Standard testbeds excluded descriptions with direction modifiers such as *far* and *central*, because the current algorithm does not have an implementation for these concepts. The Gold Standard from M2 contained 44 entries, and that from M2, 36.

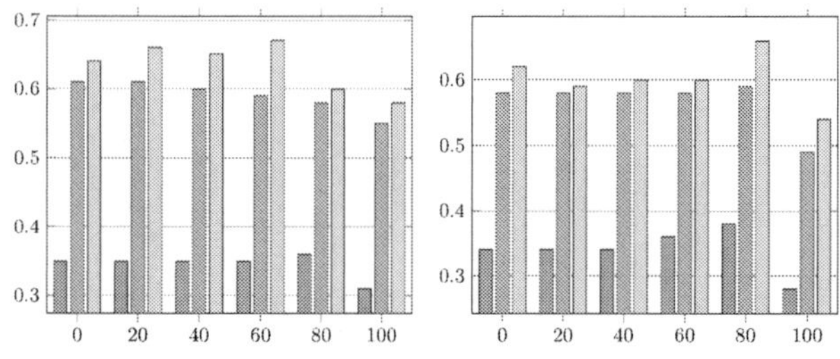

(a) Training scores (M1).　　(b) Test scores (M2).

Figure 4: DICE similarity scores when running the algorithm against both sub-corpora (M1 and M2), using 3 different operation combinations – no operation (blue), mereology only (red), and both mereology and intersection (brown) – and 5 different recall thresholds. The X axis shows the different recall thresholds in percentage. The Y axis shows the average DICE scores across all data sets.

For each testbed we ran the algorithm 6 times, one for each recall threshold of an arbitrary set of thresholds (0.0, 0.2, 0.4, 0.6, 0.8 and 1.0). The results (shown in Figure 4) suggest that there is no specific recall threshold that gives better results, but 1.00 (i.e. no false positives accepted) is not the ideal threshold as it gave the worst results in all scenarios. However, the evaluation showed that there was a consistent gain in performance after the addition of each spatial operation. The highest average of DICE scores for M1 went from 0.36 with no operations to 0.67 with both operations, whereas for M2 scores went from 0.38 to 0.66.

We can attempt to explain why some of our output differs from the human descriptions. **Geocharacter-**

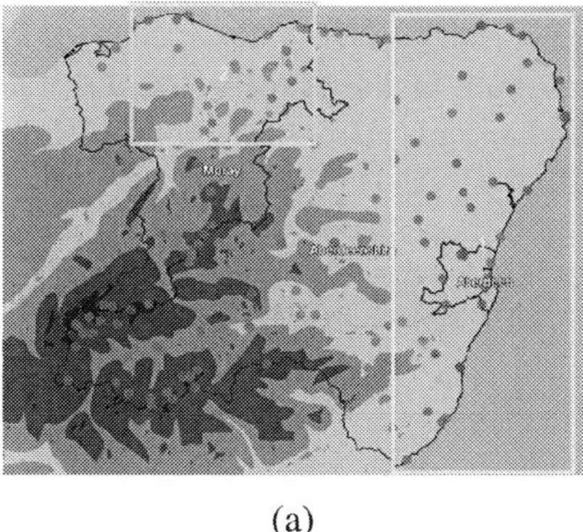
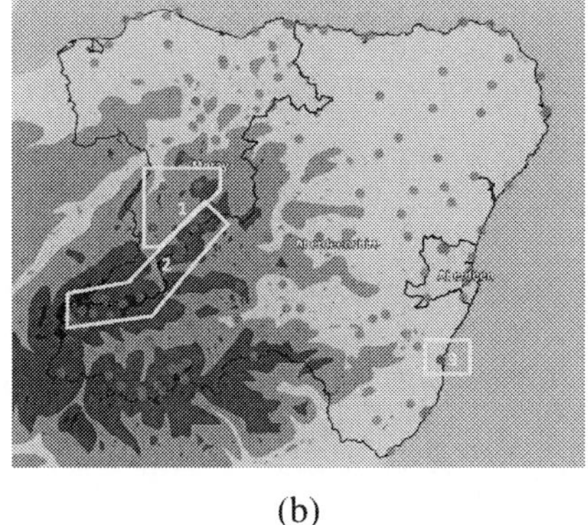

(a)   (b)

Figure 5: Examples of almost perfect match between human-generated and machine-generated descriptions.

ization: If the mental models of the humans do not align with those our algorithm uses. An example of this is the description (EAST ⊓ COASTAL) which the human M2 gave to cluster 1 of the map in Figure 5a. The winning description according to the algorithm was only (EAST), because (EAST ⊓ COASTAL) covered less of the target points. This relates also to the topic of vagueness (Van Deemter, 2009), if one assumes descriptors not to have crisp but fuzzy boundaries (Schneider, 2000; Bittner and Smith, 2003). **Weighting:** If some descriptions should be rewarded if they include certain descriptors. This is much in line with the preference order of properties from the Incremental Algorithm (Dale and Reiter, 1995). The human-generated description for cluster 2 on Figure 5b was (HIGH ⊓ (SOUTH, MORAY)) which was the second best description generated by the machine. If the algorithm rewarded descriptions that include a named area, maybe the above description would have won.

These are only some of the possible reasons. We may not forget either that discourse and brevity may also play a role. Nonetheless the results we present in this paper show how, in any scenario, an algorithm for generating geographic expressions performs better if it employs intersection and mereology than without any operation.

6 Conclusions and Future Work

In this paper we have outlined an algorithm for generating geographic referring expressions. The algorithm employs 2 spatial operations – intersection and mereology – when processing point-based data. We described the compilation of a data-and-text aligned corpus, which we used as a testbed to guide development and to test the final system. We have shown that employing spatial operations makes the machine-generated output more similar to the human-generated descriptions. We increased the overall average of similarity between the computer output and human descriptions from a 0.38 (DICE), when no operations are used, to a score of 0.66, when computing mereology and intersection.

In line with Reiter and Belz (2009), we believe that our metrics-based evaluation was valuable but only a 'development-stage' guidance. A task-based evaluation shall be more revealing of the algorithm's performance. Thus, our next study will evaluate how well users accomplish a task given the descriptions generated by our algorithm. Nonetheless we are convinced that spatial operations are employed by humans when producing descriptions, which makes the algorithm described here to be more human-like than previous approaches. Above all, our results show that relative properties are paramount when generating referring expressions in geographic domains, where mereological relations are key.

7 Acknowledgements

We would like to thank Arria NLG for sponsoring this PhD project. Our special thanks are due to the meteorologists Mr Ian Davy and Mr James Brownhill for providing examples of spatial referring expressions which guided the development of our algorithm. Many thanks to the members of the Computational Linguistics Aberdeen group for their helpful comments, especially Kees van Deemter, Steph Inglis and Daniel Couto-Vale.

263

References

John Bateman, Joana Hois, Robert Ross, and Thora Tenbrink. 2010. A linguistic ontology of space for natural language processing. *Artificial Intelligence*, 174(14):1027–1071.

Anja Belz and Albert Gatt. 2008. Intrinsic vs. extrinsic evaluation measures for referring expression generation. In *Proceedings of the 46th Annual Meeting of the Association for Computational Linguistics on Human Language Technologies: Short Papers*, pages 197–200. Association for Computational Linguistics.

Thomas Bittner and Barry Smith. 2003. Vague reference and approximating judgments. *Spatial Cognition & Computation*, 3(2-3):137–156.

Anthony G Cohn and Jochen Renz. 2008. Qualitative spatial representation and reasoning. *Handbook of knowledge representation*, 3:551–596.

Robert Dale and Ehud Reiter. 1995. Computational interpretations of the Gricean maxims in the generation of referring expressions. *Cognitive science*, 19(2):233–263.

Rodrigo de Oliveira, Somayajulu Sripada, and Ehud Reiter. 2015. Designing an algorithm for generating named spatial references. *ENLG 2015*, page 127.

Andrew U Frank. 1992. Qualitative spatial reasoning about distances and directions in geographic space. *Journal of Visual Languages & Computing*, 3(4):343–371.

Albert Gatt, Roger PG van Gompel, Kees van Deemter, and Emiel Kramer. 2013. Are we bayesian referring expression generators. In *Proceedings of CogSci*, volume 35.

Helmut Horacek. 2004. On referring to sets of objects naturally. In *Natural Language Generation*, pages 70–79. Springer.

John D Kelleher and Geert-Jan M Kruijff. 2006. Incremental generation of spatial referring expressions in situated dialog. In *Proceedings of the 21st International Conference on Computational Linguistics and the 44th annual meeting of the Association for Computational Linguistics*, pages 1041–1048. Association for Computational Linguistics.

Imtiaz Hussain Khan, Kees Van Deemter, and Graeme Ritchie. 2008. Generation of referring expressions: Managing structural ambiguities. In *Proceedings of the 22nd International Conference on Computational Linguistics-Volume 1*, pages 433–440. Association for Computational Linguistics.

Emiel Krahmer and Kees Van Deemter. 2012. Computational generation of referring expressions: A survey. *Computational Linguistics*, 38(1):173–218.

Stephen C Levinson. 2003. Space in Language and Cognition: Explorations in Cognitive Diversity. chapter 2, pages 24–61.

Inderjeet Mani, Christy Doran, Dave Harris, Janet Hitzeman, Rob Quimby, Justin Richer, Ben Wellner, Scott Mardis, and Seamus Clancy. 2010. SpatialML: annotation scheme, resources, and evaluation. *Language Resources and Evaluation*, 44(3):263–280.

David M Mark, Christian Freksa, Stephen C Hirtle, Robert Lloyd, and Barbara Tversky. 1999. Cognitive models of geographical space. *International journal of geographical information science*, 13(8):747–774.

Alejandro Ramos-Soto, Nava Tintarev, Reiter Ehud de Oliveira, Rodrigo, and Kees van Deemter. 2016. Natural language generation and fuzzy sets: An exploratory study on geographical referring expression generation. In *Proceedings of Fuzz-IEEE 2016*. IEEE.

Ehud Reiter and Anja Belz. 2009. An investigation into the validity of some metrics for automatically evaluating natural language generation systems. *Computational Linguistics*, 35(4):529–558.

Ehud Reiter and Robert Dale. 2000. *Building natural language generation systems*, volume 33. MIT Press.

Ehud Reiter. 2007. An architecture for data-to-text systems. In *Proceedings of the Eleventh European Workshop on Natural Language Generation*, pages 97–104. Association for Computational Linguistics.

Markus Schneider. 2000. Finite resolution crisp and fuzzy spatial objects. In *Int. Symp. on Spatial Data Handling*, page 5a. Citeseer.

Somayajulu Sripada, Ehud Reiter, Jim Hunter, and Jin Yu. 2002. Sumtime-meteo: Parallel corpus of naturally occurring forecast texts and weather data. *Computing Science Department, University of Aberdeen, Aberdeen, Scotland, Tech. Rep. AUCS/TR0201*.

Ross Turner, Somayajulu Sripada, and Ehud Reiter. 2010. Generating approximate geographic descriptions. In *Empirical methods in natural language generation*, pages 121–140. Springer.

Kees Van Deemter. 2002. Generating referring expressions: Boolean extensions of the incremental algorithm. *Computational Linguistics*, 28(1):37–52.

Kees Van Deemter. 2009. Utility and language generation: The case of vagueness. *Journal of Philosophical Logic*, 38(6):607–632.

Jette Viethen and Robert Dale. 2008. The use of spatial relations in referring expression generation. In *Proceedings of the Fifth International Natural Language Generation Conference*, pages 59–67. Association for Computational Linguistics.

Michael F Worboys and Matt Duckham. 2004. *GIS: a computing perspective*. CRC press.

Crowd-sourcing NLG Data: Pictures Elicit Better Data.

Jekaterina Novikova, Oliver Lemon and **Verena Rieser**
Interaction Lab
Heriot-Watt University
Edinburgh, EH14 4AS, UK
{j.novikova, o.lemon, v.t.rieser}@hw.ac.uk

Abstract

Recent advances in corpus-based Natural Language Generation (NLG) hold the promise of being easily portable across domains, but require costly training data, consisting of meaning representations (MRs) paired with Natural Language (NL) utterances. In this work, we propose a novel framework for crowd-sourcing high quality NLG training data, using automatic quality control measures and evaluating different MRs with which to elicit data. We show that pictorial MRs result in better NL data being collected than logic-based MRs: utterances elicited by pictorial MRs are judged as significantly more natural, more informative, and better phrased, with a significant increase in average quality ratings (around 0.5 points on a 6-point scale), compared to using the logical MRs. As the MR becomes more complex, the benefits of pictorial stimuli increase. The collected data will be released as part of this submission.

1   Introduction

The overall aim of this research is to develop methods that will allow the full automation of the creation of NLG systems for new applications and domains. Currently deployed technologies for NLG utilise domain-dependent methods including hand-written grammars or domain-specific language templates for surface realisation, both of which are costly to develop and maintain. Recent corpus-based methods hold the promise of being easily portable across domains, e.g. (Angeli et al., 2010; Konstas and Lapata, 2012; Mairesse and Young, 2014), but require high quality training data consisting of meaning representations (MR) paired with Natural Language (NL) utterances, augmented by alignments between MR elements and NL words. Recent work (Dušek and Jurčíček, 2015; Wen et al., 2015) removes the need for alignment, but the question of *where to get in-domain training data of sufficient quality* remains.

In this work, we propose a novel framework for crowd-sourcing high quality NLG training data, using automatic quality control measures and evaluating different meaning representations. So far, we collected 1410 utterances using this framework. The data will be released as part of this submission.

2   Background

Apart from (Mairesse et al., 2010), this research is the first to investigate crowdsourcing for collecting NLG data. So far, crowdsourcing is mainly used for evaluation in the NLG community, e.g. (Rieser et al., 2014; Dethlefs et al., 2012). Recent efforts in corpus creation via crowdsourcing have proven to be successful in related tasks. For example, (Zaidan and Callison-Burch, 2011) showed that crowdsourcing can result in datasets of comparable quality to those created by professional translators given appropriate quality control methods. (Mairesse et al., 2010) demonstrate that crowd workers can produce NL descriptions from abstract MRs, a method which also has shown success in related NLP tasks, such as Spoken Dialogue Systems (Wang et al., 2012) or Semantic Parsing (Wang et al., 2015). However, when collecting corpora for training NLG systems, new challenges arise:

(1) How to ensure the required high quality of the collected data?

(2) What types of meaning representations can elicit spontaneous, natural and varied data from crowd-workers?

To address (1), we first filter the crowdsourced data using automatic and manual validation procedures. We evaluate the quality of crowdsourced NLG data using automatic measures, e.g. measuring the semantic similarity of a collected NL utterance.

To address (2), we conduct a principled study regarding the trade-off between semantic expressiveness of the MR and the quality of crowd-sourced utterances elicited for the different semantic representations. In particular, we investigate translating MRs into pictorial representations as used in, e.g. (Black et al., 2011; Williams and Young, 2007) for evaluating spoken dialogue systems. We compare these pictorial MRs to text-based MRs used by previous crowd-sourcing work (Mairesse et al., 2010; Wang et al., 2012). These text-based MRs take the form of Dialogue Acts, such as *inform(type[hotel],pricerange[expensive])*. However, there is a limit in the semantic complexity that crowd workers can handle (Mairesse et al., 2010). Also, (Wang et al., 2012) observed that the semantic formalism unfortunately influences the collected language, i.e. crowd-workers are "primed" by the words/tokens and ordering used in the MR.

3   Experimental setup

The experiment was designed to investigate whether we can elicit high-quality Natural Language via crowdsourcing, using different modalities of meaning representation: textual/logical and pictorial MR. We use the CrowdFlower platform to set up our experiments and to access an online workforce.

3.1   Data collection: pictures and text

The data collected is intended as training input to a statistical NL generation process, but where alignment between words and the MR is left unspecified as in, e.g. (Dušek and Jurčíček, 2015; Wen et al., 2015). The input to the generation process is a pair of MR and NL reference text. Each MR consists of an unordered set of *attributes* and their *values*. The NL reference text is a Natural Language utterance, possibly consisting of several sentences, which is provided by a crowd worker for the corresponding MR. An example MR-NL pair is shown in Figure 1.

For the data collection, a set of sixty MRs was

MR	name [The Wrestlers], priceRange [cheap], customerRating [low].
NL	The Wrestlers offers competitive prices, but isn't rated highly by customers.

Figure 1: Example of an MR-NL pair.

prepared, consisting of three, five, or eight attributes and their corresponding values in order to assess different complexities. The eight attributes used in the MRs are shown in Table 1. The order of attributes is randomised so that crowdworkers are not "primed" by ordering used in the MRs (Wang et al., 2012).

Attribute	Data Type	Example value
name	verbatim string	The Wrestlers, ...
eatType	dictionary	restaurant, pub, ...
familyFriendly	boolean	Yes / No
priceRange	dictionary	cheap, expensive, ...
food	dictionary	Japanese, Italian, ...
near	verbatim string	market square, ...
area	dictionary	riverside, city centre, ...
customerRating	enumerable	1 of 5 (low), 4 of 5 (high), ...

Table 1: Domain attributes and attribute types.

75 distinct MRs were prepared in a way that ensures a balance between the number of used attributes in the final dataset. We excluded MRs that do not contain the attribute *name* from the set of MRs with three and five attributes, because we found that such MRs are problematic for crowd workers to create a natural grammatically-correct utterances. For example, crowd workers found it difficult to create an utterance of a high quality based on the MR `priceRange[low]`, `area[riverside]`, `customerRating[low]`.

The textual/logical MRs in our experiment (see Figure 1) have the form of a sequence with attributes provided in a random order, separated by commas, and the values of the attributes provided in square brackets after each attribute.

The pictorial MRs (see Figure 2) are semi-automatically generated pictures with a combination of icons corresponding to the appropriate attributes. The icons are located on a background showing a map of a city, thus allowing to represent the meaning of attributes *area* and *near*.

Figure 2: Examples of pictorial MRs. Left: for a family-friendly, Sushi/Japanese restaurant, cheap, neither near the centre of town nor near the river. Right: for a restaurant by the river, serving pasta/Italian food, highly rated and expensive, not child-friendly, located near Cafe Adriatic.

3.2 Validation procedures

There are several reasons why crowdsourcing might generate poor quality data: (1) The task may be too complex or the instructions might not be clear enough for crowd workers to follow; (2) the financial incentives may be not attractive enough for crowd workers to act conscientiously; and (3) open-ended job designs without a gold-standard reference test may allow them to simply randomly click or type "gibberish" text instead of performing the task.

In our experiment, we provided crowd workers with clear and concise instructions of each task. The instructions contained the goal of the data collection, a list of rules describing what is required and what is optional, and three examples of utterances paired with an MR. Instructions for the textual/logical MR and the pictorial MR were intended to be as identical as possible for the two conditions, with only slight unavoidable differences, such as the format of the example MR provided (logical or pictorial).

In terms of financial compensation, crowd workers were paid the standard pay on CrowdFlower, which is \$0.02 per page (each containing 1 MR). Workers were expected to spend about 20 seconds per page. Participants were allowed to complete up to 20 pages, i.e. create utterances for up to 20 MRs. Mason and Watts (2010) in their study of financial incentives on Mechanical Turk, found (counter-intuitively) that increasing the amount of compensation for a particular task does not tend to improve the quality of the results. Furthermore, Callison-Burch and Dredze (2010) observed that there can be an inverse relationship between the amount of payment and the quality of work, because it may be more tempting for crowd workers to cheat on high-paying tasks if they do not have the skills to complete them. Following these findings, we did not increase the payment for our task over the standard level.

In order to check for random inputs/"gibberish" and to control quality of the data, we introduced a validation procedure, which consisted of two main parts (see sections 3.3 and 3.4 for details):

(1) Automatic pre-validation. The purpose of the automatic validation is to block the submissions of utterances of inappropriate quality.

(2) Human evaluation of collected data. The purpose of human post-evaluation is to rate the quality of collected utterances.

3.3 Automatic Pre-validation

The first pre-validation step is to select participants that are likely to be native speakers of English. Previous crowdsourcing experiments used different methods to ensure that crowd workers meet this criteria. One option is to create a qualification exam that will screen out non-native speakers. However, as discussed by (Sprouse, 2011), this method is not reliable, as workers can re-take qualification exams multiple times to avoid disqualification. Furthermore, qualification exams severely decrease participation rates, as many crowd workers routinely avoid jobs that require qualification (Sprouse, 2011). Alternatively, Sprouse (2011) and Callison-Burch and Dredze (2010) argue for self-identification of the participants, while using their IP addresses to ensure that their geolocation information is consistent with this. In accordance with this, we used IP addresses to ensure that participants are located in one of three English-speaking countries - Canada, the United Kingdom, or the United States. In addition, both in the name of the task and in the instructions, we included a requirement that "Participants must be native speakers of British or American English".

The second pre-validation step checks whether participants spend at least 20 seconds to complete a page of work. This is a standard CrowdFlower option to control the quality of contributions, and it ensures that the contributor is removed from the job if they complete the task too fast.

As a final pre-validation step, we created four JavaScript validators to ensure the submitted utterances are well formed English sentences:

(1) The first validator checked if the ready-to-submit utterance only contains legal characters, i.e. letters, numbers and symbols "', . : ;£'".

(2) The second validator checked whether the length of the utterance (in characters) is not smaller than the required minimal length. The required minimal length was calculated as follows:

$$min.length = length.of.MR-$$
$$number.of.attributes.in.MR \times 10; \quad (1)$$

Here, *length.of.MR* is the total number of characters in the provided MR. *Number.of.attributes.in.MR* is either 3, 5 or 8 depending on the number of attributes in the provided MR. *10* is an average length of an attribute name, including two associated square brackets. Thus, $min.length$ is simply an approximation of the total number of characters used for attribute values in each specific MR.

(3) The third validator checked whether the ready-to-submit utterance contained all the required elements, e.g. the name of the described venue or the name of the venue near the described one.

(4) The last validator checked that participants do not submit the same utterance several times.

The automatic validators were tested on the data collected during a pilot test phase and were able to correctly identify and reject 100% of bad submissions.

3.4 Human evaluation of collected data

While automatic validators help reject some invalid cases, human feedback is needed to assess the quality of the collected data. In a 2nd phase we evaluated

the collected data through a large-scale subjective rating experiment using the CrowdFlower system.

6-point Likert scales were used to collect judgements on the data, via the following criteria:

1. *Informativeness.* Q1: "Is this utterance informative? (i.e. do you think it provides enough useful information about the venue?)"
2. *Naturalness.* Q2: "Is this utterance natural? (e.g. could it have been produced by a native speaker?)"
3. *Phrasing.* Q3: "Is this utterance well phrased? (i.e. do you like how it is expressed?)"

Finally, crowd workers were asked to judge whether the utterance is grammatically correct.

4 Results: Collected data

In order to maintain a balanced workload distribution between the two MR conditions, we divided the workload into two batches: each batch was posted in the morning of two different workdays. Such a workload distribution was previously described in (Wang et al., 2012) as appropriate for a between-subject design. Each batch corresponded to one of two conditions: the first batch contained only textual/logical MRs, and the second one used only pictorial MRs. The analysis presented in the following sections is based on this experimental design.

435 tasks were completed by 134 crowd workers: 70 crowd workers completed 212 tasks based on textual/logical MRs, and 64 crowd workers completed 223 tasks on pictorial MRs. This resulted in collecting 1410 utterances, 744 on textual, and 666 on pictorial MRs. 13 crowd workers completed the tasks on both types of MR. The utterances created by these 13 subjects for the pictorial MRs were excluded from the analysis, so that it would not violate a between-subject experimental design with a possible learning bias. The final dataset therefore contained *744 utterances elicited using the textual MRs and 498 utterances elicited using the pictorial MRs*, with 1133 distinct utterances. The dataset will be released with this submission.

We now use objective measures to assess the effect of the MR modality on the collected NL text.

4.1 Time taken to collect data

The data collection for the first batch (only textual/logical MRs) was completed in about 26 hours,

	Textual MR		Pictorial MR	
	Mean	StDev	Mean	StDev
Time, sec	*347.18*	*301.74*	*352.05*	*249.34*
3 attributes	283.37	265.82	298.97	272.44
5 attributes	321.75	290.89	355.56	244.57
8 attributes	433.41	325.04	405.56	215.43
Length, char	*100.83*	*46.40*	*93.06*	*37.78*
3 attributes	61.25	19.44	67.98	22.30
5 attributes	95.18	26.71	91.13	21.19
8 attributes	144.79	41.84	121.94	40.13
No of sentences	*1.43*	*0.69*	*1.31*	*0.54*
3 attributes	1.06	0.24	1.07	0.25
5 attributes	1.37	0.51	1.25	0.49
8 attributes	1.84	0.88	1.63	0.64

Table 2: Nature of the data collected with each MR. Italics denote averages across all numbers of attributes.

while the second one (only pictorial MRs) was completed in less than 18 hours.

The average duration per task was 352 sec for the pictorial MR, and 347 sec for the textual/logical method, as shown in Table 2. A two-way ANOVA was conducted to examine the effect of MR modality and the number of attributes on average task duration. The difference between two modalities was not significant, with $p = 0.76$. There was no statistically significant interaction between the effects of modality and the number of attributes in the MR, on time taken to collect the data. A main effects analysis showed that the average duration of utterance creation was significantly longer for larger numbers of attributes, F(2,1236) = 24.99, $p < 0.001$, as expected.

4.2 Average length of utterance (characters)

The length of collected utterances was calculated as a total number of characters in the utterance, including punctuation.

The average length of utterance was 101 characters for the textual/logical MR, and 93 characters for the pictorial method, as shown in Table 2. A two-way ANOVA was conducted to examine the effect of MR modality and the number of attributes on the length of utterance. There was a statistically significant interaction between the effects of modality and the number of attributes in the MR, F(2,1236) = 23.74, $p < 0.001$. A main effects analysis showed that the average length of utterance was significantly larger not only for a larger number of attributes, with $p < 0.001$, but also for the utterances created based

on a textual/logical MR which had a higher number of attributes, $p < 0.001$.

4.3 Average number of sentences per utterance

The task allowed crowd workers to create not only single sentences, but also multi-sentence utterances for any provided MR.

The average number of sentences per utterance was 1.43 for the textual/logical MR, and 1.31 for the pictorial method, as shown in Table 2. A two-way ANOVA was conducted to examine the effect of MR modality and the number of attributes on the number of sentences per utterance. There was a statistically significant interaction between the effects of modality and the number of attributes in the MR, F(2,1236) = 3.83, $p < 0.05$. A main effects analysis showed that the average number of sentences was significantly larger not only for a larger number of attributes, with $p < 0.001$, but also for the utterances created based on a textual/logical MR which had a higher number of attributes, $p < 0.001$.

4.4 Semantic similarity

We now examine the *semantic similarity* of the collected sentences. The concept of semantic similarity aims to measure how well the collected utterances cover the meaning provided in the MRs. This concept is similar to that of Informativeness (see section 5.2), as a higher value for semantic similarity shows that more information, originally provided in the MR, was expressed in the NL utterance. However, these two concepts are not interchangeable, as we will explain later in Section 5.1.

We used a semi-automatic labelling process to assess the semantics of the collected data and compared them to the given MRs. We first performed spell-checking by using Microsoft Word. Overall, about 7% of the collected utterances contained one or more spelling errors. Note that this result is in line with (Wang et al., 2012), who report 8% spelling errors for crowd-sourced utterances. We corrected these by hand. Next, we used an automated process to assess whether the collected data covers all required semantic concepts in the MR, using text similarity. In particular, we calculated a similarity score between the provided MR and the collected utterance, using the UMBC Semantic Text Similarity measure provided by (Han et al., 2013), which ranked top in the *SEM 2013 Semantic Textual Similarity shared task. This measure is based on distributional similarity and Latent Semantic Analysis (LSA), and is further complemented with semantic relations extracted from WordNet. The score was calculated using a Web API[1] to query the UMBC Semantic Similarity service.

We find that textual MRs elicit text which is significantly more similar to the underlying MR than using pictures (similarity score of 0.62 for pictures vs. 0.82 for text, $p < 0.005$, where 1 indicates perfect overlap). We attribute this difference to the fact that utterances in response to pictorial MRs are more varied and thus receive lower scores. For example, the similarity score between "cheap" (in MR) and "cheap" (in a corresponding utterance) is 1, whereas the similarity between "cheap" and "low price" is 0.36 using the UMBC Semantic Text Similarity measure.

As a next step, we normalised the results of semantic similarity on a 1-6 scale, in order to make the results comparable to the human ratings on 6-point Likert scales and compare semantic similarity to the self-evaluation results. In order to make results comparable, we labelled the semantic similarity of a corresponding utterance as *higher than average* if the result was higher than 4 (53% of all collected utterances), *lower than average* if the result was lower than 3 (4.3% of all collected utterances), and *average* otherwise (43% of all the utterances). This metric is then used to automatically assess the amount of relevant information from the MR which is preserved in the corresponding NL text, see section 5.1.

5 Results: human evaluation of the collected data

While automated or semi-automated metrics provide some useful information about the collected utterances, human feedback is necessary to properly assess their quality. In this section, we first compare the data collected using self-evaluation and crowd evaluation methods, and later we analyse Informativeness, Naturalness, and Phrasing of the collected utterances. We mostly use parametric statistical methods in our analysis. It has been debated for over 50 years whether Likert-type measurement scales should be analysed using parametric or non-parametric statistical methods (Carifio and Perla, 2008). The use of parametric statistics, however, was justified repeatedly by (Carifio and Perla, 2008), (Norman, 2010) and more recently by (Murray, 2013) as a "perfectly appropriate" (Carifio and Perla, 2008) statistical method for Likert scales that may be used by researchers "with no fear of coming to the wrong conclusion" (Norman, 2010). We therefore present and analyse mean averages (rather than the mode) for the collected judgements.

5.1 Self-evaluation vs. Crowd evaluation

In our experiment we used two methods to evaluate the quality of collected utterances: self-evaluation and an independent crowd-based evaluation. During the self-evaluation, crowd workers were asked to rank their own utterances. Note that data collected using the self-evaluation method was not intended to allow us to compare the quality of utterances elicited via pictorial and textual MRs. Rather, this data was collected in order to understand whether self-evaluation may be a reliable technique to evaluate the quality of created utterances in future studies.

In the self-evaluation, for each of their own NL utterances, crowd workers could select either *higher than average, average*, or *lower than average* values for Informativeness, Naturalness, and Phrasing.

For the independent crowd evaluation, a new CrowdFlower task was created. In this task, crowd workers were asked to look at one utterance at a time and to rate each utterance using the same procedure.

In order to compare the results of self-evaluation with the results of the independent crowd evaluation, we labelled the results of perceived Informativeness, Naturalness and Phrasing as *higher than average, average* and *lower than average* in both modes.

Cohen's kappa coefficient was used to measure inter-rater agreement between the two groups of evaluators, i.e. self-evaluators and independent crowd evaluators. The statistics did not reveal a significant level of agreement between the two groups of evaluators neither for the scores of Informativeness ($\kappa = 0.014$, $p = 0.36$), nor Phrasing ($\kappa = 0.007$, $p = 0.64$), nor Naturalness ($\kappa = -0.007$, $p = 0.62$).

The lack of agreement with the independent evaluation already indicates a potential problem with the self-evaluation method. However, in order to further assess which group was more reliable in eval-

---

uating utterances, we compared their Informativeness scores with the Semantic Similarity score of the corresponding utterances. As discussed before, the concepts of Informativeness and Semantic Similarity are similar to each other, so better agreement between these scores indicates higher reliability of evaluation results. In particular, utterances with high Semantic Similarity would be expected to have high ratings for Informativeness, as they express more of the concepts from the original MR.

The percentage agreement between the Informativeness and Semantic Similarity was 31.1%, while for the utterances evaluated independently by the crowd it was 60.3%. The differences in percentage agreements for the utterances with *good* semantic similarity was even higher: 32.1% for self-evaluators vs. 75.1% for crowd evaluators. This strongly suggests that the evaluation quality of self-evaluators is less reliable than that of the crowd. Therefore, we focus on the data collected from crowd evaluation for the analysis presented in the following sections.

5.2 Informativeness

Informativeness was defined (on the questionnaires) as whether the utterance "provides enough useful information about the venue". Also see section 3.4. The average score for Informativeness was 4.28 for the textual/logical MR, and 4.51 for the pictorial method, as shown in Table 3. A two-way ANOVA was conducted to examine the effect of MR modality and the number of attributes on the perceived Informativeness. There was no statistically significant interaction between the effects of modality and the number of attributes in the MR, $F(2,1236) = 1.79$, $p = 0.17$. A main effects analysis showed that the average Informativeness of utterances elicited through the pictorial method (4.51) was significantly higher than that of utterances elicited using the textual/logical modality (4.28), with $p < 0.01$. This is an increase of 0.23 points on the 6-point scale (=4.6%) in average Informativeness rating for the pictorial condition.

As expected, Informativeness increases with the number of attributes in the MR, in both conditions.

5.3 Naturalness

Naturalness was defined (on the questionnaires) as whether the utterance "could have been produced by a native speaker". The average score for Naturalness was 4.09 for the textual/logical MRs, and 4.43 for the pictorial method, as shown in Table 3. A two-way ANOVA was conducted to examine the effects of MR modality and the number of attributes on the perceived Naturalness. There was no statistically significant interaction between the effects of modality and the number of attributes in the MR, $F(2,1236) = 0.73$, $p = 0.48$. A main effects analysis showed that the average Naturalness of utterances elicited using the pictorial modality (4.43) was significantly higher than that of utterances elicited using the textual/logical modality (4.09), with $p < 0.001$. This is an increase of about 0.34 points on the scale (=6.8%) for average Naturalness rating for the pictorial condition.

5.4 Phrasing

Phrasing was defined as whether utterances are formulated in a way that the judges perceived as good English (see section 3.4). The average score for Phrasing was 4.01 for the textual/logical MR, and 4.40 for the pictorial method, as shown in Table 3. A two-way ANOVA was conducted to examine the effect of MR modality and the number of attributes on the perceived Phrasing. There was no statistically significant interaction between the effects of modality and the number of attributes in MR, $F(2,1236) = 0.85$, $p = 0.43$. A main effects analysis showed that the average Phrasing score for the utterances elicited using the pictorial modality was significantly higher than that of the utterances elicited using the textual/logical modality, with $p < 0.001$. This is an increase of +0.39 points (about 7.8%) in average Phrasing rating for the pictorial condition.

As the complexity of the MR increases (i.e. number of attributes) we note that the pictorial MR outperforms the textual MR still further, with an 11% boost in Phrasing ratings (+0.55 – from 3.98 to 4.53 on a 6-point scale – for 8 attributes) and a similar 9.6% (+0.48) increase for Naturalness ratings.

A Pearson product-moment correlation method was used to determine a strong correlation ($r = 0.84, p < 0.001$) between Naturalness and Phrasing, suggesting that evaluators treat these concepts as very similar. However, these concepts are not identical, as the evaluation results show.

	Textual MR		Pictorial MR	
	Mean	StDev	Mean	StDev
Informativeness	*4.28***	*1.54*	*4.51***	*1.37*
3 attributes	4.02	1.39	4.11	1.32
5 attributes	4.31	1.54	4.46	1.36
8 attributes	4.52	1.65	4.98	1.29
Naturalness	*4.09****	*1.56*	*4.43****	*1.35*
3 attributes	4.13	1.47	4.35	1.29
5 attributes	4.07	1.56	4.41	1.36
8 attributes	4.07	1.65	4.55	1.42
Phrasing	*4.01****	*1.69*	*4.40****	*1.52*
3 attributes	4.01	1.62	4.37	1.47
5 attributes	4.04	1.70	4.28	1.57
8 attributes	3.98	1.75	4.53	1.54

Table 3: Human evaluation of the data collected with each MR (** = $p < 0.01$ and *** = $p < 0.001$ for Pictorial versus Textual conditions). Italics denote averages across all numbers of attributes.

6 Discussion

We have shown that pictorial MRs have specific benefits for elicitation of NLG data from crowd-workers. This may be because, with pictures, data-providers are not primed by lexical tokens in the MRs, resulting in more spontaneous and natural language, with more variability. For example, rather than seeing *child-friendly[yes]* in a logical/textual MR, and then being inclined to say "It is child-friendly", crowd-workers who see an icon representing a child seem more likely to use a variety of phrases, such as "good for kids". As a concrete example of this phenomenon, from the collected data, consider the picture on the left of figure 2, which corresponds to the logical MR: *name [Loch Fyne], eatType [restaurant], familyFriendly [yes], priceRange [cheap], food [Japanese].*
The logical MR elicited utterances such as "Loch Fyne is a family friendly restaurant serving cheap Japanese food" whereas the pictorial MR elicited e.g. "Serving low cost Japanese style cuisine, Loch Fyne caters for everyone, including families with small children."

Pictorial stimuli have also been used in other, related NLP tasks. For example in crowd-sourced evaluations of dialogue systems, e.g. (Black et al., 2011; Williams and Young, 2007). However, no analysis was performed regarding the suitability of such representations. In (Williams and Young, 2007), for example, pictures were used to set dialogue goals for users (e.g. to find an expensive Ital-ian restaurant in the town centre). This experiment therefore also has a bearing on the whole issue of human NL responses to pictorial task stimuli, and shows for example that pictorial task presentations can elicit more natural variability in user inputs to a dialogue system. Pictorial method can also scale up to more than just single-entity descriptions, e.g. it is possible to show on a map several different pictures representing different restaurants, thus eliciting comparisons. Of course, there is a limit in the meaning complexity that pictures can express.

7 Conclusions and Future Work

We have shown that it is possible to rapidly create high quality NLG data sets for training novel corpus-based Machine Learning methods using crowd-sourcing. This now forges the path towards rapidly creating NLG systems for new domains. We first show that self-evaluation by crowd workers, of their own provided data, does not agree with an independent crowd-based evaluation, and also that their Informativeness judgements do not agree with an objective metric of semantic similarity. We then demonstrate that pictures elicit better data – that is, judged by independent evaluators as significantly more informative, more natural, and better-phrased – than logic-based Meaning Representations. There is no significant difference in the amount of time needed to collect the data, but pictorial representations lead to significantly increased scores for these metrics (e.g. of around 0.5 on a 6-point Likert scale). An error analysis shows that pictorial MRs result in more spontaneous, natural and varied utterances. We have done this by proposing a new crowdsourcing framework, where we introduce an initial automatic validation procedure, which was able to reject 100% of bad submissions. The collected data will be released as part of this submission.

In future work, we will use the collected data to test and further develop corpus-based NLG methods, using Imitation Learning. This technique promises to be able to learn NLG strategies automatically from unaligned data, similar to recent work by (Dušek and Jurčíček, 2015; Wen et al., 2015).

Acknowledgments

This research received funding from the EPSRC projects GUI (EP/L026775/1) and DILiGENt (EP/M005429/1).

References

Gabor Angeli, Percy Liang, and Dan Klein. 2010. A simple domain-independent probabilistic approach to generation. In *Conference on Empirical Methods in Natural Language Processing (EMNLP)*.

Alan W Black, Susanne Burger, Alistair Conkie, Helen Hastie, Simon Keizer, Oliver Lemon, Nicolas Merigaud, Gabriel Parent, Gabriel Schubiner, Blaise Thomson, Jason D. Williams, Kai Yu, Steve Young, and Maxine Eskenazi. 2011. Spoken dialog challenge 2010: Comparison of live and control test results. In *Proceedings of the SIGDIAL 2011 Conference*, pages 2–7, Portland, Oregon, June. Association for Computational Linguistics.

Chris Callison-Burch and Mark Dredze. 2010. Creating speech and language data with Amazon's Mechanical Turk. In *Proceedings of the NAACL HLT 2010 Workshop on Creating Speech and Language Data with Amazon's Mechanical Turk*, pages 1–12. Association for Computational Linguistics.

James Carifio and Rocco Perla. 2008. Resolving the 50-year debate around using and misusing Likert scales. *Medical education*, 42(12):1150–1152.

Nina Dethlefs, Helen Hastie, Verena Rieser, and Oliver Lemon. 2012. Optimising Incremental Dialogue Decisions Using Information Density for Interactive Systems. In *Proc. of EMNLP*.

Ondřej Dušek and Filip Jurčíček. 2015. Training a natural language generator from unaligned data. In *Proceedings of the 53rd Annual Meeting of the Association for Computational Linguistics and the 7th International Joint Conference on Natural Language Processing (Volume 1: Long Papers)*, pages 451–461, Beijing, China, July. Association for Computational Linguistics.

Lushan Han, Abhay Kashyap, Tim Finin, James Mayfield, and Jonathan Weese. 2013. Umbc ebiquity-core: Semantic textual similarity systems. In *Proceedings of the Second Joint Conference on Lexical and Computational Semantics*, volume 1, pages 44–52.

Ioannis Konstas and Mirella Lapata. 2012. Unsupervised concept-to-text generation with hypergraphs. In *Conference of the North American Chapter of the Association for Computational Linguistics (NAACL)*.

Francois Mairesse and Steve Young. 2014. Stochastic Language Generation in Dialogue Using Factored Language Models. *Computational Linguistics*, 40(4).

François Mairesse, Milica Gašić, Filip Jurčíček, Simon Keizer, Blaise Thomson, Kai Yu, and Steve Young. 2010. Phrase-based statistical language generation using graphical models and active learning. In *Proceedings of the 48th Annual Meeting of the Association for*

Computational Linguistics, pages 1552–1561. Association for Computational Linguistics.

Winter Mason and Duncan J Watts. 2010. Financial incentives and the performance of crowds. *ACM SigKDD Explorations Newsletter*, 11(2):100–108.

Jacqueline Murray. 2013. Likert data: What to use, parametric or non-parametric? *International Journal of Business and Social Science*, 4(11).

Geoff Norman. 2010. Likert scales, levels of measurement and the laws of statistics. *Advances in health sciences education*, 15(5):625–632.

V. Rieser, O. Lemon, and S. Keizer. 2014. Natural Language Generation as Incremental Planning Under Uncertainty: Adaptive Information Presentation for Statistical Dialogue Systems. *IEEE/ACM Transactions on Audio, Speech, and Language Processing*, 22(5):979–994.

Jon Sprouse. 2011. A validation of Amazon Mechanical Turk for the collection of acceptability judgments in linguistic theory. *Behavior research methods*, 43(1):155–167.

Wei Yu Wang, Dan Bohus, Ece Kamar, and Eric Horvitz. 2012. Crowdsourcing the acquisition of natural language corpora: Methods and observations. In *Spoken Language Technology Workshop (SLT), 2012 IEEE*, pages 73–78. IEEE.

Yushi Wang, Jonathan Berant, and Percy Liang. 2015. Building a semantic parser overnight. In *Proceedings of the 53rd Annual Meeting of the Association for Computational Linguistics and the 7th International Joint Conference on Natural Language Processing (Volume 1: Long Papers)*, pages 1332–1342, Beijing, China, July. Association for Computational Linguistics.

Tsung-Hsien Wen, Milica Gasic, Nikola Mrkšić, Pei-Hao Su, David Vandyke, and Steve Young. 2015. Semantically Conditioned LSTM-based Natural Language Generation for Spoken Dialogue Systems. In *Proceedings of the 2015 Conference on Empirical Methods in Natural Language Processing*, pages 1711–1721, Lisbon, Portugal, September. Association for Computational Linguistics.

Jason D. Williams and Steve Young. 2007. Partially Observable Markov Decision Processes for Spoken Dialog Systems. *Comput. Speech Lang.*, 21(2):393–422, April.

Omar F. Zaidan and Chris Callison-Burch. 2011. Crowdsourcing translation: Professional quality from non-professionals. In *Proc. of ACL*, pages 1220–1229, Portland, Oregon, USA, June.

Association for Computational Linguistics
209 N. Eighth Street
Stroudsburg, Pennsylvania 18360

ISBN 978-1-5108-3116-2